"This splendidly thorough   *ical*

"An outstanding study that significantly advances our understanding of women's lives in the late eighteenth and early nineteenth century." *Journal of American History*

"A significant and unique contribution to that growing body of literature on the War of 1812 and on women's experiences of war generally … *In the Midst of Alarms* is also a wonderful read – and I highly recommend it." **Jane Errington, Ph.D.**

"A lively account of the history of women during the time of the War of 1812 on both sides of the 49th parallel." **Katherine M.J. McKenna, Western University**

"Thanks to Dianne Graves's diligence, future scholars have a compelling new set of historical characters that they can – and must – use in any serious study of the War of 1812. Graves's meticulous recreation of the multifaceted experiences of women at war refutes the simple stereotypes of the soldier on the battlefield or the diplomat at the council table. Rather, with a storyteller's flair, she uncovers the webs of 'family' that undergird this most seemingly masculine of occupations." **Catherine Allgor, Professor of History, University of California at Riverside, author of *A Perfect Union: Dolley Madison and the Creation of the American Nation***

"This is a fascinating study of women during the War of 1812 – American, Canadian and British. It contains a wealth of stories and introduces dozens of new actors to the historical stage: rich and poor; white, black and aboriginal; urban and rural. Both scholars and the general public will find it of interest." **Holly C. Shulman, editor, <The Dolley Madison Digital Edition>, University of Virginia**

"The story that Dianne Graves tells in these pages is rich and varied. We learn how the upper classes spent the war years in places like Washington, Philadelphia and New York as well as in Quebec, Montreal and York (now Toronto).… We gain some understanding of how the wives of officers and enlisted men coped with separation, privation and loss. We learn what women thought of the war, how it changed their lives and, in many cases, what became of them.… This pioneering work does much to illuminate a little-understood dimension of the War of 1812." **From the Foreword by Donald R. Hickey, Professor of History, Wayne State College, Nebraska**

"This is a well researched, wonderfully readable book." ***Esprit de Corps* magazine**

Foreword

by Donald R. Hickey

Warfare has always been a pre-eminently male activity. Hence, those writing the history of wars have usually focused on the role of men, leaving women in the shadows of the backdrop. The old-fashioned military historians of the drum-and-bugle school were interested mainly in battles and campaigns. Women rarely entered their stories, and when they did, it was as the spoils of war when an invading army ravaged the countryside or stormed a fortress, or as camp followers who were portrayed, not entirely accurately, as assorted hangers-on, vagabonds and prostitutes. It is only in the last half century that women have broken out of their traditional roles, and that, not coincidentally, historians have started investigating their role in wars. Although we know a lot more than we once did about that role in some wars, the War of 1812 remains terra incognita. That is why Dianne Graves's book is so interesting and important.

It is not easy to do research on this topic because the sources are scattered and sparse. Although upper-class women sometimes documented their thoughts and actions in letters, diaries and memoirs, middle-class women usually did not because they were either illiterate or simply too busy to leave a written record. For women from the lower classes – servants and slaves – and for indigenous women, there is even less source material.

Graves has overcome these limitations, not only ferreting out a variety of sources penned by women but also making good use of the records left by men. Hence, she is able to shed considerable light on the history of women during the War of 1812. We learn much about their everyday lives: how they spent their time, the problems they had to contend with (especially if they were married to military personnel), the dangers and suffering they might be subjected to (particularly if living in a theatre of war) and, more broadly, how the War of 1812 affected their lives.

The story that Dianne Graves tells in these pages is rich and varied. We learn how the upper classes spent the war years in places like Washington, Philadelphia and New York as well as in Quebec, Montreal and York (now Toronto). We gain some understanding of how the wives of officers and enlisted men coped with separation, privation and loss. We learn what women thought of the war, how it changed their lives and, in many cases, what became of them after the war. In the process, we also pick up considerable social history on such topics as how women dressed, what they ate, what their gardens looked like, how they travelled and, more generally, how they coped with the challenges of living in a war-torn world.

This pioneering work does much to illuminate a little-understood dimension of the War of 1812. We can hope that it will stimulate other scholars to dig deeper into the subject to expand our understanding of the thoughts, feelings and actions of women in this age of armed conflict.

DONALD R. HICKEY
Wayne, Nebraska

Introduction

As someone who has always had a strong interest in the Edwardian period and the First World War, stepping back in time to the early nineteenth century has been a journey of immense fascination. It began some six years ago when I started to explore the voluminous archives of my husband, Donald E. Graves, an historian who specializes in the War of 1812. As my interest grew, I realized that, although the diplomatic, political, military and naval aspects of this conflict had been extensively treated in print, there was relatively little about the life and times of the women who lived through it. *In the Midst of Alarms* endeavours to fill that gap. Although I took full advantage of my husband's resources on the subject, I must stress that – apart from vociferously complaining that books he needed were missing from his library, answering in his characteristic manner my rather simple questions about the period and editing the final manuscript – this was the only assistance he gave while I was writing this book. In everything else I paddled my canoe alone on a challenging voyage of exploration through unfamiliar waters.

Most simply put, *In the Midst of Alarms* is an attempt – from an impartial standpoint in terms of nationality – to bring to life the experiences of a broad cross-section of women in North America during the time of the War of 1812, and some who viewed the war from a greater distance. It is not a history of that conflict, although to provide a framework for the experiences of women in the war, I have included below a brief chronology of its major events. Given size limitations, it has been impossible to include all the material I collected during my research; otherwise this book would have been twice as long as it is. My intention has been to provide a door into the world, now two centuries distant, in which these women lived, and a glimpse of the kind of people they were, the events they experienced and how the war affected their lives.

I should also stress that I have not written from a feminist perspective and that I have deliberately refrained from making comparisons between their time and ours by imposing a modern context on the past. From our position in the twenty-first century, at a time when western women can boast levels of independence and accomplishment undreamed of by their 1812 counterparts, such comparisons seem to me to be irrelevant. Instead, I have tried to present the lives of the women of the War of 1812 within the parameters and constraints that governed their times.

Given the huge challenges they faced in dealing with aspects of life which today have become quite matter-of-fact, these women are to be greatly admired. Not only that, but they also coped with the privations, depredations and unpredictability of war, often alone or with little support. Although women in wartime North America faced many situations that brought them face to face with the darker side of human nature, conversely, they often found kindness, goodness and generosity in time of need. And in terms of sheer willpower, there are numerous examples of women who survived against great odds by their own efforts and determination.

With regard to their surviving records, it is important to note that almost all diaries and letters extant from the War of 1812 period were written by literate women of the upper and middle classes who had time at their disposal and knowledge and ability to put pen to paper. Very seldom has an account by a private soldier's wife, a farmwife or a female servant survived – and even more rarely the words of an aboriginal or African-American woman. To a considerable extent, I have therefore had to rely on the words of literate white women, or military and civilian white men. The voices of other women are heard mainly through third-party accounts, but this does not in any way detract from their important place in the period that forms the subject of this book.

I should advise the reader of a few matters relating to terminology. To simplify the question of military and naval ranks, I have tried to use the highest rank gained by an individual during the war. I have used the term "Canadian" for English-speaking residents of British North America and *"Canadien"* for French-speaking residents. Although it was Fort Amherstburg and the village of Malden during the war, the two names were reversed in later years, and so I have used Fort Malden and the village of Amherstburg throughout. Finally, I have retained the Canadian spelling of Chippawa, as opposed to the American spelling of Chippewa.

On the question of monetary values, during the three years the War of 1812 lasted, the British pound sterling was worth, according to research done by Donald Hickey in *Don't Give up the Ship! Myths of the War of 1812* (Toronto and Chicago, 2006), between US$3.75 and US$4.25. Like Professor Hickey, I have taken the average of the three years, which works out to £1 = $3.87. A pound was composed of 20 shillings (each worth an average of 19 cents) while a guinea was one pound and one shilling, or $4.06. It should be noted, of course, that both the pound and the dollar bought a lot more in 1812 than they do today.

I now turn to the pleasant task of recording the names of those who came to my aid during the course of researching and writing this book. Let me begin by expressing my gratitude to the following for their generous assistance: Dr. Carl Benn of Toronto; René Chartrand of Hull, Quebec, and Brian Leigh Dunnigan of the William L. Clements Library, University of Michigan, Ann Arbor, both of whom were especially kind in locating or providing a number of the fine illustrations that appear in the book; Christopher George of Baltimore, Maryland; Major John Grodzinski of the Royal Military College of Canada, Kingston, Ontario; Michelle Guitard of Ottawa; Robert Henderson of Manotick, Ontario; Professor Keith Jeffery of the University of Ulster, Belfast; Dr. Faye Kert of Ottawa; Fiona Lucas of Toronto; the late Robert Malcomson of St. Catharines, Ontario; Professor Christopher McKee of Grinnell College, Grinnell, Iowa; the late Professor Emeritus John Morris of Kent State University, Ohio; Peter Osborne of Harbledown, Kent; Scott Sheads and Vincent Vaise of the National Parks Service, Fort McHenry National Monument, Baltimore; Stuart Sutherland of Toronto; Dr. Luce Vermette of Hull, Quebec; Patrick Wilder of Cape Vincent, New York; Professor Joseph Whitehorne of Front Royal, Virginia; and Wayne Wilcox of Eastport, Maine.

When attempting to trace portraits of some of the women in the book, I contacted their descendants. Unfortunately several I hoped to find – those of British women in particular – cannot be located at present even though their existence was known at one time. I am, nevertheless, most grateful to the following who were good enough to respond to my enquiries: Lord de Saumarez; The Marquis of Anglesey; Lord Townshend; Mrs. Juliet Mortensen; Sir Simon Codrington; and Mrs. Joan Hoseason. Paul Adamthwaite, a descendant of the de Rottenburg family, was good enough to respond to my questions, and to attempt, unsuccessfully, to locate the family portrait of Lady Julia de Rottenburg. Sir Christopher Prevost kindly allowed me to include the Thomas Phillips portrait of Anne Elinor Prevost; and writer Nancy Holmes did some valuable groundwork in the, to date, fruitless search for the portrait of the beautiful Catherine Norton that was formerly in the collection of the Duke of Northumberland.

In tracking down important material, I wish particularly to acknowledge the help of author Margaret Elphinstone, who generously shared with me her research on Madame La Framboise. I also owe special debts of gratitude to Patrick Kavanagh of Buffalo, who worked tirelessly at the archives of the Buffalo and Erie County Historical Society and elsewhere on my behalf, and Jay Karamales, who researched for me at the Library of Congress, Washington, D.C.

I much appreciated the assistance of the staff of the various institutions with whom I had contact: Sarah Tapper of Decatur House, Washington, DC; Stephanie Jacobe and Meg Eastman of the Virginia Historical Society, Richmond; Simon Lake, Curator of the New Walk Museum, Leicester, Britain; Clare Baxter of the Northumberland Estates, Alnwick, Britain; Cindy Olsen of the Star-Spangled Banner Flag House, Baltimore; Stephanie McGreevey, Librarian of Mackinac Library, Mackinac Island, Michigan; Alison West and Bridget Hanley of the Ipswich Record Office, Britain; Lorelei Eurto, Munson Williams Proctor Arts Institute, Utica, New York; Peter Harrington, Curator of the Anne S.K. Brown Military Collection, Brown University, Providence, Rhode Island; Paul Cox of the Heinz Archives and Library, National Portrait Gallery, London; Suzanne Morin of the McCord Museum, Montreal; Kate Johnson, Curator, Historic Hudson Valley, Tarrytown, New York; Mrs J.V. Thorpe, Archivist, Gloucestershire Record Office, Britain; Christine Turton of Gloucester Public Library, Britain; Janet Bishop of the New Brunswick Museum, Saint John; Karen Mansfield of the Worcester Art Museum, Massachusetts; Nicola Woods of the Royal Ontario Museum, Toronto; Lynda McLeod, Librarian, Christie's Archives, London; A. Bentley of the Massachusetts Historical Society, Boston; Dennis Carter-Edwards and John McLeod of Parks Canada; and Ian Bowering of the Cornwall Museum, Ontario.

I also received help and guidance from the staffs of the Library and Archives of Canada, Ottawa, in particular Pat Kennedy, who generously gave me the benefit of her time and knowledge; the National Archives of Britain, Kew, Surrey; the British Library; the Newspaper Library, the National Portrait Gallery and the National Army Museum, London; the Public Archives of Nova Scotia, Halifax; the Niagara Falls Public Library; the Williams Research Centre, New Orleans; the Historical Society of Old Newbury, Massachusetts; Historic Cherry Hill, New York; and the Massachusetts, Connecticut, Maryland and Virginia Historical Societies.

My gratitude goes to the Riversdale Historical Society, Maryland, and Margaret Law Callcott for permission to quote from *Mistress of Riversdale: The Plantation Letters of Rosalie Stier Calvert;* to the Ipswich Record Office for permission to quote from the letters of Sir Philip and Lady Louisa Broke; to the

Firestone Library, Princeton University, New Jersey, for allowing me to quote from the letters of Edward Livingston; and to the Connecticut Historical Society for use of the George Howard Autobiography and Record Book.

Others who have kindly supplied information or assistance in various ways include James Elliott, Marianne Krajicek, Robert Linden, Lori Locke, Patricia Reid, Susan Montgomery, Margaret Sankey, Linda Storrie, Katrina Wilder, Barbara Dundas and Major Helga Grodzinski, CD. Professors Catherine Allgor and Holly C. Shulman were good enough to read the final manuscript and provide jacket quotes. War of 1812 historian and author Professor Donald R. Hickey of Wayne State College, Nebraska, not only provided the foreword, but his thorough reading of the manuscript saved me from committing many major errors.

In conclusion, I wish to express my special gratitude to the Honourable Myra A. Freeman, former Lieutenant Governor of Nova Scotia, for granting me permission to photograph inside Government House, Halifax, and to artist Peter Rindlisbacher for generously allowing me to use some of his beautiful paintings. My publisher, Robin Brass, who has enthusiastically supported this project, is deserving of the greatest praise for his patience, editing and customary superb design and production work. In conclusion, it goes without saying that I am deeply indebted to the War of 1812 historian I mentioned earlier. Thank you, Don, for your painstaking and scholarly editing of my manuscript, for making it a better book in the process and for doing your best to put up with my trespassing in your territory. I should also acknowledge the other male in the house, Ned the cat, who is no less demanding but always appreciative of my efforts. If I have inadvertently omitted anyone in these acknowledgements, I hope they will forgive an honest oversight.

Dianne Graves, 2007

Note for the Second Edition

It is a happy coincidence that the second edition of *In the Midst of Alarms* is appearing, with minimal revision and in a new paperback design, as the bicentennial of the War of 1812 gets under way. I would like to express my appreciation of the efforts of my publisher, Robin Brass, to bring the book out in a fresh format for this important commemoration.

Dianne Graves
*18 June 2012, the 200th Anniversary
of the Declaration of War*

IN THE MIDST OF ALARMS:

THE UNTOLD STORY OF WOMEN

AND THE WAR OF 1812

Abigail Smith Adams (1744-1818) was the wife of former American president John Adams and by 1812 she and her husband were living at their New England estate. Unlike many of her contemporaries, Abigail could view her country from a wider world perspective, having experienced diplomatic life overseas and mixed with the great and near great. She also happened to be married to a man who respected her intellect and valued her counsel. Abigail Adams supported education for women to better prepare them for their duties as wives and mothers, and cherished a belief in separate but equal roles for the sexes. (Portrait by Gilbert Stuart, oil on canvas, gift of Mrs. Robert Homans, copyright Board of Trustees, National Gallery of Art, Washington.)

"A terrible commotion."
War Comes to North America

To meet Britannia's hostile bands	*Yankee doodle, march away,*
We'll march, our heroes say, sir,	*Yankee doodle dandy,*
We'll join all hearts, we'll join all hands;	*Yankee doodle, fight brave boys,*
Brave boys we'll win the day, sir.	*The thing will work right handy.*
Yankee doodle, strike your tents,	*Soon will the toils of war be o'er,*
Yankee doodle dandy,	*And then we'll taste of bliss, sir,*
Yankee doodle, march away,	*On beauty's lip, which all adore,*
And do your parts right handy.	*We'll print the melting kiss, sir.*
For long we've borne with British pride,	*Yankee doodle, beauty charms,*
And su'd to gain our rights, sir;	*Yankee doodle dandy,*
All other methods have been tried;	*Yankee doodle, ground our arms*
There's nought remains but fight, sir.	*Our sweethearts are the dandy.*[1]

Early on a June morning in 1812, Mary Elizabeth Clark became one of the first women in British North America to learn that her country was at war. The wife of Thomas Clark, a wealthy merchant of Queenston, Upper Canada, Mary and her husband were roused from slumber at their home overlooking the falls of Niagara to be told that a Mr. Vosburgh had arrived from Albany with very important information. The express message, which one of his employees handed to her husband, confirmed the news that no one wanted to hear – the United States had declared war on Great Britain.[2]

To many British North Americans who had been "half-expectant for the rising storm," the outbreak of hostilities came as no great surprise.[3] Indeed, there had been tension between Washington and London for a number of years and rumours of war had been constant throughout that time. Some people in both American and British territory welcomed the news and among was them was

George Hamilton, a young cousin of Mary Clark's husband. "If the Yankees come after this," exclaimed Hamilton, a militia cavalry officer, "the Devil is to them, especially when my troopers take the field we'll snip their heads off like the tops of thistles."[4]

War was certainly no stranger to the Clarks. Mary's mother, Elizabeth,[5] had survived the Revolutionary War. The eldest daughter of Sir William Johnson, Superintendent of Indian Affairs, and his famous and influential Mohawk consort, Molly Brant, or Konwatsi'tsiaiénni, to use her aboriginal and preferred name, Elizabeth had fled with her family from their home in the Mohawk Valley.[6] Her childhood memories of that escape, recounted to Mary and her siblings, were an important part of the family's heritage. Mary's Scottish father, Dr. Robert Kerr, was a pioneer physician in the Niagara region of Upper Canada and a justice of the peace who lived in the town of Newark (now Niagara-on-the-Lake). He had fought in the Revolutionary War, and although he was in his middle years by 1812, Dr. Kerr was ready to take up arms again. Mary's brothers, William and Robert, were officers in the Glengarry Light Infantry Fencibles, a regular British regiment raised in Canada, and her brother Walter was attached to the Indian Department, the military agency that oversaw contact with Britain's aboriginal allies. Finally, Thomas Clark, Mary's husband, was a lieutenant-colonel in the local militia and had been diligently drilling his regiment since the beginning of 1812.

The lives of North American women like Mary Clark had indeed long been overshadowed by war. The conflict that began in June 1812 – which forms the context of this book – derived from the ongoing struggle that Britain had been waging against France since 1793. While Napoleon, emperor of the French since 1804, had been victorious on land, he had been unable to defeat Britain, which had the most powerful navy in the world, at sea. After Vice-Admiral Horatio Nelson triumphed over the French fleet at the Battle of Trafalgar in 1805, the French leader began an economic war against his opponent, aimed squarely at Britain's maritime empire. In 1806 and 1807, Napoleon decreed that British ships attempting to import British goods into Europe would be subject to seizure. Britain responded with Orders-in-Council which prohibited any vessel carrying cargo to or from a French or French-controlled port on pain of confiscation.

This economic warfare actually had little effect on the two belligerents but it did have a doleful result for the large American merchant economy, which had profited from trade with both nations. In an effort to keep the republic out of the crossfire, President Thomas Jefferson secured an embargo in 1807 that prohibited American vessels from leaving port, but this initiative simply caused more damage to the American economy. Since Britain was a sea power it was almost inevitable that there would be friction when ships of the Royal Navy stopped and searched American flag vessels on the high seas, and the tension between the two nations was exacerbated when British naval captains impressed, or forcibly conscripted, American sailors into the Royal Navy. This tension was further amplified by a recurrence of conflict with the aboriginal nations residing in the American Northwest (the modern states of Illinois, Indiana, Ohio and Michigan) which many Americans attributed to British instigation.

By the spring of 1812, President James Madison had reluctantly decided that war was the only way for the United States to resolve its differences with Britain. Although many Americans, particularly in the New England states, were vehemently opposed, on 18 June 1812 the republic declared war on Great Britain. Ironically, at almost the same time the British government became aware of the depth of American feeling and repealed the hated Orders-in-Council – but it was too late.

The republic's motives were summarized by Andrew Jackson, a Tennessee militia officer, in a rousing call to arms which contained some idiosyncratic spelling and expression:

> We are going to fight for the reestablishment of our national charector, misunderstood and vilified at home and abroad; for the protection of our maritime citizens, impressed on board British ships of war and compelled to fight the battles of our enemies against ourselves; to vindicate our right to a free trade, and open a market for the productions of our soil, now perishing on our hands because the *mistress of the ocean* has forbid us to carry them to any foreign nation; in fine, to seek some indemnity for past injuries, some security against future aggressions, by the conquest of all the British dominions upon the continent of north america.[7]

Not all Americans were so confident. At her home in New England, Abigail Smith Adams must have regarded the coming of war as the gloomy realization of what she had long foreseen. An ardent republican and wife of former president John Adams, Abigail had lived through the Revolutionary War and never wavered in her opposition to British rule of the American colonies. Throughout that conflict, she had continued to manage the family farm and raise her children, all the while assuring her absent husband by letter that she was coping very well. "I would not have you distressed about me," she had written to him, "danger, they say, makes people valiant."[8] In the postwar years, Abigail had accompanied her husband when he was appointed the first American ambassador to Britain. John Adams's task had not been easy, but wearing the mantle of diplomatic wife with tact and simplicity, Abigail had worked hard to enhance her husband's relationship with King George III, and to promote favourable relations between the two nations.

Her experiences abroad had given Abigail Adams the opportunity to study life and make comparisons with the United States. As she saw it, the new republic had definite advantages, including personal liberty, the ease of obtaining property "and the plenty which is so equally distributed."[9] Yet she also recognized in her people "that restless spirit, and that baneful pride, ambition, and thirst for power which will finally make us as wretched as our neighbours."[10] In the summer of 1812, Abigail might well have thought to herself that it was these qualities that had led to the American declaration of war.

The United States, as Abigail Adams and her contemporaries knew it in the early nineteenth century, was already a large country. It shared a border with British North America to the north and with Spanish Florida to the south, and possessed an ill-defined western frontier along the Mississippi River. Consisting of eighteen states (Louisiana having been purchased from France in 1803 and admitted to the Union that very year) and the territories of Indiana, Illinois, Michigan, Missouri and Mississippi, it was referred to by most Americans as "these United States," although some who had a more progressive

(Facing page) **Three stages of pioneer life.** In the first image, a family of settlers has cleared a space in the forest and erected a simple log house with a stick chimney, a roof of peeled elm bark and windows covered with oiled paper. There are logs piled in readiness for a wood fire, a small shelter for some of the animals and hay for cattle and sheep. The woman of the house feeds a pig and some fowls with scraps of food from her apron.

At the second stage it is summer. More land has been cleared, a brush fence and a log bridge erected and a garden laid out for growing vegetables. A logging bee is in progress, with neighbour helping neighbour. The housewife is now a mother with a baby in her arms.

In the third image, ten years have passed. A frame house has been erected next to the original log house, with a framed barn and a picket fence enclosing the garden. More land is under cultivation, more livestock has been added and there is an orchard of maturing fruit trees. In the distance can be seen a log school house for the local children. (Engravings by unknown artist. Author's collection.)

concept of nationhood were calling it "the United States."[11] With a population in excess of seven million people in 1812, Americans boasted that theirs was the largest country in the civilized world after Russia, and the only independent republic.

Its sheer expanse gave the people of the young republic a vision of the future that encouraged bold and ambitious dreams. According to a geography text published in the U.S. in the 1780s, Americans were celebrated for "the excellence of their Constitution, which provides for political liberty and individual security," and "justly famed for their ardent love of freedom, for their hospitality and industry, and for the great attention they pay to agriculture and commerce."[12] The years from 1790 onwards marked a period of considerable change, with the creation of a new national government, the emergence of a party system and a culture based on democratic politics. Socially, a levelling process was taking place, with cheap land available to all and a sense of greater equality. By 1812, despite the economic woes caused by the war in Europe, the people of the republic felt confident that a brighter future lay ahead.

The United States at that time was still predominantly rural. About four fifths of American families were farming and their activities were tied to their homes, land, artisans' shops and stores.[13] In areas of early settlement such as New England, and Virginia and other southern states, farms, plantations and homesteads were relatively sophisticated, but in more backward and remote areas of the country such as the Michigan Territory or the Holland Purchase – a large tract of land stretching from western New York State through Ohio that had been settled within the preceding decade – life was still primitive.

The average American rural dweller and his wife worked hard and were independent, self-respecting and resourceful. These were qualities moulded by the extremes of climate and the fact that they could be cut off from the rest of the country for months at a time. As pioneers in North America had discovered, women were indispensable in such conditions, and when an attempt was made to form a bachelor settlement near Orleans, New York, the male members quickly felt the need of wives, as a poem on the subject makes clear: "The world was sad; – the garden was wild; And man, the hermit, sighed – till WOMAN smiled."[14]

Only a very small proportion of the American population lived in urban areas. Of cities with more than 10,000 inhabitants, New York was the largest, followed by Philadelphia, Baltimore, Boston, Charleston, New Orleans, Salem and Providence. New York was the leading cultural and artistic centre while

Philadelphia claimed "a certain elegance" and was known for its rich and cultivated society, university, medical school, libraries and theatres.[15] Washington, the capital of the republic, was still under construction and likened by one foreign visitor to "those Russian towns traced in the deserts of Tartary, in whose inclosures we behold nothing but naked fields and a few glimpses of houses."[16] It stood in stark contrast to nearby Baltimore, which had developed into a shipping and grain milling centre with a bustling port and a population of about 41,000 souls. Charleston, with its elegant architecture, was known for the lavish hospitality and luxurious lifestyle of its upper circle, and on the Gulf of Mexico was New Orleans, a city of strategic importance and a major trading centre, which possessed a unique character derived from its lively mix of peoples and cultures.

Rural Americans, who travelled little, often believed that the cities were evil places full of "luxury and sin" where "gaiety and pleasures … turned the heads of girls, made them worldly, and tempted them to their fall," and young men were "led into dissipation, vice, and crime."[17] More Americans were familiar with smaller centres such as Hartford, Detroit or Havre de Grace, each of which had fewer than 5,000 people but its own regional character and economy. With local farming, manufacturing, trading and other enterprises, these smaller towns were all "bustle and business" and important focal points for the surrounding population.

Whether they dwelt in town or country, American women of the early nineteenth century tended to be strong and self-reliant. This was particularly true of the remarkable generation who had lived through the Revolutionary War and whom writer Elizabeth Oakes Smith described as "brave, sturdy, intelligent."[18] In 1812, however, even an educated American woman only had slightly more control over her life than her counterpart of a half century earlier. She was bound by the continuing constraints of a patriarchal society in which men predominated, for, ironically, the conditions that had enabled the new United States of America to establish itself as an independent nation and permitted middle-class white men to achieve wealth and political power, restricted women to a more limited role.

Following the Revolutionary War, the egalitarian principles of the Declaration of Independence were at variance with the prevalent code of refined feminine behaviour. Women who had taken pride in managing families, homes and affairs during that conflict, however, were not prepared to accept without question the conventional belief in feminine weakness and delicacy. Abigail Adams

Newcomers. The Loyalists in this camp scene at Johnstown on the St. Lawrence in 1784 were starting a new life in the British provinces with the few personal effects they had been able to bring with them. Note one woman washing in a wooden tub, and another cooking using a cast iron kettle suspended over an open fire. Watercolour by James Peachey, himself a Loyalist refugee. (Library and Archives of Canada, C-2001.)

was, for the time, a leading advocate of women's rights. "I would desire you would remember the ladies," she told her husband, John, "and be more generous and favorable to them than your ancestors."[19] Mrs. Adams's plea was aimed at provoking a review of the English Common Law that still held good in the republic, and under which the statutes concerning marriage were nearly identical to those of England. A married woman was deprived of her own economic resources and her husband, with few exceptions, exerted the same unlimited power over her as was the case in Britain and the British colonies.[20]

To the north of the United States, the population of British North America, estimated to be no more than 500,000 in 1812, lived mainly in settlements clustered along the American border, which extended from New Brunswick in the east, to the upper Great Lakes in the west. The majesty of this wild country could not fail to impress, and Susan Burnham Greeley, daughter of an early

Canadian settler, tells of the "grand and solemn sound" that proceeded from "those glorious woods when the wind blew hard" and of forests so thick that "you might swing the axe here all day and not let in the light of the sun."[21] The density of the growth and the size of the trees, the largest of which were more than five hundred years old and as tall as a modern seventeen-storey building, cast a perpetual gloom "almost touching on sadness," and the sight of nature on such a vast and unspoilt scale provoked in many an "indescribable sensation of awe, loneliness and astonishment."[22]

The first white settlers in this part of the continent had been the French who had arrived in the early seventeenth century. With the French defeat in the Seven Years War, New France had passed under British control and had become the province of Lower Canada. The French-speaking population of Lower Canada, known commonly as the *Canadiens,* with their own language, culture and civil law, formed a distinct society within British North America. They outnumbered the English-speaking population until after the American Revolutionary War, which brought a wave of new English-speaking settlers – the Loyalists or Americans who supported the British Crown during that conflict.

Nearly half a million Americans had remained true to Britain, and by the end of the Revolutionary War between 60,000 and 100,000 of them had chosen to leave rather than live in a republic.[23] These Loyalists had suffered severely for their allegiance to the Crown, and to women like Hannah Showers, who had fled to Upper Canada with her husband and family, the prospect of another conflict brought the return of dark memories. Hannah never forgot the long gruelling trek from Pennsylvania to British territory, during which she and her children had braved "the hunger, the hardships, and the mosquitoes." Thanks to some "friendly Indians who helped us on our way" they had eventually reached safety and a chance to start a new life.[24] Those who came from rural backgrounds had an advantage over people from urban areas as the "man who caused a blade of grass to grow where one had not been before, was of more use to mankind, than many heroes or philosophers."[25]

From these rough beginnings, many Loyalists survived life on the frontier and, together with immigrants from Britain, the majority of whom tackled with zeal the challenges of life in the wilderness, saw their communities and families grow. Their sons matured into strong young men who could wield an axe and their daughters became self-reliant, capable women who could undertake any work required of a settler's wife. In time, such colonists became aware that theirs was a demanding life that brought the satisfaction of personal achievement and a sense of participation in the building of a new colony. As the Reverend John Stuart, a Loyalist minister who settled at Kingston, put it, "we are poor, happy people, industrious beyond example."[26]

In the years immediately preceding the outbreak of war in 1812, the Loyalist and British population of Upper Canada was augmented by an influx of American immigrants. Many chose to settle along the Niagara and Grand Rivers, on the shores of Lake Huron and further west. These more recent arrivals, encouraged by "the exuberance of the soil, the mildness of the government, and an almost total exemption from taxes," soon made a good life for themselves, and by 1812 many were living well above subsistence level.[27]

With a population described as "industrious, economical and money making," Upper Canada was a land of "stump and snake fences"; of log cabins with cellars below ground to store fresh milk, pickled pork and game pies; of chicken coops, cattle sheds and teams of oxen working the fields; and of "raw-boned men in homespun linsey-woolsey scything the tawny harvest of midsummer," with their wives beside them.[28] Some areas, the Niagara region in particular, were becoming "very populous and rich," with men like Mary Clark's husband, Thomas, enjoying considerable financial success, a comfortable life and a place in local society.[29]

While the majority of women and their families in the British colonies still lived a traditional rural existence, by the time of the war, those in the larger centres were able to enjoy a measure of sophistication. Fredericton and Saint John in New Brunswick prospered from a thriving lumber trade that supplied the raw material for the Royal Navy's shipbuilders. Halifax, Nova Scotia, with 9,000 souls and its harbour, garrison, naval base and fashionable social season, was reputed to be the liveliest port in the empire after Portsmouth. The city of Quebec, with nearly 10,000 people, was the capital of British North America and the centre of government, while cosmopolitan Montreal, with 25,000 people, was the largest and richest city in the colonies, wealthy from the lucrative fur trade.

West up the St. Lawrence and into Upper Canada were towns like Cornwall with its neat wooden houses and Brockville, described by one visitor as "the best built and prettiest" town he had ever seen.[30] Kingston, a shipbuilding centre and naval base, was known for its fine architecture and "imposing" appearance."[31] The town of Newark in the Niagara Peninsula, was said by one visitor to be "a beautiful and prospective place," while the "small, but handsome village" of Queenston, home of the Clarks, was reckoned to be a place of "considerable trade, and inhabited by a civil and rich people."[32] Towards the western end of Lake Ontario stood York, Upper Canada's young capital, later to become the city of Toronto. Muddy and unostentatious, the town nevertheless impressed some newcomers, one of whom commented that it "may be termed handsome, reared as if by enchantment, in the midst of a wilderness."[33]

At the outbreak of war, there were also women in British North America who were new arrivals from the mother country, for the protection and administration of the colonies in peace and war involved a succession of soldiers and officials, often accompanied by wives and families. From the rocky cliffs of the Gaspé peninsula to the fertile country of the Niagara or the Detroit River, North American life superimposed itself upon the standards and values of proper British society and provided experiences that tested the character and widened the perspective of these British women.

To get to North America, they had first to risk the dangerous North Atlantic. Lady Katherine Sherbrooke, wife of Nova Scotia's lieutenant-governor, made the crossing in 1811 aboard HMS *Manila* and sailed away from a nation for which war was an accepted part of life and in which those under the age of sixteen had never known anything else. The country British women left behind

Upper Canada's backwoods capital. York, shown here in 1804, had expanded somewhat by 1812 to a town of around 600 inhabitants. Its grid pattern of streets led down to the lakeshore and at the western end of the town stood its garrison of British regular troops. The residents of York lived beside the forest and were accustomed to having bears, wolves and other predators in the vicinity. (Painting by Elizabeth Hale. Library and Archives of Canada, C-40137.)

was one where visitors remarked upon its air of prosperity, for although engaged in a seemingly interminable struggle with France, Britain was proud of its self sufficiency, freedoms, system of government, commerce and overseas trade. Whatever their social condition, the British people felt secure, shielded by the might of the Royal Navy. However, by the onset of the Napoleonic Wars the old order in rural areas was starting to decline as the advent of the industrial age meant that machines could do work far more quickly and efficiently than traditional village craftsmen. Britain in 1812 was not only a country at war, it was a country undergoing major social and economic change.

Whether settler, army wife or lieutenant-governor's lady, British women who came to North America were confronted by a vastly different environment. They faced a much more rugged life in a far harsher climate, and new peoples. Most had never before set eyes on the aboriginal peoples, who were a source of abiding interest and the subject of much comment in their correspondence. Adjusting to new faces and new places came more easily to some than others, and most army wives were inured to a life of change and mobility, and to the rough conditions of garrison life abroad. British women who travelled in the more remote areas of the continent also saw the grandeur of the wilderness and nature at its most pristine. It was an environment that challenged them to find within themselves a sense of adventure, and many did. Wives like Elizabeth Procter, wife of Major-General Henry Procter, and Maria Muir, wife of Major Adam Muir of the 41st Regiment of Foot, who chose to accompany their husbands on active service, may have been familiar with the refinements of Harrogate or Tunbridge Wells, but during their time in North America they came to know the savage reality of war in the wilderness and what loyalty to their country in extreme adversity really meant. They also learned something of the native peoples – the annual pattern of their lives and the rituals and ceremonies that gave them access to spirit forces which had power over the growth of crops, the abundance of game and success in battle.[34]

What replaced the former rather settled life of these women from Britain was the unpredictable, the colourful and the primitive. The howl of wolves on a still night or the silhouette of an aboriginal woman skilfully spearing fish on

Braving the Atlantic. This painting of a ship in rough weather gives a sense of how formidable the waves could be during the journey from Europe to North America. The accounts of women who made the crossing tell of fierce storms, vessels in danger of capsizing and passengers fearful for their lives. Despite their harrowing experiences, most people eventually reached their destinations little the worse for their ordeals. (Painting by unknown artist. Library and Archives of Canada, C-126440.)

a moonlit river were far removed from riding through Hyde Park Gate in a hackney coach or sitting beneath rose-covered arbours in the "land of caps and bonnets, kings and queens, dukes, rogues and princes."[35]

As war descended upon them in 1812, most women in North America knew their lives would soon be subject to events beyond their control. Abigail Adams had no doubt about the issues at stake. As she wrote, "we have our firesides, our comfortable habitations, our cities, our churches and our country to defend, our rights, privileges and independence to preserve."[36] Beliefs were not that much different in British North America, where many feared an invasion of their thinly-populated country, and newer American immigrants felt torn between the nation they had left and the one in which they were now living. For most British North Americans, however, the matter was quite simple – they would do what had to be done to preserve their colonies, freedom and way of life.

Given the vast distances of the continent and the slow communications, news of the declaration of war took some time to spread. Louise Pothier, wife of Montreal-based fur trader Louis-Toussaint Pothier, was better informed than many as her husband and son had regular dealings with the Northwest Company, the great fur trading enterprise whose astute directors had been keeping a close eye on the American political barometer. In York, Anne Powell, a judge's wife, had also kept a weather eye on events, and to her, the signs had been ominous for some time. The previous year she had remarked on the "uneasy suspense upon the present state of politics" and the approaching crisis which she regarded as likely to "determine the fate of our Governments."[37] By early 1812, she was so filled with an uneasy dread of war that her daughters, who were "making shoes, altering dresses and endeavouring to economize" for a forthcoming dance, provided her with much-needed diversion.[38] The news of war, which was taken from Queenston to York, spread quickly through the provincial capital. It created anxiety and confusion, but not panic. "Heard that the Congress had declared War against us," wrote one inhabitant, describing how all York was "in alarm" and "every one's countenance wore the mark of surprise."[39]

Hundreds of miles to the east, the people of St. Andrews, New Brunswick, learned of the war from their American neighbours in Eastport, across Passamaquoddy Bay. Friendly relations had long existed between these two communities and after war was declared, the inhabitants of Eastport voted unanimously to maintain good relations with the folk who lived in New Brunswick.

Louise Pothier was married to Louis-Toussaint Pothier, a well-known personality in the fur trade. His connections with the Northwest Company, whose directors took precautions to safeguard shipments of furs as war approached, meant that Louise probably knew of the outbreak of hostilities earlier than many Canadian women. Hardly had the news broken than her son, Jean-Baptiste, was busy forming a corps of *voyageurs*, which took part in the capture of Fort Michilimackinac in August 1812. (Portrait by unknown artist. Library and Archives of Canada, C-39922.)

On both sides of the boundary line people were determined to "live on as amicable terms as the state of affairs would allow."[40] The commander of the British garrison at St. Andrews immediately sent word to Major-General Sir Martin Hunter, the lieutenant-governor of New Brunswick, at Fredericton, the provincial capital. "What may not a day bring forth!" was the reaction of his wife, Jean, on 25 June 1812 when she learned the news. The previous evening, the Hunters had entertained guests for dinner, and when the possibility of war was mentioned, "those who gave an opinion on the subject were sure 'Jonathan would not declare war.'"* No sooner had the Hunters retired to bed, than at "one [in the morning] we were knocked up by an express from St. Andrews to inform the General war was declared at Washington on the 17th [actually the 18th]," recorded Lady Hunter.[41]

From Fredericton, Hunter forwarded the news to Nova Scotia's lieutenant-governor, Lieutenant-General Sir John Sherbrooke, at Halifax. On Sunday 28 June 1812, he and his wife were enjoying a pleasant day at their country cottage. As Lady Katherine Sherbrooke wrote in her journal, after a leisurely walk in the garden and a short evening boat trip, "just before ten o'clock, dispatches arrived

---

* "Cousin Jonathan" or "Jonathan Yankee" was period slang for Americans in common use by Britons and Canadians during the War of 1812. The implication was that Americans were rude, bumptious country cousins of the more sophisticated members of the English-speaking world.

... to acquaint Sir John that the Americans had declared War against us on the 17th inst."[42] Lady Katherine rose at dawn the following morning and accompanied her husband on an inspection tour of the defences of Halifax. Although she rarely included remarks of a personal nature in her journal, such was the gravity of the situation that she was moved to write, "I felt very melancholy and uncomfortable," and that it was "hard" to shake off the "gloomy idea that had taken possession of my mind in consequence of the state of public affairs."[43]

Lady Catherine Prevost, wife of Lieutenant-General Sir George Prevost, Governor-General and commander-in-chief of British North America, learned the news at Quebec on 23 June. Her seventeen-year-old daughter, Anne Elinor, remembered being "summoned in the midst of my French lesson" to hear "an important piece of intelligence: – 'America has declared War against England.'"[44] Another local resident, Elizabeth Hale, the wife of a British officer, recollected that this latest intelligence left her feeling "in a very unpleasant state" and with plenty of cause for anxiety. The possibility of war and what Elizabeth described as the "impertinent free & easy manner of Yankeys" had long been topics of discussion.[45]

When word of war reached the St. Lawrence River, "the greatest alarm was immediately created on both sides of the lines, from mutual fears of hostile incursion from the other side of the boundary."[46] With the Niagara and St. Lawrence Rivers forming part of the border between the two belligerents, the new state of affairs was a total departure from the customary life of the local people, who had a long-standing tradition of trading, meeting and socializing across the border. Being suddenly cast as enemies was hard to accept, and produced fear and great discomfort in communities that were "in the habit of friendly intercourse, connected by marriage and various other relationships."[47]

Many Canadians living near the border began to move out of range of possible fighting. In late July 1812 an American newspaper reported that on the opposite side of the Niagara River,

> expecting a descent from the American army, the Canadians have, for ten days past, been removing their families and effects from the river into the interior. At Newark, Queenston, and other villages on the river, there are no inhabitants except a few civilians and officers and soldiers.[48]

Along the St. Lawrence, although many on both sides of the river knew each other well, they grew watchful of one another. It soon became clear how their lives had changed when, late in June 1812, eight schooners left Ogdensburg harbour in an attempt to escape upriver into Lake Ontario. An observant resident on the Upper Canadian side saw them and quickly gathered a group of volunteers to pursue the vessels. Two were taken unarmed and without resistance, and the "emigrant families" aboard, who had hoped to escape to distant parts, were "set on an island, and the vessels burned."[49]

On the whole, the people of the Canadas were "not pleased," wrote one woman, anxious at the prospect of their country "being devastated by fire and sword, of which they already had had a foretaste,"[50] a reference to the Revolu-

EASTERN NORTH AMERICA
IN 1812

tionary War. Those too young to remember that earlier conflict were scared at the prospect of what lay ahead. Among them was Margaret Nelles, who lived with her family at Grimsby in the Niagara area. As she remembered: "We were frightened at the declaration of war and how awfully the cannon sounded and what a fearful time it was when my father, who was a Colonel, and brother an officer in the same regiment, had to go out to defend the frontier."[51]

British regular troops were deployed to areas of strategic importance and their places filled by militiamen. As orders circulated for militia volunteers to turn out at short notice, Canadian housewives hid their valuables and checked their stocks of provisions. There was much to do but this helped distract women from the worry they felt about the safety of husbands, sons and friends who faced the prospect of battle and possible death or injury.

The anxiety many Canadians felt at the outbreak of war was shared by their American neighbours, now enemies. It being clear that the border areas, – although far removed from the causes of the war, – would be a battleground because of their proximity to British territory, many living near the border could only "lament that folly has found new victims."[52] At Fort Niagara on the Niagara River, one of the daughters of Dr. Joseph West, the American army surgeon stationed there, remembered that after they heard the news, "sleep was banished from all eyes for the remainder of that night."[53] At dawn, she was aware of the sound of "the artificer's hammer" at work as cannons were placed in position and "company after company of militia" came pouring in from all quarters, wearing "all sorts of uniforms, and as raw and undisciplined as ever." The families of the officers at the fort were sent into the surrounding country for safety, and on their way they passed a hundred or more Tuscarora warriors, all "powerful, active young men, decorated with their war paint and armed with tomahawk and hatchet," who had turned out to support the republic.

As fortifications were hastily erected and efforts made to put on a show of force to match that of their new enemies across the river, quiet Niagara villages were transformed into military rendezvous points. Days and weeks of mustering the militia followed, with men called out *en masse* as they waved goodbye to anxious wives, mothers, sisters, fiancées and daughters. The sound of fife and drum, the rattling of the wheels of baggage wagons, the crackling of muskets being fired at weapons practice, and the sight of troops arriving, parading and leaving, became commonplace as men prepared for war.

There was great fear among many Americans that aboriginal warriors allied to the British would "fall upon the settlements, then young and feeble, and lay waste the country with fire and tomahawk."[54] For a time, "every breeze that came from Canada, or from the west" brought with it disturbing rumours and at the slightest alarm, "the timid would flee into the woods." Most were wives, children and older people who had been left without the protection of their menfolk, and who were seen,

> hastening off and leaving their houses open and the table spread with provisions, and fleeing on horseback and on foot, in carts, and in wagons, laden with such articles of value as they were able to snatch in their haste; some driving their flocks and herds before them.[55]

Although on both sides there was an exodus away from the border in the opening months of war, the arrival of British and American regular troops did

Amherstburg, 1804. Amherstburg, on the Detroit River not far from Detroit, was home to Fort Malden, one of the British military posts that guarded the frontier between Upper Canada and the United States. When war broke out in 1812, the citizens of the two communities began to eye each other with suspicion, as was the case at many places along the frontier, even though the border peoples had long been trading and intermarrying with one another. (Painting by Peter Rindlisbacher, courtesy of the artist.)

A lady in her own right. In Lower Canada, the *Code civil* permitted women a greater say in their affairs than under English Common Law. This portrait shows Marie Louise Renée de Charnay, co-seigneur of Kamouraska, who was head of her family with her husband, and shared the ownership and management of the family estate. (Painting by François Baillargé, 1801-1802. National Gallery of Canada, Ottawa. Photograph by René Chartrand.)

a great deal to allay fears and it was not long before some civilians returned to their homes. The family of Dr. Joseph West was among the first to come out of hiding, and while the doctor continued his work at Fort Niagara, his wife and daughters lived at a nearby farm. There, as his eldest daughter recalled, they remained "unmolested, except occasionally by the enemy landing from their boats and plundering the hen roost."[56]

British troops were clearly visible across the Niagara River at Queenston as they fortified the wooded heights above that village. Soon there was a redoubt in place with two or three long-range artillery pieces that could strike at Lewiston on the American bank of the river. These, and other neighbouring border communities such as Brockville and Ogdensburg, Buffalo and Fort Erie, observed each other closely but there was little outward evidence of hostility. As one American soldier stationed at Lewiston wrote to his wife in mid-August 1812, "there is as much appearance of peace as war at present."[57]

When news of war reached Detroit, gateway to the Michigan Territory, it brought a "dreadful sensation," remembered Abigail Snelling, wife of an American army officer stationed there. Detroit had a stockaded fort with a sizeable garrison and hitherto, the townspeople had gone about their business confident that the 300 or so troops of the post could defend them from "any hostile efforts of the Indians, or of an enemy unprovided with artillery."[58] Nevertheless, some local citizens had anticipated the conflict, among them Amy Hawkins Witherell, wife of Judge James Witherell of the Michigan Territory, who took their children to the safety of the family home in Vermont. With a British garrison posted not far away at Fort Malden on the opposite side of the Detroit River, the inhabitants of the two towns, like other border communities, began to eye one another with suspicion. When the citizens of Detroit saw the ferryman who regularly carried people across the river taken prisoner by the British, civilians started to take sides and it was not long before "brothers seemed arrayed against each other" in a new and uncomfortable way.

Apart from Detroit, the military outposts of the Northwest frontier and their attendant civilian communities were quite accustomed to tensions between the settlers and the aboriginal peoples. From Fort Dearborn at the southern end of Lake Michigan, to Fort Wayne at the junction of the St. Joseph and Maumee Rivers, to Forts Ball and Stephenson on the Sandusky River, the white population lived in an almost constant state of alert against attacks from aboriginal bands who had resisted the tide of settlement. These peoples had listened attentively to the words of the charismatic Shawnee leader Tecumseh, whose dream was to create a native confederacy from British territory in the north to the Gulf of Mexico in the south. It was this dream that led Tecumseh to ally himself with Britain at the outbreak of war.[59]

Another influential figure who rallied aboriginal support for Britain in the Northwest was Robert Dickson, a Scot who ran a trading post at Lake Traverse in the upper Minnesota Sioux country with his Sioux wife, To-to-win. As war began to appear likely, Mascotapah or "Red Hair Man," to use Dickson's aboriginal name, was moved by a combination of "loyalty, altruism, and economic self-interest" to contribute to the defence of the Canadas.[60] With his extensive knowledge of the region and the language and customs of its aboriginal nations, he solicited their support for the British. As tension heightened in the area, the sense of dread felt by American troops and their families at the isolated military outposts in the Northwest, grew with it.

Americans living along the eastern seaboard became increasingly concerned about the prospect of a British invasion and the arrival of the Royal Navy. Near Bladensburg, Maryland, plantation owner Rosalie Stier Calvert took such a threat seriously. "Our warships are going out, preparations are being made, etc. All this is nothing yet," she wrote to her father, convinced all the same that, "the English can, with some fishing line, take all our frigates."[61]

As the level of anxiety rose, better informed members of the population took a more optimistic view of events and at Lamberts Point, Virginia, Elizabeth Kennon wrote to a friend, ever since the declaration of War, there has been a terrible commotion in the town; the people are so much alarmed already that many have begun to remove their goods and chattels out of the way of the Enemy; they appear to think the British have Aladdin's Lamp; or something as wonderful with which they can transport an army here so quick. They surely forget the little Pond they have to ferry their troops over; altho' in no laughing humour, I cannot help smiling at their folly.[62]

At the same time Mrs. Kennon, a widow with two sons and a son-in-law serving in the United States Navy, was not without anxiety for her own family and acknowledged,

the drum is at this moment rattling in my ears and reminding me that "War's dreadful blast is blown" and that there will be "many sweet babes fatherless and many widows mourning" before it is concluded. Alas "what havoc does ambition make in this poor world."[63]

Some distance away in Washington, at the eye of the breaking storm in June 1812, Dolley Madison, wife of President James Madison, appeared as serene and bright as ever. She knew full well that her husband had no wish for this war, which he had hoped to avoid, and had been concerned about the possibility for some time past. "The world seems to be running mad, what with one thing and another," had been her despairing comment to her sister, Anna, a few months earlier, adding that, "the war business goes on slowly, but I fear it will be sure."[64] In May she was still hoping that the "dreaded epoch may be some distance off."[65] Now, alas, it had arrived and she recognized that her husband faced great difficulties, one of the biggest being the fact that with the New England states adamantly against it, the republic was divided over the decision to go to war.

In this region the conflict was extremely unpopular from the outset. It was clear that not only would it have an adverse impact on maritime trade, already blighted by the prewar embargoes, and upon the economy and relations with British provinces to the north, but there was considerable sympathy for Britain in her prolonged struggle against France. Sarah Smith Emery of Newburyport, Massachusetts, remembered how tidings of war reached the town on 4 July 1812 amid the annual Independence Day celebrations. On what should have been a festive occasion, many in Newburyport found little to be cheerful about, including Sarah's husband, David, who ran a tavern close to the town. David Emery remarked gloomily, "wife, I fear I am ruined." Many years later, Sarah admitted honestly that at the time, "I did not share in this despondency," for

24

she did not fully appreciate his concern over the possible effect of war on their business.[66]

America's divisions were very evident. Within President James Madison's own Republican party there were two factions: some members opposed the war loudly while others, including a group of men whose fiery pro-war oratory had earned them the nickname "War Hawks," were just as vociferously in favour of it. At the same time, while Southern newspapers like the *Richmond Enquirer* delighted in announcing that "the government have assumed a stand to redress the wrongs and vindicate the rights of their country," and characterized Britain as "our ancient and inveterate foe," in northern states, where the opposition Federalist party held sway, many were ready to express their vehement opposition to the idea of war.[67] The call for men to join the militia in New York State's western district, which included the Niagara area, was answered by a published statement in a local newspaper asking, "why should our swords be drawn in redress of injuries which we have never felt?"[68] Furthermore, commented the author,

> the renown which you seek is not our renown ...... The wrath of God precedes it, and desolation follows in its footsteps. It delights in blood, and in fields strewn with carnage, in the tears of the widow, and the plainings of the orphan perishing of want and disease.[69]

The outbreak of hostilities, a nation deeply divided, a governing Republican party at odds with itself, and the task of winning another election in 1812, posed daunting challenges for James Madison, and behind her mask of cheerfulness, his wife, Dolley, was in a sombre frame of mind.

While Americans wondered about the strength and intent of their new adversary, across the border the inhabitants of the British provinces feared an unwelcome invasion of their thinly populated land. On both sides of the border, however, most people viewed the war in simple terms. They would defend to the best of their ability the land, life and freedom they cherished. As many civilians agonized over what lay ahead, British, Canadian and American troops and their aboriginal allies awaited their orders, and the commencement of the struggle that would determine the fate and the future of the North American continent.

The family / la famille. Prominent Quebec merchant John William Woolsey poses with his wife, Julie Lemoine Woolsey, five of their children and an elderly female relative in a portrait painted in 1809. John Woolsey served as a militia officer in the War of 1812, reaching the rank of major, and was away on active service for extended periods throughout that time. Many wives like Julie Woolsey had to cope with the duties and responsibilities thrust upon them in the absence of their menfolk, and relied upon the help and support of other family members. (Painting by William M. Berczy, National Gallery of Canada, Ottawa. Photograph by René Chartrand.)

CHAPTER ONE

"The faithful wife, without debate." The Woman's World in 1812

Hard is the fortune of all womankind
She's always controlled, she's always confined.
Controlled by her parents until she's a wife,
Then a slave to her husband for the rest of her life[1]

The lives of women in North America in 1812 were shaped not only by nationality, culture and tradition, but also by their environment, which moulded their lifestyle to a considerable extent. Beyond these considerations, a woman's life was largely a reflection of her class, religious beliefs, her husband's work or profession and of prevailing social attitudes. Common to all, however, whether they lived in a garrison, a bustling city or the remote hinterland, was the fact that their daily routine revolved around marriage, home and children. Family life, the success of which depended largely upon both husband and wife fulfilling complementary roles, provided women with a security they could seldom find elsewhere unless they chose a religious vocation.

The price paid for that security was inequality. Almost all white women in North America, where the Common Law prevailed, were subject to a legal system which restricted their economic status and independence, making them effectively chattels of their fathers before marriage and their husbands afterwards.[2] While single women and widows had the same property rights as men – with the exception of the right to vote – married women had no legal rights over property. This meant that control of any wealth or property a woman brought to her marriage was exercised entirely by her husband.[3]

A notable exception to this general rule prevailed in the province of Lower Canada where the legal system was more favourable to women. While they could take no legal action or start a business on their own, and their husbands still had absolute control over family assets, they were subject not to Common Law but to the *Coutume de Paris*, the law governing New France before the British conquest in 1763. This provided for joint ownership and regarded marriage as a partnership, with the wife retaining legal possession of properties received as an inheritance or gift from her parents. She was also invested with the right to half her husband's property and, upon her death, her children could demand half of their father's property as heirs of their mother. Any such claims made by a wife and children were given priority over those made by creditors, and children also had the right to buy back certain assets that had been sold outside the family. Finally, women in Lower Canada had the right to vote, although it was taken from them in the 1830s.[4]

A woman's role in society was clearly delineated as being subordinate to that of men. According to the French philosopher Jean-Jacques Rousseau, the role of women was "to please" and be useful to men and "to make us love and esteem them, to educate us when young and to take care of us when grown up, to advise, to console us, to render our lives easy and agreeable."[5] They were to be "submissive, amiable, and virtuous," to demonstrate in their behaviour that they were happy in their subordination, and to find contentment and personal fulfilment within their own homes.[6] Rich or poor, all women were expected to behave with propriety, and to demonstrate grace, thrift, gentleness and high ideals. Independence of thought was discouraged, and in the intellectual sense little was expected of a woman, as the following poem, published in 1813, illustrates:

> Woman's a book of tiny size,
> Suited to catch the coxcomb's eyes.
> In silks and muslins neatly bound,
> And sometimes neatly gilt around.
> But what is strange in reader's sight
> The book oft stands unletter'd quite!
> The frontispiece is gayly dress'd,
> Blank paper fills up all the rest!!![7]

Their lack of independence, both social and legal, proved difficult for many strong-minded women. Nevertheless, it seems that despite its disadvantages, most favoured marriage over single life, which brought with it social marginalization. Home and family were the *raison d'être* of most women in 1812 and Eliza Rundell, author of *A New System of Domestic Cookery*, published in 1815, advised that the duty of a wife was to "preside over the family, and regulate the income allotted to its maintenance," at the same time stressing the importance of a wife making her home "the sweet refuge of a husband fatigued by intercourse in the jarring world."[8] As his "enlightened companion and the chosen friend of his heart," Rundell assured her readers that if a wife carried out her duties satisfactorily, "happy the man" who was married to her and "blessed are the children who call her mother."

Wife or mother, daughter or sister, housekeeper or servant, the daily routine was constant and in many cases, arduous, leaving little time for being an "enlightened companion" to husbands or fathers. Indeed, it is clear that to survive and prosper in North America, women – even the more privileged – needed to be industrious, resourceful, capable and physically strong, for they had to carry out all their domestic tasks without the aid of today's labour-saving devices, while raising large families in a climate that produced extremes of weather which taxed even the fittest.

Whether inhabiting a mansion or a cabin in the woods, a woman was expected to be chatelaine or mistress of her domain and "the faithful wife without debate."[9] Her days were filled with tireless industry and she frequently undertook most of the work herself, possibly aided by another female family member. In a sizeable home the daily tasks were easier to organize, but for a wife living in a flimsy city tenement or a small log home and faced with preparing food, cooking, washing, drying clothes, spinning, weaving, and mending, often in one room with numerous children around her, it was a different story. And on the frontier, life was dependent upon what could be grown, made or traded.

Economy and attention to all aspects of running a household were considered marks of female efficiency among the rich as well as those of lesser means. This attitude is typified by Gertrude Lewis, wife of Major-General Morgan Lewis, quartermaster general of the U.S. Army during the war. The Lewises owned a "capacious brick house" with outbuildings that stood on a wooded tract of land beside the Hudson River, and Gertrude or "Gitty," as she was affectionately known to her husband, took a "hands on" approach to the running of her home, supervising "every detail of the management of the estate, as well as of the household."[10] According to her son, this capable woman was "the center round which everything revolved, and no member of her family was content until her approbation and co-operation had been secured."

As Gertrude Lewis knew well, paid help was often hard to obtain. North Americans were not accustomed to the kind of mistress-servant relationship common in Britain and Europe, as one foreign traveller discovered when he asked an assistant at a hotel to "be kind enough to tell your mistress that I should be glad to see her." "My mistress, Sir!" came the reply, "I tell you, I have no mistress, nor master either. I will not tell her, Sir, I guess; if you want Mrs. M____ you may go to her yourself, I guess," because "in this country there is no mistresses nor masters."[11]

This attitude differed markedly from customs in Britain, where polite servants were readily available and the lady of the house was not seen wielding a broom or beating a rug. When Lieutenant-Colonel Joseph Gubbins and his wife, Charlotte, arrived fresh from England at Fredericton, New Brunswick, in 1810, they discovered to their consternation that "some of the most respectable and affluent families in Fredericton are occasionally without a female domestic."[12] Furthermore, those hired in the colonies, wrote Colonel Gubbins, "will not submit to be called servants, but help or hireling, and stipulate to dine with the master and mistress whom they call Mr. or Mrs." Such a lack of respect appeared bad enough to the Gubbins, but the general shortage of staff meant that even "slatterns, drunkards or thieves" had to be considered for temporary labour.[13] Some of the domestic staff who worked at various times for another British officer, Major Jasper Grant, and his wife, Isabella, are described as having been "rather sullen," and "much disposed to darkness of character."[14] Among them was a woman named Beck, who was regarded by the major as "so impudent and lazy that she does nothing, and we must say nothing," presumably for the reason that she would have been difficult to replace.[15]

Running any household, and particularly a large one, demanded organizational ability, energy, and determination. Eliza Rundell had further advice to offer on the subject, citing as areas of "not inconsiderable responsibility," a knowledge of prices and accounts, prompt payment of bills, supervising servants, keeping good hours and maintaining a twice-yearly inventory of furniture and china.[16] Rosalie Stier Calvert, mistress of a large residence at Bladensburg, had a reputation as "one of the best housekeepers in Maryland," and whether or not she had read Rundell's book, Rosalie followed its advice, believing in attention to detail, "moderation and prudence" and the ability to economize.[17] She and her husband, like many other southern landowners, had slaves who worked in their plantations and helped in the house and gardens. The Belgian-born Rosalie felt herself at a disadvantage in dealing with her African-American servants compared to her American husband, who had grown up with them. Nevertheless, it was not long before she formed her own

The mistress of Riversdale.
Rosalie Eugenia Stier Calvert, pictured here with her eldest daughter, Caroline Maria, came from a wealthy Belgian family and was married to an American businessman. The Calverts owned several plantations and a beautiful house, Riversdale, near Bladensburg, Maryland. Throughout the war the astute Rosalie managed her household, children, staff and financial affairs with unusual acumen. She described her portrait as an "exact resemblance" of herself. (Oil on canvas by Gilbert Stuart, 1805. Maryland Historical Society, Baltimore, Maryland.)

opinion as to how best to handle them, declaring to her sister that it was not necessary to "treat these people harshly in order to be well served. You must only be firm."[18]

No doubt women like Gertrude Lewis and Rosalie Stier Calvert paid great attention to cleanliness, as did Lydia Sigourney and her mother at their Norwich, Connecticut, home. Lydia's residence was one of the "better class of New England houses" with "two parlors, a bedroom, a spacious kitchen with a wing for a pantry and milk-room" on the ground floor and "five chambers" and a large garret on the second floor.[19] This type of house was often well furnished, with family portraits on the walls, imported carpets, polished hardwood furniture, upholstered sofas, ornaments, candlesticks and perhaps a pianoforte. As Lydia later recalled, she and her mother were "very happy ... in our light and constantly recurring household occupations."[20] They were "up with the lark" and busy with broom and duster to make sure "every apartment was kept in the speckless sanctity of neatness," and the enterprising pair also "papered walls when we chose" and "refreshed the wood-work of our parlors with fresh coats of paint."

Most people lived more simply, but even the most basic dwelling could be made to feel homely, as the following 1813 description of a log dwelling in New York State indicates:

> A supply of wood was neatly piled at one side of the "clean-winged hearth." Over the mantle, which held many small articles useful and ornamental, hung a pair of antlers. Ears of maize, hunks of dried venison and rings of dried pumpkin swung from the smoky ceiling. The bare floor was as clean as hands could make it. A tall clock, reaching from floor to ceiling occupied one corner and a small flax-wheel another. There were a few splint-bottomed chairs, a settle and a home-made table.[21]

Rural dwellers in North America, both recent settlers and long-established farmers, generally lived honest and unpretentious lives. The difficulties of remote living are outlined in the New Brunswick journal of Lieutenant-Colonel Gubbins, in which he mentions the "lonesome and extremely difficult situation" of newer colonists, who were likely to have to endure "the extremes of wretchedness … for some years" before they could have "anything like plenty."[22] It was a challenge to keep animals and poultry alive in the winter and homes could often only be reached along "an execrable track, lately cut through deep swamps encumbered with roots of trees and stumps recently cut down." Travelling in such inaccessible territory carried with it the "shocking" risk of getting lost and "perishing in the vast wilderness."[23]

In the remote Northwest area of the United States life could be dangerous in a different way. Many homes often had thick wooden shutters with apertures instead of windows, as a defence against possible aboriginal attacks, and Mary Ann Brevoort, who grew up in the area, remembered how people were generally afraid to have a fire in the house because of the "delight" of local warriors in "being able to set fire to anything they came in contact with."[24] The only recourse was to "beeswax candles, lighted, and put in one of the water buckets covered with a piece of wood." Life often depended upon improvisation, and Mary's mother cooked using an oven "built of poles and clay." Vegetables had to be buried in the ground in winter to preserve them, making them hard to get at when the ground froze, and when the menfolk brought home game, it had to be hung on a "large spike" in the family's one-room cabin so that it could be dressed.[25]

Women like Mary Ann Brevoort often did their washing in the nearest stream or river and would "sit on a stool, dip the piece in the water, rub on the soap, and pound with a short handled paddle called a "battois."[26] With no running water, women had to fetch what they needed from a lake, stream, spring or the nearest well. Mary Anne Brevoort remembered that her family used to fetch their water using buckets and a wooden yoke "made to fit the shoulders and neck," because "every drop of water which we used, was carried from the river, no matter how far the house stood from it."[27]

The aboriginal peoples lived according to traditions and customs which differed from nation to nation. As an example, the Huron (or Wyandot) dwelt in villages consisting of bark cabins clustered within palisaded walls built by the men. While the men hunted, fished, traded and made weapons, the women did all the domestic work, raised their children with the help of the most senior women, bartered with traders and worked the fields using a system of cultivation, which they also taught their friends, the Ottawa. Many other skills also had to be mastered: the making of clay cooking pots and bark vessels used as dishes; the gathering of berries and nuts, and the winter's supply of fuel; the preparation of hides; the weaving of wicker grain baskets and rush mats for the floors and doorways of their cabins; and the sewing together of strips of bark for their canoes. Such traditional tasks occupied aboriginal women for months on end, but they looked forward to the fall harvest feasts and celebrations, the naming of children born in the past half-year, and the midwinter rites that marked the passing of the old year to the new and the season of darkness to the time of light.[28]

Like the native people, white North Americans who had chosen a life of farming were closely connected to the rhythm of the seasons. For them, the yearly cycle involved growing and harvesting crops, mending fences, tilling the ground without modern machinery, planting seeds by hand, cutting grass with a scythe and reaping grain with a sickle. With the autumn came harvest and Thanksgiving, the milling of grain, the collecting of firewood and the chopping of timber for winter use. Meat, game, poultry, fruit and vegetables were preserved by drying or storing them below ground in a root cellar or in the ground itself. Not a moment was wasted, and the coming of winter brought indoor tasks such as spinning, weaving, sewing, mending and repair work. Some communal activity took place throughout the year, with maple sugar-making in the spring, autumn corn-husking, and bees – occasions when neighbours met to help each other build a barn, make a quilt, spin, or pare apples.

Sarah Smith Emery, who grew up in rural Connecticut, remembered what a day was often like on her family farm. Her mother would get up "in the early dawn" to milk the cows.[29] During breakfast, "the milk for the cheese was warming over the fire, in the large brass kettle," and her aunt and mother took turns making cheese. Then came preparations for dinner, usually served at midday. Afterwards, "the cheeses were turned and rubbed," and if there was "linen whitening on the grass" in the warmer weather, "that must be sprinkled." For the afternoon, Sarah's mother put her in "a clean frock" and dressed herself, usually in blue-checked gingham, "starched and ironed to a nice gloss." During the hot weather, the women often took sewing "to the cool back room" until five o'clock, when the men came in from the fields and tea and food were served. Then the vegetables were "gathered for the morrow, the linen taken in, and other chores done." When sunset came, the cows were brought in from the pasture, milking completed and "the day's labor was ended." At nine o'clock "the house was still, the tired hands gladly resting from the day's toil."[30]

Elizabeth Oakes Prince was the daughter of a family which farmed near Yarmouth, Maine. An "austere plainness pervaded the household," she recalled, but there was also a homeliness, and "no lack of anything."[31] Her family raised and spun flax, and kept sheep for wool, which was dyed, spun and woven on the farm. Elizabeth, her mother and aunts, undertook the milking, weaving and soap-making, cheerfully "singing old ballads" as they did so. There was usually milk, cream and cheese to exchange for other necessary items, and Elizabeth remembered there being "heaps of apples in autumn" and bins of vegetables and barrels of beef and pork carefully stored in the stone cellar. Everything depended upon constant labour, for if the upkeep of a farm and its land were neglected for any reason, hardship would result.

Daughters were expected to help their mothers and the 1815 diary of Louisa Collins, whose family farmed at Dartmouth, Nova Scotia, lists, with rather variable grammar and spelling, the range of her summer and fall tasks:

August the 15
The dairy as usual takes up most of my morning ... and after finishing there I picked a baskit of black currants for Miss Beamish in the afternoon ... then went out and raked hay ... I shall retire early to night for I am tired after my days work.

August the 17
I was very busy all the morning with house work – in the afternoon I was with Mrs Beamish and picked sum berrys.

August the 30
yesterday's work – I was very busy making wine near all day, and butter. In the afternoon I picked sum berrys.

September the 1
This has bin a very busy day with me and all – we had our house to clean … and … I have bin making hay till quite dark.

September the 7
We have had a very large wash to day which keep me very busy.

September the 20
I have bin spinning all day I expect I shall grow like a weed in the shade for I go no farther than my dairy and from there to my spinning room.

October the 12
I have bin very busy nearly all day working till my fingers are sore.[32]

Other autumn work, according to the account of Lydia Sigourney of Connecticut, included cutting and drying fruit for "tarts" and "confections," wrapping apples in paper and preparing quinces "embalmed with sugar."[33] The garret floor of Lydia's house was carefully covered with sheaves of maize, among which were stored beans, pumpkins and potatoes, and herbs for "domestic pharmacopoeia" or distillation.

With such a daily workload – and frequent pregnancies – it is hardly surprising that many women aged rapidly. The burden fell especially heavily upon slave women who, in addition to caring for their families, often undertook hard physical labour in the fields, or worked very long hours in domestic service. Sally Hemings was one of the more fortunate in this respect. She worked as a household servant to Thomas Jefferson and as lady's maid to his daughter Mary (Maria), and although almost forty years of age by the war and the mother of four children ranging in age from six to fourteen, she was described by those who knew her as "very handsome" and "decidedly good looking."[34]

From time to time most country folk visited the nearest village or town. Towns were important as the focus of local and regional commerce and trade, defence and social life, and centres such as York in Upper Canada, Fredericton in New Brunswick and Detroit in the Michigan Territory formed oases of civilization on the frontier. Country wives who could not get to a larger cen-

The market girl of Quebec. Among a farmwife's normal tasks was taking produce to sell at the nearest market. This rather charming representation of a Lower Canadian woman shows her driving her cart dressed in a long skirt, blouse and jerkin, and wearing a wide-brimmed hat. Note the chicken aboard the cart, and a barrel filled with what appear to be cabbages or lettuces. (Painting by E.C. Kellogg. Library and Archives of Canada, C-41717.)

tre often had to rely on their nearest village, where there was usually a general store selling all manner of items. They were fortunate if they found one as well stocked as the "beau ideal of a Country Store" in Connecticut described in the memoirs of an American army officer.[35] This emporium contained "an immense variety of Materials calculated to meet the wants, and suit the fancies of the surrounding population." Bartering was an accepted practice and the shop in question was willing to exchange

> Calicoes – and cloths – and Watches and Brass Jewelry and Hard ware and Crockery ware and Molasses, and Rum and Apple Jack – Methelin and Salt Petre – Gunpowder and Poole Yokes – and all articles that ever bore a Name – for Butter and Eggs and Flax – for Check Linnen and tow Cloth – for Bed Ticking and flannel – for Corn and Wheat and Rye and Oats, and for all things material and immaterial.[36]

Many country people never ventured to the larger cities, believing such places to be synonymous with indulgence and sin. Indeed, a military or naval presence in a major centre, although good for business, was also the cause of much dissipation and disturbance. In ports such as Halifax, a busy staging post for troops arriving from Britain which, if the fleet was in, might have as many as 6,000 service personnel among a civil population of 9,000, there were plenty of unsavoury characters who tended to frequent the area of the docks where taverns, gaming houses and prostitutes were common. With drunkenness, theft and violence rife, it was little wonder that the housewives of Halifax "refrained from hanging out their clothes on a washing day because they saw a soldier about" and would not "venture homeward alone after dark," as "life and property were considered insecure after nightfall."[37]

There were, of course, many who preferred city life, with its easy access to shops and facilities, and opportunities for employment. In the United States, some cities offered women the chance to work in the fledgling cotton and woollen manufacturing industries. Country people might find the factories strange indeed, but did not feel their rural livelihood threatened as in 1812 many city people still subsisted on what their country cousins could produce.

Cities were also social centres, and women who occupied a prominent position in society often found that their daily life was concerned with keeping up appearances. Their wartime activities are discussed in detail later but, generally speaking, such women paid visits and received calls at their homes, entertained guests at dinner parties, hosted receptions, completed their correspondence, read a good deal and pursued private pastimes. Away from the limelight, these women treasured their quiet time. Dolley Madison, the wife of President James Madison, enjoyed her Virginia country house, Montpelier, and Lady Katherine Sherbrooke, wife of Sir John Sherbrooke, Nova Scotia's lieutenant-governor, cherished the time spent at Birch Cove, their country cottage outside Halifax. It provided her and her husband with the opportunity for quiet walks, carriage rides, boat trips and a place to relax from official duties. Katherine Sherbrooke, who used to read aloud to her husband from newspapers, books and novels, was a fan of the works of Jane Austen, noting in her journal for July 1815 that she was part way through *Mansfield Park*, "a novel we were both very anxious to see."[38]

With her keen interest in plants and the natural world, the garden of Birch Cove also occupied much of Katherine's spare time. As she noted the weather and which vegetables were planted, she also recorded varieties of flowers and knew many by their Latin names. Nature continually delighted her, be it in the

Coach travel. Although uncomfortable and sometimes dangerous, by the time of the war coach travel was being developed together with new road systems in the United States. Both there and in the British provinces, where roads were still in a primitive state, travellers seldom had anything complimentary to say about this mode of travel. This illustration shows the first stage from Baltimore to Washington waiting outside an inn. (Gaillard Hunt, *Life in America One Hundred Years Ago.*)

form of "several humming birds in the garden," which appeared to be "most partial to the woodbines," or delightful "sweet peas & Mignonette," picked to display indoors, or "some beautiful Moss," discovered in a wood.[39]

Most women spent much of their time at home and their leisure activities – when they had time for leisure – were limited. For those who liked to read, there were books to be purchased, although the cost put them beyond the reach of many. Newspapers were eagerly perused, especially those from Europe as, ironically, both American and Canadian newspapers paid almost as much attention to the war against Napoleon as they did their own conflict closer to home. In towns and cities, sales of goods and auctions of prize cargoes offered the wealthier members of the population an opportunity to contemplate the purchase of fine furniture, beautiful silks, shawls and clothing, carpets, brandy, and much more. For poorer city women there were occasions to browse in markets or gather with friends at one of the many taverns that acted as meeting places. Throughout the war years, parades and public holidays helped to boost the morale of civilians, Independence Day being one of the most important days of the year for Americans and royal anniversaries forming the major commemorations in the British colonies. More rural families did their best to maintain contact by visiting one another, but isolation was often the rule. As one farmwife declared, "I expect the sun may rise and set a hundred times before I shall see another human that does not belong to the family."[40]

For all that individual circumstances varied, certain things were common to women in both the United States and British North America: visiting friends and relatives; attending Sunday church services; sewing and spinning circles; chatting with friends over afternoon tea; evening games of cards, chequers, chess and backgammon; and dancing and singing – whether folk melodies from "the old country" or the voices of African-American slaves "welding their native chants" upon the white man's hymns, lullabies and folk songs.[41]

With the progress of settlement and thus increased leisure time for the better off, gardening was changing. By the first decade of the nineteenth century, many wealthy people in North America had turned from purely practical gardens to more elaborate designs with an eye to artistic appearance as well as functionality. They strove to recreate the formal garden style popular in England with consolidated spaces, a profusion of ornamental detailing and a mixture of plants, fruit and vegetables. Such gardens were a focus of much interest, but for most people horticulture continued to be a necessity rather than a pleasure. The majority of North American gardens were planted to provide fruit, vegetables and herbs, and were usually constructed in orderly geometric patterns with beds and intersecting paths.

By 1812 a very wide variety of herbs, plants and flowers had been introduced into these gardens, and growers advertised regularly in newspapers. Lydia Sigourney's Connecticut garden contained a courtyard planted with spruce trees and alternate columns of "fragrant eglantine and the luxuriant white rose," and surrounded by three large areas filled with an array of flowers – peonies, amaryllis, damask roses, sweet william, larkspur, pinks and dahlias, to name just a few.[42] A sizeable area was devoted to peach, apple and pear trees, and there was also a vegetable plot, a herb garden for medicinal use and some grape vines.

In the southern states, the climate allowed the growth of more exotic fruits and vegetables, and throughout the continent were to be found not only indigenous plants and flowers, but also those from Europe, South America and the

Far East. English flowers similar to those mentioned by Lydia Sigourney were found alongside tulips from Holland and orange trees from the Mediterranean, but for variety, there surely cannot have been a garden in North America to compare with that of former president Thomas Jefferson. At Monticello, his Virginia home, Jefferson worked to care for his collection of flowers, trees, shrubs and vegetables, aided by his slaves, who undertook the greater part of the manual work, and his daughter, Martha Jefferson Randolph, who also supervised the running of his household.

The first planned gardens at Monticello were nearly twenty years into their maturity by 1812, and Jefferson had garnered specimens from all over the world. Meticulously kept records indicate that there were over ninety different species of trees, seventy different varieties of vegetables, plus shrubs, vines and dozens of herbaceous plants. Martha Jefferson Randolph had only to walk the grounds to see a Kentucky coffee-tree, an Empress tree from China, an English holly tree, figs from France, squashes and broccoli from Italy, peppers from Mexico and magnificently stocked flowerbeds. Constantly collecting and experimenting, Jefferson summed up his own view of gardening when he wrote, "the greatest service which can be rendered [a country] is to add a useful plant to its culture."[43]

To find a garden diary kept by a North American woman of this time is rare, but fortunately the "Garden Book" of Catherine Claus of Newark has survived. Catherine, wife of Colonel William Claus, Deputy Superintendent of Indian Affairs for Upper Canada, was a horticultural propagator as well as a gardener and her notebook, kept from 1806 to 1810, carefully records all that she accomplished in her garden. Catherine exchanged cuttings and seeds with other keen gardeners, and her list of fruit trees indicates that she was successful at propagating specimens including "Mrs. Powell's peach," a reference to Anne Powell, noted paragon of York society. Random entries explain that among her apple trees, Catherine Claus "grafted No. 1 & 2 Newtown Pippins & Spitzenburg from Albany on stocks in the Nursery by the Quince trees" and that she sewed "two beds of peas & one of early Dutch turnips from D. Kerr," who was undoubtedly Dr. Robert Kerr, a neighbour and Mary Clark's father. At times, Catherine also obtained items for her garden from considerable distances and she records both a "New Orleans plum" and a "South Carolina Clingstone" [peach tree] in an inventory of her trees. By 1812, Catherine Claus had a fine, well matured garden.[44] *

* Extracts from Catherine Claus's garden book will be found in Appendix A.

Pole Beans,
Swiss Chard,
Cabbage,
Asparagus,
& Peas

Currants,
Beans & Kale,
Gooseberry,
Lettuce,
Cucumber
& Hops

Small Peach
&
Apple Trees

Squash,
Spinach,
& Flax

Malva Crispa,
Irish Potatoes,
Currants,
Peppers,
Onion,
& Garlic

Pumpkin,
Gooseberry,
Carrots,
Malabra,
Spinach,
Asparagus,
& Okra

Espaliered pears and peach trees growing along the stone walls.
Apple and cherry trees intermingled at the west end of the garden.

Plan of an early nineteenth-century garden. The average garden of this period was not elaborate and certainly not ornamental. Designed to provide fruit, vegetables and herbs, many such gardens were constructed in orderly patterns and contained easy-to-work rectangular beds divided by intersecting paths. In this plan, the beds are planted with fruit and vegetables and the borders provide space to grow flowers for decorative purposes. Fruit trees include free-standing specimens and espaliered varieties of pears and peaches trained to grow along the walls. (Plan by Christopher Johnson.)

Garden produce contributed significantly to meals, which for the majority of North Americans were simple. Lydia Sigourney mentions that her parents believed in "good food, neatly presented" and in the principle of not "living to eat, but eating to live."[45] Another writer on everyday life in North America at that time, however, declared that it was "not the land of the gourmand" and maintained that the diet of many poorer folk was generally bad, with fried food, bread and pastry that was "indigestible enough to ruin the character of the people."[46] Yet another commentator believed that bad nutrition produced "the cadaverous, shambling men" and the "sour-faced, flat-breasted women" who were "met with at every turn of the road in the South and often enough in other parts of the country."

Nevertheless, those housewives who were too sensible to live unhealthily were capable of producing very appetizing fare. One French visitor to Connecticut just before the war enthused over a "superb piece of corned beef, the stewed goose, the magnificent leg of mutton, vegetables in plenty, and at each end of the table an enormous jug of excellent cider."[47] This meal reflected the staple diet of North America, which tended to consist of bread, vegetables and fruits in season, game and fish. Both the white and aboriginal peoples hunted a wide variety of birds and animals such as deer or buffalo (often smoke-dried to preserve it), wild turkeys and pigeons. The aboriginals were also excellent fishermen and it was not uncommon on warm evenings to see them spearing fish by the light of pine burning in metal pots suspended on the top of wooden or iron poles. They often sold their catch at the nearest market or town.

In addition to raising crops, settlers kept livestock for meat, and probably some ducks, geese and chickens for eggs and the pot. In the south, the milder climate made it possible for livestock to thrive year round, and one wartime account by a British naval officer who served in the Chesapeake Bay area notes that "in these parts, the dinner usually consists of good wholesome joints; none of your disguised shoes stewed in beans, as elsewhere; turkeys, hams &c. in profusion."[48] The Chesapeake also produced extremely good garden produce and another newcomer to the Washington area wrote in the summer of 1813 that he had enjoyed an excellent dinner with "green Peas and huge Cucumbers and young Potatoes" and a dessert of "Strawberries as big as grape shot, and cream."[49]

The housewife of 1812 worked much harder than her modern counterpart to prepare food for the table. Her labours included baking bread, preparing wild rice, dressing game, making items such as sauerkraut and apple cider, preserving small fruits, salting, smoking or pickling meat in brine, making butter, cheese, lard, sausages, gelatine and perhaps some kind of home-made wine.[50] Such tasks were time-consuming and labour-intensive: turning a freshly-killed pig into ham, sausages or meat for roasting took several days, and bread, which formed the basis for many meals, took many hours to make. Given that tea and coffee were too expensive for many people, substitutes had to be gathered in such forms as mountain sweet, tansy or cherry bark.

Common household utensils were already being produced in the iron-manufacturing areas of Lower Canada and the Atlantic seaboard of the United States. More affluent households possessed items such as roasting pans, funnels and cheese vats, but the poorer people and those living in remote areas survived with the minimum of everything, and many a winter evening was spent whittling wooden bowls, cups and trenchers – wooden boards upon which food was served or cut.

With wood as the only source of fuel, most cooking was done over an open fire. Pots were hung from hooks on an iron crane or armature, which fitted into a wide chimney in such a way that it could swing in over the fire. The most versatile cooking implement of the day was a kettle, a deep iron pot on legs, which was suspended over the fire by hooks or placed above it on a trivet. Also very popular was the Dutch oven, made of iron with legs and a tightly fitting lid. It was usually positioned on the hearth away from the main fire and used for baking single items such as cakes or puddings. By pre-heating it before the food was placed inside and then covering it with hot coals, which might need to be changed several times during cooking to keep the temperature even, a Dutch oven would cook food steadily. Another implement commonly used for frying food was the spider, shaped like a frying pan but with long legs that allowed it to stand over the fire.

Many of the terms for household items in common use at the time have since disappeared and would be unfamiliar to most modern women. Dictionaries of the colonial period and later, remind us that a "bittlin" was a milk bowl made of pottery, pewter, glass or wood; a "cotterel" was a bar from which pots could be hung over a fire; and a "chaffern" was a vessel for heating water. A "frail" was a basket made of rushes; a "kibble" was a wooden bucket used to draw water from a well; a "runge" was an oval wooden tub with handles; and a "thibble" was the term for a skimmer or spatula.[51]

Meat for roasting was placed on a spit which could be turned while it was cooking, and a brick or stone oven, usually built into the fireplace, was used for baking. Manipulating the fire and placing the cookware correctly were the only ways of controlling temperature and were vital to successful open-hearth cooking. Women had to be very careful, as their long skirts could easily catch fire, and it was not uncommon for a woman to be severely or fatally injured when such accidents occurred. Dampening the hems of aprons and petticoats to make them less flammable was a common practice. Adequate supplies of wood for heating and cooking were vital, but during the war women often found their stores depleted as soldiers sought wood for their campfires.

A housewife was responsible for the quality of food she served and Eliza Rundell had plenty to say on the subject in her guide, *A New System of Domestic Cookery*. The "direction of a table" was a matter of concern, for Rundell believed that a woman must be mindful of "judgement in expenditure, respectability of appearance; and the comfort of her husband and those who partake of their hospitality."[52] In addition to recipes, this book contained information on a range of items, from how to carve a suckling pig or a cod's head, to how to brew strong beer, make blacking or polish for shoes, preserve blankets or prevent a door from creaking.

Cookery books published in England had found their way across the Atlantic. North American editions began to appear just before the turn of the nineteenth century, and while these were sought by wealthier members of society, in the kitchens of countrywomen or frontier housewives recipes tended to be passed from mother to daughter. For those with the money and the desire to offer a refined and generous table, however, *The Art of Cookery Made Plain and Easy* by Hannah Glasse reigned supreme. First published in London in 1747, this book remained a best seller for almost a hundred years, making Hannah possibly the best known cookery writer of the eighteenth and early nineteenth centuries.[53] The 1760 edition, one of twenty printings, presented a veritable cornucopia of recipes and reflected the wonderful variety and diversity of produce available in Britain at that time. The British were proud of Mrs. Glasse and also of another writer, Mary Cole, whose book, *The Lady's Complete Guide; or Cookery in All its Branches*, was among the first to cite ingredients of recipes in a systematic way. The works of these two women were regarded in their home country as among the best sources on the subject.

No doubt a few eyebrows were raised in Britain, therefore, when people learned that the Americans had published their own cookery book in 1796. Entitled appropriately *American Cookery*, its author was Amelia Simmons, about whom little is known. *American Cookery* went through a number of editions, printed variously at Hartford, Albany and several places in the Hudson River Valley, perhaps an indication of where Simmons may have lived.

Borrowing heavily from other sources but adapting American ingredients such as cornmeal, pumpkins and molasses to the English tradition of cooking, Amelia Simmons's book established her as a skilful cook who used herbs, wine, and roasting techniques common in Britain. *American Cookery* was also the first guide to use pearl ash as a leavening agent. In her preface, Amelia explained that it had been written "for the improvement of the rising generation of FE-MALES in America," and that women of means would understand that

> many hints are suggested for the more general and universal knowledge of those females in the country, who by the loss of their parents, or other unfortunate circumstances, are reduced to the necessity of going into families in the line of domestics, and doing those things which are really essential to … them as good wives … and useful … to society.[54]

The 1815 edition of *American Cookery* includes the first known appearance of recipes that later became famous: Johnny Cake, Indian Pudding and Pumpkin Pie. Simmons was also the first person to use the terms "squash" and "slaw," and it was she who suggested serving roast turkey with cranberry sauce, a combination that came to be regarded as quintessentially American.[55]

Collecting recipes, then as now, was popular. Hannah Jarvis, wife of William Jarvis, Upper Canada's provincial secretary and registrar, kept a book containing many recipes and practical hints. She brought some ideas with her from England – how to "make Hams the Yorkshire Way" and "prepare Bread after the London Bakers" – and on her arrival in the provincial capital of York, she began to add new recipes such as "New York Butter Biscuit" and "Rusks Mrs. Powell's Way," another reference to Anne Powell. Hannah's book also contained instructions for preparing home-made wines, spruce and molasses beer, vinegars, sauces, several kinds of yeast and many different cakes, biscuits and pies. A section on household remedies also contains diverse contributions, from "to kill Thistles" to a method to "Purify Vegetable Oil," and a way to make "black Dye, for Silk."[56] *

---

* For a selection of recipes from the cookbooks of Hannah Glasse, Amelia Simmons, Eliza Rundell and Hannah Jarvis, see Appendix B.

Hannah Owen Peters Jarvis (1763-1845), shown here with her daughters Maria and Augusta, was the daughter of a Loyalist Church of England minister from Connecticut who moved to England before the Revolutionary War. In 1785 she married William Jarvis, another Loyalist in exile, and the couple sailed for British North America in 1792. William was appointed provincial secretary and registrar of Upper Canada and the Jarvises decided to make their home at York. While raising her family, Hannah kept a household book containing many recipes and practical hints. After her husband's death, she went to live with one of her daughters but fell on hard times towards the end of her life, enduring her situation with her customary cheerfulness. (Oil on canvas, 1791, by James Earl Raise. Royal Ontario Museum.)

North American food, whether it was a substantial fish stew in Louisiana or Maine, a brace of chickens cooked in Pennsylvania Dutch style, or efforts to reproduce the "roast beef of old England" in the British colonies, presented a variety of cooking styles, as Eliza Rundell would no doubt have noted with interest. In the American Northwest, for example, the *pièce de résistance* of the backwoods menu was, by all accounts, "hog an' hominy," a dish of pork served with corn that had been boiled to remove the hulls, soaked in clear water and cooked until soft.[57] Corn was a popular vegetable in frontier garden plots, and two varieties of cornbread – Johnny cake and pone – were eaten regularly at breakfast and dinner, with cornmeal mush and milk often appearing at supper.

The residents of Washington were known to enjoy similar food and as one visitor noted, the area was known as the "land of Hog homminey & hoe-cake," with inns and taverns serving "homminey at Breakfast, homminey at Dinner & homminey at Supper."[58] Corn in season appeared at meals in British North America, and in September 1812 Lady Katherine Sherbrooke remembered, "for the first time Indian corn being brought to table – it is boiled in the Cobs, and eaten with cold butter."[59] Cornmeal was an important staple food for many aboriginal people, who prepared their version of "small homony" by grinding it with a mortar, boiling it for about half an hour, and eating it without salt or other accompaniment.[60]

In Connecticut, Lydia Sigourney recalled that baked beans were a favourite dish that appeared regularly on the supper table of "every householder who was able to compass its ingredients, at the closing day of the week."[61] Buckwheat cakes and flapjacks were eaten a great deal in the eastern United States, while hot rolls, muffins and biscuits were a standard accompaniment to meals in the southern states. The cooks of Louisiana combined the area's fruit, vegetables, fish and seafood with a range of spices to create dishes in the French or Creole style. Virginian cuisine and hospitality were demonstrated to perfection by Dolley Madison, who knew just how to alleviate the heat of summer with "wine, ice, punch and delightful pine-apples," and who, at her country home, served tasty suppers consisting of "a variety of warm cakes, bread, cold meats and pastry."[62] Her breakfasts tempted guests to "tea, coffee, hot wheat bread, light cakes, a pone, or corn loaf – cold ham, nice hashes, chickens, etc." It was a mode of living characterized by "that abundance, that hospitality, and that freedom, we are taught to look for on a Virginian plantation," said one visitor.

An interesting insight into contemporary diet is provided by the diary of Joseph Willcocks, who resided at York, Upper Canada, before the war. For three years Willcocks faithfully recorded all the items consumed at dinner in the household of Peter Russell, a prominent member of the provincial administration, who was his patron. An analysis of this culinary record makes for interesting reading, for even though vegetables and fruit were available in season, the Russell household ate a huge preponderance of meat dishes. Of the 682 meat dishes recorded in his diary, 434 consisted of beef in various forms (roast, boiled, stewed, corned, hashed, fried, steaks, kidneys, beef steak pie, beef tongue, beef head); 118 were veal; 69 were pork (corned, boiled, roast, ham, bacon rashers, pigs' trotters, cheek, head, livers); and 61 were lamb or mutton (roast, leg, stewed, boiled, hashed, loin chops, breast, pie, broiled, cold, quartered). Willcocks also recorded 192 soup dishes, 116 dishes of poultry, game and eggs, and 101 fish dishes. Of the remaining 148 main course dishes that appear in his record, 97 consisted of hash, 40 of pancakes, 3 of tripe and 2 of sausages.[63]

In contrast to this seemingly never-ending selection of meat, poultry and fish, only 17 vegetable dishes are recorded, mainly asparagus and cabbage. Among the 348 desserts listed, 56 were various puddings and 50 were pies (especially minced pies) or tarts. In the period of almost three years covered by the diary, only one dish of fruit, in the form of melon, is noted. In all, 1,609 dishes appear in Willcocks's diary and nearly half of all meals consisted of meat, hash or pancakes, a diet which today would be regarded as unbalanced and unhealthy.[64] *

For official entertaining, North American hostesses strove to impress. At the president's house in Washington, for example, Dolley Madison liked to offer a combination of North American and European dishes. Although she had a natural preference for her favourite Virginian recipes, Dolley nevertheless ensured that her chef made every attempt to include items of haute cuisine and her official dinners, served on handsome Sèvres china decorated with a bold black, gold, orange and white border, were always abundant and lavish. Sarah Seaton, who arrived in Washington in 1811, recorded that her first dinner party at the Madisons was "very fine," with many "French dishes, and exquisite wines."[65]

---

* The analysis of meals consumed in the Russell household between 1800 and 1802 will be found in Appendix C.

When it came to clothing, the average North American woman had little enough time or money to attend to dress beyond functional garments. Outside major urban centres, fashion was not of primary importance and to be a little out of date in style was merely the result of a practical sense of values. Clothing, usually handmade of homespun and woven materials such as plain, striped or checked wool or linen, was made to last and was mended and restyled to extend its lifespan. Many women owned only one dress at any given time and if they could afford a "best dress" of cotton or even silk, it was often the only thing of value they possessed. Almost without exception the early nineteenth-century housewife was able to sew well enough to make clothes for herself and her family, as well as to alter or repair hats, and knit stockings, gloves and shawls. Homemade clothing was often very well produced. Indeed, one visitor to Upper Canada during the war noticed that,

> the people here dress well at all times, but when they go abroad, or on the Sabbath, they dress very fine ... I do not mean that fancied fineness studied and practised in large cities and populous places – such as jewels, rings, ribbons, powder, paint, and the like; but with garments of the finest stuffs, with but few trinkets of any kind. The most of their clothing is of their own manufacturing.[66]

For those with time and money there was satisfaction in being able to select the latest fabrics with which to make new apparel. In Maine, Elizabeth Oakes Prince remembered that most of her family's clothing was made at home from "fine linens," or "checked and striped ginghams, broadcloths."[67] The yearly visit from "a cheery shoemaker" and periodically from a tailoress, enabled shoes and finer outfits to be acquired. In Virginia in 1814, Sally Sinclair, wife of Captain Arthur Sinclair of the U.S. Navy, asked a friend visiting Richmond to purchase a few items for her, including:

> 8 yards of six quarter cambrick; fine ... 3 pair of shoes by the inclosed measure; one black the other green, the third buff ... 6 yards of dimity ... half a yard of white crape, and three quarters of a yard of white satin ... 2 yards of plain silk lace about an inch and a half wide ... 6 yards of white satin ribbon ... ¾ of a yard of pretty grave silk, cinnamon colour if to be had.[68]

Sally was clearly planning to make dresses or have some made, and to change the lace trimmings and ribbons on existing gowns and bonnets, thereby giving them a new look. Her mother, Elizabeth, also requested items for herself, including "a checked Italian silk such as will suit my age and widowhood," and "three pounds of spun cotton … of a proper fineness for knitting common stockings."[69] At her home on the Hudson River the very able Gertrude Lewis was so adept at sewing that she made all her own clothes, even though she had the means to purchase them. It seems that "there was scarce an article in the wardrobe of a man or woman that she could not make herself or direct another how to make," and her "accurate eye and steady hand were of incalculable value to her family."[70]

Regional, climatic and cultural differences influenced modes of dress but ordinary women often wore a simple shift tied at the waist or a coarse linen or cotton chemise covered by a loosely cut bodice.[71] Skirts were ankle-length or above and full, and for added warmth a woman might wear two or three petticoats. In addition there might be a shawl or apron and a hooded cloak for outdoor wear. The French-Canadian *habitant* women of Lower Canada made dresses, short jackets, petticoats and camisoles from their own woven materials, with smocks for indoor wear and cloaks and bonnets for the outdoors. In the southern United States, the warm temperature dictated the use of cotton or other light fabrics for gowns, while the style of settlers in the Northwest long remained a cross between their own traditional clothing and that worn by the aboriginal people. "Linsey coats and gowns" were the "universal dress" of women in early times while men's attire was "partly Indian," with breeches or leggings, and moccasins instead of shoes.[72]

The dress of aboriginal women varied according to the traditions of their peoples. In addition to sewing their costumes, aboriginal women were skilled at beadwork and porcupine-quill embroidery, producing exquisite designs to adorn pouches, moccasins, boots, dresses, skirts, jackets and other items. There were also forms of decoration using feathers, fish skins and appliqué in furs. In some traditions a deity known as Spider Woman was identified as the originator of needle arts, with special symbolic signs said to have been passed by her to women in dreams. An oral tradition preserved among the northern aboriginal peoples attributed such talents as a special gift from the Great Spirit to the first native woman.

High fashion was beyond the reach of most women but society ladies of means sought to follow prevailing European styles of dress, and for those in the public eye, it was important to appear fashionably attired. During the War of 1812, Paris was at the leading edge of fashion, with London following closely behind, and news of the latest styles was eagerly seized upon when it reached

North America, often via letters, newspapers and popular illustrated fashion magazines such as *La Belle Assemblée*. The most fashionable women during the period were seen wearing the high-waisted narrow lines of the Empire style which characterized the period, usually made of a fine material such as muslin or silk. Because the desired effect of the new style was somewhat daring, with diaphanous white muslin clinging in the manner of classical sculpture, women could only wear the briefest of underclothing and many young ladies went without corsets and stays. It was considered too revealing and *décolleté* for the more conservative, and only the most confident of North American women would appear thus attired.[73]

The dedicated female follower of fashion wore different dresses at different times during the day – morning, afternoon and evening – and for different activities such as walking, riding, afternoon tea, card parties, dances and balls. A considerable range of accessories was needed to complete these outfits: gloves, parasols, muffs in winter, cashmere shawls, tunics, kid or silk slippers, boots, bonnets, and turbans or ostrich plumes for evening wear. There was also a passion for jewellery, gems and elegant embroidery, with newspapers advertising the arrival of such items as "very elegant Gold Neck Charms," "Jet Ear Rings" or "Ladies Tortoiseshell and common Hair pins."[74] Such lavish taste and the rise in interest in European fashions was condemned by American moralists, one of whom lamented the fact that "the lowest and most contemptible part" of female pride had become "a fondness for their persons, a desire of beauty, and a love of dress."[75] (For additional information on women's fashions, see the pictorial essay which follows this chapter.)

Fine fashions, much admired as they were, counted for little when a woman was faced with a domestic crisis. Sickness or complications in pregnancy were problems that, in the absence of a husband, a woman often had to handle with little or no help. Inasmuch as disease and sudden death were facts of life, women were accustomed to such challenges. Living in a city was no advantage, for there was a dread of epidemics brought in by ships. Yellow fever appears to have been one of the worst, striking centres like Philadelphia and New York annually and spreading as far north as Portland, Maine. Typhoid also appeared and in the summer of 1813, it struck one of Rosalie Stier Calvert's plantations in Maryland. Rosalie, her children and three house servants caught it, and she lost a daughter at the tender age of seventeen months. "I hope that we shall never again experience another summer or illness so terrible," she wrote to her

Tending the sick. At a time when many people lived far from such medical help as existed, most women were experienced at nursing their families and those of neighbours. In this illustration, friends and family are caring for a sick mother and her baby. (Drawing by George Balbar from Bob Foley, *The Niagara Story, Volume 1*, reproduced by permission of the author.)

father, only to contract the same disease again the following year so badly that she almost died.[76]

Smallpox, tuberculosis, rheumatism, pneumonia and "lake fever" in the north (later recognized as malaria) were frequently encountered, and in the days before professional nursing and the discovery of the causes and proper cures of these and other maladies, women were expected to know how to care for the sick. Some worked as healers and midwives, using herbal and home-based remedies, but most women at some time or other nursed their own families and helped their neighbours. Treatments proven to be beneficial by experience were often passed on, and Rebecca Almon of Halifax received a tip from her aunts in Boston that "drinking freely of a strong concoction of spanish sarsaparilla, has been found to be an excellent remedy for the rheumatism."[77] Newspapers advertised patent medicines, and one of the widest ranges available throughout the war came from Messrs. Michael Lee and Company of New Orleans. That firm's list of products included "Lee's Infallible Ague and Fever Drops," "Lee's Elixir," "Lee's Worm Destroying Lozenges," "Lee's Ointment for the Itch," "Lee's Tooth-ache Drops" and "Lee's Grand Restorative of Mustard."[78]

There were, by this time, male doctors practising and in places with a military garrison, the services of army surgeons could sometimes be procured by local civilians. Many people, however, still preferred to rely on their own treatments or the services of a woman working as a healer, and it was often only in extreme emergencies that a doctor might be summoned, even though members of the medical profession in larger cities were beginning to perform operations that saved lives. Robert Gourlay, a contemporary chronicler of the opinions of Upper Canadians, published the results of a questionnaire about midwifery he sent to the settled areas around York and Niagara. It seems that most residents of these districts did not see the need for a doctor in their area. "We have hitherto been blessed with so healthy a climate as to require little or no aid from medical men," they said, the nearest physician being located six miles away with a practice that was "none too lucrative from the country twelve miles round."[79] Much medical treatment still revolved around bloodletting and purging, and with their limited knowledge it is doubtful whether many physicians in the first two decades of the nineteenth century succeeded in treating familiar complaints any better than did healers or those using home remedies.

The aboriginal peoples were known for their healing powers and allowed instinct to guide them in administering herbal and other cures.[80] Before the war an American woman, Mrs. Stoddard, received help from the local aboriginal people when she and her husband were taken ill with influenza and their treatment, known as the "Indian sweat," involved digging holes in the ground and filling them with hot stones over which water was poured. The sick person was placed close to the steam, covered with blankets and given hot drinks. White people had faith in native remedies and one wartime officer wounded in the thigh received help from a Shawnee healer sent to him by the warrior chief, Tecumseh. The inflamed wound healed well, using "nothing but herbs."[81]

A major part of a woman's duty, wrote Eliza Rundell in yet another pronouncement on what was expected of a good wife, was the rearing of "a healthy progeny in the ways of piety and usefulness."[82] Among white women, childbirth at this time was regarded, not without reason, as a hazardous business but it was worse for slave women, many of whom lived under very difficult conditions. At that time, women had few birth control measures available apart from abstaining from marital relations. Condoms made from sheep's bladders and vaginal sponges were in use, but as a protection against venereal disease, not for contraception, and the average woman spent almost all of her earlier married life either pregnant or nursing children.[83] Endemic diseases and lack of knowledge about illness and infection resulted in a high mortality rate for mothers and newborn across North America, and it was all too common to find doleful entries in the diaries of many women such as the following: "departed this life the wife of Mr. Seth Abbott, March 17; was buried with her infant in her arms, which died a few hours previous to her death."[84] Another, on a grave at Grafton, Vermont, is a sad epitaph to Rebecca Park, who died in 1803 at the age of forty.

> Behold and see as you pass by
> My fourteen children with me lie
> Old or young you soon must die
> And turn to dust as well as I.[85]

During pregnancy, most mothers-to-be had little time for rest and received no antenatal care as they could not escape the fatigue of the relentless daily round. General debility in pregnancy was not uncommon, and malaria was a major cause of miscarriages because quinine, administered to help treat it, was an abortificient and could stimulate the uterus. Usually the most dramatic problem for pregnant women was preeclampsia or eclampsia. Physicians, not knowing the cause, would treat it dramatically with measures that included cold water or ice applied to a shaven head, extensive bleeding and mustard baths followed by doses of calomel. If a baby was stillborn, or if problems such as convulsions or haemorrhage occurred after delivery, it was cause for great concern because of the poor remedies available.[86]

When the time came for a woman to have her baby, some of those recently arrived from Europe and unused to the idea of neighbours delivering their babies, went to a city for the birth. The majority, however, monitored their own pregnancies and delivered their offspring at home, usually attended by a local midwife. The importance of cleanliness during a delivery was recognized even though there is seldom mention of boiling instruments or the use of sterile cloths. Information exists on some of the common procedures at that time, including the use of "several drops of opium" and camomile tea to lessen pain during labour,[87] although the use of laudanum or opium for pain relief was not always favoured as drowsiness could impede delivery.

Among the books then available was *A Treatise on the Management of Pregnant and Lying in Women* by Dr. Charles White, published in England in 1793. White emphasized that in general it was advisable to study the natural progression of each birth and, if possible, to "leave things to nature."[88] If a healthy young woman found herself in labour alone and without assistance, White advised her in the early stages to walk and rest when "a pain should oblige her to lie down."[89] If necessary, a purgative was administered to empty the bowels.

Positions in labour varied, with women encouraged to walk around and to keep active as long as possible. Squatting seems to have been common during the pushing stage. There is mention in one study of women being told to lie on their left side during labour with their knees drawn up to their abdomen, their feet resting against a bedpost and their legs separated by a pillow. This kind of horizontal position differed from the centuries-old tradition of kneeling or remaining upright.[90] Dr. White favoured "resting on the hands and knees" and "standing, sitting, hanging by the arms between two persons, half sitting and half lying, either upon the bed or on the knee of an assistant" in "slow, tedious labours."[91] At the same time, doctors on the Atlantic seaboard of the republic were beginning to use instruments to hasten delivery and manage difficult births. Several chapters of White's book deal with complications of childbirth arising from factors such as "tender constitutions," hereditary disorders, "improprieties of dress" and "indolence and improper diet."[92]

If she lived in an isolated place it was not unusual for a woman to be alone in labour, especially during the war, and to deliver her own baby. If she was fortunate enough to have help with a birth, female members of the family or neighbours usually remained in the house to comfort a mother during her labour and lying-in, and to help with the domestic chores until she was able to resume such tasks herself. A reasonable period of rest was considered normal and could be as much as ten days for farm women, whose workload was considerable.

The presence and experience of other women at childbirth was valued, and

Chippawa mother and child. An aboriginal mother prepares to nurse her infant, who is strapped securely into a carrying board. In aboriginal society, although males had a dominant public role, women wielded a great deal of influence behind the scenes as most aboriginal nations used consensus among their adults members as a way of arriving at a course of action. (Thomas McKenney and James Hill, *History of the Indian Tribes of North America*, 3 vols., Philadelphia, 1837-1844.)

together with the assistance of herbs or a medical book, stood many mothers-to-be in good stead. However, in the more conservative southern states, there was some resistance to change or exposure to the more progressive medical ideas and obstetric texts circulating in the northern states. In this region slaves and free black women fulfilled an important role as midwives, colour being of little significance when skilled help was needed. Rosalie Stier Calvert recorded that for one of her pregnancies, she had the services of "an old negress ... who is highly regarded, I liked her so much that I wanted only her."[93]

Childbirth customs among the native peoples varied according to whether they lived in small or large groups, inhabited communities or were nomadic. Attitudes towards birth seemed to be "hopeful rather than fearful," and according to one observer in Upper Canada, birth was "in general a very easy matter among Indian women, cases of danger or death being exceedingly rare."[94] Although most aboriginal women helped at a birth from time to time, a few in each group were recognized as the senior and most experienced midwives. In cases where there were complications, it is also known that husbands assisted at the birth, even performing the equivalent of a Caesarian section on occasion. Indications are that leading an active, outdoor life ensured that many aboriginal women were strong and healthy, bore their children patiently and well, enjoyed a normal delivery that was usually supervised by experienced midwives, and were soon up and about again.

On the whole, women endured childbirth complications and infant deaths with fortitude and faith, and often took consolation in religion, which was central to the life of most people at that time. During the war, when the good news of a birth reached a young father who was away with the military, it was a cause for celebration. This was true of Lieutenant Joseph-David Mermet, a British officer of a literary frame of mind. "Fate," he wrote, "reduces you to your bare bones: she presents you with a son. Admit it, a wife becomes more precious when she becomes a mother. Oh sentiments of a father!"[95]

With husbands and sons away on active service, many women during the War of 1812 had little recourse but to manage their homes, families, enterprises and circumstances with self-reliance, practicality and common sense. In hindsight, they might well have regarded the war years as a critical period in their lives. As yet another milestone along the long road that would lead eventually to emancipation, their wartime experiences took them a step nearer to the time when a woman would cease to be solely the "faithful wife, without debate,"[96] and become instead, "mistress of herself."[97]

The duties of a wife. In 1812, the life of the average North American woman revolved around the daily routine of running her home and caring for her family. Many women had little help, other than from a mother or daughter, but wealthier women were fortunate to be able to afford servants, although they were not always easy to come by. In this scene, a newly-married woman is addressing her housekeeper and housemaids, one of whom is inspecting her wedding ring. (Illustration by C.E. Brock from 1895 edition of Jane Austen's *Pride and Prejudice*.)

What to Wear? Women's Clothing in the War of 1812 Period[1]

Fashion for North American women in 1812 depended largely upon their station in life. The style of dress for most ordinary women had not changed much in more than two decades, their daily routine allowing little or no time to accommodate changes in style, and practicality being the main consideration. Most items of clothing had a long life, and when no longer serviceable, the material was put to use to make patchwork quilts or other useful items. Almost all ordinary women had to be able to make clothes for themselves and their families, often from home-spun or hand-woven wools or plain, checked or striped linens. Ready-made cotton fabrics were usually available only to women of means.

Typical everyday wear consisted of a coarse linen or cotton chemise – the basic article of underclothing for women of all classes until well into the nineteenth century – over which was worn a loosely-cut bodice of homespun cloth or perhaps leather, sometimes laced in front. Outer skirts were full, usually

Everyday wear. The lady of the house wears a plain grey day dress with a white fichu and white cap. Although she and her husband could afford at least one servant, this woman might have added a white apron while attending to household matters. (Print after cartoon by Thomas Rowlandson in *The Military Adventures of Johnny Newcome*.)

Shipboard fun. This scene shows port women, several of whom are dancing with the sailors. The woman in the centre wears a patterned dress, perhaps of her own making, with matching cotton fichu, an apron and flat slippers. Several of the other women are also wearing caps. (Print from cartoon by George Cruickshank)

ankle-length or a little above, usually made of wool or linen. For added warmth in winter, a woman might wear two or three petticoats, the term petticoat usually referring to an under-skirt, often pleated onto a waistband, with openings in side seams to access pockets. Cloth was home-dyed in a range of colours.

Another type of dress worn by such women consisted of a simple homespun shift tied at the waist and generally made of fine linen. It could be full, three-quarter length or short-sleeved. Partly or fully boned stays – the foundation garment at that time – were worn over the shift by poor or working women, and women of all classes wore short blouses or gowns loosely tied at the waist and flowing to the hip over a skirt or petticoat. Army women normally dressed much as described above, and period cartoons and illustrations sometimes show them wearing cast-off items, such as military coats.

Accessories commonly included a cap, a fichu (a cotton covering knotted at the front and worn over a low-cut bodice for modesty), coarse woollen or cotton stockings, an apron, a shawl and a warm hooded cloak for outdoor use. Shoes were sensible in style and made of leather with squared toes. Shoes were bought or made in identical pairs, not left and right, and were broken in by wear.

A small minority of North American women with the means to afford high fashion followed the trends of Europe. Paris was the centre of all things fashionable, followed by London, where tastes were more conservative and in keeping with the simpler North American lifestyle. The fashionable North American woman kept abreast of European innovations via letters from friends, newspaper advertisements and magazines, which provided illustrations on the latest trends. Gowns – the term for dresses in 1812 – were straight and high-waisted (following Empire styles very popular at the time) and were tailored to suit day or evening wear. Day

The other end of the social scale. Here, women are waiting with convicts to be transported to Australia for criminal activitity. Clearly of the lower orders, they are seen in skirts and blouses without the fichus normally worn for modesty. One is bare-breasted and her skirt is patched. (Print from cartoon in *Country Journal and Poughkeepsie Advertiser*, 1780.)

gowns, designed for a variety of different activities, were usually ankle-length and had full-length sleeves, which could often be detached. They might be high-necked or worn with a fichu to provide cover for a lower neckline. Materials favoured were light fabrics such as fine cotton or muslin, popular in Paris and London. A fitted, boned bodice might be worn beneath such gowns, but the more daring women went without. These gowns could be revealing in windy weather, as the cartoon "The Three Graces in a High Wind" indicates.

Clothing for a working girl. A servant girl is shown wearing an ankle-length, high-waisted dress over a shift, and a frilled cap. (Detail from "Arrivée d'une diligence," painted by Louis-Léopold Boilly, 1803. Louvre, Paris. Photograph by René Chartrand.)

For evening wear, gowns had short sleeves, lower necklines and sometimes trains, and ladies traditionally wore long gloves. The very few North American women who chose to be seen in revealing Parisian styles raised more than a few eyebrows among their more conservative peers, who were unused to such daring attire.

A wide range of items accompanied the basic day or evening gown of society women. There might be a jacket (generally short and fitted), a pelisse (a longer, looser fitting coat) or a long, cloak fastened at neck, with or without a hood. Cotton caps were worn during the day, and hats for outdoor and evening wear came in a wide range of styles, including Henry VIII caps, hussar caps, turbans, straw hats and bonnets. In the evening, when heads could be uncovered, plumes were often substituted for hats.

Taking the air on horseback. As may be seen in this print, women rode side-saddle and wore a long, high-waisted habit. The lady in question also wears a veiled top hat and is being politely greeted by an officer. (Print after Vernet. Anne S.K. Brown Military Collection, Brown University, Providence, Rhode Island. Photograph by René Chartrand.)

Flat-heeled slippers or half boots in cloth or leather, parasols, reticules (small purses), decorative shawls, gloves and a range of jewellery were also essential to the wardrobe of the fashionable lady.

Such accessories were regularly imported into North America. Storekeepers in cities and towns also offered a range of imported fabrics and dressmaking supplies for those who chose to make their own gowns or have them made by a dressmaker.

At the cutting edge of fashion. In terms of daring attire, there were few women in North America to compare with Elizabeth Patterson Bonaparte. As seen here, she is wearing the décolleté style that shocked the more conservative society ladies of Washington. (Engraving, James Parton, *Daughters of Genius*.)

A gown for a young lady. This illustration shows a promenade or evening gown with frills around the neck and hem in the same material, a practice introduced in 1810. Among her accessories are long gloves, a shawl, a closely fitting cap, pearl earrings and flat slippers. (German fashion print, 1810.)

(Right) **London fashions for 1814.** These designs for July 1814 by "Mesdames Powley and Harmsworth of New Bond Street" show a day dress of white satin trimmed with blue crepe with matching cap and a walking dress of fine white linen trimmed with wide lace frills, worn with a satin "Oldenburg" hat trimmed with ostrich feathers, a primrose silk scarf and matching boots. (*The Ladies Monthly Museum or Polite Repository of Amusements and Instruction*, Volume XVII, 1814.)

Dress in polite society. The etiquette of dress required gowns for different activities during the day. This 1815 illustration shows, from left to right, an afternoon gown for paying calls, a walking gown, a promenade gown for an assembly and an evening gown for formal occasions. (Gaillard Hunt, *Life in America One Hundred Years Ago*.)

Three graces in a high wind. In this cartoon, three young women wear gowns of thin, fine material without any kind of undergarments. When the wind blows, more of their contours are revealed than was considered seemly at the time. (Print from engraving by James Gillray, 1810.)

Pennsylvania wedding. In this charming scene, a young couple are being married by their local minister at the home of the bride's parents. Beside the bride stands her bridesmaid, and seated are the girl's tearful mother, father and younger siblings. Several other relatives stand nearer the door. Note the two doves in the cage hanging on the back wall, and two other witnesses, the family dog and cat. (Engraved print after painting by John Lewis Krummel, *Analectic Magazine*, 1820.)

CHAPTER TWO

"*Maidens here are sweetly singing.*" Love, Courtship, Marriage and Dangerous Liaisons

Tho' oft our friends have frowning said
And called it sense and reason,
'Twas time enough as yet to wed
At any future season;
But HARRY *vow'd it should be soon*
And own'd too long we'd tarried
Then fix'd the twenty first of June,
The day that we were married.

O sweetest day in all the year
The day that we were married.

Three years have pass'd in marital bliss
So maidens do not tarry
A single life is sure amiss,
So I advise to marry;
For was the time to come again,
To Church I would be carried,
And truly bless the happy day,
The day that we were married.[1]

May 1813 arrived in Halifax with a light snowfall, but warmer breezes soon carried away the last vestiges of winter. Within a few days, Lady Katherine Sherbrooke was able to walk in her garden for the first time that year and on the 8th of the month, as the mail packet from England arrived bringing welcome news from home, she and her husband, Sir John, made their way to St. Paul's Church, Halifax, for a wedding. Both bride and groom were well known to the Sherbrookes, he being the dashing Captain Lord James Townshend, RN, commanding officer of HMS *Aeolus*, and she, Elizabeth Martha, eldest daughter of Provo F. Wallis, superintendent of His Majesty's Dockyard at Halifax.[2]

Although active service deprived many women of the company of husbands and admirers during the war, to others it brought opportunities to make a good match when officers, soldiers and sailors unexpectedly arrived in their community. Wedding bells rang regularly in towns with a military or naval presence, and fathers gave away daughters with their blessing and, not infrequently, a dowry. Wartime romances saw many a young woman launched into a future that sometimes lay, as in the case of Elizabeth Townshend, far from home.

The road to matrimony in early nineteenth century North America was beset with obstacles, for marriage was not only a personal contract but also an important institution over which society had considerable influence. In British North America, where church and establishment created an atmosphere of restraint, the complex business of courtship was carefully monitored in accordance with contemporary precepts. Young people were expected to marry someone of their own background, rules of behaviour were strict, and meetings between the two sexes generally occurred only in acceptable and organized public settings such as outings, assemblies, dances and supervised gatherings. Dancing was an excellent means of bringing people together, and in the British provinces in particular, many seem to have taken to the dance floor at every opportunity.

Care, however, was always taken to tread the line of respectability since loss of reputation was disastrous for a young woman. Coquettish behaviour was not considered proper in polite British society, nor was it appropriate for well-bred American women. Eliza Southgate of Maine declared she would always "endeavour to act in a manner that my conscience will justify, – to steer between the rocks of prudery and coquetry, and take my own sense of propriety as a pilot that will conduct me safe."[3] Less acceptable aspects of feminine behaviour were well catalogued by Lieutenant Joseph-David Mermet of the British army, an enthusiastic poet who recorded in verse some of his thoughts and impressions of the society he encountered in the Canadas during the war. Mermet composed a series of pen portraits under the title "*Les Quidproquo des Coquettes*," which included the following sketches of young women he met:

> That Lucile, while plastering make-up on her face, tells me
> That someone is waiting, that she is dashing off to the theatre,
> This I can well believe;
> But if Lucile says it is an unexpected invitation,
> And that she is going there to see, rather than be seen,
> This I cannot believe.[4]
>
> That on her mother's orders, submissive Isabelle,
> Keeps her eyes lowered and walks as though in a daze,
> This I can well believe;

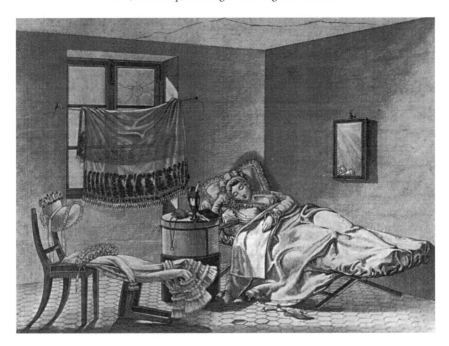

Economizing for the ball. For any young lady wishing to meet eligible men, dances, assemblies and balls were the best opportunity. Here, a young hopeful is living in spartan accommodation but is happy because she has her ticket for a ball tucked into the corner of her mirror and a new gown lying across the chair near her makeshift bed. (French print, *c.* 1818. Author's collection.)

> But that out of the corner of her eye, she does not admire
> The sweetheart who gazes at her and sighs for her,
> This I cannot believe.
>
> That her dress, which is too long, has huge folds,
> That hide the beautiful lines of her lovely body –
> This I can well believe;
> But that with a helping hand, the flirtatious hypocrite
> Does not enable it to become shorter and more clinging,
> This I cannot believe.[5]

In smaller communities behaviour had to be beyond reproach. Since she was unable to circulate at will, a young woman's home was important as a place where possible suitors called or attended gatherings under the watchful eyes of parents or guardians. Before permission to court was given, many a polite conversation took place, enabling a young man to assess his chances of success and parents to appraise the suitor. For the *habitants* of Lower Canada, courting was strictly supervised and a man could only pursue a girl if he intended to marry her. In Upper Canada, Sunday night was usually set aside for ritual courting, which was permitted by even the strictest parents. Among the French-speaking *Acadiens* of the Atlantic provinces, a young man was allowed to visit a young woman at her home on one evening a month when he could talk to her under her parents' supervision. Given the complexity of the matter, it is not surprising that long courtships were frowned upon – as these verses from a traditional *Acadien* folk song illustrate:

> Maidens here are sweetly singing,
> Maidens longing to be wed.
> Slowly through the village strolling,
> I can hear them softly whisp'ring,
> "Mother I must wed today.
> Don't say nay!"

> Hold your tongue, you little silly,
> You are hardly yet fifteen;
> Till you're old enough to marry,
> Love must tarry, love must tarry.
> Till you're sixteen, you must be
> Fancy free.[6]

For those young women who desired it, advice on general conduct, friendship, love and marriage was available. Scotsman Doctor John Gregory had many sage comments to offer in his book, *A Father's Legacy to His Daughters*, which stressed that "the power of a fine woman over the hearts of men of the finest parts, is even beyond what she conceives."[7] The complexity of courtship at that time can be seen in a letter written by Rebecca Byles of Halifax, which revealed the delicate balance required in attracting an eligible man while not appearing more eager than accepted form would permit:

> 1st what is a Lady to understand when a Gentleman tells her she looks mischievous, funny and Satirical?

> 2ndly does a Gentleman pay a Lady a compliment, or does he not, when he desires that part of the civil things he says to her may be placed to the account of her Friend?

3rd does a Lady descend from her proper dignity when she expects a Gentleman who courts her & whom she means to encourage to constantly attend her?

4th in what manner is a Lady to prevent a Gentleman who she is partial too [sic] from paying her too particular attention when he is not explicit.[8]

Insufficient encouragement could dishearten a suitor and sometimes it was only the threat of his departure which prompted the unmasking of a woman's true feelings, as this verse reminded its readers:

> How oft, if at the court of Love
> Concealment be the fashion,
> When How-d'y-do has failed to move,
> Good-bye reveals the passion![9]

Other young women, such as Maria Johnson of Montreal, were more straightforward. Her suitor, Major-General Barnard Bowes, declared that Maria had stolen "his heart his love his very soul," and wrote thus of their relationship:

> Maria meets you with a smile
> Her artless mind disdains all guile
> The chasten'd joy her eyes disclose
> Sweetly expresses love for B[owes].[10]

All in all, courtship was a tricky business in the early nineteenth century, and still is today, for that matter. Lieutenant John Le Couteur of the British army, a romantic through and through, was much attracted to the ladies but much troubled, as his low rank and still lower stock of funds made it impossible for him to marry. On two occasions during his wartime service in North America, Le Couteur inadvertently got caught in complicated situations involving young women.

The first took place in the winter of 1813-1814 when he was boarding with a widow in Kingston who had a female relative staying with her. Le Couteur found this young person attractive but being a somewhat naive youth, he did not realize the attraction was mutual until the day a friend asked

"Do you admire Miss – – very much?" "She is the nicest girl I have ever met in [North] America, very good & dear." "Is that all you think of Her?" "Oh Yes, what else could a poor Sub[altern] like me think of?" "Then take care what

Mrs. Robison's house. Kingston, Upper Canada, was the Royal Navy's main base on Lake Ontario. In this view, the house on the left with a picket fence was the home of Mrs. Elizabeth Robison, a naval widow. Lieutenant John Le Couteur boarded here during the winters of 1813-1814 and 1814-1815 and enjoyed some pleasant social occasions and not a little flirting with some of the local girls. The house, in King Street, still stands today. (Painting by Harriet Cartwright, 1833. Library and Archives of Canada, C-2751.)

you say and do. She has a heart as sensitive as it is good and you are making an undue impression upon it." ......

I hardly credited my informant, or rather examiner, but a few evenings after at forfeits, when I had to salute the young Lady as a forfeit, she trembled so much and looked so pale, though concealing her face as in jest, that I felt more uneasy than Herself. This put me on my guard not to be as studiously attentive as I had previously been. Had I been Five and Twenty and a Captain, She would have been an admirable Mother to my, or to any other man's children who might have had the good luck to marry her.[11]

Le Couteur did not learn from this experience and later found himself in a similar scrape while serving in Montreal. He and his friend Harry Le Mesurier were frequent visitors to the home of a Mr. and Mrs. Caldwell and their two daughters, Amelia and Sophia, the latter being a "haughty beauty."[12] Mrs. Caldwell, thinking Le Couteur suitable prey, offered Sophia as a potential wife but as the young officer recorded, he had nothing beyond a Guinea [$4.06] a week and My [Sub]altern's pay which was quite out of Marrying Condition. Poor Le Mesurier was very annoyed when I told him of it and said I must gradually withdraw from too much intimacy because whatever I might feel Myself, I might be unsettling the peace of mind of a very sweet girl, who thought me very agreeable. Which I did, as cautiously as propriety might admit.[13]

In the United States, behaviour and courtship were slightly more relaxed by 1812 and some parents took an increasingly liberal attitude that allowed their daughters to socialize without supervision, on the understanding that they would not behave in an improper manner. It was therefore possible, perhaps, for young American women to enjoy a greater degree of independence than their British North American counterparts and to take advantage of everyday social opportunities, especially in the case of country folk. Young people could meet while out walking, at church, at the shops or working the land where their lives and futures lay. They enjoyed riding, picnicking, berry picking, dancing, visiting friends or singing around a piano. At one tavern in eastern Kentucky in the late spring of 1812, "a puppet show had drawn together all the Lads and Lasses for twenty Miles round."[14] After the show, the young people went into a nearby tavern, where couples danced "with all their strength, dressed in their best of course." As the girls watched, the "Lads took off their Coats & Jackets" and "performed feats of activity, while the perspiration flowed copiously down their blooming faces."

Various accounts left by young American women provide glimpses into their lives. Sarah Smith Emery of Newburyport was brought up in a religious home but still allowed a reasonable degree of freedom. She recalled that it was customary for the young ladies to visit one another and give tea parties, with tea "served at six."[15] The young people of her town enjoyed evening parties and balls, where the dancers performed "contra dances" and "four-handed and eight-handed reels," pausing occasionally to fortify themselves with "jellies, various cakes, fruit, wines and hot punch."[16] On the morning after a dance or party, it was quite in order for young men to call upon their "fair partners to inquire respecting their health."

There were, of course, families where more rigid rules prevailed. The daughters of Puritan households were brought up to obey their parents and to put duty above all else. As Elizabeth Oakes Prince of Portland, Maine, remembered:

Puritan maidens were easily managed by their careful mothers and … found themselves on the road to matrimony, they hardly knew how. The Puritan maiden was as a rule expected to marry; her mother was determined that she should marry, for a kind of stigma was attached to an old maid. To be a wife, to mother children was esteemed the proper thing, the right thing and the beautiful thing.[17]

Elizabeth recalled how the "unflinching obedience" of her upbringing had the effect of making "the children not only submissive but passive," and that the "passion of a Puritan maiden existed, but was buried under a vast substratum of Duty."[18] Once freedom was tasted, of course, it was not easily cast aside. Many girls no doubt felt the same as a young American woman who found she had such fun at "balls, and quilting, and applebees" that she chose to ignore her father's admonitions about not staying out late and did not return home until the early hours of the morning.[19]

When she was finally allowed to attend dances and assemblies, Elizabeth Oakes Prince became a keen observer of the intricacies of courtship and the views of others regarding it. As she remembered:

such and such a one will make a match because they dance together, – another one is positively engaged because she does *not* dance with him. If a lady does not attend the assembly constantly – 'tis because her favorite swain is not a member, – if she does – 'tis to meet him there: if she is silent, she is certainly in love; if she is gay and talks much, there must be a lover in the way. If a gentleman looks at you at meeting you are suspected, if he dances with you at the assembly it must be true, and if he *rides* with you – 'tis confirmation strong as proof of holy writ.[20]

Her Puritan background aside, it was a time in Elizabeth's life that proved to be "such a frolic! Such a chain of adventures," that she confessed "the page of romance never presented its equal."[21]

The majority of young people married someone from within their own community. Sarah Smith Emery met her husband, David, while he was serving as an officer in the local militia regiment. Sarah Trumbull of Windsor, Connecticut, met George, her future husband, at a local gathering and married him after a lengthy seven-year courtship. As George wrote later, "I called on Miss Sarah Trumbull" and "she confessed a kindred flame – our Joyful hearts fluttered in the dawning breezes of love – the Seal of constancy cemented our plighted faith, and heaven seemed to smile at the happy union."[22]

In the choice of a mate, by 1812 love had generally become "an essential ingredient in the marital equation" and a daughter was at liberty to refuse a proposal of marriage if it was not present. Not to marry for love, said one woman, would be to "drag through life a galling chain."[23] This same observer believed that two "*souls* must be kindred to make the bands silken, all others I call unions of hands not *hearts*." Despite being free to choose a husband, most young women respected their parents enough to ask for their consent to a match. Some parents opposed the selection of a partner and in such cases, secret courtships, conditional engagements and clandestine marriages often resulted. Public opinion was inclined to hold parents responsible and a lawyer in Maine insisted that, as a general principle: "no good comes from opposition" in such affairs as "young peoples hearts are generally much wiser than old peoples heads."[24]

While love was the object of many, there were also opportunists of both sexes for whom money was the major motivating factor. When Margaret England of

Meeting the ladies. War brought a change in social life for many unattached women, with greater opportunities to meet officers and soldiers and enter into liaisons with them. In this scene, an officer and friend encounter a group of ladies in the street and stop to make polite conversation. (Illustration by C.E. Brock for 1895 edition of Jane Austen, *Pride and Prejudice*.)

Kingston, Upper Canada, married York merchant Jacob Herchmer, the Reverend George Okill Stuart thought she was "artful and I suspect has consulted her Interest rather than her Judgement, in the choice of the Husband she has married."[25] In his opinion, such marriages were "very seldom productive of conjugal felicity. Calculating women like Margaret, of course, had male counterparts who put self-interest ahead of any other motive. Joseph Willcocks of York was just such a man. In search of power, patronage and a wealthy wife, he wrote to his elder brother, Richard, about his disappointment over one local lady:

> I have met a very great loss by the removal of Col[one]l Smith from the York Garrison he was uncommonly attentive to me, he had also a very pretty sister that I would have been uncommonly attentive to if she carried more metal [money]; indeed she is a rarity for there are few Pretty Girls in the Country, but you know beauty will not make the pot boil, which consideration alone prevented me from assuming an air of Seriousness.[26]

Willcocks pursued another woman who fitted his requirements – the wealthy Elizabeth Russell, half-sister of Peter Russell, not only the adminis-

Russell Abbey was the home of Elizabeth Russell, a member of York society and half-sister to the Honourable Peter Russell, former Administrator of Upper Canada. The house, a one-storey frame structure, stood close to the shore of Lake Ontario and it was here that Miss Russell was unsuccessfully wooed by Joseph Willcocks before the war. (After an engraving in Henry Scadding, *Toronto of Old*. Toronto Public Library, J. Ross Robertson Collection, T11480.)

trator of Upper Canada but also Willcocks's patron. Having made a point of becoming the best of friends with Mr. Russell, Willcocks was soon "almost one of the household, with all the comforts that this world could possibly afford."[27] He was clearly capable of being the kind of smooth talker described in the following lines by Lieutenant Mermet:

> The flatterer is like the bee.
> Which goes from the carnation to the jasmine;
> And stings whichever arouses it;
> Is interested only in itself and its booty;
> Rejoins its friends in the morning;
> Is on watch until it sleeps;
> Buzzes as it goes about its thieving:
> But if it buzzes in your ear,
> Beware of its honey and its venom.[28]

Russell saw through Willcocks's motives and, as Willcocks himself recorded, "Mr. Russell, finding that Miss Russell and myself were pulling a cord together, immediately dismissed me and for once left me naked to the world."[29]

The war opened up a wider sphere of romantic possibilities for many young women, who met men from other parts of their continent and overseas. In British North America, the daughters of wealthy merchants and colonial officials found their social opportunities vastly enhanced by the arrival of new regiments and their officers. Wherever they went, the men in uniform left an impression, and civilian males often found themselves displaced by military suitors vying for the affection of the local belles. Thomas Ridout, a Canadian, complained to his father that, while in the Niagara in the autumn of 1813, there were several eligible young women at a local farm where he and his male friends were frequent visitors. The Canadians soon became aware that they were no longer as welcome as they once had been and that the reason for their decline in popularity was due to "an astonishing run of white cuffed ensigns and lieutenants at the house and the carpet parlor is adorned the whole day with red [coats]."[30]

Not only did young women find men in uniform more attractive than their civilian counterparts, but they quickly became aware of the importance of rank. Lieutenant John Johnston, RN, who served with the British squadron on Lake Ontario, complained in the summer of 1813 that he and his fellow junior officers

rarely went ashore in Kingston and when they did, they were not much in demand "as the ladies here are too fine" for any officer under the rank of captain.[31]
When American Major-General James Wilkinson assembled his army on Grenadier Island at the eastern end of Lake Ontario in October of that year before
moving against Montreal, the one young single woman on the island became
"the object of more interest and admiration than often falls to the lot of the most
dominant city belle."[32] Such "unexpected incense offered up to her few charms,"
according to one young officer, caused this ordinary country girl to be

> suddenly converted, by some military magic, from a Cinder-breech into a
> Cinderella, and [she] flaunted about in her linsey-woolsey gown and checked
> apron, with more airs than many a lady feels authorized to assume, even
> when arrayed in lame and tulle. She would not speak to a colonel, would
> hardly look at a captain, and would almost spit in the face of a subaltern, who
> hazarded a side-long glance of admiration.[33]

When handsome young officers and pretty young ladies were thrown together by the circumstances of war, it was hardly surprising that, as one civilian
man remarked, "the Devil has got into all the Girls."[34] Love took flame in a variety of circumstances that included winter sleighing parties, and "many a matrimonial union" had its beginning during "these icy expeditions."[35] Elsewhere,
Cupid's arrow also struck in the kitchen of a home where a young British army
bandsman met the sister of the lady of the house "while the pastry work was
going on."[36] An "admirable performer in the Kent-bugle," he proceeded to woo
her with "some favourite airs" and whether "melted by the music, or by the heat
of a roasting fire," she stole away with him. By the time she returned she was
"noosed" to her bandsman by the nearest available parson.

A pretty face was always a welcome sight to soldiers. During the American
occupation of part of the Canadian Niagara area in 1813, an officer from Albany
remembered that his brigade was approaching a neat cottage one afternoon.
"We, of the romance," he recalled, referring mostly to his fellow aides de camp,
"immediately became perpendicular in the saddle and ... adjusted our caps,"
for they had spotted flower-pots outside the door, evidence of a female presence, and were sure that "a pretty damsel was within."[37] Their instincts proved
correct when the cottage door opened and they saw a "young lady, who would
have been thought tolerably pretty any where, but who at that place, and under such circumstances, appeared absolutely handsome." Enemy or not, as the
commanding officer's horse drew level with the front gate,

Sleigh bells and romance. Winter was the main social season in the northern part of North America, and outdoor activities such as sleighing were popular. The start of many a warm friendship took place during "icy expeditions," such as the one pictured here at Halifax, Nova Scotia. (Detail, painting by William Eagar. Library and Archives of Canada, C-013362.)

this apparition of loveliness came tripping down to it … meeting in her progress a light breeze that lifted up her dark locks so as to show her face, and impressed itself on her light drapery, so as to show her form to the best possible advantage.[38]

The friendly Canadian invited the officers to enjoy some refreshment with her and her father, and by the time the troops moved on, most of the younger officers had fallen "vehemently in love" and cast "longing, lingering looks behind, until our heads had become almost reversed."[39]

Another chance meeting left an impression on the ever-eager Lieutenant John Le Couteur when, in September 1812, he found himself travelling up the Saint John River to Fredericton in a "Gun Boat … the slowest conveyance that could be imagined."[40] During the passage, he paid a visit to a veteran officer, General John Coffin, and met the general's daughter, Sophia. Le Couteur thought her "a splendid girl" and she became even more an object of his admiration when he learned that she and her father had been crossing the river one morning in a small boat, when "a great Bear attacked them, and would have swamped the boat" if Sophia had not helped her father. While the general was "battering Bruin with the Butt end of an oar," Sophia "pushed the point of the boat hook into his Eye which made Bruin scratch it and retreat." As the eighteen-year-old and impecunious young officer wistfully noted yet again: "if I had been a rich Captain, I should certainly have tried to captivate, if not capture, such a brave girl!"[41]

Sometimes love occurred spontaneously in the darkest of situations. When British troops and their aboriginal allies burned the town of Buffalo, New York, in December 1813, almost all the town's inhabitants fled. One young man, Augustus Fox, was in his sleigh when he passed the Pratt family and offered to give two of them a ride. Into the sleigh jumped Esther Pratt, "a charming young Miss," to whom he lost his heart on an otherwise dismal day.[42] That same winter, Major Mordecai Myers of the 13th U.S. Infantry Regiment was convalescing at the house of Surgeon James Mann, on the American shore of the St. Lawrence. Myers had been wounded during the Battle of Crysler's Farm on 11 November 1813, and subsequently contracted a fever that caused him to suffer "everything but death."[43] Surgeon Mann did not think he could save him, but Myers survived and spent the winter under the care of Mann and his niece, Charlotte Bailey. By the time the major was well enough to rejoin his regiment, he and Charlotte were in love and were married the following spring.

One of the most remarkable examples of love in adversity involving an officer who fought in the war began during the siege of the Spanish city of Badajoz in 1812. Captain Harry Smith, who later served at Washington, Baltimore and New Orleans in 1814, met and fell in love with his future wife, Juana Maria de las Flores de Leon, when she and her sister arrived destitute at the British camp. Smith and his friend, Lieutenant John Kincaid, were captivated by Juana's beauty, Kincaid describing her as "an angel! A being more transcendingly lovely I had never before seen."[44] Just fourteen years old and straight from a convent, Juana had about her

a delicate freshness – more English than Spanish; her face, though not perhaps rigidly beautiful, was nevertheless so remarkably handsome, and so irresistibly attractive, surmounting a figure cast in nature's fairest mould, that to look at her was to love her; and I did love her.[45]

Lady Smith (1798-1872). Juana Maria de los Flores de Leon met her husband, Captain Harry Smith, when her home city of Badajoz, Spain, was besieged in 1812. The couple were married soon afterwards and enjoyed a distinguished and happy life together. Sharing in the honour of her husband's knighthood, his service in India and his appointment as governor of Cape Province in 1848, Lady Smith gave her name to a South African town that would achieve fame in a later war. (Print after portrait by unknown artist, 1815. Author's collection.)

It was Harry, however, who won the heart of this "angel." He saw not just Juana's physical beauty, but that she also possessed a "just sense of rectitude, an innate purity of mind, a singleness of purpose which defied malice, and a soul that soared above circumstances."[46] It was not long before she became "alike the adored of the camp and of the drawing-room ... everybody's *beau ideal* of what a wife should be." Harry Smith soon married his "Juanita" and in so doing, found the love of his life – as he later wrote, a scene of "devastation and spoil" had yielded to him "a treasure invaluable."[47]

Lieutenant Kincaid believed that "only those who have been in the theatre of fierce warfare" could "fully appreciate the additional value which it gives to one's existence."[48] It is likely that a British army surgeon at New Orleans in 1815, who had volunteered to stay behind and nurse the wounded after his own army had withdrawn, would have agreed with this view. Some of the local ladies offered to help the medical staff of both armies with the task and "a belle of the city, famed for her charms of person and mind," demonstrated her concern and devotion to the wounded to such an extent that the surgeon in question "conceived a warm regard and admiration" for her. Brought together at a time of great adversity, the hero of this romantic story, Dr. J.C. Kerr, settled in New Orleans after the war, married "the Creole lady ... and became an esteemed citizen and the father of a large family."[49]

Romances survived despite the absences attendant on war that many young couples had to endure. There was an inevitable sadness when a regiment left town, and "many a fair face was at the window smiling encouragement, or looking with regret."[50] If love had conquered hearts, the sense of loss was all the greater, but love often overcame the most difficult of circumstances. Separated by the Atlantic were Captain William Mulcaster, second-in-command of the Royal Navy's squadron on Lake Ontario, and his fiancée, Sophia Van Cortlandt, living in Devon at the home of her brother-in-law. It had been agreed that the two would marry on Mulcaster's return from North America and in the meantime Sophia could only wait and pray for his safety. Mulcaster was seriously wounded during an attack on Oswego, New York, in May 1814, but recovered and arrived in England the following September. Sophia, meanwhile, had received a much-delayed report from North America that her fiancé had been mortally wounded and "sank to the ground in a swoon." Once she discovered that he had not only survived but was on his way home, she was overjoyed. The couple, happy to be reunited, decided not to delay and were married a month later.[51]

In a situation of separation by such a great distance, it was natural for a fiancée to suffer anxiety, a good deal of which was caused by slow communications. Like Sophia Van Cortlandt, Agnes Cossar, engaged to Captain Robert Barclay, RN, commanding officer of the British naval squadron on Lake Erie, also waited in England for news. Barclay, who had already lost an arm in combat, was severely wounded in action at the Battle of Put-In-Bay in September 1813 and, as soon as he was able, wrote to Agnes to describe his battered physical condition. He offered to release her from their engagement but she refused to consider it, for so relieved was she to know he had survived that, "if there was enough of him to contain his soul," she said, she promised to marry him.[52]

For Captain William Hamilton Merritt, a Canadian militia officer, the war found him on the opposing side to his American fiancée, Catherine Prendergast. The young couple kept in touch by letter and throughout the several months William spent as a prisoner of war in Connecticut in 1814, he lamented to Catherine the "unhappy situation which our countries are placed in" and which he feared would deprive him "of the greatest pleasure I have ever enjoyed, viz. seeing you."[53] Catherine replied that "if I should be separated from you for years I will ever remain the same as you left me." She also confessed that she had not dared to hope their romance would work out, explaining that "I could not help thinking at times you were like many others and it would be impossible that your mind would be the same for such a length of time."[54] William's reply assured Catherine that his sole wish was for "the peaceable enjoyment of Domestic Happiness which you only are able to bring me if Heaven will grant me this blessing." A few weeks later came tidings of the end of the war, and Catherine and William were finally wed.[55]

If a romance grew serious enough to consider the prospect of marriage, it was a matter of great consequence, for matrimony was considered to be a sacred and legal bond for life, and sex was regarded as exclusive to the married state. Physical intimacy of any kind was therefore forbidden until a couple were virtually engaged and in any case, most young people had little or no privacy in which to attempt it. Gossip ensured that the rules were obeyed, and those who transgressed found themselves the object of both criticism and ostracism.[56]

In an age of such clearly defined parameters, marriage for most young people came early. It was regarded as both a civic duty and an individual imperative, for to remain single was to be condemned, according to one newspaper, as "a roving restless being ... the sad victim of untamed passions."[57] Young men with little education and experience of the world tended to marry the first girl who awakened their mating instinct, and most girls preferred not to wait long, since outside matrimony they had little independence from their parents. For those men uncertain or unwilling to take the final step, there were salutary warnings of what life would be like as a lonely bachelor:

> The man who passes his life without a wife will contract unsocial habits, be displeased with the world, and in the winter of his years will stand like a lonely tree on an extended plain ... without a companion to soothe his troubles and wipe away the tears wrung by misery.[58]

Married status gave women protection and respectability, and by emphasizing the sanctity of marriage, churches of the early nineteenth century stressed the stability of family life. In the words of the Reverend John Strachan of York, "there's a holiness about the fireside of a well regulated family."[59] When it came to choosing a wife, there were many different views on her ideal virtues, from the high standards of women like Eliza Southgate quoted earlier, to those of a man who hoped for no more than a hard-working helpmate. A down-to-earth opinion was offered by Major-General Andrew Jackson to his ward, Andrew J. Hutchins. "One word to you as to matrimony," Jackson wrote, advising the young man to seek a wife "who will aid you in your exertions in making a competency and will take care of it when made."[60] In the general's opinion, this entailed looking "at the economy of the mother and if you find it in her you will find it in the daughter."

Not all men had the good fortune to meet suitable candidates for matrimony and some resorted to a totally pragmatic approach to the problem – they placed an advertisement in a newspaper. In May 1813, a notice appeared in *Poulson's Daily Advertiser* headed, "To Widows!" inserted by Colonel Phineas Stevens, who "having need of a wife to manage his domestic affairs, and not having leisure to go in pursuit of one," took this method of "making his wants known."[61] He invited interested applicants to write to him at his farm and added, "none need apply but such as can come well recommended." The person he was seeking "must be no *less* than 35, nor more than 50 years old – healthy, and capable of washing dishes in a neat and fashionable manner." A similar advertisement in the *Montreal Gazette* told readers in May 1814 that:

A Gentleman in possession of a handsome income, concerned in a house of respectability, of good disposition, and agreeable manners, but from the tedium and ennui of a single life, rather attached to his bottle, wishes to Connect himself to a Lady not exceeding twenty years, of a handsome person, elegant accomplishments, and pleasant temper. It is hoped that none will answer this, but those of undoubted respectability.[62]

Before a man could marry, he had to be able to support a family. For gentlemen of means, successful businessmen, government officials, officers and the like, there normally came a time when they were able to make adequate provision for a wife, but for the less well-to-do, this often meant delaying marriage. Some couples were fortunate to have parents able to provide financial assistance and a case in point was Elizabeth Grant, popular Montreal socialite and the daughter of Marie-Charles Grant, Baroness de Longueuil. For Elizabeth, romance blossomed during the winter of 1813 when she met a young Swiss officer of De Meuron's Regiment, Lieutenant Charles-Nicolas-Fortuné de Montenach. Charles-Nicolas thought Elizabeth had "everything that could fulfil my desires and flatter my opinion" and the fact that the couple shared the Roman Catholic faith proved to be "the deciding factor in her mother's consent to our union."[63] Elizabeth and her officer were married on 20 January

1814 in the church at Longueuil on the St. Lawrence. Lieutenant De Monte-nach cherished his new wife's "distinguished education, appropriate to her rank" and the "excellence" of her heart," all of which, he was happy to admit, "contribute to making my life happy." For him, the end of the war could not come soon enough, and meanwhile Elizabeth's mother presented the newly-weds with "all that could give us perfect ease of living," he wrote, referring to a generous financial allowance.[64]

After obtaining permission to marry, some couples kept their plans secret from all but close family members until the wedding day drew near. It was the prerogative of the prospective bride to set the date and she was often involved in selecting the place where she and her future husband would live. Sarah Smith Emery recalled how she and her fiancé, David, went to look at an old tavern some months before their wedding and Sarah could immediately see that an application of "whitewash, paint and paper" would "work wonders" on the sombre decor.[65] Viewing it as both a prospective business and a home for a family, Sarah felt "quite inspired" at the prospect of her new life as a tavern-keeper.

If all the hurdles had been successfully negotiated, came the great day. Ar-rangements for the wedding ceremony were not usually made until shortly before the date, and a week seems to have been the average time between is-suing invitations and the ceremony. Unlike England, where the Marriage Act of 1753 fixed times and places where lawful marriages might occur, in British North America there was no clear preference for time of day, nor for a church as opposed to a private home. In the United States a similar situation prevailed and weddings took place in churches or before a minister at the home of the bride.

Whether it was a simple affair involving two people promising before wit-nesses to live as husband and wife, or something more elaborate in front of a large assembly of guests and with bridal attendants (who were by this time becoming more common), the ceremony was conducted with solemnity and – occasionally – a touch of humour. An announcement published in the *Gazette and New Brunswick Advertiser* in the summer of 1815 stated that "Mr. Henry Cain age 34" had recently been married to "Mrs. Maxwell of Clark's Bridge, age 66," it being "the sixth time of the Bridegroom and the ninth time of the Bride's being joined in wedlock."[66] With wry amusement the notice concluded, "if Love's a flame that's kindled by desire; an old stick is surely best, because it's drier."

Society weddings in North America were accomplished with as much atten-tion to style and etiquette as circumstances permitted. Many brides-to-be in the British colonies no doubt took note of newspaper reports of society weddings in England, which were actually rather rare as it was considered bad form to disclose information on private matters. One notable exception, taken from the *London Courier*, concerned the 1812 "Marriage Extraordinary," at St. James's Church, Piccadilly, between "Mr. Pole (now Wellesley) and Miss Tylney Long." William Wellesley Pole was a nephew of the Duke of Wellington and his bride, Catherine, the daughter and heiress of Sir James Tylney Long.[67] Theirs was without doubt one of *the* London weddings of the war years and warranted the privilege of a full newspaper report of this "long talked of matrimonial alliance."[68]

To the fascination of women readers, the bride's costly outfit was described as consisting of

> real Brussels point lace ... placed over white satin. The head was ornamented with a cottage bonnet, of the same material ... with two ostrich feathers. She likewise wore a deep lace veil, and a white satin pelisse, trimmed with swansdown ... The lady's jewels consist principally of a brilliant necklace and earrings.[69]

In her stunning apparel, the new Mrs. Wellesley Pole and her husband were transported from the church in a "magnificent equipage," described as a "singly elegant chariot, painted in bright yellow, and highly emblazoned, drawn by four beautiful Arabian grey horses," which took them to the home of the bride's father at Blackheath in south London.

On the other side of the Atlantic, where life was less sophisticated, no effort was spared to ensure that a young lady of quality looked her best on the most important day of her life. When Elizabeth Oakes Prince of Portland married Seba Smith, editor and joint proprietor of the local newspaper, at her parents' house, "all the appliances were in the best style of the period." Elizabeth wore a dress of "white satin, with lace flounces, white silk hose and long white gloves," and white flowers in her long, golden brown hair.[70] At Newburyport, Sarah Smith Emery had a quiet family wedding in April 1812 and chose to wear a dress of "white India muslin, the skirt edged by an ornamental border wrought in colored worsted; bands of similar embroidery finished the neck and short sleeves, with a girdle to match."[71] As part of her trousseau, Sarah selected a "walking dress," with a "short pelisse of light drab silk, trimmed with black lace; the bonnet matched the pelisse, trimmed with bias folds of the silk bound with white satin, and white satin strings." She and her new husband having purchased their tavern, she went from her wedding to her new abode and straightaway found herself "landlady of a public house."

Among American wartime marriage announcements appeared one at Newport, Rhode Island, in which two sisters wed, if not in the same ceremony, then within a day or two of each other. As the *Connecticut Gazette* reported in May 1814, Miss Harriet B. Auchmulty tied the knot with army Captain John F. Haleman, while her sister, Miss Maria M. Auchmulty, married Marine Corps Captain Robert D. Wainwright.[72]

Weddings in the British colonies were usually family affairs, often followed by a party given by the bride's parents with food, drink and dancing. For the most part, the time of ostentatious weddings had yet to arrive, although some managed to cause quite a stir, as in March 1812 when Caroline Fairchild of Saint John married James Wood. The bride's trousseau was apparently the talk of the town, for Caroline had "forty dresses, flounced and ribboned and pleated and puffed."[73] Seamstresses worked from sunrise to sunset and fittings took days to complete.

Local tradition also played its part in wedding ceremonies. A description of a Cape Breton *Acadien* marriage between François Bourneuf and Marie Doucet tells of between two and three hundred guests at the reception, which consisted of reels and dancing which lasted a full twenty-four hours, "a liberal supply of drinkables," and a hearty meal of "all kinds of flesh and fowl boiled in the same kettle with potatoes, turnips, carrots etc."[74] An unusual feature of an Acadian wedding reception in those days was the fact that couples moved their chairs as close together as possible and threw "a blanket or coverlet over their heads," which enabled them to "say all sorts of soft things to one another" in private until they wished to dance again.

In the American Northwest, where there might be "no store, tailor, dressmaker, blacksmith or other help within a hundred miles," men often wore "moccasins, leather breeches, leggins, linsey hunting-shirts, and all homemade," to a wedding, while women's attire tended to be "linsey petticoats and linsey or linen bedgowns, coarse shoes, stockings, handkerchiefs, and buckskin gloves, if any."[75] The food might well consist of a "substantial backwoods feast of beef, pork, fowls, and sometimes venison and bear meat roasted and boiled, with plenty of potatoes, cabbage and other vegetables," or "deer, muskrat, raccoon, turkey, quail, pigeon, skunk, and porcupine with the quills on."[76] Even though the dinner table was possibly no better than a rough piece of timber, with men using their hunting knives if cutlery was scarce, "the greatest hilarity always prevailed." After a lively session of dancing reels and jigs, a deputation of women put the bride to bed about 9 P.M., often by ladder into a basic loft arranged for the purpose, and the young men did the same with the groom.[77]

At remote Mackinac Island during the war, weddings linked families of different backgrounds and cultures. One of them was between Mademoiselle Bailly, the adopted aboriginal daughter of a French fur trader, and Edward Biddle, a young American from an old and distinguished Philadelphia family. Mademoiselle Bailly was "fair-complexioned for an Indian, although her eyes were very black, and her hair equally so and of the thickest and longest," and when Biddle met this beautiful young woman, "the attachment warmed into a sincere love on both sides," although, not knowing each other's language, they could not communicate very much initially.[78]

The Biddles' wedding, recorded by a guest, Elizabeth Baird, was held at the island home of Mademoiselle's stepfather. The bride wore her traditional dress – a calf-length skirt with side pleats, "elaborately embroidered with ribbon and beads on both the lower and upper edges" and covered with row upon row of ribbon.[79] Her scarlet broadcloth leggings had wide trimmings and her moccasins were embroidered with ribbon and beads. There was also a sort of "loose-fitting garment made of silk for extra occasions," and she wore rows of beads around her neck.[80] Mademoiselle Bailly's hairstyle was "plain, parted in the middle, braided down the back and tied up again, making a double *queue*." As Elizabeth Baird wrote in summation, "Would that my pen might do justice to this wedding!"[81]

Marriages among the aboriginal peoples were also conducted according to traditional custom. Those between aboriginal women and white men who worked in the wilderness country as merchants, fur traders, lumbermen, pioneer farmers and *voyageurs*, were often *à la façon du pays* or according to prevailing custom.[82] Such arrangements lasted as long as the husband remained in the area and when a man left, his wife and children often returned to her people. Some, however, were like that of Scottish fur trader Robert Dickson and his Sioux wife, To-to-win, and lasted until his death.

Military weddings were, of course, not uncommon during the war. Lieutenant Le Couteur mentions a number of ceremonies in his journal, among which were the following:

6 February [1814]

No church to day, Our Rector having gone to York to celebrate the wedding of Captain Loring of ours and Miss Campbell, a pretty person of nineteen.[83]

17 February [1814]

Captain Henry Alexander Stewart Dobbs RN, a prime Sailor and Gentleman, having invited our Rector, the Reverend Mr. Stuart to attend for the occasion, He was united in marriage to dear rattle, Mary Cartwright, the daughter of Colonel Cartwright … at Eight o'clock this evening. The happy couple were to have gone to Montreal for their honeymoon but a rumour of an Attack coming to ear this morning … no leave could be thought of.[84]

Given the risks of active service, it is not surprising that military couples often decided to marry at short notice. Captain James Fitzgibbon of the Glengarry Light Infantry saw much action during the war and had a good reputation as a combat officer. In early August 1814, while his regiment was fighting an invading American army, Fitzgibbon, to his commanding officer's surprise, "asked [for] leave, without giving any reason for such an apparently unreasonable request."[85] Few officers would have received permission, but Fitzgibbon's record made him the exception and his commander approved a short absence.

Fitzgibbon managed to send a letter to Mary Haley, his fiancée, at Kingston 250 miles away, before securing himself passage on a ship headed along Lake Ontario to that town. According to Fitzgibbon's granddaughter, although not a society woman, Mary Haley was a person of "taste and education," and she duly appeared at the appointed time on 14 August 1814 outside the church at Adolphustown, then an important community on the road between Kingston and York. The couple were married and "the knot tied, the soldier said farewell to his wife on the church steps" and immediately left to return to the war.[86] James Fitzgibbon, knowing he would shortly be involved in heavy fighting, did not want "the girl he loved being left unprovided for" should he fall in action – and now Mary would be entitled to a pension as the widow of an officer.[87]

After a wedding, most newly married couples retired to their future home. In the Canadas and parts of the republic, this was often followed by the custom of "charivari" or "shivaree." Those involved, usually young men from the neighbourhood, wore their clothes back to front, disguised themselves in frightening masks, or blackened their faces and wore "grotesque caps on their heads, adorned with cocks' feathers and bells."[88] They surrounded the residence of the bridal couple, as they were about to retire to the sound of "tin kettles, horns, and drums, cracked fiddles, and all the discordant instruments." They would bang on the door with "clubs and staves," demanding to be let inside to drink the bride's health, or to be given money to treat themselves "at the nearest tavern." If there was no response, they would increase their awful din, "firing guns charged with peas against the doors and windows, rattling old pots and kettles" and publicly abusing the groom "for his stinginess in no measured terms." Sometimes these shenanigans might continue for several days and things could turn nasty on occasion, with serious injuries known to "arise out of an imprudent refusal to satisfy the demands of the assailants."[89]

The habit of a newly married couple appearing in church on the Sunday following a wedding was another common ritual across North America, and there were also certain proprieties to be observed among society brides. In Halifax, for example, it was customary for a bride and bridegroom from the upper strata of society to call, soon after their wedding, upon the lieutenant-governor and his lady to pay their respects, which were duly returned a few days later. As Lady Katherine Sherbrooke's journal confirms:

> Sunday 7th June 1812.
> Went to Church and afterwards to Gov[ernmen]t House, where we saw a great many Visitors, the first of whom were the Bride and Bridegroom Major & Mrs. King, who were married on the 4th of June.[90]

Most couples did not take a honeymoon as this was a later custom, and even then it was regarded as a luxury for the privileged. For those who did, events sometimes forced a change of plans, as was the case with Captain and Mrs. Dobbs, who cancelled their honeymoon because of the alarms of war. Others were luckier: after Margaret Nelles of Grimsby, Upper Canada, fell in love and married "a fine noble generous hearted" officer, Major Edward Pilkington, in February 1814, they had a short honeymoon "in a cottage" on the Niagara River "above the Falls and in sight of the American shore."[91] Margaret was so devoted to her new husband, of whom she said, "to see him was to love him," that after this romantic interlude she insisted on accompanying him "to the wars."

For many women, marriage brought their first permanent move away from the family home and the beginning of a metamorphosis into the person to whom a husband looked for "purity, piety, submissiveness, and domesticity."[92] Most new wives undoubtedly hoped that marriage would bring them happiness and good fortune, but the more realistic were aware that "fate may heave her quiver filled with poison'd darts to deaden every pure domestic joy."[93] In the early nineteenth century, marriage was regarded as a woman's destiny, but its responsibilities and worries, especially in wartime, were such that it often proved in the short term to be "a sad, sour, sober beverage," with "some joys, but many crosses."[94]

As has been discussed, there were plenty of opinions voiced about what was expected of a good wife, most frequently along the lines that she should be competent inside her home and attentive to matters outside it, and that she should express an interest in her husband's affairs but not offer advice or personal comment unless asked. There were, of course, bound to be women who resented the restrictions marriage brought, but there were also those who saw it in a positive light. One newly-married American woman wrote to a friend that

> marriage I have heard denounced as the grave of female friendship, but believe it not, Heaven never intended such an institution selfish, tho' it concentrates our interests & our feelings, it expands the heart to generous benevolence, & teaches us to love with fervor, those we before have justly prized.[95]

The duty of a good wife, this same woman believed, was that she should contribute daily and hourly to the comfort of her family and "improve the manners and dispositions of men by her society and example."[96] Moral essays or suitable books on religion were recommended as reading matter aimed at helping a wife to make the best of what Dean Swift described as "the grand affair of your life" and to help her "gain and preserve the friendship and esteem of your husband."[97] Whether this was taken seriously is debatable, but many women probably veered towards writer Hannah More's description of their gender as people who "bless, dignify, and truly adorn society."[98]

When it came to practical hints about how to accomplish the role of wife and mother, a poem written two decades before the war contained a great deal of common sense advice that was still applicable. By 1812, Mehetible Mowat, for whom the poem had been written, was a widow in St. Andrews, New Brunswick, but she had kept the verse given to her on her wedding day. The earliest days of married life, the poem began, were often filled with "childish strife" and the poet impressed upon the new wife that, in dealing with her husband,

Then is the time, by gentlest art
To fix his empire in your heart.
For should it by neglect expire
No art again can light the fire.[99]

In speaking of a wife's relationship with her husband, the poet advised:

Be sure you n'er for power contend
Or try with tears to gain your end
Sometimes the tears that dim your eyes
From pride and obstinacy arise.
Heaven gave to man unquestioned sway
Then Heaven and man at once obey.[100]

The importance of a happy disposition was also stressed:

Let sullen looks your brow ne'er cloud
Be always cheerful, never loud.
Let trifles never discompose
Your temper, features or repose.
Abroad for happiness ne'er roam
True happiness resides at home.
Still make your partner easy there
Men find abroad sufficient care.
If every thing at home be right
He'll always enter with delight.[101]

When all was said and done,

Small is the province of a wife
And narrow is her sphere of life,
Within that sphere to walk aright
Should be her principal delight.
To grace the home with prudent care
And properly to spend and spare,
To make her husband bless the day
He gave his liberty away.[102]

Not every woman, of course, could measure up to such standards, and
there is evidence of troubled relationships. Public notices from the war period
point to wives who did not manage money well, and this at a time when most

Matrimony – a man loaded with mischief. This cartoon depicts the wording on an old English tavern sign that "a monkey, a magpie, and wife is the true emblem of strife." Note the wife brandishing a glass of gin and the husband wearing a chain and padlock labelled "wedlock." (Engraved eighteenth-century print, in James Parton, *Caricature and Other Comic Art in All Times and Many Lands*, 1878.)

had no financial means of their own and had to ask their husbands for even the smallest amount. The following announcement, placed in the *Connecticut Gazette* in 1812 by one John Fitzgerald, draws attention to the overspending of his wife:

> Whereas my wife Esther has been in a habit of contracting debts greatly to my disadvantage, and embarrassment; this is therefore to forbid all persons trusting her on my account, as I will not pay any debts of her contracting after this date.[103]

On the other hand, if a husband was guilty of some misdemeanour, a wife was usually counselled to turn a blind eye. According to one account, when the misdemeanour in question was infidelity, which was generally held to be "superlatively criminal in women," it was viewed "in a far less disadvantageous light" in men.[104] A woman with an unfaithful husband should, rather than show her anger, "feign ignorance of his misconduct and by superior agreeableness and attractions win him back." Similar advice was given to Rosalie Stier Calvert by her father in a long letter he wrote to her about marriage, money and family matters. "The power of a wife over her husband," Henri Stier informed his daughter,

> is boundless when she knows how to govern with moderation and method. If he slips away now and then, it is easy to bring him back and the only secret consists in making the interests of his family dearer and more interesting to him than all other diversions, in short, in making him find true happiness in his home.[105]

Nonetheless, Elizabeth Kennon of Williamsburg, Virginia, left an account of a husband who was publicly humiliated when he tried to stray from the fold. It seems that in Williamsburg there was a somewhat notorious lady whom Elizabeth Kennon identified only as "Kitty," who had produced "two babies without the assurance of a parson" by different men.[106] One of the men still maintained a relationship with her but one night when he was away on business, a local married man decided to pay a call on "Kitty" believing she might wish to add him to her string of lovers. His aggressive behaviour annoyed "Kitty"

> to such a degree, that she wrote a note which she dispatched by her servant to his wife; requesting her to come and take her husband away; she then opened her windows and bawled out as loud as she could, begging the neighbors to make Mr. - - - go away.[107]

Naturally, the "whole affair thus became very public," and on his return home this Virginian Casanova found his wife "in dreadful fainting fits." He begged "Kitty" to write a letter to his unhappy spouse saying that "she had mistaken another for him," which she finally agreed to do.[108]

Women were certainly not always the paragons of virtue society expected them to be, as Joseph-David Mermet, the soldier-poet, noted in one of his pen portraits:

That beautiful Cloris speaks with an air of sincerity,
That she is really the mother of all her children:
This I believe;
But that her old husband, with his dry and severe tone,
Is sure that he is the father of them all;
This I cannot believe.[109]

In an age when social rules were inviolable, at least on the surface, concealment was everything. Should a man and woman enter into an affair outside marriage, discretion was essential. To fail in this respect was to be at best socially compromised and at worst, socially ruined, for if a woman's infidelity became public knowledge, the resulting scandal might cause her to be shunned. Some families made the best of things, as Lieutenant-Colonel Joseph Gubbins discovered during his travels around New Brunswick. One night he stayed at an inn where the innkeeper, a respectable man, had married his daughter to "one of the most affluent young men in the neighbourhood" but when she subsequently gave birth to "a mulatto boy," her "connexion before marriage with a Negro was easily established."[110] No divorce could be obtained, and the husband was obliged to keep his wife and her baby with him. As far as Colonel Gubbins was concerned, this was merely evidence of "the want of morals in this country."

For a married woman to be involved with a bachelor was sure to set tongues wagging. When this happened to Alicia Cockburn, a British officer's wife, she pursued the relationship in the face of any and all criticism. Alicia was married to Lieutenant-Colonel Francis Cockburn of the Canadian Fencibles and was the sister-in-law of Rear-Admiral George Cockburn, who will emerge later as the predator of the Atlantic seaboard. It was not the happiest of unions and Anne Elinor Prevost, the astute daughter of Lieutenant-General Sir George Prevost, governor-general of British North America, noted that when the Cockburns arrived at Quebec it was clear that Alicia was "an unhappy wife, and there was an expression in her countenance, and a tearfulness in her eyes that seemed to say, 'though I strive to be cheerful, I am really wretched.'"[111] Over the winter of 1812-1813, during her husband's frequent absences from Quebec on duty, Alicia began to hold regular *salons* at their residence. Among those who attended with increasing frequency was Captain Henry Milnes, aide-de-camp to Sir George Prevost, and he soon formed an attachment for his hostess. It was Anne Elinor Prevost's belief that this liaison arose from the "most amiable feelings" on the part of the young officer, who felt sorry that Alicia, seemed to have "no friend to look to for support" and that she appeared to be experiencing only "harshness and neglect" from her husband.[112] Before long, "the chief object" of Captain Milnes's life was to drive Mrs. Cockburn in his carriole in the morning and to devote himself to her in the evening.[113]

Even Cockburn's return to Quebec in February 1813 did not appear to interfere with the captain's regular visits. Milnes spent much time with the Cockburns and, according to Anne Elinor Prevost, "strange to say, the husband seemed to be perfectly pleased and contented with his wife's friendship" with the young officer.[114] By now the affair was an open secret among the city's elite and when it was pointed out to Milnes "how much pain it would give his family, to witness such folly," he "burst into a flood of tears" and promised he would return to England at the first opportunity his army service permitted.[115] Unfortunately, he was killed in action the following summer.

Although she had now acquired something of a reputation, Alicia Cockburn continued to be received socially and Anne Elinor went to some length to explain why:

> The lady has retained her place in society, though several other friendships have succeeded her fondness for poor Captain M[ilnes]. – and it is possible that she never has been more than very imprudent and very extraordinary, but most undoubtedly in the instance to which I now allude, her fascination excited such affection as not only enabled her to influence his opinions, but made him [Milnes] unhappy.[116]

Anne Elinor's mother, Lady Catherine Prevost, who was fond of Milnes, "in spite of his own sinful weakness," was much less impressed with Alicia Cockburn's conduct, which "she could not regard with any degree of compliancy."[117] Shortly thereafter, Alicia moved to Montreal, where conventions were less rigid and society was more lively.

Alicia Cockburn's situation may be viewed with sympathy, perhaps, as in the early nineteenth century an unhappy marriage normally had to be endured rather than abandoned. In June 1813 Mary Baker of Boston wrote to her sister Margaret Pacan of her own unfortunate predicament. "I am sorry to inform you that Mr. Baker is turned out to be one of the worst of husbands," she confided, adding that if it were possible, "I would go to you and leave all that is dear to me here."[118] Even though Mary was "well in property," and had many friends, not to mention two fine sons, she admitted to her sister, "I am troubled with the lowness of spirits" caused by her husband's "ill treatment."

If a woman did leave her husband, it was not unusual to find a notice placed by him in a newspaper, announcing her departure and his refusal to cover any debts she might incur. The *Royal Gazette and New Brunswick Advertiser* for 27 July 1812 contained such a notice placed by Thomas Ingleby of Saint John: "Whereas my wife Sarah has left my Bed and Board without any just cause or Complaint whatever; this is therefore to forbid all Persons from trusting her on my Account, as I am determined to pay no debts of her contracting."[119] Stephen Harris inserted a notice in the *Connecticut Gazette* about his wife in even stronger terms:

> Whereas my wife Betsey Harris has eloped from my Bed and Board, and carried away with her my daughter Mary-Ann Harris about five years old, this is therefore to forbid all persons from harboring or trusting my said wife or daughter on penalty of the law in such case made and provided, for I will pay no debt of their contracting after this date.[120]

With the exception of the aboriginal peoples, to whom divorce was simply a matter of a man or woman deciding to leave the other, the legal end of marriage was rare in 1812. Quite apart from the social stigma, the costs involved placed it beyond the financial means of the majority of women. Nevertheless, mention exists of a divorce petition lodged at New London County Court early in 1812 by Betsey Saunders of Preston, Connecticut. In it, she stated that she had been lawfully married in 1806 to Francis Saunders of Preston, but "that said Francis had committed the crime of adultery with violation of his marriage covenant, and hath absconded to some part of the world unknown to the petitioner."[121] The court ordered her to appear in the County Superior Court on "4th Tuesday of September next, when and where the respondent is required to appear and shew cause, why the prayer of said petition should not be granted."

The most famous divorce in North America of the period must surely have been that of Elizabeth (Betsy) Patterson Bonaparte of Baltimore and her husband, Jérôme, younger brother of Napoleon Bonaparte, who had married in 1803 and been forced apart by the emperor's disapproval of the match. After he annulled the union in France, Betsy was left with no alternative but to take the appropriate legal steps in the United States. Her petition to the General Assembly of Maryland was published in the *New York Evening Post* of 19 December 1812 under the title, "Madame Bonaparte's Petition for a Divorce." In it, Betsy declared that "Your petitioner deems it unnecessary, if indeed the delicacy of her situation would permit it, to recount those various considerations, that ought to influence an enlightened legislature in granting the necessary aid to dissolve a union contracted and maintained under such circumstances."[122] Having submitted her case, Betsy hoped that the Assembly, even given "the indissoluble nature of the marriage contract," would not fail to remember that "such cases may and do occur, where the happiness of individuals may be consulted without sacrificing the permanent good of society."[123] Betsy was fortunate – on 2 January 1813 a bill annulling the marriage was passed by a majority and signed by the governor of Maryland.

There were, of course, romantic relationships between men and women into which marriage, for one reason or another, did not enter. Liaisons of this nature were not uncommon but could be perilous to both parties, particularly at the higher levels of society, where avoiding scandal was of paramount importance. Nevertheless, danger did not stop men from keeping mistresses, although mistresses could be as dangerous as wives.

Consider the case of Janette Bilodeau-Parent in Lower Canada, who had long been the mistress of a certain Jude de Bonne, a man with political aspirations. When de Bonne ended their affair to make a marriage that would further his political career, Janette retaliated by publishing a letter in the newspaper *Le Canadien* because there was "no other way of obtaining justice."[124] With all the fury of a woman scorned, she added that her former lover had "the treachery to tell me that I was bringing him down" and that he had "shamelessly betrayed me" so that the public "would see him in a good light." Janette had done much to assist him in his early political career, but as she now informed the world, if "the scoundrel has got married and has suddenly become religious," this was only "to obtain your votes."[125]

Again, discretion was paramount in the matter of liaisons between unmarried couples. In the military, extra-marital affairs and mistresses were accepted so long as an officer's personal reputation and that of his service did not suffer. When they did, the results were predictable, as was the case with a Captain "C." of the 2nd U.S. Artillery Regiment, whose lover followed him to war in disguise, acting "as his waiter [servant] in men's clothes." This relationship not only embarrassed his fellow officers, it made the captain a laughing stock among his subordinates. Ultimately, the lovesick officer was court martialled and dismissed from the service.[126]

Captain James Basden of the 89th Regiment of Foot encountered similar problems after he took his mistress on campaign. When Basden's regiment was being transported up the St. Lawrence in the summer of 1813, he did not travel with his company but in the boat in which his lady friend was seated. Unfortunately, during a stop on the way, men from his company committed theft against some local farmers who complained to Basden's superior officer. Basden was suspended from duty, the first step to arraigning him before a court martial, but, as was his right, Basden wrote to the commander-in-chief, Lieutenant-General Sir George Prevost, in an attempt to explain the circumstances.

Stating that he had fourteen years of unblemished service during which it was his proud boast "not only to have escaped censure but to have done my duty," Basden confessed that the reason he had neglected his responsibilities was that he had brought a female companion to North America.[127] He was aware that this relationship might be regarded as "a blind infatuation," but to him it was an affair of the heart which "from my feelings receives a different title." Not wishing to be parted from her and "having understood from several to whom I applied for information, that women were constantly proceeding towards the Centre Division" in Upper Canada, he had taken her with him to that province. He had not intended to disobey orders, but his dereliction of duty had resulted from his "agony of mind," and Basden was sure that, when Prevost considered the matter, his "conduct will not appear in so unfavorable a point of view" and that the commander-in-chief might "be induced to mitigate the severity" of his censure.[128] Surprisingly, it actually worked and Basden was restored to command of his company and redeemed himself the following year by his conduct at the Battle of Lundy's Lane.

Probably the most notable incident involving a dangerous liaison during the War of 1812 concerned Captain James Leonard of the United States Navy. In November 1812 Leonard was posted to Sackets Harbor on Lake Ontario, where he took up his duties as second-in-command to Commodore Isaac Chauncey, commanding the American naval forces on the Great Lakes. When he arrived, Leonard was accompanied by a woman everyone assumed to be his wife, and he rented a hotel room for Mrs. Leonard in the village. Sometime later, rumours began to circulate that the woman was not who she purported to be. The hotel keeper, William Lord, told Leonard that if she was not his wife, "she must leave" but, according to Lord, Leonard replied that "he was not bound to tell me who she was, that if I got my pay for keeping her, it was sufficient for me."[129] Lord remembered that the lady in question behaved with the "decorum and propriety" expected of an officer's wife and that she received and returned courtesy calls from other officers' wives and accompanied the captain to social events. Nonetheless, the rumours increased, particularly after another woman confronted Mrs. Leonard about her relationship and received the reply that it was "nobody's business whether she was Captain Leonard's wife or his whore."[130] Tongues truly began to wag after "Mrs. Leonard" signed the name "Fanny Canfield" on a credit note issued at the store of a Mr. Lawrence at nearby Brownsville.

The woman was, in fact, Fanny Williamson, the wife of a Mr. Williamson of New York. Inevitably, the gossip reached the ears of Commodore Isaac Chauncey, Leonard's commanding officer, who had seen Fanny "sitting at the window of the house occupied by Captain Leonard."[131] Chauncey, whose own wife, Ann, had received "Mrs. Leonard" socially, told his second-in-command that the affair could not be tolerated and that the woman must go. Leonard confessed she was his mistress but gave Chauncey his undertaking that she had been sent away. It was therefore with some astonishment that a few weeks later Chauncey saw the couple "walking together publicly in the streets" of Sackets Harbor. He decided to turn a blind eye, however, and concentrate on winning the war rather than becoming enmeshed in what was now the very public private life of Mrs. Fanny Williamson and Captain James Leonard.[132]

The matter came to a head in April 1813 after Leonard took over command of a new warship, the USS *Madison*, which had just been completed. Chauncey insisted that his captains keep their ships "in a state of perfect preparation night and day to repel any attack that may be made by the Enemy," and he issued a general order that "no officer or Man on any pretext whatsoever is to sleep out of the Vessel which he belongs to without permission first obtained from me in writing or recommended by the Doctor."[133]

On the night of 12 April 1813 Leonard should have been on the *Madison*, but he had slipped ashore before dark to be with Fanny and was therefore not present when a strong wind pushed the ice against his ship and knocked her off her anchorage. According to Chauncey, it was only the "extraordinary efforts" of the crew of the *Madison* that saved the vessel from being a "total loss."[134] Chauncey hurriedly dressed and was rowed to the ship, where he spent four hours supervising efforts to secure the vessel. The *Madison* was still in "a very exposed and dangerous situation" when morning arrived, and Leonard finally came on board between 10.00 and 11.00 A.M. He apparently

Sackets Harbor, 1813. This small port was the headquarters of the United States Navy's Lake Ontario squadron, and the place where a wartime affair between Captain James Leonard, USN, and Fanny Williamson proved to be his downfall. Leonard's dereliction of duty led to his court martial in December 1813, his suspension from the navy and a public reprimand. (Painting by Peter Rindlisbacher, courtesy of the artist.)

left the ship again later same day "before she was either secured or in a place of safety" and without giving Chauncey an explanation "of his being absent from his duty."[135]

An infuriated Chauncey promptly placed Leonard under arrest for having "Slept on shore frequently" without permission, "particularly on the night of the 12th April inst."[136] The commodore then drew up charges against Leonard for disobedience of orders, neglecting his duty concerning the safety of his vessel, and, last but not least, for

> Dissolute and immoral practices – Specification – For introducing some time in December last, your Mistress, to the family of Major Samuel Brown and Suffering her afterwards to pass as your Wife and in violation of your promise

to me, you are now living with the same Woman in the most public manner, whereby you neglect your duty to your Country and to your Ship, and Set a bad example to the officers generally, and the young Midshipmen in particular one of which lives in the House with you and your Mistress.[137]

Leonard was ordered to remain in or near Sackets Harbor until a court martial could be convened, and the exasperated Chauncey deliberately took his time in making the necessary arrangements. It was not until December 1813 that Leonard was tried and, after eight days of testimony about his disobedience, neglect of duty and conduct unbecoming an officer, was found guilty on all counts, suspended from the service for twelve months and publicly reprimanded in a general order read "on board every ship in the Navy of the United States, and at every station where were naval officers serving."[138] Leonard remained in the navy but was never again given command of a warship – a high price to pay for passion and arrogance.

The women with whom officers had affairs without any thought of marriage probably accepted that such liaisons were not likely to last. Occasionally they had tragic consequences, as a popular song of the period, "The Unfortunate Miss Bailey," tells us:

> A captain bold from Halifax
> Once left his captain quarters,
> Seduced a maid who hanged herself
> One morning in her garters.
> His wicked conscience smited him,
> He lost his stomach daily,
> He took to drinking turpentine
> And thought upon Miss Bailey.[139]

Alas, the song was not far off the mark. A soldier of the 68th Foot recalled when one of the officers of his regiment kept a mistress but later rejected her "for some error in her conduct."[140] The result was "most painful, for the poor creature put an end to her existence, by taking poison." As was to be expected, the officer escaped any blame in the matter, for "the jury brought in a verdict of lunacy," and she was buried, "pitied by all who knew her."

It was not only officers who engaged in this kind of behaviour. Lieutenant John Le Couteur's soldier servant, Private Cornelius Mills, became involved with the maidservant of another officer. Again, as Le Couteur recorded, the result was tragic:

My rascal Mills played me and my friend Mrs S[hore] a vile trick by getting her maid in the family way. I and He wished to marry her but Captain S[hore] would never consent to it which I was exceedingly angry at. However both the poor girl & child died. He was very penitent and really wished to do what He ought but was prevented – shamefully, I think.[141]

P roblems and pitfalls notwithstanding, romance appears to have flourished during the difficult years from 1812 to 1815. Although there were times when stress, danger and tragedy took their toll, many couples separated by the circumstances of war were sustained by their relationships. Most cherished the hope, which sprang eternal even when conditions seemed so uncertain, that there would be a life to share when the fighting was over. In anticipation of happier times, the following verse, written by a British woman, offered comfort and consolation:

> When vexed by cares and harassed by distress,
> The storms of fortune chill thy soul with dread,
> Let Love, consoling Love! still sweetly bless,
> And his assuasive balm benignly shed:
> His downy plumage o'er thy pillow spread.[142]

German engraving, 1813.

Madeline La Framboise (1780-1846), according to those who knew her, was a woman of great energy, enterprise, charm and dignity. The daughter of a French-Canadian fur trader and an Ottawa woman, she married fur trader Joseph La Framboise, and after his death she continued their business independently and very successfully. After her retirement in 1822, Madeline La Framboise divided her time between Montreal and Mackinac Island, where she built a fine house and became involved in charitable work. This portrait of her was painted from a description. (Courtesy of the Harbor View Inn, Mackinac Island. Photograph by Jeff Dupre.)

CHAPTER THREE

"For their work continueth."
Gainful Employment

Sweet Poll of Plymouth was my dear,
When forc'd from her to go,
Adown her cheek rained many a tear,
My heart was fraught with woe.
Our anchor weigh'd for sea we stood,
The land we left behind,
Her tears then swell'd the briny flood,
My sighs increas'd the wind.[1]

Although hearth and home was the focus of life for most North American women of the wartime period, necessity, vocation and a desire for greater independence were among the circumstances which prompted some to seek employment, – domestic and otherwise. Amelia Simmons and Hannah Glasse took that step and their cookery and household books quickly became best sellers. They were not alone. According to period newspapers, there were other enterprising women engaged in a wide range of occupations. Mary Salmon of Boston ran a shop where "all sorts of Blacksmith's Work" was done "with Fidelity and Dispatch."[2] Marguerite Hastier of New York City was a silversmith, Ann Mott of Saint John, a printer, Jane Massey of Charleston, a gunsmith, and Mary Wilson of Norfolk, Virginia, a shoemaker. Jane Marion of York successfully ran the bakery established by her late husband, while Elizabeth Russell, another Charleston resident, advertised as a shipwright in the *South Carolina Gazette*. Readers of the *Pennsylvania Gazette* may have noted with interest that Mrs. Lydia Darragh made "Grave-Clothes" and laid out "the Dead, in the neatest Manner."[3]

Many women assisted in businesses owned and run by their husbands or fathers. They found that there were customers to be served, paperwork to be completed, apprentices to be supervised and a range of other ways in which a woman could usefully contribute. Margaret Jordan, whose husband ran a tannery in New Brunswick, handled all business matters during her husband's frequent absences, discussing problems or queries with the foreman and taking care of paperwork and administration. The personal papers of Lower Canadian administrators and merchants show that their wives could be authorized to participate in business negotiations and represent their husbands in legal disputes. In addition, spouses helped to cultivate the social contacts necessary to further their husbands' careers at a time when business alliances were much valued.[4] Theoretically, if a woman – other than a widow – chose to work in her husband's business she earned little more than her keep, since the law of the period did not recognize her right to control her income. In practice, however, a good husband would have been unlikely to exploit his wife's lack of access to her earnings and would have made proper provision for her.

Given the prevailing convention that a woman's place was in the home, many worked in a domestic capacity. With large numbers of people on the move during the war – officers, soldiers, families, couriers, merchants and the like – housewives often earned much-needed extra income by providing bed and board. The quality of the meal depended in part on the availability of produce, but some travellers were fortunate to enjoy excellent hospitality, as in the case of those who stayed at the home of Nancy Crysler, wife of Canadian militia officer Colonel John Crysler, who lived not far from present-day Morrisburg, Ontario. Mrs. Crysler was a hard-working and hospitable Dutch housewife. Militia Captain Jacques Viger described how she equalled her husband in "hospitality and civilities" and "all sorts of attentions," which included "most comfortable beds" and an excellent "*déjeuner à la fourchette.*"[5] Surgeon William Dunlop also stayed at the Crysler home and when the good doctor sat down to eat in the dining room, in which he observed tapestries and "bright and shining" crockery (for Mrs. Crysler also believed in keeping an immaculately clean house in the "most classic style of Dutch taste"), he faced "a variety and profusion of meat, fish, eggs, cakes and preserves" for breakfast and dinner.[6]

With so many on the move, business was brisk for boarding houses during the war. In May 1813, a Mrs. Sprowlls advertised in the *Montreal Herald* that she had moved to a "commodious house" where her attention would be "wholly devoted to the accommodation of boarders" on terms "as reasonable as circumstances will permit."[7] Mrs. Plum in New Orleans and Mrs. Bradish in New York were also known for their excellent hospitality, and Mrs. Bradish's establishment was reported to be "the best boarding-house in the United States."[8] It catered for men and women, and in the dining room up to forty at a time were seated at one huge table. The lady of the house, who presided at its head, prided herself upon her breakfasts, which were "celebrated for their profusion," and her reputation was such that she attracted high-ranking officers and officials among her guests.[9]

In the early nineteenth century, taverns in North America were many and various, and often set up in tandem with another business. At Hanford's Landing on the Genesee River in New York, for example, Abraham Hanford and his wife ran their tavern with "a store of goods." According to a young man who lived and worked with the Hanfords, Mrs. Hanford was a "fine looking, handsome" woman and her hostelry was "very pleasant."[10] Some of these taverns were managed by women working alone. A Mrs. Hunter advertised in the *Montreal Herald* in 1813 that she had "removed from the Old Market place to the New" where she continued "to keep a Tavern and Groceries, as formerly."[11] In the case of a petition lodged by Marie Antoinette Bouquin, a French woman who arrived in Lower Canada with De Watteville's regiment that year, she had formerly been in charge of the officers' mess of this unit and wished to "keep a Tavern at Montreal, until the Said Officers Shall again take her into their Service."[12]

Once a tavern was established, it could do well if properly managed. Close to the falls of Niagara in Upper Canada was a rather famous establishment that had been in business since the 1790s. It was started by Canadian Charles Willson and his wife, Debora, an American who had deserted her previous husband. When Charles died shortly before the war began, Debora and her two attractive daughters, Harriet and Statira, continued to manage the tavern, which became known colloquially as the "Widow Willson's place." Throughout the war, Willson's tavern was patronized by the officers of both belligerent armies, and Debora Willson, despite being American-born, was always careful to remain absolutely neutral. The establishment's popularity was enhanced by the presence of Harriet and Statira, the latter being so striking that one young British officer termed her the "Naiad of the Falls."[13]

During the late afternoon of 25 July 1814, Brigadier-General Winfield Scott of the American army, moving north with his brigade along the Niagara River, stopped to ask Debora Willson about the presence of British troops in the area. She gave him – as she gave the officers of both armies – perfectly accurate information that they were nearby in strength. Scott continued on his way to initiate what later became known as the Battle of Lundy's Lane, one of the bloodiest

The tavern by the falls. Debora Willson, a widow with two pretty daughters, ran a tavern in Upper Canada near Niagara Falls that was popular with troops of both sides during the war. It was situated behind the trees on the high ground to the left of this painting of Niagara Falls and did brisk business throughout the war years. (Painting by George Heriot, 1814. Library and Archives of Canada, C-12797.)

engagements of the War of 1812. That same night, Debora Willson's tavern, being close to the scene of the fighting, was pressed into service by the American army as an emergency dressing station for the many wounded.[14]

Across the border, any traveller who stopped at Cold Springs, near Buffalo, found an excellent hostelry named Hodge's Tavern. Run by the Hodge family, it was known locally as the "brick house on the hill," and Mrs. Hodge's son, William, later recorded that "all battles and events of the war were fully related and discussed in our bar-room."[15] According to William Hodge, there were two rooms on the lower floor, one of which served as a combination parlour, sitting room, main kitchen and dining-room, while the other was

> the more public one. It could not be mistaken as one looked toward the right on entering by the large front door into the hall. There the eye was caught by large black letters on an unpainted door, telling the visitor to "WALK IN."[16]

The public room contained an open fire and a bar partitioned off in one corner, to enable food to be prepared and dishes cleaned. Under the shelves of her bar, Mrs. Hodge had "the whiskey and cider barrels" as well as "kegs of brandy, rum and gin, and one or two kinds of wine."[17] In season, she offered "spruce beer, home-made, of course," and cider, which in the cold weather "was set upon coals and embers to heat." A tavernkeeper like Mrs. Hodge had to know how to prepare a mixed drink known as a "sling," which consisted of "sugar-water and brandy, rum or gin, well stirred with the 'sugar-stick.'" Hot slings were made the same way, using a heated iron "to temper them" and a sprinkling of nutmeg. According to the custom, most people were as used to drinking these "different kinds of liquors as beverages, as people now are of using tea, coffee, and even milk."[18]

Innkeeping involved the provision of adequate food and drink for guests, servicing the bedrooms – placing fresh candles in candlesticks, washing and supplying clean bedlinen, shaking up and turning the featherbeds, filling wash-stand pitchers – and arranging stabling for horses and the reception of car-riages. Inns gained a reputation for their food, service, atmosphere and the standard of the guests. Two inns at Forty Mile Creek in Upper Canada, between York and the Niagara, were the popular haunts of "every officer [who] could get in."[19] Run by Mrs. Lewis and the Nelles family respectively, both were busy during the war years and on one occasion Mrs. Lewis was run ragged by her guests, a hungry group of young officers, who "got her to put some veal on the spit, and some salmon in the pot; and these she cooked amidst repeated calls, and endless din."[20]

At a popular inn on the Credit River in Upper Canada, Assistant Surgeon Samuel Holmes of the 97th Foot found himself one of a multitude of visitors. "Every room and corner," he remembered, "swarmed with Indians, their squaws and children, with boatmen, soldiers, and some of their adventurous wives," who "were eating, and drinking, and bartering, and clamouring, and drying their clothes, and pressing round the fires in a state of semi-nudity."[21] All those present were having such a good time that one young man stood up in the midst of the throng flourishing a "lump of broiled fish in one hand, and mug of peach-brandy in the other" and cried out, "if this be war, may he never have a clean pipe at his wake that wishes for peace."

Surviving sources suggest that inns were either very good or rather bad. Among the favourable wartime accounts of such establishments was one con-cerning Rogers's Inn at Stamford, Upper Canada. "Rogers is the best in the province," was the opinion of Surgeon Holmes, who sampled a number of hostelries on his travels. He was impressed by the fact that Mrs. Rogers was quick to spot the needs of her customers and to produce a bottle of something warming with which to "expel" the "chilly sensations" after a journey.[22] Some innkeepers overcharged, and on his way to the city of Quebec, American prisoner of war Samuel White paid eight dollars (the approximate amount of his monthly pay) for a change of clothing which amounted to nothing better than two old shirts.[23] At Point au Bodet, between Montreal and Kingston, Captain Christopher Hagerman had to spend one November night at an inn which he described as "intolerable bad."[24] The innkeeper was "a Canadian Dame about 6 feet 2 inches in heighth, who is as surly as she is big and ugly, & seldom gives you any thing you ask for." In this case, however, there were compensations, for the "Dame" had two "tolerably well looking Daughters," whose "opposite dispositions to their mother's," Hagerman decided, "sometimes compensates the way worn traveller for his other discomforts and privations."

Running a reputable inn or hotel, then as now, was a demanding job requiring – to use modern jargon – culinary, management and inter-personal skills. Mallard's Inn at Saint John did brisk business during the war under the direction of Margaret Bonsall and Nancy Farquhar, daughters of Loyalists. Their parents had built the hotel with its huge kitchen, eight fireplaces, tavern, dining room, bedrooms with comfortable canopied beds, and a large room reserved for assemblies and theatrical performances, and well before 1812 Mallard's Inn had a reputation for excellence. Saint John being a busy port, it catered to a variety of visitors: travellers from the regular post chaise running to and from Fredericton; those who had ridden miles through the New Brunswick forest to reach the coast; traders from the West Indies; British military families; local officials; and captains of merchant vessels setting out for Europe with cargoes of timber. After the death of their mother, Ann, in 1812, Margaret and Nancy devotedly continued the family business at Mallard's Inn, which was well known for its good, wholesome food and its warm welcome.[25]

For one lady innkeeper the war brought unexpected prosperity. As Sarah Smith Emery of Newburyport, Massachusetts, remembered, "it is an ill wind that blows no one good," for she was able to profit from the fact that British manufacturers were running "cargo after cargo into their eastern provinces," from where they crossed the border by ox teams.[26] At Sarah's tavern at Newburyport, the "accommodations were excellent," and the teamsters used it as their headquarters. The Emerys' prosperity began one night when Sarah and her husband, David, were awakened by a knock on their bedroom window. Outside was a local man with a stagecoach "filled with merchandise, gloves, muslins, laces, vestings, ribbons, and other articles of a like description."[27] Sarah recalled that the goods were "hastily placed in my best bedroom, from whence they were gradually taken to the stores in town." As more items started to cross illicitly into New England, a weekly trade began at the Emerys' establishment that lasted until early 1815. Some evenings, Sarah counted "a dozen or fifteen" wagons drawn up outside. It was not long before the *Boston Gazette* was advertising "Liverpool ware china, imported English hats" and "elegant white Superior Long Shawls."[28]

The local collectors of customs were in the habit of frequenting the tavern and on one occasion Sarah "entertained the two old gentlemen in my parlor" while her husband loaded a team with contraband "and drove away to West Newbury without exciting the slightest suspicion."[29] When some pretty shawls arrived, Sarah made sure they reached the store of Dolly Carnes, a lady who ran a haberdashery business in Newburyport, which "brought a rush of customers to that spinster's establishment," for "shawls were in great demand with wool being scarce."[30] In spite of the risks Sarah and David Emery took they were never apprehended, and their quiet, orderly tavern remained the perfect front for a successful smuggling operation.

Women who ventured outside the traditional domestic sphere were most successful in winning society's acceptance when they engaged in charitable and religious work, or became teachers. In Boston, charity work had a long tradition and in 1801 a group of Congregational women organized the Boston Female Society for Propagating the Diffusion of Christian Knowledge. In Montreal, a secular organization of women was founded around the same time to help the sick and the poor, and to care for and educate abandoned children. This type of activity was well established by 1812, and as cases of hardship came to the notice of government authorities during the war years, benevolent societies were established in which women were employed. The Female Hospitable Society of Philadelphia offered a chance to earn money by sewing and spinning. It aimed to help all "as are not able to procure work living as domestics," and especially those with husbands who "by the Calamity of War" could not provide for their families and were "obliged to resign their wives and children" to employment "in honest industry." The women could make "Silk Stockings, Table Linen, Quilting, Bed Covers" and similar items.[31]

Those who chose to enter religious orders took their reward in their faith, the security of their life, and the knowledge that they were doing good work. In Lower Canada there were communities such as the *demoiselles de la Charité chargées par Sa Majesté de la direction de l'Hôpital-General de Montréal*,[32] better

Les Ursulines de Québec. The forty-five or so nuns at the Ursuline convent at Quebec, illustrated here, devoted themselves principally to the education of girls. To supplement their income from teaching, they also sold needlework and produce from their bakery and garden. Said to be more rigid in their seclusion than other orders, the Ursulines wore a long black robe with a black veil that made them look, according to one early-nineteenth-century traveller, like "so many walking coffins." (Painting by John Lambert. Library and Archives of Canada, C-84461.)

known as the Grey Nuns. Another order, the *Ursulines de Trois-Rivières*, had opted for a peaceful, austere, convent life structured so that women of more humble origin undertook housework, while those with a higher level of education concentrated on community work such as teaching and hospital care.

Although women made early inroads into the medical profession during the war, teaching was a sphere where they had long been involved. Since a good education was considered essential for any young lady and the trend towards a European-style education in North America was on the rise, more upper-class girls than ever were being educated in this manner, even though some people regarded it as merely providing accomplishments which were inappropriate to life in their country. Rosalie Stier Calvert of Bladensburg, Maryland, tended to this view, telling her sister in a letter, "the education of young girls here is quite mistaken at present" because they were being raised "as if they are going to marry dukes and marquises, and then [the girls] don't ensnare anybody because the men are afraid of their airs and expenses."[33]

Nevertheless, parents who wanted the latest and best education for their girls sent them to finishing schools, academies and female seminaries whose aim was to produce a lady able to mix in society at home and abroad. These establishments offered instruction in subjects such as reading, arithmetic, spelling, penmanship, geography and French. Classics were taught on occasions, and instead of history or politics, girls read plays, poetry, novels and moral tracts, and learned the skills of music, singing, playing an instrument, dancing, painting, drawing and fine needlework.

There were many women running such schools during the war, and they usually solicited students in the local newspaper. Among the more interesting, Mrs. Holland, wife of the bandmaster of the 19th Light Dragoons, advertised in the *Montreal Herald* that she and her husband had opened a "BOARDING & DAY SCHOOL, for the Tuition of Young Ladies," where girls would also learn dancing, music and singing in addition to the normal range of academic subjects.[34] Her husband taught the flute, the pianoforte and singing, and this very musical family promised that "every exertion will be made for the improvement of their Pupils." In Halifax, Mrs. Powell, married to the manager of the city's Theatre Royal, not only acted in the plays her husband staged, but she and her daughters taught dancing.[35]

The curriculum of the many schools then catering to young women students in large cities across North America can be judged from a printed prospectus of the Montreal Ladies Seminary, "under the direction of Mr. & Mrs. Andrews; Assisted By Their Son & Daughters."[36] The Andrews family advertised that

> EVERY Study comprised in a useful, literary, and accomplished education, is taught in this Establishment, by the respective Persons engaged. In Drawing and Painting, instructions are given by Mr. W.W. Andrews; and in Music, Dancing, and the various uses of the Needle, by the MISSES ANDREWS.[37]

Fees varied from 2 to 3 guineas (about $8 to $12) a quarter plus an extra 5 shillings (about $1) per quarter for pens and ink with "One Load of Fire Wood, for each Child, expected in the Winter." The Andrews also took in boarding students at 9 guineas per quarter (about $36), payable in advance, and these students were "required to furnish their own Bed and Bedding; and a Table, Tea Spoon, and Napkins for their own accommodation," and were "allowed to visit their friends on Saturdays only."[38]

Some women took up teaching out of necessity, sometimes after the death of a husband. Elizabeth Regan Fairchild of Saint John was widowed early in life and at the age of thirty-four decided to open a school for boys in her house.[39] In Montreal, it was financial need that drew Jean-Charlotte Berczy into taking on pupils. The Swiss wife of painter William Moll Berczy, Jean-Charlotte soon established herself as the city's "Mistress of Drawing," and this was not surprising, for she had spent five years studying painting in Florence and exhibiting at London's Royal Academy before coming to North America. During the war Madame Berczy remained a well-known figure in Montreal, where she taught art, music and languages to the children of the city's privileged.[40]

Another woman attracted to teaching was a former actress who became America's earliest best-selling novelist. The theatre first brought Susanna Haswell Rowson to North America, for she had been spotted in Edinburgh by the manager of the Chestnut Street Theatre in Philadelphia. After a spell as a pleasing but not particularly talented actress, Susanna decided to open a school for girls, and continued to teach near Boston throughout the war. She seemed to have found her vocation, for she was deeply committed to young women becoming "thinking citizens in a democratic nation."[41] This conviction distinguished Mrs. Rowson from her contemporaries, and she used the characters in a series of novels she wrote between 1786 and 1804 to indirectly convey such strongly-held ideas as her disapproval of snobbery, the value of hard work and independence, and the importance of being content with one's station in life.

Susanna Rowson went out of her way to encourage her pupils to study literature and fine arts and also advised them to learn their legal rights. While she continued to believe that the first duties of a woman were domestic, she did not support the prevalent degree of emphasis on romance and marriage, and cherished her own independence as a working woman.[42] It has been written of this exceptional woman that "the varied and somewhat romantic life led by that lady perhaps fitted her, better than would have been thought," to be the guide and friend of the girls she hoped to influence towards a more independent existence.[43]

Lydia Sigourney, who would also become an American writer of note, attended two of the best seminaries in Hartford and passed on the fruits of her education to others. She and a friend opened a school in Norwich, Connecticut, and were "thronged with applicants."[44] The two women realized they were considered by some to be too young to take on such a responsible venture, yet their school prospered throughout the war. Mornings were devoted to academic subjects and afternoons to the "ornamental branches" of learning such

Susanna Haswell Rowson
(1762-1824), a former actress
who became America's first
best-selling novelist, was originally from Britain. After a spell
as a pleasing but not especially
talented thespian, she opened
a school for girls near Boston,
where she taught throughout
the war. An exceptional woman
and a progressive theorist for
her times, Susanna Rowson was
deeply committed to women
becoming "thinking citizens
in a democratic nation." (Oil
on canvas by unknown art-
ist. Courtesy of Worcester Art
Museum, Worcester, Massa-
chusetts.)

as embroidery, painting and drawing.[45] Lydia and her colleague enjoyed their
work and each evening they spent time "taking counsel for the reform of those
who needed it, and for the welfare of all." The fees charged yielded "no great
pecuniary gain" to the enthusiastic pair, who were teachers as much for the love
of their work, as for any financial reward.[46]

Among those educators who believed that a more academic curriculum was
important for female students were Ellen and Rachel Mordecai of Warrenton,
North Carolina. Members of a distinguished Jewish family and, coincidentally, friends of Elizabeth Kennon of Virginia, the sisters taught at their father's
school and fully supported the type of education it offered, aimed at enabling
young women to contribute to society as the mothers of the future. The school
advertised itself as a "Female Academy" and offered a scholarly education that
included, "Reading, Spelling, Writing, Arithmetic, English Grammar and Pars-
ing, History, Geography and the use of the Globes, Astronomy, Mythology and
Blair's Rhetorick."[47] It also catered to the need of young ladies to acquire the
necessary accomplishments of music, drawing, French and "Plain and Ornamental Needle-work."

The level of education these women teachers offered was available to only
a small minority of girls in North America. Some daughters of poorer families received instruction through the church at a convent where, in addition to

religious studies, they were taught housekeeping and sewing. Many, however, received little or no formal instruction, and what they learned was often from a parent or neighbour who had some knowledge of reading, writing and arithmetic, or from an itinerant teacher passing through their district.[48] Remoter communities, in particular, fared badly but there were missionaries working as teachers, as is known from a letter written in 1813 by the Bishop of Nova Scotia, Dr. Charles Inglis. It mentions that a British and Foreign Bible Society missionary, Mrs. Margaretta Legette, a widow with a large family, had applied for the appointment of school mistress at Country Harbour, Nova Scotia, and was regarded by the Bishop as a "decent, respectable woman" and "very competent" to hold that position.[49] Bishop Inglis wholeheartedly recommended her for the post in question as he did Mrs. Anne McKensie, a fifty-year-old widow from England who had requested a similar appointment at Hubbard's River, where there were "upwards of 25 children capable of instruction without the means of obtaining it."

Many women chose to enter the clothing trade. Dolly Carnes of Newburyport was one of a number of ladies who ran businesses concerned with women's fashions. Seamstresses, weavers and corset-makers were also to be found, and many seamstresses operated from home or shared premises with their husbands. After a short, but expensive apprenticeship, usually completed before the age of nineteen, a girl was trained and ready to begin this kind of work, for which there was considerable demand. Although many women made their own clothes, wealthier ladies often hired a dressmaker to produce gowns for them.

Knowing the importance of European fashions, dressmakers were at pains to make it clear that they kept up with the latest trends. Mrs. Smith and Miss Jones, "Pelisse, Mantle & Fancy Dress Makers" of 31 Warren Street, New York, advertised in the *New York Evening Post* in 1813 that they had "received by the late arrivals, patterns of Dresses for the present Season."[50] Gowns could be made "at shortest notice," and Smith and Jones particularly assured ladies "residing in the country" that they, too, could have "their cloaths made in the newest fashion" by "sending a dress that fits." There appears to have been no shortage of materials available for dressmakers during the war years, with merchants like Messrs. M. Marks & Company of Richmond announcing that among their "Spring Goods" in 1813, were "fancy Muslins" and "striped half silks."[51] In New York that same year, Mr. Benjamin Jewell's store was offering a wide range of fabrics from "japanned and seeded cambrics" and "Irish linen" to "domestic stripes and ginghams."[52]

Given the prevailing fashions and the demand for hats and bonnets, millinery was another trade that attracted an increasing number of women. A few days after the outbreak of the war, Mary Southgate of Richmond, Virginia, respectfully informed the ladies of that city that she had "just opened a choice assortment of *Fashionable Millinery*," having made arrangements with a supplier in New York.[53] Mary's business flourished, for some eighteen months later she again advertised in the same newspaper, telling local ladies that she had "just returned from New York, Philadelphia and Baltimore" and would very shortly be receiving from those places, "a seasonable and fashionable assortment of Millinery."[54]

Dressmakers were not restricted to the major cities. Since 1808, Maria de Dieman had been running the first specialized "mantuamaking business in all its branches" at York, Upper Canada, and a year before the war she engaged an apprentice, moved premises and was clearly doing well enough to expand.[55] Another York resident, Frances Murray, opened a second mantuamaking and millinery shop in the town in 1810, and both enterprises survived the war. They, and all the other women engaged in the business of providing fashionable ladies' apparel, were pioneers in their field, for it was not until after the war that increased demand made dressmaking and millinery recognized and respectable crafts.

Women in lower income families often chose to work as servants to the wealthy, and as cooks, dairymaids, wet nurses or governesses. It was usually the eldest daughters of large families who were sent out to do such work to help make ends meet, and it is no surprise that they changed jobs frequently in an effort to find a better position. A servant girl could be hired at a young age but had to wait until marriage brought the security that enabled her to escape her daily drudge. Many were indentured or legally bound over to serve for a set period and for some, the life became so intolerable that they did, indeed, abscond. In December 1813, Jane R. Sims of Philadelphia placed a newspaper advertisement in *Poulson's Weekly Advertiser* offering a reward of three dollars for Betsey Schaeffer, her "indented servant girl," who had run away, taking "1 brown and 1 red and white striped Silk Frocks, 1 Cambric and 3 striped Cotton ditto, 2 pair Germantown toilled Stockings, 5 Aprons, and many other articles of Clothing. Also a red leather trunk."[56]

A polite, hard-working servant earned her mistress's approval and support. At Bladensburg, Rosalie Stier Calvert and her husband had some eighty slaves working on their plantations, and in their household were several who were highly regarded by their mistress. A girl called Kitty cleaned and made beds and was only about fourteen years old. She was "quite skilful," and "even puts my hair in curl-papers every night," wrote Rosalie, who regarded her as invaluable, as she did her cook, Fanny.[57] Fanny's "occasional intemperance" was balanced by the fact that she was excellent at making "all sorts of cakes, pastries, sausages, bread, etc." Another black servant, Lucie, who had accompanied Rosalie's parents to Europe on one occasion, was also described as "a very good chambermaid and conducts herself well."[58]

Good cooks were always much in demand, for a woman who could work

At the hearth. Often it was the eldest daughters of large families who were sent out to work as domestic servants. A servant girl could be hired at a young age and would remain in service until the security of marriage enabled her to escape her daily drudge. Good domestic help was valued, for it was not always easy to find in North America. In this print, a maid is taking a short break from her labours in the company of a feline friend. (Print after painting by Leslie George Dunlop, c. 1800. Photograph by René Chartrand.)

magic with the mixing bowl or the bread oven was never short of work. At Fredericton, New Brunswick, Lieutenant-Colonel Joseph Gubbins noted that when it came to entertaining, there was a constant demand for two or three local women who could be "hired by the day to dress a dinner and attend at table, and they are to be seen at all parties and their dishes recognized."[59]

In the more senior position of housekeeper, a good professional woman was valued and esteemed, and at one point Gertrude Lewis was fortunate to find a Mrs. Tillotson to help her run her home near Staatsburg, New York. Mrs. Tillotson's abilities were evidently many and varied, for she

> excelled in the domestic arts, so useful in a household, so graceful in a woman. Her hands were always ready to perform her will, whether to cut a silhouette or to stitch a wristband. Had she the opportunity to cultivate her talents, she might have been an artist.[60]

In contrast to these traditional women's' pursuits, there are also accounts of women being active in what were, at that time, male occupations. The name of a British woman, Molly Thompson, appeared among the listed owners of ship, the *Victory* of Liverpool, which was captured during the War of 1812 by an American privateer, *Viper*. Taken to Hampden, Maine, as a prize, the *Victory* was re-captured by British forces in September 1814 and restored to its owners in October of that year.[61] At York, Upper Canada, Jane Marion was actively engaged in work as a baker when the war broke out, having inserted a small notice in the *Upper Canada Gazette* confirming her intention of carrying on the family "baking business and keeping a house of entertainment," which was to say, an inn. The widowed Jane had helped her late husband and understudied him in all aspects of his craft, as well as handling customers and working as hostess and cook at their inn. Such valuable experience was now put to good use as she took on the mantle of sole proprietor.[62]

In 1814, Ann Mott of Saint John was another widow who was about to embark on a new career. Her late husband had been the official British government printer, authorized by His Majesty King George III to print all proclamations for the King's forces in the province, and Ann decided to continue his work. Being the King's Printer, as the sign over the shop doorway indicated, was no small matter and for a woman to take over such a prestigious appointment was unprecedented, but Ann Mott had also understudied her husband and worked with him to found the province's first newspaper, the *Royal Gazette and Nova*

Scotia Intelligencer. As the first woman in New Brunswick to own and operate a printing business, Ann was determined to continue both the business and the newspaper, and she changed her shop sign to "Royal Printer," since no woman could hold the title of King's Printer. The inaugural edition of her newly-named newspaper, the *Gazette and New Brunswick Advertiser*, appeared on 11 January 1815 with a paragraph explaining that she was now sole proprietor, "aided only by the exertions of her son," and an assurance that "no pains" would be spared to "render the Paper worthy" of the continued support of local readers.[63]

In her role as newspaper proprietor, it was clear that Ann Mott not only had a good head for journalism, but she was also prepared to work hard. She did much of the printing herself, including operating a press that produced one sheet at a time, and also tackled reporting, editing and screening replies to advertisements. While other women were sewing at home or enjoying dinners or card parties, Ann Mott worked by candlelight, scouring the latest London papers for articles she could insert into the *New Brunswick Advertiser*. It was not long before she was able to advertise for an apprentice to learn the business, and in time, could lay just claim to her success as a pioneer Canadian woman publisher.

Some aboriginal women also engaged in business pursuits. By 1812 Scottish fur trader Robert Dickson had been running his trading post at Fort Traverse in present-day Minnesota for twenty-five years, and the presence of his Sioux wife, To-to-win, had been most influential in forging links with the aboriginal peoples in the region. As agent and superintendent for the "Indians of the Nations to the Westward of Lake Huron," Dickson, who was anxious to co-operate in any military plan that might produce British supremacy in the region, was able to use his connections to great advantage.[64] During his many wartime absences, To-to-win's life continued to be busy at the trading post. Not only did she conduct the business of the post, but she also raised four children.

Elsewhere in the remote Michigan Territory, another woman made an extremely successfully living in the years before the war. Madeline La Framboise, or "Madame La Framboise" as she was generally known, was a *métis*, the beautiful daughter of a French fur trader and an Ottawa woman of high birth. Having married Joseph La Framboise, another fur trader, she and her husband lived and worked in western Michigan and set up their headquarters on the Grand River. Madeline's two mother tongues, her knowledge of aboriginal ways and customs, and her ability to control and handle aboriginal warriors "no matter what their condition," had proved to be important factors in making her and her husband among the most successful traders of their day.[65] She remained a "very potent factor in maintaining peace and goodwill" among the people of the territory, but tragedy struck in 1806 when her husband was murdered and she was left a widow with two children.

It was expected that Madame La Framboise would give up her business but instead she obtained her own trader's license and set up a trading post near the present-day city of Grand Rapids, a step that demanded great courage and perseverance. There, she superintended the clerks and *engagés* and satisfied herself that business was being conducted in a proper and profitable manner. Her work required much time away travelling in remote country and coping with primitive conditions, and the fact that she often faced danger qualified her as "one of those hardy Great Lakes pathfinders who prepared the way for future settlers."[66] Her success was such that, according to records, she made up to ten times more than the average trader.

Every summer Madeline La Framboise attended the annual gathering of fur traders at Mackinac Island along with two other successful women dealers, her sister, Thérèse Schindler, and Margaret Mitchell, a Chippawa woman who was the wife of a British army surgeon. The aboriginal people brought their pelts to sell from far and wide and amid a throng of traders, clerks and *voyageurs* were men from the north, for the island also gave security to the activities of the Northwest Company and the Hudson's Bay Company. As the business of trading began, the village and its surroundings became a "scene of life and animation," as *voyageurs* sang, merchants gave lavish parties and the sounds of native dancing and chanting carried on the still air of a summer's evening.[67]

At Mackinac Island, Madame La Framboise was known and respected as an extremely successful *bourgeois*, or proprietor of her own enterprise, and her remarkable success in what was an almost exclusively male-dominated world was achieved despite the fact that she could not, at that time, read or write. To those who met her she was a dignified, graceful, refined and charming woman with hair as dark and shiny as "a crow's wing."[68] This distinguished businesswoman continued her enterprise until the War of 1812 threw the region into turmoil and put a damper on the fur trade. After the American garrison on Mackinac Island fell to British forces in August 1812, the island remained under British control until the end of the war and Madeline La Framboise remained with it. She got along well with the occupying forces and probably traded little throughout that time, accepting that business would not resume until the end of hostilities. She had come to love Mackinac so much that she had a house built there which survives today as the Harbor View Inn, among Mackinac's best-known hotels.

Mackinac, winter 1812. Nestling below Fort Mackinac, which by the first winter of the war was in British hands, can be seen the village that was often referred to as the "Gibraltar of the North." This remote outpost was of great strategic importance and a busy trading centre in the warmer months, hosting a gathering of fur traders from many parts of North America. In winter, however, it suffered from isolation and supply problems. Fort Mackinac remained in British hands until after the peace, when it was returned to the United States. (Painting by Peter Rindlisbacher, courtesy of the artist.)

It stands as a reminder of one of the wealthiest and most charismatic fur traders of the early nineteenth century and a woman who, along with her sister and the intelligent "eccentric, energetic and capable" Margaret Mitchell, was a pioneer in a male-dominated world.[69]

An entirely different work environment was that of Rosalie Stier Calvert. The Maryland plantations she owned with her husband, George, grew tobacco, wheat, maize, oats and clover, and while George was engaged in other business matters, Rosalie often looked after the day-to-day running of operations in addition to the supervision of her household and the direction of work in her gardens. Although running such a venture and managing investments required skills usually attributed to men, Rosalie was blessed with a good business sense and a natural interest in commerce. Encouraged by her Belgian father, she learned to control her own financial destiny and throughout the war played an active part in the fortunes of the plantations.

Too European and affluent to be typical of plantation owners at that time, Rosalie Calvert was, nevertheless, very diligent. "We get up at sunrise," she told her father, explaining that after breakfast, her children and her household usually occupied her until late morning when "I dress for the day and work."[70] There were occasions, Rosalie confessed, when she was simply "swamped with tasks" for, in addition to her domestic affairs and the problems associated with the plantations and their slave workers, she managed to bring nine children into the world. It was no wonder that she admitted, "sometimes I am so tired by evening that I fall asleep while taking tea."[71] When war came in 1812, Rosalie watched events with the eye of an astute political observer and businesswoman who had foreseen that the conflict would seriously affect the American economy and her family's investments. She negotiated the war years with difficulty, coping with a downturn in her financial affairs and the grief that followed the loss of two of her children from illness.

I n raising their families, North American women of the early nineteenth century inevitably dealt with illness, and some exceptional women worked as healers and midwives. Theirs was a skill requiring gentleness and wisdom, not only in treating patients and delivering babies, but also in acting as "community pharmacists" who believed that nature provided cures for all manner of ailments. They experimented as they observed the healing properties of plants, and often trained other female relatives in the same art.

One of the most notable women working in this field before the war was Martha Ballard, who lived on the Kennebec River in Maine. She tended the people of her district for many years, continuing until a few weeks before her death in 1812 at the age of seventy-seven, when she rode on horseback without a pillion to reach an expectant mother. During the years she served the surrounding communities, Martha journeyed through the worst of weather and survived storms and rivers in flood – on one occasion, she noted in her diary that she had to paddle across a tidal river with "A great sea A going."[72]

Because so few women of Martha Ballard's generation – especially in her chosen profession – left a written record of their lives, her diary is a special document. Besides delivering babies, she knew how to make teas, pills, ointments, syrups and salves using plants, roots and more common household items such as molasses, vinegar, spirits, soap and flour. She was extremely knowledgeable about finding and gathering herbs, and three quarters of those mentioned in her diary also appeared in Nicholas Culpeper's famous treatise *The Complete Herbal*, a classic on the subject published in London more than a century earlier. Martha Ballard knew how to poultice wounds, administer enemas, induce vomiting, reduce swelling, stop bleeding and prepare bodies for burial. Among the many complaints she treated were frostbite, colic, measles, dysentery, sore throat and some referred to in the language of the time as "the itch," "flying pains" and "the salt rhume."[73]

Martha Ballard's example of dedication and service was also to be found among other midwives and healers. At York in Upper Canada, Isabella Bennet, a "midwife from Glasgow," had a sign outside her home. Like Ann Mott of Saint John, Isabella was the wife of the King's Printer in the town and she was able to pursue her work while her husband pursued his.[74] In Clinton County, New York, Elizabeth Keese Smith had a distillery where she utilized "the medicinal properties of herbs and roots," having learned to make medicines and potions under the instruction of her mother, Ruth Hull, who was "a skilled botanist and understood these things."[75] Mother and daughter "practiced midwifery all over that part of the country as long as they were able," and like Martha Ballard, Elizabeth Keese Smith continued her work into old age. "She would get on horseback and ride over the mountains," her son recalled.

> I remember her telling me of going through the woods at night with a torch of birch bark in one hand and medicine in the other on roads marked only by blazed trees, while wolves and panthers were howling around her on all sides; they did not touch her because of the light.[76]

Typical of the local "healing women" in small communities and rural areas was the redoubtable Margaret Bruce, better known as Peggy Bruce, who ran the St. Andrew's and St. Patrick's Inn in Cornwall, Upper Canada. Peggy had eloped with her soldier husband during the Revolutionary War and, after her husband's death, had continued to run the business while raising four children and tending the sick and injured in the village. According to Surgeon William Dunlop of the British army, who lodged with her for some time, Peggy was "one of the best and most original characters" he had ever met, possessing many virtues but also a hair trigger temper, often displayed with guests she did not like. On occasions, she had resort to "all powers, offensive or defensive, by tongue or broom, as the case in hand rendered the one or the other more expedient."[77]

Although Surgeon Dunlop was in Peggy's favour, the relationship had its drawbacks because she insisted on dragging him to the bedside of anyone ailing in Cornwall at any hour of the day or night. When he remonstrated against being appointed "physician-extraordinary to the whole parish," particularly as there was a local doctor – whom Peggy considered "measurably inferior to any

Army medical man who wore His Majesty's uniform" – she had the perfect retort: "what the d ---- does the King pay you for, if you are not to attend to his subjects when they require your assistance."[78]

Having marched Dunlop to the home of an ailing person, Peggy was apt to first scold the lady of the house for not calling her sooner, and then to argue with Dunlop's diagnoses, her main medical *dictum* being that it was always essential to "support the strength."[79] This meant not only cramming the invalid with "every kind of food that by entreaty or importunity he could be prevailed upon to swallow," but also an insistence on a hot bath "infused with herbs," with which Dunlop agreed, as it would "most likely do good, and the herbs no harm." At the conclusion of a consultation, the indomitable Peggy would usually fish around in a pair of apron pockets "the size and shape of saddle bags," from which she would produce a couple of bottles of wine, which she "deemed might be useful to the patient." After these unwanted (to Dunlop at least) house calls, Peggy always rewarded him with "something comfortable kept warm" in the oven of her inn and a "stiffish horn of hot brandy and water."[80]

Besides serving as healers and midwives, women also worked as nurses. With the outbreak of war, civilian women joined army wives in working for the armies and many volunteered, or were co-opted, to look after sick and wounded soldiers. To fully understand the work of nursing assistants, it is necessary to know something of medical practice during the War of 1812. Many soldiers died from disease during the conflict and their treatment should have been a matter of the highest priority, but the Napoleonic period was, alas, not a time when the medical profession was noted for great efficiency, expertise, organization or hygiene.

Nursing assistants worked under the direction of male army surgeons who, with their surgeons' mates, dealt with wounds following battle, and with disease

The keeper of the St. Andrew's and St. Patrick's Inn.
Peggy O'Sullivan Bruce was one of the first Loyalist settlers in Cornwall, Upper Canada. The widow of a former soldier, during the War of 1812 she ran a log tavern in the town successfully enough to provide a living for herself and her four children. Peggy was known for her Irish wit and caustic humour, and for her round-the-clock care of the sick. She had no compunction about waking the nearest military surgeon and dragging him off in the dead of night to attend to a patient, but many had reason to be grateful for her care. (Silhouette, courtesy of Cornwall Museum Archives.)

and a range of medical conditions at all other times. When the call to arms came and the military forces on both sides increased, it became necessary to set up large camps and to consider where both temporary and permanent hospitals should be established. The British already had hospitals near some of their garrisons at Montreal, Halifax, Kingston, Quebec and York. The American army had no real medical department at the start of the war and began by treating sick and wounded soldiers in field tents. The cold northern climate dictated the need for proper hospital accommodation, and it was soon built at locations such as Greenbush and Lewiston in New York and Burlington in Vermont.[81]

In the camps, illness and death from natural causes often resulted from unhealthy or unsanitary conditions, which few medical experts of the day associated with disease. Nurses would typically encounter throat and chest infections made worse by exposure to the weather and sleeping in wet uniforms or tents. Intestinal complaints such as diarrhoea or dysentery were common and usually stemmed from drinking contaminated water or eating bad food. In summer, heat exhaustion, typhoid and malaria laid many soldiers low, and tuberculosis was ever present. Simple measures such as the regular inspection of food or proper drying and airing of tents could lead to a significant improvement in the general health of the troops, and in time of peace, officials could insist on such measures. In the chaos of war, however, these guidelines often went by the board, and, as a result, nurses were kept busy tending the sick.[82]

Since women were accustomed to tending family and neighbours in time of sickness, nursing was a natural activity for them in 1812. As Hannah Jarvis of York wrote, "I think the Practice I've had will intitle me to the Name of a good nurse – for I can assure you that I am seldom without some one who calls for my assistance."[83] Hannah's comments held true for the vast majority of women, but this in no way prepared them for the scale of the problems they faced in the war. After the American victory at the Battle of New Orleans in January 1815, for example, one British officer described "the piteous cries of my poor countrymen undergoing various operations … I cannot describe the strange and ghastly feelings created by seeing a basket nearly full of legs severed from these fine fellows, [of the 93rd Regiment] most of which were still covered by their hose."[84] Civilian women helped to nurse the wounded at New Orleans and the city's Ursuline nuns opened their convent when the military hospitals became overcrowded. "Mistress and maid, creole and quadroon, white and black," rose to the challenge, gave of their time and compassion freely, and watched at the bedside of many a wounded soldier day and night.[85] At Fort Erie in September

1814, American women worked as nurses at temporary field hospitals, performing a variety of thankless and distasteful chores and remaining, according to their pay vouchers, throughout a siege that lasted nearly two months.[86]

Following a major battle, an army surgeon's work was grim and fatiguing. As Surgeon Dunlop of the British army put it: "There is hardly on the face of the earth a less enviable situation than that of an Army Surgeon after a battle – worn out and fatigued in body and mind, surrounded by suffering, pain and misery, much of which he knows it is not in his power to heal or assuage."[87] When casualties were very heavy, surgeons persuaded women to do orderly duties. Any reluctance on their part would have been understandable, given the sights and sounds they had to face in military hospitals. According to one American military surgeon,

> nothing but the Groans, of the wounded & agonies of the Dying are to be heard. The Surgeons, wading in blood, cutting [off] arms, legs & trepanning heads to rescue their fellow creatures from untimely deaths – hear the poor creatures, crying – Oh, Dear! Oh Dear! Oh My God! my God! Do, Doctor, Doctor! Do cut of[f] my left! my arm! my head! to relieve me from my misery! I can't live! I can't live! would have rent the heart of Steel & shocked the insensibility of the most harden'd assassin & the cruelest savage.[88]

Miss West, daughter of American army surgeon Dr. Joseph West at Fort Niagara, remembered the wounded being brought back to the fort after the American attack on York in April 1813. Day and night she heard "the groans of the sufferers" and after having visited the hospital, was compelled to write:

> oh, what scenes of sorrow and suffering! Here lay a poor soldier without an arm, or the hand gone and the arm hanging loosely by his side; there one without a leg; there one with most of his face shot off. Many died.[89]

The condition of the patients in such hospitals was bad enough, but still worse was the fact that basic hygiene was often lacking, with results that were occasionally tragic for the nurses as well as patients. Consider the case of one British army nurse, who "pricked her finger with a pin left in one of the bandages, caught the infection, her finger was first amputated, then her hand, the sluff appeared again in the stump, she refused to undergo another operation, the consequence was she soon died."[90]

The tender mercies of nurses and helpers were important in a variety of ways, whether in comforting the wounded or by staying close to the fighting, even though it was impossible to care adequately for all the casualties on a battlefield. Surgeon William Horner of the American army, who tended many wounded men after the bloody Niagara battles of 1814, noted that his patients seemed to respond better to women nurses or female family members and that, under their care, "recoveries took place which would scarcely have followed in the ordinary hospital practice."[91] Nursing and hospital work was possibly the most arduous and distressing employment undertaken by women during the war, but it was work that desperately needed to be done.[92]

Some women made a living in less orthodox ways. Among them was "Madame Hooper" of Newburyport, Massachusetts. According to Sarah Smith Emery, Madame Hooper had run a school in the town before achieving notoriety as a "famous fortune teller, rivalling in celebrity Moll Pitcher of Lynn."[93] Apparently "born and bred in good society," Madame Hooper was "short and stout, with a strongly marked countenance" and "glittering gray eyes."[94] She possessed a very expensive and handsome wardrobe of antique gowns which she wore with a unique bonnet of her own making. This costume, combined with an "oracular, sibyllic manner," was "calculated to inspire credulous people with the awe and wonder she coveted." Madame Hooper's home was "visited by persons of all ages and classes from near and far," seeking a glimpse into the future, an incantation to banish a troublesome neighbour, or, perhaps, a little "magic" to keep a husband or sweetheart safe during the war. This fashion-conscious soothsayer was somewhat highhanded but few in Newburyport ventured to cross one "possessing supernatural powers,"[95] and she made a very good living throughout the war.

There were many women involved in the entertainment business, among them a certain Mrs. Sickles who staged puppet shows with her husband. At a tavern at Scipio, New York, just before the war, one young man recollected "seeing Punch and Judy shows (as exhibited by Sickles and his wife)" and pantomimes such as "the Babes in the Woods."[96] Mrs. Sickles appears to have been multi-talented as she was capable of "dancing blindfolded among eggs laid on the floor in a particular manner while Sickles played the violin."

The Powell family of Halifax also possessed diverse and useful talents. Mr. and Mrs. Charles Powell and their two daughters taught dancing to the town's elite and occasionally took to the stage at the Theatre Royale, which Charles Powell managed, with a repertory of comic songs, readings or sketches, and a little Shakespeare and serious poetry thrown in for good measure. A typical Powell performance might include reading an act from "Hamlet," a couple of short and humorous presentations such as "Darby Logan's Passage from Dublin to London" or a "Critical Dissertation on Noses," all to be followed by a song "giving a whimsical description of the Battle of the Nile ... Sung in the Character of a French Officer."[97]

More serious theatre was popular in North America and playhouses were to be found in most major cities. Much is known about the North American theatre of the period thanks to the memoirs of William Dunlap, a British dramatist, theatrical manager and critic, and William Burke Wood from Nova Scotia, also a manager. Many of the leading performers on the American stage at that time were British, but they were no less appreciated by American audiences despite the war, for the London theatre was highly regarded. As a result, many British actors and actresses crossed the Atlantic to the republic and were glad, according to William Dunlap, to be in a country where they were not "degraded by the presence of a privileged order," who did not appreciate the artistry in what was often deemed an unworthy profession.[98]

Some of the most popular actresses on the American stage during the war had begun their careers a number of years earlier, among them the Misses Juliana and Eleanora Westray. These two talented British women, together with their younger sister Elizabeth, had arrived in the republic in 1796. They soon made a name for themselves and by 1812 Juliana, who had become the wife of William Burke Wood, was described as a lady "whose public talents and private virtues have raised her to a very high rank in public estimation."[99] Juliana's sisters, Eleanora and Elizabeth, also married actors, Eleanora's husband, John Darley, having turned to the theatre after service as an officer in the United States Marine Corps. Dunlap described Eleanora as among the country's top performers who, in many of the parts she played, "shone beyond compeer [sic]."[100] Commended for her looks, acting ability and stage presence, Eleanora Darley became one of the most popular thespians of the War of 1812.

Husband and wife teams were commonplace in the theatre at that time but there were also women working alone who merited Dunlap's praise. Sarah Ross from Nova Scotia, "evinced a dawning of talent" that was to make her one of the best performers on the American stage, while English actress Mrs. Powell possessed such "beauty and talents" that she soon found herself "at the head of her profession in the theatres of New England."[101] There was also a Mrs. Johnson, who had made her debut some years before the war and was so "accomplished and elegant" that she elicited bitter animosity on the part of other actresses in a profession rife with "strife and bickerings."[102]

By 1812, although both Eleanora Darley and Juliana Wood were mothers of young children, it did not prevent them from fulfilling a busy acting schedule. City dwellers looked to the theatre to provide distraction during the war years but summer disease epidemics sometimes delayed the opening of the theatre season and forced managers to find safer venues. Nevertheless, plays and players continued to be in demand, and Mesdames Wood, Darley, Young, Johnson and others remained firm favourites with their audiences along with Agnes Holman, another notable new arrival from London in 1812. The talented Agnes was soon so highly regarded that she was able to command a great deal of money.[103]

Eleanora Darley was working in Boston in 1812 where, on 16 December, the *Boston Gazette* announced her appearance in an entertainment to "celebrate the late capture of the *Macedonian* by Commodore Decatur," one of a series of naval victories gained by the American navy.[104] It proved such a success that Eleanora was invited to New London in January 1813 as the star of another evening to commemorate the victory but this time, the triumphant Decatur himself was in attendance. The *New York Evening Post* reported on the occasion, which was billed as "a theatrical performance with entertainments called 'Fraternal Discord,' together with "a patriotic sketch entitled, 'America, Commerce and Freedom.'"[105] The theatre was "filled to overflowing," and by the time Decatur arrived, his sailors were seated in the pit. They gave twelve cheers for their commanding officer and then, as the curtains of the stage parted, Eleanora Darley emerged. At first there was "dead silence," and then voices were heard

Juliana Westray Wood (1778-1838) was the eldest of three talented actress sisters who performed through the war years for American audiences. Originally from Britain, Juliana married actor, director and theatre manager William Burke Wood and settled in Philadelphia. (Oil on canvas, *c.* 1811 by Rembrandt Peale. National Portrait Gallery, Smithsonian Institution.)

Eleanora Westray Darley, the second of the Westray sisters, was born in 1780 and married John Darley, an officer in the United States Marine Corps, in 1803. John took up his wife's profession and together they were one of the most successful acting duos of the war, performing across the northeastern United States. The couple later settled in Philadelphia and one of their sons, Felix Octavius Carr Darley, be-came one of nineteenth-century America's most famous illustrators. (Engraving by J.W. Steel from a painting by J.C. Darley. Manuscripts, Archives, and Special Collections, Washington State University.)

from different parts of the pit, exclaiming, "Oh God, what a pretty, pretty girl! How I should love her? How I do love her."

Even though appreciating the sketch required, as the *Evening Post* some-what airily remarked, "a much greater exertion of intellect" than sailors were "disposed to make," the talented and lovely Eleanora obviously captured the hearts of her audience.[106] To complete the evening, patriotic songs were sung and then Eleanora sang "Poll of Plymouth in an excellent stile," to "an abun-dance of shouting and cheering."[107] To have performed and sung for one of America's greatest naval heroes was something Eleanora Darley doubtless re-membered for a long time to come. She, her sisters and their contemporaries provided comedy, tragedy, the wit and wisdom of Shakespeare and a good deal else besides, for the American public throughout the war years.

Whatever their reasons for pursuing the challenges of employment during the War of 1812, many women took this step away from the conventions of the time. In so doing, they faced and overcame the prevailing climate of opin-ion and, sometimes, the stigma of working in a male-dominated world. Those who succeeded were trailblazers for the generations who would follow them in the years that span their time and ours. They deserve to be acknowledged,

> For their work continueth,
> And their work continueth,
> Broad and deep continueth,
> Greater than their knowing![108]

Paddling into the wilderness. Canoes such as those shown in this nineteenth-century artwork were the vital communication link from the St. Lawrence to the upper limits of the Great Lakes and beyond. Many a military wife travelled to distant outposts using this mode of transport for considerable stretches of the journey. (Print after painting by Frances Ann Hopkins in Edwin O. Wood, *Historic Mackinac*.)

CHAPTER FOUR

"A stirring and restless life."
Army Officers' Ladies

A damsel possessed of great beauty,
She stood by her father's own gate,
The gallant hussars were on duty,
To view them this maiden did wait;
Their horses were capering and prancing,
Their accoutrements shone like a star,
From the plain they were nearest advancing,
She espied her young gallant hussar.

It was there she conversed with her soldier,
These words he was heard for to say,
Said Jane, "I've heard none more bolder,
To follow my laddie away."
"O fie!" said young Edward, "be steady,
And think of the dangers of war,
When the trumpet sounds I must be ready,
So wed not your gallant hussar.[1]

"How is it possible," enquired a young American woman of a male friend who was an army officer,

that you can ... subject yourself to a life of exposure, in some out of the way half civilized region ... if you have a wife and family leaving them at some forlorn place, in anxiety and distress among unpitying strangers, or what would be almost as bad, dragging them about from pillar to post with you suffering all the various, discomforts, privations and deteriorating influences of campaigning and garrison life, and finally terminating this inglorious career, in some ignoble skirmish ... leaving a destitute wife and family to the short lived sympathies of your brother officers, and the cold charity of the world.[2]

An eventful dinner. British officers' wives travelling to North America often endured rough crossings. Here, George Cruikshank, the well known Georgian cartoonist, has captured the hazards of dining at sea in bad weather. As he describes it, the "efforts of a heavy lurch after dinner" have sent officers, wives, food, bottles, chairs, mess staff and children flying in all directions. (Cartoon, George Cruikshank, 1818. Author's collection.)

This unpromising view of life for an officer's wife in the American army raises the question why any woman would choose such an existence. Tough and rigorous, military service often consigned American officers to remote and inhospitable posts, and British officers to long periods of foreign service in hostile or disease-ridden places. Most importantly, active service in wartime – the *raison d'être* of armies – always carried the risk that a single moment could transform a wife into a widow.

Although there were considerable social pressures for a woman to marry during this period, she needed strong motives to wed a man whose life involved such uncertainty and hardship at a time when life was, in general, more precarious. Love was undoubtedly foremost but there were also notions of patriotism, duty, honour, a woman's wish to prove to her husband that she was equal to the task, or simply a taste for adventure. Any or all of these incentives were sufficient to impel some early-nineteenth-century ladies to agree to such an unpredictable and unsettled future.

Among the many challenges that awaited army officers' wives was the discomfort of travel. In the spring of 1812, "Mrs. P.," a British officer's wife, found herself bound for North America aboard the brig *Anns* to join her husband. Hardly had she acquired her "sea legs" than the weather grew stormy and as the passengers attempted to eat dinner, according to one of their number, they had to hold onto something firm with one hand, "while the other was employed in steadying the Soup, Leg of Mutton or dumplings – and occasionally snatching a mouthful during a level."[3] When the wind picked up, the *Anns* began "rolling gunwale under," and the lamps hanging from the deck overhead were swinging so hard that they were banging on the beams. At this point, away went the seats and with them, in the words of the young officer,

> Soup, Mutton, dumplings, crockery, knives, forks, Mustard Pepper, Sauces and such like. The Lady [Mrs. P] screamed, as well she might, the Gentlemen shouted. I grappled a berth, and laughed heartily, snatched hold of the Lady when, again at the next roll, away went the others, with all the implements of industry in an alarming confusion and mess. All our chairs were broken, our table cloths cut, the Cook ill or sulky.[4]

For some British officers' wives with previous experience of life overseas, going to a province like New Brunswick was not the ordeal it might otherwise have been. Flexibility and adaptability were valuable assets, as Lady Jean Hunter, married to Lieutenant-General Sir Martin Hunter, the lieutenant-governor of the province, proved on her arrival. Lady Hunter was accustomed to makeshift conditions, having lived some years earlier in Gibraltar. "We lie on the floor," she had written at that place, "not having anyone to unpack our furniture and beds, and were most handsomely bit by bugs, house-ants, mosquitoes, and all sorts of company of that sort" but "we have all been laughing at one another, and enjoying our house with all its inconveniences.[5]

Despite its remote location, the government and military community of Fredericton, capital of New Brunswick, was a good deal more sophisticated than the province's remote fishing and lumbering outposts, and Jean Hunter threw herself into her duties with gusto. The regiment her husband had raised, initially named the New Brunswick Fencibles and later the 104th Foot, kept husband and wife busy as they worked to make sure things went smoothly. "We are all anxiety, and are brushing up to look as smart and beautiful as possible," wrote Lady Hunter prior to the arrival of a senior officer from Halifax to inspect the regiment.[6]

Lady Jean Hunter (1774-1844) was Scottish by birth. A well-travelled and experienced army wife, she thrived on the challenges of life in the somewhat primitive setting of Fredericton, New Brunswick, and gave birth to five of her eleven children while in North America. Jean Hunter proved to be a great asset and support to her husband after his appointment as chief military officer of the province, and in the raising of what became the 104th Regiment of Foot. The Hunters left North America at the end of Sir Martin's tour of duty in late August 1812. (Print after portrait by unknown artist. Author's collection.)

Lady Hunter was one officer's lady who recognized that she could not always afford to stand on ceremony in a colonial backwater, but must adapt to local conditions. With the coming of winter and inevitable shortages of certain supplies, Jean Hunter considered herself and her husband fortunate to have "as much wood as we can burn, bread and salt pork" and beef, plus basic essentials such as "teas, rice, salt, butter, and candles."[7] Able to make the best of things, she braved the weather to go dancing and feasting even in the severest conditions, declaring, "I suppose it is the effect of frequent transplanting which makes we folks so young and gay."[8]

Another enthusiastic new arrival in New Brunswick was Charlotte Gubbins, who arrived from England in 1810 with her husband, Lieutenant-Colonel Joseph Gubbins, and their young family, "knowing nothing of the country, with fine carriages, fine furniture, etc. etc." According to Jean Hunter, Colonel and Mrs. Gubbins were "quite new-fangled" and delighted with their surroundings, and although she perceived the new arrivals to be "fine, dashing characters, Bath people, quite the *haut-ton*," she also found them "agreeable" and "willing to make the best of it."[9] Like Jean Hunter, Charlotte Gubbins loved the Canadian winter, declaring that she "never saw anything so beautiful" as the snowy landscape of New Brunswick, and that "no description can do it justice – quite Fairyland." Jean Hunter was delighted to find a kindred spirit and was pleased that Charlotte apparently did not seem to mind "flying up here – ten miles – even to pay a morning visit, with a strong north-west wind and the glass below zero."

Life for an officer's wife depended much upon the size and location of her husband's station. Duty in cities such as Halifax, Montreal, Quebec, New York or Baltimore invariably saw wives comfortably lodged close to all the services available. Those posted to smaller garrisons such as York in Upper Canada or Fort Niagara on the American side of the Niagara River also enjoyed a fairly comfortable lifestyle and the company of other military families. Although officers and their wives were expected to mix with the local civilian population, the military had its own intimate social circles with entertainments that were "more like a family reunion than a gathering of strangers."[10]

It was those wives who opted to accompany their husbands to the most isolated locations who had to make the greatest adjustments. Consider the journey of Mrs. Maule, wife of Lieutenant-Colonel John Maule of the 104th Foot, who took her children from York to join her husband on Drummond Island in Lake Huron. After the first thirty miles overland, they crossed Lake Simcoe by boat and then had to undergo "a Portage of eight or nine miles more."[11] Almost at the end of their long journey by boat up Lake Huron, their vessel ran aground on a rocky reef with a big swell running. Firing muskets, the ship's crew attracted the attention of the troops on nearby Drummond Island and during the night Colonel Maule "with a Bateau of Officers and Soldiers" came to the assistance of the vessel, towing her off the rocks and rescuing his family.[12]

American officers' wives with husbands sent to the country's distant frontier posts in the years leading up to 1812 also endured long and often hazardous journeys to reach these forts spread throughout Ohio, the Indiana, Michigan and Illinois Territories, and along the Mississippi. The son of one officer's wife remembered the time he and his mother travelled the waterways from Detroit to his father's new command. Some of the rivers were so narrow that the trees almost met overhead and snakes were very plentiful. "In several instances," he recalled, "they fell into the Boat, once a large rattlesnake nearly falling into my Mother's lap."[13] The daughter of another family travelling to Fort Wayne in the Indiana Territory remembered a night when, as they huddled beside a roaring fire, she could see "the eyes of the wolves all around us."[14] Not only that, but a wandering party of aboriginal warriors took most of their remaining provisions, leaving them barely enough for the final leg of their journey.

Those women who ventured into the interior of the North American continent encountered what one historian has referred to as "the privations and loneliness" of a life "so remote from the civilized part of the world" that it could only be understood by those who had experienced it.[15] Mail, supplies and

Fort Wayne in 1812. This engraving of the fort, on the Maumee River southwest of Lake Erie, clearly shows how an American military outpost in hostile territory was constructed. The position of the stockaded enclosure, set upon a hill, helped to provide a better defence in the case of attack, and the two blockhouses at opposite corners would have been manned around the clock. The interior of the fort contained a parade ground, barrack blocks, officers quarters and other buildings for the use of the garrison and its families. (Lossing, *The Pictorial Field-Book of the War of 1812.*)

news came by way of traders and couriers but only during the months when the waterways were navigable. In winter, outlying garrisons were often cut off completely. An American inspecting officer who regularly visited the Northwest described how he frequently found himself at the location of "a small Detachment where an uninterrupted Silence reigned, giving it the resemblance more of a Convent … than a place of Arms."[16]

Most families lived within the bounds of the post, usually a stockaded fort. Fort Dearborn, on the site of present-day Chicago, consisted in 1812 of a barracks block, two blockhouses, workshops and other accommodations built around four sides of a quadrangle and enclosed within two protective wooden palisades. Most officers and their families were housed within the barracks block. With set allowances for quarters and baggage, a captain in the American regular army might be allocated one room for himself and his family and share a kitchen with six other officers. Officers' wives did all they could to make their surroundings pleasant, and bright curtains, a few well chosen pieces of furniture or a picture, contributed to making a living space acceptable. Officers usually took full advantage of their rank, which entitled them to at least one servant and, in the case of the more senior officers' wives, due deference and chivalry on the part of the regiment's younger officers.[17]

An officer's wife was expected to entertain regularly and to offer her guests a good table. At a remote post she had to keep a constant eye on practicalities, planning a long way ahead to ensure that food and other necessary items were ordered and delivered before the winter. Other challenges at such stations included lack of facilities, boredom, loneliness in isolation, and fears for the health and safety of children in the absence of adequate medical provision. In 1812, Rebekah Heald, wife of the commanding officer of Fort Dearborn, was expecting her first child. She had made the long journey to the fort on horseback, and was respected for her positive outlook and willingness to fit into a frontier community. On 4 May 1812, Rebekah gave birth to "a son born dead for the want of a skilful Midwife," but being a resilient woman, she put her misfortune behind her and carried on.[18]

Life in the wilderness was not always dull. The ladies of the American garrison on Mackinac Island had a lively time every summer when the island hosted its annual gathering of those involved in the fur trade, and women like Margaret Hanks, wife of Lieutenant Porter Hanks, the commanding officer of Fort Mackinac, and Mrs. Whistler, the half-Scottish, half-French wife of another officer, could not help but be caught up in the atmosphere of the trading jamboree.

For those wives in more civilized locations, life could be agreeable. Isabella Grant, wife of Major Jasper Grant of the 41st Foot, spent the best part of a decade before the war in Upper and Lower Canada. She enjoyed her husband's different postings, beginning at Sorel, where she shared her "little peaceful abode"

The mouth of the Niagara River as seen from Lake Ontario, showing the American Fort Niagara on the left, and Fort George on the right. In the foreground is the lighthouse where the keeper's daughters met invading American troops in the spring of 1813 and took advantage of circumstances by making a steady income from doing the laundry of their enemies. (Lossing, *The Pictorial Field-Book of the War of 1812*.)

Inside Fort George. The layout of Fort George, the palisaded British military post on the Niagara River, is clearly visible in this 1805 painting by a British officer who served there. Of note are the blockhouses on the perimeter, a guardhouse to the extreme right, barracks blocks and officers' quarters in the centre, and the esplanade, upon which soldiers are drilling. Dogs and tame bears are also shown within the precincts of the fort. (Painting by Edward Walsh, surgeon of the 49th Regiment of Foot. William L. Clements Library, University of Michigan.)

with bears, raccoons, wolverines, wolves, lynxes and martens, and then at Fort George on the Niagara River.[19] Moving to Upper Canada from the lower province was not easy, particularly since everything there was "two hundred per cent dearer" than at Montreal, and Isabella felt obliged to take all her possessions with her.[20] Thus, keeping her company on her journey were all her items of furniture, plus "6 cut pint Decanters" and "2 doz'n and 8 cut water glasses fit for the prince of Wales."[21] Even though on arrival at Fort George Isabella Grant had to face the usual summer outbreak of "Lake fever, or fever and ague," and acclimatise as quickly as possible to temperatures of "94 in the shade, and 98 exposed," she coped.[22]

It was her move to Fort Malden at Amherstburg in 1808 that brought Isabella Grant most closely in touch with the kind of world her American counterparts knew at their remote frontier posts. She, her husband and children settled into a log house beside the Detroit River where the air was filled with the fragrance of forest, orchard and the proximity of the water. The green-fingered Isabella managed two gardens from which she harvested "an abundance of vegetables of every kind" and adjacent to which were two fields where she kept "a horse, two cows, and as many sheep as supply our wants."[23] As the wife of the post's commanding officer, Isabella hosted many visitors, including the aboriginal peoples who gathered at Fort Malden in 1808 to greet the governor of Upper Canada, Sir Francis Gore. On that occasion she witnessed the ceremonial gift-giving that was an important part of native-white diplomacy, and clearly proved such an asset to her husband that he wrote, "the Governor dined frequently with Bell and me, and would not dine elsewhere. He expressed himself most highly pleased with my command at this Post."[24]

Being the wife of a commanding officer sometimes fell upon the shoulders of younger and less experienced women than Isabella Grant. Lieutenant-Colonel John Murray of the 100th Foot, newly married in 1810, brought his wife with him when he took command of Fort George. Mrs. Murray and her husband lived in a single-storey building which was well equipped with furniture, china and curtains of a superior quality, and able to accommodate overnight guests.[25] Without the extremes of isolation and danger of the remoter American garrisons, a post such as Fort George enabled officers and their wives to live in a manner that more closely reflected their background.

Mrs. Murray quickly became popular and was described by Major-General Isaac Brock as a "charming little creature, full of good sense and spirit."[26] Although life on the Niagara was thought by some to be "uninteresting and insipid," one suspects that Mrs. Murray would have been far from bored.[27] Garrison social life was active and the fort happened to be located near the busy town of Newark with its shops, Turf Club and regular dances. During the summer, picnics and visits to local beauty spots were *de rigueur*, and at harvest time, officers and their ladies might well be invited to local farms to sample the new crop of corn. In winter, younger officers put on plays as entertainment, and there were frequent skating, sleighing and tobogganing parties. In addition to the dinners, dances and assemblies held by the local community, most garrisons organized dances of their own, and Mrs. Murray probably acted as Brock's official hostess when he gave a ball to the *"beau monde* of Niagara and its vicinity" at Fort George in January 1811, an occasion which, according to her cousin, Colonel James Kempt, she described as "splendid."[28]

When military entertainments were offered, they were usually well organized. A "Ball & Supper," for example, was given by the 88th Foot in February 1815 at Sorel in Lower Canada which, according to a newspaper account, "in point of splendour, Taste & Changement, far exceeded any thing of the kind, ever

witnessed in either Provinces of Canada." The generous claim was substanti-
ated by descriptions of the "effulgent glow, of interesting and vivid beauties,
who at once gave lusture [sic] & gaiety to the Room," the spirited dancing and
an impressive supper "composed of all the delicacies and rersties [rarities] that
the season would admit of."[29]

As a commanding officer's wife, Mrs. Murray would have attended garrison
weddings and christenings, and participated actively in the social custom of
receiving and returning calls from other ladies. She probably visited Mary Clark
in her fine house overlooking the falls of Niagara, and at Newark she would
have met Catherine Claus, wife of Colonel William Claus, Deputy Superintendent General of the Indian Department. At York, accessible by road when the
weather permitted, Mrs. Murray would have encountered the wives of the York
garrison, among them Elizabeth Derenzy, wife of Captain William Derenzy of
the 41st Foot, and Angelica Givins, married to Major James Givins of the Indian
Department. And there were also the *grandes dames* of York society such as
Anne Powell and Elizabeth Russell, still unmarried and known as an independent lady of means in the town.

If other military posts were nearby, officers and their ladies sent and received invitations to their respective social functions. Before the war, officers
from Fort George on the Canadian side and Fort Niagara on the American side
of the Niagara River visited each other regularly. Miss West, whose father was
surgeon at Fort Niagara, remembered how that fort used to be

> lit up for festive hours, enlivened by the smiles of beauty, the cheering voice
> of friendship, mingled with the strains of gay music; the old walls decorat-
> ed with our country's banners; the eagle's broad wing chalked beneath our
> feet; and manly forms ready to use them, (if need be,) flitting past in the gay
> dance.[30]

A posting to stations such as Fort Niagara or Fort George might have lacked the
glamour of larger city garrisons, but it was certainly a great deal livelier than life
in the isolated outposts on the western frontier.

To fully understand the lives of army officers' wives during the war period,
it is helpful to look at their husband's respective services. For its part, the
British army had changed little in the previous century and, according to one
authority, British military wives fitted into distinct groupings:

women who follow an army may be ordered (if they can be ordered) in three ranks, or rather classes. The first shall be those who are ladies, and are the wives of the general and other principal commanders of the army, who for the most part are carried in coaches … The second class is those who ride on horseback …The third class is those who walk afoot, and are the wives of inferior officers and souldiers [sic].[31]

British army officers were often the younger sons of upper class families who needed to earn a living, and for whom a life in the military was regarded as a perfectly respectable career. Commissions were available by purchase, an archaic system which, despite periodic attempts to reform it, was open to abuse by the unscrupulous or the "needy and greedy." A man's ability to buy his commission and subsequent promotion up to the rank of lieutenant-colonel did not, of course, mean he was intelligent or fit for the job, and it was no surprise that the intellectual capacity and talent for command of many officers left a great deal to be desired. By 1812, however, after nearly two decades of warfare against the French, most of the incompetents had been weeded out, and more promotions were gained by merit or seniority than by purchase.

Not without good reason, a military treatise of the period urged would-be British officers to pay attention to education, and if a young man's intellect was not up to the task, "the idea of his being put into the army ought instantly to be abandoned."[32] Although the same commentator was firm in the opinion that it was "by learning alone that individuals rise to eminence and power, from the inferior ranks of society," in practice, it would be many years before this would come about in the very conservative British service. In their free time, officers enjoyed active pursuits such as riding, shooting, hunting and walking. Some also read – more often military manuals and non-fiction than novels – and a few talented souls sketched, played musical instruments or sang. Since officers regularly attended social functions at home and abroad they were expected to behave appropriately, but there were always men holding the King's commission who, whether or not they had the funds, loved gambling, liquor, duelling and womanizing. Most officers desired higher rank, and because it was often long in coming, the traditional toast "Here's to a bloody war and swift promotion!" did not originate by accident.[33]

Typical of the younger officers in the British army during the War of 1812 were those who were prisoners of war in Connecticut with Captain William Merritt of the Canadian militia in 1814-1815. Merritt, a perceptive man, left thumbnail sketches of his fellow prisoners in the diary he kept. He thought Royal Marine Lieutenant William Vinicombe "a very fine steady young man," who "employs his time in reading, writing &c., and makes the most of it; very temperate; in short he possesses every good quality."[34] Captain George Eliot of the 103rd Foot was "a most daring, enterprising, and active officer," while Captain Henry Gore of the 89th Foot struck him as a "very gentlemanly, active, and handsome man."[35] It would appear that these qualities were not uncommon, as a period manual for British staff officers lists "temperance, courage, perseverance, moderation in prosperity" and "constancy in adversity" as officer-like attributes and, according to Merritt, the men he spent time with possessed most of them.[36]

Although the U.S. Army was younger and less hidebound than its British counterpart, American officers were also expected to be gentlemen. Indeed, George Washington insisted that the regular officer corps should consist of "young Gentlemen of good families, liberall education, and high sense of honour."[37] Although money was useful, promotion could not be obtained by purchase as in the British army, but was instead the province of the government. It was politics, not money, that often influenced American military appointments, and when the Republicans came to power in 1801, young men hoping to gain commissions in the army or navy needed to demonstrate a political affiliation to the ruling party.

In the spring of 1812, the tremendous expansion of the regular army resulted in hundreds of men, including some Federalists, receiving commissions. Senior regimental officers entering the army at that time were typically lawyers, merchants, farmers, planters, holders of local and state office, and Republican activists. As prominent men in their communities, they were well placed to know the congressmen who influenced decisions about commissions. Many such officers were former state legislators, local office holders or had held rank in the militia. With political connections rather than suitability for command being so often the criterion for obtaining a commission, it is no wonder that Winfield Scott, a prewar regular officer, later commented that "many of the appointments were positively bad, and a majority of the remainder indifferent. Party spirit of that day knew no bounds, and, of course, was blind to policy."[38]

Whatever its flaws, the American army did not develop into the closed elite that marked the British officer corps. Within the American military framework, many men without wealth, formal education or social standing had a chance to advance themselves in keeping with their nation's egalitarian ideals, and the

An American officer's lady. The attractive Mary Sicard David, wife of Lieutenant John T. David, 15th U.S. Infantry, posed for this portrait, which, from her dress and hairstyle, is likely to have been completed shortly before or during the war, possibly on the occasion of her engagement or marriage. Mary was one of the lucky wives, for her husband returned safely from active service in 1815. (Print after painting by Thomas Sully in a private collection. Photograph by René Chartrand.)

officer corps of the republic mirrored the country's geographical distribution and social diversification. A Virginian planter's son might not have much in common with the son of a mill owner from Pennsylvania, yet both had their place. No matter what their background, however, army regulations demanded that the behaviour of its officers should meet the level expected, and penalties for transgressions were stern.

As a general rule in both armies, officers were discouraged from marrying until they held an appropriate rank and could maintain an expected lifestyle. In the British army, for more than a century after the War of 1812, the unspoken rule was that "lieutenants never marry, captains may marry, majors should marry, and colonels must marry." Once the decision had been made, the financial demands of married life – suitable quarters, entertaining, a wife's wardrobe, the purchase of a horse and trap (the hallmark of social standing for any couple of quality) – were considerable. In sum, the considered wisdom in the armed forces of both Britain and the United States held that for an army officer, marriage was not a step to be taken lightly.

Officers, even junior officers, did marry of course, and the lady of choice was expected to behave in a manner befitting her newly-acquired position in society. Looks and personality were every bit as important as breeding, at least in the mind of one commentator who firmly believed that "a pretty girl, a good dancer and a showy rider" would fare far better than "Lady Drystick, with her ancient pedigree and aristocratic airs."[39] Also important, as is clear from the example of women like Jean Hunter and Rebekah Heald, was a willingness to fit into a tightly regulated society and the ability to cope with less than ideal living conditions. It was also a great advantage to possess a personality and constitution that could withstand the rigours of a life that was, to say the least, unpredictable.

As has been stressed, travel was very difficult and hazardous. When war was declared, Lydia Bacon, married to Lieutenant Josiah Bacon of the 4th U.S. Infantry Regiment, was with her husband's regiment on the move in the American Northwest. Lydia kept a journal that provides a clear picture of the life of an officer's wife in rough country and uncertain times. At one point, while travelling through Michigan, Lydia had good cause to be apprehensive, for as she wrote:

> we are expecting an attack from the Indians 'ere we reach Detroit, God only knows our fate, but my fervent Prayer is that such a calamity may be averted from us, it would be dreadful, such a number of Women & Children along... Officers & men sleep with their clothes on & their implements of War by their side.[40]

Lydia wondered how her friends at home in Massachusetts would feel in her predicament, but concluded, "I believe that people in perilous situations do not realize their danger for I feel somewhat composed & those around me appear so too."[41]

The trials of Lydia on her odyssey included troublesome mosquitoes, heavy rain that made the road an "entire swamp" and the travellers "repeatedly wet through," and the difficulty of holding the horse's reins in one hand and an umbrella in the other while trying "to keep the bushes from scratching my eyes out, & tearing my bonnet off my head."[42] There was also the challenge of fording rivers where the current was so strong that, as Lydia recorded, "oft times, it is almost impossible to gain the opposite shore." Having to carry personal possessions required some ingenious arrangements, and on one occasion the young Mrs. Bacon realized she looked "really laughable" as she trotted along carrying a large bag "containing some necessary articles, a Bible, Homer's Iliad, & A huge Sponge cake presented by one of our kind Friends the morning of departure."[43]

Not all aspects of frontier life were bad. Lydia Bacon enjoyed being in the open, riding on horseback and sleeping on "a bear skin for our bedstead & a Buffaloe Robe for our Bed." She also commented frequently on the beauty of her surroundings, spotting along the way "strawberry vines full of fruit" and "wild roses and various other flowers."[44] To her, "our American Wilderness," as she termed it, was something to marvel at, especially when it also provided such culinary delights as fresh fish from the rivers and "a dish of garlics" growing wild at one of the campsites. When Lydia arrived at Detroit, the worst danger she had experienced on her journey was the time when she "heard the report of a gun & felt the wind or something pass close to my ear." This had turned out to be an accidental discharge from a soldier's gun, the bullet narrowly missing Lydia, who believed herself to be "constantly preserved through dangers seen & unseen."[45] Ironically, it was to be at Detroit, where she supposed herself to be safe, that Lydia would encounter real peril.

Travelling with the army was usually eventful, and on rare occasions, rather pleasant. The anonymous wife of a British subaltern who arrived with her husband at Kingston, Upper Canada, in 1813, enjoyed sleeping under canvas. She remembered that her husband, Charles,

> asked me whether I would prefer taking my chance for a night and a day in a tent or remaining in the waggon until he could dispose of the men and return to find a lodging for us. I was quite charmed with the alternative and declared for the tent ... and so we took possession of our tent by the light of a brilliant moon – can you imagine anything more delightful or novel than being there at the end of a long day's journey in a very crowded wagon. I could not tear myself away from the door of my tent for hours.[46]

This young woman was fascinated by the scenes of the camp around her: "the snow white canvas tents with the bustling soldiers assembling their campfires for cooking their suppers, or resting on the grass, or posting sentinels."[47] When it came time to eat, once the "kettle was boiled and our camp table spread," she and her husband "opened our provision basket" and began their meal. The evening passed happily, for both appreciated the pleasures of their improvised living. "Never," declared this lady, "did two lighter or happier hearts join in thanksgiving for the blessings of good shelter and rest."

River and lake transport being the most common mode of travel in the interior, officers' wives were accustomed to taking to the water. Moving them, however, was sometimes not an easy matter, according to Lieutenant John Le Couteur of the British army. In 1815, he was assigned the unpopular task of supervising the transport of his regiment's wives and children down the St. Lawrence from Kingston to Montreal. In his journal, he complained that this involved being responsible for "all the women, children, Sick, sorry or lazy, besides all the heavy luggage of a strong Reg[imen]t. on a permanent move."[48] During the voyage, Le Couteur was inundated with requests from the officers' wives: "see to my luggage. Do place an awning to the batteaux. See to my children. See to the Baby," and so on. "Never was I so pestered," he commented by the time he got his charges safely to Montreal, where the exasperated young officer was "heartily delighted to land my light baggage and my fair friends, the Ladies and women and chicks of the Regiment – leaving them I must say ungallantly to their own resources – and marching my detachment ... to the barracks."

British Lieutenant John Lang recalled a pleasant, if noisy, voyage on the St. Lawrence when some of the junior officers and wives of his regiment travelled upriver in the spring of 1813. Accommodation aboard their boat was crowded, with nine people sleeping in a cabin equipped with only two berths. Mattresses were laid on the floor but nobody slept much because there was "such a noise of talking, laughing, scolding & singing that it was totally impossible to rest."[49] The senior officer present tried in vain to keep order, but "he had no sooner worked out his God damns than he was saluted by a volley of pillows & bolsters" from his subordinates and their wives. After a lively night, Mrs. Rathbone, wife of Lieutenant James Rathbone, ordered everyone "upon deck until she would get breakfast prepared," which turned out to be "a most sumptuous meal of the fresh eggs & milk we had procured the day before."

The presence of wives sometimes produced scenes out of the ordinary. During the summer of 1812 when one rather plump lady was unwilling to get her feet wet by wading ashore from her vessel on the St. Lawrence, an officer in another boat offered to take her on his back. "They were both particularly stout, bulky people," recorded an observer, and they had not got very far when the officer, "owing to his heavy burden, sank so deep in the soft mud that he actually stuck fast," and could not move a step further:

> "Pon my honor, Mrs. O – " said he, puffing and blowing, "I'll be under the necessity of putting you down!" She had scarcely time to exclaim "Oh dear, Mr. T – !" in reply than she found herself up to her knees in water; and sure in such a plight "such a pair was never seen."[50]

Onlookers watched with considerable amusement as this "great fat fellow, in long red coat and cocked hat, up to his knees in water" led by the hand, "very cordially" but in a great hurry, "as fat a lady, with flowing garments lightly floating on the silver wave." As they splashed along through the mud, they were "all the while in terrible dread of being shot," but fortunately reached the shore unscathed.[51]

Army wives had an advantage over their naval counterparts in being able, when conditions permitted, to occasionally visit their husbands while they were on campaign. In the spring of 1813 Marie-Anne-Julie de Salaberry, not long married to Lieutenant-Colonel Charles Michel de Salaberry, the commanding officer of the *Voltigeurs Canadiens,* travelled to her husband's headquarters at Saint Philippe, Lower Canada. The dark-eyed Marie-Anne, daughter of a wealthy Lower Canadian landowner, was fairly advanced in pregnancy when she had the opportunity to join her husband. If de Salaberry worried about his wife making the journey in her delicate condition he did not say so and was happy to find her in good health on her arrival, despite her "often complaining, but that is easily accounted for."[52]

In Montreal at around the same time, Agathe Nowlan, wife of Lieutenant Maurice Nowlan of the 100th Foot, was anxious to visit her husband, who was stationed at Kingston. The Nowlans were newly married but with the country in "so very disturbed a state," Maurice told his wife not to think about joining him. A series of letters between the two ensued, each trying to persuade the other. "You could not find a place to put your head," Maurice told Agathe, further explaining that "the common necessities of life are so very extravagant that it would be impossible to Scrape up the least Comfort here."[53] He also pointed out the difficulties she might have as a woman alone, and was unwilling for her to put herself in any compromising situation.

Marie-Anne-Julie de Salaberry (1787- 1854), wife of Lieutenant-Colonel Charles Michel de Salaberry, commanding officer of the *Voltigeurs Canadiens,* came from a wealthy Lower Canada landowning family. They were married only two months before war broke out and she joined him on active service when conditions permitted. Marie-Anne gave birth to the eldest of their seven children in 1813. When the war ended, the family occupied a new mansion beside the Richelieu River at Chambly, their seigneury. After her husband's death in 1829, Madame de Salaberry doggedly continued to raise her family alone. Three of her children predeceased her. (Photograph of painting by unknown artist, courtesy of Patrick Wohler.)

In the summer of 1813 after the 100th Foot was ordered to the Niagara frontier, Maurice and Agathe found themselves separated by an even greater distance and the protective Maurice was more adamant than ever that his lady should not travel. Sickness and danger were prevalent and he endeavoured to explain other problems. "You may think it hard that I try to prevent your coming near me my only Life," he told Agathe, adding, "it's not known the moment we may be in the utmost confusion, and what would become of me if I was to leave the only one dear to me in this world to the care of Strangers?"[54] The thought of having to abandon his "jewel" "in the open field destitute of any support," only to have her "exposed not only to officers but to the worst of Soldiers," was unbearable. Hard though it was, Maurice urged Agathe to "content yourself" and await further news.[55]

Lieutenant William MacEwen of the 1st Foot was also serving in the Niagara while his wife remained in Montreal, and his letters made it equally clear that it was no place for a lady. "We are in the centre of woods, which are wild in the extreme," MacEwen told his wife. "There is nothing to be had for money and we must live on our rations, which are bad, and, I may say, too little for any man in good health." In addition, "the Americans are in our front, strongly fortified in Fort George, and if reports are correct they have mines in readiness to blow the place up as soon as our army gets into the garrison."[56] A few weeks later the news was no more encouraging, for the officers and men were encamped upon damp, bad ground and many, including MacEwen himself, were ill with "fever and ague." "Where I am obliged to live," he told his wife, "the people would not sell me a fowl nor a potato."[57] It was not until the following spring, after American troops had retreated, that Mrs. MacEwen finally received a more heartening letter from her husband, telling her,

> I am getting into a barrack … the only one in the place, and will have it ready in a few days for your reception if you are determined to abide by a stirring and restless life. I am afraid this will be the case throughout the summer, as the Americans are determined to beat us from the place very soon … Bring some spirits and everything you want, as there is nothing here.[58]

One of the hardest things for officers' wives to bear was lack of news. Their husbands often did not have time to communicate and many women found themselves in the same position as Madeleine-Charlotte de Léry, married to militia officer Lieutenant-Colonel Louis-René Chaussegros de Léry, who was anxiously awaiting news of her husband in the autumn of 1813. It was not until

Madeleine-Charlotte's brother, Lieutenant Thomas Verchères de Boucherville, arrived home "literally in rags" after the Battle of the Thames in late October 1813 that she knew for certain her husband was safe.[59] In rare cases where a man kept detailed records of the events he witnessed, a wife was very well informed. Captain Jacques Viger of the *Voltigeurs Canadiens* wrote copiously about his experiences in letters to his wife, Marie-Marguerite, intending to publish them at some future date. Another woman who knew a good deal about the wartime activities of her spouse was Catherine Claus of Newark. Through long involvement with the work of the Indian Department, Catherine understood the need to maintain good relations between the British army and its native cohorts and was used to having aboriginal visitors at her home, especially when they were hungry. "I have not unfrequently witnessed," wrote one onlooker, "every morsel of pork in Mrs. Claus' house consumed by the subsequent arrival of Indians," but the perceptive Catherine knew that the Indian Department would "forfeit every claim to their good will" if she allowed her visitors to "rest without a meal."[60]

At this time, discussion of the politics and the conduct of the war were generally the prerogative of men, but the letters of one British officer's wife demonstrate an intelligent grasp of events. Alicia Cockburn spent much of the war in Quebec and Montreal while her husband was absent on active service. Quite apart from the social life of these centres, she was fascinated to be able to get, as she phrased it, "all the political news red hot from the Governor's forge."[61] Alicia spent part of the summer of 1814 with the British garrison at Fort Chambly on the Richelieu River, where she was the house guest of a general. As she wrote to her cousin in England, time spent in his home afforded her the credit of "becoming somewhat au fait" with the "*theory & practice* of War."[62] By all accounts, "nothing else was heard, or thought of, from morning till night," and as Alicia recorded, "to examine military plans, & look over maps of the places about to be attacked, were considered amongst the *most peaceable employments* we had."

Alicia Cockburn was one of those army wives who seemed to thrive on a sense of adventure. Not having any children, she was free to travel and in the summer of 1814 relished the prospect of a change of scenery:

> I am at present meditating a journey to Upper Canada, and even a trip into the United States under a Flag of Truce, which to do the Yankees justice they treat with uncommon civility especially when borne by Ladies whom they allow to go much farther, & peep about much more, than we should do in a similar case, whatever might be their beauty & accomplishments.[63]

A far cry from the North American wilderness. British officers' wives were often accustomed to homes like this one in the village of Harbledown, southeast England, where Alicia Cockburn lived before her marriage. After her genteel life in the English countryside, Alicia and many like her had to adjust to the challenges and changing conditions of military service. From the moment she arrived in British North America with her husband, Lieutenant-Colonel Francis Cockburn, Alicia thrived on the more rugged aspects of life and did all she could to make the best of her time. (Photograph by Dianne Graves.)

When her husband assumed command of the British garrison at Cornwall, Upper Canada, Alicia was invited to join him and was pleased at the prospect of the journey, albeit in the intense summer heat. She did not subscribe to the prevailing fashion for women to maintain pale complexions and remain well sheltered from the sun, and told her cousin, "I am so *beautifully* brown, & my hair grown so dark that I propose sitting for my picture in the character of an Indian Princess without more delay."[64]

Although there was always the hope among wives that leave might be granted to their husbands, officers were usually discouraged from taking it in wartime for a number of reasons, not the least being the exigencies of the service. When it was granted, it was often short, particularly in the British army, as the views of the Duke of Wellington on the matter – that no officer should receive more than two days leave as forty-eight hours was "as long as any reasonable man can wish to stay in bed with the same woman" – held sway.[65] In some cases, the temptations caused by long separations proved too much. Major William Dunlop, surgeon to the 89th Foot, spent the winter of 1813 at Fort Wellington on the St. Lawrence. The officers of the 89th were, according to Dunlop, a "fine jovial unsophisticated set of 'wild tremendous Irishmen'" prone to enjoying themselves. The captain and senior lieutenant at Fort Wellington, recorded Dunlop, were, "as Bardulph hath it, better accommodated than with wives" – in other words, the two men had mistresses with them.[66]

When orders were received for a regiment in a garrison station to go on campaign, some officers' wives accompanied their husbands. The anonymous wife of the British officer who earlier described her pleasant evening at the campsite at Kingston faced the prospect of being left behind when her husband was ordered at short notice to the Niagara peninsula. The idea of a lonely vigil at Kingston thousands of miles from home with no friends and relatives, upset her so much that as she wrote, "the risque and discomfort would be all our own and balanced against reputation and the various expenses in securing us a lodging," if her husband could find one, "the alternative of going or staying was not long in being decided in my mind."[67]

However, when she saw the small, cramped sloop in which her husband's regiment was to travel up Lake Ontario, "swaying and creaking in the wind," she had to force herself not to show any outward "expression of alarm," and to suppress her "momentary conviction to turn the white feather."[68] She therefore stepped on board with her baby daughter, Tilly, and found "a corner of the deck upon a pile of greatcoats which I had arranged for my own accommodation." No sooner was she settled than a senior officer espied her in her burrow and accosted her:

> "Hallo, what the devil have we here?" was his first exclamation, "here is a woman on board … walk off Madam if you please, who in the name of wonder brought you here or gave you leave to come." "I am here with my husband" was my reply. "Your husband! My goodness are you a mad woman to talk of Husbands and think of following them in an affair as this. Walk off, Madam, go on home and thank your stars that I found you before it was too late."[69]

Despite her protestations and those of Charles, her husband, the officer insisted she must disembark and there she was,

> under the growing clouds of a stormy evening on a wharf crowded with soldiers and Sailors with baggage and myself the only female in sight and my poor child sleeping in my arms and the only human being upon whom I had depended now flying from us toward the wild Lakes in a vessel which seemed

clearly incapable of weathering the coming tempest, I stood still for a moment watching the receding sail … trying to collect my thoughts and decide
what next was to be done.[70]

This touching scene of a wife alone, far from home and not knowing if she
would see her spouse again, was not uncommon. Abigail Snelling, an American
army wife, was only sixteen and pregnant when her husband was taken prisoner
after the fall of Detroit in August 1812. Like the British officer's wife at Kingston,
Abigail had to fend for herself and make arrangements to have her baby. When
she was born, Abigail's little daughter, Mary, became her mother's great consolation and "beguiled many an anxious hour of separation." Baby Tilly probably
did the same for her mother at Kingston.[71]

Some officers' wives came close to the battlefield. Love, devotion and loyalty
were among the factors that made them step resolutely into the path of danger.
A good example is Elizabeth Procter, wife of Major-General Henry Procter,
British commander on the Detroit frontier in 1813. Elizabeth and her children
were living at Fort Malden when war broke out and she decided to remain
there. Mrs. Procter was soon accustomed to her days and evenings being taken
up with the affairs of war and was well informed about events on the frontier.
Among the many visitors to the fort was the great aboriginal leader Tecumseh, who joined the Procter family for dinner on several occasions. When an
American naval victory on Lake Erie in September 1813 forced her husband to
abandon Fort Malden and withdraw his troops to the east, Elizabeth and her
children accompanied him. It is no wonder Henry Procter cherished his wife
and family, who for many months had shared with him the hardships of campaigning on the frontier. Unfortunately for the loyal Elizabeth, Procter was not
the best of commanders and was later court martialled for his actions during
this campaign. He was found guilty and sentenced to be suspended from the
service for six months.[72]

Another wife who was never far from her husband during the war was Catherine Norton, or Karighwahcagh to use her aboriginal name, a woman said to
have been of English, French, Delaware and Mohawk blood. On 27 July 1813
Catherine married Captain John Norton, a half-Scottish, half-Cherokee aboriginal leader who was regarded as a war chief among the Mohawk people.[73] Also
known by his native name of Teyoninhokerawen, Norton fought alongside the
British, and he and his wife left an impression on those who met them. Lieutenant John Lang of the 19th Dragoons mentions in his diary of August 1813, "we

met the Indian Chief Norton with his wife, who is the prettiest Squaw I ever saw."[74] Catherine and John Norton were a striking couple in the dual world they inhabited.

Other wives who went on active service did not always, alas, create such a favourable impression. Mrs. Mullins, wife of Lieutenant-Colonel the Honourable Thomas Mullins, commanding officer of the 44th Foot, was among those who accompanied the British expeditionary force to New Orleans in 1814. Mullins was the son of an Irish aristocrat and his wife was very confident of her position in life. According to one historian, she was a forceful woman who was proud of her aristocratic connections and "constantly bragging of her husband."[75] For her, sailing with the expedition was very much a question of status.

By the time the British ships reached the coast of Louisiana late in 1814, Mrs. Mullins had taken it upon herself to preside over the officers' wives and made it her business to be "friendly with the most promising of the future officials," men whom the British confidently expected to place in positions of power after New Orleans had been conquered.[76] "Condescending to the lesser officers' wives, full of her aristocratic connections, proud of her husband's brilliance, confident of his future promotion," Mrs. Mullins, however, was headed for a fall, for contrary to all expectations, the British suffered a devastating defeat at New Orleans in January 1815. After the fighting had ended, she was horrified to learn that her husband had been branded a coward for his actions during the battle. She confined herself to her cabin aboard ship and later refused to believe the accusation, insisting that her husband had been maligned. When Lieutenant-Colonel Mullins was dismissed from the army after being found guilty by a court martial, Mrs. Mullins was said to have been troubled ever after by violent headaches that would not respond to any treatment.[77]

As individual as the men to whom they were married, many army officer's wives of the war set an example worthy of respect. Offering strength and support, beauty and brains, courage and determination, they demonstrated their worth and often proved to be assets to their husbands. A seventeenth-century British commentator wrote that "the fittest man to make a soldier is a perfect gentleman; for generous spirits are ever aptest for great designs."[78] Without doubt, these officers' ladies more than complemented the "generous spirits" with whom they had chosen to share a life of danger, adventure, separation, adversity and, on occasion, celebration.

The soldier's wife. British wife Mary Anne Hewitt is representative of many women who accompanied their husbands in the Napoleonic Wars. She survived much hardship, was described as a "virtuous, honest, well-principled young woman" and was much respected as an excellent and skilled nurse. In this engraving, she is pictured in mid-nineteenth-century clothing at Elvas, Spain, leaning on the regimental drum of her husband's regiment, the 48th Foot, with the camp to the rear. (From Richard Cobbold, *Mary Anne Wellington: The Soldier's Daughter, Wife and Widow*.)

CHAPTER FIVE

"Their fate unpitied, and unheard their name."
Soldiers' Wives and Women

Poor husbands they are gone for soldiers,
It's the truth, you really do know;
Heaven protect them in their journeys,
To beat America, their daring foe.

Poor wives they think a month longer
Than they used to think a year,
Because they've lost husbands and father
Who cannot their children hear.

Children prattling to their mothers,
"When will father come?" they cry;
Which sets the tears a-flowing
From each tender mother's eyes.

Ask relief, then the parish grumble,
It's the truth you really do know;
And when they can't keep house no longer
To the workhouse they're bound to go.[1]

In his memoirs, a British veteran of the Napoleonic Wars reflected on the "trouble and misery many lovely young women of respectable connections" brought on themselves by marrying soldiers. After a battle, he complained, there were "so many of these damned women running and blubbering about, enquiring after their husbands," that he wondered why they did not "stop at home where they ought to be."[2]

It was a good question, because life with a man whose duty required constant movement, sometimes overseas, and all too frequently resulted in death or

155

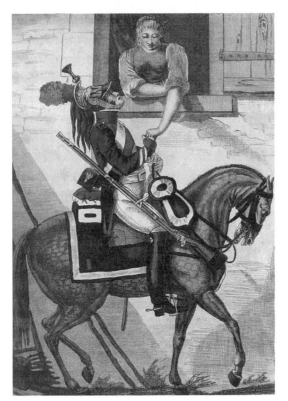

The girls do love a soldier. Although the subject is European, this drawing illustrates well the attraction a uniform – particularly a splendid uniform such as that worn by this French dragoon – could have on the opposite sex. Military recruiting posters of the period were at pains to stress this fact and to use it when seeking to entice young men into the army. (Print after Martinet. Anne S.K. Brown Military Collection, Brown University, Providence, Rhode Island. Photograph by René Chartrand.)

serious injury, was not something to be entered into lightly. It is small wonder that parents were usually dead set against their daughters marrying soldiers, especially as the army, in Britain at least, had a reputation for debauchery, heavy drinking and violence such that a decent man "had but to don the red-coat to be dubbed a lewd profligate wretch."[3] Irrespective of the army's poor reputation, however, a man in uniform – a common sight at that time – held a strong appeal. "Women adore a martial man," noted one commentator, and there is no doubt that a handsome soldier turned many a female head.[4] Indeed, British army recruiting officers emphasized the power of a uniform to win over a maiden's heart; a recruiting poster for the Glengarry Light Infantry Fencibles, raised in Canada during the War of 1812, declared with utter assurance that "flinty must by the heart of that Damsel, and vain her pretensions to taste, who could resist a *Light Bob of the Glengarry's* when equipped in his new *Green Uniform*, which will unquestionably be *the neatest in the Service*."[5]

Once a woman had allied herself to a soldier, sooner or later the question of marriage would arise. The American and British armies did not forbid their enlisted men from marrying – that would have been impossible – but they did not make it easy. "Marriage," stated one British manual, "is to be discouraged as much as possible" and officers were directed to explain to their men "the many miseries that women are exposed to, and by every sort of persuasion they must prevent their marrying if possible."[6] Since a British enlisted man had to have the permission of his company commander for his wife to live in his quarters and receive rations, and as that officer wanted as few women in the barracks as possible, he had a great deal to say about the matter. Company commanders were advised to make diligent enquiries into "the morals of the Woman" and to ascertain "whether she is sufficiently known to be industrious, and able to earn her bread" as unsuitable liaisons often resulted in "distress and ruin."[7] If a proposed match "appeared favourable, it was thought wise to approve it," as "honest, laborious Women are rather useful," said one manual, and the soldier should be "indulged, as far as can be in the power of Officers to extend their favour, whilst his behaviour, and that of his Wife deserves it."[8]

On the other hand, if a company commander discovered that a possible bride had a bad character – "which too often is the case of those, on whom the Soldiers fix their affections" – he was advised to strongly discourage "a connection which must, in a short time, inevitably destroy the ease and happiness" of the man. If, despite all cautions, the soldier persisted in marrying a woman deemed unsuitable by his commanding officer, who, it must "incontestably be allowed," was "a cooler judge" than the couple,

> such contempt and insolence, should, as much as possible, be discouraged, by obliging him, not only to mess [eat], but lie [sleep] in the Quarters of the Company he belongs to, at the same time, that his wife is prevented, from partaking of any advantage either from his Pay or Quarters: this severity, of course, must soon expel her from the Regiment, and be the certain means, of making other Soldiers cautious, how they attempt such acts of disobedience.[9]

It is difficult to ascertain exactly how many soldiers married without permission, but it appears to have happened often enough for orders to have been repeatedly issued on the subject.

In the years immediately preceding the War of 1812, the U.S. Army also condoned but restricted the marriage of enlisted men. The regulations were clear that only four wives were permitted per company "when organized and completed agreebly to the establishment" and these authorized wives were to be issued "one ration each" per day.[10] During the war, the permitted number of

Farewell to the ship. When British regiments went overseas on active service, the number of wives allowed to travel with them was strictly limited. A system of drawing lots was often used, and the unlucky wives were left behind to face an uncertain future. In this scene, a young wife with babe in arms waves farewell to her husband aboard his departing ship. (Anne S.K. Brown Collection, Brown University, Providence, Rhode Island.)

women was raised to five per company, meaning that if an American regiment was at full strength, as many as fifty women would be receiving rations, but no mention is made of rations for their children.[11]

Regular regiments raised in the Canadas came under British regulations and wartime colonial units raised under the authority of the governments of Upper or Lower Canada seem also to have followed these regulations. For example, the records of the Incorporated Militia of Upper Canada (which despite its title was more a regular than a militia unit) reveal that in March 1814 the number of wives per company varied between five and twelve. Among the names recorded, Christeen Mills, Darcus Boon, Charity Wintermot, Anona Forbes and Elizabeth Robertson headed the numbers with six children each.[12] The records of the *Voltigeurs Canadiens*, a regiment formed in Lower Canada, point to the fact that wives were often with that unit even though the living conditions were spartan. There appear to have been some industrious and capable women with the *Voltigeurs* who, in addition to other tasks, were required to assist in making uniforms and were paid for their work at the same rate as a tailor. A memoir by Captain Jacques Viger mentions by name "Mesdames Porugais, Panquet, Lavigue, Barbeau and *caquet-bon-bec* Delorier," and describes Panquet and Delorier being "especially hard-working" as they "acquired the washing of the garrison of Cataracoui."[13]

American and Canadian militia units were sometimes accompanied by wives and camp followers but more rarely than was the case with regular troops. Since militiamen usually served not far from their places of residence or came from established backgrounds with farms or businesses, it was more common, when they were called out for service, for their wives to remain at home.

Once they married a soldier, British and American army wives learned that theirs was a life subject to orders. In the British service, only those women on the Married Roll of a regiment – the authorized wives – were permitted to reside in barracks. Military couples lived and slept with the single soldiers in large rooms and as a rule their only privacy was a screen of blankets or a canvas sheet. With, at best, just two single beds to call their own, they were expected to accommodate any children they might have and make some sort of family life.

In such a setting, wives had to accustom themselves to the coarseness of their surroundings and witness their sons and daughters being exposed to language and behaviour that was not favourable to a proper upbringing. One historian has described soldiers' children as "for the most part, stunted, gnome-like little creatures" who "trundled round wearing cast-off army garments, tightened tunics and cut-down trousers," and who were very adept at "the use of furious oaths." Those as young as five or six years old could be seen "pulling at evil-smelling short clay pipes … and swilling frightening quantities of ale, porter or canteen beer."[14] Just before the War of 1812, efforts began in the British army to set up regimental schools for these children, who, in addition to their lessons, were instructed "in the means of making themselves useful and gaining their Livelihood."[15] Girls were taught needlework and knitting and boys, tailoring and shoemaking. An inspection of the regimental school of the 62nd Foot at Halifax in 1815 reports that "the greatest care is taken in the religious instruction of the children."[16]

American military couples also lived in barracks with no special quarters for their dependants. The lack of space and privacy led, at times, to problems. In 1805 at Fort Wayne, Indiana Territory, Sergeant William Bailey was demoted to private partly because of his "brutal Treatment of his wife." Mrs. Polly Bailey, whether from her husband's conduct or her rough ways, was judged to be "quarrelsome, & frequently making use of abusive and unbecoming language to the men in the room where she lives."[17] Garrison life could be tough and un-savoury, and one soldier imprisoned for drunkenness at Detroit in 1810 begged to be released because he was concerned that in his absence, his wife and chil-dren would be "exposed in an open barrack to the insults of a parcel of wild soldiers."[18] Dangers might be lurking outside a frontier post, but there were also problems within.

Polly Bailey, with her bad language and quarrelsome ways, is reminiscent of the female "old campaigners" in the British army. As the term implies, these were older wives who knew all there was to know about army life and, tough-ened by years of communal living and active service, they formed a rather un-manageable part of almost every British regiment. An eminent historian of the Napoleonic wars has left an apt thumbnail sketch of these veterans. They were

> as hard as nails, expert plunderers, furious partisans of the supreme excel-lence of their own battalion, much given to fighting. Many of them were widows twice and even thrice over – for when a married man was shot, and his wife was a capable and desirable person, she would receive half a dozen proposals before her husband was forty-eight hours in his grave. And since the alternative was a hazardous voyage back to relatives in England or Ireland, who had probably broken off with the girl "who ran away with a soldier," most of the widows concluded to stop with their battalion, with a new spouse and a new name.[19]

Other witnesses attested to blasphemy, fisticuffs and sundry other problems caused by meddling with certain of these pugnacious "old campaigners," and for the newly-married soldier's wife of a gentler disposition, barracks life must have come as a rude awakening.[20]

Kitchens, with several wives attempting to cook for their husbands and families at the same time, were places where tempers could become as hot as fat sizzling in a pan. At Fort Niagara in 1813, a problem arose concerning Mrs. Sowders, a cook whose son was serving in the same garrison. Trouble boiled over in the kitchen one day when a Corporal Heafer entered it to get some meat and initiated a fracas that led to a court martial. At those proceedings, Corporal Henry, "being duly sworn, says, Heafer was not drunk, that Heafer called Mrs. Sowders an old heifer, that she took up a stick when Heafer kicked the stick." At this point, Mrs. Sowders's son, Jacob, "collared Heafer and ran him against the wall, when Corp[ora]l. Henry took him away."[21] Another witness, Corporal Levy Penington, stated that

Corporal Heafer who was not drunk came into the room when Mrs. Sowders told him they wanted no drunkards there. Some words passed between them, when Mrs. Sowders took a pan handle to strike Heafer, he said he would not strike a woman. She then took up a stick appearingly to strike him. Heafer appeared to defend himself when Jacob Sowders flew at him, and collared him. Corporal Henry relieved him, when Mrs. Sowders called a file of men to take Heafer under guard.[22]

Private Steven Carmichael gave evidence that

Heafer was not drunk, that when Corporal Heafer come into the room Mrs. Sowders ordered him out, that he would not go until he drew his meat. She then slapped him in the mouth, appearingly in anger. Heafer called her an old heifer, and if not a woman he would kick her. She then attempted to strike him with a pan handle. She then attempted with a stick; he tried to defend himself, when J. Sowders jumped at him and choked him; Corporal Henry relieved him.[23]

Whether Heafer was drunk or not, Mrs. Sowders was clearly someone who would brook no nonsense, but in the end it was her son, Jacob, who was punished and not his feisty mother. For assaulting a non-commissioned officer, Jacob Sowders received two weeks' hard labour followed by confinement in the guardhouse.[24]

Soldiers' wives were subject to disciplinary measures not much less severe than those meted out to their menfolk. A British wife could be turned out of the barracks for repeated offences of drunkenness, fighting in quarters or using foul language. If she was found guilty of prostitution, she was likely to be drummed out of her regiment, barracks or camp and sent for trial, since such behaviour often led to internal conflicts, not to mention the fact that sexually-transmitted diseases could seriously hamper fighting effectiveness. In its efforts to handle such problems, American regulations specified that, "women infected by the venereal disease shall, in no case, nor on any pretence, be allowed to remain with the army, nor to draw rations."[25] There was also concern about wives consorting with soldiers other than their husbands, as this led to tension and fighting in the ranks; in August 1813, a General Order was issued at Camp Meigs that "Any married woman who has or shall abandon her husband and be found strolling about camp or lodging in the tents of other men shall be drum'd out of Camp."[26] Larceny on the part of women in both armies was severely punished, as in the case of a soldier's wife stationed at Gibraltar, who was "whipped through the streets of the town for theft, receiving one lash every fifty yards," before finally being turned out of the garrison.[27]

Clearly, there were dishonest, disorderly soldiers' wives, and during the War of 1812 "plunder and Robbery" was committed by some of the women who travelled with the British army that invaded the Chesapeake in 1814. Rear-Admiral Edward Codrington, RN, recorded that their crimes were perpetrated upon "even the poorest" American civilians and that "women from some of the Transports have been guilty of enormities shocking to humanity."[28] As a result, the admiral ordered that "no persons beneath the Rank of Field Officers [majors] and Captains of the Navy be allowed to go on shore except upon duty or by permission of a Flag Officer or the General," and that furthermore, "none of the Women are to be permitted to leave their ships."

In the likely vain hope of promoting better behaviour among soldiers and their families, the armies of both nations stressed the importance of religion as part of military life. The U.S. Army recommended "all officers and soldiers diligently to attend divine service."[29] The British army believed regular worship to be important in helping to suppress "all Sorts of Immoralities among the Soldiers" and in controlling the "natural profligacy of the lower class of Men" and their wives, who exhibited "total ignorance in religious matters."[30]

In spite of all they had to contend with, some soldiers' wives managed to preserve both their decency and their dignity. It was recognized that the presence of the better type of woman in a regiment was an incentive for the men to behave well. She might find herself comforting a new recruit, mothering a soldier's sweetheart, or perhaps offering advice to a newly married wife ignorant of army life. If she happened to be among the literate minority, such a wife could also help men who wanted to learn to read and write. Whatever complaints may have been levelled at these women as a whole, it seems that by and large their presence was not resented and that sensible, useful soldiers' wives were viewed as an asset.

The life of an army wife in the early years of the nineteenth century centred upon the basic needs of her family. One of her priorities was to provide meals for her husband and children, and since army rations were monotonous, it was expected that they would be supplemented by provisions purchased or foraged. Soldiers with sober, industrious wives who could "be depended on for eating well" were allowed to take their food with their families rather than their companies.[31] A good diet, according to British advice, was beneficial to soldiers in correcting "drunkenness, and in a great measure prevents gaming, and thereby Desertion,"[32] but in reality the diet of the average British soldier and his family consisted mainly of variations on ration salt pork, bully beef, potatoes, pea soup, biscuits, bread and cheese. In addition to the daily allowance of rum, brandy or whisky, light beer was often available, brewed mainly to ensure that the water used was safe to drink. In the British army, a wife's ration entitlement was half that of her husband, although the traditional army bugle call that announced meals indicated otherwise:

> Officers' wives get puddings and pies
> And sergeants' wives get skilly
> But a private's wife gets nothing at all
> To fill her poor little belly.[33]

American wives fared slightly better, for their ration allowance was larger and a wife's share was determined by her husband's rank.[34]

Wives did their best to supplement the daily menu by various means, and it was common for them to grow fruit, vegetables and cereals in the garden of a garrison. Many were conscientious, capable and skilled at improvising. One British officer remembered the soldiers' wives setting up "a piggery, to have a little nice winter bacon, and I have heard it said, that they go so far as to have a bit of garden to furnish greens for ditto" and a " fowl-yard, which is frequently a foul-yard, they are sure to manage."[35] The same officer described these "barrack ladies" as "for the most part very clever – good hands at a dish of scandal now and then, as well as getting up a dish of mutton chops."

As a soldier's pay was abysmally low in the armies of both belligerent nations, money for items such as his family's clothing or cooking utensils came most likely from what his wife could earn. She was expected to work, and if she was not willing to provide for herself and her children and was found to be a drain on her husband and his rations, she was liable, as mentioned earlier, to be turned out of a regiment. There were several ways in which British and American army wives were employed. They could work as cleaners or servants to the officers, or help care for the sick of the regiment. Some took in sewing and some worked as cooks, usually in the messhouse of a garrison where they prepared food for the officers and anyone else willing to pay them.[36] Male army cooks were generally held in scant regard, for "the good God sends the food and the devil sends the cooks," was an popular soldier's saying of the time. If a wife could improve upon that sad state of affairs, she was much valued.[37] In 1813,

Captain Viger of the *Voltigeurs Canadiens* employed a Madame Désprès as his cook for a short period. The woman who normally performed this task, a Mrs. Maid, whom he thought as "lovely as life itself," and "*propre* as a pearl," had just produced a baby son and the captain was anxious to restore the rosy-complexioned Mrs. Maid to her "triple function of *Ménagère, Cuisinière et Laveuse* in my Hotel; duties she has always fulfilled to my complete satisfaction."[38]

In both armies, the most common employment for wives was that of laundress, a service constantly in demand. In the U.S. Army they were paid at set local rates and responsible for ensuring the wash house was kept clean. Each summer after 1 June when the weather was warm enough, they had to do their washing under a "Bowery built near the river." Laundresses, often wives of senior enlisted men, had a considerable amount of work as American regulations stated that soldiers "will not wear their Fatigue Frock & Trowsers more than three Days without washing." Company commanders sought to allocate work so that every woman had a fair proportion of washing, thus ensuring that they did not neglect the needs of the garrison "in order to wash for people not of the Garrison" and avoiding complaints that some women got more work and pay than others. The rules were firmly maintained and any transgressor was turned out of her garrison and "not suffered to enter it again."[39]

A colourful description of laundresses at Fort Sill, Oklahoma, later in the nineteenth century, would probably also have applied to the War of 1812 period. According to the author, "east of the sewer outlet was 'Soap Suds Row,' a collection of huts, old tents, picket houses and dugouts.[40] Here lived the "company laundresses, together with troops of shock-headed children, prowling curs and scavenging chickens." A study of their work during the period they were employed by the army reveals that some laundresses were dishonest, some were troublemakers, and others were "of easy virtue," but the majority appeared to be, in the words of one American general, "good, honest, industrious" women "ever-ready for a fight, yet kind of heart in a rough manner, always ready to assist in times of distress."[41]

Information about the work of laundresses in the British army appeared in a popular military treatise published before the War of 1812. It suggested methods to ensure that they did their work properly and stated that the women who washed for soldiers had to be "punctually paid," without which "they are unable to provide that quantity of soap, the linen must require."[42] The author advised that "Pay-Serjeants should be directed to stop for washing, from those, who are so idle to neglect a punctual Payment, and every week clear off the Women, who, by this method, can have no excuse, for not doing justice to the Linen."[43] Senior officers could set prices for laundry work, and in one example the rate was two pence halfpenny (about four cents) for each shirt washed. This fixed price could not be changed, and any woman "refusing to wash for the above sum will be struck off the rations."[44]

Working in military hospitals was another source of employment for soldiers' wives. American army regulations specified that "every hospital and infirmary, shall be supplied with one or more female attendants, at the discretion of the senior surgeon."[45] A wardmaster was appointed to be "responsible for the cleanliness of the patients and the wards," and to ensure that "the nurses and attendants are kind and attentive to the sick and wounded. All the attendants shall be considered as under his immediate direction."[46] In addition to tending the patients, nurses were also expected to "scour and cleanse the bunks and floors, to wash the blankets, bed sacks, and cloths of the patients, to cook the victuals of the sick, and to keep clean and in good order the cooking utensils." For this work they were paid not more than "six dollars per month, and one ration per day." On the official scale of pay for American army personnel, nurses were not listed although "Hospital Stewards" were shown as entitled to pay of $20 per month.[47]

British regulations for hospitals during the period stipulated that

> there is to be one decent, sober woman nurse, who shall receive at the rate of one shilling [about 20 cents] *per diem*, whose duty will be to prepare the slops and comforts for the sick, and occasionally to assist in administering medicines, cooking the victuals, washing, &c. and for every ten men confined to bed by fever, an additional Nurse and Orderlyman should be allowed.[48]

Over and above regulations covering hygiene and the handling of infectious and convalescent patients, a British army nurse also had to ensure that patients were kept "extremely clean" and that the clothes they brought with them "should be purified."[49] Each patient was to be issued a clean shirt and a clean pair of stockings" if he can sit up, twice a week or oftener if necessary," and was to be shaved two or three times a week. Nurses were also expected to comb their patients' hair and wash their hands and faces every morning, and "their feet once a week in warm water."[50] They were directed to prepare food for their charges under quite specific dietary instructions: the sick were to be "furnished with bread made of the finest wheat flour, and fresh meat, perfectly good and wholesome," but with regard for "the greatest oeconomy" to "laying out money" for such items.[51] In certain instances a nurse had to be prepared to find, in addition to the usual foods, special items, such as "Mutton, Fish, Chicken Broth, Wine, Porter, Cyder, Brand, Tea, Potatoes, or Vegetables," for those patients "whose cases the attending Surgeon may think will require such Indulgencies."[52]

As described in an earlier chapter, during hostilities a hospital had to cope with a wide range of wounds and conditions resulting from combat. Without modern medical advances the work of a nurse in a War of 1812 hospital was gruelling and challenging. Whatever she had to face, a military hospital was one place where she could be sure of not encountering disorderly conduct, for it was specified in the British regulations that "every species of gaming is strictly forbidden" and any patient who was "convicted of swearing, disorderly behaviour, insolent and provoking conduct towards the attendants, or of any deviation from the hospital regulations, must be severely punished."[53]

Since army life, despite all its problems, offered regular pay and rations, and the chance for a couple to live some sort of family life, most British soldiers' wives reasoned that it was better to go with their husband's regiment if it was transferred overseas than to be left behind with little or no means of subsistence. A life following the drum was hard, but given a choice, the prospect of a tent in some foreign field was preferable to poverty, charity or starvation at home.

When a British regiment was on home soil, wives could live in barracks, but when it received orders for field or overseas garrison service, their number had to be limited. Furthermore, only legally married wives (those having wed with the consent of a soldier's commanding officer) were eligible for consideration. Before 1813 the maximum number of wives permitted to accompany a regiment embarking for foreign service was six per one hundred men, but in the spring of 1813 a general order was issued permitting up to twelve women per company to embark with a regiment for foreign garrison service. However, only six per company were permitted if a regiment was warned "for active Field Service" – or none at all "according to the nature of the Service for which the Regiment may be destined."[54] All such quotas, however, were subject to the discretion of the commanding officer and he might decide to take no wives at all. If he did take them, he was advised that those selected to accompany the unit should be "of good Character and having the inclination and ability to render themselves useful" and that it was "very desirable that those who have children should be left at home."[55] Much less is known about the children of a British regiment but, as the number of authorized wives and the number and sex of their children was normally included on a regiment's twice-yearly inspection return, a perusal of these documents for five British regiments that served in North America during the War of 1812 reveals that for each wife, there was an average of 1.5 children.[56]

There were always more wives wanting to accompany their husbands than the regulations permitted. Despite the official advice given to commanding officers, the selection was usually made by having them draw lots – at least in the British army and probably in the U.S. Army – as it was the fairest system. This draw was often delayed until the night before the regiment sailed to allow the wives to enjoy the benefit of hope for as long as possible. Not surprisingly, most of them dreaded this process, which was usually carried out in public with tickets marked "To go" or "Not to go" placed in a hat. Each woman then took her turn to draw her fate.

There is a description of this ritual when the 94th Foot was ordered to Portugal during the Napoleonic Wars. As the wives in question each drew a ticket, a lucky pick fell to "Old Meg," an "old campaigner" and an "outrageous virago, who thought nothing of knocking down her husband" and was greatly disliked by everyone in the regiment.[57] As Meg triumphantly waved her scrap of paper in the air, shouting that she would "live to scold more of you round the fireside," some of the onlookers were heard to curse the "old wretch" who had "the devil's own luck and her own." Unfortunately, among the losers was a young woman, "wife of a young man who was much respected in the company for his steadiness and good behaviour," who was utterly distraught at knowing she would not be able to accompany her husband.[58] With a cry of "Oh, God help me!" she "sank fainting" on her husband's shoulder and her agony "drew tears from every eye in the room," apart from the redoubtable "Old Meg" who shouted out, "what are ye a makin' sic a wark [noise] about? … I suppose she thinks there's naebody ever parted with their men but her, wi' her faintin'; and her airs, and her wark."[59] The young wife and her husband are said to have sat all night holding hands before he embarked and, with the parting words, "farewell Sandy! we'll maybe meet in heaven," the wife and her child watched him go aboard the waiting transport.[60]

Such distressing scenes were common. When the 23rd Foot prepared to leave Colchester for North America, nobody got much sleep the night before the regiment departed as the "wailings" of the abandoned wives "resounded in the barrack yard."[61] Lieutenant William Keep of the 28th Foot remembered that when his regiment embarked for foreign service, among the wives left behind was "one poor creature" who had been with the unit for years. Keep last saw her perched on a rock, "giving vent to her lamentations … the tears rolling over her weather beaten features, and her fists clenched in a wild paroxysm of grief and heroism, crying out 'fight 28th – fight boys – fight 'em.'"[62]

One of the worst such cases of marital break-up occurred in the spring of 1814 when selected regiments from Wellington's army embarked at Bordeaux for the war in North America. During six years of campaigning in the Iberian Peninsula, hundreds of Portuguese and Spanish women had taken up with the men of the Duke's army, but only six wives per company were permitted to embark with the units destined for North America. Worse still, Wellington issued a General Order stating that all women with the army who could not prove that they were legitimately married – which meant most of the foreign women – would be refused transport to the British Isles. He attempted to soften the blow somewhat by permitting commanding officers to take a few "who have proved themselves useful and regular" on board "with a view to being ultimately married," but the greater part of these unfortunate women and their children were ordered to be returned to their respective homelands.[63] Sergeant Joseph Donaldson of the 94th Foot remembered that:

> The generality of them were not married, but the steady affection and patient endurance of hardship which they exhibited, in following those to whom they belonged, would have done credit to a more legal tie. Being here ordered to return to their own country with the Portuguese army, and strict orders given to prevent any of them from proceeding farther, the scene which ensued was distressing, – the poor creatures running about concealing themselves, in the vain hope of being allowed to remain; but it was all to no purpose: although they were willing to have sacrificed country and relations to follow us, the sacrifice could not be accepted.[64]

On the other hand, some soldiers used the opportunity of active service to deliberately abandon a wife and family. This was only to be expected as, in the British army, recruiters actually emphasized that enlisting was one way to get out of marital responsibilities. The 14th Light Dragoons, for example, urged all those "with too much wife" to join their ranks while the Lincolnshire Regiment advised that "Spirited Lads of Size, Character & Qualifications" might "acquit themselves of all women Labouring with Child and young Children & enter into the direct road to Honour and Preferment."[65] Given the mobility of military life, such men could remain out of reach of their families for as long as they chose. Some American women, however, took measures to "retrieve" their menfolk and one army wife, Rosanna Hickman, petitioned the secretary of war claiming that her husband, George, had enlisted while he was drunk. With several acquaintances able to certify that she and her children would be "reduced, to the Most abject want and distress" unless Hickman was released from his enlistment, her case received a sympathetic hearing.[66] Mrs. Mary Maloney, wife of Peter Maloney, who had worked as a tailor in Philadelphia before enlisting, also asked for his discharge and her petition was supported by the Board of Managers of the Philadelphia Almshouse, which had been helping Mary and her three children since her husband's enlistment.[67]

Not surprisingly, many soldiers' wives left behind experienced great hardship and their difficulties could lead them into bad company, prostitution, and even suicide. Out of the need for basic survival some of them, reasoning that in time of war their husbands might not return, decided to seek security with someone new. This sometimes caused complications, as in the case of a British woman, Rachel Heap, who, believing her soldier husband to be dead, remarried. She had three children by her second husband before her first spouse showed up, very much alive.[68]

In Britain, soldiers' wives left behind when their husbands went overseas were granted a travel allowance if they chose to return to their home village or town. A wife first had to obtain from her husband's commanding officer a duplicate of the list for the regiment, battalion, corps or detachment to which her husband belonged, with his signature to certify that she was indeed "the Wife or reputed Wife of a Soldier in his Regiment, Battalion, Corps or Detachment."[69] Having shown this to a magistrate, she would then receive a certificate stating her destination and the route to be travelled, and an amount not exceeding "Two-pence per mile" (about three cents). She was required to present this certificate to "any Overseer of the Poor of any Place" through which she passed, in order to receive additional funds to get her to the next city or town within a radius of eighteen miles, and so on.[70] At her destination, she surrendered her certificate to the local overseer of the poor, and all too often ended up in the poorhouse herself. Any wives not complying with these regulations were to be "treated as Vagrants."[71]

Those British soldiers' wives who were fortunate enough to accompany their husbands came under strict discipline. For example, if the wives travelled on a troop transport, there were regulations relating to the "cleanliness, discipline, regularity in messing, and general attention to the treatment and conduct of soldiers."[72] At eight o'clock each evening, except for men on watch, every soldier – and therefore every woman – had to be in a berth and married couples were not to be allowed to make separate berths all over the ships, by hanging blankets, which obstruct the circulation of the air; but are to have adjoining berths in some one part of the ship; and the women, as well as the men, are to be most strictly subject to the order of getting up at six o'clock A.M. when all their partitions must be cleared away for the day.[73]

Once everyone was awake, bedding had to be aired on deck if the weather permitted, and the berths and decks swept, scrubbed and scraped, work in which the wives assuredly participated. Divine service was held every Sunday as it was judged to "produce and promote cleanliness and good order among the soldiery."[74]

Women and children who travelled on British warships, as opposed to transports, were entered on the vessel's pay list. Thus, it is known that in the spring of 1814, twenty-four wives and fifteen children of the 1st Regiment of Foot travelled on the frigate HMS *Leopard* from Britain to the city of Quebec. Among them were Ann West with her children, John and Mary; Jesse Butcher and her daughter; Elizabeth McArtney with her son, Thomas; and a Mrs. Dobbin with three offspring. Aboard warships army dependants were, according to regulations, "victualled at half allowance of all Species for the times and from the dates set against their respective Names in the Said List," meaning that they were allowed half the normal ration issued to sailors. Their children received one quarter of that amount.[75]

No matter the vessel, travel by sea was seldom uneventful. In 1812, the 28th Foot encountered serious storms while crossing the Bay of Biscay and an officer thought how "deplorable" it must have been for the soldiers' wives to be "tumbled together, somewhere below decks, half drowned and stifled."[76] Other memoirs tell similar tales of women cooped up in overcrowded, leaky, rat-infested hulks and "rolling into the lee-scuppers when the ship would take a lurch that way."[77] The army wives who had been to sea before tended to fortify themselves against the rigours of such voyages and were often so drunk by the time of embarkation that they had to be hoisted aboard.

The voyage to North America was always dangerous. Huge seas developed in stormy conditions and one group of wives endured terrible weather in October 1812 when their ship, battered in a fierce gale, lost its mainsails, yards and rigging and nearly capsized. Nevertheless, the vessel remained afloat and as one passenger wrote, "we have had ten children born in the convoy since we left England … ladies all well again."[78] It was at times like this that humour helped people to survive such ordeals and not every day was bad; when the 23rd Foot crossed the Atlantic, the regimental band played "country dances, and the soldiers with such women as were embarked, danced till past midnight," an event "repeated whenever the fineness of the weather permitted."[79]

Women who accompanied their husbands on campaign during the War of 1812 faced arduous land travel, often across hostile country in miserable weather, illness and anxiety over spouses engaged in battle – hazards which all too often resulted in widowhood. An account of army life at Quebec in 1759 could equally well have applied to 1812:

> the swarming flies, short rations, dysentery and scurvy were as plaguing as the painted Red Indians, prowling around the old posts with tomahawks and scalping knives. The only relief was in the almost lethal spirits provided by the women sutlers.[80]

Rough country and bad roads were common, as the 19th Light Dragoons found when they continued westward in the direction of Kingston in 1813. In warm June weather they had to march through "a swamp totally impassable for any kind of wheel carriage and nearly so for horses." At one point the ground was so boggy that officers, soldiers, and wives were "obliged to keep out in the Lake to avoid being smothered in mud, up to our saddle skirts in water and

La bagage de campagne (Campaign baggage). In this satirical 1815 cartoon, French artist Eugene Delacroix portrays with some comic exaggeration a British military couple. The soldier has a loaf of bread stuck on his bayonet, washing drying on his musket and a large barrel of spirits hung around his neck while he holds one of his children by the hand. For her part, his wife carries a nursing infant in her arms and also that night's meal. (Author's collection.)

often swimming the horses for quarter of a mile." As everyone struggled on for another eighteen miles, the rain came down "the whole way in torrents." Walking in such conditions required great effort and if progress were too slow the officers knew that "the women, children and heavy impedimenta" accompanying a regiment might have to be left behind to enable it to make faster progress.[81]

When Lydia Bacon marched to Detroit with her husband's regiment, the 4th U.S. Infantry, in the spring of 1812, her feelings were

> somewhat tried seeing the poor Soldiers wives trudging on foot, some of the way mud up to their knees, & a little Child in their arms, only 4 or 5 Waggons allowed to carry the baggage, the poor women of course have to suffer, I should think it would kill them.[82]

If marching was bad, camping could be worse. An American officer has left a description of one army camp at Lewiston on the Niagara River in the autumn of 1812:

> We have lately had the most tremendous storm of cold rains and worst wind that I ever saw at this season of the year ... terrible hail, lightening, thunder and the whole army of terrors seemed pressed into requisition ...... Many tents blew up and over ...... I had not a dry thread to brag of ...... O, the glorious life, and the innumerable comforts of Soldiers![83]

Such words evoke an image of poor army wives, skirts sodden, desperately trying to keep the camp fire alight and the bedding dry so that there would be some warmth and cheer for themselves and their husbands.

Summer in the northern theatre of war brought with it illness in many forms and there were the inevitable plagues of insects. One officer camped at Kingston in May 1813 recalled that it was common for his tent to be invaded by "myriads of flying things" that included gnats, sandflies and mosquitoes, and by spiders, woodlice and toads. He concluded, "what a paradise this spot would be for an entomologist."[84] Winter in the northern theatre usually resulted in a suspension of hostilities until the following spring, and the troops settled into quarters for the cold season. For those who had to travel at that time of year, conditions could be very harsh. An American officer marching with his unit to winter quarters at French Mills, New York, in December 1813, wrote of a morning that was "the coldest I ever felt."[85] He described soldiers "chilled to the heart" and mentioned one poor child who, despite the best care its mother could provide, was "frozen as stiff as a poker" and had to be "poked under the

The baggage train. When troops were on the march, the baggage wagons normally travelled at the rear of a column. Here, women can be seen aboard the last two wagons, and in the one at the back, a woman and her children are pictured sharing it with soldiers, bedding, a chest, a regimental drum, tent poles and other paraphernalia. (Print after drawing by W.H. Pyne, 1802.)

snow without ceremony." So desperate was the plight of the troops that at a village along the way, a soldier stole a child "and sold it for a pair of shoes and a quart of whiskey" to fortify himself against the bitter weather. The child's mother, who naturally refused to be reconciled to her loss, was given "one dollar and fifty cents to redeem her child."[86]

When a unit neared an area where action was likely, some wives might remain with the troops but more often they were left at a garrison or post in the rear. Jane Ferguson, a British soldier's wife who travelled to Lower Canada with the 100th Foot, stayed in garrison at the city of Quebec while her husband and his regiment proceeded up country. Due to an administrative hitch, Jane was issued her normal food ration but none of the pay her husband had signed over to her. She had to help with laundry, mending, cooking, and cleaning in order to earn enough to survive but fortunately, as a devout Methodist, her church connections brought forth all the help she needed and she suffered "but little of

"Soldiers on a march to Buffalo." Life on the road was often very hard, involving arduous marches across rough, inhospitable country. In this cartoon, American soldiers and regimental women are seen crossing a stream. Whilst one woman at the front is being carried (note the kettle and pan hanging from the stock of her soldier's rifle), most must hitch up their skirts to get through the water, at the same time looking after their children. (Cartoon based on Thomas Rowlandson's *Women and Children on the March. Old Buffs 1808*. Courtesy, William L. Clements Library, University of Michigan.)

the privations and hardships of a soldier's life." As a woman of strong faith with a "practical nature and plucky spirit," Jane was heard to remark on one occasion when things were difficult, "what is all this, if we only get to heaven at last!"[87]

When they knew a battle was impending, soldiers' wives felt the understandable emotions associated with their situation. If they had managed to remain with their regiment, the sight of the wounded being carried to the surgeon for treatment brought home a cruel reality. Some women close to battle were able to render useful assistance, but they were usually regarded as encumbrances. On 22 July 1814, shortly before the bloody Battle of Lundy's Lane in the Niagara Peninsula, Major-General Jacob Brown of the U.S. Army issued instructions that all women with his division were to be sent to Buffalo, and that "Necessity urges to this measure."[88] They were provided with transportation and rations when they arrived there, where they were to "be employed in the Hospital." Some women, however, stayed with the army when it went into battle. Major Mordecai Myers of the 13th Infantry Regiment recorded that, after he was wounded in the arm at the Battle of Crysler's Farm in November 1813, he was fortunate enough to find a horse to carry him to the rear and was "led part of the way by a camp woman."[89]

Women who remained close to their men when they went into action often faced the unenviable task of finding a missing husband among the dead or wounded after the fighting was over. Surgeon William Dunlop of the British army remembered an American soldier who was so badly wounded that Dunlop could do little for him. The man's wife came through the lines under a flag of truce to find her husband "lying on a truss of straw, writhing in agony, for his sufferings were dreadful."[90] As Dunlop recalled, "such an accumulation of misery seemed to have stunned" the poor woman, who sat down on the ground and,

> taking her husband's head on her lap, continued long, moaning and sobbing, while the tears flowed fast down her face; she seemed for a considerable time in a state of stupor, till awakened by a groan from her unfortunate husband, she clasped her hands, and looking wildly around, exclaimed, "O that the King and the President were both here this moment to see the misery their quarrels lead to – they surely would never go to war without a cause that they could give as a reason to God at the last day, for thus destroying the creatures that He has made in his own image."[91]

Half an hour later, she was a widow.

Some of the grief-stricken British army wives whose husbands were killed at New Orleans in January 1815 found a good Samaritan in Rear-Admiral Edward Codrington. Codrington was moved to help a number of these bereaved women, one of whom actually had a baby "in the jolly boat" alongside his ship, HMS *Blake*, "before any other help than Nature's could reach her!" The kind-hearted admiral was anxious to assist the new mother, especially after he learned that her husband was among the dead, and he extended this help to the other recently-widowed army wives, explaining in a letter to his wife, Jane, that before long he had "a regular harem, including nurses" under his protection.[92]

I n both armies there were also camp followers, women who followed the army but were not married to soldiers and thus not "on strength." Some camp followers took in sewing, fetched firewood and water, foraged for extra supplies when needed and seized opportunities as they came along – their livelihood being dependent upon whatever they could make. Others among them worked as sutlers – military traders who were authorized to sell food and other items to soldiers – and a well-stocked sutler might carry cheese, cured meat or sausages, coffee, tobacco and similar provisions. These traders were subject to their own regulations, and those of the United States army specified that no sutler was

> permitted to sell any Kind of Liquors or Victuals, or to keep their Houses or Shops open, for the Entertainment of Soldiers, after Nine at Night, or before the Bearing of the Reveilles, or upon Sundays, during the Divine Service or Sermon, on the Penalty of being dismissed from all future Suttling.[93]

As civilians, sutlers received no pay and lived off their earnings but they were subject to "orders, according to the rules and discipline of war."[94] Officers were responsible for ensuring that they supplied the soldiers with "good and whole-some provisions, or other articles, at a reasonable price, as they shall be an-swerable for their neglect."[95] Controlling costs was important, for when soldiers bought items from civilians and not sutlers, there were "perpetual quarrels" over payment, given that the "avaricious and unreasonable civilian natives" were not normally subject to the military regulations governing prices.[96] In the American army, annoyed by the price-gouging inflicted on the enlisted men, senior officers often stepped in to set fair prices which sutlers had to follow on pain of losing their authorization to sell. At Fort Meigs in the spring of 1813, for example, the set prices ranged from 25 cents for a "Common dipped" candle, 50 cents for a pound of tobacco to $3 for a gallon of "Maple & dissolved sugar Molasses."[97]

A lasting image of British army sutlers comes from an account of their work in Spain during the Peninsular War. It recounts how they had obtained a number of pigs, one of which was "being killed in the street, with its usual mu-sic on such occasions," while another was roasting nearby over a straw fire.[98] As some of the sutlers were busy "cutting up and selling pieces of other pigs killed a few hours before," others "with their Don Quixote wineskins all about," were pouring out wine to the "half-boozy, weary soldiers" and peddling "apples and pears, gourds for soup, sour plums, &c."

Life for soldiers' wives during the War of 1812 was characterized by a certain camaraderie and a strong sense of purpose, loyalty and belonging, but it could also be harsh, insecure, unpredictable and dangerous. One veteran army wife later described her experiences and what she said would have found an echo in the hearts and minds of many women who were affected by the conflict. In the end, she wrote, after the "pride, pomp, and circumstance of glorious war" were gone, what remained was a memory of the reality of "death and destruction, in their most appalling forms."[99]

Most of the soldiers' wives of the war, illiterate and unnoticed, remain as anonymous today as the unsung heroes of the conflict – their husbands. The truth of their life could be said to be contained in the following verse:

> Gods! let a spent or rambling ball
> Touch but a Prince's hat or coat
> Expanded are the hundred mouths of fame.
> Whilst braver thousands but untitled wretches
> Swept by the sword, shall fall like paltry vetches,
> Their fate unpitied, and unheard their name![100]

These women, however, must not be forgotten. If the generals in North America shared the view of the Duke of Wellington that the army would have been worse off without its women, then those stalwart ladies received some of the recognition they deserved.

Daughter of the regiment. Sutlers were military traders authorised to sell provisions, food and drink at reasonable prices, and they were subject to military regulations and discipline. Some of these women also took in sewing, fetched firewood and water, foraged for extra supplies when needed, and provided companionship for the men they served. This engraving of a sutler shows her standing in front of a British encampment with a barrel of what was probably brandy in one hand, and a glass in the other. (Engraving by Henry Lemon. Author's collection.)

The livelier side of port life. The streets and alleyways of most major ports were perpetually alive with commerce, sailors, grog shops, brothels, taverns and the like. In this cartoon by Thomas Rowlandson are to be seen, among other things, a one-legged fiddler, a sailor and his girl dancing to the music, an officer and his wife saying their farewells outside the "Ship" tavern, a busy money lender's shop, a drunken man being carried off the street, and a man smoking a long clay pipe from an upper window as he contemplates the entire riotous scene. (Print of cartoon, 1811.)

CHAPTER SIX

"The lass that loves a sailor."
Naval Wives and Women

The moon on the ocean
Was dimmed by a ripple
Affording a chequered delight;
The gay jolly tars
Passed a word for the tipple,
And the toast –
For 'twas Saturday night:
Some sweetheart or wife
He loved as his life
Each drank, and wished
He could hail her
    But the standing toast
    That pleased the most,
    Was "The wind that blows,
    The Ship that goes,
    And the lass that loves a sailor!"[1]

The origins of the War of 1812 were largely found on the high seas, and the conflict involved considerable naval action. By the time the war began, after more than a century and a half of professional development, and following nearly two decades of continual fighting in which it had vanquished the fleets of France, Holland and Spain, Britain's Royal Navy ruled the waves. This prompted some justifiable fear and trepidation on the part of the families of American sailors at the prospect of their loved ones facing such a supremely powerful enemy on the water. By comparison with its venerable British counterpart, the American navy was a tiny but highly professional service, with superb ships expertly manned, and which had been tested in the Quasi-War with France in 1798-1800 and the campaigns against the Barbary pirates in 1801-1805.

American and British naval wives knew that their futures would linked to one of these services. Not that the navies of either nation encouraged their officers to marry, for they generally followed the dictates laid down in one period treatise which warned officers that falling in love meant encountering "the most dangerous of all the passions; mistrust yourself in this passion more than in any other, for it has often effected the ruin of the bravest characters." Instead, aspiring young heroes were urged to cultivate "a thirst for glory and renown, and you will tear yourself without much difficulty from the allurements of love."[2] Men being men, and women being women, this advice was routinely ignored.

In peacetime or war, a naval officer's wife normally remained at home with her family or found temporary lodgings at a port where her husband's ship might be expected to return. The transition from peace to war is likely to have affected naval wives less in practical terms than their army counterparts, since they were already accustomed to long, lonely vigils in the absence of their husbands. For British naval wives, whose menfolk had been serving at sea throughout the French and Napoleonic Wars, which had begun in 1793, danger and uncertainty were an accepted part of life. These women knew that their husbands belonged to a service of impressive size, power, tradition and the highest sense of honour and duty. The Royal Navy was far more successful than the British army in attracting officers, in part because no money was needed to buy a commission. Instead, its recruits began as young midshipmen who underwent a rigorous, cost-free training that involved years of practical seamanship.

For many a young man of intelligence and ambition who liked the sea and sought a life that was challenging and venturesome, the lure of the navy was irresistible despite the fact that it offered little leisure time and extended periods away from home and family. With social and educational standards rising during the period before the Napoleonic Wars, British naval officers were often cultured gentlemen who not only knew how to command ships but could also speak more than one European language. Some played musical instruments such as the violin or harpsichord, some were excellent artists and draughtsmen, and some were sufficiently interested in art or sculpture to become collectors.

Senior naval officers who hoped to recruit and keep young men in the Royal Navy had to demonstrate that they could, and would, advance the careers of their protégés. When an officer was promoted to command of a ship, he could name some of the men he wished to take with him, thus giving young officers of talent and ability a chance to rise swiftly on merit. The long period of warfare with France had produced a brilliant flowering of officers of the highest calibre who were expert ship commanders and fearless in engaging the enemy. Their exploits and professionalism, from Vice-Admiral Horatio Nelson down, made them a select group whose achievements have probably never been equalled. Dashing and courteous in their blue and white uniforms and gold braid, British naval officers proved, for the most part, to be as gallant and mannerly as they were professional.

In comparison, the United States Navy was barely twenty years old when war began, but it was fast making up for lost time. Even if it did not embrace all the customs of its British model, by 1812 it had grown to become a competent and professionally cohesive service. Many American naval officers had spent their formative years in the merchant marine or had served as officers in the merchant service while on half-pay. This kind of service was considered useful for building character and securing training. Even though the republic held fast to its vision of a democratic, egalitarian society, the lives of its people were still imbued with a sense of the inherent order of things – that some were placed high and others low – and this held true among naval officers. As in the Royal Navy, a demanding and effective training system for young midshipmen underpinned the United States Navy. Only the very best candidates were selected, thereby promoting a high degree of efficiency and commitment among those who progressed to the junior and middle ranks of the service. Gentlemanly they were, and ready to show their British counterparts how wrong they could be if they chose, some-what derisively, to refer to their American opponents as "Cousin Jonathan."

There were a number of outstanding American naval officers who were a match for their British opposite numbers, and who were complemented by wives of beauty, elegance and spirit. All naval wives being separated from their husbands by varying distances – thousands of miles in the case of most British wives – contact was maintained by letter as far as possible. These women also kept in touch and sought to boost one another's spirits. As Ann Hull, wife of Commodore Isaac Hull, USN, put it in a letter to Minerva Rodgers, wife of Commodore John Rodgers, in 1813, she hoped that "this will find you well & with such increase of *courage* as the times call for."[3]

Some naval wives had the benefit of years of experience and tradition. At the start of the war, Lady Maria Cochrane, wife of Vice-Admiral Sir Alexander Cochrane, had been married to both her husband and the Royal Navy for nearly a quarter of a century. Cochrane had already distinguished himself in battle against the French and Maria was to see little of him until 1815. Other wives, like Lady Warren, wife of Vice-Admiral Sir John Borlase Warren, commanding officer of the Royal Navy in North Atlantic waters at the outbreak of war, had spent much time in overseas colonies, while a few, like Lady Anne Hardy, married to one of Britain's most famous officers, Captain Sir Thomas Hardy, had actually been to sea in their husbands's ships. During the war, Hardy commanded the British ships blockading the American coast as far south as New York and was fortunate to have a wife who understood his life, for Anne Hardy was herself the daughter of a senior naval officer. Lady Jean Hunter, who knew Anne and had attended her wedding, thought her a "charming girl" who "very wisely accompanies her husband to sea and is just the kind of young person that will never, in any situation, be the least trouble, having no airs, or whims, or *nerves*."[4]

From a similar mould came Jane Codrington, wife of Rear-Admiral Edward Codrington, RN, commander of the squadron that formed part of a British expeditionary force to North America in 1814. Like Anne Hardy, Jane had joined her husband at sea some years earlier on the British expedition to attack the island of Walcheren off the Dutch coast in 1809. After the operation had ended, Jane, six months pregnant but undaunted, survived a dramatic journey across the English Channel when her ship ran aground on a sandbank in stormy weather and lost its rudder. Although at home in England during her husband's service in North America, Jane exchanged letters with him, keeping as closely in touch with events as communications would allow. This beautiful and charming woman had always been ambitious for her admiral and had supported him at every step in his career, particularly after his participation in the Battle of Trafalgar, which led to her attendance at the funeral of Admiral Lord Nelson. For Jane Codrington, there was "proper pride and exultation" at being one of the "wives of Trafalgar," and her gratification in being the lady of a prominent naval officer far outweighed the trials of long separations.[5] It was, she believed, worthwhile as she watched her husband rise in "increased estimation and distinction in the noble service."[6]

Not knowing how long this new war would last, naval wives prepared themselves for painful partings and brief reunions. Remaining at home in Newport, Rhode Island, was Elizabeth Perry, wife of Commodore Oliver Hazard Perry, one of an exclusive band of American naval officers who gained resounding successes against the British during the war. Elizabeth had many admirable attributes, and to her charm and good looks could be added "intelligence and talent," and "a thousand rare qualities of truth, simplicity, fortitude, and warm-hearted affection" that enabled her to cope with the unexpected change in her life that came in 1813. In September of that year her husband won a major victory on Lake Erie and Elizabeth found herself the wife of a national hero. Two years earlier while on her honeymoon, she had listened to his predictions of war, but that she should now be the wife of an officer of national acclaim was something neither of them could have foreseen. As one historian later wrote, Elizabeth Perry was clearly held in highest regard by her husband, whom she viewed as "my guardian angel on earth."[7] In graciously accepting the honours bestowed upon him when he made his triumphant way back to Newport, Commodore Perry freely acknowledged his regard for his wife.

Lucy Ann Macdonough, wife of Master Commandant Thomas Macdonough, was more fortunate than most naval wives in being able to spend much of the war with her husband. This was possible because Thomas Macdonough commanded the American squadron on Lake Champlain. While he took his little fleet into winter quarters late in 1812 and set about improving its fighting capabilities, Ann, as she was known, was nearby in their pleasant home with its view across the lake to the mountains of Vermont. Isolated it might be, and quieter than the Connecticut town where she had grown up, but Ann was content simply to be with Thomas, who was widely regarded as a courteous, gentlemanly and "most amiable man, not less loved than esteemed by his officers and crew."[8] He likewise delighted in his wife's companionship for, according to a poem written about Ann by her cousin, "her charms can ev'ry scene improve."[9] When Thomas Macdonough won a decisive victory over a British squadron at the Battle of Lake Champlain in September 1814, Ann Macdonough joined that exclusive circle of American naval wives married to heroes. She felt "particularly solicitous" that her husband was safe and she accepted, amid the celebration of his victory, promotion and the birth of a new baby, that her quiet days on Lake Champlain were a thing of the past.[10]

Of all the ladies of American naval officers, however, it would be hard to find a more glamorous example than Susan Decatur, wife of Commodore Stephen Decatur. Not only was Susan beautiful and accomplished, but she was married to a man regarded by many as the "most dashing and romantic officer ever to hold an American naval commission, and one of the most intelligent as well."[11] By 1812, the couple had been husband and wife for a little over five years and the citizens of Susan's home town of Norfolk, Virginia, still remembered their passionate courtship and wedding. The whole town had turned out to see the "accomplished and much admired Miss Susan Wheeler" wed her gallant beau.[12] Decatur had told Susan that he was pledged to serve his country first and foremost, and that if he should break that pledge he would be unworthy of a wife who possessed a "fine mind highly cultivated," more than "a common share of good sense" and great "amiability of disposition."[13]

When war broke out, Susan travelled to be with her husband wherever his ship was in port, be it Newark (New Jersey), New York or New London. A British sailor who was taken prisoner by Decatur and knew many of his crew told of how the "old tars" who were sentenced to be flogged for their various misdemeanours would sometimes approach "the commodore's lady with some piteous tale, begging her to intercede for them." This Susan evidently did with "almost constant success," causing the sailors to say, "good luck to her – she has a soul to be saved." If the story is to be believed, Decatur's love for his wife was such that he found it hard to refuse her even if it was prejudicial to discipline.[14]

The Decaturs seem to have been the perfect naval couple, and after Stephen's portrait was painted by the artist Gilbert Stuart, a poem appeared in a New England newspaper in 1813 entitled, "Lines to Gilbert Stuart Esq., Upon his intended portrait of the beautiful wife of one of our Naval Heroes, having already completed that of her illustrious husband." This of course refers to Susan Decatur, of whom the poem says:

> Stuart I charge thy genius, try
> To catch the enchantment of that eye;
> Let her – the fairest of the fair –
> The myrtle leaves of VENUS wear,
> While round her happy hero's brow,
> The laurels of a nation flow.
>
> That neck let floating curls entwine,
> Make all its pearly treasures thine,
> Be thy creative thought obeyed,
> And call to life the featured shade.
> Just touch the cheek with dawning red,
> Soft as the leaf from roses shed.
>
> But from the deeper lip prepare
> The rubied bud that ripens there –
> Since never to the critic eyes,
> May there an earthly equal rise;
> I charge thy genius, let it be,
> REFLECTING her, and SPEAKING thee.[15]

"The fairest of the fair." Susan Wheeler married Commodore Stephen Decatur of the U.S. Navy in 1806. Beautiful and elegant, she was the daughter of the mayor of Norfolk, Virginia, and perfectly complemented her dashing husband. The Decaturs, one of the most glamorous couples of the war, later settled in Washington. After Stephen was killed in a duel in 1820, Susan remained prominent in Washington society, maintaining the reputation of her late husband. She died in 1860. (Oil on canvas, attributed to Gilbert Stuart, on loan to the Stephen Decatur House Museum, an historic site of the National Trust for Historic Preservation in the United States.)

Glamorous and confident, Susan Decatur was not at all averse to being in the limelight. When Stephen Decatur fought and won a single-ship action against the Royal Navy's HMS *Macedonian* in late 1812, she found herself almost as much an object of attention as her husband. What made this victory even more interesting is the fact that Susan had met the commanding officer of the defeated British ship that same year, a few months before the war broke out. The *Macedonian* had put in at Norfolk on official business in February 1812 and her captain, John Carden, had been a dinner guest at the Decatur home. That evening, there had been plenty of good-natured banter over the diplomatic situation, behind which lay the possibility that the two officers might well end up as enemies if their two countries went to war. On September 1812, by sheer chance, as Stephen Decatur and his ship, the USS *United States*, were out in search of action, they met HMS *Macedonian* in the Eastern Atlantic. The ambitious Decatur was determined to carry off a victory that would outshine his brother officers, and after defeating the *Macedonian*, he became the only American officer during the War of 1812 to bring a British frigate into port as a prize of war.[16]

Not all naval officers' wives were able to take life as much in their stride as Susan Decatur. Louisa Broke, wife of Captain Philip Broke of HMS *Shannon* – serving in North American waters when war broke out – felt her husband's absence acutely. Unlike Jane Codrington or Susan Decatur, Louisa Broke was not ideally suited to being the wife of a naval officer and her husband regarded it as his duty to protect her from the harsh realities of war. As he wrote to his mother, Louisa was "one of those daughters of Eve who seem to have been formed as the helpmates of man but who need his support."[17] Even though she was "equal to the duties of a wife and mother," she was a shy person who relied heavily on her husband and was never comfortable when he was absent. In addition, she suffered from headaches that were to plague her for many years, possibly caused by the worry and anguish she felt but seldom showed.

Wartime worries. Sarah Skipwith Sinclair (1790-1827) was married to Captain Arthur Sinclair of the United States Navy. With her husband away almost continually on active service during the war years, Sarah spent the time living with her mother, Elizabeth Kennon, in Virginia, and caring for her young family. She missed her husband greatly, suffered much anxiety for his safety and found the long separations hard to bear. (Portrait by unknown artist. Virginia Historical Society, Richmond, Virginia.)

"A poor decrepit hobbling piece of antiquity" is how Elizabeth Beverley Kennon (1762-1830) described herself later in life with characteristic self-deprecating humour. A naval widow with two sons and a son-in-law serving in the United States Navy during the War of 1812, Elizabeth was able to balance her natural concern with a strong religious faith. She corresponded regularly throughout the war years with her friends Rachel and Ellen Mordecai, teachers in North Carolina, and her warm, philosophical personality and wide outlook are endearingly evident in her letters. (Portrait by unknown artist. Virginia Historical Society, Richmond, Virginia.)

Another naval wife uncomfortable in her wartime role was Sally Sinclair, a young mother in her early twenties and the wife of Captain Arthur Sinclair, USN. Sally was from a naval family in which partings were a regular feature of life, but she had not experienced war before and was expecting her third child when the war broke out. With a husband and two brothers away on active service, Sally, who, according to her mother, "used to be the livelyest [sic] of our set," was

> prey to conjugal and maternal uneasiness; for her husband is on the boundless Ocean, she knows not where; and in his absence she expects to bring into the world a little innocent; who may perhaps be fated never to see its Father. She has to reflect on the dangers her husband is exposed to; and a husband so fondly loved too she is really I think to be pitied.[18]

The passing of time did not ease Sally's concerns and in October 1812 her mother wrote,

> poor Sally is gone to bed; to forget in the comforts of sleep her sorrows, and cares; she has been quite low spirited all day, in consequence of letters from her husband, informing her that he was to sail in a day or two; she supposes he is now on the ocean; and she is again assailed, by the same fears she experienced during their last cruize.[19]

For Sally Sinclair and Louisa Broke the war was one long, agonizing wait, as it was for the wife of Captain Charles Stewart of the USS *Constitution*. Newly married in 1814, Delia Stewart became, according to a friend, a different person from the previous winter when, still single, she had been "without a care and now she is a very anxious wife & has given up society entirely."[20]

We know less about wives of the lower naval ranks. Neither the Royal Navy nor the United States Navy prohibited sailors from marrying, but they were strict about the presence of women on warships at sea. The British *Regulations and Instructions Relating to His Majesty's Service at Sea* forbade commanding officers of warships to take any woman to sea, "either as passengers, or as part of the crew," unless they first obtained permission from their superiors.[21] The Royal Navy, somewhat grudgingly, did permit women on board warships in port but only if they were "the wives of the men they come to, and the ship not too much pestered even with them."[22] American regulations expressly stated that the commanding officer of an American warship was "not to carry any women to sea without orders from the navy office, or the commander of the squadron."[23] Despite these official *fiats*, there is evidence that women went to sea on warships, particularly on British vessels, which tended to remain at sea longer than their American counterparts.

Some British captains took their wives to sea with them, a practice that, although officially frowned on, seems to have been regarded as a perk of a commanding officer. There is fragmentary evidence, however, that it was not uncommon for the wives of lower-ranking crew members to be present on operational voyages, but it is rarely official evidence as these women were "invisible," not being listed on the ship's books or pay documents. For example, in 1803, despite American naval regulations, a Mrs. James Low, the wife of the "Captain of the Forecastle" of the frigate USS *Chesapeake* gave birth to a son "in the Boatswain's Store Room."[24] The child "was baptiz'd in the Midshipmen's apartment" and the mother being unwell, "Mrs. Hays the Gunner's Lady, officiated" but

> The other Ladies of the Bay – The Forward Most part of the Birth [sic] Deck – viz. Mrs. Watson: the Boatswain's Wife, Mrs. Myres the Carpenter's Lady – with Mrs. Crosby the [marine] corporal's Lady: got drunk in their own Quarters out of pure spite – not being invited to celebrate the Christening.[25]

There were thus at least five women on the *Chesapeake* during this cruise and while it might be argued that this was nearly a decade before the War of

1812, there is other evidence, often from courts martial or courts of inquiry, indicating that the presence of wives and women on board warships, while not common, was not unknown.[26] In December 1813, Commodore Stephen Decatur, commanding the USS *United States*, signed Mary Allen and Mary Marshal, both wives of crew members, onto his ship as nurses – a most unusual event as these women now had official status. In 1814, Catherine Martin and Sarah Bond, and their children, Arthur and Mary Martin and William Bond, were listed on the books of the British squadron on Lake Champlain, the women to receive two-thirds ration allowance and the children one-third. In September 1814, the wife of the steward of the British frigate HMS *Confiance* was killed by a roundshot as she tried to aid wounded men during the naval battle on Lake Champlain.[27]

Evidence seems to indicate that while such women were sometimes the wives of ordinary sailors, more often they were married to warrant officers. These were technical specialists such as the gunner, carpenter, sailmaker, cooper and boatswain, who frequently remained with a ship after it had finished a commission or cruise and the commissioned officers and many of the crew had left the vessel. Serving on the same ship for many years and having small cabins in the forward part of the vessel, it was natural that their wives lived with them in port and some may have stayed on board when the ship put to sea. Four of the five women mentioned above as being on the *Chesapeake* in 1803 were married to warrant officers while the fifth was the wife a non-commissioned officer of marines.

It was much less common for the wife of an ordinary or able seaman to be on board, not only because it would probably not have been permitted, but because most seamen in both navies were young, single men. A landmark study of the Royal Navy during the eighteenth century has concluded that of the great majority of the able and ordinary seamen and landsmen (or raw recruits), nearly 80 per cent were under the age of twenty-five and that, overall, only about a fifth of the enlisted personnel were married. For the Royal Navy, these statistics had most likely not changed much by the early nineteenth century and the age and marital status of the personnel of the USN would probably have been similar.[28]

The wife of a sailor was usually condemned to spend months or years at her home, which tended to be near one of the major ports. If she was lucky, a British sailor's wife would receive a portion of her husband's pay in his absence, but many sailors chose not to send their pay home, and their wives had to find other means to support themselves and their children. Evidence from a sample of nineteen ships' pay books of the Royal Navy during the eighteenth century

The work of the press gang. Forced conscription was a standard practice of the Royal Navy during the Napoleonic period, and in this drawing by Thomas Rowlandson one woman has fainted and two others are clinging to their menfolk, who are about to be marched away to sea. (Cartoon by Thomas Rowlandson. Author's collection.)

has revealed that fewer than five per cent of the total complement of these vessels made any remittance to their wives or families, and of that small percentage, only just over half went to wives or women with the same surname. There were certainly married men who tried to send money to their wives, but there were also many who spent it on drink and other pleasures.[29] According to Samuel Leech, who served aboard HMS *Macedonian* during the War of 1812, the average tar behaved in port rather like "an uncaged bird" and would "follow the dictates of passions and appetites, let them lead him whither they may."[30]

In Britain, there was a second category of sailors' wives – those unfortunate women whose husbands had been impressed or forcibly conscripted into the navy. Britain could not maintain her maritime empire without the use of conscription to man her large fleet, and in fact the practice by some British captains of forcibly impressing American seamen was one of the contributory causes of the War of 1812. While Britons took great pride in the deeds of their navy, relatively few wanted to serve in the lower decks of His Majesty's warships with their crowded living spaces, harsh discipline and the ever-present threat of death by disease, combat or the perils of the sea. Many were exempt from the press, including middle and upper class males, tradesmen, merchant sailors, fishermen, ferry-men and civil servants, so its burden fell largely on the ranks of the unemployed and labouring people.

In Britain the press was active throughout the war with France, which lasted, except for a brief eighteen-month period, from 1793 to 1814, and there were many sad tales of men literally torn from the arms of a loving wife. Cartoonists depicted such women fainting as a husband or sweetheart was forcibly marched off to the fleet, and brides being deprived of their bridegrooms on their wedding day. Although gentlemen, or those purporting to be, were generally exempt, one such cartoon shows a respectable-looking man being taken and a woman on her knees in front of the pressing officer imploring, "for goodness sake, dear your honour, set him free, he maintains his father, mother, sister and wife!" The officer's callous response is: "let them starve and be damned. The King wants men. Haul him on board, you dogs."[31]

Any woman who associated with a sailor, whether legally married or not, was therefore subject to a life of uncertainty, long waits and brief reunions. Most common sailors saw little of their spouses during their service and since the majority of sailors and their women could not write, long intervals without news took their toll. For women at home it required resolve, self-denial and a vast amount of patience to remain true to their menfolk in such circumstances. While some achieved the almost impossible, many simply painted their faces and set off for the docks to find alternative company when the next ship dropped anchor. There was certainly no shortage of vessels putting in at major naval bases such as Norfolk, Bermuda, Halifax, New York, Plymouth and Portsmouth during the war, and there must have been many females who convinced themselves that after a man had been gone for a year or more, it was not unreasonable to seek other companionship.

For most naval women, home, family and employment occupied their time. Some worked as nurses in port hospitals where they quickly made friends with their patients Here they sometimes had a chance to witness how professional care, improved diet and time away from the temptations of drink wrought minor miracles. The records of the Royal Navy Hospital at Kingston, Upper Canada, during the war reveal that nearly half the nurses employed were women. They received only 2 shillings per day (about 40 cents) in contrast to their male counterparts, who were paid three times as much.[32] At Plymouth naval hospital, visitors were amazed to discover how many "husbands" the nurses claimed to have among the inmates. As one sailor remembered, some had several husbands "or men they called by that name, all living on board different ships." As it was rare that any more than one of the ships would in port at the same time, these enterprising women "equally enjoyed the caresses of the pliable spouses in happy ignorance of their dishonour." In his opinion, such women were "exceedingly bold" and he confessed he had "a great deal to do to repulse the temptations I met with from these sirens."[33]

Although most sailors were young and single, whenever a British warship entered a port, a surprising number of naval "wives" suddenly appeared. Because of desertion, shore leave was rarely granted in the Royal Navy during the Napoleonic Wars, but, by long-standing custom and official blessing, a sailor was permitted to have his wife on board when his ship was in port. A simple verbal declaration by a sailor that a woman was his wife was all that was required. Thus, when a ship dropped anchor, scores of women boarded the "bum boats" – the small watercraft whose occupants sold items to the warship crews such as silk handkerchiefs, fancy shoes, buckles, watch chains, jewellery, clothing, clay pipes, food and, occasionally, liquor – to go out and greet it. For men who had not set eyes on females for months or even years, the sight of the women approaching was "truly gratifying, and a grand treat."[34] One memoir left by a sailor who served in a large ship of the line recorded how, as soon as the bum boats were allowed alongside, the crew "flocked down pretty quick, one after the other, and brought their choice up," so that there were shortly as many as 450 women below deck.[35]

Since British sailors usually received their long overdue pay when they reached port and since some might have acquired prize money as well, they often had funds to spend. For this reason, when the naval "wives" of Gosport ran down to the docks to greet a newly-arrived warship, they sang a little ditty:

> Sailors they get all the money,
> Soldiers they get none but brass;
> I do love a jolly sailor,
> Soldiers they may kiss my arse.
> Oh! my little rolling sailor,
> Oh! my little rolling he;
> I do love a jolly sailor,
> Soldiers may be damned for me![36]

I do love a jolly sailor. There were always women in port ready to go aboard a newly-arrived ship to keep the sailors company. Here, a boatload of painted ladies, already in cheerful mood, is being rowed out to a vessel at anchor. Note the woman at the bow with flagon and glass in hand and several others manning the oars whilst the ferryman plays his violin. Casks of brandy and gin are being towed behind the stern of the boat, doubtless to be enjoyed later by the women and the sailors they are going to "wed." (Print after caricature by W. Elmes.)

Such women were the most visible members of their sex to be found at any major naval base. Often they were lively young things with the kind of charm that earned them nicknames like "Pretty Nancy" and "Sweet Poll of Plymouth," and made them the subject of ballads and sea songs. However, behind the bright exterior, according to a period sailor's memoir, they were usually "most pitiable" and had become "callous; indifferent to speech and behaviour, and so totally lost to all sense of shame, that they seem to retain no quality which properly belongs to a woman, but the shape and name."[37] In his memoirs, Seaman Samuel Leech of HMS *Macedonian* recalled the "boat-loads of defiled and defiling women" who arrived at his frigate, and how a sailor only had to select "whoever best pleases his lustful fancy," to be able to keep her on board until the ship sailed. Leach described these women, who crowded the

Accommodation at Portsmouth. In this cartoon by Thomas Rowlandson, a sailor and his companion, who is not his wife judging from the miniature portrait of another man worn around her neck, arrive at the door of a lodging house adjacent to the harbour which offers accommodation for "single men and their wives." The term "wife" was used very loosely in many short-term relationships enjoyed whilst a ship was in port. In the background another sailor is also availing himself of some female companionship. (Courtesy, William L. Clements Library, University of Michigan.)

major naval bases, as being "lost, unfortunate creatures" and "fallen beings."[38]

Once a sailor had chosen his companion, she usually remained with him throughout his stay in port, where he shared his pay and rations with her and often bought her gifts. Naval women saw a great deal of inebriation aboard ship, for to be in a state of "beastly intoxication," as the moralizing Samuel Leech described it, was considered the "acme of sensual bliss" by the men.[39] Sailors loved their beer as well as grog, which was watered-down rum, and the women often managed to smuggle additional alcohol on board despite scrutiny by men-at-arms, the forerunners of the modern shore patrol. Drinking invariably led to singing, dancing and carousing below decks, and discipline inevitably lapsed. Drunken women were known to assault officers, to swear and complain, and even to wave "their petticoats to the flagship," which in all probability was carrying the commanding officer of the fleet.[40]

Little wonder that the sight of "dirty women, the objects of sailors' affections, with beer cans in hand," and the "abominable" smells and "disgusting" sights below decks came as such a shock and disappointment to one new midshipman boarding a warship for the first time that he was reduced to tears. At bedtime on his first night on board, young Frederick Chamier tried to climb into his hammock, lost his balance and fell out, whereupon, he remembered, "I was instantly seized by a *lady*, who had some right to be in that part of the ship from her connexion with one of the midshipmen, placed properly in bed, tucked up ... had a kiss, which savoured much of rum; and then was left, not in the dark or entirely [to] my own reflections."[41]

When the time came for a ship to sail, many of these women appeared heartbroken but behind the façade there was often not a great deal of sentiment. Partings were generally taken in good spirit by those whose hearts were "not very sensible of the tender passions," and all concerned were accustomed to "such gambols."[42] The last day in port was often the time for a "good deal of merry, black-guardly banter, a good deal of drunken squabble, and very energetic wrangle over the sailor's money."[43] Before the sun set that day the women were ferried ashore and discipline was restored.

For females such as these, it was usually a case of "out of sight, out of mind," as there was always new company to be had on another vessel. Not all encounters were transient, however, and some rough beginnings led to romance and marriage as, on occasion, sailors grew so tired of their rootless life that they became determined to marry. In one account, a sailor proposed to the first girl he met ashore and, having married her, returned to his ship without even knowing where she lived. He would have discovered her whereabouts soon enough, however, as his new bride would have been anxious to receive a copy of the marriage certificate plus some of his pay. Having a marriage certificate in a major British naval base was useful protection against the occasional order of the local mayor to "turn all the loose single women out of the town."[44]

Whatever life had to offer the average sailor in the American and British navies of 1812, many of them acquired a strong sense of duty even if they were pressed men rather than volunteers. For the wives and sweethearts they left at home, however, it was far from an easy life. Yet when all was said and done, the women who took up with seamen recognized, as did the wives of naval officers, that a sailor's heart, though "it might have been pledged to his darling inconstant girl" back home, was first and foremost at the disposal of his ship, the king or president, and his country.[45]

Putting pen to paper. Letters were the main means of communication for most literate people during the War of 1812. The capture by enemy privateers of packet ships carrying the mail and the vagaries of war were two of the reasons why letters did not always reach their destination. Those that did were much cherished by family members, friends and lovers and did a great deal to maintain morale. (Drawing by George Balbar from Robert Foley, *The Niagara Story, Volume 1*, reproduced by permission of the author.)

CHAPTER SEVEN

"*The sensations of a wife, and mother in times such as these.*"
Binding Ties and Keeping in Touch

Love, to thee my thoughts are turning
All through the night
All for thee my heart is yearning,
All through the night.
Though sad fate our lives may sever
Parting will not last forever,
There's a hope that leaves me never,
All through the night.[1]

"I have no less than seventeen of my family now in the service; sons, grandsons, including three sons-in-law," wrote John Askin of Sandwich, Upper Canada, to a friend in January 1813. "Yet as long as God gives Mrs. Askin, myself and family health," he continued, "I think her spirits and mine never will fail us, and although when the lives of our children are at risk we feel anxiety, yet we would suffer much more did any of them shrink from doing their duty."[2]

Like any conflict, the War of 1812 cut a swathe through family life, bringing innumerable partings and extended separations as husbands, fathers, sons, brothers and other male relatives departed for service in the armed forces of their respective nations. Couples and families tried hard to keep in touch and letters – eagerly anticipated and much treasured – were the principal means of doing so. It was a time when people wrote thoughtfully and eloquently, and surviving correspondence helps to shed considerable light on family relationships, the pressures put upon them by war, and the bonds that sustained them. Mail was slow, taking weeks or even months to reach its destination, and sometimes failing to arrive at all. Letters sent by women to male family members were often lost through the vagaries of war, and it is therefore more common to find those sent home by male relatives than those written by wives, mothers, daughters or sisters.

To the Byles family, which was scattered across the English-speaking world, letters were a lifeline. Catherine and Mary Byles of Boston had a brother, the Reverend Dr. Mather Byles, in Saint John, New Brunswick, and nieces and neph-ews in Nova Scotia and Britain.[3] One of the Reverend Byles's daughters, Rebecca, was married to a physician, Dr. William Almon, who was surgeon-general to the military forces in Halifax, and she had a son and two sisters living in England. Members of this widespread family wrote to one another regularly, Rebecca Alm-on and her two aunts being devoted correspondents. When war was declared, Catherine and Mary Byles in Boston told their niece Anna, in England, that "the situation of affairs is now truly distressing & we most severely feel our separa-tion from our beloved relations."[4] They saw little prospect of anything to "raise our spirits which indeed are greatly depressed," and wrote to Rebecca Almon that "our hearts are quite full," not only because of the war but also because "we seem now to be shut out from any intercourse with our dear absent relations."[5] At Halifax, Rebecca sympathized with her aunts, joining them in lamenting a "cruel and unnatural war" and praying for "a speedy termination of it."[6]

For the Byles clan, the last two years of the war were particularly difficult. In February 1813 Rebecca was obliged to pass on to her aunts the news that the son of her sister, Anna, had accidentally drowned while trying to rescue a friend in difficulties in the sea off the Devon coast. Rebecca herself then succumbed to illness and many weeks elapsed before she was able to write again to the Misses Byles that "I was so extremely out of Health that I found it necessary to go im-mediately to the Country."[7] After a few trouble-free months and the happy news early in 1814 that Rebecca's son, William, had married a Miss Laliah Johnson, a "lovely girl," March of that year brought further sad tidings of the death of the Reverend Dr. Mather Byles.[8]

Throughout their wartime separation the Byles family, and in particular Rebecca and her aunts, always found strength in their faith and in their family ties. "How grateful and consoling is the reflection both to you and to us," wrote Catherine and Mary to Rebecca, believing that "many waters cannot quench love, neither can the floods drown it."[9] To them, "the Storms" which "for a time separate our persons" only served to "unite our souls more affectionately." The three women were overjoyed at the confirmation of peace in 1815, not least because Rebecca and her husband could now plan to visit the aunts in Boston. Until that happy time arrived, the two sisters wrote, they would continue to visit all their beloved relations "in idea [in letters]," as they had done throughout the war years.[10]

When circumstances broke up families and kept couples apart, letters helped to maintain morale on the home front. *Canadien* militia wife Louise Pinsonnant received regular correspondence from her husband Paul-Théophile, a captain in the *Chasseurs de Saint-Philippe*, as did Clotilde Weilbrunner, wife of Pierre Weilbrunner, a lieutenant in the 2nd Battalion of the *Milice d'Elite et Incorporée*. "Take courage my dear friend," wrote Paul-Théophile Pinsonnant to Louise, "and hope with me that heaven will watch over and preserve us. He has not given us the children we have, for us to leave them at so young an age."[11] He urged Louise to "be strong" and to "pray for me my dear, for I don't have the time." Pierre Weilbrunner's letters were generally of a practical nature, and Clotilde Weilbrunner received many requests for items her husband needed. Not only was she to despatch his "account book" but also the "big trunk that has all my clothes, hats, blankets, tassel and plume, in a word all my company concerns."[12] Finally, so as not to forget the inner man, Clotilde was to make sure she included "some cabbages, and onions and a little bit of butter." Remembering his fellow officers, Pierre also requested "two gallons of rum to give to the rest of the quarter." Over and above all that, "I will ask nothing more from you," he told his Clotilde, "than to desire the pleasure of embracing you."

Another *Canadien* militia officer, Louis-Joseph Papineau, felt a strong sense of responsibility towards his mother, father and sister, Rosalie. The Papineau family lived in the peaceful Lower Canadian countryside and, as Louis said, "be assured that there is less danger where you are than anywhere else."[13] He gave his mother and sister sound advice, urging them to

> make the most of your situation; amuse yourselves, occupy yourselves and keep boredom at bay, harden your souls and your hearts, take care not to give in to the unhappiest and least useful of states of mind, that of getting involved in others' misery when you cannot be of any help.[14]

While he was on active service, young Papineau visualized the two women at the family home, "busy at one end of the house," while "here we continue killing men and not marrying off our daughters, these are hard times."[15]

Rosalie Cherrier Papineau (1758-1832) was the wife of Joseph Papineau, a notary public, who sat for the constituency of Montreal in the first Parliament of Lower Canada. The couple had four sons and a daughter, named Marie Rosalie after her mother. One of their sons, Louis-Joseph Papineau, who fought as a militia officer in the War of 1812, wrote regularly to his parents and sister during the conflict. He later led an insurrection in Lower Canada in 1837. Madame Papineau was a woman of "much amiability of character." She died of cholera at the age of seventy-four. (Print from portrait by unknown artist, in Henry James Morgan, *Types of Canadian Women and of Women who are or have been connected with Canada, Volume I*.)

Not surprisingly, the stress of wartime separation made many mothers ambivalent about the war. In Kentucky, when recruiting parties were searching for volunteers to join the militia, one mother could hardly bear the idea of her teenage son going to war, although she admitted that "I would despise him, if he did not want to go!"[16] She therefore sent him with her blessing. Another woman, Mary Pruitt of Abbeville, was moved to tell her sons, "I will not say one word … to oppose your wishes – go and serve your country like men."[17] When they were ready to leave, she saw them off with the injunction not to shed a tear but to "go in God's name – and if you fall in your country's cause I will not regret it – be virtuous, faithful and honest, and my tears are at an end."[18] Such conduct, stated the newspaper which reported it, was admirable, and it added: "let those who think lightly of female virtue and patriotism read this and blush for shame" because "in the revolutionary war our females acquitted themselves well, and so will their daughters of the present day."[19]

Many mothers were resigned to the absence of their offspring. Elizabeth Kennon of Virginia, for example, was a naval widow who had two sons and a son-in-law in the navy and third son anxiously awaiting the day when he could become a midshipman. In the spring of 1812, as the United States moved towards a declaration of war, Elizabeth was in a state of "fearful anticipation" that "the poor Sailors will have to bear the first Brunt."[20] Once hostilities began, her thoughts were preoccupied with her menfolk, especially in view of the "gigantic strength" of the Royal Navy, but she put her trust in "the wisdom, power, goodness and mercy of the Almighty."[21]

Elizabeth was also concerned for her daughter Sally, wife of Captain Arthur Sinclair, USN, who appeared to be falling "prey to conjugal and maternal uneasiness" about her husband.[22] "May you never know," Elizabeth wrote to a friend, "the sensations of a wife, and mother in times such as these; when objects so dear to them, are engaged in the horrid conflict."[23] By November 1813 it had been six months since Elizabeth had received news from her midshipman son Beverley and seventeen months since she had seen him, but she found some levity in the fact that "nautical mania seems to pervade my family to such a degree" that her eldest son, George, a naval surgeon, confessed he would not be surprised if he heard of his mother "applying for a commission of some kind or other."[24] Elizabeth Kennon knew better than many what was required of sailors in their dangerous profession and wrote to a friend, "blest be the Names of our valued seamen; those ornaments of our country. I hope they ... will always be venerated by their grateful and applauding countrymen."[25] When Christmas 1814 came and most of the men in her family were still at sea, she finally admitted that she no longer worried if she did not hear from them for prolonged periods. She now realized "how wisely and mercifully are we organized ... that we can thus conform our hopes and wishes, fears and anxieties all to our situations."[26] Although the war had brought greater worry to Elizabeth, it had also brought an acceptance through faith of circumstances outside her control.

Across the Atlantic, when Jane Johnston bade farewell in England to her son, John, in the spring of 1813, it was in the knowledge that the young midshipman was bound for North America. Johnston was to join Commodore James Yeo, RN, who was assuming command of the British naval forces on the Great Lakes. The Johnstons were a prominent and well-connected family and were friends with Lord Melville, First Lord of the Admiralty, who had promised John Johnston a speedy promotion. Jane learned from her son's letters, however, that naval life was not what he had been led to expect. Commodore Yeo, who had "talked so smoothly in London quite altered his tone in Blue Water," John complained to his mother, describing the trials and tribulations of the trans-Atlantic voyage and his somewhat uncomfortable introduction to life as a midshipman.[27] Powerless to do anything to cheer him in his "Griefs," the best Jane could do was to endeavour to fulfil his request to "try & get a commission sent out" in the hope that promotion would end his miseries.[28]

The spirits of many prominent military and naval husbands were boosted by the support of their wives. Major-General Jacob Brown, perhaps the most successful wartime American commander, freely admitted that it was his wife, Pamela, who sustained him through the rigours of the conflict. Ten years married when the war broke out, Brown was a pioneer settler of northern New York State, while Pamela, the daughter of a Utica lawyer, was an educated and accomplished woman. Like many women in her position, Pamela Brown grew accustomed to her husband being away from home, and she appears to have been the force that held the family together. She concentrated on managing her household, caring for her children and supporting her husband in his absence, and by all accounts, succeeded admirably.

Although Pamela Brown was a cornerstone of the success that eventually came her husband's way, unfortunately few letters between them have survived. From those that have, it is clear that the Browns were devoted to each other, Jacob declaring to Pamela that he was anxious to hurry home "to your embraces and ... our dear children."[29] Probably the best testimony to Pamela's influence comes from letters her husband wrote to others. "No person living merits happiness more than she does," Brown told his brother-in-law, Nathan Williams, because, "in the gloomiest moments of my life I have found her my best consolation and firmest friend."[30] "I often reflect upon the course of my life and the agency my wife has had in producing whatever love we have en-

Pamela Williams Brown (1785-1869). After her wedding in 1802 to Jacob Brown, Pamela Brown apparently rode off on a white horse and carried a tea kettle with her – an early hint, perhaps, of the efficiency with which she later managed her family and household. Described as a woman of strength of character, self possession and fortitude, she was deeply loved and respected by her husband, who described her as "my best consolation and firmest friend." (Oil on canvas, 30x24 ca. 1818, by Ezra Ames. Munson-Williams-Proctor Arts Institute, Museum of Art, Utica, New York.)

The residence of Jacob and Pamela Brown at Brownsville, New York. Work began on the construction of this house in 1811, to accommodate a growing family that eventually comprised nine children. The twenty-two-room limestone structure, completed in 1815 and still standing today, was set on eight acres of treed lawns. It included a twenty-foot-square living room and two large connected rooms used for parties and dancing. In 1817, they were the scene of a special dinner attended by President James Monroe. (Benson Lossing, *The Pictorial Field-Book of the War of 1812*.)

joyed," he declared to Williams, adding, "I can truly say that her indulgent, *firm, magnanimous*, and intuitive mind had offered me the only support that could sustain me amidst the many difficulties and dangers with which I have been envisioned."[31]

Marie-Anne-Julie de Salaberry was another wife much cherished by her husband, Lieutenant-Colonel Charles-Michel de Salaberry, commanding officer of the *Voltigeurs Canadiens*. Madame de Salaberry had brought to her marriage the gift of the seigneury of Chambly, on the Richelieu River, where the coupled planned to build a home after the war. "I pine for such happiness," Charles-Michel wrote to his wife, acknowledging his "good fortune" in being united with her and telling her that as far as the army was concerned, "the married man is not cut out for such a profession." For his own part, he believed that "one must just be patient and resign oneself to a lifestyle that one cannot avoid."[32] Even as he prepared for a major engagement in October 1813, de Salaberry missed his wife and felt "wretched, my dear friend, to be parted for so long from all that one holds most dear. What Misery!"[33] A few days later de Salaberry triumphed at the Battle of Châteauguay, fought on 26 October 1813, and as soon as he could, he wrote to Marie-Anne,

> Just a few lines to let you know that the enemy started retreating yesterday. I think we have saved Montreal for this year …… It is certain that we fought against the entire American army. Its loss is considerable, much greater than we thought when I wrote to you earlier. I hope it will give us a chance to rest, and that I shall have the good fortune to see you again soon. I am very tired.[34]

His victory ensured de Salaberry's place in history but he would assuredly have acknowledged the support of his "dear friend," Marie-Anne, who backed him in all his endeavours.

Another wife who was always behind her husband was Jane Codrington, married to Rear-Admiral Edward Codrington, RN, who served on the Atlantic seaboard during the war. Codrington believed that Jane was his "pole star of comfort and content," and such was the Codringtons' relationship that in his letters to his wife Edward did not hesitate to discuss and even criticize British command decisions and operations.[35] After their defeat at New Orleans in January 1815, he wrote openly of his sadness at "throwing away the most valuable soldiers of our country by an assault bordering on desperation."[36] Few wives can have had the confidence of a husband in so complete a manner, and the Codrington correspondence is a record not only of the triumphs and tragedies of the British side of the war, but of a deeply cherished relationship between a distinguished officer and a devoted wife.

In a similar vein, Major-General Andrew Jackson regarded his wife, Rachel, as his mainstay, and she seemed to feel the same way::

> My thoughts are forever on thee. Wherever I go, wherever I turn my thoughts, my fears and my doubts distress me. Then a little hope revives again and that keeps me alive. Were it not for that, I should sink. I should have died in my present situation but my blessed Redeemer is making intercession with the Father for us to meet again, to restore you to my bosom where every vein and very pulse beats high for our health, your safety, and all your wishes crowned …… Think of me your dearest friend.[37]

Rachel Donelson Robards Jackson (1767-1828). The daughter of the co-founder of Nashville, Tennessee, Rachel Robards married Andrew Jackson in 1794 after a supposedly legal divorce from her first husband. When Andrew and Rachel discovered that the divorce had not been legally finalized, they had to re-marry. Andrew Jackson's professional and military duties often took him away from home, and in his absence the capable Rachel raised their adopted son and ran their Tennessee plantation. In later years, Jackson entered politics as a candidate for the presidency but the press found out about his premature marriage and accused Rachel of adultery, attacking her mercilessly. She died of a heart attack on 22 December 1828, two weeks after her husband's election to the presidency, and was buried in the white gown she had bought for his inauguration. (Engraving by J.C Buttre. Library of Congress)

It was Rachel who ran the Jacksons' Tennessee plantation during the war, and when in December 1814 Andrew Jackson was tasked with defending New Orleans from British attack, he reached out to his wife. By this time, he was close to physical collapse and asked Rachel to come to him. "I was taken verry ill," he informed her, "the Doctor gave me a does of Jallap & calemel, which salavated me, and there was Eight days on the march that I never broke bread."[38] Knowing his wife was on her way buoyed up the tired general, but by the time Rachel arrived at New Orleans, he had secured a resounding victory. Finding fame and fortune thrust upon her did not change Mrs. Jackson, who remained the same capable, devoted wife she had always been. Beneath all the glamour and trumpeting, Rachel Jackson had the assurance of her unshakeable relationship with her husband and her strong religious faith.

Major-General Robert Ross of the British army was also sustained by a loyal spouse. Ordered to lead the British expedition to the Chesapeake in the summer of 1814, Ross had sailed from Bordeaux in France, leaving behind his wife, Elizabeth, who was very concerned that he had not fully recovered from a serious wound sustained in Europe just a few months before. Elizabeth had campaigned with Ross in Spain and helped to nurse him to recovery, but his departure for North America was a matter of particular anguish as she suffered a "presentiment that she never would see her husband again."[39]

Robert Ross's letters convey a sense of the couple's mutual affection. After learning from Elizabeth that she had been forced to remain at Bordeaux because of illness, Ross expressed his deep regret at having to abandon his beloved "Ly" as he called her, in "a foreign Country with Careless Servants."[40] Were it in his power to leave the army, he continued, "I would without hesitation fly to you." Reminding Elizabeth that she was his "Prop and must support me," he assured her, "this War cannot last long, and we then meet my Ly, *never* again to separate."[41] Sadly, the happy reunion never came to pass, for Robert Ross was killed in action at Baltimore in September 1814.

Another pair were Edward and Louise Livingston of New Orleans. When he was absent from home, Edward Livingston missed his wife dreadfully. "I want your society always," he informed her, admitting he could find "no expression adequate to the Love, the tender friendship and exalted Esteem which every year of our intercourse has increased, and which nothing can lessen or Destroy."[42] On one occasion when Louise herself was away, the sight of one of her gloves lying on his desk "brought tears to my eyes!" confessed Edward. In his next letter he asked her, "is it folly? Romance it cannot be at my age. No, dear Louise! they are tears of the tenderest affection that I am obliged to drop and wipe off, that I may see to write to you."[43] As he pointed out, "upon the affection of one depends the sole happiness which the other can know."[44]

Edward Livingston's sister, Gertrude, the wife of Major-General Morgan Lewis of the U.S. Army, appeared to enjoy a similar relationship with her husband. Gertrude and Morgan Lewis wrote to each other regularly, although she was apparently "not fond of scribbling," doubtless finding that the task of running of their household occupied most of her time. Her husband, however, reminded his "dear Love" that, "immersed as I am in business the only pleasure I have is to hear that those whom I most love are at ease and happy."[45] Time spent together was precious, and on one occasion when he was able to get to Albany, where "Gitty," as Gertrude was called, had been visiting with a friend, Lewis arrived only to find that he had missed her by a few hours. He freely admitted how much it had upset him:

> I need not say how much I was disappointed on entering Mrs. Ludlow's house, to find that you had departed. The cause was an afflicting one, and produced sensations which the exertion of all my philosophy could not bear me up against. I was completely unmanned, and do not believe I could at that moment have looked an English army in the face.[46]

The strength of affection and devotion that existed between such couples was evident, and none more so than with Commodore John Rodgers, USN, and his wife, Minerva. For John Rodgers, the conflict was measured by a series of happy reunions and sad partings, and sustained by the love he shared with his wife. Home and family were close to his heart and he was fortunate in Minerva to have a refined, educated woman who adored him. By 1812, the tall, dark John and the pretty, golden-haired Minerva had been married for some six years and their correspondence forms a unique husband-wife archive of the wartime period.

Minerva Rodgers was a woman who appreciated that she was blessed with a happy marriage and, unlike Elizabeth Ross, she felt optimistic about the future, telling her husband in June 1812 that "something whispers me that you will be returned to me in safety."[47] Although she hated the long separations brought about by her husband's naval service, she believed they did much to "animate and keep alive our affections," and she counted her blessings.[48]

John and Minerva corresponded with such openness that two centuries later it is impossible not to warm to the personalities that emerge from their letters. Minerva's regular epistles to her husband talked of life at home, including news of family and friends, while his to her concentrated on his cruises and the people he met. As a naval wife, Minerva occasionally wondered whether "all the anxiety, doubts, and privations" of their life brought more pain than pleasure, but took great consolation in her husband's feelings towards her – which he sometimes concealed in his letters "thro' the medium of Double Entendres," and which, she said, made her "perfectly tremble."[49] Minerva clearly had a similar effect on her husband, for he confessed that she had it in her power "to make me cry by the mere assistance of a goose quill."[50]

Like the other wives of senior officers, Minerva Rodgers was well aware of the importance of her husband's service and although she was conscious that during his time at sea he would be "exposed to dangers which will doom my poor heart to a tumultuous warfare between hopes & fears," she assured him she would, "always endeavour to look upon the bright side of the picture."[51] Determined to "believe nothing good or bad till I have it from under your own hand," Minerva remained ever optimistic, convinced that "much happiness is yet in store for us."[52] While John was absent, she occupied her time at their home in Havre de Grace, Maryland, caring for their two young sons and indulging her love of music, reading, the theatre and the company of friends. When life seemed dull, she dreamed of the future and pictured John and herself, "side by side jogging soberly along, smoothing for each other the uneven surfaces of life, trampling on ambition and all the various cares which exist in his train, and attending to the innocent prattle of ten or a dozen little urchins."[53]

It helped when, in 1813, Minerva was able to visit John, and she made three journeys with her children to see him that year when his ship was at Boston and Providence. Meeting the wives of other naval officers, among whom were Susan Decatur and Ann Chauncey, wife of Commodore Isaac Chauncey, made her realize that she was not alone in her concerns, especially when she found Mrs. Chauncey looking "thin & pale & very anxious about her husband," sentiments with which Minerva sympathized only too well.[54] These wartime reunions were joyful for Commodore and Mrs. Rodgers, but partings were hard and when she said goodbye on one occasion, Minerva declared herself to be bereft of happiness and a "poor lifeless inanimate being without you & your feelings."[55] John, in turn, admitted it was difficult to describe the emotions that took "possession of my soul, Heart & Mind at the moment I took leave of you."[56] When she set off from Providence in the spring of 1813, Minerva told her husband it was like "tearing soul from body," but soon after her arrival at Havre de Grace, her thoughts were distracted from her distress by finding the townspeople "all in commotion in consequence of the appearance of some British Frigates off Turkey Point."[57] Minerva did not share their anxiety, telling John that "I am not to be frightened by idle threats, and shall feel myself perfectly secure." A little over two weeks later, British naval forces attacked Havre de Grace and Minerva Rodgers, who always feared for her husband's safety but not her own, came face to face with the reality of the war.

A gap in correspondence leaves us none the wiser as to Minerva's experience of that attack, although it is known that she was in Havre de Grace when it took place. Her husband had just departed on a five-month cruise that was to take him across the Atlantic to the British Isles and as far south as the Azores, and that resulted in the capture of twelve British vessels. Once he learned of the British attack, John Rodgers became anxious for his family's safety, but Minerva had already decided to distract herself from the painful reality of recent events by immersing herself in the wedding plans of her sister, Maria. Worse was to come, however, in the summer of 1814 when a force of British troops under the command of Major-General Robert Ross, who was as devoted to his wife as John Rodgers was to Minerva, captured Washington. As word of the British attack on the capital spread, Minerva Rodgers wrote anxiously to John:

The most disastrous news reached us ... I am led to hope that it is greatly exaggerated yet cannot flatter myself that it is groundless ... Oh my husband! Dearest of men! All other evils seem light when compared to the danger which threatens your precious safety. When I think of the perils to which your courage will expose you, I am half-distracted, yet I would not have you different from what you are. I have just heard that Washington is in ashes. I am bewildered & know not what to believe but am afraid to ask for news ... May God preserve and bless you![58]

With British warships still in the Chesapeake Bay after the fall of Washington, tension remained high and some two weeks later a highly agitated Minerva wrote to her husband that she had just glimpsed a large enemy force proceeding up the Bay. "There are now visible from the top of the house, about 25 or 30 sails," she scribbled hastily, adding that "we have had here a full view of the British fleet."[59] This time, the British were heading for Baltimore, where Rodgers was patrolling, and Minerva could think of little else but his safety. "God preserve you my Lover," she wrote, knowing

> how much will devolve upon you & your brave seamen yet I endeavour to be composed – I find all my fortitude is insufficient for the various calls upon it. Whenever you have a moment drop me a line! If I should hear a cannonading from Baltim[o]re Good Heavens what will become of me![60]

The sound of artillery fire from the direction of Baltimore was indeed audible in Havre de Grace and Minerva was left to wait and wonder. In the event, the British attack proved unsuccessful, and when the enemy expeditionary force moved out of the Chesapeake to head south, its departure brought a sense of relief to the local people. Minerva Rodgers's hunches proved correct, for her husband survived the war. As for Minerva herself, she remained one of the wives to have personally experienced an enemy attack on her home town during the conflict, a fact that made her postwar years all the more precious.

To testify to the bleakness of separation – and the power that images of home and a loving wife could exert over a man – one need look no further than the account of Ensign William K. Beall, an American officer captured at Detroit in August 1812. As he proceeded to Amherstburg in Upper Canada aboard a British ship, Beall was deeply depressed and lay awake at night beset by images of his wife at their home in Kentucky. "In my sleep the air drawn figure of my Melinda often rises to my view: beauteous as an Angel, gentle as the spring, smiling on me with enchanted tenderness and yielding to my fond embrace," he recorded.[61] "In dreams, with rapturous fondness, I have pressed her to my bosom, felt her soft touch, heard the sweet accents of her voice, and gazed upon her lovely countenance till every sense was lost in ecstasy and love."

Such passion could be a positive force for a couple separated by war, as it was for John and Minerva Rodgers, but it could also be disruptive. Consider British Lieutenant Maurice Nowlan and his wife, Agathe, newlyweds who were separated by the conflict after only six months of marriage. The depth of feeling between the two and the distress their separation caused is evident from Maurice's letters, in which he poured out his heart to Agathe, assuring her that he would far sooner be alone and reading her letters "than go amongst this gay society," which he could not enjoy "when I am separated from the only one that is dear to me in this World."[62] But as much as he longed for his bride, Nowlan was of the firm opinion that an army camp was no place for a woman. Agathe was still coming to terms with her new life as an officer's wife and complained at not hearing from Maurice as often as she wished, unaware that on active service there were many other demands on his time. Despite such reproaches, Maurice Nowlan loved Agathe very much, telling her that "my jewel you are my only care if it was not for *you my jewel my Heart my Soul my every thing thats dear* on Earth I believe I would run Headlong at times."[63]

The situation was not helped by the fact that in the autumn of 1813 Nowlan's regiment, the 100th Foot, was sent to the Niagara, making the distance between Maurice and Agathe at Montreal even greater. "Nothing on Earth could give me more pleasure than to have the infinite happiness of pressing you to my Heart," Maurice assured her on their first wedding anniversary in June of that year, hoping fervently that "Kind Heaven will shortly relieve us and send us once more together, my Love what joy and comfort I promise myself when that happy day comes."[64] Throughout his wife's ordeal, Nowlan tried to reassure and calm her. "Try to be a little more patient," he begged, at the same time asking, "what can I do my dear so far away?"[65] Perhaps, as he suggested to her, "kind fortune may do some thing for me shortly."

On 10 December 1813, Lieutenant Maurice Nowlan had a serious matter to convey to his spouse. He was to take part that night in a risky attack on Fort Niagara and although he was confident that he would survive, he still found it difficult "to bid my dear and loving wife adieu and perhaps the last time." He tried hard to reassure her:

My dearest jewel don't torture yourself with grief if you should chance to get this before I have time to write you again. Hope for the best, my only Heart. You know you are my only care, it's but for you I live, may the Almighty bless you, my only wife.[66]

Sadly, Maurice Nowlan was killed in action during the attack. There is no record of how Agathe Nowlan coped when she learned of her husband's death but she could perhaps take some small consolation in having been loved by a devoted husband and a brave officer.

Another army wife who found separation hard to bear was Sarah Howard of Windsor, Connecticut. Her anxiety was tempered by the fact that she knew her husband was enjoying army life. A prewar merchant, George Howard had found his daily routine monotonous but, as the likelihood of war grew, he later admitted that "my nightly visions were all of the Army – I determined to seek renown."[67] George was quick to accept a captain's commission in the 25th Infantry Regiment in March 1812, leaving Sarah to run their business and care for their one-year old daughter, Julia. "Be not Unhappy," he urged his wife, "I will soon see you and My friends – My Country, and the beloved of My Soul."[68]

In the spring of 1813, while serving on the northern frontier, Howard sent his wife a graphic description of having to sleep in the open "upon a Bed of Snow six feet deep." He seemed to thrive upon the experience, however, for as he added, "we bore it like Men who wished to Meet a foe." A few months later, Howard fell seriously ill and was granted leave to convalesce at home. On his arrival at Windsor he wrote in his diary: "I threw myself into the Arms of a Wife – Father and Mother – and folded to My bosom a lovely Daughter."[69] By the spring of 1814 George Howard was back with his regiment and, although he told his wife, whom he described as the "Harbinger of light to the Eye of darkness," that his duty was "severe and somewhat dangerous," he also had to admit, "to me it is delightful," especially since, when alone,

the Abstract intellect wanders from scenes of Watchful care, and dubious strife and seeks repose in the abodes of Conjugal Affection. These are the Moments of unalloyed delight, which invigorate the Body and render Man impervious to toil or danger.[70]

A letter from Sarah in April 1814 provides an impression of how she was coping with his absence and the gaps between his letters:

Dear Howard,

We this Morning received a long letter from you dated the 8th of April – we have some almost every Week – but they are so long coming that we feel just as anxious to hear again – but it is a great consolation to Me – to have them when I do, and I embrace this as it is the first opportunity I have had to write you a line, that you may know you yet have a Wife and child that mourns the absence of a loving Husband and Parent. My health is good, but spirits rather low – the ensuing Season appears long and tedious as I more than ever feel the want of a bosom friend. O My dear Howard, that you May soon return to this humble dwelling is the most constant wish of your

Affectionate Sarah.[71]

She added a postscript:

Julia is a fine girl – goes to school every day – learns finely and talks much of her poor Papa – She says Ma, if you wont cry, Pa will come home again. I have No News of importance. Your friends wish to be remembered to you That the Almighty may have you in his holy keeping is the fervent prayer of your Affectionate Wife.

Sarah's prayers were answered as, after seeing action in the summer of 1814, George Howard was sent on a recruiting assignment that kept him out of harm's way until the end of the war. Sarah could rest easy in the knowledge that, having fulfilled his wish to follow the drum, her husband would return home safely.

Another loving marriage subjected to long separations was that of Captain Philip Bowes Vere Broke, RN, and his wife, Louisa. The Brokes, both from Suffolk county families with comfortable livings, had known each other from childhood, and Philip was devoted to his fair-haired young wife with her lovely blue eyes. After their marriage in 1802 children followed, together with long years of absence for the capable Broke, many of which were spent on blockade duty off the French coast. Letters meant a great deal to this staunch pair and it is evident from their surviving correspondence that Broke wrote to his wife almost weekly and never hesitated to tell her how much he missed her, nor from helping and comforting her as much as he could. These letters were all the more important as Louisa was a somewhat retiring person who was not well suited to being a sailor's wife and needed constant reassurance from her husband to keep her spirits up.

Three devoted husbands. Commodore John Rodgers, USN, (top) Lieutenant-Colonel Solomon Van Rensselaer, United States Army, (below left) and Captain Philip Broke, RN, (below right) all wrote very regularly to their wives. The correspondence of these couples illustrates very clearly the close bonds that existed between them, and how much letters mattered. This was especially so for Solomon Van Rensselaer and his wife, Harriet, in 1812, when they had to cope with the tragic loss of a child. (Engravings from Lossing, *The Pictorial Field-Book of the War of 1812*.)

When war came in June 1812, Broke had been at sea nearly six years, during which time there had been precious few reunions with his wife and family. He was the commanding officer of HMS *Shannon* and whilst engaged in long, dreary spells of blockade duty, he had made his ship one of the crack frigates in the Royal Navy. To Broke, a first class seaman and naval officer, serving his country was a matter of the highest duty, and he wrote to Louisa confidently that he, his ship's company and their "wooden mistress" were fully prepared and ready to do "all we can for the splendour of the *proud old flag*."[72]

This confidence was not exaggerated – after a series of stinging British naval defeats in single-ship engagements in the opening months of the war, on 1 June 1813 Broke and the *Shannon* met and captured the American frigate USS *Chesapeake* in a short but bloody action off Boston. During the hand-to-hand fighting that took place, Broke received a serious wound from a sword cut to his head. Forced by his injury to give up command, he arrived back in Halifax as a convalescent and told his "beloved Loo" in a badly scrawled letter that the *Shannon* had "at last gained a glorious victory" that would allow him to "very soon return to my affectionate Loo's arms."[73] Throughout his naval service, Broke had always kept with him a lock of his wife's hair in a small blue satin bag, and it remained beside his sick bed during the long period of recovery.[74]

When news of the *Shannon*'s victory reached Britain, Louisa Broke was staying at the seaside town of Budleigh Salterton, Devon, and was on her way to church with friends. The date was Sunday, 11 July 1813, and as she read the newspapers in her carriage, Louisa realized that the man she had married was a hero. "This has been a day of great trials to me my beloved Husband," she told him, putting pen to paper that very day.[75] Louisa was gratified to learn that her spouse was so highly thought of by the whole country, but knowing him as she did, she also knew his riposte would be, "it is enough to make me proud that I ever was & had reason to be of use." Beyond all else, she was profoundly thankful that "so valuable a life" had been saved "when in the midst of so many & great dangers."

In October 1813 Captain Philip Broke, still recovering but now able to resume his command, sailed for England. By this time, Louisa had received countless letters of congratulations and knew that honours were awaiting her husband on his return. Not only would he receive the Freedom of the City of London and a sword valued at a hundred guineas (about $420), but artists were requesting the privilege of painting his portrait and poets were publishing laudatory poems about him. To Louisa this adulation was of less importance than the return of the man she loved, and when he arrived at Portsmouth in early November to a hero's welcome and the "thunders of fort and fleet," one of the first things the couple did was to go to church with their children and give thanks for their blessings.[76] Philip Broke had always expressed to his wife his firm belief that they would eventually be safely reunited, and the Brokes were able to see that wish fulfilled.

Unfortunately, there were couples whose marriages were already suffering from a strain that war only compounded. Such was the case for Solomon and Harriet Van Rensselaer of Albany, New York. When Lieutenant-Colonel Van

Rensselaer left his home in the late summer of 1812, he and his wife were still coming to terms with a terrible personal tragedy. A month earlier, a deranged man had shot and killed their six-year-old son, Van Vechten, while he played in a meadow near their home, and when Solomon was ordered to report for duty, his grief was still great.

Having had to leave a distraught Harriet, who also happened to be pregnant, Van Rensselaer took up his duties at Lewiston, New York, expecting to hear from her, but when there was no letter by the end of August he grew concerned. "What under the Heavens is the reason you do not write to me," Solomon asked her, "I have written from almost every place I have been at, without receiving a line from you."[77] He confided in another friend his concern that the "recollection of the late overwhelming event at home" had proved too much for his wife.[78]

In early September, when Harriet Van Rensselaer finally felt able to put pen to paper, she told her husband of her "poor afflicted heart, which has been so excessively oppressed" and which had felt "no comfort since that trying hour when the most awful of all our many calamities befell us."[79] She had tried to take her mind off her son's death by work of various kinds, but could still picture the "awful, the distressing sight" of Solomon carrying him into the house, and the little boy, "bleeding and dying in your Arms!" His loss was enough to "harrow my very Soul," she wrote in anguish, describing herself as a "most miserable wife," and almost envying her husband the distraction of military service, which, as she said, "must be of course, some relief to your depressed spirits."[80]

In October, as he completed plans for an attack across the Niagara River, Solomon Van Rensselaer was recovering from a bout of fever but managed to write to Harriet in loving terms. "Of course I shall be compelled to expose myself in a high degree as an example to them [the soldiers] to do their duty" in the forthcoming assault, he informed her. "I will succeed or fall. If the latter, let me beg of you to meet the event with fortitude, and do not unnecessarily repine at my loss."[81] He prayed he would see his wife again, for as he told Harriet, "never in my life have I been so impatient to return home to comfort you under your affliction." At the Battle of Queenston Heights on 13 October 1812, the very day that Harriet Van Rensselaer gave birth to another son, Lieutenant-Colonel Solomon Van Rensselaer was wounded five times but survived. By the second week of November, he was well enough to return to the home where his presence was so sorely needed.

The importance of letters, or lack of them, is conclusively highlighted in the unhappy tale of Private John Patterson of the 22nd U.S. Infantry Regiment. In the autumn of 1812, Patterson's unit was stationed at Lewiston, New York, and most of his erratically-spelled correspondence was sent to his wife, Levina, in northern Pennsylvania. In his first missive, dated 16 August 1812, Patterson informed his "dear and loving companion," that he was well and that "in about 6 weakes i shall have 16 dollers comeing to me – then i shall be able to cend some home."[82] Patterson told Levina that when not on duty, he spent his spare time reading, writing and preaching the gospel to his comrades and hoped that "you will pray for me – and i hope that the friends will not dispise you or me because i am a souldier." This reference to "friends" may indicate that Patterson was a Quaker.[83]

Nearly a month passed before Patterson wrote again and although he had not yet received a letter from Levina, he had received a message from her via another soldier, Private Cook, who had been granted leave and had visited the place where she was living. Presumably from Cook, Patterson learned that Levina had reproached him "becose i did not come with cook," and he proceeded to explain that he "had no money and thea would let [only] so many on furlow at once so far ... so dont blame me for not comeing or think i dont care for you for i do think as much of you as ever i did."[84] Counselling her to "remain in the cause of god and bee contented," Patterson hoped he would receive a reply and signed himself "your loveing companion."

In a third letter written at the beginning of October 1812, Patterson promised Levina that he would "try to git a furlow and come home this winter," but that he was, meanwhile, "respected among souldiers and officers."[85] It is clear that Levina made no response to this letter, and by February 1813 John Patterson was becoming concerned about his wife's silence. "I have heard nothing from you," he complained, "this is the forth letter sence i have been at niagary and i want to hear from home and how you are."[86] Two months later, when there was still no word from home, Private Patterson told Levina sadly:

i have wrote six letters to you and received none and i have wrote 8 letters sence i inlisted and received but one ... i do beegin to think hard of it – i do some times think you have for got me or do not care any more about me – i dont think i shall write you till i receive one – but if you have forgot me i hope that you have not forgot god ... my fellow souldiers receive letters from 50 to 6 or 7 hundred miles all most every weak and i receive none and am so near home – about 150 miles – and i hope that you will write to me how you are and all the rest … so no mo[re] at present but my love to you all.[87]

Unfortunately, a few weeks later Private John Patterson died from illness. It is not known whether his family received this last letter. In it he included a description of himself "standing guard five miles out of the fort in sight of the british farmes and their buildings."[88] If she received this letter, Levina Patterson was left with a lasting image of her husband on duty within view of the enemy, pensive and alone.

English woodcut, early nineteenth century.

"Queen of Hearts." Dolley Madison (1768-1849), wife of President James Madison, was an immensely popular and much loved First Lady whose charm and great personal warmth earned her the above-mentioned nickname. Her wartime hospitality, including dinners, receptions, balls and her famous weekly soirées, was famed across America, and her effortless style and dignity drew praise from all quarters, for she was also known for the many beautiful and fashionable outfits she wore during her husband's presidency. (Print from painting by Gilbert Stuart.)

CHAPTER EIGHT

"The windings of the mazy dance."
High Society

Some ladies and gentlemen, Friday night last,
Had a ball, which for splendour all others surpassed;
With the spruce Captain Benson next Lydia appeared;
The Captain is more to be loved than be feared
He charms all hearts with his graces and airs
When he simpers and smiles and leaps over the chairs
Says Benson to Lydia, "Pray dearest Miss Brown,
How can you exist in this hole of a town?
No opera, no concerts, no balls are there here
Nor anything lively but twice in the year.
One cannot e'en lounge on the Dyke or Parade
But you mix with detestable people in trade."
"True, captain," says Lydia, "there's nothing can charm me
But such lively fellows as you of the army;
They're always so pleasant, so thoughtful, and gay,
Their very appearance drives vapours away."[1]

Picture the upper gallery of a richly-furnished and stately Louisiana residence where guests relax after a splendid repast of crabs and crawfish prepared in the Creole fashion. Imagine the lantern-lit quarterdeck of one of His Majesty's warships where ladies, clad in pale muslin, dance with their dashing naval officer escorts on a warm summer evening. Or an official reception at the White House, where the warm glow of hundreds of candles, sparkling conversation and the pleasing tones of an orchestra, create an ambience that is uniquely Washington. Throughout the war years, despite attacks and alarms, rumour and blockade, high society across North America brought gaiety and glamour to a continent in conflict.

From New Orleans, scene of the war's last major battle, to Halifax, the warden of the north, the highest social circles of cities and towns large and small formed exclusive groups to which admittance was based on such factors as pedigree, position, wealth, military rank or accomplishment, and connections. In these circles, manners, good behaviour and lively discourse counted for much, and young women who aspired to a place in society had to be able to display such attributes, as well as a cultivated mind, good taste and a fashionable appearance.

Education played an important role in the making of a society lady, as did proper behaviour. Concerning deportment, one writer on such matters stressed that

> one of the chief beauties in a female character is that modest reserve, that retiring delicacy, which avoids the public eye, and is disconcerted even at the gaze of admiration ...... People of sense and discernment will never mistake such silence for dullness. One may share in a conversation without uttering a syllable. The expression in the countenance shews it, and this never escapes an observing eye.[2]

A young lady of quality was also encouraged to cultivate such personal traits as propriety, restraint and common sense, the lack of which, as the writer Jane Austen was at pains to point out in her novel *Persuasion*, might well result in unwise decisions and sorrow.[3] Austen's heroines demonstrated pride, delicacy, moderation, self-discipline, a willingness to bear the dullest and most wearying burdens for family and relatives, and a quiet, resolute opposition to all things coarse and unrestrained.

Gentleness was another feminine ideal, as an emerging young poet, John Keats, extolled in verse:

> Ah! who can e'er forget so fair a being?
> Who can forget her half retiring sweets?
> God! she is like a milk-white lamb that bleats
> For man's protection.[4]

Gentle they might be, but in Britain well-read women were no longer regarded as unusual in the upper strata of society, and they were beginning to make their presence felt to a greater degree. North American women were already comfortable with this change, stemming as it did from republican principles in the United States, and from the influence of Loyalist mothers in British North America, not to mention the self-reliance necessary for life on the continent. As we know, education for the "better" class of young woman in North America was regarded as important, and Eliza Southgate, daughter of a physician and judge in Scarborough, Maine, was among the young ladies of her generation who were taught to think independently and form their own opinions. In Eliza's case this was hardly surprising, as she attended the boarding school near Boston run by the progressive Susanna Rowson, who encouraged a liberal outlook. Parents such as Eliza's, who had wealthy connections, could afford to launch their daughters into society, and as part of her "finishing," Eliza Southgate was taken on an escorted tour of New England to enjoy parties, visits, horse riding, dances, tea parties and romance. It was, she declared, as "elegant and pleasant" an *entrée* into her future adult life as she could have wished, and there were many other young women like her in North America who harboured similar ambitions.[5]

In the United States, any discussion of high society must begin with Washington, capital of the young republic but still very much under construction in 1812. The emerging landmark buildings, monuments, unfinished walkways and broad avenues of wartime Washington were the setting for a lively social life which, although many residences still had grazing cattle as neighbours, already exhibited a certain stylish flair. Almost everyone of distinction could afford to build or rent a fine house and own a carriage with four horses, even if the streets were unpaved, major public buildings were surrounded by untidy wasteland and forest still covered much of the area.

At the beginning of the War of 1812, Washington's population consisted of some 5,900 whites, 850 free persons of colour and numerous slaves working on the new public buildings and in many of the households. The city, noticeably southern in spirit, was a natural hub for the growing domestic slave trade caused in part by the expansion of cotton cultivation in the lower South, while its free African-Americans were represented in a wide variety of skilled trades and service occupations. White inhabitants consisted mainly of elected government officials, army and naval officers, government clerks, a small diplomatic corps and a few wealthy landed families. Society in the capital operated on two principles: first, that in government service any man of senior rank was entitled to corresponding prestige and privilege in his private life; and secondly, that any member of a family which had enjoyed social prestige for generations had a right to continue to do so. Under former president Thomas Jefferson, Washington protocol had been somewhat republican with a degree of informality that surprised many foreign visitors, but under James Madison there was a marked difference.[6]

On the evening in March 1809 when President Madison and his wife, Dolley, held their first official reception, the streets leading to the presidential mansion were busy with carriages bringing more than four hundred guests. As they entered the main reception room, known as the East Room, the new arrivals were met by the soft glow of hundreds of candles flickering in glass chandeliers. It was the most glamorous evening Washington had witnessed and the presidential couple were gracious hosts. Dolley Madison,[7] one observer recorded, looked beautiful in a "plain cambrick dress with a very long train, plain around the neck without any kerchief," and a "bonnet of purple velvet, with white satin and white plumes."[8] Dolley was a remarkable woman with "a supreme social graciousness," and was so beloved and successful in her role that, in the words of one biographer, she "left an imprint which no other President's wife has ever made."[9]

The position of First Lady was one for which she was uniquely suited, even though it was far removed from the life that she had known as a girl growing up in Virginia. The road that had brought her to the social pinnacle of her country began in 1794 when, as a young widow living in Philadelphia, she married James Madison. Dolley Todd, as she was at that time, had been born into a large, comfortable Quaker home in the Virginia tidewater country, where her father owned a plantation. Her first marriage to lawyer John Todd had ended prematurely with his death from yellow fever, leaving Dolley to cope alone with their young son, and when she was introduced to the Princeton-educated James Madison, seventeen years her senior, their courtship became the talk of Philadelphia.[10]

In 1801, Dolley's life took a different turn when President Thomas Jefferson appointed James Madison as his secretary of state. The Madisons' move to Washington, a developing city "capable of every improvement," placed Dolley at the centre of a world of politics, power, duty and responsibility.[11] She enjoyed life in the young capital, however, and as she began to acquire a wide circle of friends and acquaintances, she was also preparing for her future duties by serving as hostess to the widowed Jefferson at many official functions. By the time James Madison became the fourth president of the United States in 1809, Dolley was able to discharge her responsibilities as president's lady with great skill.

Washington in 1812 was still small enough for "all the great folk to be gathered together in one drawing-room," and with Dolley Madison at their head, social gatherings in the evening blossomed.[12] She was perfectly fitted to shine at any kind of function. The secret of her success, said one commentator, was her "exquisite tact, true kindness, great adaptability, and personal charm."[13] Whether she was meeting a senior officer or government official, a society matron or a distinguished newcomer, Mrs. Madison had an extraordinary ability never to forget a name and was always able to address people personally even after a long interval between meetings. She carefully studied the individual tastes of her guests, serving strong whisky punches to attract politicians, daintier morsels to the ladies and regional or European specialities to overseas visitors. Her choice of food and drink and her reputation for always having attractive young ladies among her guests acted as a considerable lure to gentlemen, and even political opponents somehow managed to forget their rancour at Dolley's soirées.

As the president's lady, she never allowed the gravity of high office to subdue her warm and open nature, which contrasted with, but complemented, the more reserved manner of her husband. Indeed, Dolley Madison's charm was so effortless that she seemed to impel Washington from its rougher beginnings into a new, genteel era. Behind her demeanour lay an innate ability to discern character and evaluate situations, and she was able to react sensibly no matter how complex the circumstances might be. When it came to politics, Dolley refused to be drawn into its machinations and her neutral stance is evident from the comment that, "by her deportment in her own house you cannot discover who is her husband's friends or foes."[14] The sheer force of her poised, pleasant manner enabled Dolley to assuage hot political tempers and adapt herself to people and situations "with an intuition that has never been matched" in the history of the White House. No doubt she had also taken to heart her husband's advice to "be always on your guard that you become not the slave of the public nor the martyr to your friends."[15] Above all, Dolley realized that her own and other people's personal affairs paled into insignificance in comparison to what was going on around them – the momentous business of guiding and developing a nation that was, for the present, at war.

What individual impressions did Mrs. Madison leave upon those who knew her? By the time her husband took office, she was a tall handsome woman in her late thirties. To the author Washington Irving, who met her in 1811, she appeared as a "fine, portly buxom dame, who has a smile and a pleasant word for everybody."[16] Irving was struck by her regal dress and relaxed manners, and by the way in which she happily entered into "a constant round of banqueting, revelling and dancing." Artist Eastman Johnson, who painted her portrait, described her as having a "countenance full of benignity and gentleness. She talks a great deal and in such quick, beautiful tones. So polished and elegant are her manners that it is a pleasure to be in her company."[17] Washington socialite and commentator Margaret Bayard Smith decided early that she liked Dolley for her "good humour and sprightliness, united to the most affable and agreeable manners." She recognized Dolley's genius in being "charming and discreet, gifted and sensible" and a "foe to dullness in every form, even when invested with the dignity which high ceremonial could bestow."[18] But it was a New York politician who gave Dolley Madison her lasting unofficial title. Senator Samuel Mitchill declared:

> She has a fine person and a most engaging countenance, which pleases, not so much from mere symmetry or complexion as from expression. Her smile, her countenance and her manners are so engaging, that it is no wonder that ... with her fine blue eyes and large share of animation, she should be indeed, a QUEEN OF HEARTS."[19]

Dolley Madison's style and fashion sense also drew praise from all quarters. Dressing well was, then as now, expected of those in the public eye, and women aspiring to a place in society were taught how to present themselves. Paris was the global fashion centre and Dolley regularly consulted Madame Serrurier, wife of the French ambassador, as well as the wives of the American ambassadors posted to foreign capitals abroad. She obtained imported items through the good offices of friends such as Phoebe Morris, the daughter of a close associate, and wrote on one occasion to her "beloved Phoebe" asking her to look out for a *"fascinating* Head-dress – I enclose you 20$, my darling, and you will add to the Bonit [sic]or Turban some artificial Flower or fruit for the Head."[20] For a year or so before the war, Dolley was also able to enlist the assistance of Joel Barlow, the American ambassador to France, and his wife, Anna. As special friends, she wrote to them asking if they could send her "by safe vessel, large headdresses, a few flowers, feathers, gloves, and stockings, black and white, with anything else pretty, and suitable for an economist, and let me know the amount."[21] Anna Barlow took to the task with relish and sent Dolley a wealth of gowns, headwear, "flowers, trimmings, and ornaments."[22] With such finery, Dolley maintained a reputation as the "leader of everything fashionable in Washington."[23]

Behind the scenes, Dolley Madison remained a simple person at heart, as was evident in matters of housekeeping. In the morning, she would often don a grey dress, white apron and white kerchief which she swapped only later in the day for the elegant outfits called for by her role as society hostess. She chose and supervised well her servants, all of whom were important in ensuring she could offer impressive standards of hospitality and cuisine to influential visitors. Her famous weekly receptions, evenings of "blazing splendour," according to Washington Irving, would not have been as successful without meticulous planning and great expense.[24] Even on quiet days the presidential mansion was full of people – often family and female friends – with whom Dolley could discuss books or events, or perhaps chat about parties, gowns or other matters of mutual interest away from the public gaze. It was in private that she relaxed the "deliberate and somewhat stately demeanour" which always characterized her public persona, while retaining the affability for which she was known and loved.

Dolley Madison was all "unassuming dignity, sweetness, grace" at the inaugural ball in 1809. She appeared in a dress of buff-coloured velvet with a "very long train, but not the least trimming, and beautiful pearl necklace, earrings and bracelets."[25] She loved turbans, much in vogue at the time, and that evening wore one from Paris made of matching buff velvet and white satin with "two superb plumes, the bird of paradise feathers." The overall effect, combined with the new First Lady's general bearing, caused one guest to declare that Dolley Madison "in manners and appearance answered all my ideas of royalty," and that as far as she was concerned, it was impossible for "any one to behave with more perfect propriety."[26]

After that famous first evening, the presidential residence during the Madison presidency became *the* gathering place for high society and a new "grace and vitality" was evident in the nation's leading social circle.[27] Winter was the season of diplomatic dinners and dancing assemblies, at which beautiful ladies indulged in conversation and discreet flirtation and demonstrated their vivacity on the dance floor with ambassadors, military and naval officers and politicians. Pretty young women, mainly from Virginia and Maryland, converged on Washington to attend these events, which led to the capital's growing reputation as a marriage market.[28] Summer was for picnics, dances, outdoor entertainments, music, and visiting friends while conditions were at their most favourable for travel.

One of the First Lady's earliest projects was to refurbish her official residence with the aid of an allowance granted by Congress. She chose yellow for the satin and damask curtains, chairs and sofas of the drawing room, in which she would hold many functions. Elaborate mantlepieces, fine oil lamps, a lovely gold and crystal centrepiece for the state dining table, a pianoforte, the best table linen, china and glassware all found a place in Dolley Madison's new décor, and her taste was admired, particularly by those familiar with the European *haut monde* who appreciated a little old-world glamour.

On a day-to-day basis, society wives and daughters gave and attended social functions in the evenings and paid formal calls on each other in the mornings, adopting the practice of using calling cards to announce their arrival. A complex code of etiquette determined the length and frequency of calls, whether a call should be returned or not and the kinds of people to whom one was "at home." Mrs. Madison, for example, did not initiate calls but returned those made by other ladies, and held or attended private parties for wives of prominent citizens, cabinet officers and foreign ministers when their husbands were absent on business. Society ladies in Washington, as one period commentator noted, were "taking a station ... which is not known elsewhere" in the United States.[29]

Many of these prominent women had long been friends. Among them was Margaret Bayard Smith, wife of Samuel Harrison Smith, the first proprietor of the National Intelligencer newspaper and now president of the Bank of Washington. There was also the beautiful heiress Marcia Van Ness, whose husband John had entered Congress, and whose dignity, "great sprightliness of mind, and amiableness of disposition" placed her among "the first in society."[30] Anna Maria Thornton was the wife of Dr. William Thornton, who had designed the Capitol building and was a district commissioner. A newer arrival was Sarah Seaton, the wife of William Seaton, who succeeded Samuel Harrison Smith at the National Intelligencer. Sarah was witty, intelligent, charming and energetic, and displayed "admirable self command," which endeared her to Dolley Madison and others.[31] A fine pianist, Sarah was often invited to entertain Mrs. Madison and discuss with her "books, men and manners, literature in general, and many special branches of knowledge."[32] Another leading member of society was Elizabeth Kortright Monroe, the elegant, accomplished wife of Secretary of State James Monroe. A tall, dark beauty who had acquired considerable sophistication during several diplomatic postings to Europe, Elizabeth and her two daughters were regarded as authorities on the fashions of the beau monde of Paris and exponents of its "latest fancies."[33] In high society, where there was always a fascination for ladies familiar with European ways, Madame Serrurier, the fashionable and attractive wife of the French ambassador, and Sally McKean of Philadelphia, married to Don Carlos Martinez de Yrujo, the former Spanish ambassador to Washington, were highly regarded.

These women were among the elite of the capital but it was often graced by younger women, including many from other parts of the republic who wintered in Washington. Pretty Harriet Stoddert, daughter of former secretary of the navy Benjamin Stoddert, made her debut at one fancy-dress party at the Ottoman legation, wearing a "ravishing costume of orange-colored Canton crape."[34] Her charms "so wrought upon the susceptible heart of her oriental host [the

Ottoman ambassador] that he followed her from room to room, and finally, to her great dismay, asked her to be one of his wives." Julia Wingate, daughter of Major-General Henry Dearborn, said to be "one of the most beautiful women that Maine ever produced," was admired in Washington for her looks, her facility as a gifted conversationalist and her "dignified though captivating manner."[35] Margaret Armstrong, daughter of Secretary of War John Armstrong, was described as "handsome and intelligent," while Maria Mayo from Richmond, Virginia was considered by Dolley Madison to be "even more beautiful and talented" than several of the more prominent society belles.[36]

The women of Maryland were celebrated at that time for their looks and charm and three young ladies from the Old Line State – Hortensia Hay, Mary Ann Caton and Elizabeth Patterson Bonaparte – were stars in "a famous constellation of beauties."[37] Mary Ann and Hortensia were exceptionally graceful and elegant young women but even they were eclipsed by Elizabeth Patterson Bonaparte. Elizabeth, or Betsy as she was known, created a stir whenever she appeared and a contemporary left a description of this renowned lady:

> How I wish you could see Madame Bonaparte in all the splendor of dress, and all the attractions of beauty. I think I never beheld a human form so faultless. To the utmost symmetry of features is added so much vivacity, such captivating sweetness! and her sylphic form "thinly veiled" displays all the graces of a Venus de Medicis. She appears particularly lovely in a fine crepe robe of a beautiful azure color interwoven with silver, in this attire she is truly celestial, and it is impossible to look on any one else when she is present.[38]

Betsy Patterson Bonaparte's story was as fascinating as the woman herself. The daughter of a wealthy Baltimore shipping magnate, Betsy, just eighteen years of age, had met and married Jérôme Bonaparte, the younger brother of the French emperor, in 1803 when he happened to be in the United States. The couple travelled to France but, though Betsy was approved of by most of the Bonaparte family, Napoleon refused to recognise the union and had it annulled. Realising that the Emperor would not change his mind, Jérôme dishonourably abandoned his young bride, who was forced to take refuge in Britain. There, she gave birth to a son and returned to Baltimore, "the most wretched of women."[39] Rosalie Stier Calvert of nearby Bladensburg had watched the affair unfold and was always dubious about the outcome. "I don't know how this story will end," she recorded, describing Betsy as "the most extraordinary girl, given to reading … the rights of women, etc., in short, a modern *philosophe*."[40]

Elizabeth Patterson Bonaparte (1785-1879). As the former wife of Jérôme Bonaparte, younger brother of the French emperor, "Betsy," as she was known, spent much of the war in Baltimore and Washington, where she took society by storm with her daring mode of dress. In this portrait she is wearing a white empire gown with gold trim and her hair is secured by a gold pin. She has chosen to wear a double row of pearls and matching drop pearl earrings from her extensive collection of jewellery. (Oil on canvas by Franciscus Josephus Kinson, 1817. Maryland Historical Society, Baltimore, Maryland.)

Having been the wife of a Bonaparte, it was impossible, Betsy believed, "ever to bend my spirit to marry any one who had been my equal before my marriage," or "to be contented in a country where there exists no nobility."[41] She measured all society by the imperial French yardstick, demanding to be treated as she felt she deserved, and Washington society was the closest thing Betsy could find to the sophisticated life she craved. In a city where women prided themselves on being fashionable and the president's wife often stole the show in one of her elegant gowns, Betsy wore dresses so daring for the time that on one occasion at a select and elegant party, her appearance threw the entire company "into confusion."[42] Margaret Bayard Smith, who was present, recalled that

> no one dar'd to look at her but by stealth … Her dress was the thinnest sarcenet and white crepe without the least stiffening in it … there was scarcely any waist to it and no sleeves; her back, her bosom, part of her waist and her arms were uncovered and the rest of her form visible.[43]

Washington society, nowhere near ready for "an almost naked woman," as Margaret described Betsy's appearance, was shocked. Rosalie Stier Calvert, who was also present that famous evening, reported less dramatically that Madame Bonaparte was "wearing a dress so transparent that you could see the color and shape of her thighs, and even more."[44] Several horrified ladies "made a point of leaving the room, and one informed the belle that if she did not change her manner of dressing, she would never be asked anywhere again."[45] The erring Betsy was told plainly that if she wished to be accepted in society, she must promise in future to "have more clothes on."[46]

Undaunted, Betsy continued to favour the *décolleté* style of dress, by which she set the fashion. She also dazzled onlookers with her magnificent jewellery, some of which had been given to her by her former husband and his family.[47] It was said by one contemporary that, although many Washington belles strived to imitate this most striking of women, they did so "without equal éclat, as Madame Bonaparte has certainly the most transcendently beautiful back and shoulders that ever were seen."[48] Betsy dazzled everyone – in Europe as well as the United States. When she had been in Paris, she had met the famous Madame Récamier, a celebrated beauty herself, who had been the subject of two fine portraits by the artists Jacques-Louis David and Théodore Géricault, but even this acclaimed woman felt herself eclipsed by Betsy, whom she described as "the most beautiful woman in the world."[49] Not surprisingly, Madame Bonaparte had many male admirers, and among her personal papers is a poem in French entitled "*Rose d'amour et de bonheur*" or "Rose of love and happiness," of which the first verse, here translated, sings its subject's praises liberally:

> How beautiful is my Rose:
> And how inspiring her appeal!!
> Everything about my rose charms and pleases,
> Her perfume is intoxicating.[50]

The war brought unwelcome changes to the social life of the capital. Many men disappeared from the city, others appeared in uniform, the gravity of affairs of state became more marked and the working day of the president – an industrious man at the best of times – grew even longer. Despite the heavy responsibility he carried, James Madison still regularly attended social events. Society kept abreast of the progress of the war and, despite military defeats and many problems, everyone was cheered by American victories at sea during the early part of the conflict. In December 1812, as Washington society prepared to attend a ball to celebrate the victory of the USS *Constitution* over HMS *Guerrière*, another victorious American warship arrived at Newport with its trophies. Commodore Stephen Decatur, captain of the USS *United States*, had just captured HMS *Macedonian* and knew that at the *Constitution* ball Dolley Madison would be presented with the flag of the *Guerrière*. Decatur visualised what a stir it would create if the First Lady were also to be presented that evening with the flag of the *Macedonian* and promptly despatched one of his officers.

The scene was dramatic. The *Constitution* victory ball was held at Tomlinson's Hotel on Capitol Hill and attended by a glittering assemblage of Washington society, with congressional leaders, cabinet members, Supreme Court justices, the diplomatic elite, officers, belles and matrons. The ballroom was dominated by the flag of the *Guerrière* suspended across one wall, with the orchestra beneath it. All was laughter and gaiety until, in the midst of the dance, an unexpected arrival brought a hush to the proceedings. Decatur's officer entered the ballroom, the music stopped and the crowd gave way as the lieutenant from the USS *United States* walked towards Dolley Madison. When he reached the First Lady, he triumphantly unfurled the flag of HMS *Macedonian* on the floor before her. The ecstatic crowd burst spontaneously into song with "Hail, Columbia," and the evening proceeded in an atmosphere of high elation.[51]

Washington society remained carefree throughout the fall of 1812. It was an election year, and divisions within President Madison's own Republican party were so marked that his re-election was in doubt. Madison needed every friend and vote he could get, and his wife did everything in her power to assist her husband. When Dolley was dressed in one of her many splendid outfits and radiating friendship, sympathy, admiration, humour – whatever was appropriate to the moment – it was a hard-hearted guest who would not set politics aside in her captivating presence. Her efforts paid off, and Madison gained a second term.

In 1813 the arrival of British warships in the Chesapeake added a certain edge to life, but the threat remained far enough away to be dismissed with the swirl of a ball gown. Certainly, it did not tarnish the patina of society pleasures and in the early summer of 1814, with enemy vessels now present in strength in the bay, the elite of the capital continued to enjoy picnics, open air theatre performances, receptions and dances. By August 1814 Washington was so accustomed to rumours of possible invasions that there was little apprehension of danger when disaster struck. But, after the capital experienced its "baptism of fire" (discussed in chapter 10), in which the government was forced to flee, Washington rose phoenix-like from the ashes. Although the President and First Lady had to live in borrowed accommodation after the destruction of their official residence, the social round gradually regained momentum. It can truly be said that the war years in Washington belonged to the people who made them, but most of all to James and Dolley Madison, who did much to create an atmosphere in which harmony flourished and discord gave way to enjoyment. The capital's society of that time has been described as "genuine and national" in its newness, and more "real" than in later years.[52]

Washington may have owned the republic's highest social circle but there were others not far below it. Philadelphia, the national capital of earlier times, remained one of the liveliest cities on the continent despite some of its former Quaker austerity. It had a long tradition of brilliant, sumptuous entertainments, receptions, assemblies and dances, the latest of which were taught to eager young men and women by European dancing masters. Philadelphia also had its own constellation of beauties, some of whom made their mark in wartime Washington.

For its part, Boston possessed a *coterie* of cultivated men and women who compared favourably with those "of any court in the Old World," and Bostonians managed to arrange almost as many society entertainments as New York.[53] Boston society was evolving with the fast-growing city, and although the overall tone remained aristocratic, it was also fun-loving.

New York gatherings were equally animated, with dances often held in the assembly room of the City Hotel, the largest establishment of its kind in the country. New York, too, could boast its own belles – young women such as Anne Allen, who was likened by her younger sister, Mary, to "a brilliant luminary which seemed to animate everything within its influence, and I was the modest satellite shining with a reflected lustre."[54] Mary, however, was being too modest for she, in turn, was described by the eminent physician Dr. Benjamin Rush as "one of the most beautiful and charming women of her time."[55]

When it came to hosting social events, New York prided itself on its high standards, which are clear from the descriptions of celebrations held in the city to mark the two naval American victories already mentioned. A formal dinner was followed by a ball honouring the victorious captains, Commodore Stephen Decatur of the *United States* and Captain Isaac Hull of the *Constitution*, and this event, according to *Niles' Weekly Register*, was without parallel.

> On Thursday evening last a ball was given to the commanders and officers of our victorious frigates, which for splendor of decorations and brilliancy of company has never been equalled in this country on any public occasion. The city assembly room was ornamented with transparencies, and by a profusion of colors displayed in a most beautiful and tasteful manner.[56]

The supper room was "intended to appear like the cabin of a ship of war, every part of the walls being covered by a flag or a transparency," and one immense standard formed a canopy over the dining tables. Adding to the decor in no small way, it seems, were the ladies. The *Weekly Register's* account continues:

> on no occasion in this country has so large a number of beautiful and elegantly dressed females been seen; nearly 300 ladies sat down to supper, all of whom were splendidly dressed. The supper was plentiful and elegant, but owing to the smallness of the room no gentlemen (excepting guests and the managers) were permitted to enter whilst the ladies supped, so that the *coup d'oeuil* was beautiful beyond description. Among the guests were Commodore and Mrs. Decatur, Captain Hull, Lieutenant Nicholson and General and Mrs. Armstrong. This splendid entertainment was conducted with remarkable regularity.[57]

Smaller towns in the north held dances, dinners and parties, and even in New England, where an economc depression gripped the region in 1814, there were oases of good cheer to be found, of which Portland, Maine, and Salem, Massachusetts, were two. Salem thrived through the success of its privateers and remained buoyant throughout the war. In the winter of 1813 the town enjoyed a series of "cotillion parties," wrote one young woman to a friend, further explaining that "last evening was the first party, and 3/4ths of the Company were Brides, or engaged ladies."[58] The war and the growing British blockade of the American coast did not prevent romance and amusement from flourishing in that particular town.

Not to be outdone, the social elite of the southern Atlantic states and Louisiana competed with their northern neighbours. Southern society was developing a style of luxurious living with beautiful country seats and elegant town homes. Hospitality was gracious, and Charleston, South Carolina, in particular was unrivalled in this respect. The members of its ruling circle lived like landed nobility and were treated as such, and it was the custom for each to host a large ball every year. However, it was the city's dinner parties which became its most famous events, occasions at which gentlemen and their ladies sat down to lavish menus accompanied by the best wines. The exceptional and cultivated conversation that held sway on these occasions warranted a description of the table talk as "better than it can be in an age of hurry and incessant employment."[59]

The father of one Charleston society belle, Isabel Barron, commissioned an artist to paint her miniature shortly before the war. Edward Green Malbone was the man chosen, but his subject so bewitched him that when Isabel's father discovered the pair were becoming romantically linked, he stopped all contact between Malbone and his muse. Fortunately for posterity, Malbone completed his work and a superb portrait of the lovely Isabel remains a testament to his feelings for her.[60]

New Orleans, despite being located in unhealthy bayou country, enjoyed a deserved reputation as a pleasure-loving city. The city's Spanish and French past and its blending of nationalities, which in addition to the aforementioned included Anglo-Americans, Germans, Irish and free people of colour, had produced a lively population of mixed blood and a society which loved to dance. Its members assembled weekly for the purpose, and with a surplus of women in the city, young ladies were always looking for eligible dancing partners. These

The artist's muse. Shortly before the war, the artist Edward Green Malbone, was commissioned to paint Isabel Barron, a society belle of Charleston, South Carolina. After discovering Malbone had fallen in love with his daughter, Isabel's father forbade any further contact between the pair. The completed work, however, remains a testament to Malbone's ability to capture the beauty of his muse. (Print after miniature by Edward Green Malbone, author's collection.)

regular gatherings were attended with an "inconceivable avidity," wrote one observer, adding, "the passion for dancing is at its height." It was a time for "dressing up, for games, for love,"[61] and in winter, especially, everyone took to the floor "in the city … in the country … everywhere," and "if not with much grace, at least with great ardor."

The balls of New Orleans were of two kinds: the Quadroon Balls, to which white men, but not their ladies, were admitted, and which became famous as "one of the great mistress markets of the world"; and the subscription balls, which were exclusively for whites of both sexes. These were rather grand affairs and conducted with "all the propriety possible in a city where the smallest disagreement provoked a duel." For that reason no alcohol was served, only "orange-flower sirup and *eau sucrée*," and since not many people in New Orleans owned carriages, ladies often walked to these events "in their satin slippers," preceded by slaves carrying lanterns.[62]

The men of New Orleans generally preferred outdoor pursuits to more cultured activities but the ladies, particularly the Creole women – descendants of European or black settlers in the Caribbean – were elegant and beautiful with an appreciation of fashionable clothes. As a song of the immediate postwar period put it:

> You've heard, I s'pose, how New Orleans
> Is famed for wealth and beauty,
> There's girls of ev'ry hue it seems,
> From snowy white to sooty.[63]

Louisiana governor William C. C. Claiborne appeared on occasion with his beautiful Spanish Creole wife, Sophronie Bosque, as did Louise Livingston, married to a prominent lawyer, who was one of the city's most striking Creole society ladies. Indeed, it was at one of the many dances held in New Orleans that Louise had first met her husband, Edward Livingston. As a widow of French descent from the island of St. Domingo, she captivated Edward, who came from an old, politically-powerful New York family, with her grace, looks and intelligence. The couple was soon married. Such was the speed at which the French-speaking Louise improved her knowledge of English and acquired an appreciation of her husband's literary, personal and professional pursuits that Edward came to trust her good taste and judgement in many things.

It became a tradition at the Livingston home to hold "open-house" breakfasts, enlivened by literary talks and readings, in a broad courtyard shaded by orange and fig trees.[64] Guests drank coffee and ate "calas," a local breakfast cake, or other delicacies filled with nuts or fruit, such as *confiture figues, pralines pistache* or *pralines pacanes*. Evenings at the Livingston house were spent on the balcony, which acted as a kind of *salon en plein air*, where guests could enjoy the finest Creole cooking seasoned with animated discussion. The sound of laughter and earnest conversation in French, Spanish or English drifted on the sultry air along with the perfume of jasmine and oleander. Louise Livingston's *salon* rapidly became the "resort of every notable stranger who visited New Orleans," many of whom took away with them a vision of the "distinction of manner and brilliant powers" of their mesmerising hostess. As the "presiding genius of her table," Louise Livingston had the gift of "drawing out the talents of her guests" and "could hold her audience quite enthralled."[65]

In late 1814, Major-General Andrew Jackson, charged with defending New Orleans from an impending British attack, arrived in the city and soon came into contact with the Livingstons. It was the start of a lifelong friendship and the general immediately appointed Edward to be his secretary, translator, confidential advisor and local mediator.

After Jackson's victory over the British on 8 January 1815, the months that followed were among the liveliest and most memorable seen by New Orleans society. Concerts, plays, dances and other events were eagerly attended, and when Rachel Jackson joined her husband she found the lively social scene a marked contrast to the quiet life she normally led on their plantation in Tennessee. Rachel did not have a wardrobe suitable for society but Louise Livingston came to her rescue and arranged a selection of dresses for the wife of the city's distinguished hero. Louise and the other fashionable ladies of the city warmed to Rachel Jackson's gentle disposition and kindliness, and their initial secret amusement at her unsophisticated appearance gave way to genuine affection, marked by their gift to her of a set of topaz jewellery.

At a grand dinner and ball held to commemorate George Washington's birthday in February 1815, the Jacksons and the Livingstons led the way to the ballroom. To open the evening, Andrew and Rachel Jackson danced "a most delicious pas de deux" country-style.[66] As one guest later described it, to see General Jackson, "a long, haggard man, with limbs like a skeleton, and Madame La Generale, a short, fat dumpling, bobbing opposite each other like half-drunken Indians, to the wild melody of 'Possum up de Gum Tree' and endeavoring to make a spring into the air" was a sight he would not soon forget.

Let us leave "Old Hickory" and Rachel enjoying themselves in Louisiana and travel north to the possessions of His Majesty King George III. In British North America, high society was to be found at the provincial capitals of Halifax, Fredericton, Quebec and York, as well as the commercial city of Montreal. Society was dominated by the wives of the governing British officials such as Lady Katherine Sherbrooke in Nova Scotia, Lady Jean Hunter in New Brunswick and Lady Catherine Prevost in Quebec. These women took their roles seriously and, like Elizabeth Patterson Bonaparte, often had experience of upper social circles across the Atlantic. This was certainly the case with Lady Katherine Sherbrooke, wife of Nova Scotia's lieutenant-governor, Lieutenant-General Sir John Coape Sherbrooke.[67] As a distinguished officer highly regarded by the Duke of Wellington, Sherbrooke had a military record that had secured him an invitation in June 1811 to dine at Carlton House in London, the official residence of George, the Prince Regent, who, in face of his father's continuing madness, was Britain's head of state.

One can get a sense of the splendour of such occasions from a report of the

Government House, Halifax, was the official residence of the lieutenant-governor of Nova Scotia, who during the War of 1812 was Lieutenant-General Sir John Sherbrooke, accompanied by his wife, Lady Katherine. The Sherbrookes hosted numerous official functions here, spending their private time at Birch Cove, their country cottage. (Painting by John Woolford. Library and Archives of Canada, C-003558.)

Carlton House dinner published in *The Times*. To house all the invited guests "four superb marquees" in Chinese style were erected with additional rooms for dancing, and the gardens, full of beautiful blooms, were hung with "garlands and festoons of roses of every colour, honeysuckle, pinks, carnations, and tulips."[68] Coach after coach deposited guests at the main entrance of the Prince Regent's imposing residence and spectators marvelled at the sight of splendid-looking men in military attire or "court suits, richly embroidered," and beautiful women, all trying to outdo each other in the latest fashions. *The Times* correspondent was ecstatic at how the "waving plumage – the elegant variegated dresses – the sparkling diamonds, – and, still more, the native beauty and grace of the Ladies, gave a sort of enchanting perfection to the whole of this brilliant, courtly exhibition."[69] When supper was announced, the guests made their way under an illuminated arch into the marquees adjoining the Prince Regent's gothic conservatory, where no expense had been spared to provide a magnificent banquet. Their host and his most distinguished *invités*, including members of the exiled French royal family, sat at a separate table in the main conserva-

Inside the vice-regal residence. This reception room on the ground floor of Government House, Halifax, shown as it is today, could well have been a venue for the receptions that preceded formal dinners hosted by Lieutenant-General Sir John and Lady Sherbrooke during the war years. (Photograph by Dianne Graves, by kind permission of The Honourable Myra Freeman, former Lieutenant Governor of Nova Scotia.)

tory. Down the middle of the Royal table, covered in gold and silver plate, was "a serpentine babbling brook of real water occupying a central space" filled with "gold and silver fish" and edged with "moss and flowers."[70] Such splendour had seldom been seen, even at Carlton House, and the opulence of the occasion was remembered as presenting "a grandeur beyond description."

For Lady Katherine Sherbrooke, having experienced the Prince Regent's hospitality, society on the other side of the Atlantic was a somewhat different affair. When her husband was appointed lieutenant-governor of Nova Scotia in 1811, she accompanied him to Halifax, the provincial capital, which was to be her home for more than a decade. As the summer station of the Royal Navy's North American fleet, Halifax was home to some 9,000 civilians and, depending on the season, between 4,000 and 6,000 military and naval personnel. The town was a somewhat wild place, boasting a drinking establishment for every one hundred persons but in contrast, a school for only every one thousand. The presence of naval and army officers added a certain *éclat* to the town's rather

The inconveniences of a drawing room. The joys of an overcrowded assembly are seen in this period cartoon. Where one officer is treading on a lady's train, elsewhere another couple are colliding, and in the doorway a corpulent lady and gentlemen are trying, unsuccessfully, to pass one another. (Cartoon by George Cruikshank, 1818.)

tight society, in which even the smallest daily activities revolved around rank and precedent. One had to know one's place and a resident gleefully recalled the occasion when "the Bishop's lady once swept out of the ball-room with her daughters, because she saw the wife of a baker who had made money coming in the door."[71]

The better streets on which were to be found the homes of wealthy Haligonians were no great distance from the seedy harbour alleyways, but they were two distinct worlds. High society in Halifax went about its daily round in relatively close proximity to the disreputable and dissipated. While brawling and drunkenness occurred daily, Halifax society enjoyed the genteeler pursuits of cards and conversation, tea parties, carriage rides, assemblies and balls where "such a show of beauty as hardly any other town could exhibit" was to be seen.[72] The two worlds rubbed shoulders: the refined with the squalid and immoral; the assemblies with the grog shops, taverns and dancing houses. Every Sunday, while the rougher elements of society sobered up from Saturday night, much of the administration and military garrison, led by the Chief Justice of Nova Scotia in his scarlet and ermine robes and the senior army and naval officers, marched to St. Paul's Anglican Church to attend worship.

Winter was the principal social season, and with no military exercises, entertainments abounded. Officers and fashionable ladies travelled in sleigh parties to nearby frozen lakes and inlets, and as one of their number wrote, "these sleighs filled with elegantes and driven by monstrous-looking exquisites, muffled up to the eyes," dashed along "at a wonderful pace," their bells ringing frantically to warn pedestrians.[73] The ladies seemed not to mind the cold, for there was often the beautiful winter sky to admire and an opportunity for romance. Indeed, as one observer remarked, "though a nose may be frost-bitten – there are no cold hearts" on these snowy winter rides.

As the head of both Nova Scotia's government and its society, Lieutenant-General Sir John Sherbrooke wore a very public mantle and his wife, Lady Katherine, was mistress of two domains: Government House, her husband's official residence in the town, and Birch Cove, a pleasant country cottage a short distance outside it. The former was an imposing two-storey Georgian mansion with a splendid ballroom and a series of elegantly-furnished day rooms on the lower floor for receiving and entertaining. A wide staircase at either end of the house led upstairs to bedrooms whose windows overlooked the harbour.

By the outbreak of war in June 1812, Lady Katherine had held her position as lieutenant-governor's lady for just eight months. She tackled her social duties with gracious dignity and her journal, kept throughout the war, contains many fascinating insights into society activities in the provincial capital. It catalogues the kinds of functions that she hosted and attended: balls, soirées, levees (formal receptions held by the Sovereign or his official representative), troop reviews and various regular official functions. After church on Sundays, Sir John invariably hosted a levee at Government House mainly for gentlemen, while his wife carried out a series of house calls, as important a custom for her as it was for Dolley Madison. Indeed, for Lady Sherbrooke to make nine calls in a day was not unusual and sometimes the number was even higher; on 9 January 1812, for example, she recorded that she paid thirteen visits in the morning, while on 4 November 1812, after shopping and making calls, she returned to Government House only to find "innumerable" calling cards awaiting her.[74] Lady Sherbrooke's journal entry that "Mrs. George was so obliging as to make me out a list of the Ladies whose visits I had to return" gives a sense of the degree of obligation attached to this ritual.[75]

Many evenings at Government House were taken up with hosting dinners, and for Lady Katherine and her husband to spend an evening alone was so unusual as to merit a mention in her journal. Invitations to dine with the lieutenant-governor were usually extended to local officials and their wives, aides-de-camp and visiting senior army and naval officers, and on some of these occasions Lady Sherbrooke was the only woman present. She was required to take an interest in current affairs as well as military and naval matters, and although she never mentioned the subject in her journal, she doubtless learned much of importance from the conversations that took place at her table.

This near non-stop dining had to make way for other important occasions in the annual calendar such St. Andrew's Day and Christmas, with its round of parties, official receptions and visitors. Taking precedence over all else, however, were the yearly rituals marking royal birthdays. The King's official birthday sparked off several days of celebrations: a *feu de joie*[76] was fired by the garrison and Sir John Sherbrooke reviewed the regular troops and the militia. Then, while her husband held a levee, Lady Sherbrooke attended formal afternoon tea with a select group of ladies. The celebrations usually came to an end with a ball and fireworks.[77] As one visitor to the town recorded, formal social occasions at Halifax were conducted "in the same manner and style as English etiquette and fashion have established," and were "so much akin to England," that "there were few who could honestly say that they were not in the mother country."[78]

Across the Bay of Fundy from Nova Scotia lay New Brunswick, and although settlement had only begun to nibble at the edges of that province's dense forests, a burgeoning social life was already to be found in the towns of Fredericton and Saint John. At Fredericton, Lady Jean Hunter and her husband, Major-General Sir Martin Hunter, had done much to set the tone of local society. The kind of ball that remote Fredericton could mount is well described in accounts of a pre-war event held to mark Admiral Lord Horatio Nelson's victory at Trafalgar. That evening, the ballroom was "brilliantly lighted, and ornamented with infinite taste," and the dancing presented a striking and rather romantic spectacle, marked by the presence of several splendidly-attired aboriginal women.[79] Partnering the ladies in their delicately-trimmed Empress-line evening gowns and feathered headdresses were the officers in their white trousers, silk knee-length stockings, silver-buckled pumps and long-tailed scarlet coats cut away at the waist and handsomely embellished with buff facings and silver buttons. Supper was served at tables amid pillars linked by evergreen arches and "enlivened by artificial flowers, and lighted by innumerable lamps," creating a scene of "such enchantment" that it momentarily "arrested the attention of all present from the rich profusions of rare and delicious viands and liquors with which the supper tables were loaded, and the novel and beautiful devices with which they were adorned."[80] When the dancing resumed and couples moved around the floor under candle light, it seemed incongruous that the backdrop to this elegant evening was the seemingly endless forest, the Saint John River and the rough, muddy track that led in and out of the provincial capital.

By 1813 a new lieutenant-governor of New Brunswick, Major-General George Stracey Smyth and his wife, Amelia, were the leaders of Fredericton society. Amelia Smyth, who, according to Lieutenant John Le Couteur of the 104th Foot, had "glowing auburn hair," soft grey eyes, a "matchless complexion" and a voice "so musical it was a seraph's when singing," presided with charm over social events that were "very gay" that year.[81] As Le Couteur recorded in his journal on New Year's Eve, 1812, "some idea may be entertained of the Society at Fredericton when I relate that I was at Thirty five dinners, evening parties, or balls since I came up here on the 4th of Sep."[82] This increase in activity certainly pleased Penelope Winslow, one of the town's most prominent young ladies and daughter of Judge Edward Winslow of the Supreme Court of New Brunswick. The lively Penelope heartily approved of the new animation that the arrival of young officers stationed in New Brunswick during the war brought to the little provincial capital.[83]

Doyenne of Saint John. Elizabeth Hazen Chipman (1766-1852) was the wife of Ward Chipman, a Loyalist lawyer who became Attorney-General for New Brunswick. He and Elizabeth lived in an expensively furnished Georgian mansion, where she offered gracious hospitality. Mrs. Chipman was famous for her dinner parties, her afternoon tea parties and her popular musical *soirées*, all of which made her home one of the liveliest venues for Saint John society. (Portrait, oil on panel, painted in 1817 by Gilbert Stuart. Acc. 91.23.3, The New Brunswick Museum, Saint John, NB.)

Downriver from Fredericton at the busy port of Saint John, life revolved around maritime affairs but despite the fact that it could boast few of the amenities of Halifax, Saint John had its own upper circle. Evening parties or "Gregories," as they were known, were occasions at which, according to one British officer, "the ladies sit round the room and entertain one another with whispers," followed by a "substantial supper" and "songs too bad to even laugh at."[84] To some, such amusements were considered tiresome but to local people whose lives revolved around the sea, or the "forest and fowling piece," they were perfectly acceptable.[85]

In Saint John, a notable and expensively furnished Georgian mansion was the home of Ward Chipman, attorney-general of New Brunswick, and his wife Elizabeth. A brilliant Harvard-educated lawyer who had come to the province as a Loyalist, Chipman had been responsible for drawing up the town charter and Elizabeth Chipman was accustomed to gracious entertaining. She could number statesmen, clergy and even royalty among her visitors, and her dinner parties were famous affairs at which guests ate at her great mahogany dining table, set with fine silver cutlery and glassware. Elizabeth Chipman's drawing room was also regularly patronised and her lady callers relished the opportunity to discuss the arrival of the latest fashions from London as they sipped tea from their hostess's exquisite Crown Derby tea service. Saint John, like Fredericton, had its share of dances and receptions in winter, and evening concerts were fashionable. Mrs. Chipman hosted many of these musical evenings at her mansion, a select venue for the town's society during the war years.

The city of Quebec housed the official residence of the governor-general and commander-in-chief of British North America, Lieutenant-General Sir George Prevost. In his dual roles, he presided over society together with his wife, Lady Catherine, who was described by her daughter, Anne Elinor, as a very kind person of great "goodness of heart" who reached out to help others regardless of their station in life.[86]

Lady Catherine's kindly approach endeared her to those she met, from the wives of local clergymen to popular young ladies about town like Christine Nairne, the daughter of a Scots officer who owned property at Murray Bay near Quebec. "Rusty," as Christine was often known (presumably because of the colour of her hair), had been educated in her father's country and had acquired a taste for the Edinburgh elite. On her return to Lower Canada she was allowed to winter at Quebec, where her father wanted her to have a place in society and where he judged the gentry to be "vastly hospitable Civil and well-bred."[87]

Military families came and went in Quebec, but among the senior wives of long standing was the respected Elizabeth Hale, wife of John Hale, deputy paymaster to the British forces and a niece of Lord Jeffery Amherst, prominent in the Seven Years' War. The sophisticated, vivacious and ambitious Elizabeth had met Major-General Isaac Brock before the war and she and her husband were close friends of the general. A talented amateur artist, she was also known for her paintings and sketches of the city and its surroundings.[88]

Quebec, with its northern location, had a reputation as one of the coldest cities in the Canadas. In winter, when the St. Lawrence froze and the roads were nearly impassable, communication with the outside world almost ceased and its residents settled in for an enjoyable social season of balls, dances, dinners, skating, snowshoeing and excursions by sleigh or *carriole*. Although liveliest during the cold months, the people of Quebec also made the most of the summer and many were the occasions for horse riding, races, picnics, balls and parties on board British warships in the harbour.

The journal kept by Lady Catherine Prevost's daughter, Anne Elinor, is very informative about life as she knew it in the capital of British North America. A teenager by the time she arrived at Quebec, Anne Elinor kept a daily account which she later destroyed, describing it as a "very silly sort of performance."[89] However, before doing so, she extracted from it an account of "any thing worth recording, either in the way of events and feelings." What remains today is a composite of her journal and her retrospective observations, written with the benefit of hindsight and maturity.

As a young lady who was both honest and shrewd, particularly in her judgment of people, Anne Elinor provides a fascinating, if subjective, commentary on high society before and during the war. As the threat of conflict drew nearer, Quebec, like Washington, was in merry mood and New Year's Day 1812, which also happened to be Anne Elinor's seventeenth birthday, was marked with a dance in her honour, complete with the presentation of a birthday cake baked by the nuns of Quebec's *Grand Hôpital*. She now assumed a unique position in society as the governor-general's daughter, and joined her mother in hosting a series of official events and receptions, much as Dolley Madison did in Washington. These were evenings with music and refreshments, to which "all came who had any pretence to being introduced, or were already our acquaintance." Anne Elinor described them as "much like a Grand Rout at Bath or London."[90] In addition to attending private balls almost every week and innumerable assemblies and suppers, the Prevosts hosted dinners every Tuesday and Thursday attended by local dignitaries, members of the aristocracy and military personnel. Also invited were other representatives of provincial society such as Mrs. Charles Grant, better known as Marie-Charles-Joseph, Baroness de Longueuil,[91] and her daughter, Elizabeth, who visited the city during the winter from their home near Montreal.

In keeping with her position in the social hierarchy, Anne Elinor Prevost was permitted chaperoned walks, visits to the shops and excursions by snowshoe and *carriole* with those female friends who were deemed suitable company

Artist and mother. Elizabeth Frances Amherst Hale (1774-1826), wife of Colonel John Hale, Deputy Paymaster to the British forces, lived in Lower Canada in the years before the War of 1812. The mother of a growing family, she also found time to draw and paint, completing a number of studies of the Quebec, the St. Lawrence and the country homes she and her husband owned at Sherbrooke and, later, Ste. Anne de Beaupré. Elizabeth was the only officer's wife of the Quebec garrison to be pregnant when the war broke out. Her husband sent her and their children to England. She returned to Lower Canada in 1816, where she died of cancer ten years later. (Portrait painted in 1799, possibly by Francis Ferrière. Library and Archives of Canada, C-112017.)

River landscape. Elizabeth Hale enjoyed painting river scenes, and although the location of this view is unspecified, it is almost certainly the St. Lawrence. Other paintings by Elizabeth Hale appear on pages 14 and 381. (Watercolour by Elizabeth Hale. Library and Archives of Canada, C-13082.)

for the governor-general's daughter.[92] The girls seemed to enjoy themselves as much as British army wife Alicia Cockburn, who spent the early part of the war at Quebec and declared herself to be fond of the "wild graces of this charming Country" and of carrioling or walking across the frozen St. Lawrence. "Tho' I have been frost bitten," recorded Alicia, "the velocity with which we bound over rocks & mountains of Ice is indeed wonderful, & surprised me not a little at first."[93]

The news of war in June 1812 sent a chill through Quebec society. Elizabeth Hale, the only senior military wife in the city expecting a baby, was sent home to Britain with her seven other children until the fighting was over, and Rusty Nairne, who was recovering from a rheumatic complaint at her family home, was unable to join in the light-hearted "feasting, dancing, fun and frolic" encouraged by Sir George and Lady Prevost as a relief from the "many days and hours of anxiety."[94] During her father's frequent absences from Quebec on military duties, Anne Elinor Prevost helped her mother to fulfil her social obligations and to host the usual twice-weekly dinner parties. Despite the anxieties of war, the winter of 1812-1813 at Quebec, according to the governor-general's daughter, seemed to be the most enjoyable of the four she spent there. Her

Fête given by Sir James Craig at Spencer Wood. This event, hosted by the governor-general of the Canadas at his estate two miles west of the city of Quebec in 1809, would have been one of the most exclusive gatherings in the provincial summer social calendar. Note the military band of the 100th Foot, who were stationed at Quebec at the time, playing in the shade of the trees to the left, and the group of ladies listening to them. (Print after watercolour by George Heriot, 1809. Author's collection.)

friend Elizabeth Grant arrived to enliven the atmosphere with her animated conversation, jokes and sense of fun, and the young ladies enjoyed the company of some charming officers, among them Captain Henry Milnes, aide-de camp to Sir George Prevost. The list of social events included "an immense party"; a "large levee" with "festivities" the following day; a dance, a dinner, a ball, and more.[95] "I think I never danced so much as during this gay and happy winter," wrote Anne Elinor, and the mood continued into a summer of riding, dinners, evening entertainments, dancing to the pianoforte, expeditions in the countryside and parties on the river.[96]

Just as American victories were celebrated in Washington, so British victories were the subject of festivities at Quebec. This was particularly true after the defeat of the American offensive against Lower Canada in the autumn of 1813 when "many gay parties ensued."[97] As far as Anne Elinor Prevost was concerned, the highlight of the Quebec season that second year of the war was a grand ball and supper on 7 January 1814 given in her father's honour by the officers of the garrison. "I never thought so much of any ball in my life," she wrote, particularly as it was arranged that she should open the dancing with Lieuteunant-Colonel Joseph Morrison," the triumphant British commander at the Battle of Crysler's Farm fought the previous November. "Dear Colonel Morrison!" recorded Anne Elinor, "more interesting and agreeable than ever – our victorious Hero!"[98]

Andrew Cochran, Sir George Prevost's somewhat shy assistant civil secretary, attended the same event but did not enjoy himself as much as his patron's daughter:

> I was at the Grand Wonder of Wonders, the Garrison Ball, which was certainly an elegant thing. I did not dance at all for really and truly, even if I had been induced to do so I should have found an insuperable objection in the temperature of the atmosphere which was pretty nearly the same as that which is to be felt in an oven after the bread is baked. There were about 400 people and for these a most sumptuous supper was prepared, however all of which could not sit down and I was among those who were doomed to shift for themselves.[99]

Even on such pleasant occasions, however, the war could intrude; one young lady who was not present at the January 1814 ball at Quebec was Rusty Nairne, in mourning for her brother who had been killed at Crysler's Farm.

The Governor-General's daughter. Anne Elinor Prevost (1795-1882) was the daughter of Lieutenant-General Sir George Prevost, governor-in-chief of the Canadas. She left an account of her time in North America which provides a lively insight into high society at Halifax and the city of Quebec, and comments on the war as it affected her family, particularly in its latter stages. (Portrait by Thomas Phillips, courtesy of Sir Christopher Prevost.)

During the summer of 1814, Lady Catherine Prevost took her children to Montreal to join her husband at his temporary headquarters there. Montreal was the largest, richest and most cosmopolitan city in British North America, and its prosperity was based on its function as the international entrepot for the lucrative fur trade, one of the major economic enterprises in the world at that time. In warm weather, the wharves of its harbour were crowded with ships loading furs and unloading all kinds of imported goods from Europe and the West Indies. Fur had brought the city real wealth and the men who ran the trade became legends in their own lifetime. The names of the North West Company and the Hudson's Bay Company became synonymous with power, money and the commercial empires that held "lordly sway over the wintry lakes and boundless forests of the Canadas, almost equal to that of the East India Company over the voluptuous climes and magnificent realms of the Orient."[100] The fur barons lived in splendid residences on the slopes of nearby Mount Royal, which saw many an elegant dinner and many an evening of intense mercantile discussion. "If you enjoy good eating, card playing, dancing, music, and gaiety," remembered a visitor to the city, "you will find an abundance of all."[101]

On Sunday mornings before and during the war, a procession of walkers on fine days and carriages in wet weather made their way to church, among them members of the city's English-speaking society, an interesting blend of local aristocracy, wealthy merchants and businessmen, and officers and their wives from the garrison. Of the upper stratum of Montreal society, one of the most prominent members with one of the finest houses in the city, was Sir John Johnson, the superintendent of the Indian Department. Sir John and his wife, Lady Mary, or "Polly" as she was more often called, lived a busy life. With most of her large family having left home and her husband busy with the affairs of his department and his responsibilities as a militia colonel, Lady Polly Johnson contented herself with the company of her single daughter, Marianne, and her widowed daughter, Catherine Maria, the wife of Major-General Barnard Bowes, killed in Spain. The three Johnson ladies were much admired in polite Montreal society, as was the Baroness de Longueuil, who lived in a "lovely house surrounded by nice gardens and walks" on her own island in the St. Lawrence across from the city.[102] High society also included senior military and civilian personnel, among them Lieutenant-General Francis de Rottenburg and his wife, Julia, Judge Isaac Ogden and his wife,[103] and wealthy French-Canadians like the St. Ours family, whose connections made them part of English-speaking society.

Lieutenant-General de Rottenburg, born Franz von Rottenburg in Danzig, was a European soldier of fortune who had entered the British army in the 1790s. In his fifties by 1812, de Rottenburg was perhaps the most experienced British senior commander in the Canadas during the war. The baron's appearance on the Canadian social scene as an aristocrat with a distinguished military reputation gave him an entrée to society wherever he and his beautiful and much younger wife were stationed. Julia de Rottenburg, the daughter of a Neapolitan general, made a great impression from the moment she set foot in British North America, captivating nearly every officer who met her, as well as most men in general. Colonel Edward Baynes, one of Sir George Prevost's senior staff officers, recorded that the lovely Julia

> made a complete conquest of all hearts. She is in reality remarkably handsome, both in face and figure, and her manners uncommonly pleasing, graceful, and affable. There is, I fancy, a great disparity of years. They both speak English very fluently, and with very little foreign accent.[104]

When Lieutenant John Le Couteur encountered Julia de Rottenburg, he was much taken by her "lively brilliant countenance."[105] Yet another officer spoke of the "general admiration and estimation" accorded this famous beauty who was

> young ... fair, beautiful, – lively, discreet, witty, affable, – in short, so engaging, or rather so fascinating, that neither the courier nor my paper will admit of doing her justice; however, from what I have said it is necessary further to add and explain, that it is not my opinion alone but that of the public.[106]

Julia did have competitors. In 1814, John Slade, a civil employee of the British army, recorded in his journal that a Mrs. Braybrook, who had travelled with his party from Britain, attended a ball in Montreal where "people were divided in the opinion, which was preeminent she or Mrs De Rottenburg ... who was esteemed the most beautiful that was ever seen in Canada."[107] Nonetheless, throughout the war Julia de Rottenburg remained the reigning belle in Montreal, not an easy accomplishment as the women of that city were regarded as "remarkably pretty" and very fashionable.[108] With her beauty and lively nature it is hardly surprising that, like Elizabeth Patterson Bonaparte, Mrs. de Rottenburg had many admirers.

In Montreal at the same time as Julia de Rottenburg was Alicia Cockburn. The wife of Lieutenant-Colonel Francis Cockburn, Alicia came to the city in 1813 after her husband was appointed an inspecting field officer of militia. She soon began to host her own *salon*, and it was not long before she met Julia. With their husbands absent on active service during much of 1813, the beautiful, charming, refined Julia and the spirited, astute Alicia, who soon found the city much to her liking, enjoyed the best of what wartime Montreal society had to offer. Meeting the Bishop's wife, Judge Ogden's daughter or the ladies of the fur barons was all part of the social round, but the two women discovered they had more fun in each other's company.

In May 1813, the 19th Regiment of Light Dragoons arrived in Montreal and the dragoon officers, as one remembered, quickly "got acquainted with all the principal society of the place."[109] Lieutenant John Lang recorded in his diary that he received an invitation to the Longueuil ancestral home on their island across from the city, where the baroness and her daughter, Elizabeth, entertained. In warm weather, the island was an ideal spot for breakfasts, evening picnics, dancing and pleasant walks enjoyed by both English and French-speaking guests. As the 19th Dragoons was the only regular British cavalry unit to serve in the Canadas during the war, society found them more attractive than the more pedestrian infantry regiments that made up the greater part of the British army in North America. Thus, when General de Rottenburg inspected the regiment, Lang recorded that "all the beauty and fashion of the place were assembled for the occasion on horseback" which, he noted, was "the usual mode for the Canadian Ladies to take the air in summer."[110] Towards the end of June, Lang encountered the unforgettable duo of Julia and Alicia when he went "to spend the evening with Mrs. C[ockburn]." There, as he wrote, he also met "Miss G[rant] and Mrs. De R[ottenburg]. a beautiful & charming woman of our acquaintance."[111]

An invitation soon arrived for Lang and his commanding officer, Lieutenant-Colonel John O'Neill,[112] to join these ladies for an evening "'Pic Nic dinner party' on Nun's Island," so named for a convent there, and after a delightful boat trip on St. Lawrence the happy group arrived at their destination.[113] The nuns supplied the party with "Strawberrys cream and ices" and watched the revellers dancing on the grass, appearing not to have any "objection to the music" or band "which we had brought with us and which opened their hearts to such a degree that they came out and looked on," remembered Lang. The older nuns, however, were "very much shocked at the indecency of our dress," Lang continued, and they went on to tell Julia de Rottenburg of their dismay at the ladies "going about without any skirts to their coats" and of their particular offence at Lieutenant-Colonel O'Neill's "thin silk pantaloons." Even in hot weather, "some of the Ladies who were rather thinly clad did not escape censure from these good *religieuses*."[114]

For Lang and the 19th Dragoons, the fun came to an end when they were ordered to Kingston in early July. Not surprisingly, he and Colonel O'Neill chose to spend their last evening in Montreal with "Mrs. De R[ottenburg]. Mrs. C[ockburn]. and Miss G[rant]. who has been particularly kind and attentive during our stay."[115] All three ladies clearly impressed the men who came into contact with them, including a certain discerning observer of Montreal society who happened to be a student of Shakespeare, and rather cleverly matched quotations from his favourite plays to Alicia, Elizabeth and Julia:

Marie-Charles Joseph De Moyne de Longueuil (1756-1841), fourth Baroness in her own right, married Captain David Alexander Grant of the 94th Regiment of Foot, by whom she had two sons and a daughter. A well-known figure in Lower Canada society and much loved by her family and friends, she was known as the "Mimi" Baronne. (Watercolour by unnamed artist. Toronto Public Library. J. Ross Robertson Collection: T16549.)

"A lovely house surrounded by nice gardens and walks" was how one young officer described the home of the Baroness de Longueuil on an island in the St. Lawrence near Montreal. It was here that she and her daughter, Elizabeth, hosted many parties during the summer of 1813, to the delight of all who attended them. (Watercolour by Anthony Reynolds Vyvyan Crease. Toronto Public Library. J. Ross Robertson Collection: T15594.)

Mrs (L[ieutenant] Col[onel]) Cockburn
Pray thee, take pain
To allay with some cold drops of modesty
The skipping spirit; lest, through thy wild behaviour,
I be misconstrued in the place I go to,
And lose my hopes.[116]

Mrs (Gen'l) De Rottenburg
[O,] she doth teach the torches to burn bright!
It seems she hangs upon the cheek of night
Like a rich jewel in an Ethiop's ear.[117]

Mrs De Montenach [Elizabeth Grant]
Bring forth men-children only!
For thy undaunted mettle should compose
Nothing but males.[118]

Montreal, while the target of the American campaign of 1813, was never seriously threatened by attack and partied on throughout the conflict, but things were different in the communities of Upper Canada, which suffered several American invasions. The society of the provincial capital of York was not only more backward but also more rigid than its counterparts in Lower Canada, comprising senior government officials, army officers and professional men such as lawyers and doctors, below whom were the rest of the population. Among the members of an elite that closely guarded entry to its ranks were Justice William Dummer Powell, a judge of the Court of King's Bench, and his wife, Anne, York's formidable *grande dame*; Elizabeth Russell, half-sister of the wealthy former administrator of the province, who lived in a fine home on the waterfront; William Jarvis, Upper Canada's provincial secretary and registrar, and his wife, Hannah; Dr. William Baldwin, a local physician who also practised law; Colonel Aeneas Shaw, the adjutant-general of the militia and his wife, Margaret; and Dr. John Strachan, prominent Anglican divine in Upper Canada and chaplain to the garrison at York, and his wife, Ann. Army officers such as Major James Givins of the Indian Department and his wife, Angelica, were also welcomed in society.

The remoteness of the provincial capital made its members a distinctly inward-looking group who set great store by the minutiae of manners and customs, and who measured everyone else according to their standards and rules.

Polite society. *Le thé anglais*, or "English Tea," was the original French caption to this delightful near-caricature by the French artist Basset, done in Paris in 1815. Cups of tea and polite conversation were the order of the day, and gentlemen callers, such as those pictured here, frequently joined the ladies at these afternoon social rituals. Note the officer in the cut-down cocked hat who has hung his sword and sword belt over the arm of his chair. (Print after Basset. Anne S.K. Brown Military Collection, Brown University, Providence, Rhode Island. Photograph by René Chartrand.)

Within the limited resources of a pioneer society, great attempts were made to impress neighbours and to recreate the life of the English privileged classes, albeit with rigid and often-outdated habits and customs, and the "bungling aid of under trained servants."[119] Comical scenes might ensue when the proud ladies of York, who one minute were admiring each other's gardens, found that the very next, pigs, which ran wild in the town, were rooting up the grass and despoiling all their efforts.

Even though it was not completely closed, it was difficult to gain admittance to York's high society from "below." When French merchant adventurer Laurent Quetton de St. George[120] asked permission to pay his addresses to one of Anne Powell's daughters, the redoubtable Mrs. Powell dismissed his "presumptuous suit" and decisively rejected his overtures, considering him a wholly unacceptable suitor.[121] Monsieur de St. George happened to have fallen foul of one of the arbiters of social standards in the town; all who accepted Mrs. Powell's invitations to dinner, issued twice a week, were scrutinized. In a society where formality was everything and the most casual or spontaneous action could be misconstrued, Anne Powell informed her brother that "the follies of little York" would serve to entertain him "for an hour's ridicule."[122] She realized how such "follies" would appear to an outsider, but could not help lording it over others, adding that as far as her neighbour was concerned, "wherever I am, she is below me."[123]

Most members of York's small upper crust entertained at their sizeable and well-furnished homes set on extensive holdings of land and referred to nonchalantly by their owners as "cottages." Before the war, their sons were sometimes sent to England or travelled in Europe to complete their education and their daughters, armed with a new and expensive wardrobe of clothes, often went to finishing schools in Lower Canada or the United States to learn French, drawing, embroidery and deportment. Despite the intense rivalry and differences of background and outlook that divided the people of the town and were the cause of a great deal of dissention, jealousy and jostling for position, conversely, a shared view of their own self-importance united the members of York society. They actually believed that the town was the "envy and opprobrium of the rest of the province."[124]

York was twice occupied by the American army during 1813, and in the aftermath the town was badly in need of some comfort and cheer. A new series of fortnightly subscription assemblies began early in 1814, attended by civilians, officers from the garrison and their wives, military doctors and others who had been displaced by fighting and enemy occupation. With music provided by the musicians of the Canadian Fencible regiment, wine by "Mr. McIntosh" and cakes by "Lackie the Baker," wartime York set out to recapture some of the gaiety lost the previous year, and to reassure itself that things could, and would, get better.[125]

Newark and Kingston, the two other Upper Canadian centres that found themselves close to active military operations, managed for part of the war to maintain a social life. Newark had a tradition of holding excellent assemblies until it, too, was occupied and burned by the Americans in 1813, after which such social events were transferred to York. At the opposite end of Lake Ontario, fashionable society in Kingston was restricted to a comparatively small section of the population. Yet again, the military garrisons played a significant role in the life of both towns and their busy social programmes of seasonal activities included party balls with a restricted number of guests, and assemblies or subscription balls which often began at dusk, or "early candle light" as it was known, and continued after a hearty supper until dawn. Most of the social life of Kingston, however, occurred in private homes and, as Lieutenant John Le Couteur recorded in January 1814, the "great day of festivity" was New Year's Day.[126]

> The Ladies sit in state, like girls sitting as Bridesmaids at home to receive wedding suits. Cake and Wine and Kisses are privileged to be taken together – many a young fellow has lost his heart on this great day when the too near contact of eyes and lips has formed the first link of a chain destined never to be broken. Red Coats were not deemed sufficiently intimate for the blessing, generally, but I managed now and then to succeed [with a younger woman] by commencing an attack upon some respectable dowager as a Hornwork [outer work in a fortress].[127]

Society ladies added interest and much-needed glamour to the tenor of life during the War of 1812. Those with beauty, accomplishment, charm and intelligence were remembered as bright lights during a dark time. When an officer enjoyed feminine company at cards, indulged in a lighthearted *tête à tête* at dinner or swept a beautiful woman across a dance floor, he could, in "the windings of the mazy dance," forget for a short time what awaited him when he returned to the field.[128] Military personnel and civilians alike were cheered at the prospect of diversions from the seriousness of the conflict through which they were living, and such opportunities afforded, at the very least, a reminder of what benefits could still be found in an hour or two of lighthearted enjoyment.

The bombardment of Detroit. On 16 August 1812, British forces opened fire on Fort Detroit from the Canadian bank of the Detroit River, and the two ships pictured here, HMS *Queen Charlotte* and HMS *General Hunter*, gave covering fire for British troops crossing to the American side. The inhabitants of Detroit had to make the unpalatable choice of facing a British bombardment if they remained in the town, or hostile aboriginal warriors in the surrounding forest if they left. Of those who decided to stay, many terrified women and children later took refuge in a deep ravine at a farm some distance from the fort. (Painting by Peter Rindlisbacher, courtesy of the artist.)

CHAPTER NINE

"*Vicissitudes and commotions.*"
Women and the War
in the Northern Theatre

All the brave are taking up arms,
Farewell! I must leave this abode,
In the midst of alarms I take with me
The memory of our love.
And what is my watchword? Loving you faithfully,
Madame, it shall be honour!
For if I fight for that,
I know victory will be mine.[1]

In March 1812, Major-General Henry Dearborn, the senior officer of the United States Army, wrote to his daughter, Julia, telling her to inform her neighbours "that they may prepare for war; we shall have it by the time they are ready."[2] When the conflict commenced in June, women across North America faced challenges that included additional workloads, financial hardship, separation from loved ones, shortages, and in some cases, serious danger when they were caught up in the actual fighting. It is now time to consider more closely how these women fared in the midst of war's alarms, and our examination begins in July 1812 at the officers' quarters in the American fort on Mackinac Island, located in the Michigan Territory near the neck of Lakes Huron and Michigan.

Even though war was declared on 18 June, a month later the news had still not reached Fort Mackinac. The island's fort was under the command of Lieutenant Porter Hanks, who was fortunate in his remote posting to have the company of his wife, Margaret. Life continued peaceably enough until the morning of 17 July, when some unwelcome visitors arrived in the form of a force of British regulars, armed *voyageurs* from the Northwest Company and aboriginal warriors, all under the command of Captain Charles Roberts. Roberts had learned of the outbreak of war a week earlier and had been ordered to seize Mackinac Island, which occupied a strategic location. He approached the American post under a flag of truce and, informing Lieutenant Hanks that war had been declared, summoned him to yield his post. Outnumbered, outgunned and totally unprepared, Hanks had no choice but to surrender.

Roberts quickly took over the island, whose inhabitants were assembled to have an oath of allegiance to the Crown administered, which "most of them willingly took."[3] The American garrison and their dependants were taken by ship to Detroit, and as they set off down Lake Huron they saw many canoes. The aboriginal people of the area had already started to flock towards Mackinac to demonstrate their friendship to the British and receive a share of the goods captured at the fort. Although Margaret Hanks was accustomed to the ways of the native peoples, she knew that the war would not only incite the warriors but also divide them, and that it could mean only one thing – serious trouble in the Northwest.

That trouble was not long in coming and it surfaced, among other places, at Fort Dearborn, the site of what is now the city of Chicago. The commandant of the fort, Captain Nathan Heald of the 1st United States Infantry, believed that he was on good terms with the aboriginal people in his area and that his post was safe and secure. When news reached him on 10 July 1812 that war had broken out, he was confident he could withstand any possible aboriginal attack on his fort. After another messenger brought the bad tidings that Fort Mackinac had fallen to the British, however, Heald was ordered to evacuate his garrison and its dependants and to distribute all government stores to the local aboriginal people as he thought proper.

Most of the wives at Fort Dearborn were self-sufficient women, some of whom had spent a substantial part of their lives on the frontier. Margaret Helm, married to Lieutenant Linai Helm, was the daughter of a local trader, while Captain Heald's wife, Rebekah, was used to the wilderness and accounted "very expert" in the use of a rifle.[4] As they began packing, a friendly Potawatomi chief, Win-ne-meg or the Catfish, urged Heald to disregard the evacuation order and remain at the fort. Having learned that Brigadier-General William General Hull's army, which had briefly invaded Upper Canada, was in retreat, Win-ne-meg knew that such an indication of American weakness would rouse the aboriginal people in the Fort Dearborn area and make overland travel dangerous. Heald unfortunately chose to ignore this wise advice.

Rebekah Heald (1790-1857), the wife of Captain Nathan Heald, commanding officer of Fort Dearborn. Rebekah was one of several wives caught up in an attack and massacre by Potawatomi warriors near Fort Dearborn on 15 August 1812. An expert in the use of a rifle, Rebekah was badly wounded but managed to stay on her horse. She was fortunate to survive the attack, during which she was taken prisoner with her husband. She was later released and after the war moved to Missouri. (From a daguerreotype made in later life, in Milo Quaife, *Chicago and The Old Northwest, 1673-1835.*)

By 12 August 1812, all was ready for the evacuation. Having decided to destroy the remaining liquor and firearms in his stores rather than distribute them to friendly local warriors, Heald received another warning from Black Partridge, a chief with whom he had hitherto been on good terms. The message was that "linden birds have been singing in my ears to-day; be careful on the march you are going to take."[5] Once again, Heald ignored the advice, and on the morning of 15 August 1812 fifty-four men and their families, plus many of the civilians from the nearby trading settlement and a party of some fifty friendly Miami warriors, left Fort Dearborn to commence an overland march to Fort Wayne, about 140 miles to the east.

Just two miles south of the fort, the party was ambushed by a force of some 500 Potawatomi warriors under their chief, Assignack, or Black-bird. The Miamis fled and the Americans found themselves facing a force almost ten times their size. In the short, desperate conflict that followed, all, including the women, fought bravely, knowing their survival depended upon it. Rebekah Heald used her rifle effectively and Mrs. Holt, another wife mounted on horseback, laid into her attackers with her husband's sword. Mrs. Corbord, a soldier's wife, was tragically killed while resisting other warriors and Margaret Helm was dragged off to a nearby lake, where the men who had seized her attempted to drown her.

In a very short time, only twenty-eight Americans remained on their feet. They succeeded, however, in breaking through the ranks of their enemies, who

THE NORTHERN THEATRE

0   50   100 miles
0   50   100   150 km

■ fort   ● town/village or battle site

N

Lake Superior

St. Joseph I.

■ Fort Mackinac

Lake Michigan

Georgian Bay

Lake Huron

Penetanguishene

Nottawasaga Bay

L. Simcoe

UPPER CANADA

Bay of Quinte

MICHIGAN TERRITORY

Fort York ■ ●York   Lake Ontario

Soc

Stoney Creek   Burlington Bay   Ft. Niagara   Batavia   Charlott

St. Clair R.   Ft. George Queenston   Canandaigua

Grand R.   Niagara R.   Ft. Erie ■   Canandaigua

Malcolm's Mills   Ft. Erie ■

Moraviantown   Buffalo

Thames R.   Port Dover   Port Ryerse   N E W

Detroit   Dolsen's Mills   Lake Erie   Fredonia

Sandwich

Detroit R.   Long Point

Amherstburg (Fort Malden)

Raisin R.   Frenchtown   Erie

Put-in-Bay

Fort Miami   PENNSYLVANIA

Fort Meigs

Maumee River   Fort Stephenson   ●Cleveland

Fort Defiance   Sandusky R.   Allegheny R.

BLACK SWAMP   O H I O

●Pittsburgh

●Urbana

●Dayton   VA.   VA.

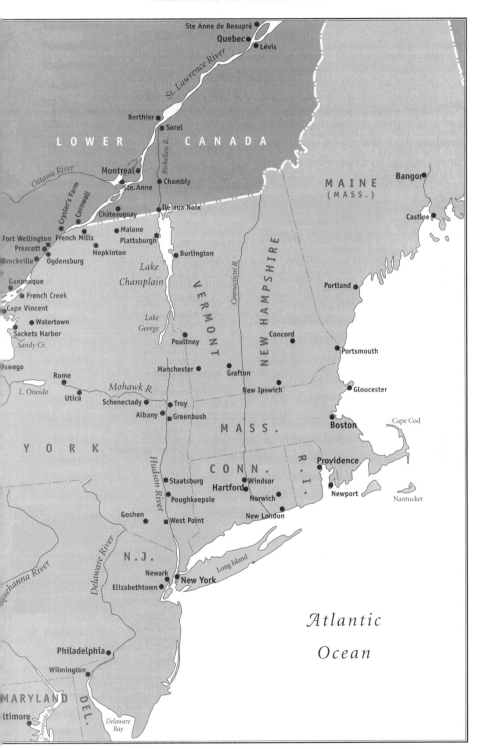

gave way and showed signs of a willingness to parley. Captain Heald met with Black-bird to arrange terms of surrender and it was agreed that all arms should be given up and the survivors should become prisoners of war, to be exchanged for ransom as soon as practicable. After being taken to the Potawatomi encampment near Fort Dearborn, the prisoners were distributed among their attackers and the fort was torched. In this tragedy in the wilderness a total of twelve children, plus all the male civilians, three officers, twenty-six private soldiers and one woman were killed.

At about the same time, Margaret Hanks of Mackinac Island reached Detroit safely with her husband only to find Hull's army in its stockaded fort under siege by a British force commanded by Major-General Isaac Brock. The civilians sheltering inside Detroit were fearful of Brock's aboriginal allies, as well they might be. The warriors, who may have numbered as many as 800, presented "an extraordinary spectacle," according to one eyewitness who had seen their preparations for battle, "some covered with vermillion, others with blue clay, and still others tattooed in black and white from head to foot."[6] To anyone unfamiliar with the ceremonies and rituals of the native peoples it was, he said, like "standing at the entrance to hell, with the gates thrown open to let the damned out for an hour's recreation on earth."

As Lieutenant Porter Hanks was preparing to face a court martial for the surrender of Michilimackinac, Brock was making ready to bombard Detroit. Margaret Hanks was now trapped in a town full of people who, according to local resident Mary McCarty, appeared gloomy and listless, the men gathering in small groups to talk, the normally active housewives, "languid and depressed," and the old women rocking to and fro in their chairs as they "recalled their superstitions and prophesied evil at hand."[7] When a warning was received that the British batteries would shortly open fire, "all was panic and confusion," with "crying infants clinging to their half-distracted mothers," as they hastened to pack their valuables, and "older children everywhere but where they should be."[8]

The civilians of Detroit faced the unhappy choice of British artillery if they remained in the town or the dangers of the surrounding forest which "swarmed with Indians," if they chose to leave.[9] At noon on 16 August 1812, the women and children who had decided to depart gathered in a deep ravine outside the town and at 4 P.M. the British artillery opened up, firing for the rest of that day and at intervals through the following night. Mary McCarty, huddled in the ravine with the others, listened to the sound of shells exploding in a nearby orchard and worried about the proximity of those that "also burst near us harmlessly."[10] Around midnight, the civilians outside the fort were moved to a large stone root-house for warmth and protection as the fort was overcrowded with troops and terrified civilians who, despite the bombardment, preferred the dubious security of the stockaded post.

Lydia Bacon, the wife of Lieutenant Josiah Bacon of Hull's staff, was one of those inside Fort Detroit. As the enemy artillery began its work, Lydia recorded in her diary that

> the enemy's shot began to enter the Fort, & as some Ladies were making cylinders (bags to hold the powder) & scraping lint in case it should be wanted, a 24 pound shot entered the next door to the one they were in, & cut two Officers who were standing in the entry directly in two their bowels gushing out, the same ball passed through the Wall into a room where a number of people were & took the legs of one man off & the flesh of the thigh of another.[11]

Unfortunately, one of the two officers killed was Lieutenant Porter Hanks. After another roundshot entered the hospital quarters, severing the head of one patient and killing his attendant, everyone realized that "the enemy had got the range of the Fort so completely, that it was considered dangerous for the Women & Children to stay any longer in the Quarters." Lydia relates that they all hurried to the same root house as the other civilians. "Never shall I forget my sensation," she recorded,

> as I crossed the Parade ground to gain the place of safety ... my feelings had been under constant excitement for many weeks & now were wrought up to a high pitch, *weep* I *could not, complain* I *would not,* & my eyes raised upward to catch a glimpse of the bombs shells & balls that were flying in all directions.[12]

Some women were so "petrified with affright" that they had to be "carried senseless to the bomb-proof vault for safety." Several of them were "bespattered with blood," and when Lydia reached the root house she found it

> nearly full of Women and children, one Lady so sick she was obliged to be carried there in a bed. What a scene was here presented, such lamentation & weeping I never heard before, & I sincerely hope I never shall again, among all this number but three appeared composed & they felt more than can be described.[13]

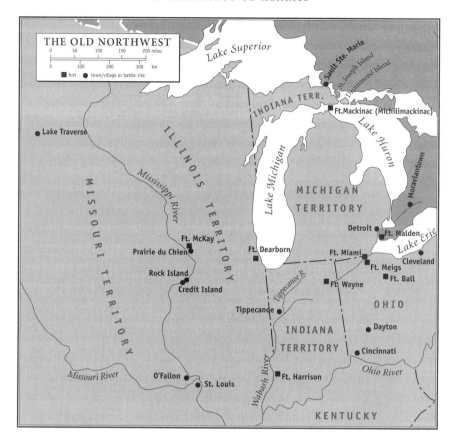

Margaret Hanks, who had seen the corpse of her husband, was for a time "bereft of reason."[14] She was probably the woman Lydia Bacon described as being in "an agony of grief" and asking "amidst her lamentation … what she *had done* to deserve this sore trouble."[15] According to another account, when Margaret Hanks was "placed among the sufferers" in the bombproof vault, the picture of anguish and distress was "complete."[16] With her was Abigail Snelling, married to another American officer, Captain Josiah Snelling, who managed to get to the vault to see his wife. "My dear," he apparently told her, "I know not what moment I may be shot down; I have come to say farewell, and ask you to make me a promise, that in case I fall you will *never marry an Englishman*."[17]

Among other wives likely to have been caught in the bombardment of Detroit were Sarah Sibley, married to a member of the territorial legislature, and Adelaide Dequindre Campau, whose husband, Joseph, was a local merchant. They, together with women such as Adelaide Askin Brush, wife of Elijah Brush, a farmer and officer in the Michigan militia, and Marie-Thérèse Berthelet Lasselle, a refugee from earlier frontier fighting, had to decide whether to attempt to escape from the town or remain and face the consequences.[18]

As night fell, Mary McCarty, who had not been in good health for some time, was among the women sheltering in the root house. The combination of "fright, fatigue, and bad air of the crowded-root-house" brought on an illness "so violent" that her friends had to carry her to a nearby house, where she was placed in an upper room in "a most dangerous position, as, it being nearly daybreak, the firing was more frequent."[19] Sick though she was, Mrs. McCarty was concerned for the safety of her two children in the root house and sent her mother to check on them while she lay alone, listening to the "booming cannon," and now and then "starting and shrieking as a ball whizzed by the house."[20] By this time, Mary felt certain that "the next shot would terminate my existence." As day dawned, the cannonading stopped and Mary's mother returned to tell her that the British were coming across the Detroit River. "Now," said she, "we shall be between two fires, and where to go for safety I cannot tell."[21] All Mary could do was pray, and hope for the arrival of her husband and father, who were fighting with the Michigan militia.

Fearful of an aboriginal massacre, Hull decided to surrender Detroit to Brock and his regular troops. Once the town was in British hands, American prisoners of war watched uneasily as hostile aboriginal warriors began "singing and dancing their war dances."[22] Many soldiers and civilians feared they were "preparing [to] murder our fellow creatures and not only the soldiers but the helpless women and children." There was, however, no massacre after the surrender of Detroit and one young woman witness from the town later remembered that the British were "very kind," and gave "free passage to the frightened people who wished to leave the frontiers."[23]

Among the incidents which did occur, Major Henry B. Brevoort of the United States Army was seized by enemy warriors and forced to begin walking on all fours towards the woods. His very anxious wife suddenly found herself approaching his captors and pointing to the sky as she spoke to them of "their great Father the 'Manitou,'"[24] the mention of whom had an immediate effect.[25] The men "let fall their weapons, shook hands, and all said, 'ta-yaw, ta-yaw,' which means great, brave." They left, enabling Mrs. Brevoort to take her husband to safety.

Ottawa warriors captured a Mrs. Snow and her nine children, who lived in Cole Creek, Huron County. This poor woman became so weak that her captors killed her, and it was her unfortunate husband, who had gathered a group of men to accompany him in pursuit of his family, who found the body. Her experience is illustrative of "many unfortunates whose names tradition has not preserved," and, as a postscript to this event, warriors who later arrived at Detroit carrying "a woman's scalp upon a pole," had with them "a family of nine children, their clothes all torn to shreds."[26]

The fall of Detroit, Mackinac and Fort Dearborn broke American military power in the Northwest. The aboriginal nations of this area, who had been resisting white settlement for more than two decades, now hastened to become British allies. Their decision to do so was influenced by Tecumseh, the Shawnee war chief whose dream was to form a confederacy of all native nations between the Great Lakes and the Gulf of Mexico that would be able to preserve their lands from the floodtide of American settlers. With the prospects of success looking bright, Tecumseh sent messengers to all the nations in the Northwest inviting them to join him in the "complete expulsion or utter extermination" of their American enemies. The Winnebago, Potawatomi, Kickapoo, Ottawa, Shawnee and less powerful nations listened, and young warriors began the "war-dance."[27]

After the fall of Detroit, Tecumseh decided to mount a series of attacks on the remaining American posts in the Northwest: Forts Harrison, Madison and Wayne. These attacks took place in the first days of September 1812 and all were unsuccessful. At Fort Wayne, an estimated twenty-five women and children were removed to safety just before the attack began, but it seems that at least one woman, Emeline Sheptaun, remained inside the fort during the assault, which occurred on 6 September. Emeline was of French ancestry and had come to know the aboriginal people of the area through her trader grandparents. Having learned their language and become "a great favourite" with them, once war broke out Emeline was protected by her past associations but was eventually taken into Fort Wayne for her own safety.[28]

As soon as the government in Washington learned of the disaster in the Northwest, it undertook steps to regain Detroit and the lost territory, but it took Major-General William Henry Harrison more than a year of campaigning to evict the British from American soil. By October 1813 Harrison had recaptured Detroit, occupied the Canadian side of the Detroit River and, with his victory at the Battle of the Thames in Upper Canada, not only secured the Northwest from further British incursions but also ended the aboriginal threat, for Tecumseh was killed in the battle.

Detroit, meanwhile, suffered British occupation from late August 1812 to September 1813. During that period Mary McCarty, who returned to her home near the town, recorded how her residence and that of her father were plundered of all their valuables not just once, but several times. Looting was widespread, and as she wrote sardonically, "we fared quite as well as our neighbours."[29] There was, however, a more terrifying side to the raiding for she also related that just as people began to feel "secure in the enjoyment of their comforts," aboriginal warriors "would enter the house, and carry off everything that tempted their cupidity." Under such circumstances, Mary could not help thinking that "happy were the helpless families if they escaped with life."[30]

According to Mary's account, the British occupying force instituted a procedure whereby the civilians were directed to paint "a red mark on their sheep and cattle, and red doors to their dwellings" to prevent depredations on the part of the invaders' aboriginal allies.[31] Many Americans, including Mary's husband, refused to comply. This was a cause of concern to his wife, who had been informed by a friendly warrior that she and her relatives were "safe, because you are French, and have black eyes and hair," but that her husband with his fair hair should seek protection in Detroit. McCarty, however, stubbornly refused to mark his possessions. "No British red for me," he told his wife, even "if I die for it."[32] Fortunately he did not. The British occupation of Detroit was, in Mary McCarty's words, "a long weary year," and when the town was repossessed by American forces, it and the surrounding area were "in a most deplorable condition," having been "devastated by war, overrun by tribes of hostile savages, and very thinly settled."[33]

Another local resident, Marie Navarre, became accustomed to warriors passing by with their "war-whoop," and to seeing them "painted red around the mouth, a sign that they wanted to drink blood."[34] She refused to be intimidated and accepted them into her home, where they would sit on the floor and make a great display of producing the scalps they had taken. Being of French extraction and having taken the trouble to learn their language, Marie Navarre was known and accepted among Britain's warrior allies, and she was not alone in having the courage to befriend a potentially dangerous enemy in the interest of self-preservation. Mrs. Williams, wife of a tavern keeper and postmaster at Fredonia, New York, took much the same attitude. Described as "a dauntless little woman," she also became a "great favourite with the Indians," because she fed them and was brave enough to allow warriors she did not know into her house.[35] It was not unusual for her to be turning a piece of meat on the spit in her open fireplace or lifting "a pudding, steaming and fragrant," from her iron cauldron and "the next moment be confronted by a stalwart Indian, who would eye the dinner hungrily." She always offered food to aboriginal visitors and in so doing, preserved a good name with them.

Not all the battles fought over that year in the Northwest were victories for the republic. A major American force was defeated and captured at the Battle of Frenchtown on the River Raisin in January 1813, and from that engagement comes a telling anecdote. The British officers stationed at Fort Malden at Amherstburg, Upper Canada, were holding a ball in Draper's Tavern on 18 January 1813 and all in attendance were "full of dance and fun." Suddenly, in walked Colonel Thomas St. George,[36]

> equipped for the field. "My boys" said he, in a loud voice, "you must prepare to dance to a different tune; the enemy is upon us, and we are going to surprise them. We shall take the route [set out] about four in the morning, so get ready at once."[37]

According to an account of the evening, despite the "confusion and surprise," all the men present seemed to "like the fighting as much as the dancing," with the result that the ball "broke up at once, and every man was at his appointed post at the proper time."[38] St. George marched his troops out and they fought a successful action at the River Raisin. Unfortunately, that victory was blighted when the British commander, Major-General Henry Procter, failed to restrain his aboriginal allies and they murdered American prisoners.

Tecumseh was not present at the River Raisin, which was unfortunate because he always tried to prevent such atrocities. A charismatic man, admired by his enemies as well as his allies, Tecumseh has been the subject of much historical writing but considerably less attention has been paid to his remarkable elder sister, Tecumapease, who played a major part in raising this great aboriginal leader. Described as a superior, intelligent person, she was the "principal female chief" in the band – the Shawnee recognizing women as leaders. It is likely that Tecumapease, whose name means "Flying Over the Water," was born in 1762. She grew up in a village on the bank of the Scioto River in what later became Ohio. The Scioto Shawnee were a fiercely independent people and under the leadership of her father, Pukeshinwau, they flourished. Her mother, Methoataakee, was an enlightened woman who encouraged her daughter as she grew into a young woman of proud bearing.[39]

Of her three brothers, Tecumseh was the one with whom Tecumapease had

Tecumapease (*c.*1762-*c.*1817), sister of the Shawnee aboriginal leader Tecumseh, was a member of an aboriginal delegation from the western nations invited to visit Sir George Prevost in the city of Quebec in 1814. In this representation, the faces of the warriors appear to have been caricatured, but Tecumapease may be one of the two female figures on the left of the painting. (Watercolour by Rudolph Von Steiger. Library and Archives of Canada C-134461.)

a particularly close relationship as, when their parents parted company, she raised him. Their father had witnessed a shooting star on the night of Tecumseh's birth and, because of it, predicted his son would become a great leader. It was Tecumapease who played a major role in Tecumseh's formative years and as he matured, she was on hand to see him grow into a successful provider and war chief, and to witness the emergence of his characteristic qualities of judgement, integrity, commitment and erudition. By 1795, at the age of twenty-seven, Tecumseh had shown enough leadership ability to form a separate community of some fifty warriors and their families. Tecumapease stayed with him as the leader of the women and her position was cemented when she married Wahsikegaboe, or "Stands Firm," a warrior who eventually became a chief and a leading supporter of Tecumseh. According to one person who met her, Tecumapease was someone who was "sensible, kind-hearted and uniformly exemplary in conduct," and she is said to have "exercised a remarkable degree of influence over the females of her tribe."[40] Her exact appearance is not known, and the one illustration of her that exists today is only a representation.

When war broke out in 1812, Tecumseh joined the British and proved a formidable ally. While he was engaged in the war, Tecumapease was involved in rearing his son, Paukeesaa, whose mother had died soon after he was born, and he remained with her until manhood.[41] Tecumapease and the other Shawnee wives accompanied Tecumseh on his wartime campaigns. She was nearly fifty years old by that time and must have wondered how long it would be before her husband, brother and seventeen-year-old nephew finished fighting the Americans. She and Paukeesaa, along with the other dependants of Tecumseh's confederacy, joined the British army when it retreated from the Detroit River in the autumn of 1813 and, at the Battle of the Thames, Tecumapease lost not only her brother Tecumseh, but also her husband, Wahsikegaboe. The survivors of the aboriginal force set off towards to Burlington Heights on Lake Ontario, where the women and children remained while the warriors continued to wage war against the United States.

At the invitation of Lieutenant-General Sir George Prevost, Tecumapease and Paukeesaa travelled to Quebec in early 1814. There, Tecumapease received some condolence presents from Lady Catherine Prevost and was much moved when Sir George spoke of the sorrow he had felt upon hearing of Tecumseh's death. That same year the Prince Regent, as a mark of respect for Tecumseh, sent a handsome sword to Paukeesaa.[42] The British paid compensation to the widows of warriors killed fighting for the Crown in the war, and on 25 April 1815, Tecumapease received the sum of $50 and made her mark on a receipt acknowledging payment. After the war she returned to the Detroit area, where she is thought to have died about 1817. By raising the great native leader Tecumseh, this remarkable aboriginal woman, who has long been neglected by historians, played a major part in her brother's struggle for his people to maintain "a common and equal right in the land as it was first, and should be now, for it was never divided."[43]

Although the Northwest suffered during the war, no part of North America witnessed heavier fighting and no area suffered from worse devastation than the Niagara peninsula. Throughout the conflict, more regular troops from both belligerent nations were deployed in this area than any other, and it experienced intense combat – pitched battles, sieges, raids and skirmishes – during thirty months of hostilities. The civilians living on both sides of the Niagara River, which formed the international border, paid a stiff price for a quarrel that was not of their making and whose origins were far removed from their lives.

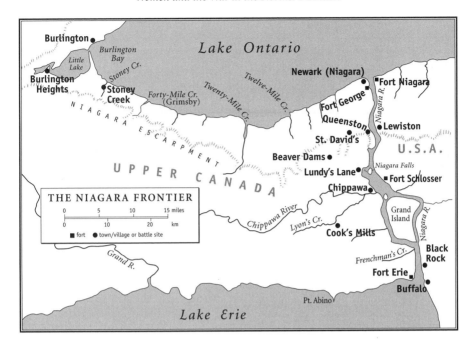

During the first four months of hostilities the Niagara was fairly quiet, although excited American and Canadian militiamen exchanged occasional potshots across the river. This changed in October 1812 when an American army of regular troops and New York militia crossed the river during the night of 12 October and seized the little Canadian village of Queenston. Major-General Isaac Brock, whose headquarters were at Fort George near Newark, a few miles north of Queenston, immediately marched with what force he could gather to dislodge the invaders. The battle continued through 13 October and ended in a British victory that cost Brock's life.

The people of Queenston found themselves in the middle of the fighting, and some left the village. Among them was Laura Secord, whose husband, James, was in action with his militia company. Mrs. Secord took her children and headed towards the village of St. David's, three miles west, where she had relatives. Those who could not escape found shelter in the root cellars of their homes or took refuge with neighbours. Later in the day when the sound of the firing began to lessen, Laura Secord could no longer sit idly at St. David's and, leaving her children with her family, headed back towards her village. There she was faced with the sight of wounded men of both armies lying everywhere, and she found her husband among them, wounded badly in the shoulder and the knee. She attended to him as best she could and with the help of a British officer, carried him to their home where he would spend much of the rest of the war convalescing.[44]

Towards the end of that day there were still women to be found close to the fighting. Captain John Norton, the Mohawk war chief, remembered that as his warriors pursued the retreating enemy they met two women who had been taken by force from their homes. The sight of Norton's men in their black and red paint, symbolic of life and death, must have been alarming to these ladies but as they ran towards the warriors "with Tears in their Eyes," Norton and his people "assured them in passing, that the Enemy should soon be repaid for their insolence."[45]

One of the American soldiers captured at Queenston was an artilleryman named Doyle who had been stationed at Fort Niagara. His wife, Fanny, remained at that place and was there on the morning of 21 November 1812 when British gunners at Fort George on the Canadian side of the river commenced a heavy bombardment of Fort Niagara. It was answered by the Americans and the exchange continued throughout the day. In her husband's absence Mrs. Doyle, an army wife to the core, was determined to take his place at the guns of her husband's post. With no regard for her own safety, she worked alongside his comrades as he would have done and her bravery came to the notice of Major George McFeely, the commandant of Fort Niagara. "During the most tremendous cannonading I have ever seen," he reported, Fanny Doyle "would take the ball tongs from any of the men, run to the fire, take up a hot shot, put it in the cannon, and run for another.[46] She kept this up "for the whole of the day," serving a 6-pdr. gun mounted on top of the fort's stone messhouse and displaying "fortitude equal to the maid of Orleans," or Joan of Arc. Another account states that Fanny continued to do her husband's duties, "regardless of the shot and shell that fell around her," and "never quitted her station until the last gun had been fired."[47] The courage of this army wife made her a household name in the United States.

Unfortunately, the Battle of Queenston Heights and the bombardment of Fort Niagara were just preliminaries. In late May 1813, following their successful attack on York (described later), American forces under the command of Major-General Henry Dearborn crossed the Niagara River and took Fort George and the neighbouring town of Newark. Some civilians fled the area but most stayed, and a local man, Lieutenant William H. Merritt of the Canadian militia, remembered that "it was really painful to see, and hear the distress of the women. I was stopped every few moments to satisfy their inquiries as to

"Fortitude equal to the maid of Orleans." While her husband was a prisoner of the British, Fanny Doyle helped to serve the artillery of Fort Niagara in November 1812 as they fired hot shot across the Niagara River in answer to British artillery at Fort George. She continued to work an entire day regardless of the shot and shell that fell around her, and her bravery drew comparisons with that of Joan of Arc. This is a representation of Mrs. Doyle at work by nineteenth-century artist T. Walker. (Anne S.K. Brown Military Collection, Brown University Library, Brown Unniversity, Providence, Rhode Island.)

the safety of some husband, father, brother or son."[48] The anxious women collected in groups in every public place through the countryside but Merritt was able to quiet "the fears of those for whom I had the highest regard." As British troops retreated to Burlington Heights (modern-day Hamilton), Merritt went with them, feeling totally wretched about the "unhappy situation of my family, whom we left totally unprotected." There were a great many others in a similar situation, for in his neighbourhood "every Man had left to join the forces."[49]

Not all Canadian women were panicked by the invasion. When the Americans landed at Newark, heavy fighting occurred near a lighthouse and the invaders were intrigued to discover that the structure contained non-combatants in the form of "two or three pairs of tolerably bright eyes, belonging to the daughters of the keeper," Mr. Henry.[50] The girls and their mother had not run away but had decided instead to hide inside the lighthouse, which offered better protection than their small cottage nearby. These "Pharos-Belles," as they were termed by an American officer who met them, were not at all intimidated by the presence of the enemy, who, "entering into conversation with them" felt a "very natural curiousity" to know more of "the dangers they had passed." While Mrs. Henry served refreshments, her daughters engaged in conversation with the invading officers and were "soon enlisted as the laundresses of as many wardrobes as their tubs and lines could accommodate." Not only that, but they "patched and darned themselves into a very handsome income; still maintaining reputations, so far as we know, as fair and spotless as the linen they did up with all the skill of accomplished clear-starchers."[51]

Part of the Canadian side of the Niagara remained under American occupation throughout much of 1813 and constant skirmishing took place between the two armies. Young William Merritt recorded the names of several women who underwent unpleasant experiences, one of them being a Mrs. Cain, who was detained with her daughter by an American picket at the village of St. David's and "came off in a very great fright, fearing they might be re-taken."[52] On another occasion, when "two or three hundred enemy dragoons and infantry" plundered all the farms within reach, most of the local ladies fled to "Mrs. McNabb's" on the Lake Road to find safety in each other's company. During a skirmish close to the Ball family farm, "the ladies were eye witnesses from J. and P. Ball's windows." Although the U.S. regulars were generally well-disciplined, a number of New York "volunteer" units that accompanied them proved to be enthusiastic looters, even though civilians took care to secrete their most precious possessions. One careful housewife chose to bury her silver teapot beside a spring of water where the "mud could be stamped down over it and show no suspicious traces."[53] Another family had a great deal of specie, which they "hid in a barrel and buried, and made doubly secure by placing a heavy cider press over the spot."[54] Sixteen-year-old Mary Secord remembered that when American troops burst into her home,

> there was a rush for the pictures and bric-a-brac. One soldier seized something that he said he would take to his wife, another to his sister or sweetheart. Grandmother made herself busy gathering the articles she wanted and the soldiers laughingly commended her enterprise."[55]

Things became so bad that "riotous looters got at the stores, cut open feather beds and pillows and flung with yells the feathers to the winds."

It is small wonder that many civilians lived in fear but the names of two very brave Canadian women, Julia Defield and Jane Kerby, have emerged from this dark time. In June 1813 Captain James Fitzgibbon was commanding a small but elite British force which harassed the occupying American army. One day he rode out alone, trying to locate a party of enemy raiders near the falls of Niagara, when he encountered Jane Kerby, wife of militia Captain James Kerby. Jane warned Fitzgibbon that the enemy had just passed, and Fitzgibbon noticed a cavalry horse tethered outside Defield's Inn, which was nearby. He rode up to the inn with Jane Kerby in pursuit and as soon as he dismounted, was attacked by two Americans who had seen him approach. The three men fought hand to hand and after Jane called for help, "another fearless woman," Julia Defield, wife of the innkeeper, emerged from the building and "adroitly disarmed" one of the Americans, enabling Fitzgibbon to take them prisoner.[56]

That was how Jane Kerby remembered it but William Merritt has left a slightly different version of the incident. According to him, after seeing a horse tethered outside a private house Fitzgibbon went inside only to find two Americans, a "Rifle Man and a Soldier."[57] He pretended to be "an old acquaintance," which threw the soldiers off their guard, and he managed to seize the weapons of both men. He then "pulled and pushed them both out of the House," all the while demanding their surrender, "whilst they were retorting the same on him." Mrs. Kerby, one of several people nearby, "begged and threatened them by turns to no effect," and after a struggle the rifleman drew Fitzgibbon's sword from its scabbard and

> was in the act of thrusting it into his breast, when the woman of the House, Mrs. Duffield [Defield], who was standing at the door with a Child in her Arms, kicked the sword out of his hand. He stooped down to recover it, she threw the Child on the floor, ran out and wrenched it completely from him, hiding it in the House.[58]

According to Merritt, Julia Defield's husband came back a few moments later and disarmed one man while Fitzgibbon did the same to the other. Both Americans were taken prisoner and "upon the whole," wrote Merritt, "it was a most gallant and daring proceeding."[59]

A third version, written by James Fitzgibbon's granddaughter, describes Merritt going into the tavern and seizing the musket of an American dragoon but having to fight a second dragoon before wresting the muskets from both men. In retaliation, one of the Americans managed to draw Fitzgibbon's sword and "attempted to cut him over the head with it," but failed.[60] The American then grasped it as a dagger and tried to impale Fitzgibbon, but as he raised his arm to strike, two small hands "seized it from behind, grasped the wrist, and the sword was wrenched from his hold by a woman," who was Julia Defield. An old man, who happened to come along at that moment helped Fitzgibbon to take both Americans prisoner.

The *Montreal Gazette*, which reported on the incident, confirmed Jane Kerby's part in the proceedings, stating that Fitzgibbon "called upon two men who were looking on to assist him in disarming the two Americans, but they would not interfere."[61] Jane Kerby, "apparently distracted, used all her influence, but in vain," and it was left to Julia Defield to seize the sword as the rifleman made to strike Fitzgibbon and pull it from his grasp. Even given the variations in detail, all the accounts are unanimous that Jane Kerby did her best to warn Fitzgibbon and to seek help, while Julia Defield actually seized the arm of the man wielding the sword. It was a service that Fitzgibbon did not forget and which he would repay many years later.

The courage displayed by Laura Secord during the American occupation is discussed in a later chapter, but matters generally became worse for all the Canadian civilians in the occupied area in September 1813. That month, American regular troops were withdrawn and replaced by a brigade of New York militia. Canadian Joseph Willcocks, mentioned earlier, had turned renegade and was appointed "Police Officer" for the occupied area, and his small unit of fellow turncoats not only engaged in widespread looting, as did the New York militia, but also arrested many locals guilty of no other crime than the fact that Willcocks did not like them. Willcocks and his men waged a vendetta against their former countrymen and women, burning and pillaging the farms of those who had once been neighbours and friends and even committing murder on occasion.

The depredations so provoked the British commander, Lieutenant-General Gordon Drummond, that he began to squeeze the American forcing occupying the area around Fort George into a smaller and smaller perimeter. The American commander, New York Brigadier-General George B. McClure, became somewhat panicky and decided to withdraw across the Niagara River into American territory. McClure had orders from Secretary of War John Armstrong that, if it was necessary for the defence of Fort George, he could destroy neighbouring Newark. Even though he decided to give up the fort, McClure also made up his mind to destroy the town on the pretext that "the British would not find quarters in it during the winter."[62]

Of an original population of a thousand or so, there were only about four hundred people left in Newark, most of them women, children and old men. On the morning of 10 December 1813, a blustery, snowy day, those who had remained were told to leave their houses and take their personal effects with them as the town would be torched that afternoon. One resident recalled that they were given "four hours notice" and had "no Carts, horses, not ten friends and those divided." Many refused to believe that McClure's order would be carried out. Those who did scramble to remove some of their belongings sat beside them in the snow at one o'clock that day as the burning party, armed with torches and lanterns and led by Joseph Willcocks, set about its appalling work. In half an hour the town "was a sea of fire," with much of the furniture that had been moved into the streets burning along with everything else. As one person remembered, what was saved was "nearly Destroy'd" and the Americans themselves pilfered the "small remains."[63]

The torching of Newark was accomplished so hastily that the American sutlers who had stores in the town barracks did not have time to remove their goods. Moreover, Willcocks and his men showed no mercy to the sick and the weak. Charlotte Dickson, the wife of local lawyer William Dickson, was alone and ill in her house, but was carried outside in her bed and left in the snow. Others suffered a similar fate, including Mrs. Campbell, widow of Captain Donald Campbell, former fort major of Fort George, who had died almost a year earlier. Mrs. Campbell and her children were evicted into the cold of the Canadian winter and set out to walk several miles in search of shelter. Tragically her youngest child, just a toddler, died of exposure on the way.[64]

In the town, weeping women and children stared as their world was consumed by flames. Their immediate concern was shelter, and while some refugees began to build crude structures using half-burnt boards, others started walking to neighbouring farms to find sanctuary. A force of British troops under the command of Colonel John Murray, seeing the glow in the night sky, entered Newark to find the streets littered with furniture and every building except one a pile of glowing embers. Ironically, McClure and his troops had left Fort George in relatively good order, but when dawn broke on 11 December 1813 the grey light revealed Newark as "a ruin, nothing to be seen but brick chimneys standing ... of the once beautiful town."[65] Not far away, snowdrifts yielded up the frozen bodies of women and children who had succumbed to the cold while trying to reach safety during the previous night.

People living in the surrounding countryside were profoundly touched by

Homeless in the depths of winter. The winter of 1813-1814 was one of great hardship for the people of communities on either side of the Niagara River. After the burning of Newark by American troops in December 1813, the British retaliated by crossing the river and laying waste to villages as far south as Buffalo. In this illustration, a mother safeguards her child and her few remaining possessions while in the background can be seen the smoke of burning buildings. (Drawing by George Balbar from Bob Foley, *The War of 1812: Niagara Story Volume 2*, reproduced by permission of the author.)

the sufferings of the homeless. Mrs. McFarland, whose large brick house stood on the river road to Niagara Falls, provided food and hot drinks for the refugees while others came with sleighs to take them to their own residences, where they were given shelter and cared for until the hard times were over.[66] Some women and children from the town, however, were forced to spend that winter living in root houses, cellars or other makeshift structures, and most had to rely on help from their relatives, or to accept charity.

Secretary of War John Armstrong, acting for the American government, officially disavowed responsibility for the destruction of Newark, attributing it to the unauthorized conduct of McClure. Armstrong sent a copy of the order he had given McClure to destroy the town only if necessary for the defence of Fort George to Major-General James Wilkinson, the senior American commander in the north, and told him to transmit it to Sir George Prevost, the British commander-in-chief. Wilkinson did so, enclosing a copy of the order in a letter stating that the "outrages which have ensured the unwarranted destruction of Newark, have been carried too far, and present the aspect rather of vindictive fury than just retribution," actions that were "reputed more to personal feelings, than any settled form of policy."[67] This was a direct reference to the involvement of Joseph Willcocks in the matter, but it by no means satisfied Prevost and Drummond, the latter deciding coldly that "retributive justice demanded of me a speedy retaliation on the opposite shore of America."[68]

That retaliation was not long in coming. On 19 December British and Canadian troops crossed the Niagara River and captured Fort Niagara in a daring night assault. A Mrs. Gillett, whose husband and eldest son were on militia duty, was alone with her remaining children at nearby Lewiston when the British attacked. She knew from a "strange, confused noise from the direction of the river" that something was wrong, and as she finishing her milking, British warriors appeared and started to search her property for plunder.[69] One of her sons, Orville, managed to escape, leaving his mother and her two remaining children to endure what followed. The house was ransacked and one of the warriors opened a demijohn of whisky, from which he "imbibed freely and seemed to like it exceedingly." As more warriors arrived they began to quarrel over the whisky and then "behaved like fiends," even threatening to "brain the children." While they were still arguing amongst themselves over who should have the demijohn, Mrs. Gillett dashed out of the house with her young ones, intending to seek the protection of a British officer whom she could see some distance down the street. One of the warriors followed her, killed one of her sons and scalped him in front of her.

For the next few days, Mrs. Gillett was held prisoner but managed to escape with her two remaining children – one just a baby, and the other four years old – while her native guard was in a drunken stupor. "Homeless, friendless, penniless, distracted by grief," fearing her captors would come in pursuit and thinking of the "ruins of her once happy home," Mrs. Gillett and her little ones trudged through the winter snow in an effort to reach her father's home, all of 270 miles distant.[70] Often begging for a lift on a farmer's sleigh or asking for food and shelter, the distraught mother experienced a great deal of kindness from people she met during her long journey, including a good-hearted farmer who gave her a temporary home when she was in danger of collapsing. Late in February 1814, the little family finally reached Mrs. Gillett's parents, who were sad to see the daughter who had left twelve years earlier as a happy bride returning in such a deplorable condition.

Once Fort Niagara was taken, Drummond let his troops and aboriginal warriors loose on the American side of the Niagara and they destroyed almost every building along the thirty-five-mile stretch of the river from Fort Niagara to Buffalo. Warned of the British approach, the people of Buffalo barely had time to pack a few essentials before fleeing. Mrs. Anna Brayman, whose husband, Daniel, did not believe the warning, only departed in haste when "Major Miller came to our house and rousing us up told us that we must leave."[71] All Anna Brayman could do was to put "her bake-kettle with bread in it, some pork and other things" into her husband's wagon before they set off.

Not all were as fortunate as the Braymans. Another couple, John Haddock and his wife, had no wagon and struggled out of town on foot with their six children. They managed to walk fifteen miles on the first day, carrying the youngest of the family and "wearied almost to death."[72] That night, they slept on the floor of a kind stranger, "with only two blankets, which was all we had saved from the fire and the sword." Generosity and kindliness were in evidence elsewhere too, as a farmer on his way to Buffalo with a wagon-load of cheese for market encountered a frightened group of women and children a short distance out of town. He immediately "threw his cheese out upon the ground, abandoned it, and loaded his wagon with the most helpless" to assist them "in their flight."[73]

When the British forces entered Buffalo on 30 December 1813, a village described by one American soldier as "a nest of villains, rogues, rascals, pickpockets, knaves & extortioners," they proceeded to plunder and destroy the place.[74] Among the townspeople who had chosen to stay was Margaret St. John, "a stout, resolute woman," whose husband had died leaving her with nine children, a home and a hotel to run.[75] Mrs. St. John was among those Americans who had denounced the burning of Newark as an "exhibition of wantonness only fit for savages," carried out with "a bravado that only belonged to cowardice."[76] She had decided to guard her home, declaring, "here is all I have in the world, and I will stay and defend it." Having managed to evacuate most of her children to safety, she remained with her two eldest daughters, Martha and Sarah.[77]

Opposite Mrs. St. John lived Sarah Lovejoy, "a spirited woman, about 35 years old," whose husband was fighting with the militia and whose son had fled

Widow St. John. One of the few houses left standing in Buffalo after the British attacked the town and set fire to most of the buildings in late December 1813 belonged to the widowed Mrs. Margaret St. John. She had disapproved of the American burning of the Canadian town of Newark a few weeks earlier and decided to remain in the Buffalo to protect her property. Several accounts indicate that the British officer commanding the Buffalo raid, Major-General Phineas Riall, sent a soldier to watch over her house. (Print in Frank H. Severance, *Publications of the Buffalo Historical Society, Volume IX.*)

into the woods for safety.[78] There are differing accounts about what happened to Sarah Lovejoy when the enemy arrived, but all agree that warriors forced their way into her house, where Sarah is described as having "protested angrily" at the intrusion.[79] In the ensuing struggle, a warrior "raised his tomahawk and cleft her skull."[80] Another version describes the St. John women watching from their house as Mrs. Lovejoy "engaged in an altercation with an Indian over a shawl which he was trying to pull from her hands" and mentions that one of the St. John girls called to her to "let the Indian have the shawl" and come across to the safety of their house. Sarah Lovejoy did not comply and a little later they witnessed her killing.[81]

There is also an account of this murder by one of Margaret St. John's daughters, Martha, who remembered that

> my mother said she saw an Indian pulling the curtains down from the window of the Lovejoy house opposite, and saw Mrs. Lovejoy strike his hand with a carving-knife, and saw the Indian raise the hatchet; but as the door closed she could not know for certain that he killed her. She did not dare to go and see.[82]

Martha St. John also noted that her mother warned Sarah Lovejoy, "do not risk your life for property," to which Mrs. Lovejoy answered, "when my property goes, my life shall go with it."[83] Mrs. Lovejoy's body was apparently "dragged into the yard, where it lay until the departure of the troops." Later, Judge Ebenezer Walden of Buffalo, helped by the St. John girls, carried the dead woman's body into her house and placed it on a bed. Despite the different versions of the incident, what is clear is that Sarah Lovejoy died that day.[84]

The British withdrew from Buffalo but two days later, on 1 January 1814, another detachment arrived and destroyed almost all of the remaining buildings, including the St. John hotel and Mrs. Lovejoy's house. Amid the smoking ruins of the town, only Margaret St. John's home survived together with the jail, the frame of a barn and Reese's blacksmith's shop, spared because it had become the village morgue. Elsewhere, British raiding parties struck the village of Cold Springs and burned Hodge's Tavern. Mr. and Mrs. Hodge were long gone when the enemy arrived, leaving behind them a stash of merchandise including "casks of liquor," which had belonged to merchants in the village and been placed "in store there for safety."[85]

Many civilians now found themselves homeless in bitter winter weather and the roads were crowded with refugees. Groups of women and children on foot marched with retreating militiamen and Seneca warriors, and altogether they made up a "strong current of dismay, rout and flight," amid further dismal rumours that hostile warriors were "just in the rear, tomahawking men, women and children indiscriminately."[86]

Batavia became a rallying point for the New York militia and the homeless citizens of the frontier. Private houses were thrown open, barns and sheds were used as accommodation and families who had been separated in their hasty departure from Buffalo were reunited, "their scattered members, male and female, dropping in one after the other."[87] Such was the demand for food that "bread, meat and drinks soon vanished from the log taverns on the routes" and were shared with those most in need. All along the Niagara frontier were the "blackened remains of once happy homes, scathed and desolated," and there was,

> a gloomy stillness brooding over the scene, so profound, that the gaunt wolf, usually stealthy and prowling, came out of his forest haunts at mid day, and lapped the clotted snow, or snatched the dismembered limb of a human corpse that in haste and flight had been denied the right of sepulchre.[88]

In January 1814 Sir George Prevost issued a proclamation declaring that British forces would refrain from such acts of destruction in the future if American forces did the same. Such was the devastation on both sides of the Niagara River, however, that there were few civilians still living near the waterway. Of those who remained on the Canadian side, some had become so inured to war that even the invasion in July 1814 of Major-General Jacob Brown's American army was not enough to dislodge them. Captain William Merritt urged his mother to abandon her home west of Newark but "she could not be prevailed upon to leave the House," and his sister, Susan, decided to remain with her.[89] With enemy troops approaching, properties looted or abandoned, and evidence of damage from the former American invasion, the Canadian side of the Niagara was in such a sorry state that Merritt could only write in his diary, "the Country never was more destitute than at this time."[90]

Chance placed one British officer's wife, Hannah Jenoway, directly in the path of the American invaders. Hannah had just brought her family from Kingston to near Queenston, where her husband was stationed, when the enemy crossed the river. As she wrote to her sister-in-law in England:

> I had only been there a fortnight when five thousand of the Yankees landed above Fort Erie. Mr. Jenoway was left to command Queenston and the fortifications he had constructed, but unfortunately our army had to retire after a hard battle, with only fifteen hundred of the British to oppose so many of the enemy.[91]

Hannah was describing the Battle of Chippawa, fought in fields near the Niagara River on 5 July 1814. As she went on to explain,

> about nine o'clock in the night, I was obliged to make my retreat with the children. When we got back four miles from Queenston, six Indians rushed out of the bush and asked me for my money. The servant was so frightened that he durst not speak to them, but I had courage enough to make them understand I was an officer's lady, when they immediately went away. You may easily suppose what a tremor I was in.[92]

Hannah's fright notwithstanding,

> On we went towards the Twelve [Mile Creek]. Before we got within six miles of it our servant upset us [overturned their carriage]. Fortunately we had no limbs broken, only much bruised. We were near a Mr. Thompson's, where we staid three weeks, with the Yankees within four miles of us, and [they] came a few times within a mile-and-a-half of us. After the Americans had retired to St. David's and Queenston, my dear husband fetched us to Fort George, made the family a present of twenty dollars and drove off.[93]

Hannah coped throughout this dramatic episode only to have two of her children become "alarmingly ill of the ague and lake fever." Throughout her ordeal, she demonstrated the sort of inner strength that enabled many women to survive.

Hannah's resolution echoes a Peninsular War account of a woman at the Battle of Rolica, Portugal, in 1808. Dressed in a riding habit and straw bonnet, and carrying a parasol and a large basket, this lady was riding along a road bordered by dead and wounded men when a British officer, Captain George Landmann, encountered her. He urged her to go back, it being hardly a suitable place for a woman. "Upon this," he remembered, "she drew herself up and with a very haughty air," and with what appeared to be "a perfect contempt of the danger of the situation," she replied, "mind your own affairs, sir. I have a husband before me."[94]

While the American Northwest and both sides of the Niagara suffered the most during the war, the conflict occasionally intruded into other areas adjacent to the international border. There were infrequent raids or landings and sometimes an important action, but although the war affected the way of life of everyone to some extent, major military operations were intermittent and their effect less devastating.

Although western Upper Canada had been briefly invaded by Hull's army in July 1812, which prompted much anxiety, it was not until September 1813 that the war arrived to stay. An American naval victory over the British squadron on Lake Erie gave the United States control of that body of water and permitted Major-General William Henry Harrison, commander of the Northwestern Army, not only to regain Detroit but to contemplate an invasion of British territory across the river. His British counterpart, Major-General Henry Procter, badly outnumbered and with his supply lines threatened, began to plan a retreat from his position at Fort Malden to Burlington Heights on Lake Ontario. In preparation, he sent ahead the women, children and invalids:

> My sick are on the Thames, as are my women ...... I have sent Mrs. Procter off and I fear she will have much to encounter. My eldest daughter was ill and but little recovered when she went off three days since. What a sudden, what a complete reverse![95]

Although Tecumseh urged him to stand and fight, Procter's mind was made up and on 27 September 1813, his army began to withdraw from the Detroit

Retreat along the Thames. With the defeat of a Royal Navy squadron on Lake Erie in September 1813, the British decided to evacuate Fort Malden ahead of an expected attack by American troops. The garrison, local settlers, allied warriors and their families retreated along the Thames River on foot and by boat, to begin the long march eastwards to Burlington Heights. (Painting by Peter Rindlisbacher, courtesy of the artist.)

frontier. The women and children had been sent on ahead and after the army caught up with them, the entire force made camp near Moraviantown. It was here on 5 October that it was brought to ground by Harrison at the Battle of the Thames and practically destroyed in a short but vicious battle in which, as stated earlier, Tecumseh was killed.

The women and children who were with Procter's army were in a desperate situation. Some surrendered to the victorious Americans while others tried to make their way to Burlington Heights. One such was Maria Muir, whose home at Fort Malden was now under enemy occupation and whose husband, Major Adam Muir of the 41st Foot, had been taken prisoner in the battle. Maria Muir gathered up her children, secured a wagon and set off, unescorted and unprotected. After a long and arduous journey through wild country she reached York, and it was there that Thomas Verchères de Boucherville, a young militia officer, encountered her. He was full of admiration, later stating that:

I must remark in passing, that women as courageous as she was are extremely rare. She had not hesitated a moment to set out in a wagon with her young children, to go forty or fifty leagues [120 or 150 miles] through a country almost devoid of settlers, with steep hills difficult to descend and much more so to climb, and this in a time of war when savages were roaming the woods ready to scalp anyone they met. I cannot praise too highly the spirit of that remarkable woman.[96]

The disaster at the Thames left the Detroit River in American hands and for the remainder of the war, much of Upper Canada between that river and Fort Erie was a "no man's land," visited by the troops of both nations but never securely in the possession of either belligerent. It suffered a number of American raids, some led by another Canadian traitor, Andrew Westbrook, who commanded a unit of "rangers" which occasionally swept through the area. In early April 1814, Westbrook raided the hamlet of Oxford, intent upon capturing the local militia commander, Major Sykes Tousley, whose unfortunate wife awoke in the middle of the night to find Westbrook standing beside the couple's bed pointing a pistol at her sleeping husband's head. Seeing the terrified woman was about to cry out, Westbrook warned her: "If you scream, I shall blow your husband's brains out."[97] Mrs. Tousley managed to control herself and watched while Westbrook took her husband away as a prisoner of war.

A more serious incursion took place about a month later when a force of American regulars and militia crossed Lake Erie from Pennsylvania and attacked the small settlement of Dover on the north shore of the lake. Under the deliberate order of the American commander, Lieutenant-Colonel John B. Campbell, these raiders not only destroyed legitimate targets of war but also considerable private property. The reason, he said, was to make the inhabitants "feel the effects of that conduct they had pursued towards others," a reference to the burning of Buffalo.[98] Amelia Ryerse, sixteen years old at the time, never forgot the day the Americans arrived at her widowed mother's farm:

My Mother and myself were at Breakfast, the Dogs made an unusual barking. I went to the door to discover the cause. When I looked up I saw the hillside and the fields as far the eye could reach covered with American soldiers. ...... Two men stepped from the ranks, selected some large chips, came into the room where we were standing and took coals from the hearth without speaking. My mother knew instinctively what they were going to do. She went out and asked to see the commanding officer, a gentlemen rode up to her and said he was the person she asked for. She entreated Him to spare her property and said that she was widow with a young family. He answered her civilly and respectfully and regretted that his orders were to burn, but that he would spare the house, which he did and said in justification the buildings were used as barracks and the mill furnished flour for British Troops. Very soon we saw a column of dark smoke arise from every building and what at early morn had been a prosperous homestead, at noon there remained only smouldering ruins.[99]

According to Alexander McMullen, an American militiaman who participated in the raid, most of the civilians around Long Point were "permitted to carry out [of their houses] the valuable part of their moveable property" and nothing else.[100] By the time the raiders re-embarked, McMullen commented, they were "generally disgusted with the conduct" of their own commanding officer.

Samuel White, another American militiaman who took part in the Long Point raid, left an interesting postscript to this event. As White was marching with his unit along the lakeshore, he noticed that

in many places along the road the houses were literally crammed with ladies, collected there to see us as we passed through ... and here I would strongly recommend all who may be in want of handsome wives to visit the borders of Lake Erie, for I have never seen, before or since, in any part of the country, more beautiful and elegant looking ladies.[101]

The raiding in western Upper Canada continued for the remainder of 1814. In early September, Westbrook briefly occupied the Talbot Settlement on the north shore of Lake Erie, staying on the farm of a militia officer, Captain Daniel Rapelje. Rapelje's high-spirited young daughter, Aletta, remembered the unwanted visitors "piling the fencing in heaps" to build campfires for the night and such was their work that in the morning the Rapelje farm was a scene of desolation: "the wheat and hay scattered over the fields, and corn taken out of the crib, the sheep were all slaughtered."[102] One of the raiders dressed himself in clothing belonging to Aletta's brother and then had the gall to ask her opinion on the fit. "The clothes are well enough," shot back the young woman, "but they are on a very bad man just now."[103] Just before the intruders left, Aletta accosted Westbrook, calling him "the worst kind of thief and scoundrel."[104]

The American and Canadian shores of Lake Ontario witnessed a number of intrusions by both sides, the most serious being the American attack on York in April 1813. As the six hundred or so residents of the provincial capital prepared to go to bed on the evening of Monday, 26 April, fourteen American warships were sighted on the lake. As dawn broke the following day, the American fleet approached the shore west of the town and British regulars and Canadian militia marched out to oppose a possible landing. Despite imminent danger, Mary Baldwin, a resident of York, could not help remarking that "nothing could equal the beauty of the fleet coming in – it preserved the form of a crescent while the sails were white as snow."[105]

Mary and several other women "assembled together to take measures for the flight of the ladies," but not all the women wanted to leave. Ann Strachan, wife of the Reverend John Strachan, and society matron Anne Powell chose to remain, as did others including Penelope Beikie, wife of John Beikie, Sheriff of the local area. Penelope's husband and son had volunteered to help defend the town and she was worried for the safety of "her two poor fellows in the heat of the battle."[106] She found comfort and strength in the words of Psalm 91: "He that dwells in the help of the Highest shall abide in the protection of the God of Heaven etc." As she later wrote to a friend, her faith gave her "more strength and fortitude than all the other females of York put together; for I kept my Castle, when all the rest fled."[107] This was not quite true, for others such as Anne Powell and Angelica Givins, wife of Major James Givins of the Indian Department, had remained to guard their houses while Elizabeth Derenzy, wife of Captain William Derenzy of the 41st Foot, was nursing her seriously ill father, Prideaux Selby, at his home.[108]

The invaders landed in the face of stiff British and Canadian resistance but the defenders were forced to retreat to the town. As the Americans approached York, the warships began firing at the garrison or barracks, which "obliged the females, children &c., to leave it," and one officer's son remembered how he, his mother and the other families "retired into the country to the house of an officer of militia."[109] Soon afterwards, to the terror of all those who had chosen to stay in York, a portable powder magazine in one of the British batteries exploded, killing and wounding a large number of men. The defenders of the town were overwhelmed by superior numbers and, after holding out for several hours, were forced to retreat. Major-General Sheaffe, the British commander, ordered the grand magazine in the garrison to be blown up to prevent British munitions and gunpowder from falling into enemy hands. Lieutenant Ely Playter of the militia went to collect his greatcoat from the officers' quarters and found Mrs. Chapman, a woman who usually cooked for the officers, still in the building. Playter advised her to leave and they had only just passed through the garrison gates when the grand magazine blew. The explosion was so great that it was heard and

Ann Wood McGill Strachan (1784-1865) was the daughter of Montreal businessman and politician James McGill and wife of the Reverend John Strachan, Church of England rector of York. After the American attack on York in April 1813 John Strachan sent Ann and their children to Cornwall, thinking it would be a safer place than the Upper Canadian capital. Unfortunately, the pregnant Ann was robbed and molested by American troops when they occupied Cornwall toward the end of that year. As a result of her experience, she suffered physical and emotional problems that lasted for many months. (Silhouette, November 1807. J. Ross Robertson Collection, Toronto Public Library T13800.)

felt as distant as Fort Niagara, while to the north of the town Mary Baldwin and her companions "all sat down on logs and stumps frightened out of their wits."[110] Many tons of debris were caught up in the blast, which ballooned up into the sky and then began to fall to earth again, damaging people and property.

When the Reverend John Strachan heard the terrible noise, he went to "look after the Ladies," and found his wife, Ann, in a state of terror.[111] After despatching her and their children to the home of a friend outside York, he began helping the wounded to the hospital. By now the British troops had retreated, the terms of the town's surrender had been completed and American soldiers and sailors were engaged in widespread looting. Houses were robbed – among them that of Angelica Givins, who was almost shot by the invaders and suffered considerable loss and damage to her property. In "great distress," Angelica approached the American commander, Major-General Henry Dearborn, to ask for protection for her family and property, but he informed her he was unable to grant this to anyone connected with Britain's aboriginal allies, her husband being an officer of the Indian Department.[112]

When American soldiers tried to rob the Beikie house, they found Penelope Beikie a formidable foe. Greatly relieved that her husband and son had survived the fighting unscathed, Penelope had "the temerity to frighten, and even to threaten some of the enemy" who arrived at her door and thereby preserved most of her possessions.[113] She noted with satisfaction that all the empty houses in the town were ransacked while she lost only "a few things, which were carried off before our faces; but as we expected to lose all, we think ourselves well off." Mrs. Beikie was sanguine about the whole affair. "I really attribute this visit to the vengeance of heaven on this place," she wrote, blaming it on the fact that quantities of stores, farming utensils and other items sent from England years earlier, instead of being distributed, had been kept "in the King's stores." As Penelope said, "now our enemies have them, to do with them as they please. I think we deserve all we have got."[114]

Elizabeth Derenzy's father had died of his illness and she was too full of grief in the aftermath to think of much else. Some of the other ladies of York, however, had more than a little to say about the disaster that had befallen their town and there were dark mutterings about Major-General Sheaffe's conduct of the battle. According to Anne Powell, the reigning matriarch of the provincial capital, the word "mismanagement" was "a more gentle term that is generally applied to the disastrous event."[115] Anne Powell's formidable presence in her residence had preserved it from harm but her feelings ran high and she wrote about the Americans:

> I hope that the time is not far distant when their hateful Flag will yield to the British Lion; such an event will be some alleviation to the chilling reflection that a lawless Mob can boast of having obliged our gallant Troops to retreat before them.[116]

To Anne, the American occupation of York was a turning point in her life. She worried that her little town would never recover from the destruction it had suffered, nor from the disgrace, which "is I fear indelible."[117] "At best our actual situation is almost hopeless," she wrote to her absent husband, William. She wished that the British defenders of Upper Canada had "one ray of the spirit of Wellington." As far as she was concerned, "only a miracle alone can extricate us," but lest William Powell should think his wife weak, she made a point of assuring him that her resolution was not giving way. "We have endured privations," said Anne firmly, "we can endure greater."

The news of what had happened at York spread rapidly throughout Upper Canada and thereafter the sound of gunfire was enough to spread alarm along the shore of Lake Ontario. A British attack on Sackets Harbour on 29 May 1813 panicked the people of Kingston, who listened "in breathless trepidation to the distant roar of Guns & musquetry" while the action lasted.[118]

To the east along the St. Lawrence River, the first eight months of the war witnessed a series of tit-for-tat raids. In September 1812, American troops from Ogdensburg raided the Canadian village of Gananoque, where the militia was commanded by a Colonel Joel Stone, a prominent Loyalist who was "particularly obnoxious to the Americans."[119] The invading force surrounded his house and fired into it, slightly wounding the colonel's wife. One local resident, see-ing the humour in the situation, described how the "unmannerly" musket ball struck Mrs. Stone, a keen dancer, "so hard upon the tender, she is no longer able 'to trip it on the light fantastic toe.'" That same month, a boat from the Canadian shore landed near Sturgeon Point on the American side of the St. Lawrence and a number of soldiers entered the house of a family that had fled, seizing any clothing, furniture and provisions they could find. Not content with their haul, they then proceeded to raid two other houses before staggering back to the boat with their booty, hoping their craft would stay afloat until they were safely back on their own shore.[120]

The raid on Gananoque prompted a British retaliatory attack on Ogdens-burg in October 1812 but this was decisively rebuffed by the defenders, com-manded by New York Brigadier-General Jacob Brown. Quiet reigned along the St. Lawrence until February 1813, when an American night raid on Brockville took that town by surprise. A party of some 200 American soldiers and citi-zen volunteers crossed the frozen river, supposedly to rescue a group of fellow citizens being held in the Brockville jail. They met with little resistance and all the prisoners, with the exception of one man being held for murder, were freed and returned to Ogdensburg. With them went supplies, arms and forty-five of Brockville's most prominent citizens. The captives were soon released to their homes but the British decided it was time to teach the Americans across the river a lesson.

Later that same month, a force of 800 British troops and Canadian militia crossed the icebound St. Lawrence and, after a stiff fight, took Ogdensburg. The people of the village were thrown into confusion and alarm and many of them were seen hastening away at great speed. After seizing two schooners, artillery and other war stores, the attackers dismantled the town fort and burned the barracks. Once again there was looting, although it is unclear whether it was carried out by troops or Canadian civilians who crossed over in their wake. Mrs. York, a resident of Ogdensburg who fled the town, reported on the raid and informed her brother that

> our house was plundered of almost every thing, and my husband a prisoner
> on the other side. You can easier imagine my feelings than I can describe
> them. They did not leave any article of clothing, not even a handkerchief
> – they took all my bedding but left the beds; they broke my looking glasses
> and even my knives.[121]

Jane Okill Stuart (1752-1821). The Reverend John Stuart and his wife, Jane, were early Loyalist settlers in Upper Canada who made their home at Kingston with their seven children. After the reverend's appointment as chaplain of the garrison and later as bishop of Kingston, the Stuarts led busy lives until John Stuart's death in 1811. Throughout the War of 1812 Jane lived in the town with her unmarried daughter of the same name and suffered many shortages and privations. (Portrait by unknown artist. Library and Archives Canada, C-11058.)

Mrs. York's husband, who had been taken back to Prescott on the Canadian side as a prisoner, was known for his patriotism and "partizan spirit," which may have made his residence a special target. His plucky wife decided to head over the river under a flag of truce to rescue him. "My journey was not lost," she told her brother, "I procured the release of my husband, who was paroled and returned with me." Mrs. York also bears witness to the fact that much of the looting at Ogdensburg was done by civilians, not soldiers. "You will be astonished," she wrote, "when I tell you that ... the women on the other side came across, and took what was left." Her statement is corroborated by the account of a Canadian militiaman who participated in the attack, and who

> in crossing during the day, was met by a woman returning with a large mirror, which she said she had stolen from the Yankees. She had scarcely spoken, when her feet slipped on the ice, which threw her prostrate, and her ill gotten booty was lost, while boasting of her success in obtaining it.[122]

Eight fairly quiet months followed along the St. Lawrence but, in October 1813 a large American army gathered at Sackets Harbor in preparation for an attack on Montreal. The plan called for this force to move down the river in an armada of more than 300 small boats and to join up with another force advancing from the south, but its strength and intentions became known to British commanders, who prepared to resist them. At Kingston, directly across the lake from Sackets Harbor, concern and tension grew. Jane Stuart, the daughter of Anglican minister John Stuart, wrote to her brother that we have been in a continual state of alarm and apprehension this week past, expecting an attack daily and hourly. Two nights since at nine o'clock eight or nine guns were fired which terrified me more than all our former alarms united.[123]

The wind on Lake Ontario strengthened, however, and according to Jane, "blew a perfect tempest which gave us security for the night," as American warships would not attack during such weather. She and her aged mother still felt vulnerable and the situation was not helped when, next day, news came that a number of boats crowded with American troops had been seen in the vicinity of Grenadier Island across the lake. Soon afterwards, when rumours began to spread of "ten or twelve thousand men in readiness to attack Kingston," a number of the town ladies left hurriedly for greater safety. Among them was a Mrs. Macauley, evidently someone not easily scared, for as Jane Stuart commented, "danger must have been ascertained to be very near before fear would

Night passage on the St. Lawrence. As American troops, led by Major-General James Wilkinson, set off in late October 1813 along the St. Lawrence with the aim of invading Lower Canada and taking Montreal, they travelled in the kind of boats depicted in this painting. The sight of more than 300 of these vessels filled with soldiers provoked great alarm in the town of Kingston as the terrified local inhabitants expected an enemy attack. (Pencil sketch by Peter Rindlisbacher from Donald E. Graves, *Field of Glory: The Battle of Crysler's Farm, 1813.*)

have induced her to desert her house and all the comforts attached to her own fireside."[124] When word came that the Americans had bypassed Kingston and moved down the St. Lawrence, Jane and her fellow Kingstonians were "relieved from apprehension for a time."

The American army, about 7,000 strong, was commanded by Major-General James Wilkinson. The armada set off from Grenadier Island on 3 November and moved steadily down the St. Lawrence toward Montreal. On 6 November, most of troops were landed on the Canadian shore of the river in preparation to move on land. Although Wilkinson issued a general order to his soldiers that, as "nothing is so abhorrent as rapine and plunder," he would punish marauding by death, and that he was "solemnly determined to have the first person who shall be detected in plundering an inhabitant of Canada ... made an example of," some of the troops did not get the message and began to raid local homes.[125]

According to the postwar loss claims submitted by civilians, the most attractive items taken were foodstuffs, fence rails, clothing and alcohol, which is not surprising given that Wilkinson's troops were half-starved, frozen and wet. The Americans also lifted china, silver and, in one case, a sleigh. Officers tried to control their men, and after one Canadian farmwife complained that a beehive had been stolen from her barn, a search of the boats revealed the hive in the lap of a soldier, securely wrapped up in a blanket. The officer present decided to make the punishment fit the crime and the miscreant was ordered to return the hive to its owner. The man carefully unwrapped his plunder and then ran straight for the barn, but the bees, "very impatient of the restraint," attacked him and by the time he returned, his face was so swollen with bee stings that he was nearly blind and "a good object for the doctor's ointment and the gibes of his companions."[126]

The American campaign against Montreal was brought to a halt by twin British victories at Châteauguay on 26 October and Crysler's Farm on 11 November. After this, the two armies went into winter quarters and for the remainder of the war the St. Lawrence remained under British control and relatively peaceful.

Until the last summer of the conflict, Lake Champlain was a secondary theatre of war. Both nations constructed squadrons of small warships on the lake but the loss of two American ships, the USS *Growler* and *Eagle,* in June 1813 permitted Britain to control the lake for a brief period. In late July of that year, an expedition under the command of Lieutenant-Colonel John Murray made an amphibious raid on Plattsburgh to destroy military and naval stores. The town was occupied on 31 July and the work of destruction commenced, but although many stories were later circulated about looting and damage to private property, one citizen of the town stated without equivocation that

> we have seen in the papers accounts of the pretended barbarities committed here by the British, which we of this place never heard of until we saw them in the papers. Hundreds of witnesses can testify that nine in ten of these accounts are gross and infamous fabrications, and written probably by wretches who ran away on the approach of danger, and who invented the lies to apologize for their cowardice. – In all military operations there will be irregularities; but the conduct of Col. Murray and his officers, while here, as it respected a desire to preserve individual property, was deserving the praises of magnanimous enemies.[127]

Another resident recorded that: "those who staid at home found no difficulty in preventing their houses from being plundered."[128] Colonel Murray even took the trouble to search out the home of Lieutenant Sidney Smith, USN, who had been captured a few months earlier on the *Growler*. As an eyewitness remembered:

> Old Mrs. Smith moved and left her house alone, with the principal part of her furniture – Col. Murray, who commanded the expedition called at her house, and on finding that it had been deserted, enquired whether it was not the residence of Sidney Smith, when at home, and on being informed that it was, placed a centinel at the door, with instructions to protect every thing appertaining to it from harm; and Mr. Bleecker informs me, that every thing was found by the family when they returned, exactly as they were left – that no person had been in the house.[129]

In the last summer of the war, northern New York became the stage for the largest British offensive of the conflict, aimed at the capture of Plattsburgh. In the first days of September 1814, Lieutenant-General Sir George Prevost led an army of just over 10,000 men across the border and moved south. On 4 September the British occupied the little village of Chazy, New York, and used the law office of Julius Hubbell as their headquarters. When they left the next morning, according to Hubbell family tradition, Mrs. Hubbell accosted one of her unwanted visitors with the comment: "Good-bye, sirs, for a very little while, but I know you'll be back and hanging your heads as you come." She received the somewhat irritable reply: "If a man had said that, I would call him out; but since it is a fair lady ... I reply that when your prophecy comes true, every officer here shall throw his purse on your door step as he passes."[130]

Two days later, Prevost and his army reached Plattsburgh, which they occupied, and waited for the arrival of their naval squadron. Word of their approach had reached the town well in advance and many women and children had already hidden in cellars, fled to the woods, or packed up what they could take, buried what they could not and taken passage by boat down the lake. On 11 September, the Royal Navy squadron appeared and engaged the American naval squadron on the lake, commanded by Master Commandant Thomas Macdonough. At the same time, the British land forces moved against fortified American positions at the south end of Plattsburgh. The naval engagement commenced at 9 A.M., and the roar of the broadsides could be heard across the lake in Middlebury, Vermont. It ended two and a half hours later with the British naval commander dead and all his vessels flying the Stars and Stripes. The

The Battle of Lake Champlain, 1814. This view of Lake Champlain, scene of an American victory over the Royal Navy in September 1814, shows the lighthouse on Cumberland Head. To the right and rear of the lighthouse lies a bay, along whose eastern shore British troops with their batteries of artillery were poised to do battle with an American force. After the British naval defeat, Lieutenant-General Sir George Prevost, in command of the British troops, ordered a retreat. (Benson Lossing, *The Pictorial Field-Book of the War of 1812.*)

land attack had just commenced when Prevost received news of the defeat on the lake and he immediately called it off and ordered a retreat.

Many of the people in Plattsburgh retained vivid memories of that memorable day in September 1814. Mary Sheldon, just eight years old, recalled hearing

> cannon and muskets at the time of the battle ...... I saw British soldiers frequently ...... Some of the women with the British army stopped ... and did their washing. They came up to our house and borrowed an iron kettle of us, which they never returned ...... Two women brought two large mules and kept them in our barn one night at least. They expected to live here and take possession of the country clear to New York, but they didn't.[131]

Mary Williams, aged eighteen at the time, recalled a neighbour telling her, "the British are coming, You must get out!" Mary and a friend rode off to "keep the British from getting their horses."[132] Then they heard that a British captain and sergeant were lying dead in a nearby barn and went to see for themselves. Sure enough,

> The captain was shot behind the ear, but the bullet did not come through his head ... The sergeant was shot in the mouth. Blood was oozing from his mouth like beer ... A militia man took off the captain's shoes and stockings and put them on his own feet, saying that he needed them the most.[133]

As the downcast British army retreated through Chazy, Hubbell family legend has it that several officers threw their purses on the doorstep of the family home.

Admiral Cockburn burning and plundering Havre de Grace. Rear-Admiral George Cockburn was sent to North America in 1813 to inject new life into British naval operations. He embarked on a series of raids in the Chesapeake Bay area as part of his orders to "capture and destroy trade and shipping" and in early May 1813 attacked Havre de Grace, Maryland. The local people could not raise the $20,000 ransom demanded for the preservation of their town, and this scene, sketched during the raid, shows property on fire, British marines and sailors looting furniture and personal belongings, and local citizens remonstrating with Cockburn's officers. (From a sketch made on the spot by an unknown artist. Anne S.K. Brown Military Collection, Brown University Library, Providence, Rhode Island.)

CHAPTER TEN

"The anguish of such hours."
The Atlantic and Gulf Coasts

The Star that in thy Banner shine,
Shall rain destruction on thy foes,
Yet light the brave of ev'ry clime,
To Kindred friendship and repose;
Rise, Columbia! brave and free!
Thy thunder, when in battle hurl'd,
Shall rule the billows of the sea,
And bid defiance to the world.[1]

Despite widespread trepidation along the Atlantic seaboard of the United States that the war would bring a British blockade and landings, initially at least this did not turn out to be the case, and a succession of American naval victories over British warships in the early months of the war caused fear to be replaced by rejoicing. Britain was slow to respond to the American war because it still had a huge military commitment in Europe and did not want to discourage the shipment of American grain to British troops in the Peninsular War nor deflate New England's opposition to the War of 1812. Hence, the Royal Navy did not blockade most of the Middle and Southern American states until 1813 and New England until 1814.

Not that evidence of war was entirely absent from the region. In September 1813, Elizabeth Oakes Smith of Cape Elizabeth, Maine, was present when the brig USS *Enterprise* returned to Portland with her prize, HMS *Boxer*, after defeating that ship in battle. Elizabeth hurried into town to find anxious wives waiting on the quayside. As the two ships approached the harbour to solemn gun salutes, she observed "the blackened hulls, the shattered masts, the burnt and riven canvas," and even stains where blood had streamed down the sides of the vessels. She also saw "a row of objects … over which were folds of canvas and shattered flags. These were the bodies of the noble dead."[2]

The British blockade was gradually expanded, however, until by April 1814 it covered the entire Atlantic coast of the United States. Along the northern reaches there were frequent landings to procure food and water, and the occasional attack. In the spring of 1814, Lieutenant Henry Napier was an officer in the frigate HMS *Nymphe*, patrolling off New England with the task of destroying American coastal trade. The *Nymphe* was successful in creating alarm along the entire seaboard as far north as Boston, "particularly the unfortunate women and children, who had least reason to be alarmed."[3] Sympathetic to their plight, young Napier commented that "making prize money resembles killing a sheep; one likes to eat it but cannot bear the distress of the animal's death."[4] The considerate Napier always tried to treat American civilians well and on one occasion chose not to burn a captured vessel because she "belonged to an old man who had a wife and eight children and had lost $20,000 within two years."[5] As Napier commented, "Destroying this, his last, would have ruined him."

In June 1814, Napier encountered a courageous young American woman. He was after a herd of cattle that had been observed from the *Nymphe* and led a party of eighteen sailors – with visions of fresh beef preoccupying them – ashore near Gloucester, Massachusetts. The animals managed to outrun the sailors, leaving Napier and his men with no alternative but to "make use of our muskets."[6] The entire episode was witnessed by a "fine little girl" to whom the cattle clearly belonged, and she "very gallantly came and drove them away in the face of about eighteen armed men and a great gun." As Napier commented, "very few females, or even boys, would have done this, which shewed as much goodness of heart as intrepidity of mind."[7] He had to admire her even though she thwarted his plans and caused him and his men to return to their ship empty-handed.

Maine, which was then part of Massachusetts, was subjected to a more serious incursion in June 1814, when a British amphibious force seized Eastport on Moose Island in Passamaquoddy Bay. For years, Eastport had enjoyed a "somewhat dubious prominence" through a flourishing international commerce in contraband goods that had attracted "many shrewd and hard-bitten Yankee traders."[8] The town had maintained what amounted to a virtual truce with British North America since the start of hostilities, and under British occupation life in the seaport continued much as usual. The day the British arrived, the women of the town remembered the streets being bright with "scarlet and naval blue, and the wharves piled high with cannon and armaments." Curious, the townspeople watched as the British naval commander came ashore with due pomp and ceremony, and whispers passed among the spectators that he was a man of great repute. They were witnessing the arrival of Captain Sir Thomas Masterman Hardy, a close friend of the late Admiral Horatio Nelson and commanding officer of Nelson's flagship at the Battle of Trafalgar. The women of Eastport who met Hardy at one of his frequent receptions, held at his quarters ashore or on his ship, HMS *Ramillies*, found the "tall and rather corpulant" officer with his "mild and dignified manner" to be a charming host.[9]

The defences of Eastport were soon strengthened and a garrison of 800 British regulars, along with their camp followers, took up residence. They behaved correctly. A school was set up for the officers' and soldiers' children, the rights and property of civilians were scrupulously observed, and justice was meted out promptly. The citizens of Eastport were asked, however, to take an oath of allegiance to the Crown or face deportation, in which case their property would be disposed of as the occupiers saw fit. Such an oath troubled many Americans but most took it after Captain Hardy made the wise suggestion that it should be

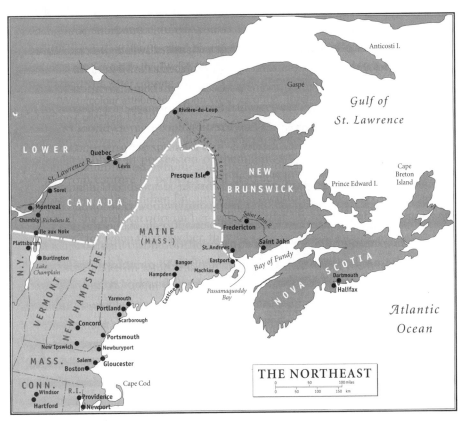

regarded as "an oath of neutrality" rather than one of "perpetual allegiance."[10] Eastport actually fared well under the Union Jack. In legal terms, the British army commander acted as chief administrator, judge and jury. He was assisted by his town major, who functioned as the chief of police, and by the garrison and barrack quartermaster-sergeant, serving as town constable. There was little serious crime or plundering by the invaders. In October 1814 a new commander arrived – Lieutenant-Colonel Joseph Gubbins, whom we have met before and of whom it was said by the American population that "on the whole he was very fair."[11] Gubbins, his wife, Charlotte, their seven children and their servants took over one of the finest properties on Moose Island, a two-storey federal-style mansion. It may have been Charlotte Gubbins who made a gift of "a small old-fashioned gold brooch, embellished with garnets and seed pearls" to a local woman. It became the highly prized heirloom of an American whose great-grandmother had received it as a gift from the wife of an English officer living at Eastport during the war.[12]

Business and entertainment flourished in the town under British occupation and the scarlet-coated officers became the local social magnets. They set up their mess in the main tavern, which was soon a daily gathering place for the most important people on the island, and brought the tavern-keeper so much business that he and his wife were able to retire shortly after the occupation ended, "saying they had made enough money."[13] The townswomen of Eastport were fascinated when they visited the quarters of the British officers and their families, where they observed a lifestyle very different from their own. They were full of admiration for the fine furniture and accoutrements, the courteous manners of their hosts and the gentility of their wives. The British mixed freely, spent freely and settled debts without delay or dispute, and although the people of Eastport did not relish being under a foreign flag, the occupation was marked largely by mutual respect and amicability on both sides. It also brought home the fact that the war did not reflect the true feelings of the common people of both belligerent nations. One suspects that, when Moose Island was returned to the United States after the war, the ladies of Eastport may have voiced some regret that the days of dinners, balls and other entertainments were at an end, for peacetime life would not be nearly as lively.

A similar situation prevailed at Castine, Maine, which was occupied by British forces in September 1814. The sight of enemy warships off the little coastal town initially instilled fear in the hearts of the local ladies. "So formidable an appearance did this fleet offer" that the American troops defending fled before the invaders could land and the "whole population turned out to witness the sight, though not without feelings of dismay."[14] Having occupied not only Castine but several neighbouring places, including Hampden, Bangor, Frankfort and Bucksport, Lieutenant-General Sir John Sherbrooke, the British commander, issued a proclamation. This assured Americans that if they would surrender their arms, remain quietly in their homes, pursue their normal daily lives and "refrain from communicating intelligence" to American forces, he would not only support their civil legal machinery but also ensure their "protection and safety" as long as he could buy supplies for his troops.[15]

The local people soon adjusted to the new situation. They became accustomed to the sight of a dozen or more British warships in the harbour and British troops repairing and strengthening the town's defences. Some enemy soldiers actually worked for local civilians although this was "soon forbidden under severe penalty."[16] Housewives made extra cash selling produce to the occupying force but this activity was also stopped when it was found that the British troops were selling their rations in exchange for liquor with the result that, as it was later recalled, there was "a disgraceful amount of drunkenness among the soldiers, and more liquor was used among the inhabitants than would be deemed well at the present day."[17] The good folk were subject to "very many inconveniences and annoyances" until the British left in April 1815, but in general, the occupation seemed to work to the satisfaction of all concerned.

In marked contrast was the experience of Americans living in the Chesapeake Bay area. The bay, an enormous natural gulf bordered by salt water wetlands, shallow creeks and inlets, and fed by numerous rivers, was a vitally important part of the republic. At its entrance stood the well-defended naval base of Norfolk, Virginia, while further up the bay lay Washington, the American capital, and Baltimore. Most of the communities on the Chesapeake, however, were smaller towns and villages engaged in fishing and farming the rolling, fertile countryside to produce grains, tobacco, fruit and vegetables. Life in the bay proceeded peacefully until the first few days of April 1813, when the sight of British warships surveying the coast set alarm bells ringing. In overall command of these ships was Rear-Admiral George Cockburn, a man who would become notorious in the United States for his depredations.[18] Cockburn, an aggressive naval officer with an outstanding record (and brother-in-law of Alicia Cockburn), had orders to blockade the Chesapeake Bay, obtain intelligence on American vessels and "capture and destroy trade and shipping."[19] His presence

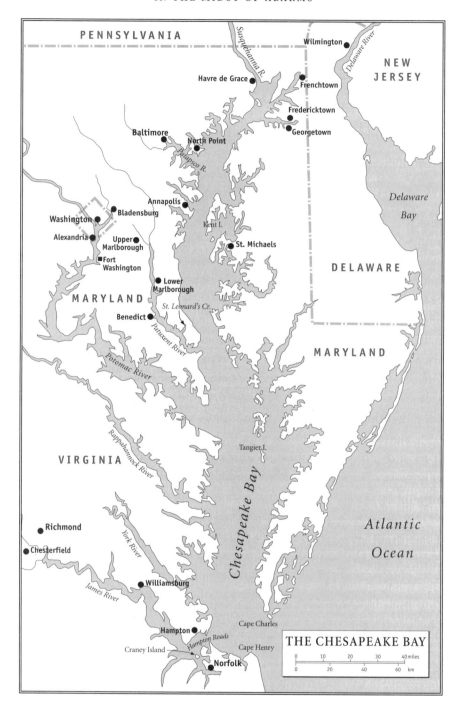

THE CHESAPEAKE BAY

was part of a British strategy to create a diversion on the Atlantic seaboard in an attempt to draw American forces away from the northern theatre of war and relieve the threat to British North America.

On 29 April 1813, Cockburn landed on an island near the head of Chesapeake Bay. At the sight of the enemy, local fisherfolk hurried off in terror, but when they were well treated by the British, who "appeared very peaceable and friendly with all," the island wives willingly provided the enemy naval officers with accommodation and meals of freshly caught fish. What the Royal Navy took it paid for, to the relief of the inhabitants, who watched as the dashing British "amused themselves with shooting and fishing."[20]

This behaviour soon changed. When Cockburn's squadron passed the nearby town of Havre de Grace[21] at the mouth of the Susquehanna River in the last days of April, the townspeople somewhat rashly opened fire with artillery. Annoyed, Cockburn saw this response as a challenge and decided to attack the little place, which consisted of only fifty to sixty dwellings, one of which was the home of Commodore John Rodgers and his wife, Minerva. Havre de Grace was inhabited by "many pleasant families, which made the society a very agreeable one, especially as they were all hospitable and fond of gaiety," but this happy existence came to an abrupt end on the beautiful, clear early morning of 3 May 1813.[22] A force of fifteen to twenty boats and barges, packed with British troops, was seen approaching, and while drums beat to call out the local militia and the frightened inhabitants rushed half-dressed into the streets, rockets and explosive shells started to rain down. The invaders soon put the militia to flight and the town fell to Cockburn.

Cockburn demanded a sum of $20,000 in ransom, and when the people of Havre de Grace replied that they could not raise that amount, they were told that their town would be destroyed within the hour. In the meantime, British sailors and Royal Marines separated into squads and set to work plundering the contents of local homes. Mrs. Sears, who owned the Columbian Inn but had wisely left it, lost "two boxes of dry goods" to the enemy, while Mrs. Phillips lost "the entire of her furniture, new and elegant," all her "wearing apparel" and some property belonging to her naval officer brother.[23] Mrs. Moore, "wife of Will[ia]m Moore who tends at the Ferry," said later that the raiders "stripped from her shoulders a large silk shawl, took her children's clothing" and even her washing, "but no matter, it was plunder."

One house, that of a Miss Polly McCaskey, a shopkeeper, was set on fire three times, but as one onlooker remembered, the fire was extinguished on each occasion "by a faithful, resolute young negro girl, belonging to" Polly, whose "conduct on this day, in many respects, deserves lasting consideration."[24] Miss McCaskey had every reason to be grateful for the loyalty of her slave and for the fact that she had a lucky escape, for "while in bed, an eighteen pounder [round shot] passed through the wall where she lay." An unfortunate woman with "an infant at the breast" was so "horror-struck by the outrageous proceedings around her," that she sat down to await her fate. It appears that the British troops "despoiled her and her child of their clothes" and "one villain actually tore from her neck, and carried away, the handkerchief that covered her bosom." The author of these accounts concluded with the rhetorical question: "Are these the 'religious' and 'liberty-loving' English?"[25]

When the British sailors and marines reached a large, elegant brick house on high ground overlooking the village, they were met by three ladies who had taken shelter there, among whom was Minerva Rodgers. Minerva, her sister-in-law, Mrs. Pinckney, and a Mrs. Goldsborough sought out Rear-Admiral Cockburn, begging him to spare the house and the remainder of Havre de Grace. Their entreaties must have had some effect as the destruction ceased, but when the women returned to the mansion they found it had been plundered and set on fire.[26] The post road from Baltimore to Philadelphia passed through Havre de Grace, and one lighter moment in the raid came when the regular stage coach between the two cities stopped at the Colonial Inn to find British troops awaiting it. Among the passengers were merchants, tradesmen and some ladies who were "milliners with the latest fashions from Paris." All survived "without

Minerva Rodgers's home on Main Street.
During the British attack on Havre de Grace, Minerva Rodgers, wife of Commodore John Rodgers, was among several local women who met with Rear-Admiral George Cockburn and urged him to discontinue burning homes in the town. Her courageous intervention saved her property from destruction, and from its dormer windows in September 1814 an alarmed Minerva espied a fleet of enemy ships carrying the British expeditionary force, fresh from its invasion of Washington, towards Baltimore. (Benson Lossing, *The Pictorial Field-Book of the War of 1812*.)

loss," except a luckless milliner from Georgetown, some of whose finery "had been purloined by an individual who ought to have known better."[27] Whoever that individual was, he was reprimanded by Cockburn, who insisted that he return "the spoils *in propria persona* to the forlorn damsel."

A comprehensive description of what happened that day is contained in a letter written by an unnamed woman at Havre de Grace to her brother in Philadelphia:

> Since I wrote you last, Havre de Grace has been visited by a terrible bombardment. It commenced on Monday the 3d at daylight. Such a scene I never before experienced. On the report of guns we immediately jumped out of our beds; and from the top of the house could plainly see the balls and hear the cries of the inhabitants. We ran down the road, and soon began to meet the distressed people, women and children, half naked; children enquiring for their parents, parents for their children, and wives for their husbands. It appeared to us as if the whole of the town was on fire. I think this act, committed without any previous warning, has degraded the British flag.
>
> The enemy robbed every house of every thing valuable that could be carried away, leaving not a change of raiment to one of ten persons; and what they could not take conveniently, they destroyed by cutting in pieces or breaking to atoms. The admiral himself was present at this work of destruction, and gave orders for it to his officers.[28]

The woman concluded: "such wanton barbarity among civilized people, I have never heard of," but she was able to report that "the whole squadron left our waters yesterday, to our unspeakable joy."

Cockburn considered the raid on Havre de Grace a success but American newspapers expressed understandable outrage and described the British as "wantonly villainous and deliberately cruel and base" to have reduced many of the residents of the little town to "houseless wretchedness and pressing want."[29]

The British raids on Maryland continued. In attacks on Georgetown and Fredericktown at the mouth of the Sassafras River on 6 May, many people in both places lost their homes and possessions. A Mrs. Miers, who kept a small grocery at Fredericktown, suffered "much pillage, and in clothing," while a Mrs. Bunker watched as her home and coachmaker's shop were burnt.[30] In Georgetown Miss Anne Pierce lost her house, as did Mesdames Down, Wilson and Freeman, all widows. Mrs. Mary Henny lost a storehouse, Mrs. Mary Everet's carriage house was torched, and Widow Percie's dwelling was "plundered and furniture destroyed."[31] Finally, the enemy "took from the ears of Mrs Williamson, who lives at the mill, her earrings."

Standing alone in the face of the enemy invaders took a good deal of nerve in the prevailing climate of war, but some women seem to have been determined to show that they were anything but shrinking violets. Kitty Knight, the daughter of a prominent citizen of Georgetown, is credited with saving a number of homes from being burned by the British during the raid. Since most able-bodied American men were serving with their local militia, only older men, women and children remained in Georgetown when the British landed. Beside two fine brick residences they encountered Kitty Knight, by all accounts a beautiful and accomplished woman, whose "tall and graceful" form had been seen in earlier years dancing with President George Washington himself at a ball in Philadelphia.[32] Under a flag of truce, Kitty stood her ground and asked Rear-Admiral Cockburn not to give the order to set the two houses alight. The British had already put the torch to one of the buildings but Kitty is reported to have "stamped the flames out twice" before managing to convince the admiral to stop the wanton destruction.

Given Cockburn's reputation, it seemed unlikely that he would respond positively to such a request, but Kitty Knight's entreaties moved him to the extent that he ordered his troops to retreat, leaving a church and several houses still standing. The surviving buildings of Georgetown became monuments to the memory of Kitty Knight's "noble and hazardous act."[33] She was not forgotten, and after her death a newspaper article credited "her heroism at the burning of Georgetown" with saving "several families from being made homeless and friendless by the fire and sword." The following verse, which commemorated brave Kitty, was later published:

> A maiden fair, with courage bold,
> With spirit pure and high,
> Displayed her flag of truce, and all
> For poor humanity.[34]

Apparently, Kitty Knight was not the only plucky woman in Georgetown. Under a flag of truce two others, a Miss O'Neill and a Miss Oliver, went on board a British ship to plead for the return of their property. They witnessed the gallant side of their enemies as they were "received with much attention, and every refreshment and comfort offered by the officers."[35]

Such friendly exchanges were not uncommon, but worse was to come in the Chesapeake. After receiving reinforcements, Cockburn attacked Craney Island at the entrance to Norfolk harbour on 21 June but was decisively rebuffed. Angered, on 25 June he attacked and captured the village of Hampton, Virginia,where the British not only looted freely but some of them assaulted several local women, the worst incident of its kind during the war and one that is more fully discussed in the next chapter.

Following a quiet spell that lasted over the winter of 1813-1814, Cockburn resumed his raiding operations in the spring. Dolley Madison was deeply concerned about the British threat to the area, feelings which were far from misplaced. As she informed a friend: "I will yet hope we may have no more war" but, "If we do, alas! alas! we are not making ready as we ought to do." In her view, the Congress seemed to "trifle away the most precious of their days, – days that ought to be devoted to the defence of their divided country."[36]

When British ships returned to Chesapeake Bay in 1814, among them was the thirty-eight-gun frigate HMS *Menelaus*, commanded by Captain Sir Peter Parker, who had served at Trafalgar on board HMS *Victory* and was cousin to the poet Lord Byron. Parker spent much of the summer probing the defences of the bay area, gathering intelligence and making small incursions. According to one his officers, he landed at St. George's Island near the mouth of the Potomac River one afternoon with a party of sailors and surrounded a house near the beach, which he knew to belong to an American militia officer. So stealthily did the British approach that the occupants, "three young ladies sitting quietly round a tea-table" with their sewing, had not the slightest idea that they were about to entertain unwelcome guests.[37]

The arrival of the armed party brought a "hasty scream of terror and astonishment," but Parker, one of "the handsomest men in the navy," treated the American girls with every courtesy.[38] He explained with regret that since their father was an active militia officer, it was his duty to set fire to their house but he would give them ten minutes to remove their most valuable personal effects. The young ladies, "endeavoured, by all the arts of their sex," to make the British naval captain change his mind. They "threw themselves on their knees, begged, implored, urged," Parker to "respect their forlorn, unprotected situation, and to leave them to their home, their wretchedness, and their tears." One sister seized his arm in desperation and pressed against it, the second watched his every expression and the third knelt like "a supplicating angel" at his feet, but to no avail. When the ten minutes had expired, Parker gave the order to set the house on fire and then "wept like a child" as he watched the conflagration along with the distraught young women.[39] As one of his officers later wrote, "no man will say that the ladies were not handsomely denied."

One of the most significant events of the War of 1812 witnessed by women was the British occupation of Washington in August 1814. On the morning of Thursday, 18 August 1814, news that a large number of British ships had anchored in the Patuxent River galvanized the people of Washington and set off a panic. Many inhabitants began to pack their bags and the roads out of the city in all safe directions were soon full of people determined to escape with as many possessions as they could take. On 20 August, British troops under the command of Major-General Robert Ross began to disembark from their ships and two days later, to advance on the capital.

As Tuesday 23 August dawned and the city's mayor dealt with enquiries from anxious citizens, Eleanor Jones, wife of Secretary of the Navy William Jones, wrote a tactful note to Dolley Madison begging to be excused from an engagement that evening. "In the present state of alarm and bustle of preparation," said Mrs. Jones, it might be "more convenient to dispense with the enjoyment of your hospitality today."[40] Dolley Madison was only too ready to forgo the arrangement, being preoccupied with the safety of her husband and his people. Knowing the president had gone to be with American troops preparing to face their enemy outside the city, she waited and wondered, and well she might, for that day at Bladensburg, not far from the capital, Major-General Ross and his men met the American defenders of Washington in battle.

Dolley was determined to remain at the presidential mansion until she was sure her husband was safe. She only had her gardener, her French doorkeeper and a handful of loyal African-Americans for company, including her maid, Sukey, and her butler, John Freeman, and his wife. These people were devoted to the Madisons, and along with the one hundred or so other slaves kept by Dolley and James Madison in Washington and at Montpelier, their country home, they were well treated. Paul Jennings, personal retainer to the president, "never knew him to strike a slave; neither would he allow an overseer to do it." They "generally served him very faithfully," as they did Dolley, who was as beloved by her servants as by everybody else in Washington.[41] On this, one of the most unforgettable days of her life, Dolley passed the time by writing a letter to her sister, Anna Cutts. "Since sunrise," she wrote, her pen dashing hastily across her notepaper, "I have been turning my spy-glass in every direction and watching

Before the burning. The official residence of President James Madison and his wife, Dolley, as it looked before the British invasion of Washington in 1814. With the city still under construction, the house stood with open space around it. Inside, Dolley Madison had completed an ambitious programme of tasteful refurbishment and the house contained many fine furnishings, fixtures and fittings. (Gaillard Hunt, *Life in America One Hundred Years Ago*.)

with unwearied anxiety, hoping to discern the approach of my dear husband and his friends."[42] By now she had received two despatches from the president, the latest of which was "alarming." The enemy "seemed stronger than had been reported," and President Madison had alerted his wife to be prepared "at a moment's warning to enter my carriage and leave the city."[43]

As British and American troops engaged at Bladensburg, the Americans, superior in number, used their artillery to good effect. Among them were sailors and marines, many of whom were "tall, strapping negroes" who "fought splendidly," but it was not long before they began to give way in the face of their enemy.[44] Rosalie Stier Calvert's home was close to the fighting, which she could glimpse from her windows. As she commented later, "I saw several cannonballs with my own eyes," and her husband, George, helped to bury the dead after the battle.[45] By 3 P.M. on 23 August 1814 news of the American defeat had reached Washington, and as Dolley Madison scribbled urgently to her sister, "two messengers, covered with dust, come to bid me fly."[46]

Mrs. Madison had already packed "as many Cabinet Papers into trunks as will fill one carriage" and had also crammed it full with "the plate and most

valuable portable articles" from her official residence.[47] By now she was resigned to the fact that her private property must be sacrificed and that people
would blame her husband for the disaster that seemed likely to befall the capital. Among treasured items in the president's house was a portrait of George
Washington, and as the minutes ticked away, Dolley Madison wrote to her sister,
Anna,

> I insist on waiting until the large picture of General Washington is secured,
> and it requires to be unscrewed from the wall. This process was found too
> tedious for these perilous moments; I have ordered the frame to be broken,
> and the canvas taken out. It is done! and the precious portrait placed in the
> hands of two gentlemen of New York, for safe keeping.[48]

Knowing she must leave the city before "the retreating army will make me
a prisoner in it," Dolley concluded her letter to her sister, not knowing "when I
shall see you or write you, or where I shall be to-morrow."[49] As her butler and
his wife set off with a feather bed, the only major item of furniture to be saved
from the presidential mansion, Dolley and her servant, Sukey, were driven with
all haste to Georgetown Heights. When her husband returned briefly to his
residence, it was deserted. He set off again in the hope of finding his wife, but
Dolley was already well on her way to the home of a friend, Mrs. Love, who lived
a few miles beyond Georgetown.

Much has been written about the British occupation of Washington. Among
the most detailed accounts were those left by women who witnessed it, in particular the diaries of Washington commentator Margaret Bayard Smith and
Anna Maria Thornton, wife of architect Dr. William Thornton. Mrs. Thornton's eyewitness description traces events from 18 August until 10 September
1814.[50] The Thorntons were among those who decided to remain in the city in
the hope of saving their property, as did Mary Hunter, wife of a minister, the
Reverend Andrew Hunter. Mrs. Hunter had long since despatched her husband
and children to the country and was rather a "formidable lady," who was determined not to see her home despoiled.[51]

Washington's most eminent physician, Dr. James Ewell, his wife, Margaret,
and their daughters were also at their house when American troops galloped
into town shouting, "Fly! Fly! The ruffians are at hand! If you cannot get away
yourselves, for God's sake send off your wives and daughters."[52] It was too late
to escape from the city and as Dr. Ewell heard his panic-stricken wife crying
distractedly, "What shall we do? What shall we do? Yonder they are coming," he

Anna Maria Brodeau Thornton (*c.*1775-1865) was the wife of Dr. William Thornton, inventor, superintendent of patents and the architect who designed the Capitol building in Washington. A member of the city's high society, Mrs. Thornton's eyewitness account of the British invasion of Washington in August 1814 is an important record of this notable event. (Print from a watercolour by Dr. William Thornton. Author's collection.)

decided that the safest place for the ladies would be the house of Mrs. Orr, a bedridden neighbour, who had already sent word that she would be grateful for company. Dr. Ewell reasoned that the enemy would behave with some decency towards a sick woman and those caring for her.[53]

Knowing that the American commanding officer, Brigadier-General William H. Winder, could not defend the city, one soldier reported seeing women and children running in the streets "in a state bordering on distraction" as they asked themselves, "what is to become of us all?"[54] Yet amid the panic, Washington's free black people were seen conducting themselves "with the utmost order and propriety," as "became patriots," and with "scarcely an exception of any failing to be on the spot."[55] By mid-afternoon on 23 August 1814 Washington was silent. Anna Maria Thornton's journal noted that "nearly All the moveable property taken away – offices shut up & all business at a stand." She and her husband decided, late in the day, to make for the Georgetown Heights, where they joined a number of other people they knew.[56]

As the light faded on the evening of 23 August 1814, Major-General Robert Ross and his men marched into Washington unopposed, accompanied by the man that everyone feared the most, Rear-Admiral George Cockburn. Columns of British troops entered Pennsylvania Avenue and passed the homes of two neighbours, Mrs. Bender and Mrs. Varnum, whose husbands had gone to fight with the militia and whose servants had long since fled. When she saw British soldiers coming down the street in their red coats, a terrified Mrs. Bender hurried to her neighbour's house "clutching a camphor bottle in one hand and a handkerchief in the other."[57]

Apart from some sporadic musket and rocket fire, there was little general disturbance but attention was soon drawn to a far bigger conflagration to the south where the city's naval yard had been set alight to prevent public stores and shipping from falling into enemy hands. Then, to the horror of the few remaining city residents, the British applied torches to the Capitol building and all that it contained, and sparks from the fire began to spread. The burning of Washington's public buildings was, to a degree, a retaliation for the American burning of Newark and other Upper Canadian villages the previous year, and the sight of many of its official structures on fire had an enormous impact upon Washingtonians. As the redoubtable Mrs. Hunter wrote after watching the scene from her house, "no pen can describe the appalling sound that our ears heard and the sight that our eyes saw."[58]

Dr. James Ewell and his wife were still with their bedridden neighbour when they discovered that the British officers, Ross and Cockburn, had decided to use their house as a headquarters. The general told Dr. Ewell politely that he would try to be "as little trouble as possible" and that Mrs. Ewell should be told that it was perfectly safe for her to return home for the night. "I am myself a married man, have several sweet children, and venerate the sanctities of the conjugal and domestic relations," Ross is said to have told the doctor, who felt reassured that his family and property would be unharmed.[59]

Mrs. Barbara Suter, a widow with a boarding house on the corner of Pennsylvania Avenue and 15th Street, also received a visit from Major-General Ross that night. Her lodgings were among those closest to the presidential mansion and it was late in the evening when she realized that British troops had surrounded the place. For Mrs. Suter, it had been a week of "great trouble, hardly sleeping at night, and all the day time spent in fright," and when General Ross entered her house and explained that he had "come, madam, to sup with you," a very nervous Mrs. Suter told him she had no food to offer and encouraged him to try a hotel nearby.[60] Ross, however, insisted that he would return to eat later, leaving Mrs. Suter to hastily kill and cook some chickens, and warm some bread.

The general and his men made their way to the president's house where they toasted their success with some excellent Madeira wine and sampled some of the hurriedly abandoned food that had been intended for dinner that day. Ross had told Dr. Ewell, "I make no war on ... ladies" and had sent a note addressed to Dolley Madison in which he promised her "an escort to whatever place of safety she might choose."[61] He had heard "so much praise" of Mrs. Madison that "I would rather protect than burn a house which sheltered so excellent a lady." However, with the house deserted and the lady long gone, the order was given to burn it and as the flames took hold, they began to destroy all the fine furnishings and fittings Mrs. Madison had so carefully chosen.

To the residents of Washington who remained in the city, that night was one of dismay and terror. Few civilians in or near Washington could sleep and most, like Anna Maria Thornton, watched the "conflagration of our poor undefended and devoted city," as the British continued to set fire to its public buildings.[62] Mary Hunter contemplated the extraordinary brightness of the fires from her upper windows for, as she wrote, "few thought of going to bed."[63] A little later, restless and having joined several other ladies in the street, a surprised Mrs. Hunter met Rear-Admiral Cockburn, who appeared more chivalrous than his reputation had led her to believe. He asked her and all the ladies present,

> in a very particular manner if they had sustained any injury – if any of the soldiers had come into our houses, or taken any thing from us. He intreated us if any thing of that nature occured that we would immediately complain, and they should be punished.[64]

The destruction was not quite at an end, however, for Cockburn insisted on burning the office of the *National Intelligencer*, Washington's newspaper, whose editor had for many months attacked him in print for his depredations in the Chesapeake. Cockburn was dissuaded by civilians who told him that the newspaper building was a rented property and that its destruction would harm an innocent man. While a local mob ransacked what was left of the Navy Yard and embarked on a bout of looting private homes, British troops, who generally respected private property, set fire to other targeted official buildings and disposed of quantities of munitions at a government arsenal.

Throughout that day the weather had been sultry, and in the early hours of 24 August 1814 a violent storm broke over Washington. British Captain John Gleig described how the "flashes of lightning vied in brilliancy with the flames which burst from the roofs of burning houses," while the thunder "drowned for a time the noise of crumbling walls, and was only interrupted by the occasional roar of cannon, and of large depots of gunpowder, as they one by one exploded."[65] The weather only added to "a night of terror and dismay" which the residents would never forget.

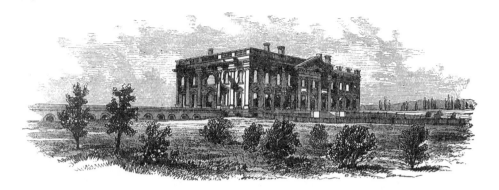

After the burning. A shell was all that remained of the president's house after British troops invaded Washington and set many of its public buildings alight in late August 1814. Contrary to popular belief, the term "White House" was in use before the war as the building had been whitewashed before 1812. It was rebuilt in the postwar years and eventually became one of the most prominent official residences in the world. (Benson Lossing, *The Pictorial Field-Book of the War of 1812*.)

When Major-General Ross returned to his headquarters at the Ewell house, he spent much of the remainder of that night commiserating with Dr. Ewell on the hardships of war. Ross told him he very much regretted having to bring such calamity upon the American capital in retaliation for the burning of towns and villages in Upper Canada, and he repeated his regret to Mrs. Ewell when she returned to her home early the next morning.

As the day progressed, storm clouds gathered and in the early afternoon of 24 August another tempest even more ferocious than the first unleashed itself on the city. The sky was so dark that it looked to Captain Gleig "as if the sun had long set, and the last remains of twilight had come on."[66] With the noise of the wind and thunder, the "crash of falling buildings, and the tearing of roofs as they were stript from the walls," the result was "the most appalling effect I ever have, and probably ever shall witness," he wrote. From her Georgetown eyrie, Anna Maria Thornton later recorded that it seemed "as if the Elements were conspiring to make the scene & times truly awful."[67]

With the coming of dusk that evening, Ross began to move his troops out of the city and back to their ships in the Patuxent. The operation was carried out stealthily, leaving campfires burning and a handful of soldiers who gave the impression that the army had settled for the night. In strict silence the main body of the invasion force made its way out of Washington and was back at the river before anyone in the city realized it.

Four days later Dolley Madison returned to Washington and went straight to the home of her sister, Anna, where she and the president would remain until more permanent living arrangements could be found. Dolley's feelings on seeing the devastated city were predictable. "I cannot tell you what I felt on re-entering it," she later wrote to her friend Mary Latrobe. "Such destruction – such confusion."[68] People came to pay their respects to her, and when Anna Maria Thornton arrived she found Mrs. Madison "very violent against the English."[69] This was no surprise, for the president's house, which Dolley had furnished with so much thought and care, was a sad sight. As Margaret Bayard Smith observed: "Mrs. M. seemed much depressed, she could scarcely speak without tears."[70]

Washington remained in a state of alarm for days to come, and every rumour and sound of gunfire threw the city into panic. "What will be our fate I know not," lamented Margaret Bayard Smith, "the citizens who remained are now moving out, and all seem more alarmed than before."[71]

After their success at the capital, Ross and Cockburn moved on to their next objective, the city of Baltimore. On 12 September 1814, Ross's army landed on North Point, east of the city, and advanced on Baltimore, but the British commander was killed when his army encountered an American force under the command of Major-General John Stricker of the Maryland militia. Although the British were able to push the defenders back, their advance halted when they encountered a line of fortifications on the eastern outskirts of Baltimore. Lacking the numbers or the heavy artillery necessary to launch a successful assault, unable to attack and not wanting to withdraw, the invaders held their position while the British fleet bombarded nearby Fort McHenry, hoping to penetrate the defences of the city from the water. This attack, which opened with a heavy assault by shot, shell and rockets fired by a dozen warships, commenced at 7 A.M. on 13 September and lasted more than twenty-four hours.

The bombardment of Fort McHenry was witnessed by many people. To Deborah Cochran of Baltimore, the sight of rockets and shells exploding "like continued flashes of lightning" through the night of 13 September filled her with fright, and as she longed for daybreak she thought "the hours would never roll around."[72] There is some evidence that a woman was among those killed at Fort McHenry. One account, unsigned and undated, speaks of the "wife of a soldier," who "whilst talking to her husband before the tents outside of the Fort was cut in two pieces."[73] Captain Frederick Evans of the U.S. Artillery stated that a woman had just brought water for the officers and men in the fort when a "bombshell hitting her exploded and she was blown to atoms."[74] Other historians who have studied the bombardment in detail believe the woman was from a tavern that stood near the fort, and that there may have been two women, one outside the fort and one inside. If the woman in question was a civilian, perhaps a laundress or even a prostitute, it would explain why her name was not listed among the casualties. Current thinking is that there were more casualties sustained at Fort McHenry than appeared in the official report, and that probably one woman was killed outside the fort during the attack.

At dawn on 14 September when the British ships, having fired between 1,500 and 1,800 projectiles, gave up and sailed away, Fort McHenry remained in American hands – a fact confirmed by the very large national flag flying over it. That proud banner was the handiwork of Mary Pickersgill of Baltimore. More than a year before, the commandant of Fort McHenry, Major George Armistead, had requested that a flag be made for his post "so large that the British will have no difficulty in seeing it from a distance."[75] Shortly thereafter, a deputation of officers called on Mary Young Pickersgill at her house on Albemarle Street in Baltimore. Mary was an excellent seamstress and the widow of John Pickersgill, an English merchant who had been a prominent importer in the city. After his death in 1805, she had set up a flag-making business with the help of her daughter, Caroline, and her mother, Rebecca Young.

Mrs. Young had herself been widowed at a relatively young age and had supported her family of five by making flags and other military items. It was she who had made the first American national flag under George Washington's direction. Pooling their talents and resources, Rebecca and Mary launched their new enterprise in July 1807 with a newspaper advertisement informing the "Military Gentlemen of Baltimore" that they could be "supplied with Silk Standards & Cavalry and other colors of every description, finished in compleat order."[76] The two women worked hard, and it was not long before their business had established a fine reputation. By the outbreak of war, many of the banners made by Mary and Rebecca were to be seen flying from the masts of Baltimore's merchant ships.

The officers who visited Mary Pickersgill in 1813 ordered a large flag to be made for Fort McHenry. Mary accepted the commission, and over the next few weeks she and her daughter, Caroline, worked steadily to cut and measure material from red, white and blue bolts of wool bunting. The flag consisted of

Mary Young Pickersgill (1776-1857), the proprietor of a successful flag-making business in Baltimore, was commissioned in 1813 to make a flag for the city's Fort McHenry. It had to be large enough to be seen by the British if they should decide to launch an assault, and when this occurred in September 1814 the flag became a symbol of hope and defiance. Following her success in business, Mrs. Pickersgill later promoted social causes such as housing, employment and financial aid for disadvantaged women. This picture is from a daguerreotype made in 1850. (Star-Spangled Banner Flag House Collection.)

eight red and seven white horizontal stripes, each two feet in depth, and fifteen white stars that measured two feet from point to point. Sewing all the pieces together required more space than Mary possessed, but fortunately she was able to use the empty malthouse of a nearby brewery. It was here that mother and daughter spread out their cloth and, often working by candlelight, carefully basted together all the different parts of the flag before meticulously stitching them. Caroline later recalled that the flag contained "I think four hundred yards of bunting and my mother worked many nights until 12 o'clock to complete it in the given time."[77] Caroline remembered that her mother was often "down on the floor" of the brewery "placing the stars," each in its correct position, and that she "superintended the topping of it, having it fastened in the most secure manner to prevent its being torn away by balls." Mary's mother, her nieces, Margaret and Jane Young, and probably her servants, all assisted in finishing the flag in six weeks. When completed, it measured 30 feet on the hoist and 42 feet on the fly, and for her work Mary Pickersgill was paid $405.90, according to the official receipt.[78]

When the British attacked Baltimore in September 1814, Mary's flag had been flying above Fort McHenry for more than a year. It was clearly visible over the beleaguered fort on the morning of 14 September and became a symbol of defiance and hope on the part of a young nation. When the frustrated British withdrew, Baltimore and Fort McHenry were safe. Francis Scott Key, a lawyer who had witnessed the bombardment, was so inspired by the sight of the flag aloft that morning that he wrote a poem which opened with the following lines:

> O! say, can you see, by the dawn's early light
> What so proudly we hailed at the twilight's last gleaming?
> Whose broad stripes and bright stars, thro' the perilous fight,
> O'er the ramparts we watched were so gallantly streaming?

Set to music, this poem eventually became the National Anthem of the United States. Fortunately, the Armistead family kept the original flag until 1907, when Eben Appleton, grandson of Major Armistead, donated it to the Smithsonian Institution in Washington, where it can be seen today.

Sewing the republic's most famous flag. Mary Pickersgill is depicted in this fictional representation stitching the stars on the blue canton of the flag she is making for Fort McHenry. She is assisted by her daughter, Caroline, and her niece, Margaret Young. The three American officers looking on are Major George Armistead, commanding officer of the fort, Brigadier-General John Stricker, commander of the local militia, and Commodore Joshua Barney, commander of the United States Navy's Chesapeake flotilla. (Oil on canvas by R. McGill Mackall. Star-Spangled Banner Flag House Collection.)

After the war, Mary Pickersgill and her business prospered. She was soon able to buy the house she had hitherto been renting and in later years, became actively involved in social issues such as housing, employment and financial aid for disadvantaged women at a time when such matters were generally ignored. Mary Pickersgill, who died in 1857, retains an important place in her nation's history for creating the famous flag that played such a prominent role in the defence of Baltimore, and in the shaping of the United States.

As for the attack on Baltimore, Major-General Ross's death seemed, as one of his aides remembered, "to have disorganized the whole plan of proceedings, and the fleet and army rested idle, like a watch without its main spring."[79] The troops re-embarked on 14 September and a few weeks later sailed for Louisiana.

In the autumn of 1814, the focus of the war shifted to the south. By now the war in the north had deteriorated into a stalemate, while on the Atlantic coast, apart from the occasional landing or raid, the Royal Navy contented itself with maintaining a blockade of all major American ports. Following the rebuff at Baltimore, the British naval commanders, Vice-Admiral Sir Alexander Cochrane and the rapacious Rear-Admiral George Cockburn in particular, argued for an attack on New Orleans. Although their army counterparts were less enthusiastic, in November 1814 a combined force headed into the Gulf of Mexico intent on the capture of the "Crescent City."

The Louisiana Territory had only been part of the United States since 1803 when Napoleon sold it to Washington for $15 million and Louisiana retained much evidence of its colonial past. It owed its foundation and many of its customs to the French, and a lot of its public buildings and fine houses to thirty-four years of Spanish rule. Many people there remained persistently French in their language, allegiance and thought and prided themselves on their European culture. They greeted the news that Louisiana was now American with little joy and much resentment.

New Orleans, a major port, slave market and gateway to hard labour in the sugar cane fields, was the largest city in Louisiana. Surrounded by water and swamp, it was a breeding ground for a host of deadly diseases. Despite this danger, the people of the city were considered carefree and fun-loving. When Major-General Andrew Jackson's forces gathered in the city in December 1814 to defend it against attack, the "fair sex" made their support felt. They "animated the ardor of their defenders, and with cheerful serenity at the sound of the drum," they presented themselves at the windows and balconies to applaud the troops going through their evolutions, and to encourage their husbands, sons, fathers, and brothers, to protect them from the insults of our ferocious enemies, and prevent a repetition of the horrors of Hampton."[80]

The British approached New Orleans in mid-December but were thwarted by a well-constructed defensive line that blocked the most direct route to the city. On 8 January 1815, ironically fifteen days after a peace treaty between the belligerents had been signed, the British launched a major attack on Major-General Jackson's defences but were decisively repulsed with heavy losses. Among the British dead was their new commander, Lieutenant-General Sir Edward Pakenham, the brother-in-law of the Duke of Wellington. A few days later, the attacking forces withdrew and New Orleans celebrated. Louise Livingston, who watched some of the military operations from the upper floor of an old plantation-house, described the British attack to her sister-in-law:

Aware of your anxiety to learn our fate, I take up my pen, notwithstanding my agitation, to give you glad tidings. Louisiana is still American. God has granted us a brilliant victory, and has spared the lives of those dear to us.

NEW ORLEANS AND
THE GULF OF MEXICO

Louise D'Avezac y Castera Livingston (1782-1860) was the wife of lawyer Edward Livingston, who was appointed aide to Major-General Andrew Jackson during the Battle of New Orleans. After the fighting was over, Louise set aside her mantle as the leading Creole woman in New Orleans society to help nurse the wounded. In later years when her husband entered politics and was appointed Secretary of State under President Jackson, Louise's popular Washington *salon* became the focal point for foreign society in the capital. (Oil on canvas after an older miniature, attributed to Theobald Chartran. Historic Hudson Valley, Tarrytown, New York.)

On the 8th [of January 1815] the enemy attacked our army and advanced to the base of the rampart, intending to take our lines by assault, but the God of Battles was with us and their defeat complete ......

Indeed, my dear sister, there never was a more glorious victory, nor one that cost less blood. Not a single father of a family was killed, and the joy of the people, thanks be to God, is unalloyed by private sorrow.

Everyone thinks this battle will end the war, and that the enemy will at once re-embark. Should this prove the case, it is impossible to conceive a more brilliant success for American arms or one more full of disaster for the English. I have in the house one of their officers, badly wounded, and it is not without satisfaction that I have received as a prisoner one who came to conquer ......

I will not dwell on all I have endured during the four different engagements of anxiety and terror. Such feelings cannot be described. The battle-ground is only a league from the city, and I could not only hear the booming of the cannon, as the house shook each time, but every musket could be heard also.

All I can say, dear sister, is that people do not often die of it, however great the anguish of such hours.[81]

Once Jackson was sure the British were gone, he brought his troops back into the city, where they were greeted by the entire populace. According to Louise Livingston, the aged, the infirm, the matrons, daughters and children, all went out to meet their deliverers, the saviours of their country. Every countenance was expressive of gratitude – joy sparkled in every feature on beholding fathers, brothers, husbands, sons, who had so recently saved the lives, fortunes and honor of their families.[82]

As for the soldiers, "they once more embraced the objects of their tenderest affections, were hailed by them as their saviours and deliverers, and felt conscious that they had deserved the honorable title." Everyone shared in "the most exquisite sensations of inexpressible joy."[83]

New Orleans celebrated by staging a splendid pageant. It featured a select group of young ladies, "representing the different States and territories … all dressed in white, covered with transparent veils, and wearing a silver star on their foreheads."[84] Each held in one hand a flag inscribed with the name of the state they represented, and in the other, "a basket trimmed with blue ribands and full of flowers." Jackson was congratulated in an address given by a Miss

Scene of thanksgiving. On 21 January 1815, Major-General Andrew Jackson and the main body of his victorious army entered the city of New Orleans and were cheered by almost the entire population. Two days later, Jackson proceeded to the square, pictured here, for a victory ceremony and a performance of the *Te Deum Laudamus* inside the cathedral. Among those in attendance were Louise Livingston, her husband and daughter, Cora. (Benson Lossing, *The Pictorial Field-Book of the War of 1812.*)

Kerr, who was chosen to represent Louisiana, and then walked amongst the young ladies "who strewed his passage with flowers." After that "the day and night were given up to pleasure both by the soldiers and the people."[85]

The experiences of women caught up in the war in the north, and on the Atlantic and Gulf coasts, are a testament to their courage, adaptability, humanity and capacity to endure. As the next chapter will reveal, such qualities were put to an even sterner test when some women, by choice or chance, found themselves playing more active and daring roles in wartime events.

Laura Secord (1775-1868) walked more than twenty miles across rough country in June 1813 to warn British troops of an impending American attack. She lived long enough to receive belated recognition for her contribution and is today one of Canada's best-known female historical figures. Here, she is depicted in later years. (Benson Lossing, *The Pictorial Field-Book of the War of 1812*.)

CHAPTER ELEVEN

"Boldly I did fight ... although I'm but a wench."

Women as Combatants, Agents and Prisoners of War

I was brought up in Yorkshire and when I was sixteen
I ran away from home, me lads, and a soldier I became
With a fine cap and feathers, likewise a rattling drum
They learned me to play upon the rub-a-dub-a-dum.

And it's many is the pranks that I saw among the French
And boldly I did fight, me boys, although I'm but a wench
And in buttoning up me trousers so often have I smiled
To think I lay with a thousand men and a maiden all the while.

And they never found me secret out until this very hour
For they sent me up to London to be sentry at the Tower
And a lady fell in love with me and I told her I's a maid
And she went unto me officer and me secret she betrayed.[1]

In a time when the idea of a female combatant was unthinkable, there were a few women who disguised themselves and fought as men on land or sea. Those who answered the call to arms apparently did so because of a thirst for adventure, love, necessity or a desire to escape from their homes or domestic situations. Among them was Sarah Roberts from England, who enlisted under her father's name as a soldier in the British army in the 1790s and served for more than a decade, attaining the rank of sergeant before she was unmasked after falling ill.[2] A well-known woman warrior from the Napoleonic period is

Nadezhda Durova, a Russian girl who enlisted as a man in a Cossack regiment in 1806, fought in several battles, was commissioned as an officer and won a medal for gallantry.[3] There are also several cases of women sailors in the Royal Navy in the eighteenth and early nineteenth centuries, one of the most remarkable perhaps being that of a black married woman who, in 1804 at the age of twenty-one, used the alias of William Brown to enlist. She served at least twelve years, attaining the important position of captain of the foretop on the 104-gun ship of the line HMS *Queen Charlotte*.[4] British newspapers also published the story of two unnamed sisters, the daughters of a bankrupt English merchant who, being "too ashamed to beg," dressed as men and joined the crew of a troop ship going to the West Indies, where they "served with credit in two or three actions in those seas."[5]

Are such accounts to be believed? In the case of Sarah Roberts, after her disguise was revealed she married a fellow soldier and bore him several children. As Mrs. Taylor she followed her husband throughout Wellington's Peninsular campaigns, ending up, for a brief period, as a French prisoner of war. She returned to live with her parents in Manchester after her husband's death and her mother "fully corroborated all the circumstances of the daughter's story" to the reporter who wrote about her. After listening to her dramatic tale, he noted that Sarah "is in full hope of obtaining the pension allowed to soldiers for long and faithful services."[6] There is no doubt about Nadezhda Durova, as not only do the official records support her story, but she also published her memoirs, which are available in English translation. "William" Brown's story is also confirmed by naval records and newspaper accounts. The reporter who interviewed her described Brown as a "smart, well-formed figure, about five feet, four inches in height, possessed of considerable strength and great activity" who "in her manner ... exhibits all the traits of a British tar and takes her grog with her late messmates with the greatest gaiety."[7]

To date, the research for this book has uncovered no women disguised as men who served in the ranks of the British or Canadian military or naval forces that fought in the War of 1812. At least three women disguised as men, however, were on American fighting ships during the conflict. In September 1812, Surgeon Usher Parsons of the United States Navy, while accompanying a draft of seamen proceeding to the Great Lakes, recorded in his diary that "We this day discovered among the crew a female clad in sailor's apparel."[8] Unfortunately, Parsons does not say what became of this woman, but she was not the only female combatant to go to sea during the war.

There was also Eliza Romley from New Ipswich, New Hampshire, who was captured while serving in the American squadron on Lake Champlain in 1813. Eliza Romley was listed as prisoner number 240 in the British prisoner of war facility at Quebec, where the entry described her as being nineteen years of age, five feet, six inches tall, with an oval face and tanned complexion, brown hair, blue eyes and a scar on her upper lip. She was documented as arriving at the facility on 9 June 1813, along with other American sailors captured on the US ships *Growler* and *Eagle* after a stiff three-hour battle on 3 June. When the British authorities discovered that Eliza was a woman, she was discharged from custody on 25 June 1813.[9]

Eliza's story is confirmed by the official British records, and the living conditions of her imprisonment were described by Abraham Walter, the pilot of the *Growler*, who managed to escape. Walter swore an affidavit before Judge Henry Delord of Plattsburgh, in which he complained that the prisoners from the two vessels were confined on a prison ship where conditions were "more disagreeable than will be imagined."[10] They received only "spoiled bread" and "exceedingly bad Meat which in almost any other situation would be absolutely not Eatable." Even worse, they were issued "no Liquors, no soap to prevent themselves from becoming Lousy, no candles & none of the other comforts of Life," and Walter maintained that "it was the opinion of all the prisoners that many of them had actually starved to death not being able to eat the Provisions."[11]

Despite his complaints, it sounds as if Walter and his comrades were given standard British rations, which were no great delight to anyone who had to eat them. Even if Eliza Romley served only briefly on a warship, she experienced a naval battle and a short captivity.

Another American woman sailor was on board the American privateer *Revenge*, which was captured by a British warship in 1813. Her case made news on both sides of the Atlantic, for when the woman in question learned she was going to be sent to the naval prison at Portsmouth in England, she unmasked herself. Her story was that she was an orphan who had begged her way to the nearest port, found employment as a landsman on a vessel and then transferred to the *Revenge* at the start of hostilities. "She has about $200 in wages and prize money and wants to be sent home to the United States," reported *Niles' Weekly Register*. "She has a comely face," the paper continued, "sunburnt as well as her hands; and appeared when in men's clothes, a decent well-looking young man."[12]

The idea of women combatants was an intriguing one to many people on both sides of the Atlantic and spawned a number of books, perhaps the most famous being the story of Lucy Brewer, the "female marine," also known as Louisa Baker. *The Adventures of Louisa Baker*, published in Boston in 1815, purported to tell the story of young woman who, after being seduced and abandoned, ran away from home. When she learned she was pregnant, she found a place to stay in Boston only to discover it was a brothel. Following the birth of her baby, Louisa Baker was forced to learn the "trade" and pay her way, but by disguising her sex and calling herself "George," she escaped and enlisted in the United States Marines. After serving on a frigate and seeing much action during the war, Louisa finished her term of enlistment without her sex being detected and eventually returned home to her family to recount her adventures. The book sold well and was followed by two sequels and a rebuttal entitled *A Brief Reply to the Late Writings of Louisa Baker*, supposedly written by the madam of the Boston brothel where Louisa or Lucy had been employed. All four books were popular among young women eager to learn more of the life of this racy heroine, but modern research has revealed that they were actually works of fiction written by one Nathaniel Hill Wright, employed by the Boston publisher Nathaniel Coverly, who received a handsome profit from their sale.[13]

A number of women were employed as intelligence agents, spies or secret messengers during the War of 1812 and seem to have been very successful in these roles. It has been said that women were a "preferred risk" for such assignments in the nineteenth century as, given the conventions of the time, they were not searched as thoroughly as men and, if apprehended, were usually not executed – the standard fate for their male counterparts.[14] Of those women active in intelligence work during the war, most were British or Canadian, possibly because American forces in the northern theatre were on foreign soil.

Among Canadian women, Catherine Pool of the Niagara area "carried provisions to a party of Militia" stationed in her neighbourhood under dangerous conditions and "gave intelligence of the approach of the enemy."[15] Another Niagara resident, Anna Maria Grenville, attested after the war in a land claim she submitted that she had risked her life at the request of Surgeon William Kerr by "conveying important intelligence to his Majesty's Army from said Surgeon Kerr respecting the intended motives of the Buffalo and Genessee Indians" and was "on that account promised a grant of land."[16] After the Battle of Stoney Creek in June 1813, British and Canadian troops combed the countryside for the retreating Americans, and Canadian Captain William Merritt commanded a small force which laid an ambush for "one hundred riflemen and a party of horse."[17] Merritt decided to use an unlikely spy – an older woman whom he persuaded to "reconnoitre and ascertain their number." Unfortunately she was seized and detained by the Americans, but she clearly had an inventive mind, as, according to Merritt, "by an excellent stratagem she got released," returned safely and "told me their situation."[18]

One of the most famous women to act in an intelligence role was Laura Secord of Queenston, Upper Canada, who, in June 1813, undertook a twenty-mile walk through American-occupied territory to deliver vital information to British forces. Laura Secord was a thirty-seven-year-old mother with fair skin, "abundant light brown hair" and "expressive dark eyes."[19] The daughter of a Loyalist from Massachusetts who had settled in the Niagara area, she had married James Secord, a prosperous merchant, and by the outbreak of war the couple and their five children were living "in easy circumstances" in a pleasant house below the Niagara escarpment.[20]

As mentioned in an earlier chapter, James Secord was badly wounded at the Battle of Queenston Heights in October 1812 and had still not recovered when American forces invaded the Niagara area in May 1813. British and Canadian forces withdrew to the area of Burlington Bay but, following their victory at Stoney Creek on 6 June, they established a loose blockade of the American position at Fort George and Newark. There was much skirmishing in the "no man's land" between the two armies. Lieutenant James Fitzgibbon of the 49th Foot was prominent in these activities, operating from a base he had established at De Cou's house, about eighteen miles west of Queenston at the place known as the Beaver Dams. Fitzgibbon's mission was to report on American movements and harass the invaders, and he seems to have set his sights on a unit of mounted volunteers commanded by Captain Cyrenius Chapin of Buffalo, who were guilty of plundering. Chapin, aware of Fitzgibbon and his operations, planned with Colonel Charles Boerstler, commanding the 14th U.S. Infantry Regiment at Fort George, to destroy Fitzgibbon's stronghold at De Cou's house. Chapin believed this mission could be accomplished by "five hundred men with a couple of field pieces."[21] Boerstler was not impressed by Chapin, whom he considered a "vain boasting liar," but was ordered by his superiors to lead a force to "capture or dislodge" Fitzgibbon. On the evening of 23 June 1813, Boerstler set out with a force of about 500 men, composed of Chapin's volunteers, a troop of regular light dragoons, two pieces of artillery and his own 14th Infantry Regiment.

Somehow Laura Secord learned of the plans of Boerstler and Chapin and set out by herself to warn Fitzgibbon. How she came by this intelligence remains unclear, as both Laura and her husband were circumspect in their postwar accounts. In later years Laura would only say that "it was while the Americans had possession of the frontier, that I learned the plans of the American commander."[22] In a memorial written in 1860, she added rather vaguely that she had "frequent opportunities of knowing the moves of the American forces" and "thus was enabled to obtain important information."[23] Her son, Charles, wrote in 1845 that his mother had "frequently met with the American officers" and had overheard one saying to another that they intended to surprise and capture the British troops at the Beaver Dams.[24] Her granddaughter recorded how Laura had told her that some Americans had "come to the house and asked her for something to eat." Having prepared a meal for them that included alcohol, she then listened outside the window and "overheard them say that they would surprise Colonel Fitzgibbon at Beaver Dam."[25] This latter account accords somewhat with that of Charles Secord.

To get from Queenston to the Beaver Dams across rough, swampy country was not an easy undertaking. Not only were there the rigours of the journey itself, but there was also the possibility of rattlesnakes, bears or aboriginal warriors who, even if they were allies, could still be formidable. Much has been written about Laura Secord's famous walk. In February 1820, James Secord, in a petition to the government for compensation for his wife, stated that she "embraced an opportunity of rendering some services, at the risk of her life, in going thro' the Enemies' Lines to communicate information to a Detachment of His Majesty's Troops at the Beaver Dam in the month of June 1813."[26] Some twenty years later, Laura wrote another petition for compensation which was corroborated in full by Colonel James Fitzgibbon, the officer to whom she delivered her information. It stated that "at great Risk peril & danger," she had travelled "on foot & partly in the Night by a circuitous route" through "the enemys lines & Indian Encampments to give important intelligence of a meditated attack of the Americans upon our troops."[27] She did not give a motive for her act, no doubt assuming that people would understand that it stemmed from a willingness to serve Crown and country. Both these petitions were intended to meet specific needs and they suggest that details of the Laura Secord story "changed depending on the narrator and his or her audience."[28]

In 1853, Laura Secord wrote a further account in which she stated that, having learned of the American plans, she determined to "put the British troops

Laura Secord's eventful walk. This scene shows the place where her cross-country route brought Laura Secord to the Twelve Mile Creek (modern-day St. Catharines, Ontario) on 23 June 1813. After crossing it, she proceeded to the British headquarters at Beaver Dams. (Watercolour attributed to John Wesley Cotton. Toronto Public Library, J. Ross Robertson Collection T17102.)

under Fitzgibbon in possession of them, and if possible to save the British troops from capture or perhaps total destruction."[29] This version gives more information on the "Indian Encampments" mentioned previously, as Laura related that she met warriors on her walk and that "by moonlight the scene was terrifying," for when they saw her, they

> all arose and with some yells said "Woman," which made me tremble. I cannot express the awful feeling it gave me, but I did not lose my presence of mind. I was determined to persevere. I went up to one of the chiefs, made him understand that I had great news for Capt. Fitzgibbon and that he must let me pass to his camp, or that he and his party would all be taken. The chief at first objected to let me pass, but finally consented, after some hesitation, to go with me and accompany me to Fitzgibbon's station, which was at the Beaver Dam, where I had an interview with him. I then told him what I had

come for and what I had heard – that the Americans intended to make an attack upon the troops under his command and would, from their superior numbers, capture them all.[30]

Fitzgibbon, forewarned and thus forearmed, succeeded in attacking and capturing Boerstler's entire force at the Battle of the Beaver Dams on 26 June 1813. In the meantime, an exhausted Laura had made her way home, wondering later how she could have "gone through so much fatigue, with the fortitude to accomplish it."[31]

Many questions have arisen over the events surrounding Laura Secord's famous walk, and this author does not propose to speculate further on them. It is also known from the diary of Lieutenant John Le Couteur, who was stationed near the Beaver Dams, that on 24 June 1813, "about half an hour before day break, an Indian brought me a message from their Chief intimating that a strong force of the Enemy with Guns and Cavalry were moving upon us by De Cew's." In other words, news of the American movement reached British troops from an aboriginal source, as well as from Laura Secord.[32]

Laura Secord's walk brought her lasting fame. When the Prince of Wales, later King Edward VII, visited British North America in 1861, she came to his attention when hers was the only female name on a list of veterans of the War of 1812 attached to an address read to the prince when he was at Queenston. The prince had come there to lay a stone to commemorate the death of Major-General Sir Isaac Brock on Queenston Heights, and his interest in Laura led to her receiving a gift of £100 (about $387) in gold. This proved to be the only financial reward she was ever given, nearly half a century after her walk to Beaver Dams.[33]

Laura's famous journey has taken on wider dimensions and greater significance in more modern times. A recent analysis of the evidence concerning her deed maintains that it is symbolic of "the entire pioneer woman's experience in Canadian history" and reflective of individual concepts of "Canadian womanhood."[34] Recently, Laura Secord was chosen as one of only two women among many men to be commemorated with a bronze bust as part of the "Valiants Memorial" in Confederation Square, Ottawa, which is dedicated to those who, through loyalty and courage, contributed to building the Canadian nation.

From New England comes an account of an American woman who proved to be a superb intelligence agent. In that region there was much dissatisfaction with both the war and the Madison administration, and Captain Sir Thomas

Hardy, RN, commanding the British blockading forces at New London, Connecticut, in the summer of 1813, resolved to take advantage of it. He enlisted the aid of James Stewart, the British consul and prisoner agent at New London. An Anglo-Irishman, Stewart was described as "one of those charming types so typical of the Regency period, displaying the manners of a courtier, the scruples of a highwayman, and the social buoyancy of a cork."[35] Because the Royal Navy was regularly seizing American merchant ships, privateers and fishing boats, Stewart's work brought him into frequent contact with Hardy and placed him in an ideal position to undertake intelligence work. Despite the fact that American officials in the New London area were suspicious of his activities and took steps to curb his contact with the blockaders, Stewart provided a stream of accurate and timely information to Hardy.

In the summer of 1813 New London was under a particularly tight blockade because three American warships – the frigates *Macedonian* and *United States* and the brig *Argus* – under the overall command of Commodore Stephen Decatur, were sheltering near the port. Decatur hoped to put to sea again, but while he waited he received few of the invitations from New London society that a national hero might have expected. The New Englanders resented the fact that they were under such close observation by the Royal Navy and held Decatur responsible for interfering with the profitable illegal trade they had previously carried on with British vessels. Decatur, in turn, was very aware of suspicious activity at sea and on shore and, in a mood of frustration and annoyance, complained to the secretary of the navy about the constant communication kept up with the enemy:

> One person has been detected in going alongside of the enemy's ships, he is now confined by order of the Marshall, there is little doubt that he was employed by Mr. Stewart the Agent for Prisoners at this place. It appears by his own acknowledgement that he is an Alien Enemy. I do trust this man may be tryed [sic] as a spy; something should certainly be done to put a stop to this communication.
>
> Mr. Stewart the gentleman above spoken of, appears to have great influence here, he has it in his power, & it is said uses it, to do much injury.[36]

In July 1813, Stewart was ordered to leave New London under suspicion of spying. His departure was reported in *Niles' Weekly Register*, which stated that (like other enemy aliens) he had been "ordered into the interior, where he ought to have been long ago."[37] This development caused a problem for Captain Hardy

No ordinary town. The port of New London, Connecticut, was the scene of much unusual activity during the War of 1812. It served as the base for an intelligence network led by Elizabeth Stewart, daughter of a prominent local family, whose work was of great assistance to the Royal Navy's fleet blockading the coast of New England. Her efforts hampered the escape of Commodore Stephen Decatur's warships. (Benson Lossing, *The Pictorial Field-Book of The War of 1812.*)

but he was quick to take action and managed to engineer Stewart's resignation as a consul, after which he was brought on board HMS *Valiant*, ostensibly to await the next packet ship to Halifax or Bermuda. Stewart, however, left his wife, Elizabeth, and their seven children behind in New London.

American-born Elizabeth Stewart was a native of the town and the daughter of a prosperous local merchant. She was also a woman of considerable standing in the community with a reputation for hosting elegant functions at her father's residence. In a centre that was a natural magnet for anti-government sentiments, Elizabeth's sympathies were well known and her husband's absence in no way curtailed her social activities, under cover of which she apparently assumed control of Hardy's intelligence network, making New London the conduit for a steady stream of information going to the British blockaders.

Towards the end of November 1813 Decatur, still trapped at New London, learned that the Royal Navy was diverting some of its vessels to other points along the coast, and saw an opportunity to escape. He chose the moonless, overcast night of 12 December 1813, the conditions being right for his two frigates to make a cautious attempt to run the blockade. Moving a large ship of war without lights in pitch darkness on a tidal river required a high degree of skill and judgment. Nevertheless, all seemed to be going well until suddenly, near the river mouth, a small blue light was seen ashore. Decatur decided it was a signal and that someone was trying to warn the British that he was attempting to break out. It seemed pretty clear that Elizabeth Stewart's spy network had been doing its work, and after a second blue light was seen on the opposite bank of the river, Decatur called off the attempt.[38]

Angry, Decatur decided to use the press to shame the people of New London and draw attention to the traitors in their midst. A few days later, the *New London Gazette* published a report on the "blue light incident" and declared that "decisive measures have been taken" to detect and bring to punishment the "traitorous wretches who dare to give the enemy every advantage." This report only annoyed the New Londoners, who were angry at the publisher for printing such an article. The incident was denied in a Rhode Island newspaper, which was adamant that it was "blue lights *from the enemy's ships*" that were seen, and none "*proceeding from the land*."[39] Decatur pressed his case in both the local and national press, but his effort did not have the desired effect and Elizabeth Stewart and her network continued to further the British cause by making sure that blue lights kept Decatur and his ships bottled up in port. Eventually, in utter frustration, Commodore Decatur was forced to leave his two frigates trapped near New London and travel overland to New York to take up a new command.

Elizabeth Stewart probably committed treason from love of her husband and hatred of the war. There were other women who acted in a similar manner during the war and the question arises as to their motives. After the Battle of the Thames in October 1813, when American troops pursued a retreating British force to a hamlet known as Dolsen's Mills, a few redcoats and warriors took up ambush positions to fight off the enemy. Their location was given away by an unnamed Upper Canadian woman who informed the advancing Americans, one of whom referred to her as a "guardian angel" because of the value of the intelligence she gave.[40] Another Canadian woman offered her enemies a hospitable welcome in her home, and in July 1812 one resident of Dover, Upper Canada, entertained a group of American officers who were foraging for supplies. They "cheerfully accepted to have supper with her" and "a sociable evening with the invaders" apparently followed.[41]

The experiences of women in or near battle have been treated in detail above but it may be appropriate here to briefly discuss the experiences of some who became prisoners. Lydia Bacon, whose account of the fall of Detroit in August 1812 was quoted earlier, witnessed the lowering of the American flag and the raising of the Union Jack at that place while an artillery salute was fired "from the very cannon, taken from them [the British] in the revolutionary war" and enemy musicians played "God Save the King" in "the most lively manner."[42] Lydia remembered that a little girl in her charge that day was impressed with "the fine uniform of the British Soldiers and expressed her delight in Broken accents, for she could not speak plain, calling them *pretty*." Lydia was put on board a British warship with other captured officers and their wives and, after some delay, taken to Fort Erie at the eastern end of the lake, where they transferred to a coach which took them to Fort George on Lake Ontario. At this point, Lydia's husband, Lieutenant Josiah Bacon, was paroled, as were the other officers whose wives accompanied them. As she noted, this "provoked some of the Batchalors [sic] very much, & made them almost promise, they would get married directly, if they could find anyone to have them."[43] Lydia and her husband were sent across the Niagara River under a flag of truce and a few weeks later she reached her family home in Boston, where she "once more had the pleasure of embracing those I dearly loved."[44]

There was a fairly constant traffic of civilian women going across the border between the two belligerent nations during the war. An American woman, Lydia Hayward, suffered what she thought was a terrible ordeal, but in retrospect her experience could have been worse. When the war broke out, Lydia Hayward and her husband, Joshua, both American citizens, had been living on the north shore of Lake Ontario near Kingston for about three years. Joshua was a Methodist preacher and he and his wife were deeply unhappy about being on the wrong side of the boundary. They discussed their predicament with others of like mind "in secret, by the light of the luminaries of the night" and when Joshua Hayward was called upon to take the oath of allegiance to the Crown he decided to leave his family and clandestinely return to the United States, hoping to bring them across the border later.[45] Not wishing to be alone, Lydia took her two young daughters to live with an uncle and aunt in the neighbourhood until she could manage to rejoin her husband.

After hearing that he had reached American soil safely, Lydia went to Kingston to ask for permission to cross Lake Ontario to Sackets Harbor, where she believed Joshua to be. She was informed that all communication between Kingston and Sackets Harbor was prohibited and, tearful and discouraged, she returned to her relatives. In November 1812 she learned that new regulations had come into effect, whereby American citizens in Upper Canada might be permitted to leave the province if they applied for a passport to a "council of officers" presiding at Kingston.[46] This proclamation "faintly revived" Lydia's hopes and, after an interview, she duly received her passport. She then faced a journey of sixty miles to Prescott, the closest post from which enemy aliens could leave Upper Canada. This was a daunting prospect in wartime for a vulnerable woman but, nonetheless, she set out, "a young female with two children, traveling in the winter season, unprotected by husband, relatives or even acquaintance; in an enemies' country, in time of war, and on the frontiers, where vice reigned almost without restraint."[47]

At Prescott, Lydia appeared before the local British commander, who interviewed everyone trying to leave Upper Canada. His questions being satisfactorily answered and her baggage searched "to see if we had any private papers that would give information of the circumstances of the army, or any contraband goods," Lydia and her children were allowed to cross by boat to Ogdensburg on the American side of the river.[48] When she saw a company of American soldiers drawn up on the opposite bank, Lydia felt that "they appeared like friends and neighbours, while my prejudice against the British was so great, I thought their soldiers appeared like savages."[49] Although elated to be back on home ground, "sorrow again rushed like a flood upon my mind," she wrote, still feeling forlorn without her husband. Fortunately for Lydia, just as she was contemplating another long journey to Sackets Harbor, the door of her hotel room opened and in walked Joshua. "I flew to his embrace in transport, regardless of spectators or ceremonies," recorded a joyful Lydia, whose emotions immediately soared from "the depths of sorrow, to the summit of happiness."[50]

On another occasion, a bitterly cold February day in 1813, three American women were crossing the Niagara River under a flag of truce when their boat got into trouble in a strong current. When the boat finally reached the shore, one of the ladies was "so overcome with the cold that she could not speak, indeed she was to all appearance dead," but she was nursed back to health by Surgeon Joseph West at Fort Niagara.[51] She had been taken prisoner by warriors "somewhere in the neighbourhood of Mackinaw [Mackinac]," had spent four months in captivity during which she was well treated by the native people, and was finally sent to Fort George, whence she had been escorted across the river.

Sometimes women prisoners found themselves being used as pawns in the war. In September 1813, the safe conduct of two American lady prisoners to American-occupied Fort George provided a perfect cover for Lieutenant John Le Couteur to engage in some intelligence gathering. He was sent to Fort George, "with a Flag of truce and two American Ladies, Prisoners *par mes garde*, Mrs. Binsh and Miss Rogers," with orders to observe the enemy's troop strength and positions – to carry out, in other words, "*espionage en Uniforme*."[52] Once the ladies were safely delivered Le Couteur succeeded, with his usual charm, in not only accomplishing his mission but also securing for himself an invitation to an excellent lunch with a friendly American officer.

Some captured women were fortunate to be the recipients of extraordinary acts of kindness on the part of the enemy. In October 1813, after the American victory at the Battle of the Thames near Moraviantown, the women and children of the defeated British army were in a state of terror, rending "the air with sobs and lamentations."[53] An American officer, seeing that in one "woe-worn group," there was a young woman "with a pair of twin babies, one of which she carried on each hip," reassured the ladies that they had nothing to fear from the victors or their native allies, and persuaded them to head to a nearby village for shelter.[54] This officer happened to meet Commodore Oliver Perry, commander

Hero of the Republic: Commodore Oliver Hazard Perry (1785-1819). Perry entered the USN as a midshipman at the age of fifteen and had risen to the rank of master and commandant by 1812. In November of that year he took command of the naval squadron on Lake Erie and in September 1813 won a notable victory over the British squadron there. Perry was present at the Battle of the Thames in October 1813 and, after it was over, gave money to a young Canadian mother with twin infants and arranged transport for her back to her home. The young mother described Perry as "the kindest and most generous gentleman in the world." He died of yellow fever in the West Indies in 1819 at the young age of thirty-four. (Benson Lossing, *Pictorial Field-Book of the War of 1812*.)

of the American squadron on Lake Erie, and Perry, when told of the plight of the young mother of twins, sent her some money and paid for a wagon to take her home to Amherstburg, a distance of more than a hundred miles. "May God bless and prosper him," said the woman, reduced to tears at finding out the identity of her benefactor; "he is the kindest and most generous gentleman in the world, and has been an angel of mercy to me and my poor babies."[55] "See," she continued, "he has not only paid this man to take us home, but has given me all this money to buy clothes for these dear little ones, now that their poor father is a prisoner and going to be sent away into the States."

It took a very cool head and a lot of nerve for a woman to act as a spy, given the risks and possible consequences, and it took a very unusual kind of woman indeed to go into actual combat. In both cases, those concerned either sought, or were presented with, an opportunity to experience conflict at the "sharp end," placing them in an almost unique situation in relation to the vast majority of their peers. Those who found themselves prisoners of war faced the uncomfortable experience of being in enemy custody and the uncertainty of not knowing how long it would be before they would enjoy freedom again. To the average woman of the time, the very idea of any or all of these experiences would have produced, at the very least, a sense of dismay or disbelief, and these ladies take a deserved place alongside all the women so far acknowledged for their bravery in the War of 1812.

A wife's anxiety. Some wives would not wait to learn if their husbands had survived a battle or engagement, and those who followed the troops sometimes had the unhappy task of searching for their loved ones among the wounded. Here, a wife has found her husband alive but wounded and in need of medical attention. (Drawing by George Balbar from Bob Foley, *The War of 1812: Niagara Story, Volume 2*, by permission of the author.)

CHAPTER TWELVE

"Worthless is the laurel steeped in female tears."
Privations, Poverty, Bereavement and Crime

When Boney commanded his armies to stand,
He levelled his cannons right over the land;
He levelled his cannons his victory to gain,
And my bonny light horseman in the war he was slain
> *Broken hearted I'll wander, broken-hearted I'll remain,*
> *Since my bonny light horseman in the wars he was slain*

If I was a small bird and had wings to fly,
I would fly o'er the salt sea where my love does lie;
And with my fond wings I'd beat o'er his grave,
And kiss the pale lips that lie cold in the clay.
> *Broken hearted I'll wander …*

The dove she laments for her mate as she flies,
"Oh where, tell me where, is my darling?" she cries;
And where in the world is there one to compare
To my bonny light horseman who was slain in the war.
> *Broken hearted I'll wander …*[1]

For many old enough to remember the Revolutionary War, the outbreak of hostilities in the summer of 1812 brought forth painful memories. It was not easy to forget the death, hardship, poverty, crimes and atrocities that had marked the first Anglo-American conflict and which had blighted so many lives. The fundamental nature of warfare had not changed, and those who contemplated the darker side of armed conflict often found it a sobering experience.

Saying their goodbyes. Partings were an inevitable consequence of war. In this scene, a militiaman is saying his final farewell to his wife and family before leaving to go on active service. (Drawing by George Balbar from Bob Foley, *The War of 1812: Niagara Story, Volume 2*, by permission of the author.)

Given the work involved in running a home, raising children, caring for live-stock and growing crops, one of the first effects of the war to be felt by women in North America was the departure of husbands, brothers or sons called away to serve in the militia. As the men left, those who remained behind knew they would have to bear the brunt of the extra work and there was much truth in the observation made by one British officer that "in any family unit, every member was vital to its success."[2] As he saw it, the value of land in North America consisted of "the labour which the proprietor can bestow upon it from within his own family, rather than from its own intrinsic worth."[3]

That labour now fell to wives, daughters, young sons and aged parents. As harvest time approached in the late summer of 1812, Lieutenant-Colonel Benoni Wiltse, a Canadian militia officer, referred to "a certain calamity that must befall us if the Militia are thus continued to be cawled [sic] from their families." He added that, if these men were absent for up to six weeks from their farms,

> they can put no spring grain in the ground and the consequence will be that their families must inevitably suffer[.] the famine even threatens before the ensuing harvest when there is but little sown that can be rept [reaped.] if the farmers are prevented from putting in spring grain the famine will un-doubted be dreadful.[4]

Wiltse's view was shared by another observer who remarked that it would not be long before some women would be "suffering for bread, as their husbands are on the lines, and they and their children have no money nor credit, nor can they get any work to do."[5] Considering the importance of harvesting and spring planting, particularly in British North America, which was barely self-supporting in foodstuffs, the militia, when circumstances permitted, were often released from service to return to their fields.

Once war broke out, there was concern over shortages of food in the border areas and a run on available items as people tried to stockpile what they could. Salt and flour were soon in short supply because "the harvest was very wet & the Farmers away from their homes so that much of the wheat had sprung before it was got into the Barn," and on 29 August 1812 one man in York, Upper Canada, wrote that "every article in the grocery line is very scarce here."[6] Since foodstuffs had to be supplied to the troops, measures were taken to conserve certain items and in Upper Canada, for example, "the governor laid an embargo on all the flour, wheat, and pork then in the province, destined for market."[7]

At Amherstburg, shortages drove militia officer and merchant, Thomas Verchères de Boucherville, to make a long and arduous journey to Montreal to fetch a consignment of goods. No other trader had dared to make this risky trip in wartime but Thomas managed to collect his order and, with aborigi-nal help, move his valuable cargo past American ships on Lake Erie by a safe route. When he reached Amherstburg at the end of his seven-month journey, he was immediately "so busy at the store" that he did not even have time to properly unpack his goods and put them on the shelves.[8] The local ladies were waiting outside when he opened his doors and soon "customers were all about the place, inside and out" he wrote, for as he said, "by this time they were in need of everything and no one wanted to miss such a splendid chance." Keep-ing supplies of food in reserve became especially important during the war: a potato bin in the cellar, a barrel of pork in brine, stone jars of butter, home-made cheeses, shelves of preserves – perhaps wild plum jam, apple butter or crabapples preserved with the molasses of pumpkins – gave people a feeling of security in uncertain times.

As the conflict dragged on, maintaining normal food production and consumption grew harder in British North America. The demands of the army commissariat, the branch of the service responsible for supplying the troops, increased, and speculation on the part of merchants selling to the army brought handsome profits while at the same time depriving civilians of staple items. In both the United States and the British provinces many shops, encouraged by the presence of the armies and the extra money in circulation, began to stock luxury items and offer credit. The result was that the temptation to spend created a problem in the artificially-inflated Upper Canadian economy, where "every one forgot his distresses, and thought himself on the high road to wealth, when he found he could sell any thing he possessed for double its real value, and have his pockets stuffed with army bills, as a recompense for some trifling service done to government."[9]

It was a problem that, directly or indirectly, sprang from "the incredible Expense of living enhanced by the demands for the Army."[10] Add the threat of privateers to incoming supplies and the difficulties of planting and harvesting in the absence of many of the men and it is hardly surprising that civilians found it increasingly difficult to cope, especially in towns with a military presence, where there was "much distress from scarcity of provisions at various times." At York things became so critical that when socialite Elizabeth Russell invited an officer to dinner, she discovered that there was "literally nothing" to give him.[11] An upset Miss Russell was saved from an embarrassing situation when a small boy happened to knock on the door with "a string of fish to sell."[12] By 1813, British troops passing through Lower Canada found bread so scarce "that it was only by paying the locals "exorbitant prices" that they "could prevail on them to part with a single loaf."[13]

As inflation mounted, poorer people struggled to meet basic needs. It did not help that the rate of pay for men on active service in the militia of both nations was considerably less than their average earnings in peacetime. Among those who felt the pinch were Catherine and Mary Byles, elderly sisters living on a small income in Boston. They were forced to economize and, in such troubled times, "we drink Souchong tea," they declared with reluctance, only allowing themselves "upon particular occasions" to indulge in "a little Hysen."[14] Jane Stuart of Kingston wrote to her brother about the cost of wood, which had become "really an expensive article."[15] Jane and her widowed mother only had enough to keep one fire alight in the main room of their property, without which, wrote Jane, "we should have been half perished." Even so, she noted,

> the winter has been severe – you may have some idea of the temperature of our chamber when I tell you the moisture my breath produced upon the pillow was frozen – a large space quite stiff – the part of the sheet that was near me turned over was in the same situation. A light warm shawl which I throw over the bed is also covered with frost in the morning.[16]

In New England seaports, where commerce had ground to a standstill, many people could barely afford basic items. Before the war the harbour of Newburyport, Massachusetts, had been busy with coastal, foreign and West Indies trade but after June 1812 its wharves grew silent. Sarah Smith Emery, whose tavern in the town continued to flourish, wrote that "many a noble man became a mere wreck of humanity, and many a delicately bred lady descended into an unthrifty, slatternly household drudge" as their offspring, "half clad and half fed, mixed unrestrained amongst the very dregs of the population."[17] Although "all kinds of country produce was cheap," fabric, household items and meat were not, and Sarah recorded that she and her husband were "in the habit of giving away livers, heads, and the cheap pieces" to those in need.[18]

Phebe Hammond of Newport, Rhode Island, had a sad tale to tell her cousin John Champlin, a New York merchant, in March 1813:

> Coussen [sic] Champlin,
> Sir nothing but my own experience of your goodness and your universal good character of helping the distressed could embolden me to take the liberty of begging the favour of a little of your assistance this horrid War has thrown my children all out of business that I have none to help me neither Sailor nor mechanic can get a days work to do I have been sick all winter havn't been able to earn a cent I need not be particular to say what I want anything you have in your family to eat or drink will be acceptable.[19]

Phebe appealed to Champlin in the hope that he and his wife would remember how in the past she had looked after his grandfather "in his last sickness," and hoped that Mrs. Champlin would be willing to give her "some little notions out of her family that is needed in every family particularly when one is sick such as a little tea coffee or shugar [sic] anything of that kind will be acceptable." It was clearly hard for Phebe to write such a letter, and she asked her cousin to be "so good as to pardon the liberty I have taken and believe me nothing but sickness and the greatest necessity could have induced me to do it."[20]

With poverty knocking on the door, civilians understandably took it hard when the enemy deprived them of stocks of essential items. During the tit-for-tat raids across the St. Lawrence, British troops captured some 300 barrels of flour stored in a barn at Hopkinton, New York, in February 1814. Since flour was regarded as a provision of war, the troops destroyed what they could not take away and, according to Harriet Sprague, whose father was the town doctor and witnessed the event, they moved the barrels to the top of a hill and let them roll down it, splintering them so that their contents poured out. The locals, mostly women, complained of "such waste and destruction" and begged the British to stop. Finally, the British officer in charge told the angry women that "they could have the flour that did not get out of the barrels," turning as he did so to Dr. Sprague and remarking, "ain't I a generous man?"[21]

For those suffering hardship, bartering was often the only way to obtain necessary items. Many a housewife managed to exchange farm produce such as eggs or butter for something else, and in the case of one Canadian family in the Niagara, years later their descendants still possessed "a side saddle and a china dinner service" for which "butter was traded at Niagara in 1812."[22] Mothers and daughters would go to town with carts or wagons laden with goods, as witnessed by one Connecticut resident:

> In either side of the *Saddle Bags,* a nice box of *Butter* – Some *knittin yarn* – half doz[en] pair of *Mittins* and a bundle of *Goose-quills.* A bundle of cleanly hetchelled *flax* and the empty *Wooden Molasses Bottle* – behind, a roll of *home spun;* and ... a basket of fresh laid Eggs. Thus Mounted and Equipped, they conveyed the fruits of their honest and untireing industry to Watsons Store – where they could *swap* for such notions as their wants demanded.[23]

The governments of both combatant nations began early in the war to impose new bureaucratic controls on the civilian population. Residents of Upper Canada were required to take an oath of allegience to the British Crown and

> to forbear all communication with the enemy or persons residing within the territory of the United States, and to manifest their loyalty by a zealous co-operation with his majesty's armed force in defence of the province, and repulse of the enemy.[24]

Since many citizens of the province were Americans who had been lured to Upper Canada before the war by free land, they faced the choice of taking the oath or abandoning their property and removing themselves to American territory. To do that legally – and thus have a chance of reclaiming their property when peace returned – they had to appear before a number of boards or committees appointed in various parts of the province to get the proper exit visas. Given the difficulty and expense of wartime travel, many could not appear before these boards.

The American government imposed its own controls. The U.S. Department of State decreed that all British aliens living in the United States were to report to the marshal of the state or territory in which they resided. Records show that there were more than 2,000 British women resident in the republic during the war years. The numbers vary considerably from state to state but the highest concentration was in New York, where a substantial number of the 733 British male aliens listed in a return made for 20-25 July 1812 were shown to have wives.[25]

Most British women mentioned in these returns were married, but occasionally the name of a single woman appears. Records for the District of Maine note that a Rose Banks, who reported on 19 October 1812, was twenty years of age and had only been in the United States for a few weeks. Margaret Core, who reported on 12 August 1812 at Portland, had arrived just four days earlier, and another unnamed single British woman appeared in the 1814 Pennsylvania return as a maid servant to Edward Legatt, a farmer at Lower Providence. Among the married women listed was Margaret Bell, wife of Samuel Bell, blacksmith of Boston, who had come to America in October 1811 with her two small daughters.[26] Mrs. Cheesman, mother of three children and wife of William Cheesman, a sailmaker, resided in New York, while Mrs. Murray, wife of physician Michael K. Murray, lived in Chesterfield, Virginia. The Murrays, who had been in America for twelve years and were respected members of their community, clearly felt an allegiance to the United States, for a note about Dr. Murray in the April 1813 return for Virginia declares "his attachment to this Country, well known." Many other British aliens appear to have created a favourable impression with the authorities, and remarks in the records include phrases such as "peaceable and inoffensive" or "expressed themselves in a friendly and Patriotic spirit."[27]

By 1812 those British aliens who had not yet made application for American naturalisation, found that if they wished to move to another part of the country, they had to have a passport from Secretary of State James Monroe. As the Royal Navy began a blockade of the eastern seaboard and concern mounted about posssible fraternization with the enemy, a federal government order dated 6 February 1813 directed that any British aliens living within "forty miles of tide water" had to obtain a passport to "retire to such places, beyond that distance from tide water as may be designated by the Marshals."[28]

War, of course, made no allowance for personal problems – however distressing they might be. After American troops occupied part of the Niagara peninsula in the spring of 1813, civilians were exposed to dangers and difficulties that weighed heavily upon them, particularly the family of Canadian militia officer Captain William Hamilton Merritt. Merritt's sister, Caroline, and her husband, James Gordon, had left their home at Newark after the arrival of the invaders and that autumn, when the greater part of the American occupying force moved to the east, Caroline and James decided it would be best for them and their children to travel by boat to the safety of the British military headquarters at Burlington Bay. According to Merritt, "the two children were unwell," and James "by no means recovered from a long fit of illness."[29] The Gordons were accompanied by William's youngest sister, Susan, and once afloat, they "encountered a violent gale of wind, with a heavy sea; on making the shore, they had nearly all been drowned." After their ordeal on the lake, Susan Merritt was taken seriously ill and William recorded that,

> her life was despaired of. All the doctors were sent for within reach ...... My tender mother went up and remained until she recovered; she was as ill as possible without dying – her burial robes were even made.[30]

When the young officer had leave, he immediately rode to his sister's sickbed, "expecting to find her a corpse," but to his great delight, discovered she was much improved.

The next Merritt family crisis occurred when William's father, Thomas, fell sick and after much persuasion agreed to stay at home. He was cared for by another daughter, Maria, but felt very vulnerable, for "everything remained exposed in the house for the first marauding party to plunder."[31] Susan Merritt continued to be unwell, probably from malaria, as did her mother, the Gordons and their two children at Burlington. When his leave expired, Captain Merritt could only tell his suffering family was that he was "on the way wherever fortune chose to bear me," and he returned to duty not knowing if he would see any of his closest relatives alive again.

In the middle of November 1813, when young Merritt was sent to the American-occupied Fort George "with a flag or truce, and, if possible to get some information of their strength," he learned that his father, Thomas, had been made a prisoner of war.[32] William tried to secure his release just as the Americans were about to withdraw from Upper Canada and threatening to "burn every house in their power on the approach of our army."[33] Despite the danger, William managed to free his father and take him to the house of friends, discovering along the way that his mother and sister Susan had both recovered from their sickness and returned to the family home. Still concerned for their safety, the young captain was told firmly that "they had become quite old soldiers as to alarms and disturbances."[34] It was not until late in 1813 that William Hamilton Merritt was able to pay a longer visit to his family, now reunited at their home. After months of danger, sickness and separation which they had, at times, despaired of surviving, everyone in the family was relieved to have come through so many ordeals.

Sometimes war brought a welcome opportunity for a soldier or sailor to be united with his wife or family. In August 1814 Captain Harry Smith, adjutant-general to Major-General Robert Ross, found himself in this fortunate position. Smith had last seen his beautiful Spanish wife, Juana, at Bordeaux the previous spring and had not forgotten the "awful trial" of having to leave her there. "Oh! the heaviness of my heart," he recalled, at saying farewell to "my affectionate young wife of seventeen years old!"[35] After the British occupation of Washington, Harry Smith was unexpectedly sent to London with Ross's official despatches. Thus, "wife, home, country, all rushed in my mind at once," he remembered as he began to picture Juana with her "dark eyes possessing all the fire of a vivid imagination," her profusion of "the darkest brown hair," her fine figure, and the "incomparable elegance and simplicity of her manner."[36]

Such was the importance of the good news he brought that upon his arrival in London Captain Smith was summoned to an audience with the Prince Regent. Buoyed by the promise of a promotion, Smith raced to his father's home in Essex for a reunion he described as "an embrace of love few can ever have known, cemented by every peculiarity of our union and the eventful scenes of our lives."[37] Husband and wife were soon aboard a stage coach bound for a belated honeymoon at Bath, where Captain Smith was listed in the "Fashionable Arrivals" column of the *Bath Chronicle* for Thursday, 17 November 1814, the very day on which the first Fancy Dress Ball was held in the city's new Assembly Rooms.[38] As Elizabeth Ross, the wife of Smith's commanding officer, was staying nearby with her husband's family, Harry and Juana Smith interrupted their idyll to pay her a courtesy visit.

Unfortunately, all too soon Smith received orders to return to North America, which meant another "horrible scene of parting was again to be endured." On that sad day, the unhappy Smith admitted that his heart was "ready to break."[39] Fortune smiled upon him, however, for he survived the war and hastened back to England in 1815, stopping only to buy some presents in London for his beloved wife before proceeding to his father's home. Juana was at church the day her husband arrived, and when she interpreted the sight of servants sent to fetch her as meaning that Harry had been killed, she collapsed "senseless, but quickly recovered to be joyously reunited with the love of her life." This young couple had survived so much, together and apart, but as Harry recorded, they were "all now happiness."[40]

Most wives had little opportunity for travel, but for those who did there were sometimes occasions when they could visit absent husbands. If such women happened to be pretty, witty and elegant, their presence was especially welcomed by men starved of female companionship. However, journeys by road in North America were often dreadful. "Oh, the roads," wrote Susan Burnham Greeley, an early settler in Upper Canada. "You would need some experience before you could imagine what the roads were."[41] A young Canadian militia officer, Thomas Ridout, told his family that he frequently had to "go middle deep in a mud hole" to help unload wagons stuck and then "carry heavy trunks 50 yards waist deep in the mire" before a vehicle could be freed and reloaded.[42]

In the United States, roads were somewhat better but still far from satisfactory. Coaches, bumpy and uncomfortable, were required by law to travel at six miles per hour and carry the mail, but highway robbers were numerous and drivers carried weapons for protection. Minerva Rodgers, wife of Commodore John Rodgers of the United States Navy, who was returning home by road and steamboat from a reunion with her husband in 1813, wrote that "I have good reason to feel more confidence in the excellent quality of my ship, than I have any reason to have in a crazy stage coach, conducted by a drunken driver over bad roads, on a dark night."[43]

In the interior of the continent, waterways were the preferred method of travel. Voyages on the Great Lakes, like those on the high seas, could be dangerous when bad weather hit; one traveller caught in a storm on Lake Erie remembered how the boat would "now rise on the summit of a huge billow, now plunge into a deep abyss" and told of enormous waves breaking and half-filling the craft.[44] River travel often involved obstacles such as rapids and portages, stretches of the journey which had to be covered by foot owing to the perilous conditions. Those travelling down the St. Lawrence River often made the trip in flat-bottomed boats built to withstand the five formidable sets of rapids between Prescott and Montreal, by which the level of the water dropped nearly 250 feet. Such hazards were frightening to the inexperienced, and it is no wonder that one traveller thought it quite "impossible" that a vessel could traverse the rapids "without being instantly engulphed, or dashed to pieces."[45]

During the war years, many women had to cope with death and bereavement. In January 1813, American and British forces fought at Frenchtown on the River Raisin south of Detroit. The Americans were defeated, and more than a hundred of their troops were killed during the battle or died later at the hands of aboriginal warriors. Many of the fatal casualties were volunteers from Kentucky, and when news of the disaster reached Frankfort, the state capital, it happened to be an evening when most of the townspeople were at the theatre. The sad tidings quickly spread through the gathering and by the end of the third act of the play,

> the whole audience had retired. Here you see fathers going about half distracted, while mothers, wives and sisters are weeping at home. The voice of lamentation is loud; the distress is deep; yet neither public nor private distress can damp the ardor of the people. Already they propose raising a new army to revenge the loss of their brave countrymen.[46]

Among the wives who learned that their menfolk had died on the River Raisin were Susannah Price, wife of Captain James Price of the 5th Kentucky Regiment; Anna Hart, wife of Captain Nathaniel Hart; and Jane Allen, wife of Lieutenant-Colonel John Allen of the 1st Kentucky Rifle Regiment. For these three women, their losses proved to be more than they could bear. Susannah Price died only a few years later, leaving four orphaned children, while Anna Hart was so inconsolable that her worried family sent her to New Orleans "hoping that a change of scene would tend to alleviate her sorrow." Unfortunately it did not, and Anna Hart died on 10 July 1818 in her twenty-seventh year.[47] Jane Allen remained "long hopeful" that her missing husband was held prisoner and that one day "despite assurances from all that he was no more," he would return. For eight years she waited and each night would open "the window shutter facing the north and place a candle on the sill." Finally her grief and hopelessness "wasted her strength" and Jane Allen died in February 1821, leaving four teenage daughters.[48]

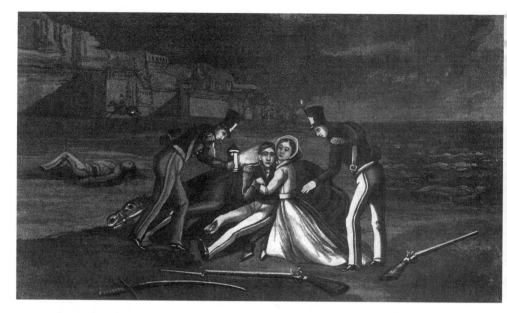

Close to battle. There were times when wives were to be found near the battlefield and in this illustration Mary Anne Hewitt, the wife of a soldier of the 48th Foot, is seen caring for one of her husband's friends after the Battle of Albuera, Spain, in May 1811. Unscrupulous women were often seen stripping the wounded and leaving them almost naked after a battle, and Mrs. Hewitt was among those who formed a company of stalwart defenders against such looting and who helped to move the suffering soldiers to where they could receive medical care. (Richard Cobbold, *Mary Anne Wellington: The Soldier's Daughter, Wife and Widow*.)

These poor women evidently succumbed to their heartbreak. Such an outcome would have been understandable for a British wife and mother whose son, Lieutenant Henry Moorsom, was killed at the Battle of Lundy's Lane in 1814. Mrs. Moorsom's other four sons, all officers, had been killed earlier, and although British families had been coping with such tragedies for more than two decades, the loss of her remaining son was a dreadful misfortune that left Mrs. Moorsom and her daughters with the kind of grief that few are called upon to bear. They may have taken some small comfort from the lines written in the scrapbook of a fellow officer after Moorsom had been buried at Fort George:

> Thou didst with honor, press th'ensanguined plain,
> But not unhonored lie amidst the slain,
> By noble Brock's, thy gallant body rests,
> Thy worth and virtues in thy comrades' breasts.[49]

Lady Polly Johnson, wife of Sir John Johnson, would have understood the feelings of Mrs. Moorsom and her daughters. During the year 1812 she lost her eldest son, William, and her daughter, Mary, to illness, and a younger son, Captain James Johnson, and a son-in-law, Major-General Barnard Bowes, both killed in action in Spain. Unfortunately for Lady Johnson, her misfortunes were not yet over, for in March 1813 her third son, Captain Richard Johnson, drowned while trying to cross the flooded Richelieu River. Her husband, Sir John Johnson, wrote to a correspondent on behalf of his wife and grieving family that "time, and a patient Resignation to the will of God must contribute to restore us to that Calm and Peace of Mind so necessary under all our afflictions and disappointments."[50] Lady Polly died before the War of 1812 ended.

The families of most British soldiers knew they would never be able to visit the last resting place of a loved one so far from home. Families living in North America were more fortunate, for they could perhaps travel to pay their last respects. Sometimes, especially in winter conditions, a body was not located for some time, and one American wife had to wait months before her husband's remains were found. Job Hoisington of Buffalo, New York, fought in the state militia when the British attacked Black Rock on 30 December 1813. As the British advanced towards his home, his wife and their six children were forced to flee with other civilians. Mrs. Hoisington received no news from her husband

Lady Mary Johnson (1753-1814), known as "Polly," was the wife of Sir John Johnson, the most prominent Loyalist in the Canadas. After a number of extended visits to England, Lady Polly had settled into life in Montreal by 1812, and while her husband was actively involved in the affairs of the militia and Indian Department, she and her daughters entertained at their fine mansion. Lady Johnson had to bear the loss of four of her children and her son-in-law during the War of 1812 and did not live to see the end of the conflict. (From an original oil painting by an unknown artist. Toronto Public Library, J. Ross Robertson Collection: T30758.)

and it was not until the snow melted the following spring that his body was found. Job Hoisington had been shot through the head and scalped, but his empty musket proved that he had died fighting. The plight of his wife is recorded in a poem from which the following verse is taken, summing up her loss and that of many others like her:

> But when the battle's done,
> I look for the return
> Of my dear husband, Hoisington,
> But I am left to mourn.[51]

A number of men and women experienced a sense of foreboding about their own death or that of someone dear to them. Elizabeth Ross had a strong feeling that she would never again see her husband, Major-General Robert Ross, when he sailed for North America in the summer of 1814, and her fears proved well founded, for he was killed in action near Baltimore in September 1814. Ursula Woodcock of Fredonia, New York, remembered how in 1813, when her family heard of Commodore Oliver Hazard Perry's naval victory on Lake Erie, her mother, Asenath, seemed to know that bad news was on the way. She hurriedly began her housework, telling Ursula she wanted to complete it "before the mail comes, for it may be, I can't work then."[52] Ursula's brother, Abner, an army officer, had been on board the brig USS *Lawrence* during the battle, and since her father had the contract to carry mail from Buffalo to Fredonia, it was he who brought a letter addressed to the family from Commodore Perry. As Mrs. Woodcock had feared, it reported her son's "bravery in the fighting, after he was wounded; till finally he was cut in two by a cannon ball."[53]

Ursula Woodcock recollected that her parents walked out of their house, through the garden and into a peach orchard, where they

> sat down on a log. There they gave vent to their pent-up grief. I followed them and stood by my mother, and such a prayer as she prayed to her God, that he would give them strength to bear up under that crushing blow, I never heard before.[54]

Ursula admired her mother, whom she remembered as "always the same persevering woman – always doing good; visiting the sick; helping the needy, and giving of her substance to the poor."[55] It was hard to have to watch her grieve, and the vision of her heartbroken parents in the peach orchard was to remain with Ursula for the rest of her days.

Lieutenant-Colonel John Macdonell, aide to Major-General Sir Isaac Brock, had a premonition of death before the Battle of Queenston Heights in October 1812. Macdonell was an ardent suitor of Mary Powell, one of the daughters of Anne Powell of York, but she studiously avoided his advances. After his death, a small notebook was apparently found containing the following poem entitled "My Mary," which conveys Macdonell's abiding devotion to her. Despite her rejection of his advances, Mary Powell was evidently deeply affected by his loss.

> Adieu! Adieu! and is it so,
> And must I from my Mary go?
> O Mary! say "Adieu" once more,
> And I'll repeat it o'er and o'er,
> Until the gale that wafts me through
> The lake shall hush my last "Adieu"!
> And still "Adieu" sweet Mary, say,
> And I will stay, and every minute,
> Shall have an age of rapture in it.
> I'll gaze upon thine eyes of blue,
> And murmur while I gaze "Adieu"!
> "Adieu"! I'll murmur with a sigh,
> And tell thee that I now must fly,
> While every sigh will speak so true,
> My heart is torn with that adieu.[56]

There were other soldiers who shared MacDonnell's sense of impending doom. Lieutenant-Colonel William Drummond, commanding officer of the 104th Foot, who was killed during a night assault on Fort Erie in August 1814, experienced "a presentiment that he never would come out of that day's action." At breakfast, he told his officers, "Now boys! we never will all meet together here again; at least I will never again meet you. I feel it and am certain of it; let us all shake hands, and then every man to his duty."[57]

Captain Sir Peter Parker, RN, also seemed to know when his time had come. Shortly before he was due to lead an attack on an American camp in the Chesapeake Bay area in 1814, he lost his cocked hat overboard and in a manner far different from his normal ebullience said quietly, "My head will follow this evening."[58] From that moment, remembered a fellow officer, Parker was "more thoughtful and reserved" than usual. He prepared his will, destroyed his letters, made "several allusions concerning his wife and family" and "in short, spoke

Honouring victory. After the successful defence of Baltimore against the British attack in September 1814, the grateful citizens of the city erected a monument the following year. It comprised a cenotaph surmounted by a short column symbolic of the Union, upon which were engraved the names of the city's fallen. This painting of it is rich in detail – servants or slave women carrying baskets on their heads, the cobbled street, a U.S. Mail coach preparing to depart. (Painting by John Rubens Smith, 1828. Library of Congress.)

Honouring the fallen. A monument was raised to Major-General Robert Ross at the place where he was killed in action near Baltimore on 12 September 1814. For his widow, Elizabeth, there was the consolation of knowing he was remembered in America, as well as at his birthplace in Ireland and on a memorial in St. Paul's Cathedral, London. (Benson Lossing, *The Pictorial Field-Book of the War of 1812*.)

like a man who had some apprehension of impending fate." That night, "a kind of melancholy settled on his countenance; and every feature indicated some secret foreboding."[59] When Parker was killed during the attack, his cousin, Lord Byron, wrote a poem as stylish as the man it commemmorated, which included the following verse:

> Yes, gallant Parker: thus enshrin'd,
> Thy Life, thy fall, thy fame shall be,
> And early Valour glowing find,
> A Model in thy Memory![60]

Captain Parker's widow, Lady Marianne Parker, was thus provided with a permanent memorial to her husband by one of the most renowned poets of the age. Yet her most treasured keepsake must surely have been a letter her husband wrote the day before his death:

My darling Marianne,

I am just going on desperate service, and entirely depend upon valour and example for its successful issue. If anything befalls me, I have made a sort of will. My country will be good to you and our adored children. God Almighty bless and protect you all!

    Adieu, most beloved Marianne, adieu,

    P. Parker

P.S. I am in high health and spirits.[61]

If at all possible, a soldier or sailor killed during the War of 1812 was given a military burial in the presence of his comrades. Such occasions were solemn, particularly when the deceased was a senior officer of note and, as was the case with Major-General Robert Ross, admired by his subordinates. After his death in September 1814, Ross's body was carried aboard HMS *Tonnant*, the flagship of the British fleet, and taken with great ceremony and solemnity to Halifax. As the *Tonnant* entered the great harbour Lady Katherine Sherbrooke, wife of the lieutenant-governor of Nova Scotia, on hearing that the general's remains were aboard, immediately cancelled the formal dinner she was to host that evening.

On the following day, 29 September 1814, Halifax witnessed its largest public funeral of the war when Major-General Robert Ross was buried with full military honours. Lady Sherbrooke recorded the events of the day:

> Three o'clock was the hour appointed for Major General Ross's funeral – Miss Addison and I were employed during the greatest part of the morning in putting [black] crape on the sword and hat that were to be laid upon the Coffin, and also upon the accoutrements of the horse that was led immediately after the corpse, and upon the hat and sword Sir John [her husband] wore. Our carriage conveyed two wounded officers who came here in charge of the Body and attended it to the grave as mourners. The coffin was landed at the King's Wharf from the Tonnant; minute guns being fired from the ship during the time it was waterborne and when it landed. Minute guns were fired from the Fort till it reached the burial ground ... all the officers of the staff & Garrison, and most of the Navy attended with Sir John and [Vice-Admiral] Sir A[lexander]. Cochrane [Royal Navy commander in North America] – There was an amazing crowd which prevented my seeing much of the procession – three salvos were fired over the grave – the funeral was over by half past four.[62]

Equal solemnity accompanied the burial of Major-General Sir Isaac Brock at Fort George on 16 October 1812. His aide-de-camp, Major John Glegg, felt that "no pen can describe the real scenes of that mournful day" and that a "more solemn and affecting spectacle was perhaps never witnessed." Anne Ilbert, who had known the general in Quebec, wrote to an acquaintance that "the conquest of half the United States would not repay us for his loss" and "by the faces of the people here you would judge that we had lost everything, so general is the regret everyone feels for this brave man."[63] As far as she was concerned, Brock's death was "the first real horror of war we have experienced," and she concluded, "God send it may not lead to a train of others."

After Captain James Lawrence, USN, was killed in the action between his ship, the USS *Chesapeake*, and HMS *Shannon* in June 1813, his body was also taken to Halifax, where arrangements were agreed between the British and the Americans to transport it to Salem, Massachusetts, for the funeral. Lawrence had been married for several years and his wife, Julia, was pregnant with twins at the time of his death. For the sake of her health and well-being, the news was kept from her for several days. Mary Williams, who lived in Salem with her mother and sister, remembered that the funeral included "a great parade."[64] The church, she recorded, was "hung with black, bordered with spruce or hem-lock, much like cypress, in deep festoons from column to column, – the gallery hung with black, and all the columns twined with black and green." The altar was also decorated for the occasion and the overall effect was so "magnificent and solemn beyond conception" that Mary Williams had to admit, "I could not have thought that appearance only could have such an effect upon my feelings."[65]

Such were the last rites for notable officers, but some women were left to mourn male relatives who met a more ignominious end. A Vermont militia-man, for example, was condemned to death by a court martial after he tried to desert in 1813. When his wife learned of his circumstances, she hurried to Plattsburgh and was permitted to visit the man in his cell. A soldier guarding the condemned man recorded that,

> never shall I forget the scene that followed …… his wife entered, and with-out speaking a word she fell at his feet, and for some time they both seemed to have lost the power of speech. She choked, sobbed and cried; and her grief and sorrows seemed more than a young and delicate female ought to bear.[66]

Soon after this, the wife pleaded for mercy before her husband's commanding officer "with all the strength of a woman's love, for the life of her husband." Her efforts were in vain, and he was executed."[67]

Another American wife whose husband suffered a similar fate was Mrs. Harris, the mother of nine children and wife of Samuel Harris. Her husband, "a poor illiterate Baptist preacher," had only enlisted in the militia because his son was keen to fight. As a member of Major-General Andrew Jackson's forces in action against the Creeks in 1814, Harris was accused of being one of the ringleaders in a mutiny that occurred at Fort Jackson, Mississippi, on 19 and 20 September of that year. The trouble arose over the length of service for the militia, some of whom believed that "there was no law to compel them to serve longer than three months," even though one of their officers consulted copies of laws relating to the matter and "satisfied himself of the right of the government to retain his men in service six months."[68] As the end of their three-month term approached, one man refused to do duty and another collected the names of those intending to leave. Samuel Harris, accused among other things of inciting his comrades to mutiny, turned in his musket and left the fort on the day his three months expired, "conscious of having done his duty."[69]

All the men involved in the matter were arrested, court martialled and condemned to death. Harris's sentence was due to be carried out at Mobile, Alabama, on 21 February 1815, by which time news of the end of the war had reached some parts of North America, but not the Gulf Coast. Mrs. Harris received a letter from her husband written the day before his execution, in which he said that he had not expected "to have this awful news to write you" and that "to-morrow I have to encounter death."[70] Distraught, Harris told his wife that his situation will "be a grief to you," but that he wished her to "meet this awful turn of events with as much fortitude as possible." Above all, he begged her to do "all in your power to keep my children together" and counselled her to "be careful of what kind of company you keep, and never bring yourselves to any disgrace." Harris and his fellow mutineers were shot the following day in front of a "great concourse."[71]

The year 1814 also saw a series of trials held that spring at Ancaster, Upper Canada, of Canadians accused of committing treasonable acts. Known as the "Ancaster Bloody Assizes," they resulted in fifteen men being convicted of high treason, eight of whom were condemned to death. Their property was confiscated by the Crown, leaving their wives and families homeless and penniless. While these women were trying to cope with this disaster, they were ordered by

Thomas Merritt, father of Captain William Merritt and Sheriff of the Niagara District, to assemble with their families at Chippawa preparatory to being "sent across to the American side" of the Niagara River. They were to be expelled from British territory for their husbands' crimes.[72]

One of the men convicted and sentenced to death at the Ancaster Assizes was Noah Payne Hopkins, a farmer from Queenston. Hopkins was charged with acting as "a Commissariat for the Americans," since he had supplied the enemy forces with a considerable amount of food after they invaded the Niagara Peninsula.[73] Before the sentence was carried out, petitions from his family and friends were sent to the authorities, and his wife, Polly, appealed for clemency for the sake of her four children. Seven of her neighbours supported her appeal, claiming they knew "circumstances favourable" to the condemned.[74] Although a local justice of the peace also certified Hopkins to be a loyal citizen, he and the seven other condemned men were hanged on 20 July 1814. A sizeable crowd turned out to watch the hangings and among them was Polly Hopkins, who witnessed "the contortions of the poor men," her husband included.[75]

Some women were victims of criminal acts: theft, looting, property destruction and, sadly, rape and murder. Such acts were perpetrated not only by enemy forces but also by civilians and troops of their own nations. In April 1814, at Thurlow, Upper Canada, soldiers of the 19th Light Dragoons committed theft and assault against a Canadian family. A local resident, James McNabb, when asked to find billets for these dragoons and shelter for their horses, sent them to the house of a Captain John Meyers and his wife, the only people in the vicinity with stables. Once in the Meyers residence, the dragoons "procured liquor and became troublesome in the House & demanded Provisions in the Kitchen." Three of them, all drunk, entered the bedroom where Captain Meyers and his wife lay ill and under the care of a neighbour, Eunice Richardson.[76]

According to Captain Meyers, the three intruders demanded that he get up and provide them with food. When he said he could not do so, one of the men left the room saying he would fetch his sword and cut off the captain's head. Meyers managed to get up, seized his gun and herded the other two soldiers out the door, threatening to shoot them if they tried to re-enter. They forced their way back in, and when the captain saw that one man had a sword, he fired a shot, hoping it would scare them. This man, Private Sylvester Burns, "drew his Sword" and badly wounded Meyers "in several places about his body."[77] At this point, Meyers must have passed out, for he only remembered finding himself "out of his house at his Gate," where he received "three Blows on his Body" from either a stick or a sword. What he did not know was that the drunken soldiers had struck his sick wife "also very much with a Club, or Stock," and severely wounded Eunice Richardson "with a Sword [blow] in the head." As McNabb later reported, this wound was so serious that "her life, I conceive to be in danger."[78] Eventually, the three men were taken into custody and placed in jail to await trial.

Other serious crimes did, alas, take place. Murder was more common in the back streets and alleyways of cities, and when it occurred in a law-abiding rural neighbourhood and the perpetrator was a woman, it made very readable news. Just one week after the declaration of war in June 1812, an American woman was convicted and condemned to be executed for a crime which appalled the readers of the *Connecticut Gazette*. Under the title "Horrid Murder," the news-paper's edition of 17 June 1812 contained an account of the trial of Cornelius A. Cole and his wife, accused of killing her mother, Mrs. Agnes Thuers. Mrs. Thuers's body had been found "under the floor of the house where these people lived," and had been concealed there since the previous winter.[79] Mrs. Cole, who was convicted "upon the plainest evidence (principally her own confessions)," admitted she "struck her mother with the head of an axe, which knocked her down, and she then cut her throat." Her husband was acquitted of murder but found guilty of concealing it.[80]

During the British occupation of Eastport, Maine, a soldier of the 102nd Foot was indicted for murder. The victim, Jane Evans, a "refined young lady," was governess to the children of the British military governor, Lieutenant-Colonel Joseph Gubbins, and a companion to his wife, Charlotte. Somewhat ironically the guilty man, Private John Shea, had been assigned the duties of servant to the regimental chaplain, and Jane Evans allegedly "made complaint of some neglect of duty on his part."[81] According to a history of the town, Jane Evans was raped and murdered by Shea on the evening of 7 December 1815 and her body was discovered near the homes of two local residents. At his court martial in the spring of 1816, Shea was convicted and sentenced to be shot, but the day before the sentence was due to be carried out, he committed suicide by hanging himself in his cell.[82]

Although rare, there were other accusations of rape during the war. Lieutenant-Colonel Joseph Gubbins, during his time as Inspecting Officer of Militia in New Brunswick, mentions in his journal that in July 1811 a Sarah Blue of West-cock had "sworn rape against I. Smith of Sackville."[83] It was exceptional for a woman to publicly charge a man with sexual assault at a time when chastity was an essential virtue in society. In the ensuing legal proceedings it was Sarah Blue's behaviour that was called into question, not that of her assailant. As this type of crime was often committed in private, it was difficult for a woman to procure witnesses to testify on her behalf. The result was that few rape cases came to trial and, of those that did, few assailants were found guilty, the majority being dismissed for lack of evidence. The statistics of the Old Bailey, one of the busiest courts in London, a city of nearly a million people, bear this out. Between 1785 and 1815 that court heard only seventy-five rape cases, and of these twelve men were found guilty, ten were found not guilty and the remainder were dismissed, mostly because of a lack of evidence.[84] The fact that the twelve guilty men were sentenced to death by hanging (one being recommended for mercy on account of his previous good character) is an indication of how seriously the crime of sexual assault was regarded during the period.

The difficulties a woman could face in such circumstances are illustrated by the case of Susannah Davids, who worked in Montreal as a servant to the Roussel family. One night in 1813, while Madame Roussel was away visiting her relatives, her husband entered Susannah's room and assaulted her. Although Roussel tried to stifle Susannah's cries by choking her, the noise awoke the Roussel children, whom she calmed and persuaded to stay in their beds. Susannah Davids then claimed that Roussel raped her "with violence and by force."[85] Unfortunately for Susannah, Roussel had a reputation as a highly respectable man and found eleven people to testify on his behalf, while his victim could only find one person to speak for her – a woman neighbour who gave her shelter the day after the assault.

Susannah Davids was a servant but even a higher position on the social scale did not protect women from sexual predators. Such was the predicament of Ann Strachan, daughter of one of the weathiest merchants in British North America and wife of one of the most prominent religious figures in Upper Canada. In the autumn of 1813, the Reverend Dr. John Strachan, Church of England rector at York and chaplain to the garrison, became worried about his wife, Ann, a woman described by her husband as being very attractive. American troops had attacked York twice in the last six months, and as Ann was in the early stages of pregnancy he decided to send her and their two children to Cornwall, which he thought would be a safer place. Unfortunately, instead of finding sanctuary, Ann Strachan encountered worse danger when American soldiers occupied Cornwall in early November. Several of the invaders entered the house where she was staying and not only raped but also robbed her. Not surprisingly, the traumatic ordeal left Ann so distraught that for some time, there was concern whether she would survive it. She eventually recovered and gave birth to a daughter early in 1814.[86]

The irony of this incident is that the American soldiers who committed the crime were under the command of Brigadier-General Jacob Brown, an officer who did not tolerate the mistreatment of civilians, even enemy civilians. At the time, of course, Brown had no knowledge of the assault on Ann Strachan, which was the work of isolated individuals – if it had been brought to his attention there is no doubt that the culprits would have suffered very severe punishment. In July 1814, Brown dismissed a colonel from his army when troops under that officer's command burned the little village of St. David's. Even though the officer had nothing to do with the destruction of the town, Brown held him responsible for the conduct of his men. Most professional soldiers subscribed to the same belief and, with few exceptions, the behaviour of the regular troops of both nations was good throughout the war – although the same cannot be said for American and Canadian militiamen. This being so, it is hard to comprehend the actions of Colonel Thomas S. Beckwith, a British officer with an exemplary combat record, concerning the worst incident of sexual assault to take place during the War of 1812.

The crime took place at the village of Hampton, Virginia, in June 1813. Beckwith was commanding a force of about 2,400 men attached to Rear-Admiral George Cockburn's squadron, which was raiding in the Chesapeake Bay area. This force was composed of two battalions of Royal Marines, a battalion of regular infantry and two companies of "Independent Foreigners." The latter were recruited from French deserters and prisoners of war and were intended for use as garrison troops in the West Indies. Such was the shortage of manpower in the British army, however, that they were instead sent to Beckwith for operations against the Atlantic seaboard of the United States. The Independent Companies of Foreigners were, without a doubt, one of the most unsavoury collections of men ever to serve the British Crown. Beckwith himself had doubts about their reliability, reporting to London that the "Officers seem to know nothing of their Men & speak ill of them – the Men on their side hint, what I fear is true, that the Officers have made away with their pay."[87] During an unsuccessful British attack on Craney Island in mid-June 1813, many of the Foreigners, officers and men, deserted when put ashore. Therefore, it is all the more puzzling that they were included in the force that landed on 25 June 1813

Hampton, Virginia. This postwar view shows the creek upon which was situated the village of Hampton, the capital of Elizabeth City County, Virginia. Early on 25 June 1813, a British force landed, overpowered the local militia, and during the plundering that ensued, one elderly man was murdered, several other civilians wounded and several women raped in what was the worst incident of its kind in the War of 1812. (Benson Lossing, *The Pictorial Field-Book of the War of 1812.*)

near Hampton, brushed aside the militia assembled in its defence, and occupied the village on 25 June 1813.

Almost as soon as they stepped on shore, the Independent Foreigners slipped the bonds of discipline and ran amok. They began to plunder houses some distance from the village and from theft, their behaviour degenerated, probably under the influence of alcohol. They murdered an elderly man, wounded several other civilians and raped between five and seven women. The initial reports on these crimes in Maryland and Virginia newspapers were so dramatic – and, in the case of the rapes, so detailed as to border on the salacious – that some editors found them hard to believe. One such report, under the title "The Monsters at Hampton," described the abuses as acts that would "forever disgrace the *British* name" and protested that

> The enormities at Hampton will never be fully known. Their features are of that horrible description that those who suffered will forever conceal them, if concealment be possible; and this will also be the common object of their relatives and friends … no *husband, father or brother* is willing to have it embodied in history that his *wife, daughter or sister* was so served.[88]

The *Norfolk Herald*, which had taken its account from "several gentlemen of respectability and intelligence," described the plight of several "unfortunate females who had not the means of effecting their escape from the town" and who were "literally hunted down by these fiends in human shape, and made the victims of indignity and brutal outrage."[89] The newspaper's staff were "unwilling to admit that even an enemy whose conduct in war is characterised by inhumanity, could have committed acts, at the bare mention of which, the blood runs cold, and the heart sickens." The *Norfolk Ledger* referred to "these black deeds, which will ever remain an indelible stain on the character of the British nation."[90]

Undoubtedly, the majority of women victims would have shared the feelings of a lady from nearby Norfolk who wrote about the raid to a friend in New York. She was distraught to think that "most of these unfortunate females (now rendered wretched for life, by the *Bulwark of our Religion*), are well known, and are beautiful beyond description."[91] When she pictured them having had to flee, "in all directions, with children in their arms, pursued by these savages," she confessed, "my heart bleeds for these unfortunate females" and she wished that "the thunderbolts of heaven strike these wretches, and clear the earth of such monsters." Not surprisingly, anxiety in the entire Bay area was high, fuelled by rumours that there would be further raids and that British had told their men they would receive "twenty five pounds a piece, three days' plunder! and all the pretty women as long as they wanted!!!!" if they took the port of Norfolk.

Since most of the outrages at Hampton had occurred in a relatively isolated area, there were few witnesses. Nonetheless, enough concrete evidence was gathered for an American officer to visit Beckwith under a flag of truce, present it to him and request that he either discipline those responsible or turn them over to Virginia for punishment. Although deeply embarassed by the matter, Beckwith did neither, even though he had the authority to convene a field court martial to try the guilty parties. Instead, he resorted to a classic bureaucratic tactic and transferred the two companies of Independent Foreigners out of his command, sending them to Halifax, where they committed further breaches of indiscipline before being broken up. Beckwith's failure to punish the miscreants is all the more surprising as he had served for many years under the Duke of Wellington in Portugal and Spain and knew well the Duke's attitude towards mistreatment of civilians – in the Peninsular army a soldier convicted of assaulting or killing a civilian was, almost without exception, condemned to death. The fact that the perpetrators at Hampton were largely French, not British, did not come into the equation – they wore British uniforms and were officially part of the British army. Beckwith's failure to do his duty not only left a stain on the reputation of that army; it also blighted a fine personal reputation.[92]

The popular American periodical *Niles' Weekly Register*, which printed many of the accounts about the Hampton raids, also provided information about another case of rape by British soldiers. This was supposed to have taken place during a British raid across the border into Vermont in the summer of 1813. The editor of the *Weekly Register* stated that he had received "depositions of several persons" attesting to trespass, "wantonness of destruction" and looting – British troops had apparently "stolen any thing and every thing – bowls, spoons, *woman's shirts*, sitting hens and looking glasses," leaving "many houses destitute of every necessary or convenience of life."[93] Worse still, according to the deposition of a "Mrs. Asselstyne,"

> the barbarians seized 'a young woman by the name of – – , about fourteen or fifteen soldiers took her, carried her by force into another room, her screeches were unavailing, they shut the door and were there with her a considerable length of time, the young woman told the deponent, they did by force, what they desired to do; she was extremely abused, and but one out of the number appeared to have any mercy on her.[94]

Even more shocking is the fact that a British officer "assailed" a Mrs. Manzer, but "she repelled him." As the editor of the *Register* concluded, "the English appear to have lost the characteristics of *Christians or men*."[95]

The behaviour of soldiers at Cornwall, Hampton and, if true, in Vermont in 1813 is cause for reflection on the darker side of human nature. If there is one bright aspect to these woeful events, it is that they were infrequent, as most soldiers in the armies of both belligerents behaved properly towards women. As for those who did not, and those who failed to punish their crimes, General Robert Taylor of the Viginia militia perhaps said it best when he wrote to Beckwith that "worthless is the laurel steeped in female tears and joyless the conquests which have inflicted needless woe on the peaceful and unresisting."[96]

Many lesser crimes were committed during the war, most occurring in cities, particularly ports. By the end of the conflict, having suffered from a continual flow sailors and soldiers, Halifax appeared, according to one citizen, to combine all the worst features of the back streets of London and Portsmouth, as "no man's liberty was safe and no woman's person secure."[97] In these places, robberies took place in broad daylight, market stallholders could find their goods rifled at any moment, house-breaking was so frequent that elaborate precautions had to be taken, and forgery was rife.

Wherever criminal activity flourished were to be found men like James Hamilton, an American soldier condemned to death in 1818 for shooting an officer. Hamilton had engaged in a life of crime for at least a decade, and shortly before his execution, he wrote an account of his wrongdoings which reveals that women as well as men were active in the criminal underworld. Hamilton served briefly in the wartime regular army but deserted and supported himself by theft. When imprisoned at Goshen, New York, for stealing a pocket watch, he met Rosannah Hitchcox, who was also serving time for theft. After their release, this couple embarked on a crime spree and at Hamilton's suggestion travelled to Albany, where he proposed to sell a land warrant he had obtained from his wartime service. Along the way, Hamilton wrote, Rosannah, being skilled at her craft, "stole in my presence a piece of calico and another of silk" and then "sold the same after making for herself a gown from each" and bought herself a shawl and a pair of shoes.[98] There was money enough left over for the light-fingered Rosannah to give James "in cash five dollars."

Fired up by this success, Hamilton then stole a bonnet which he had heard "valued at 2 dollars," whereupon he and his accomplice went out and got drunk.[99] Rosannah Hitchcox, however, was still sober enough to do a little pilfering that evening and as Hamilton noted, "put into my hands an elegant gold repeating watch," which created "an outcry" on the street. By swapping the gold watch for a silver one and some money, James and Rosannah had enough cash to reach Albany. Once there, James sold his land warrant while Rosannah continued with her usual activities, and when he returned to their boarding house, he found under the bed "two hats and a great coat," which he supposed had been "stolen by my wife," as Hamilton now referred to his partner in crime. Word soon reached the two that they were wanted for theft, so they headed for Troy, where they parted company. James returned to their lodgings one afternoon to discover that Rosannah, who had clearly been up to no good in his absence, had been "apprehended with one Josiah Bullard."[100] At this point, Hamilton decided to leave his rascally lady friend to her fate.

Rosannah Hitchcox was not the only woman who made a living out of petty theft. At Utica, New York, a man named Finney left his wife and seven children "in great distress, through the wiles of a base woman, who here he called his wife."[101] According to a description of this Jezebel, the said woman has a fine curling lock in the front of her forehead, which she admires much more than she does honesty, she being a very great adept at the slight of hand, as known by various articles missing from Doctor Stoyells's Tavern, where they put up until their departure.[102]

The lady of the curling lock also managed to steal "a favourite Dog of the name of PERO," which could perform various tricks, and its owner advertized that whoever found the dog and the woman, would be "handsomely rewarded for their trouble, and highly thanked if the harlot is in the place where she ought to be," which is to say, in jail.[103]

Some women, like Mrs. Whittlesey of Watertown, New York, went about crime in a more calculating manner. Towards the end of the war, when her husband was appointed paymaster to his brigade of militia, he found himself in possession of $30,000 as wages for the troops. He was "induced by the machinations of his wife – a woman of education, but thoroughly depraved, who worked upon his fears" – to report that he had been "robbed of all, in order to secure the money for themselves."[104] Whittlesey offered a reward of $2,000 for the apprehension of the thief and made "other demonstrations of honesty" but many did not believe him. Eventually, two men who had pledged to stand surety for him, a Mr. Fairbanks and a Mr. Keyes of Watertown, "decoyed him into a lonely place and extorted from him a confession, and the assertion that a larger portion of the money might be found with his wife." Sure enough, much of the supposedly missing cash was located at the Whittlesey home, where it had been hidden "between beds and quilted in a garment." The couple were arrested but "in a moment of confusion" Mrs. Whittlesey managed to escape by jumping into the Black River. Her body was later fished out of the water but there was little sympathy for her as "public opinion fastened all the guilt" on Whittlesey's "wretched wife."[105]

In wartime the oldest profession flourished in most North American cities. Women resorted to prostitution for many reasons, among them poverty, seduction and accidental pregnancy, alcohol, and the fact that illiteracy, ill health or the responsibilities of small children made it hard for them to make a living. Once they fell from grace they were often disowned by their families and shunned by society, and found themselves in brothels with others who had been reduced to the same state.

In the period of the War of 1812 there were clear rules in relations between the sexes. Flirtation and playfulness were acceptable but seduction was not, and

Whittlesey Rock, Watertown, New York, is said to be the place where the wife of Paymaster Whittlesey jumped into the Black River and drowned. Her weak-willed husband had a large amount of money in his possession to pay the wages of his brigade of militia, but Mrs. Whittlesey persuaded him to pretend he had been robbed so that they could keep the money. Paymaster Whittlesey eventually confessed to his crime. (Lossing, *The Pictorial Field-Book of the War of 1812.*)

to cross the line was to court disaster. It was expected that men would behave in a licentious manner and that women would keep them at arm's length – as one father advised his daughters, "men will always be ready to take more than you ought to allow them."[106] If women did not heed this advice they were liable to end up like the pretty young single mother British Surgeon Samuel Holmes met near the village of Hallowell, Upper Canada. She had "committed the inexpiable sin" of allowing herself to be seduced and had been left with "a sickly infant."[107] Although she had a gentle manner and the appearance of having been highly respectable in "more prosperous as well as more innocent days," Holmes knew her future would be bleak. "Who will now receive her, robbed of her good name, friendless and pennyless?" he asked, predicting that if this woman went to a town or city she could well end up as a "street polluting, crack voiced trull, shaking in the convulsions of a gin hiccough."[108]

Wherever there was a military presence, there were opportunities for prostitutes. The sex trade flourished from Halifax to New Orleans and there is even mention of an apparent prostitute looking for customers during the brief occupation of Washington in August 1814. She appeared, dirty and blood-stained, before some British officers shouting, "oh, I am killed, I am killed! A British sailor has killed me!" Her wounds were superficial but the matter was regarded as serious and the troops were mustered on parade for identification. When faced with lines of men in uniform, the woman was unable to identify her supposed assailant.[109]

In his confessions, James Hamilton mentions that despite being a married man he could not resist visiting brothels, and he named two prostitutes he knew in the Boston area, Sally Smith and Charlotte Hatch, who "handsomely supported me," often "contending and fighting on my account."[110] Hamilton also enjoyed himself in the brothels of New Orleans, and in the disreputable back streets of New York, where, according to another observer, there were women "bloated with rum, rotten with disease, drugged on opium, and victims of brutality and every kind of excess."[111] He described the city's prostitutes as "flashy, untidy, and covered with tinsel and brass jewelry," and that in their short dresses with "arms and necks bare," their appearance was "as disgusting as can be conceived."

Because of venereal disease, prostitution was regarded as a serious problem by both armies and an attempt was made to control it, at least in the vicinity of military camps and garrisons. Prostitution could also lead to other problems. When Peter Wheeler, a Canadian militiaman, was court martialled for desertion, his defence was that a woman of low morals, Sarah Cudney, had "enticed him to Lewiston in the State of New York and then kept him in a state of continual intoxication until after his furlough had expired."[112] There may have been financial rewards, but, as one prostitute later confessed, she resented the fact that "if I have a row with a fellow, he's always the first to taunt me of being what he and his fellows have made me."[113]

The vocabulary of those who lived at a certain level of society in Britain and its colonies contained many interesting and colourful expressions. A bawdy house or brothel was known as a "cavaulting school," and a "fire ship" – an expression commonly used for a ship that was deliberately set on fire and sent to destroy enemy vessels – was a woman with venereal disease. A "three-penny upright" was a prostitute who performed her tasks standing against a wall. If a woman had a good "apple dumplin' shop," she had an ample bosom, and if she had "sprained her ankle," it meant she was pregnant. "Dishclout" was a term for a dirty, greasy woman, and to be a "wagtail" was to be known as very lewd. A "rantipole" was someone who was dissipated.[114]

Not all the women who were engaged in this trade were passive victims of circumstances. There were those who negotiated their own prices, established networks to support each other and worked in pairs to protect themselves from violent customers. Several New York prostitutes were very successful by the time of the war, and Maria Williamson, who was reputed to run "one of the greatest whorehouses in America," was doing well enough to contemplate expanding her business. Eliza Bowen Jumel was another wealthy prostitute from Providence, Rhode Island, who had begun at an early age and later married a prosperous

French wine merchant. After his death, Eliza took over his affairs and proved to be an excellent businesswoman.[115]

In British North America, there were women who had done well enough to be able to open their own establishments in the larger centres. Depending on local attitudes, they might be arrested and charged, the most common accusation being the keeping of a bawdy house or brothel. In Montreal, one of the more lively cities in British North America, the newspapers published regular reports on the work of the courts, and thus these entries were to be found:

> Marie Danis (Widow Salois) of Montreal, on conviction of keeping a disorderly house, was sentenced to be committed to the house of correction, there to be kept at hard labour for the space of six months, at the expiration of which, to give security for her good behaviour, and to be confined until such security given.

House of ill repute. Brothels or bawdy houses could be extremely squalid backstreet affairs, but this illustration is of a higher-class establishment. Gentlemen and bare-breasted prostitutes are pictured drinking, playing cards, flirting and preparing to enter the bed chamber. (Engraving by an unknown artist. Author's collection.)

The delights of the demi-monde.
The British officer shown in this drawing, made in Paris in 1815, seems more taken with the lady than she with him. This, and her somewhat flamboyant but fashionable dress and turban, might indicate that she is a member of the *demi-monde*. During the War of 1812, such women were to be found in every major garrison town or city. (Print after Gentry. Anne S.K. Brown Military Collection, Brown University, Providence, Rhode Island. Photograph by René Chartrand.)

Marguerite Beauchamp, Rosalie Desjardin, Thèrese Desjardin and Betsy Stevens, were committed to the house of correction for twelve months, as being idle, disorderly women and incorrigible vagabonds.[116]......

Pierre St. George and Marie Lucier, his wife, convicted of having run a disorderly house, and condemned to stand in the pillory on Friday 30th from 11 a.m. to midday in front of the New Market. Pierre St. George is also to be placed in the city prison for two months, and Marie Lucier in the House of Correction until 20 January next, and given labour of the hardest sort.[117]

Vice and crime have existed throughout history, adverse social conditions and necessity often being the catalysts that have set people upon a downward path. Like most wars, the War of 1812 tended to exacerbate such circumstances by breaking the continuum of normal life and creating an environment in which privation and poverty escalated and self-preservation became critical. These darker aspects of the war, along with partings, separation and bereavement, were inevitable consequences of the conflict and it is little wonder that by 1815 the people of North America longed for an end to the fighting.

The soldier's widow. Whilst pensions for the widows of officers usually provided a living, soldiers' widows faced an uncertain future. Mary-Anne Hewitt, pictured here with her daughter and her husband's sword, suffered hardship in the years after his death. She petitioned for financial assistance and the Reverend Richard Cobbold, who learned of her plight, wrote an account of her life and experiences to help publicize her case. (Richard Cobbold, *Mary Anne Wellington: The Soldier's Daughter, Wife, and Widow*.)

CHAPTER THIRTEEN

"The blessings of peace."
The End of the War and Afterwards

Columbia and Britannia
Have ceased from Warfare wild;
No more in battle's rage they meet,
The parent and the child.
Each gallent nation now lament
The heroes who have died
> But the brave on the wave,
> Shall yet in friendship ride,
> To bear BRITANNIA's ancient name
> And swell COLUMBIA's pride.

For now the kindred nature
Shall wage the fight no more,
No more in dreadful thunder dash
The billows to the shore;
Save when in firm alliance bound
Some common foe defied;
> Then the brave on the wave
> Shall there in friendship ride;
> To bear BRITANNIA's ancient name
> And swell COLUMBIA's pride.[1]

One of the ironies of the War of 1812 was that almost as soon as it had begun, diplomatic initiatives were launched to end it. Most of these efforts came to nothing until, in the summer of 1814, British and American negotiators met at what was then the Dutch city of Ghent to discuss a peace treaty. Discussions dragged on for more than four months, but on 24 December 1814 the Treaty of Ghent was finally signed. It restored the *status quo ante bellum*, while all the major issues that had given rise to the conflict were set aside for later discussion. Unfortunately, news of the treaty did not reach North America before one last major battle was fought at New Orleans on 8 January 1815, an action that brought a resounding victory for Major-General Andrew Jackson and a British withdrawal from Louisiana.

On 11 February 1815 many British wounded were still being treated in hospitals in New Orleans when the sloop *Favourite* docked at New York. Among the first passengers to step ashore was Henry Carroll, secretary to Henry Clay, one of America's envoys at Ghent, carrying with him an official copy of the Treaty of Ghent. The news spread fast and within twenty minutes cheering crowds with lighted candles were parading through the streets of New York to the sound of church bells and the celebratory thunder of artillery salutes. As messengers prepared to set off in all directions, newspaper editors worked into the early hours to get word out to a war-weary public. Although hostilities would not end until the United States had ratified the treaty, everyone assumed that the war was over, and the celebrations continued.

At 4 P.M. on 14 February 1815, Carroll's coach arrived in Washington and deposited him outside the Octagon House, home of James and Dolley Madison after the burning of the presidential mansion the previous summer.[2] The Madisons were entertaining and, when it became known that Carroll had brought confirmation that the war was at an end, a "radiance of joy" lit Dolley Madison's face.[3] "With a grace all her own," she reciprocated the heartfelt congratulations offered to her, and immediately instructed her staff to arrange something special to eat and drink to mark the occasion. Soon she was "dispensing with a liberal hand to every individual in the large assembly the proverbial hospitalities of that house." As the butler poured wine for all present, the president emerged from his office shortly after 8 P.M. to pronounce the peace terms satisfactory and the American capital went into a frenzy of celebration.

As often happens with major historical events, people remembered how and when they heard the news of peace. Susan Burnham Greeley was spending the winter with relations in Manchester, Vermont, when she "saw the stage come in, on runners, with the word 'Peace' painted in large white letters on both sides of it."[4] At Portland, Maine, Elizabeth Oakes Smith recalled being "awakened at midnight by the ringing of bells," and people running in the streets. While women wept, children screamed with delight and everyone "shook hands with each other."[5] Lamps and candles illuminated houses in Portland throughout the night and all the "forlorn ships" that had stagnated in the harbour, as in many other American ports along the blockaded eastern seaboard, "carried long strings of lights, and flags fluttered all day in the breeze."

At Hartford, Connecticut, Mrs. Howard, mother of Major George Howard, was reading John Bunyan's "Pilgrim's Progress." The major, who was spending a few nights at home during a recruiting drive in his home state, was seated by the fire and "marking out the programme of another campaign in the ashes on the hearth" for Sarah, his "all attentive yet trembling Wife."[6] Suddenly, the Howards heard the "uproarious cry of *peace! peace! peace!*" coming from the "brazen throat of an overjoyed *Stage driver.*" When the family realized what it meant, Sarah Howard "fell motionless" upon her husband's chest while his mother raised her arms in the air and cried, "GOD be thanked."

No sooner had the celebrations commenced in nearby Hartford than two men rowed out to the seventy-four-gun ship of the line HMS *Superb*, which was anchored on blockade duty in Gardiner's Bay. The men were "full of sympathetic enquiries as regard the comforts of their friends of the fleet" and requested the honour of conveying some of the British naval officers ashore, where a host of Hartford worthies would be only too happy to shower them with "the free will offerings of *Women and Wine* of *fun and frolic* and the best of feed."[7] The British accepted, and the first officer of the Royal Navy to put a foot on dry land received "the languishing attention of the fair daughters of Federalism and the worship of admiring sycophants," complained Major George Howard. Before the young man returned to his ship, "many of the fair damsels solicited as a keepsake a button from his uniform."

Eliza Susan Quincy, one of five daughters of Josiah Quincy, prominent Massachusetts Federalist and later president of Harvard College, had more reason than most to be joyful at the turn of events. Eliza had noted in her journal for 12 February 1815 that some gentlemen visitors to her house agreed that "there was no prospect of the war with England ending – for a long time to come."[8] The very next morning, as she and her mother were "pursuing our usual employment," they heard church bells ringing and a friend burst into their home exclaiming to Eliza's mother: "Mrs. Quincy! – do you know what those bells are ringing for – Peace! Peace!" With the whole of Boston in an uproar, "we ordered the carriage or rather the sleigh," wrote Eliza, "and drove the length of the town." So thick were the crowds that "you might have walked on the people's heads," she remembered, watching as people hurried to embrace one another and shake hands. "The joy of the poorer classes of society who had suffered most from the war was very touching," Eliza recorded, adding that "it was a scene and a day never to be forgotten by anyone who enjoyed it."[9]

Eliza's father headed the official procession through Boston on 15 February 1815 and that night, fireworks

> were exhibited from night-fall to half past nine o'clock; during which nearly 400 fine rockets were thrown from the upper terrace of the [State] House; and Beehives, etc, let off from the yard. At the close, the splendid pyrotechnical Sun, the Temple and Arch of Peace, the Pine trees were seen exhibiting, for some minutes, a great variety of beautiful colors, when in the centre of the arch a brilliant Star appeared with "PEACE" in transparent letters; and a full blaze of all the other works.[10]

The following evening Eliza attended a Peace Ball at the Boston Concert Hall. It was a special occasion and the fashion-conscious Miss Quincy went to a great deal of trouble with her appearance, styling her long hair in "braids, bandeau and curls," and choosing a dress with a "sheer dotted muslin skirt trimmed with three rows of plaited white satin ribbon," as well as "white lace round the neck, a bouquet, gold ornaments, chain, etc."[11] Eliza observed that

> The Hall was decorated with transparencies from the State House, representing pillars between the window, the buildings illuminated within and without and decorated with flags, and flowers, etc., etc. The effect was beautiful. The band played as we entered stationed in a balcony above. A high seat surrounded the floor of the hall on which my mother and I secured seats with Mrs. S.G. Perkins and her daughter and Mrs. R. Sullivan and had much amusement in observing the company.
>
> Several British Officers in full uniform were actively employed in flirting and dancing not in the most graceful manner, – but still seemed favorite partners among the young ladies ......
>
> I danced several cotillions, contrary to my expectations, as I was acquainted with few of the beaux of the day.[12]

In British North America, meanwhile, Halifax was the first city to learn of the peace. On Sunday, 19 February 1815, Lady Katherine Sherbrooke noted in her journal:

> An Express received from Castine with news from New York of the arrival of a British Man of War with a Treaty of Peace between Great Britain and America

signed on the part of the former on 26th December [actually 24 December] and awaiting only Mr. Madison's approval. We went to church and had many visitors afterwards.[13]

There were smiling faces in the congregation at St. Paul's Church that day and Halifax, brightly illuminated like its American counterparts, was quick to organize a public dinner that lasted into the early hours of the morning. Haligonians had every reason to celebrate, for that dinner not only marked the end of the war but also the end of a recent smallpox epidemic. When Sir John Sherbrooke received an official copy of the treaty, and "a Cartel came in from Salem with an account of Mr. Madison having ratified the Treaty of Peace," a delighted Katherine Sherbrooke sat down with her husband to a special dinner of "plum pudding and some hashed caribou."[14]

Soon afterwards, word reached Upper and Lower Canada and was likewise greeted with joy and relief. Former neighbours on either side of the Niagara River

The château, harbour and river, Quebec. News of peace reached the city of Quebec on 1 March 1815. This view shows the château, formal residence of the governor-general of the Canadas, who throughout the war was Lieutenant-General Sir George Prevost, and his family. In the distance is the Île d'Orléans and the south shore of the St. Lawrence. (Watercolour by Elizabeth Hale. Library and Archives of Canada, C-13096.)

resumed their personal and business relations, determined to put the past behind them, and within days Americans crossed over into British territory to sell

> oxen and grain in Canada, where the stock was much exhausted. A crowd, too, of pedlars and hawkers came over with tinwares, cotton goods, French silks, wooden clocks, and other articles manufactured in the State of New York; which they soon disposed of among their old customers.[15]

According to Surgeon Samuel Holmes of the British army, who observed this commerce, the Americans were "received as old friends, and many an enquiry was made about kindred and acquaintance on the other side of the waters."

At Kingston on Lake Ontario, the news was received on 24 February 1815. The following day, a party of American officers crossed the lake from Sackets Harbor and were welcomed to dinner by their British opposite numbers, who insisted on a regimental band playing "Yankee Doodle" and drinking President Madison's health.[16] Lieutenant John Le Couteur was ordered to take official word of the peace treaty from Kingston to Montreal, and as he journeyed along the shore of the St. Lawrence he spread the news of peace. A Dutch couple, who ran a large and prosperous farm where Le Couteur went late in the evening to get fresh horses, were "in alarm" as he approached, thinking he might be the enemy. Convinced that peace had finally come, the entire family was jubilant, the father shouting: "Oh I zall zee my two boys dat are in de Militia. Oh My boys, my boys! Horsen! Yees, You zall have de best horsen. Mysell I will droive You! My boys, thank God, Peace!"[17]

It took time for word to reach the remote interior of the continent and the southern states. The British army which had been defeated at New Orleans was camped at Fort Bowyer near Mobile and received the news on 5 March. It came in a letter brought by the crew of an American barge, whose arrival was cheered "over and over" by hundreds of British troops and a group of relieved wives.[18] There was "unfeigned joy," remembered one officer, "at the prospect of returning once more to the bosom of our families."[19] As late as April, Captain Andrew Bulger, a British officer in command of the remote Fort McKay at Prairie du Chien in the Northwest, was preparing to meet an American force proceeding up the Mississippi. Just before he marched, an express arrived with the glad tidings that meant the cancellation of his planned operation.

Even if many did not entirely agree with the terms of the peace treaty,[20] Americans by and large paid heed to President Madison's proclamation of 11 March 1815 that, by government resolution, "the second Thursday in April next," was to be observed by the people of the United States "as a day of thanks-giving and of devout acknowledgements to Almighty God, for his great good-ness, manifested in restoring to them the blessing of peace."[21]

Britons and Canadians also gave thanks. At York, a special service was held early in April, led by the town's Anglican minister, the Reverend Dr. John Stra-chan. All present sat attentively to hear the good reverend talk of a divine pur-pose in the horrible, almost continuous warfare that had engulfed the world since 1793, but which had culminated in Britain's triumph over her enemies. It was a victory which had not seemed possible in June 1812 when Britain, still struggling with Napoleon, had faced a new conflict with the United States. The subjects of King George III had, Strachan argued, "abundant cause to give thanks to Almighty God for the successful issue of the contest; that we are a free and happy people; have never bowed to a foreign yoke; and have preserved in all its vigour our most excellent constitution."[22]

Communities from Halifax to New Orleans marked this historic moment in their lives. Holidays were declared, shops closed, bands and bunting were seen in many villages, and the streets were full of smiling, cheering people. Typical of the celebrations were those held in Troy, New York, where Judge Masters gave a "grand entertainment" – a dinner and ball "in handsome style" that was enjoyed by army officers and local civilians.[23] At New London, Connecticut, a ball to mark the end of hostilities was attended by most of the British officers whose ships had been blockading that port – and by Commodore Stephen Decatur and his lovely wife, Susan. As former enemies enjoyed an evening of candlelit dancing and fine food the commodore, after his fundamental disagreement with the townspeople and the notorious "blue light" incident more than a year earlier, decided to let bygones be bygones.[24]

Early in March 1815 an officer of the 100th Foot, Lieutenant-Colonel George Hay, the Marquess of Tweeddale, hosted a masquerade "Victory Ball" in Mon-treal for over two hundred guests. No expense was spared, and as everyone arrived in all manner of fancy dress, a correspondent from the *Montreal Herald* was present to report on this prestigious social occasion. Julia de Rottenburg, the city's reigning beauty, outshone the competition when she arrived on her husband's arm dressed as an "interesting Squaw" and her costume "in vain at-tempted to hide the Symmetry of her Person."[25] Among others, Mrs. Wallace, wife of Major Peter Wallace of the Royal Artillery, appeared as a flower girl, and Marianne McGillivray and Anne Richardson, daughters of two wealthy Mon-treal businessmen, were respectively a "New Market Jockey of feather weight," and a "Columbine of the old Theatre." As part of the evening's entertainments, the charming "Mrs. Colonel Murray," who had spent much time in Montreal after the fall of Fort George, put on a "display of various talents in several characters; all of which were supported with spirit," and rendered "more interesting still by her songs; accompanied by the pleasing sounds of the tinkling Guitar."

The fun continued into the early hours, when everyone enjoyed a splendid repast. According to the *Herald* reporter, it was an exceptional meal, for "all the delicacies of the *maître de cuisine* were laid out in a style seldom before witnessed in this country."[26] During supper, "when the fair revealed their charms," and masks were removed, the newspaper again singled out Julia de Rottenburg, whose "beauty was conspicuous" and "shone forth unrivalled." Lieutenant John Le Couteur, who was present, remembered that

> there was a beautiful Pandora's box in the Centre of the table which some lady was desired to open. She did so to distribute its favours or evils – when out flew a number of Canaries and other birds that flew at all the Candles and almost left us in darkness, charging and extinguishing them in succession. Such roars of laughter. I never was at a more lovely or elegant party.[27]

It was not until the "brightness of the sun eclipsed the dim light of the Chandeliers" that Tweeddale's guests brought the affair to a close by promenading "in masks thro' the streets; to the wonder of the industrious peasant, as he came to market."[28]

Not to be outdone, in Kingston Commodore Sir James Lucas Yeo, the British naval commander on the Great Lakes, staged a ball on board his flagship, HMS *St. Lawrence*, the 102-gun vessel that was the largest warship ever constructed on the inland waters. As the local newspaper reported, it too was a grand affair:

> Yesterday an elegant fete was given on board His Majesty's Ship St. Lawrence by the officers of the wardroom to the gentry of Kingston and its vicinity. The entertainment commenced at one o'clock [P.M.], with an exhibition of fire works, and dancing until four o'clock, when upwards of Ninety Ladies and Gentlemen descended to the middle deck of this beautiful Ship, fitted up in an appropriate manner, and partook of a sumptuous dinner; after which dancing re-commenced, and with the assistance of a late supper kept up the brilliant liveliness of this (to us handsome) naval scene of festivity to an early hour the next morning; when all retired highly gratified with the hilarity of the occasion and the polite attentions of their entertainers.[29]

As the months passed, people had time to reflect on the war and their experience of it. For some, there were powerful memories of the troops marching and of "battles and cannonading and takings and retakings of forts, burning of towns, marchings and countermarchings."[30] There were also memories of "towns on fire, and graybeards, and helpless children, and distracted mothers with infants in their arms, hungry and tired and tattered, flying from the brutality of human bloodhounds."[31] For others, the conflict conjured up images of the "carts of wounded brought home" and of the aboriginal peoples who "seemed to have the tomahawk suspended over the heads of friends as well as foes."[32]

At Halifax, Rebecca Almon wrote to her aunts, Catherine and Mary Byles, in Boston, hoping that "the Olive Branch may be extended & that the Period arrive when the Nations shall learn War no more."[33] In Virginia, Elizabeth Kennon was glad to be able to "hail the return of those Halcyon days, we knew not how to value as we ought, until fatal experience taught us the difference."[34] Elizabeth anticipated the homecoming of her menfolk, as did many other women, but some were not entirely comfortable about the future. At York, Anne Powell felt her wartime experiences had served to "hasten the infirmities of age and destroyed many of those hopes and prospects which, if realized, would have smoothed my passage to the grave."[35] Anne and her neighbours had struggled through "the difficulties which surrounded us," and while she certainly acknowledged her gratitude that "*all* has not been wrested from me by the evil

The indomitable Mrs. Powell. Anne Murray Powell (1758-1849), daughter of a Scottish physician, married lawyer William Dummer Powell in 1775. They lived at York, Upper Canada, and had nine children, three of whom died before the War of 1812. As her husband's career blossomed, leading to his eventual appointment as Chief Justice of Upper Canada, Mrs. Powell assumed an unassailable position in the tight upper circle of York society, from where she pronounced on manners, behaviour and the progress of the war. A woman of great strength of character, principle and common sense, she lived to the ripe old age of ninety-three. (Print after painting of Anne Powell in later life, attributed to Owen Staples, Toronto Public Library, J. Ross Robertson Collection: T15180)

inflicted on this once happy and flourishing colony," she still could not help feeling that the outlook remained uncertain. Near Bladensburg, Maryland, the business-minded Rosalie Stier Calvert was no more optimistic than Anne Powell, telling her brother Charles that "it is very fortunate for this country that peace was concluded, as otherwise the national bonds, banks, etc. would have gone to nothing."[36] To her father Rosalie wrote,

> I am afraid that we shall enjoy only a precarious peace. As long as the Democratic party continues to manage America's destiny, we have everything to fear ... at this point there is no stable price for anything ... the government could not pay the last dividends on the public bonds ... If our envoys had not signed the peace when they did, our government would not have been able to continue for six months.[37]

Even if its finances were in a parlous state, America could take pride in its wartime record. By the end of hostilities, the United States Army had proven itself equal to hardbitten British regulars and the United States Navy had won a number of notable victories over the Royal Navy on both the high seas and the inland lakes.

As British North America took stock of the war there was the recognition, first and foremost, that His Majesty's provinces had been preserved. The militia, who had fought most valiantly, had grown both in stature and confidence, and in spite of widespread condemnation of Rear-Admiral Cockburn's raids in the Chesapeake, some good had resulted, for as many as 4,000 slaves had been given their freedom.[38] The conflict became a watershed in Canadian history, and a British traveller to Upper Canada in the 1820s noted that people dated every occurrence "before or after the war."[39] A Kingston newspaper editor saw something even more significant emerging – the fact that "proofs of loyalty everywhere given ... and even by the American emigrants" had confirmed and strengthened the population in their British allegiance, making the "line of separation" between Upper Canada and its republican neighbour even more distinct than before the war.[40]

For the aboriginal peoples who had fought on the British side during the conflict, there was rather less joy. Treaties of "peace and friendship" were signed between some tribes and the United States in the late summer of 1815, and near Detroit the remnants of Tecumseh's confederacy – the Wyandot, Delaware, Seneca, Shawnee, Miami, Ottawa, Ojibwa and Potawatomi peoples – gathered to make their marks and receive ceremonial gifts. If there were those among them

Catching fish the aboriginal way. Many participants in the war left descriptions of aboriginal people fishing during the evening, silhouetted in the light of the flaming torches that helped to illuminate the waters of a lake or river. In this painting two women are at work – part of a way of life that was ultimately to disappear. (Painting by Denis Gale. Library and Archives of Canada, C-40179.)

who could recall warnings made before the war by their prophets, they might now have reflected on how true such predictions had proved to be. A Mohawk woman named Coocoochee, who lived among the Shawnee and was greatly esteemed for her "powerful incantations and her influence with the good spirits," had warned of the whites' "increasing strength and power, their insatiable avarice, and their continuing encroachments on the red men."[41] Similar words of caution had been uttered by a Delaware woman, a prophet of her people who had spoken in 1806 of the danger that a "whirlwind would wipe out the people completely."[42] In 1815, their military power broken, the aboriginal peoples east of the Mississippi were firmly launched on the sad and tragic road that would lead, ultimately, to the disappearance of their way of life.

In Britain the cessation of hostilities was welcomed, marking as it did the end of more than two decades of nearly continuous warfare. Unfortunately trouble flared up again when "that monster Bonaparte," as one Scottish woman

England at peace. After more than twenty years of war with France, victory at the Battle of Waterloo finally brought an end to the Napoleonic Wars. The signing of the Treaty of Ghent, which ended the War of 1812, and peace in Europe, were the cause of great jubilation throughout the land. South coast ports that had seen the constant traffic of war for so long were soon peaceful again, as this scene shows. (Print from etching of Ramsgate, Kent, *c.* 1820. Author's collection.)

described the former French emperor, escaped from Elba in the spring of 1815 and "raised the standard of rebellion in the south of France."[43] It was not until the following June that the Battle of Waterloo brought lasting peace to a Europe which had been at war, with few pauses, since 1793.

The return of peace to North America brought a slow but steady return to prosperity. Trade was resumed in the depressed Atlantic ports of the United States, but although peace had been restored, evidence of the war's destruction would long remain in the areas most affected by the fighting. The Niagara was "truly a most pitiful sight," with "homes in ashes, fields trampled and laid waste, forts demolished, forests burned and blackened" and everything reflecting "distress and poverty."[44] Both sides of the Niagara River were devastated, as were communities on the north shore of Lake Erie, and in parts of western Upper Canada the picture was one of ruin and desolation. Amherstburg and Detroit were in a miserable state with the surrounding countryside ravaged by the depredations of war and former farmland in as poor a condition as in the Niagara. It would take time and industrious hands to repair the damage.

Many women, particularly widows and their families, were experiencing real hardship, and attempts to relieve their distress were made in both British North America and the United States. In Upper Canada financial assistance had been provided during the conflict to civilian and militia families. When the Niagara militia were called upon to fight without having either proper weapons or suitable clothing, the shortage had been solved by "a private subscription, aided by the personal labour of the young Ladies" of York.[45] This drew attention to the fact that families deprived of the support of their menfolk were inevitably suffering, and a decision was made by prominent citizens in Upper Canada to create the Loyal and Patriotic Society of Upper Canada, which held its first meeting in York in February 1813. Membership was by subscription, and in answer to newspaper advertisements, financial donations came from as far away as Britain and Jamaica. The purpose of the society was to provide relief to families experiencing "particular distress" as a result of the death or absence of "their friends & relations employed in the militia service." The society also provided assistance to "such militia-men as have been, or shall be disabled from labour, by wounds or otherwise in the course of the service aforesaid."

Between 1813 and 1817 the society disbursed financial aid to 855 militiamen and their families and its efforts meant that many women – wives, widows and dependants – received the means to live. Every petition for assistance was considered, and funds were paid out if deemed appropriate. Mrs. Campbell, widow of the late Captain Donald Campbell who died in 1812, received £50 (about $200). One of the victims of the burning of Newark, she had lost "her house and property by fire. The enemy burning it in the most wanton manner, leaving her and her helpless children in great distress."[46] Mrs. E. Haines, whose husband was killed at Moraviantown and who was soon afterwards "delivered of twins, and left in great distress," received £8 (about $30).[47] In Mrs. Haines's case, although her husband had been an NCO in the regular army, the society waived its principle of assisting only militiamen and their families. Mrs. Isa Hill, a widow at Newark who lost two houses when the town was burned, was said to be a lady of "cultivated understanding and agreable manners, having seen much of the world," but her losses proved too much for her and she decided to leave Upper Canada for a new life in Jamaica. The society gave her £50 "to assist in carrying her there."[48]

Most recipients were both grateful and deserving, but there were some who took advantage of the society's benevolence. A widow from the London district, Mrs. Ruth Marks, received a widow's payment of £20 (about $80) on 15 May 1815 but then applied again in December of that year. It somehow escaped notice that she had already received an allowance, and another £20 was voted to her and she thereby obtained "double what the widows got."[49] In the spring of 1816, Mrs. Marks and a companion journeyed to York to apply for government widows' pensions but because they did not immediately receive them and were apparently "unable to get home," the society "ordered them each, £10 (about $40) to enable them to return."[50] Not content with this, Mrs. Marks availed herself of its bounty a fourth time when the London District was awarded a separate £72 (about $275) grant to be shared among eight recipients – one of whom was Ruth Marks. This time, however, she was caught out, the treasurer noting in his record that, although "this woman's husband was killed" in the war, she had clearly "imposed on the Society."[51]

The records of the Loyal and Patriotic Society noted numerous other widows who were left without means of support, who had lost property, clothing and, in the case of one black woman, "every thing."[52] Wartime kindness found reward too, as in the instance of a Widow Clarke, who received three payments in 1815 for the help she gave during the conflict in "caring and boarding" of people, and also "for burying Betty Feathers and other humane actions."[53] In 1817, after much good work, the society's surplus funds were turned over to the new Society for the Relief of Strangers in Distress, inaugurated at York to provide systematic care for travellers and newcomers to Upper Canada.

This charitable work was mirrored in the United States where efforts had begun during the war to assist those in difficulty. In January 1814, the New York Legislature appropriated $50,000 to relieve wartime distress and at the same time passed a law enabling the monies to be distributed by the supervisors of towns and villages such as Buffalo and Schlosser, which had suffered most. At Canandaigua, New York, an organization calling itself the "Committee on Safety and Relief" held its first meeting that same month. Dedicated to general defence and guarding the frontier from depredations, its members were also concerned with "promoting the safety and relief of this part of the country."[54] With funds raised by subscription and contributions from across the state, the committee sought the names of "such as may have suffered," whose homes had been "burned or plundered," or families where members had been killed or taken by the enemy.

The first payment was made to a Mrs. Farwell "late of Buffalo," who received just over $75, and to Mrs. Anna Baxton, whose husband had been killed or taken prisoner of war and who had "lost her all."[55] Thereafter, the committee dispensed assistance regularly with grants averaging $25. According to its minute book, from January to April 1814, it assisted twenty-five widows and forty-two wives, many of whom were living in the area destroyed by British troops in the winter of 1813-1814.[56]

A list of those distressed American residents of the Niagara frontier, prepared soon after the burning of Buffalo, reads much as do the records of the Loyal and Patriotic Society of Upper Canada. Recipients included: Agnes Greensitt, a widow with a large family who lost her husband in the summer of 1813 and later, her house and furniture, "destroyed by the enemy"; Marianne Alvord, another widow and the mother of four small children, whose house and barn had been burned, and who was dependent upon the charity of her brother-in-law; and a Mrs. Lewis, a widow with four small children, who was "supposed to be near Aurora in Cayuga and as poor as can be conceived."[57]

In 1816 Congress passed an act which provided a deadline by which sufferers from the effects of the British invasion of the Niagara frontier might seek compensation from the federal government. Under its provisions, payment could be made for buildings destroyed by the enemy and applicants could apply for loans not exceeding $1000 to assist in rebuilding their homes. They were required to supply "proof of destruction of the buildings," and any aid dispensed was in the form of a loan repayable within seven years.[58] Among the inventories of those who suffered on the frontier, many detailed the "poor possessions which often constituted the claimants all," and were "pathetic in their exhibition of brave need and patriotic penury." A few, however, were more substantial. Mrs. Serena Grosvenor of Buffalo itemised all her household effects "pilfered or destroyed by the British on the 30 Dec 1813," and her list included platters, pitchers, wine glasses, water tumblers, kettles, bedsteads, bottles, bowls, mats, pails, candle snuffers and candlesticks, chairs, tables, tea trays, decanters, a coffee mill, coffee pots and "1 Cotton Umbrella" valued at $1. In total, Mrs. Grosvenor estimated her items to the value of $181. Another woman, Mrs. LeCouteulx, was clearly married to a wealthy man, as her husband submitted an inventory of losses containing such items as "2 pairs of Brass Andirons – elegant," as well as "4 Cherry Tables," one "Black Walnut Close [Clothes] Press" and an "Engraving of Bonaparte [in] gilt frame."[59] In all, claims valued at $350,000 were filed for 334 houses and other structures destroyed by the British raids, those of Buffalo alone totalling $100,000.

In 1818, the U.S. House Committee on Claims examined a mass of testimony in an effort to decide whether 158 cases claiming compensation in and around Buffalo were "of such a character as to entitle the claimants to relief."[60]

After much debate Congress decided against the claimants. Unwilling to accept this decision, many of them continued to petition the Committee of Claims for relief. Even the passing of a new law did nothing to help them. In 1824, an act authorising a transfer of the debts of the sufferers" – those unable to repay their loans in the given seven years – was passed, but the issue of compensation continued for many more years. As late as 1840, Helen Taylor, heir of Samuel Taylor, received $289.28 for "a house of said Taylor, destroyed by fire on the Niagara frontier during the war," and one claim even dragged on until 1859, when a recommendation was made that it "be not paid."[61]

In British North America, the government of Upper Canada also tried to compensate those who had suffered significant property losses. More than 2,200 claims for compensation were submitted in Upper Canada alone, the majority from areas which had suffered fighting, depredation and burning. Again, some claims were substantial. At Port Talbot on Lake Erie, fifty families had lost "all their horses, and every particle of wearing apparel and household furniture," leaving the sufferers "naked, and in the most wretched state."[62] Records show that Colonel William Claus and his wife, Catherine, requested compensation for the loss of their home and property at Newark that totalled £3,160 3s. 4d., (about $12,125), including horses, a wagon, a phaeton, household and kitchen furniture worth over £500 (about $2,000), three "pleasure Sleighs" and "upwards of 500 Volumes of Books."[63] James and Angelica Givins, whose home was plundered during the American attack on York in April 1813, sustained losses of some £338, including carpets, calico curtains, furniture and fittings and crockery.[64] The "whole of the Wearing Apparel of Mrs. Givens & 7 children" was also taken, amounting to £100 (about $400), and "Wines and other Liquors," valued at £30 (about $120).

Given the amounts involved, Upper Canada looked to Britain for financial assistance but, having fought a long and costly war with France, the British government initially hoped that money could be raised through the sale of the confiscated estates of Canadian traitors. It soon became clear that this source would not be enough even after the claims had been drastically scaled down, and as in the United States, negotiations dragged on for years before even partial payments were made. Some women, particularly widows, were forced to struggle in poverty until they received a settlement. Susannah Jessup of Prescott, for example, was left in reduced circumstances until 1837, when she received the sum of £533 (about $2,000) as restitution for the destruction caused to her property by the building of Fort Wellington.[65]

Both the American and British governments also provided compensation to former soldiers, militiamen and sufferers in the form of land grants. The United States made provision for 160 acres of bounty land to be "designated, surveyed and laid off at the public expense," for men who had fought for their country, or their widows or heirs.[66] The militia of Upper Canada and their dependants were given grants of Crown land in the province but, again, it took a long time for claimants to receive them.

The widows of American, British and Canadian soldiers and sailors killed in the war received pensions from their respective nations. In most cases the amount was based on their husband's rank, and, in the case of enlisted personnel, it was not generous. Furthermore, all three nations legislated that if widows remarried, their pensions were forfeit. The temptation for a woman to remarry must have been considerable, but this had to be weighed against the disadvantages she faced under law of losing control of all her property to her new husband and forfeiting her pension as well. Perhaps because an annuity – even if it did not provide totally for the needs of an average family – allowed a measure of independence for a woman, many chose to remain single.

The business of restoring relations between Britain and the United States fell substantially upon the shoulders of Sir Charles Bagot, the first British ambassador to Washington after the war. Bagot arrived in March 1816, and as he immersed himself in his important work his wife, Lady Mary Bagot, began her

"Well, here we are," wrote an excited Mary Boardman Crowninshield (1778-1840) when she arrived in Washington in November 1815 to join her husband, Benjamin, after his appointment as Secretary of the Navy. Her subsequent letters, addressed mainly to her mother at Salem, Massachusetts, provide a window on Washington high society in the post-war months, and unusually detailed accounts of the fashionable attire worn by the women she met. (Print from a portrait by John Vanderlyn painted in 1816, Francis Boardman Crowninshield, *Letters of Mary Boardman Crowninshield*.)

own efforts to win the hearts and minds of the capital's elite. As a diplomatic wife, Mary Bagot impressed those who met her, particularly Mary Boardman Crowninshield, wife of the new secretary of the navy. Mrs. Crowninshield had a keen eye for fashion and carefully noted the ladies' costumes at the President's New Year reception in January 1816. Dolley Madison wore a gown of "yellow satin embroidered all over with sprigs of butterflies" and a "white bonnet with feathers"; Pamela Brown, wife of Major-General Jacob Brown, was in an orange dress "with a deep border and a shawl to match"; Susan Decatur looked lovely in a gown with a "blue lustre trimmed with satin ribbon" and a white hat "turned up in front."[67] Predictably, when the Bagots called on her, Mrs. Crowninshield's eye did not miss a single aspect of Mary's Bagot's outfit. "She looked elegantly," reported Mrs. Crowninshield to her mother,

> with braids, and curls, a muslin dress over satin trimmed with a thread lace a quarter wide, most elegant, with two rows let in front; two narrow rows of lace round the neck, rather high; no handkerchief, a bead or pearl necklace, and a gold watch chain round her neck; long sleeves with several rows of gold chain, clasped with a large emerald bracelet … and just above, two rows of beads or pearls, – looked more like beads, – a scarlet shawl thrown over her shoulders, no bonnet or veil.[68]

At the Madisons' next reception, Mrs. Crowninshield recorded that Lady Bagot was

> dressed in white, a figured lace over satin, very much trimmed at the bottom, long sleeves. The short ones very full and trimmed below, very close, and the same ornaments I had seen before, but round her neck a diamond necklace, and ear-rings. Her hair dressed, a narrow gold band, and nine white ostrich feathers. Looked very beautiful indeed.[69]

Charles Bagot and his lovely wife charmed Washington. They went out of their way to observe local customs and to be pleasant and courteous to everyone. "Mr. Bagot, the English ambassador, and his lady, are particularly assiduous in their attentions to all classes," wrote a British observer, Henry Fearon, during a visit to the capital, "and maintain a strict conformity with the habits of the place."[70] Their efforts were reciprocated by the Madisons at a presidential dinner in April 1816 which, in Mary Boardman Crowninshield's opinion, was "very handsome, more so than any I have seen." Once again, Lady Bagot impressed her in a pale green dress. "She has the whitest neck I ever saw," Mary enthused,

Postwar emissary. Lady Mary Bagot (1786-1845) was the eldest daughter of the 4th Earl of Mornington and married the Right Hon. Sir Charles Bagot, GCB, in 1806, by whom she had three sons and five daughters. Sir Charles was appointed British Minister Plenipotentiary to Washington in 1816, where he and Lady Mary created a very favourable impression. In later years, Mary Bagot returned to North America when her husband became governor-general of British North America in 1842, and upon his death the following year, she was the first wife of a governor-general to assume the title of "Her Excellency." (Print from portrait after a miniature by John Hoppner, R.A., *c.* 1806. H.J. Morgan, *Types of Canadian Women and of Women who are or have been connected with Canada.*)

"for she has black eyes and hair and her hair dressed very high." Mary also liked the "wreath of red roses and purple and white flowers" that Lady Bagot wore around her head with her hair arranged in "a great wave on the top." As a final mark in favour of the ambassador's wife, Mary pronounced disdainfully that "all the other ladies [were] in old dresses."[71]

With her style and personality, Mary Bagot contributed in no small measure to her husband's success. As their country's first postwar diplomatic representatives, the Bagots helped to establish better relations between the former enemies. In the half century that followed, there would occasionally be tensions, most having to do with the northern border, but Britain and the United States – and Canada when it achieved nationhood in 1867 – eventually drew closer together to form a firm alliance that was to prove crucial in the conflicts of the twentieth century and the first decade of the not-much-less-violent twenty-first century. It was well that Americans, Britons and Canadians celebrated the end of what one British officer called "a hot and unnatural war between kindred people."[72]

"Their fate unpitied, and unheard their name." Many women who
lived through the War of 1812 are known only by a name on a
tombstone. In this instance the name is that of Dorothy Fawson, a
woman in her fifties during the war, who died in February 1819. She
was laid to rest in the Old Burying Ground at Halifax, Nova Scotia,
not far from the grave of Major-General Robert Ross. (Photograph
by Dianne Graves.)

"A chaplet of unfading laurels."
The Fates of Women and Men

O f those women who had lived through the war, some found new homes as the western United States began to open up, while many of the British wives braved the Atlantic once more, this time with the prevailing winds in their favour, to return to their homeland. For most, the postwar years meant picking up the threads of the life they had known before 1812. Military wives continued to move with their menfolk, and naval wives resumed their lengthy vigils, albeit marking time in the knowledge that their husbands were now serving on peaceful missions. Those who had begun to enjoy success in business continued in their chosen professions while society ladies became ever more sophisticated as the cities and towns in which they lived continued to expand and evolve. For slave women the postwar years brought manumission to some, but the time of emancipation still lay many years ahead for the majority. Elsewhere, as the native people had feared, a wave of settlement and development continued to encroach upon the wilderness, and many frontier dwellers realized that their days of rugged isolation would soon be a thing of the past. Indeed, such was the pace of progress after 1815 that the first two decades of the nineteenth century soon receded into the past, overtaken by the onset of the industrial age and with it, a rapidly changing world.

A s for those women who have appeared in these pages, Abigail Snelling, who was in Detroit when it fell in 1812, remained an army wife. Her husband, Josiah, was appointed commander of the 6th Infantry Regiment and Abigail and their children accompanied him until his death in 1828. In his honour, Fort

St. Anthony was renamed Fort Snelling. In 1841 Abigail remarried the Reverend J.E. Chiplin and lived at White Pigeon, Michigan. She passed her final days in Cincinnati.

At Staatsburg, New York, Gertrude Lewis welcomed home her husband, Major-General Morgan Lewis, in 1815 and was at his side in the years to come, when he held a number of public positions. Morgan and Gertrude Lewis remained a respected and popular couple in New York.

Margaret Hanks, who saw the British flag raised at Fort Mackinac in July 1812 and was widowed at Detroit, outlived her husband by fifty-seven years, dying in December 1869 at the age of eighty-three.

Sarah and George Howard left Connecticut and moved to New York, where George started an unsuccessful dry goods business. With glowing testimonials from his wartime commanders, however, he was appointed to the position of Inspector of Customs in the city's revenue department, a post in which he remained for many years. George, Sarah, their three daughters and one son lived happily until Sarah's death, after which George remarried and returned to Connecticut. He died there in 1851.

Rachel Jackson, wife of Major-General Andrew Jackson, never forgot the hospitality she and her husband received after his victory at New Orleans. Andrew Jackson remained in the United States army until 1819 and then devoted himself to politics, ultimately becoming the seventh president of the United States in 1829. Unfortunately, Rachel never had the opportunity to become First Lady. Newspaper articles published during the election campaign persistently referred to the circumstances of her divorce from her first husband and caused her great distress. As a result, her health suffered and she died of a heart attack on 23 December 1828, two weeks after Andrew Jackson's election victory. She was buried in the garden of "the Hermitage," the Tennessee plantation that had been her home for many years.

Sally Sinclair, wife of Captain Arthur Sinclair, USN, who had missed her husband so much during his wartime service, was overjoyed at his return. The couple eventually produced a family of four daughters and four sons, three of whom served in the navies of the United States and the Confederate States during the Civil War. Sarah died in 1827 at the young age of thirty-six, survived by her mother, Elizabeth, and by her grieving husband, who only outlived her by four years.

Two of the great American naval heroes of the War of 1812, Oliver Hazard Perry and Stephen Decatur, died within a matter of months of each other, plunging their wives into early widowhood. Perry's death from yellow fever in South America in 1819 devastated his wife, Elizabeth, as he had been her "guardian angel on earth" and she felt she was much too young to have her "dearest happiness so soon destroyed."[1] Thereafter, Elizabeth Perry devoted herself to her daughter and three sons, one of whom followed his late father into the navy.

Stephen Decatur was mortally wounded in 1820 when he fought a duel with another naval officer and former friend, Captain James Barron. Susan Decatur was distraught at her husband's death but she outlived him by some forty years. She returned to Washington and became a shining light in society, working to maintain her husband's reputation. She rarely attended public gatherings lest she meet the man responsible for his death. Susan Decatur died at Georgetown in 1860.

Ann Macdonough moved with her husband, Thomas, to Portsmouth, New Hampshire, in July 1815, when he was appointed to command the navy yard in that city. Throughout the decade that followed the war, Ann and Thomas faced serious health problems, both apparently contracting chronic tuberculosis. Ann's continued pregnancies – she gave birth to ten children – and the loss of five of them in infancy had a debilitating effect on her and she grew weaker as time passed. Captain Macdonough hoped that sea duty would restore his health and sailed in 1825 as commanding officer of the USS *Constitution*. While in the Mediterranean that year, he learned that Ann had died, and the news seemed to rob him of his will to live. He relinquished command at Gibraltar and secured a passage home on a merchant ship but died during the voyage, leaving five orphaned children. One of his last requests was that he should not be buried at sea, but that his body should be laid to rest beside that of his wife in her home town of Middletown, Connecticut.[2]

Minerva Rodgers and her husband, Commodore John Rodgers, enjoyed a happier postwar life. After Rodgers became the senior officer in the navy, the couple moved to a house at Greenleaf Point, Maryland, and it was in that "dear old place," as one of Minerva's daughters remembered, that five more children were born, and the family "grew and sported for many years."[3] John Rodgers died in 1838, survived by his adored Minerva, who outlived him by almost forty years.

Dolley Madison left Washington after her husband's second term as president ended in 1817, but not before the citizens of Georgetown gave a ball in her honour. They summarized their gratitude to this beloved lady in verse:

A charming WOMAN, still we find,
Like the bright SUN, cheers all Mankind,
And like it, is admired by all![4]

The Madisons moved to Montpelier, their handsome Virginia home, where Dolley continued to dispense charm and hospitality to all those fortunate enough to visit her. After the death of her husband in 1836, she found country life too quiet and returned to Washington, where, at her residence on the corner of Lafayette Square, she remained a renowned and popular hostess despite financial difficulties later in her life. Dolley Madison died in 1849 and was buried near her husband at Montpelier.

The charming and beautiful Elizabeth Kortright Monroe, wife of James Madison's secretary of state, succeeded Dolley Madison as America's First Lady in 1817. James Monroe's term of office was observed by social commentator Margaret Bayard Smith, who continued to write about Washington society until at least 1841, and who watched with interest the progress towards matrimony of Maria Mayo, one of Dolley Madison's society favourites. In 1816, Maria married Major-General Winfield Scott, a hero of the war, and dutifully produced seven children, but her restless spirit took her on extended trips to France. Meanwhile, her husband continued his military career until 1861.

Rosalie Stier Calvert recovered sufficiently from the two serious bouts of typhoid she suffered during the war to give birth to her ninth and last child in 1816. The years 1817-1819 proved the high point in Rosalie's life as Caroline,

Margaret Bayard Smith (1778-1844), writer and Washington social commentator, was the wife of Samuel Harrison Smith, founder of the *National Intelligencer* newspaper. In addition to her private correspondence, which provides a fascinating entrée into Washington life, she was also a contributor to the literature of the day, mainly through articles, moral essays and stories. (Drawing after a portrait by Charles Bird King in Gaillard Hunt, *The First Forty Years of Washington Society*.)

her eldest daughter, was presented to Washington society and Rosalie became preoccupied in selecting her daughter's wardrobe and in cultivating suitable contacts. Such was Rosalie's excellent taste that both mother and daughter were much admired and envied around the capital. Tragedy struck in February 1820 when Rosalie lost two more of her children within a week of each other, the symptoms suggesting diphtheria. Late that year Rosalie became bedridden, suffering from heart failure, and in March 1821 she died at the age of forty-three, deeply mourned by her husband and five surviving children.

The beautiful and fascinating Elizabeth Patterson Bonaparte lived much of the rest of her life in Baltimore, but not before taking an opportunity, after 1815, to make a longed-for return visit to France. In some ways she regretted not having "vegetated as the wife of some respectable man of business" but she confessed that "nature never intended me for obscurity, and that with my disposition and character I am better as I am."[5] When her father, William Patterson, died, he left an immense fortune but Betsy inherited little because of what he termed the "anxiety and trouble" she had caused him.[6] He did, however, provide her with some nine properties in Baltimore, to be passed on to her son, Jérôme Napoleon Bonaparte, on her death. Even in old age, Betsy Patterson Bonaparte remained "a beautiful woman with a ready repartee and untiring haughtiness," who was still "capricious, but fascinating despite age and reversed fortunes." She outlived most of her contemporaries and talked of her past without reserve until her death in 1879.[7]

After the Battle of New Orleans, society hostess Louise Livingston discovered that she had an aptitude for tending the sick and wounded and was among a group of ladies who helped to nurse the victims of an epidemic of yellow fever. Her future took a different course after her husband, Edward, entered politics and was elected to the United States Senate. When Andrew Jackson became president in 1829, Edward was appointed to be his secretary of state and the Livingstons moved to Washington, where they spent a good deal of time at the White House. Louise and their daughter, Cora, became great favourites of the widowed Jackson and occupied a special place in Washington society. Edward Livingston was appointed to be America's ambassador to France in 1833, and Louise and her husband lived in Paris until 1835, where she was as popular as she had been in New Orleans and Washington. Following Edward's death in 1836 she retired to Montgomery Place, the beautiful Livingston estate on the Hudson River, and remained there until she died in 1860.

In the 1820s, Elizabeth Stewart, spy *extraordinaire,* and her husband, James, went to Britain, where they received a pension, chiefly in recognition of their outstanding espionage work during the war.

Writer and teacher Susanna Rowson continued to run her school near Boston until her retirement in 1822. Able to reflect with satisfaction on her varied life and accomplishments, she died in 1824.

The actress sisters, Juliana Wood and Eleanora Darley, trod the boards for a number of years after the war. Juliana worked mainly in Philadelphia, where her husband William was a theatre manager. She died in 1838 but William continued in the entertainment business until his retirement in 1846. Eleanora Darley and her husband, John, also settled in Philadelphia, where she performed while continuing to raise their eight children. One of her sons, Felix Octavius Carr Darley, born in 1821, was among nineteenth-century America's most famous illustrators.

Madeline La Framboise, pioneer fur trader, continued to run her business until some time after the War of 1812. Her retirement was spent mainly at her pleasant house overlooking Mackinac harbour, where she devoted her life to working for the Catholic Church. Having taught herself to read and write, Madeline instructed young people in the catechism and used her wealth to support the work of the parish priests, while also giving generously to the poor. Sadly, her son and daughter died a few years after the war, but Madeline found consolation in her charitable work, the company of her granddaughter Harriet, and the many visitors who made the long journey to Mackinac Island. The writer and editor Margaret Fuller, who visited Madeline La Framboise in 1843, described her as "very ladylike in her manners. She is a great character among them [the people of the island]."[8] Madeline La Framboise died in 1846 and was

The former home of Madame La Framboise.
After the end of her career as a fur trader, Madeline La Framboise lived the remainder of her life on Mackinac Island, where she built a fine house and devoted herself to charitable work for the Catholic church. Her former home is now the Harbor View Inn, which offers picturesque vistas of the lake. (Photograph courtesy of the Harbor View Inn, Mackinac.)

buried beside her daughter at the church of Sainte Anne, Mackinac. A monument at present-day Ada, Michigan, marks the site of her trading post and her house on Mackinac Island, now the Harbor View Inn, continues to welcome visitors to the island.[9]

Of the women who survived the attack near Fort Dearborn, Rebekah Heald led a life after the war "of quiet usefulness, like that of her sister pioneers."[10] Despite the memory of her ordeal, she remained attached to the frontier country and settled with her husband at O'Fallon, Missouri. They built a farm, where Rebekah lived until her death in 1857. Of her and those like her, it has been written that

> one may well be excited at the heroism and sufferings borne with such sturdy fortitude, of the pioneer women whose lot was cast in the midst of the troubles upon the frontier. Yet their attachment to this wild, unsettled life was still more remarkable; for as the country became settled, they would encourage their husbands or sons to "sell out" and remove still further into the wilderness.

Abigail Adams was seventy years old when the war ended and she and her husband, former president John Adams, continued to live at their home in Massachusetts. The war had not been without its sorrows, for in 1813 the couple had endured the loss of their daughter, Nabby (Abigail), from cancer. Mrs. Adams, who outlived her daughter by five years, found consolation in a "firm persuasion" that everything was part of "a divine plan." She died in 1818, a few days short of her seventy-fourth birthday.[11]

Lydia Sigourney of Connecticut and Elizabeth Oakes Smith of Maine, both young, intelligent and studious during the war years, matured into nationally-acclaimed writers. Among their works are fascinating accounts which provide insights into aspects of American social history in the last decade of the eighteenth century and the first two decades of the nineteenth.

Most of the British women who came to North America before and during the War of 1812 returned home, but not all. Jane Ferguson remained in Upper Canada with her husband, George, who began a new life as an itinerant Methodist preacher. For the next quarter of a century Jane, George and their family moved as his work demanded. Jane eventually produced thirteen children, whom she raised despite her husband's prolonged absences, without the support of any relatives, and with slim financial resources. After retiring from their arduous life in 1843, the Fergusons settled in Peel County, Upper Canada, where Jane outlived her husband, finally passing away a few months short of her seventy-fifth birthday.[12]

Maria Muir, wife of Major Adam Muir, who braved the wilderness to take her children to York in October 1813, returned to Britain with her husband. In 1816 Adam Muir sustained a serious hip injury in a riding accident and was forced to resign his commission. He received a modest pension and decided to take Maria and their family back to North America. They settled at Quebec but Muir found it difficult to find work with his injury and the family experienced acute financial hardship. He died in 1829, leaving Maria struggling to support their ten children.

Lady Katherine Sherbrooke and her husband, Sir John Sherbrooke, remained in British North America until 1818. They returned to Britain and lived in the Sherbrooke family home in Nottinghamshire, where Sir John died in 1830 and Lady Katherine in 1856. Before their departure, Lady Sherbrooke and her husband were among the first guests to stay at the Mansion House Hotel, a new luxury hotel for steamship passengers in Montreal owned by businessman John Molson. Molson paid tribute to Katherine Sherbrooke by naming the fourth vessel in his growing steamship fleet after her, and the town of Sherbrooke, Quebec, is among the places where her name is commemorated to this day.

Lady Jane Hunter and her husband, Major-General Sir Martin Hunter, that delightful pair who were "lovely and pleasant in their lives," enjoyed many happy years after they left New Brunswick in 1812.[13] In 1823, Sir Martin was appointed governor of Pendennis Castle in Cornwall and in 1825 reached the rank of lieutenant-general. He retired as governor of Edinburgh Castle. Jane Hunter died at their home, Antons Hill, Berwickshire, in September 1844, and her husband followed her two years later. Both lie in the family plot at nearby Medomsley church.

Amelia Smyth, wife of General George Stracey Smyth, the lieutenant-governor of New Brunswick during the war, was destined never to see her homeland again. In 1817 at the age of thirty-two she died of tuberculosis and was buried at St. Paul's Church, Halifax.

Charlotte Gubbins and her husband, Lieutenant-Colonel Joseph Gubbins, left Eastport in 1816 and returned to England with their seven children. Gubbins retired from the army and Charlotte died in 1824 in the south of France, where she had gone for health reasons. Her husband outlived her by another eight years.

Julia's daughter. Lady Frances Paget, (*c.* 1805-1875) was the daughter of Lieutenant-General Sir Francis de Rottenburg, KCH, and his wife, Julia. Born in Canada, she married Captain William Paget, RN, by whom she had three sons. In the absence of a portrait of Julia de Rottenburg, her pretty daughter's face is the only clue to what Julia may have looked like. (Print from a miniature by an unknown artist, likely painted around 1827, the year Frances married. H.J. Morgan, *Types of Canadian Women and of Women who are or have been connected with Canada, Vol. I.*)

Alicia Cockburn and Julia de Rottenburg, leading lights of wartime Montreal society, became titled ladies when their husbands were knighted after the War of 1812. Before she left Canada, Alicia composed the inscription for a tablet to her late lamented friend, Captain Henry Milnes, which was erected in St. George's Anglican Church, Kingston. Lady Alicia Cockburn, as she later became, accompanied her husband in the colonial service, in which he served as governor, first of Curaçao and then of the Bahamas. On their return to Britain the Cockburns settled in Dover, Kent. Their home, in an elegant row of three-storied Georgian terraced houses beneath the town's East Cliff, overlooked the harbour and from their upper windows on clear days could be seen the busy sea traffic and the coast of France. When Alicia died in 1854 at the age of seventy-two, the couple were within months of celebrating their golden wedding anniversary. Francis Cockburn continued to live at Dover until his death fourteen years later. He and his wife are buried in the churchyard of St. Michael & All Angels, Harbledown, Canterbury, where Alicia had married her dashing officer in 1804. They lie beside the grave of Alicia's mother, Lady Frances Benson, and that of Augusta Hoseason, Sir Francis's niece, and daughter of his elder brother, Rear-Admiral Sir George Cockburn, wartime scourge of the Chesapeake.

Julia de Rottenburg remained in North America for some years after the war with her husband, Lieutenant-General Francis de Rottenburg. After his knighthood and their return to England, Sir Francis and Lady Julia lived in Hampshire, where he died in 1832. He was commemorated by a memorial in Portsmouth Cathedral, which was lost when the building suffered damage during a German air raid in the Second World War. Julia's son George, Baron de Rottenburg, and her grandson, Lieutenant-Colonel William Paget, one of the three sons born to her daughter, Frances, served in the British and Indian armies respectively.

Julia's later life was not without worry, however, because of her daughter's marriage. As much a beauty as her mother, Frances de Rottenburg married Lord William Paget, a naval officer and second son of Field Marshal Henry William Paget, 1st Earl of Anglesey, in 1827. William proved to be not only a wastrel and a spendthrift but accused Frances of being unfaithful, citing Lord Cardigan, later to achieve fame as the commander of the Light Brigade in the Crimean War, as correspondent. In the notorious court case that followed, the jury found in favour of Lord Cardigan, and after more serious financial problems, William was forced to flee to France in 1846 with his family. Not until the last few years of his life, it seems, did Lord William Paget lead a comparatively respectable existence, sparing his father and his wife for a short time "the appalling tension and excitement" to which he had so long subjected them.[14] For Lady Julia de Rottenburg, it cannot have been the peaceful progression into old age she had every right to hope for.

Lady Catherine Prevost returned to England with her husband, Lieutenant-General Sir George Prevost, in 1815, when he was asked to explain the withdrawal of his force from Plattsburgh after the British defeat on Lake Champlain. Sir George demanded a court martial to clear his name but died shortly before it was to sit. He was buried in the churchyard of St. Mary the Virgin, East Barnet. Lady Catherine had a monument to him erected in Winchester Cathedral. The Prince Regent not only approved the monument but also the addition of armorial bearings to the family coat of arms. Catherine Prevost did not long survive her husband and died in August 1821 at Belmont, the family home in Hampshire. She was buried with her husband at East Barnet and their grave is today sheltered by mock orange blossom and watched over by oak, ash and yew trees. Anne Elinor Prevost, who died in 1882, was much respected by all who knew her but never married.

Juana Smith, wife of Major Harry Smith, was another wife who entered into colonial service when her husband completed his distinguished army career. Harry Smith was eventually knighted and became one of the heroes of Victorian Britain. In 1848 he was appointed Governor of the Cape Province in South Africa, and Juana gave her name to the town of Ladysmith in the Transvaal, which was to achieve fame in a future war. Sir Harry Smith died in 1860 and Lady Juana Smith, in 1872.

Final resting place. Like most British women of the War of 1812, Lady Catherine Prevost (1766-1821) returned to her homeland. Lady Prevost lies buried beside her husband in a quiet corner of the churchyard of St. Mary the Virgin, East Barnet, Hertfordshire. Their grave stands in the back left-hand corner of this picture. (Photograph by Dianne Graves.)

Instead of accepting a posthumous knighthood for her husband, Elizabeth Ross, widow of Major-General Robert Ross, proposed that the family name be titled "Ross of Bladensburg." Her request was granted and she was present at the unveiling of monuments to her late husband in St. Paul's Cathedral, London, and at Rosstrevor, Ireland, his family residence. By the time she died in 1845, Elizabeth had seen her late husband honoured by a grateful nation and her sons serving with distinction in the British army.

Of the naval wives, Sophia van Cortlandt rejoiced that Captain William Mulcaster, whom she married in 1814, recovered from the serious wounds he had sustained in North America. William and Sophia Mulcaster spent the first few years of their married life at Plymouth. Sophia produced a daughter and two sons, both of whom chose the army as a career and rose to the rank of general, the younger serving mainly in India.

Lady Jane Codrington enjoyed another twenty-two happy years with her husband, Admiral Sir Edward Codrington, before her death in 1837, leaving Edward to watch proudly as his sons continued the family tradition of service in the Royal Navy. One of Jane Codrington's great grandsons was the Honourable Denys Finch-Hatton, second son of Henry Stormont Finch-Hatton, the 13th

Earl of Winchelsea and Jane's granddaughter Anne, Countess of Winchelsea. Denys Finch-Hatton was to achieve fame through the pen of the Danish writer Baroness Karen Blixen. As the great love of her life, he appears in *Out of Africa*, the account of her experiences in Kenya.

Captain Philip Bowes Vere Broke, a hero after his victory over the USS *Chesapeake* in 1813, was made a baronet in September of that year and a Knight Commander of the Bath in January 1815. Louisa, his wife, proudly shared the tributes paid to him and together they resumed life at Broke Hall, their Suffolk home, where two more sons were born after the war. Although Sir Philip enjoyed the duties of country gentleman, fond husband and father, he maintained a strong interest in his former profession and continued to promote the development of naval gunnery to such an extent that he later became regarded as the father of this branch of the service in the Royal Navy. Louisa unfortunately suffered a decline in her health and was an invalid for the latter part of her life. She had produced eleven children, six sons and five daughters, but suffered great grief over the fact that seven of them died young. Two of her surviving sons became senior naval officers and a third served as an officer in the Royal Engineers. Lady Broke survived her husband, who, despite being troubled by his wartime head wound, remained active until his death in 1841. Louisa died two years later and both are buried in the family vault at Nacton church, near Ipswich, Suffolk.

Of the naval wives who were in Halifax during the War of 1812, Lady Elizabeth Townshend, wife of Captain Lord James Townshend, was left a widow in 1842 when her dashing husband died at the age of fifty-six. Two years later, she married another naval captain and lived for an additional thirty years, finally passing away in July 1873. Her brother, Provo Wallis, who served on HMS *Shannon* under Captain Philip Broke, became the longest-serving naval officer in the history of the Royal Navy.

Marie-Marguerite Viger, wife of Captain Jacques Viger of the *Voltigeurs Canadiens*, whom he referred to as "ma Belle" and to whom he wrote many wartime letters, spent most of her postwar life in Montreal. Her husband worked on his lengthy memoirs, and the couple produced three children. In 1833, "ma Belle" became the first mayoress of Montreal when Jacques was appointed to the new office of mayor of the city.

Marie-Anne de Salaberry and her husband, Lieutenant-Colonel Charles-Michel de Salaberry, resided at the fine house they built at Chambly on the Richelieu River after he resigned from the army. They and their steadily increasing family lived there contentedly until a fire broke out in one of the outbuild-

The house on the Richelieu. After the War of 1812, Lieutenant-Colonel Charles-Michel de Salaberry took up a new full-time role as Seigneur of Chambly, the estate given to him and his wife, Marie-Anne, as a wedding gift by her father, Jean-Baptiste Melchior Hertel de Rouville. Charles-Michel and Marie-Anne oversaw the building of an impressive stone manor house on the bank of the Richelieu River. After her husband's death in 1829, Marie-Anne remained in this house to raise their children. The house still stands today. (Photograph by Dianne Graves.)

ings in 1823, almost ruining them. Charles-Michel's health began to decline and he died in 1829, leaving left Marie-Anne with seven children to raise. With the support of her friends and relatives, she watched them grow into adulthood.

Catherine Maria Bowes, widow of Major-General Barnard Foord Bowes and daughter of Sir John and Lady Polly Johnson, became her father's companion after the death of her mother in 1814. She is said to have acquired an admirer in the person of Lieutenant-Colonel (later Major-General) the Honourable Frederick George Heriot, who was related through a cousin to Lord Byron. If the story is true, nothing came of this romantic interest, for neither of them married. In later years Maria Bowes could be proud of the fact that, like Major-General Robert Ross, her late husband had a monument to his memory in St. Paul's Cathedral, London, which paid tribute to his "deeds of valour" and "meritorious actions" and placed him "among the foremost in the list of those gallant heroes who have bled in defence of their King and Constitution."[15] Maria Bowes moved to England and died in London in 1850. She is buried at Highgate Cemetery, north London.

Rebecca Almon of Halifax was finally reunited with her aunts, Mary and

Catherine Byles, in the summer of 1815, when she and her husband, Dr. William Almon, travelled to Boston. She outlived him and died in 1853 at the age of ninety, and a plaque in St. Paul's Church, Halifax, commemorates her life.

That industrious businesswoman Peggy Bruce ran her inn at Cornwall until advancing age forced her to retire. Frances Murray of York, whose millinery business had done well throughout the war, was even more successful in the ensuing years. New Brunswick publisher Ann Mott eventually sold her newspaper and returned to the land of her birth, living in New York City until her death at the age of eighty-seven.

Rachel and Ellen Mordecai, who taught at their father's North Carolina school, continued as teachers after the war. In 1821 Rachel married Aaron Lazarus, a widower, and together they raised his seven children and another four of their own. Rachel died in 1838. Ellen Mordecai fell in love with the son of a fellow teacher and planned to marry him but her brother, Moses, objected so strongly that she ended the romance. Apparently never regretting her decision, she later helped to keep house for Moses and outlived her sister by forty-six years. She died in 1884.

Catherine Claus, the assiduous gardener whose home was destroyed when Newark was burned in 1813, lost a son and daughter during the war years. After 1815, she and her husband, William, continued to live at York, where they were members of the town's upper social circle. They eventually returned to Newark, where Catherine remained after William's death in 1826.

Anne Powell spent much of the remainder of her life in Upper Canada and was proud to see her husband, William Dummer Powell, succeed to the position of chief justice of the province in 1816, thereby guaranteeing his status-conscious wife even greater prominence. After his death in 1834 Anne lived another fifteen years, finally passing away in 1849 at the age of ninety-three.

Hannah Jarvis lost her husband, William, in 1817, just as her son, Samuel, was in jail charged with murder in a fatal duel. She spent much of the rest of her life visiting her daughters, one of whom married Alexander Hamilton, cousin of Thomas Clark. After 1830 Hannah lived mainly with her at Queenston, and remained energetic and cheerful into old age. When circumstances reduced the family to poverty, she was forced to undertake the kind of domestic work she had always delegated to servants. Hannah Jarvis died in 1845 in her eighty-second year.

Catherine Norton, the beautiful aboriginal wife of Captain John Norton, who fought with the British throughout the war, sailed to Britain with her husband in the summer of 1815. They went first to Scotland, where Catherine took English lessons. By all accounts she was a "very keen student" who could "hardly be prevailed on to quit her Spelling book and writing for anything else."[16] While in Britain both John and Catherine Norton had their portraits painted and Catherine's was on display for many years next to that of her husband at Syon House, the London residence of the Duke of Northumberland. Its present whereabouts is unknown.

In late 1816 the Nortons returned to Upper Canada and made their home on the Grand River, where John Norton settled on land granted to him as a retired army officer. They lived there until 1823, when their life together came to an abrupt end. According to John Norton, a young aboriginal man, whom Norton had fostered from childhood, was at their home during haymaking. This man's behaviour towards Catherine caused her to complain that he had "offered her the grossest insult a woman can receive," but it seems that she may have succumbed to his charms because a neighbour had seen the two together and informed Norton of the liaison.[17] Full of anger and grief, John Norton told both Catherine and her lover to leave his property, but the young man challenged Norton to a duel, and Norton killed him. A distraught Norton offered himself for trial, was found guilty of manslaughter, fined £25 and discharged. He refused ever to see Catherine again but left her a share of his pension.

In a pathetic note Catherine wrote afterwards, she begged Norton not to believe what people said about her and pleaded for his pardon, but Norton was unmoved and headed for American territory, where he is believed to have died in the 1830s.[18] It appears that Catherine subsequently made her way to Fairfield on the Thames River as, a few years later, missionary reports from that area describe how a "Brother Luckenback called to [see] an Indian woman of the Monsey tribe who had formerly been married to a certain Captain Norton," who was dangerously ill.[19] The report mentioned the "wild and dissolute life" that Catherine and her husband had led before their break-up and described the woman who had once been beautiful and the apple of her husband's eye as having become a "dirty old squaw." The missionaries reported that Catherine died in 1827.

Julia Defield and Jane Kerby, whose bravery saved the life of Captain James Fitzgibbon in 1814, continued to live in the Niagara region. Jane's first child, a daughter born in January 1815, was named Mary Margaret Clark Kerby after Mary Clark of Queenston, a family friend. Jane Kerby died in 1845. During the 1830s, Julia's son, David, joined a movement known as the Patriot Hunters – Americans and Canadians dedicated to liberating the rest of North America from British rule. He took part in an abortive attack on the village of Prescott in November 1838 and was captured and imprisoned. By coincidence, James Fitzgibbon, on whose behalf Julia had acted so bravely nearly a quarter of a century earlier, was present at his trial and spoke on his behalf. As a result of Fitzgibbon's testimonial to Julia Defield's courage, her son was released.

Laura Secord's courageous journey to the Beaver Dams during the tense summer days of 1813 ensured her a place in the history of Canada. She died in 1868 at the age of ninety-three, her efforts having brought her fame late in life that lasts to this day. Her home at Queenston is now an historic site.

Of the original Loyalists, Hannah Showers survived the War of 1812 and died in 1825 aged eighty-seven. Mehetible Mowat continued to live a quiet widow's existence at St. Andrews, New Brunswick, and in old age she looked back on memories of her flight to British North America and her happy years with her handsome sea captain husband, David. She died in 1860 at the age of ninety-two leaving possessions that had survived all her adventures: her family furniture and silverware, and most importantly, the family Bible. Like all Loyalist women, Mehetible had witnessed the passing of an era, a time when, in the words of another elderly Loyalist, Susan Burnham Greeley, the "grand music of the woods is heard no more."[20]

Catherine White, yet another Loyalist pioneer who lived through the war, had little patience with some of the newfangled labour-saving inventions of later years and offered a word of caution to the flighty young "modern" females of the younger generation:

> Give me the social spinning Wheel days when girls were proud to wear a home spun dress of their own spinning and weaving. Not thinking of high heeled Boots and thin shoes. Nor rigged out in hoops and Criniline [crinolines], [or] Salt cellar Bonnets, which have occasioned a great demand for Doctors which were almost unknown in my young days.[21]

Ending this book where it began, Thomas and Mary Clark of Queenston, Upper Canada, could well have argued that the Bible verse "the Lord gave and the Lord hath taken away" had been written with them in mind.[22] After his prewar success as a merchant, the mills which Thomas Clark owned stood in ruins in 1815, torched by American troops. There was, however, much to be proud of. All Mary Clark's male family members had served in the war: her husband in the militia; her father, Dr. Robert Kerr, as a surgeon tending the wounded of both sides; and her brothers, Robert, Walter and William, in the major battles on the Niagara front, Robert and Walter having been wounded and William and Walter taken prisoner. Few families contributed more.

After 1815 Thomas Clark resumed his business life, was active in public life and was made a life member of the Legislative Assembly of Upper Canada. He and Mary continued to entertain at Clark Hall, the fine home to which Thomas had taken "the amiable and all accomplished" Mary after their wedding in 1809. There they lived a genteel life waited upon by servants.[23] They had no surviving children and Mary died in 1835, Thomas following two years later. The Clark fortune went to Thomas's sisters in Scotland and his property was left to a business partner. Clark Hall was later acquired by Sir Harry Oakes, a millionaire entrepreneur, who tore it down and erected a splendid new residence called Oak Hall on the site. Today, it is the headquarters of the Niagara Parks Commission, which is charged with preserving both the natural beauty and the heritage of the Canadian side of the Niagara River.

For all the women named in these pages, there are countless others known only to their descendants or by a name on a gravestone. Dorothy Fawson, for example, rests in the Old Burying Ground in Halifax, not far from the grave of Major-General Robert Ross. She lived a few years beyond the end of the war and died on 11 February 1819, at the age of fifty-seven. Charity Esseltine, wife of Richard M. Esseltine, died on 21 April 1860 and lies in the Market Street Cemetery of Cape Vincent, New York. Mary Loucks, wife of Peter Loucks, lived on the Canadian side of the St. Lawrence and died on 12 December 1866 at the age of seventy-three, according to a stone at Upper Canada Village. And at Buffalo's Forest Lawn Cemetery, a marker commemorates Aurelia Bemis, wife of Asaph Bemis, who died on 29 December 1883 at the age of ninety. To them and so many more "noble mothers and daughters," belong, in the words of a young Kentucky militiaman, "a chaplet of unfading laurels."[24]

The women whose names appear in this book must represent those who remain nameless, yet whose collective efforts are an overlooked chapter in North American history. Young or old, all the wives, sisters, mothers and daughters who lived through the war would surely have echoed the belief of one British army wife that, "as long as ambition is the idol of men, so long will the sword continue to be the scourge of the world, and drive peace and contentment from the valleys of the earth."[25]

The Niagara River. This view, painted in 1816-1817 and looking north from Queenston Heights toward Lake Ontario, shows how narrow was the river that separated the two antagonists during the War of 1812. The village of Queenston nestles beneath the high ground on the left. (Painting by Francis Hall, National Library and Archives of Canada, C-3240.)

Major Events
of the War of 1812

1812

17 June – United States Senate adopts war bill.

18 June – President Madison signs war bill and War of 1812 commences.

19 June – President Madison issues proclamation confirming that a state of war exists.

23 June – The British government revokes its Orders-in-Council.

25 June – News of war arrives at York, Fort George and Quebec in Upper Canada and Sackets Harbor, NY.

27 June – News of war reaches Fredericton and Saint John, New Brunswick, and Halifax, Nova Scotia.

28 June – News of war reaches Amherstburg, Upper Canada.

30 June – News of war reaches Kingston, Upper Canada.

9 July – News of war reaches New Orleans and St. Joseph Island, Upper Canada.

17 July – News of war reaches Mackinac Island, Michigan Territory.
 – British troops capture Fort Michilimackinac.

30 July – News of war arrives at London, England.

25 July – General Hull invades Upper Canada across the Detroit River.

5 August – The Battle of Brownstown, Michigan Territory.

9 August – General Henry Dearborn and Lieutenant-General Sir George Prevost agree to an armistice.

15 August – Massacre at Fort Dearborn, Illinois Territory.

16 August – British capture Detroit.

19 August – US frigate *Constitution* wins an action against HMS *Guerrière* in the North Atlantic.

5-12 September – Siege of Fort Wayne, Indiana Territory.

8 September – United States cancels armistice.

21 September – American troops raid Gananoque, Upper Canada.

13 October – The Battle of Queenston Heights. Major-General Isaac Brock is killed in action.

17 October – USS *Wasp* wins an action against HMS *Frolic* in the North Atlantic.

25 October – USS *United States* wins an action against HMS *Macedonian* in the North Atlantic.

29 December – USS *Constitution* wins an action against HMS *Java* off the Atlantic coast of Brazil.

1813

22 January – The Battle of Frenchtown, River Raisin, Michigan Territory.

23 January – Massacre on the River Raisin.

6 February – British proclaim blockade of Chesapeake and Delaware Bays.

22 February – British troops raid Ogdensburg, NY.

19 March – Sir James Yeo appointed

commander of British naval forces on the inland lakes in the northern theatre of war.

23 April – British raid Spetsutia Island.

27 April – Battle of York, Upper Canada – American troops capture the town.

3 May – British troops raid and burn Havre de Grace, Maryland.

26 May – Britain announces blockade of major ports in middle and southern United States.

27 May – American troops capture Fort George, Upper Canada.

29 May – Battle of Sackets Harbour, NY.

1 June – HMS *Shannon* wins action against USS *Chesapeake* off Massachussetts coast.

3 June – British troops capture USS *Eagle* and USS *Growler* in the Richelieu River, Lower Canada.

5-6 June – Battle of Stoney Creek, Upper Canada.

19 June – Major-General Francis de Rottenburg appointed as president and administrator for Upper Canada.

22 June – British attack Craney Island, Virginia.

22-23 June – Laura Secord's journey to the Beaver Dams.

24 June – Battle of Beaver Dams, Upper Canada.

25 June – British raid on Hampton, Virginia.

5 July – British raid Fort Schlosser, NY.

8 July – Battle of Ball's Farm, Upper Canada.
– British raid Black Rock, NY.

17 July – Skirmish at Ball's Farm, Upper Canada.

21-28 July – Second siege of Fort Meigs, Ohio.

31 July – American raid on York, Upper Canada.

31 July-1 August – British troops raid Plattsburgh, NY.

1 August – British troops raid Swanton, Vermont.

10 September – Naval Battle of Lake Erie.

27 September – British evacuate and burn Fort Detroit.
– American troops enter Amherstburg, Upper Canada.

4 October – Skirmish at Dolsen's farm, Upper Canada.

5 October – The Battle of the Thames, Upper Canada – Tecumseh killed.

17 October – General Wilkinson's army embarks for the St. Lawrence.

26 October – Battle of Châteauguay, Lower Canada.

11 November – Battle of Crysler's Farm, Upper Canada.

10 December – Americans evacuate Fort George and burn Newark, Upper Canada.

12 December – British troops reoccupy Fort George.

13 December – Lieutenant-General Gordon Drummond appointed as president and administrator of Upper Canada.

19 December – British troops capture Fort Niagara, NY.

19-21 December – British troops burn Lewiston, Youngstown and Manchester, NY.

30 December – British troops raid and burn Black Rock and Buffalo, NY.

1814

2 April – British proclamation urges slaves in Chesapeake to join British forces.

5 April – American troops raid Oxford, Upper Canada.

25 April – British announce blockade of New England.

28 April – Napoleon Bonaparte abdicates and is exiled to Elba.

14-15 May – Americans raid Port Dover, Upper Canada.

20 May – Americans raid Port Talbot, Upper Canada.

23 May-21 June – Treason trials at Ancaster, Upper Canada.

3 July – American troops invade Upper Canada and take Fort Erie.

5 July – Battle of Chippewa, Upper Canada.

18 July – American troops burn St. Davids, Upper Canada.

24 July – British expeditionary force arrives at Bermuda from France.

25 July – Battle of Lundy's Lane, Upper Canada.

4 August – Americans attack Fort Mackinac, Michigan Territory.

8 August – Commencement of peace negotiations at Ghent in Holland.

15 August – British attack on Fort Erie, Upper Canada.

19-20 August – Troops from British expeditionary force land at Benedict, Virginia, to begin marching on Washington.

19 August–17 September – British troops lay siege to Fort Erie.

24 August – Battle of Bladensburg, Maryland.

24 August – British enter Washington.

24-25 August – British burn Washington.

28 August – British troops capture Alexandria, Virginia.

1-11 September – British troops occupy Maine coast from Eastport to Castine.

12 September – Naval Battle of Lake Champlain (naval).
 – Skirmish at Long Point, near Baltimore. Major-General Robert Ross killed in action.

13-14 September – British bombardment of Fort McHenry, Maryland.

20 September – American troops raid settlements in western district of Upper Canada.

16 December – Major-General Andrew Jackson proclaims martial law in New Orleans.

24 December – Treaty of Ghent signed by Great Britain and United States of America.

1815

2 January – HMS *Favourite* departs England with the Treaty of Ghent.

8 January – Battle of New Orleans, Louisiana.

11 February – HMS *Favourite* arrives New York City with the Treaty of Ghent.

14 February – Treaty of Ghent brought to Washington.

16 February – President Madison ratifies the Treaty of Ghent bringing an official end to the War of 1812.

24 February – News of peace reaches Kingston, Upper Canada.

1 March – News of peace reaches Quebec, Lower Canada.

6 March – News of peace reaches New Orleans.

28 March – News of peace reaches London, England.

24 April – News of peace reaches Mackinac Island.

18 June – Battle of Waterloo.

22 June – Napoleon Bonaparte abdicates throne.

8 September – United States signs peace treaty with Chippewa, Ottawa and Potawatomi peoples .

20 November – European allies and France sign Treaty of Paris, officially ending the wars in Europe after more than two decades of conflict.

"Peach trees of a very fine kind."
Extracts from the Garden Book
of Catherine Claus

E arly gardens in North America were generally modest, functional affairs, constructed in orderly geometric patterns with intersecting paths. They were usually dedicated to the production of vegetables and fruit for the table, and herbs for cooking and medicinal purposes. As the eighteenth century progressed, an increase in wealth and leisure led to the creation of more elaborate gardens with an eye to pleasure as well as practicality.

The different climate zones allowed for cultivation of crops suited to regional conditions. By 1812 many kinds of fruit and vegetables were being grown, among them varieties familiar today – marrowfat peas, savoy cabbages and Spanish onions to name but three. Popular among fruits were two varieties of apples, the long-lasting Newtown pippin, regarded by many authorities as the best-tasting American apple, and Spitzenburg, a spicy dessert apple with yellow and red stripes.

Many flowers and plants had been introduced into North American gardens by this time. Bulbs such as crocuses, garlic, chives, snowdrops, English bluebells, hyacinth, Madonna and other lilies, daffodils, jonquil, narcissus and tulips were to be found. Among favourite perennials listed in 1812 were the common anemone, aster, lily-of-the-valley, cyclamen, showy lady's slipper orchid, delphinium, cottage pink, dogtooth violet, geranium, blue and yellow flag, purple foxglove, dianthus, carnation, rose campion, hollyhock and wild sunflower. Annuals were equally diverse, and included many familiar today: sweet pea, larkspur, cornflower, morning glory, sunflower, wallflower, snapdragon, marigold, and scented candytuft. Shrubs, from lilac to honeysuckle, azalia, and assorted roses, were common in gardens and in 1815, the year the war ended, two new shrubs were introduced into America – the cherry crab apple and the Carolina rhododendron.

In Upper Canada, winter brought long periods of freezing weather, followed by a brief spring in which snowdrops and late tulips might well flower together. The short, hot summer season allowed for the cultivation of foodstuffs, such as sweet peppers and okra, normally associated with warmer climates. This was especially so in the Niagara region, bounded by Lakes Erie and Ontario and sheltered by a ridge, which enjoyed milder winters than elsewhere in the province, making it especially suited to the cultivation of fruit trees. Major Jasper Grant, a British officer who served at Amherstburg shortly before the war, pointed out that there were good growing conditions on the Detroit frontier as well, mentioning the "abundance of vegetables," the "peach trees of a very fine kind" and "melons of the first quality growing before my door without trouble or much cultivation."

Catherine Claus was the wife of William Claus, Deputy Superintendent General of the Indian Department. The family lived at Newark (modern Niagara-on-the-Lake) until the War of 1812, and the town boasted a good and profitable market that attracted farmers from a distance of thirty or forty miles. William Claus was a keen horticulturalist and particularly proud of his fruit and vegetable gardens, among the best in the region. Catherine was also a keen gardener who kept a journal over several years in which she noted that in Newark "there are several squares of ground in this village adorned with almost every kind of precious fruit."

The following extracts from Catherine Claus's Garden Book illustrate the kind of work she did. She and others like her swapped cuttings and worked hard to create gardens of great variety. Given the short, intense growing season in Upper Canada, many of her entries concern work carried out in the spring. Almost all the people mentioned are other keen gardeners, most of whom lived in or near Newark. They include Dr. Robert Kerr, father of Mary Clark of Queenston, and Julia, Catherine Claus's daughter.

1806

March

21st: Put out along the Centre walk several cuttings of the White & black Currants from Mr. Crooks also in other parts of the Garden & in the Nursery, one slip of Mrs. Servas'[Servos] yellow Clingstone [peach].

22nd: Began to trim the trees in the Garden.

26th: Sewed in the asparagus beds Celery, Cauliflower, Salad Radish & early Sugar Loaf.

29th: Grafted on the apple tree to the right of the Egg plum with Dr. Muirhead large plum graft.

31st: Grafted No 1 [Newtown Pippin apple] 2 [Red Winter Pippin apple] & 3 [Yellow Pippin] – 10 of them in the Garden & No 4 [Blue plum].

April

4th: Put out a budded peach of my budding in the bed of the centre walk – two in the Garden orchard – Some in the front court orchard.

15th: Sewed a bed of early pea from Mr. Newell, between the Spinach & Asparagus beds. Put an Egg plum under the apple trees to the right of the gate.

16th: Sewed 4 beds of White Onion seed from Albany and set out two layers of the Carnation Musk Melon.

17th: Sewed flower beds, Carrot bed square and Musk Melon square.

May

1st: Sewed one bed of Salsify in the old Water Melon square.

2nd: Next to the above sewed one bed of carrot and one bed pea along the new walk by the bees on the right, the Lima Bean & on the left the common running bean.

8th: Sewed the Ladies Fingers, potato from St. Joseph.

13th: Sewed in the Grape Vine bed, Battersea Red Cabbage, Lavender, Green wild Endive, Brown lettuce & Salmon Radish: in the Water Melon Square between the peas and onions one bed of round Spinach in the new Water Melon spot nine hills of the Blackeyed Water Melon seed: Sewed some Celery and under the Louise tree in the Nursery – Tongue grass in the new Water Melon bed.

17th: Planted 26 cabbage plants behind the asparagus bed from Captain Neill.

21st: Sewed the Guinea Pepper in the long border to the left of the Gate – in the Water Melon Square one bed with red Beet and long orange Carrot, another next to the above with round Spinach & Mr. Price's parsnips and a large bed next to the last with early Dutch Turnip Salad, white & red Turnip, Radish.

22nd: Sewed next the gate to the left 3 rows of Grape Seed & a row of Orange.

25th: Sewed in the long border to the left of the Gate Celery & Cauliflower of my own seed; 4 rows of Peppers Brown Lettuce from Albany & the Salmon, White Turnip and Salad Radish. Hive[d] the first swarm of bees in the Grass Hive.

26th: The peas sewed the 15th began to show themselves.

June

9th: Planted the corn that old Basstick gave me, behind the Lima Bean in the garden.

17th: Put out in the Cabbage square 24 early Green Savoy 33 early Sugar loaf 24 early York & in a bed of the old Musk Melon Square by themselves 9 Dwarf.

25th: Finished taking in my Hay from the ground around the house 5 Wagon loads.

27th: Put out 22 Cauliflower plants in the bed with the Spinach next the Turnips.

July

8th: Planted out 60 head of Cabbage in the large Square.

9th: Began to cut the hay in the field … Sewd a bed of Prussian Pea next the asparagus bed. Cut about one ton of hay in the lot.

August

8th and 9th: Budding Apricots, Mrs. Powell's peach, Red peach, Secord's peach, Egg Plum … Orleans plum, Green Sage Pine Apple Clingstone [peach] … South Carolina Clingstone one budded from the peach under the Hickory Trees.

1807

April

20th: Grafted two lions of the Orange Peach on two stocks near the Nutmeg Peach. Two lions one of the New Town Pippin & one of Spitzenburg [apple] on the small stocks among the Quince Trees also one of Mr. Coffin's Garden Pippin's [apple] from Col. Talbot. Same plan also in the two potato Squares on large Trees Nos 1 & 2.

25th: Put out a number of Pine roots in the garden. Rain.

28th: Grafted on a tree next to the red clingstone [peach] in the long Border one of Dr. Kerr's Newtown pippins. No. 1 [Newtown pippin] also on a tree in the bed with the Red Grapes. Sewed two beds of White Spanish Onions and one bed with Spinach both next the Asparagus beds.

29th: Dr. Kerr set out for Albany. Sewed one bed of Marrowfat and one bed of early Charlton Pea in the Asparagus Square and in the long border to the right … Early Cauliflower Celery and Early Green Savory. I sewd to the right of the walk of the Vines early Potatoes.

30th: In the same border Green wild Endive, savory and Turnip and Radish.

May

2nd: Grafted a number of peaches of different kinds & apples & pears.

5th: Grafted on one stalk in the old musk melon square six kinds of plums cherries peaches apricots and ... on other stocks about the garden also some of Mr. Crooks' Cherry, Mr. Clark's Plum and D[r.] Kerr's New Town pippins on apples in the front courts.

6th: Sewed in the square to the left of the Gate one Row of Marrowfat [peas] and Two rows of Early Charlton [peas] and sewed some of Mrs. Manius's flower seed in the border of the square to the right of the gate. Sewed in the square behind the out house some of De Polee's early potatoes.

9th: Sewed beets.

June

7th: Sew'd one and a half bed of Green onions, one chard, ditto of Red onions & the remainder of the Square with White Spanish Onions.

9th: Grafted apples in the Garden old Scott's New Town pippin, Spitzenburg & Dr. Kerr's New Town.

1810

April

2nd: Removed the Nutmeg. Julia's small Nectarine. Put out 3 of the New town pippin & Spitzenburg 1 in the garden in the place of Julia's tree 1 behind the beehives & one in front of the house near the Nutmeg Peach.

9th: Sewed early Spinach.

11th: Dressed the asparagus beds and sewed Turnip and ... Radish.

13th: Sewed flower seed in the little tubs.

17th: Put on 50 of the Patagonian Ras[p]berry from Mr. Coffin & some cut[t]ing of the White Currants from Major Halton. Two men of the artillery began to dig in the garden & a young man to clear up the field.

18th: Sewed Carrots, onion, parsnips.

24th: Planted out a young orchard by Waters.

25th: Finished the orchard. Planted a few ... early potatoes. Write to William.

Sources
Michael Weishan, *The New Traditional Garden*, New York, 1999, 149-150, 227-283.
Library and Archives of Canada, Ottawa: MG24 F128 vol. l, Grant Papers, Jasper Grant to Thomas Grant, 7 August 1808; MG19 F1, Claus Papers, vol. 4, Garden Book of Catharine Claus.

"Dry Whortleberries scattered in, will make it better."
Recipes from the Time of the War of 1812

The luxury of preparing meals using the kind of recipes featured in this appendix was enjoyed by only a small minority of people in 1812. In poorer households where life was frugal, the average diet was monotonous. Whilst fresh produce was readily available to the people of the more southerly regions of North America, families living in the north of the continent ate very much according to the seasonal cycle, with fresh produce in the warmer months and stored, preserved food in the winter. During the cold season, the range of food supplies in the early nineteenth century was constrained by the available techniques of preservation – mainly drying, salting or smoking and, for root crops, underground storage. Few people enjoyed regular supplies of fresh meat, and most ate it only when livestock, such as pigs, were slaughtered in the fall. For the rest of the year they lived on salted meat, or they went without. Asa Sheldon of New England remembered that for his family, "brown bread and milk was the constant food" in summer, and "beef-broth, with brown bread crumbled in, and for change, bean porridge" in winter.

Crops were grown according to climatic conditions, and two of the major staple foodstuffs were corn and pork, the latter appearing on the dinner tables of people of all classes. Game and fish were available to those living in the vicinity of woods, lakes or rivers, but by 1800 a dietary transformation saw a move towards greater consumption of vegetables and fruit as people realised the protection they provided against diseases caused by nutritional deficiencies. In addition, imported foodstuffs were increasing in variety, and for those who could afford them, storekeepers were able to offer a range of items such as wines, tea, coffee, sugar and spices.

The recipes in early cookbooks were organised sequentially but not in the same form as the step-by-step instructions familiar today. The following table indicates the modern equivalents of rough measurements, and translates period measurements into modern quantities:

A *dash* equals ⅛ teaspoon

A *pinch* equals ¼ teaspoon

A *gill* equals ½ cup

A *pint* equals 2 cups

A *teacup* equals ¾ cup

A *porringer* was a small pewter or metal soup dish about 6 to 8 inches in diameter and 1½ to 3 inches deep. Depending upon its size, it contained approximately 3 to 5 cups.

A *pound* equals 16 ounces (a pound of flour was about 3 to 3½ cups but the pound varied and could be as much as 4½ cups. A pound of sugar was 2 to 2½ cups)

A *quart* equals 2 pints (4 cups)

Then as now, housewives collected recipes and exchanged them with friends and neighbours. Hannah Jarvis of York left a recipe and housekeeping book which is of particular interest since it was kept by one of the first upper-class women to settle in Upper Canada. She kept detailed accounts in her book, which included instructions for preparing food, soaps, perfumes, health care remedies, cleansers, and dyes for colouring yarns. Hannah and her daughters germinated seeds indoors, planted and harvested vegetables, preserved and cured their own meats and raised their own poultry. Some of her entries came from England, where she lived for a time before her marriage, while others were given to her by women she knew. The fact that she was able to afford spices, wine and brandy is evidence that she and her husband lived well .

Crumpets
Set two pounds flour and a little salt to the fire till quite warm – Mix warm milk and water – till it is as stiff as you can stir it with a spoon – as hot as you can bear your finger in – three Eggs – well beaten – three spoonsful of yeast – add a cup of warm milk and water to the eggs – beat all well together with as much milk and water – as will make a thick Batter – cover close, set by the fire to rise.

Mrs. Bambridges way to make Gingerbread. H. Jarvis's favorite
Two pounds and a half of Flour – Ten ounces of Butter – half pound sugar – two
ounces of Ginger, one and a half pound of Treacle – melt the Butter with the
Treacle – roll thin – bake crisp – if you like them Hotter of spice add more Ginger
– some cloves – and some Mace.

To Pot Beef to eat like Venison
Put ten pounds of Beef into a deep pan – pour over it a pint of Port-wine – let it
be in it for two days – then season it with Mace, Pepper and salt – put it into a pot
with the wine it was steeped in – add to it a wine glass more of Wine – tie it down
with paper and bake three Hours in a quick Oven – when you take it out – beat it
in a mortar or wooden Bowl – clarify a pound of Butter and put it in as you see
it requires – Keep beating it till it is a fine Paste; then put it into your Pots – lay a
paper over it and a weight to pack it close – the next day pour clarified Butter over
it – and keep it in a dry cool place.

Plum Pudding
Half a pound bread crumbs – half a pound Flour, one pound of raisins, three
pounds Currants washed and stoned and chopped – seven Eggs – one and a half
pound suet chopped fine (if you wish it very rich) otherwise one pound – quarter
of an ounce each Mace Cloves, Ginger & a little Nutmeg – Candied Lemon – Orange & Citron each a quarter of an ounce – a glass of Brandy – as much Milk as will
just wet the Flour – a little Salt. Boil four hours – give little or no room to swell.

A Dish of Snow
Put twelve large apples into cold water – boil till soft – pulp them through a sieve
– beat the whites of twelve eggs to a froth. Add half a pound of loaf sugar made
fine – beat all well together – till stiff – add a little grated lemon peel – heap it up
on the dish.

Pickle Salmon as they do in Scotland
Boil the salmon until fit for the table – to every quart of the water the salmon was
boiled in – put one pint of good vinegar – first laying the salmon in some tight
vessel and sprinkling it with salt – then put on as much of the liquor of the above
described – till the fish is sufficiently immersed – apply pepper, allspice, cloves,
mace, as you choose.

Amelia Simmons was not the first American cookery writer to be published,
but she was one of the most popular and influential, demonstrating that
early American cookery, in the words of food historian Karen Hess, was about
"the continuation of traditional cookery on foreign shores, making do with

native ingredients" when they suited the recipe. In the 1815 edition of her book, *American Cookery, or the Art of Dressing Viands, Fish, Poultry and Vegetables and the best mode of making puff-pastes, pies, tarts, puddings, custards and preserves and all kinds of cakes from the Imperial Plumb to plain cake. Adapted to this country and all grades of life,* Amelia Simmons often chose recipes in the English tradition but substituted American produce. Maize, which early colonists called Indian corn, was used in place of oats, and having learned about the use of maple sap from the native peoples, she frequently included syrups. The following recipes from Miss Simmons's book feature the use of herbs and other North American ingredients such as cranberries, squash and cornmeal, and of fruit such as whortleberries and gooseberries, which appear to have been more readily available in 1815 than is often the case today.

Alamode Beef
Take a round of beef, and stuff it with half pound pork, half pound butter, the soft part of half a loaf of wheat bread, boil four eggs very hard, chop them up; add sweet marjoram, sage, parsley, summer savery, and one ounce cloves pounded, chop them altogether with two eggs very fine, and add a gill of wine, season very high with salt and pepper, cut holes in your beef, to put your stuffing in, then stick whole cloves into the beef, then put it into a two pail pot, with sticks at the bottom; if you wish to have the beef round when done, put it into a cloth and bind it tight with 20 or 30 yards of twine, put it into your pot with two or three quarts of water, and one gill of wine, if the round be large it will take three or four hours to bake it.

To Stuff and Roast a Turkey or Fowl
One pound soft wheat bread, three ounces beef suet, three eggs, a little sweet thyme, marjoram, pepper and salt, and some add a gill of wine; fill the bird therewith and sew up; hang down to a steady solid fire, basting frequently with butter and water, and roast until steam emits from the breast, put one third of a pound of butter into the gravy, dust flour over the bird and baste with the gravy; serve up with boiled onions and cramberry [sic] sauce, mangoes, pickle or celery.

2. Others omit the sweet herbs, and add parsley done with potatoes

3. Boil and mash three pints potatoes, moisten them with butter, add sweet herbs, pepper, salt, fill and roast as above.

To Keep green peas till Christmas
Take young peas, shell them, put them in a cullender [colander] to drain, then lay a cloth four or five times double on a table, then spread them on, dry them very well, and have your bottles ready, fill them, cover them with mutton suet fat when

it is a little soft; fill the necks almost to the top, cork them, tie a bladder and leather over them and set them in a dry cool place.

To Dress a Bass

Season high with salt, pepper and cayenne, one slice salt pork, one of bread, one egg, sweet marjoram, summer savery and parsley, minced fine and well mixed; one gill wine, four ounces butter; stuff the bass – bake in the oven one hour; thin slices of pork laid on the fish as it goes into the oven; when done pour over dissolved butter; serve up with stewed oysters, cranberries, boiled onions or potatoes. The same method may be observed with fresh shad, codfish, Blackfish and salmon.

A Whipt Syllabub

Take two porringers of cream, and one of white wine, grate in the skin of a lemon, take the whites of three eggs, sweeten it to your taste, then whip it with a whisk, take off the froth as it rises and put it into your syllabub glasses or pots, and they are fit for use.

Gooseberry Tart

Lay clean berries and sift over them sugar, then berries and sugar, till a deep dish be filled, intermingling a handful of raisins, and one gill of water; cover with paste No. 9 [pastry], and bake somewhat more than the other tarts.

PASTE NO. 9: ROYAL PASTE. Rub in Half a pound of butter into one pound of flour, four whites beat to a foam, two ounces fine sugar; roll often, rubbing one third, and rolling two thirds of the butter is best, excellent for tarts.

A Crook neck or Winter Squash Pudding

Core, boil and skin a good squash and bruise it well. Take six large apples, pared, cored and stewed tender, mix together, add six or seven spoonfuls of dry bread or biscuit, rendered fine as meal, one pint milk or cream, two spoons rose water, two of wine, five or six eggs beaten and strained, nutmeg, salt and sugar to your taste, one spoon flour; beat all smartly together, bake one hour. The above is a good receipt for pumpkins, potatoes or yams, adding more moistening, or milk and rosewater, and to the two latter a few black or Lisbon currants, or dry whortleberries scattered in will make it better.

Independence Cake

Twelve pounds of flour, fifteen pounds of sugar, ten pounds of butter, four dozen eggs, one quart of wine, one quart of brandy, one ounce nutmeg; cinnamon, cloves, mace of each three ounces, two pounds citrons, currants and raisins five pounds each, one quart yeast, when baked frost with loaf sugar, dress with box and gold leaf.

Johnny Cake, or hoe cake
Scald one pint of milk & put 3 pints of Indian meal and ½ pint of flour; bake before the fire. Or scald with milk ⅔ of the Indian meal, or wet ⅔ with boiling water, add salt, molasses and shortening, work up with cold water pretty stiff, and bake as above.

Eliza Rundell, author of *A New System of Domestic Cookery*, in addition to much wise, practical advice, also presented many inventive and tasty recipes. The following four are excellent examples, and readers will note that in two instances even Miss Rundell was moved to state how good they were.

An Excellent Soup
Take a scrag or knuckle of veal, slices of undressed gammon or bacon, onions, mace, and a small quantity of water; simmer till very strong; and lower it with a good beef-broth made the day before and stewed till the meat is done to rags. Add cream, vermicelli, almonds (blanch a quarter of a pound of sweet almonds and beat them to a paste in a marble mortar with a spoonful of water to prevent their oiling), and a roll.

Fried Patties
Mince a bit of cold veal, and six oysters, mix with a few crumbs of bread, salt, pepper, mutmeg, and a very small bit of lemon peel – add the liquor of the oysters; warm all in a tosser, but don't boil; let it go cold; have ready a good puff-paste, roll thin, and cut in round or square bits, put some of the above between two of them, twist the edges to keep in the gravy, and fry them of a fine brown. This is a very good thing; and baked, is a fashionable dish. Wash all patties over with egg before baking.

A French Salad
Chop three anchovies, a shallot, and some parsley, small; put them in a bowl with two table-spoons of vinegar, one of oil, a little mustard, and salt. When well mixed add by degrees some cold roast or boiled meat in *very thin* slices; put in a few at a time not exceeding two or three inches long. Shake them in the seasoning, and then put more; cover the bowl close, and let the salad be prepared three hours before it is to be eaten. Garnish with parsley, and a few slices of the fat.

Orange Fool
Mix the juice of three Seville oranges, three eggs well beaten, a pint of cream, a little nutmeg and cinnamon and sweeten to your taste. Set the whole over a slow fire, and stir till it becomes as thick as good melted butter, but it must not be boiled; then pour into a dish for eating cold.

According to food historian Karen Hess, *The Art of Cooking Made Plain and Easy by A Lady* by Hannah Glasse was both "the most English of cookbooks" and "the most American of cookbooks." First published in London in 1747, it went through twenty editions, making Hannah the most successful culinary author of her era. Hannah did not identify herself until her book was in its fourth edition, when she described herself as a "Habit maker to HRH The Princess of Wales, in Tavistock Street, Covent Garden." The book included an enormous range of dishes using a veritable cornucopia of produce that testified to the abundance of a country at the peak of its agrarian prowess.

The first American edition was published in Alexandria, Virginia, in 1805, and found its way onto the bookshelves of George Washington and Thomas Jefferson, whose granddaughters still had recipes attributed to Hannah Glasse. A number of American ingredients had already entered the English repertory and she offered an appendix to her book which contained new recipes "adapted to the American mode of cooking." These included Indian pudding, buckwheat cakes, pumpkin pie, cranberry tarts, maple beer, waffles and crullers. The following recipes, however, indicate the versatility of Mrs. Glasse's ideas, and they include an early recipe for ice cream. As Hannah Glasse said in her introduction, "I believe I have attempted a branch of cookery which nobody has yet thought worth their while to write upon."

To Roast a Turkey the Genteel Way
First cut it down the back, and with a sharp penknife, bone it, then make your force-meat thus: take a large fowl, or a pound of veal, as much grated bread, half a pound of suet cut and beat very fine, a little beaten mace, two cloves, half a nutmeg grated, about a large tea-spoonful of lemon-peel, and the yolks of two eggs; mix all together, with a little pepper and salt, fill up the places where the bones came out, and fill the body, that it may look just as it did before, sew up the back, and roast it. You may have oyster-sauce, celery-sauce, just as you please; put good gravy in the dish, and garnish with lemon, which is as good as any thing.

To make Salmagundy
Mince two chickens, either boiled or roasted, very fine, or veal, if you please; also mince the yolks of hard eggs very small, and mince the whites very small by themselves; shred the pulp of two or three lemons very small, then lay in your dish a layer of mince-meat, and a layer of yolks of eggs, a layer of white, a layer of anchovies, a layer of your shred lemon pulp, a layer of pickles, a layer of sorrel, a layer of spinach and shallots shred small. When you have filled the dish with the ingredients, set an

orange or lemon on the top; then garnish with horse-radish scraped; barberries and sliced lemon. Beat up some oil with the juice of lemon, salt and mustard, thick, and serve it up for the second course, side dish, or middle dish, for supper.

To Dress Haddocks after the Spanish Way

Take a haddock, washed very clean and dried, and boil it nicely; then take a quarter of a pint of oil in a stew-pan, season it with mace, cloves, and nutmeg, pepper and salt, two cloves of garlick, some love apples [tomatoes], when in season, a little vinegar; put in the fish, cover it close, and let it stew half an hour over a slow fire. Flounders done the same way are very good.

To dress Asparagus

Scrape all the stalks very carefully till they look white, then cut all the stalks even alike, throw them into water, and have ready a stew-pan boiling. Put in some salt, and tie the asparagus in little bundles. Let the water keep boiling, and when they are a little tender take them up. If you boil them too much you lose both colour and taste. Cut the round of a small loaf, about half an inch thick, toast it brown on both sides, dip it in the asparagus liquor, and lay it in your dish: pour a little butter over the toast, then lay your asparagus on the toast all round the dish, with the white tops outwards. Do not pour butter over the asparagus, for that makes them greasy to the fingers, but have your butter in a basin, and send it to table.

To make Ice-Cream

Pare and stone twelve ripe apricots, and scald them, beat them fine in a mortar, add to them six ounces of double-refined sugar, and a pint of scalding cream, and work it through a sieve; put it in a tin with a close cover, and set it in a tub of ice broke small, with four handfuls of salt mixed among the ice. When you see your cream grows thick round the edges of your tin, stir it well and put it in again till it is quite thick; when the cream is all froze up, take it out of the tin and put it into the mould you intend to turn it out of; put on the lid and have another tub of salt and ice ready as before; put the mould in the middle, and lay the ice under and over it; let it stand four hours, and never turn it out till the moment you want it, then dip the mould in cold spring water, and turn it into a plate. You may do any sort of fruit the same way.

To Make a Lemon Honeycomb

Take the juice of one lemon, and sweeten it with fine sugar to your palate; then take a pint of cream, and the white of an egg, and put in some sugar, and beat it up; and as the froth rises, take it off, and put it on the juice of the lemon, till you have taken all the cream off upon the lemon; make it the day before you want it, in a dish that is proper.

Marmalade of Cherries

Take five pounds of cherries, stoned, and two pounds of hard sugar; shred your cherries, wet your sugar with the juice that runneth from them; then put the cherries into the sugar, and boil them pretty fast, till it be marmalade; when it is cold, put it up in glasses for use.

To make India Pickle

To a gallon of vinegar, one pound of garlick, three quarters of a pound of long-pepper, a pint of mustard-seed, one pound of ginger, and two ounces of turmerick; the garlic must be laid in salt three days then wiped clean and dried in the sun; the long-pepper broke, and the mustard-seed bruised: mix all together in the vinegar; then take two large hard cabbages, and two cauliflowers, cut them in quarters, and salt them well; let them lie three days and dry them well in the sun. N.B. the ginger must lie twenty-four hours in salt and water, then cut small, and laid in salt three days.

Sources

Hannah Jarvis's recipes may be found in Archival and Special Collections, University of Guelph Library, Guelph, Canada: John Macintosh Duff Collection, XRIMSA210088, Housekeeping book, 19, 20, 27-28, 56.

Amelia Simmons's recipes are taken from her *American Cookery*, published by Paraclete Potter at Poughkeepsie, New York, in 1815.

Eliza Rundell's recipes are contained in her book, *A New System of Domestic Cookery, formed upon the principles of Economy and adapted to the use of private families throughout the United States by a Lady* published in New York in 1815.

Hannah Glasse's recipes appear in her *Art of Cookery Made Plain and Easy*, reprint edition, Bedford, Massachusetts, 1997.

On the subject of cooking in North America in the late 18th and early 19th centuries, see the historical notes by Karen Hess in the 1997 reprint of Hannah Glasse's *Art of Cookery Made Plain and Simple* and Jack Larkin, *The Reshaping of Everyday Life 1790-1840*, New York, 1998.

Joseph Willcocks: The Inner Man
The Diet of a Prosperous North American Family in the Early Nineteenth Century

Joseph Willcocks (1773-1814) was an Anglo-Irishman who arrived in York, Upper Canada, in early 1800 to seek his fortune. Through the good offices of a kinsman, he received a position in the household of Peter Russell, administrator of the province in the absence of the lieutenant-governor, but was dismissed from Russell's employ in August 1802 after making undue advances to that gentleman's sister, Elizabeth. Willcocks then embarked on a stormy political career as a newspaper editor and elected member of the Legislative Assembly of Upper Canada and became an outspoken critic of the British Crown and its appointees. In June 1813, Willcocks formed a unit of renegades, the Canadian Volunteers, who joined the American army. He and his men were responsible for much distress and looting in the occupied area of the Niagara in late 1813, culminating in the wanton destruction of the village of Newark in December of that year. The following year, the Canadian Volunteers fought in every battle on the Niagara front until September 1814, when Willcocks was killed near Fort Erie and the unit was disbanded.

Joseph Willcocks kept a diary during his early years in York which is of interest as he obsessively recorded every meal served in the Russell household between May 1800 and August 1802, a total of 26 months. These entries form a record of the daily diet of a fairly wealthy North American household of the time of the War of 1812. What follows is a recapitulation of the meals served. The large number of meat dishes in comparison to vegetable and fruit dishes is striking – but typical of the period at this social level .

SOUP

Total dishes		192
Turtle	3	
Mock turtle	2	

MEAT

Total dishes		682
Beef, total dishes		434
Roast	192	
Boiled	61	
Stewed	49	
Corned	46	
Hashed	42	
Beef tongue	11	
Cold roast	9	
Fried	7	
Beef steaks	7	
Beef kidneys	4	
Broiled	2	
Beef head	2	
Beef steak pie	1	
Beef kidney pie	1	

Veal, total dishes		118
Roast	59	
Minced	16	
Stewed	10	
Boiled	10	
Filet	3	
Loin	3	
Calves' liver	3	
Calves' heart	3	
Calves' feet	3	
Hashed	2	
Cutlets	2	
Calves' head	2	
Cold	1	
Calves' cheek	1	

Pork & pork products, total dishes		69
Pork	29	
Corned	8	
Boiled	8	
Roast	13	
Ham	13	
Rashers (bacon)	12	
Pig's cheek	10	

Roast pig	1
Pig's feet	1
Pig's head	1
Pig's livers	1
Pork griskins	1

Mutton & lamb, total dishes		61
Roast	23	
Leg	8	
Stewed	7	
Boiled	7	
Hashed	5	
Chops	3	
Loin	2	
Breast	1	
Pie	1	
Broiled	1	
Lamb pie	1	
Cold lamb	1	
Lamb (quarter)	1	

POULTRY & EGGS

Total dishes		116
Duck, total dishes		34
Stewed	7	
Roast	5	
Hashed	1	
Other	21	

Chicken, total dishes		29
Stewed	9	
Boiled	5	
Cold	2	
Roast	2	
Giblets	2	
Fricasseed	1	
Other	8	

Eggs, total dishes		21
Poached	4	
Fried	2	
Pigeon	15	

Fowl (not specified), total		16
Roast	7	
Boiled	5	
Stewed	3	
Cold	1	

Goose	6	
Turkey	5	
Partridge	2	
Pheasant	3	

SEAFOOD

Total dishes		101
Fish (unspecified)	45	
Salmon	31	
Corned	1	
Trout	15	
Eels	4	
Whitefish	4	
Herring	1	
Perch	1	

MISCELLANEOUS MAIN COURSE DISHES

Total dishes		148
Hash (not specified)	97	
Pancakes	40	
Cold meats (unspecified)	3	
Tripe	3	
Sausages	2	
Hare	1	
Patties (unspecified)	1	
Black pudding	1	

VEGETABLE DISHES

Total dishes		17
Asparagus	7	
Cabbage	6	
Peas	1	
Turnips	1	
Carrots	1	
Rice	1	

DESSERTS

Total dishes		348
Pudding, total dishes	56	
Bread pudding	28	
Custard pudding	19	
Plum pudding	3	
Rice pudding	2	
Apple pudding	2	
Cherry pudding	1	
Peach pudding	1	

Pies, total dishes		31
Peach pie	2	
Apple pie	3	
Cranberry pie	1	
Minced pies	25	

Tarts, total dishes		19
Currant tart	1	
Gooseberry tart	1	
Mince tarts	1	
Unspecified	16	

Apple dumpling		2
Peach dumpling		1
Trifle		1
Unspecified		238

FRUIT DISHES

Total dishes		1
Melon	1	

MISCELLANEOUS OTHER DISHES

Total dishes		4
Toast	1	
Bread & butter	1	
Boiled bread & milk	1	
Cheese	1	

RECAPITULATION

Soup dishes	192
Meat dishes	682
Poultry & egg dishes	116
Fish dishes	101
Misc. main course dishes	148
Vegetable dishes	17
Dessert dishes	348
Fruit dishes	1
Miscellaneous other dishes	4
Total number of dishes	1609

Source

National Library and Archives of Canada, Ottawa: MG 24, C1, Diary of Joseph Willcocks, May 1800-August 1802.

APPENDIX D

"Every virtue and every excellence." Extracts from *A Father's Legacy to His Daughters* by Dr. John Gregory

John Gregory (1724-1773) was a physician, philosopher and man of letters. A native of Edinburgh, Scotland, he wrote *A Father's Legacy to His Daughters*, which was first published in 1774, in the hope that in the absence of their deceased mother, he could offer his daughters some guidance that would stand them in good stead as they embarked on the path towards adulthood and matrimony. The following are extracts from his book. The headings are his.

Conduct and Behaviour

One of the chief beauties in a female character is that modest reserve, that retiring delicacy, which avoids the public eye, and is disconcerted even at the gaze of admiration ...... This modesty, which I think so essential in your sex, will naturally dispose you to be rather silent in company, especially in a large one. – People of sense and discernment will never mistake such silence for dulness. One may share in a conversation without uttering a syllable. The expression in the countenance shews it, and this never escapes an observing eye. ...... When a girl ceases to blush, she has lost the most powerful charm of beauty. ...... (pp. 26-27)

I should be glad that you had an easy dignity in your behaviour at public places, but not that confident ease, that unabashed countenance which seems to set the company at defiance. (p. 28) ......

Converse with men of the first rank with that dignified modesty, which may prevent the approach of the most distant familiarity, and consequently prevent them from feeling themselves your superiors. (p. 30) ......

Wit is the most dangerous talent you can possess. It must be guarded with great discretion and good-nature, otherwise it will create you many enemies. (p. 30) ......

Humour is a different quality ... but be cautious how you indulge it. – It is often a great enemy to delicacy, and a still greater one to dignity of character. It may sometimes gain you applause, but will never procure you respect. (p. 31) ......

Be ever cautious in displaying your good sense. It will be thought you assume a superiority over the rest of the company. – But if you happen to have any learning, keep it a profound secret, especially from the men, who generally look with a jealous and malignant regard. (p. 31) ......

Consider every species of indelicacy in conversation, as shameful in itself, and as highly disgusting to us. ...... Virgin purity is of that delicate nature, that it cannot hear certain things without contamination ...... No man, but a brute or a fool, will insult a woman with conversation which he sees gives her pain. ...... There is dignity in conscious virtue which is able to awe the most shameless and abandoned of men. (pp. 34-36) ......

Have a sacred regard to truth. Lying is a mean and despicable vice. (p. 37) ......

There is a certain gentleness of spirit and manners extremely engaging in your sex; not that indiscriminate attention, that unmeaning simper, which smiles on all alike. (p. 38) ......

There is a species of refinement in luxury, just beginning to prevail among the gentlemen of this country, to which our ladies are as yet as great strangers ... I hope, for the honour of the sex, they may ever continue so: I mean, the luxury of eating. It is a despicable selfish vice in men, but in your sex it is beyond expression indelicate and disgusting. (p. 39) ......

Let me now recommend to your attention that elegance, which is not so much a quality itself, as the high polish of every other. It is what diffuses an ineffable grace over every look, every motion, every sentence you utter. ...... In a word, it is the perfection of taste in life and manners; – every virtue and every excellence, in their most graceful and amiable forms. (pp. 44-45) ......

I wish you to possess the most perfect simplicity of heart and manners. I think you may possess dignity without pride, affability without meanness, and simple elegance without affectation. (pp. 45-46) ......

Amusements

I would particularly recommend to you those exercises that oblige you to be much abroad in the open air, such as walking, and riding on horseback. This will give vigour to your constitutions, and bloom to your complexions. If you accustom yourselves to go abroad always in chairs and carriages, you will soon become so enervated, as to be unable to go out of doors without them. (pp. 48-49) ......

The intention of your being taught needle-work, knitting, and such like, is not on account of the intrinsic value of all you can do with your hands, which is trifling, but to enable you to judge more perfectly of that kind of work, and to direct the execution of it in others. Another principle end is to enable you to fill up, in a tolerably agreeable way, some of the many solitary hours you must necessarily pass at home. – It is a great article in the happiness of life, to have your pleasures as independent of others as possible. (pp. 51-52) ......

The domestic oeconomy of a family is entirely a woman's province, and furnishes a variety of subjects for the exertion both of good sense and good taste. If you ever come to have the charge of a family, it ought to engage much of your time and attention. (p. 52) ......

Dress is an important article in female life. .... Good sense will regulate your expense in it, and good taste will direct you to dress in such a way as to conceal any blemishes, and set off your beauties, if you have any, to the greatest advantage. But much delicacy and judgment are required in the application of this rule. A fine women shews her charms to most advantage, when she seems most to conceal them. The finest bosom in nature is not so fine as what imagination forms. The most perfect elegance of dress appears always the most easy, and the least studied. (pp. 55-56) ......

In dancing, the principal points you are to attend to are ease and grace. I would have you dance with spirit; but never allow yourselves to be so far transported with mirth, as to forget the delicacy of your sex. (p. 57) ......

Friendship, Love, Marriage

It is a maxim laid down among you, and a very prudent one it is, that love is not to begin on your part, but is entirely to be the consequence of our attachment to you. (pp. 80-81) ......

A man of taste and delicacy marries a woman because he loves her more than any other. A woman of equal taste and delicacy marries him because she esteems him, and because he gives her that preference. (p. 83) ......

The effects of love among men are diversified by their different tempers. An artful man may counterfeit every one of them so easily as to impose on a young girl of an open, generous and feeling heart, if she is not extremely on her guard. The finest parts in such a girl may not always prove sufficient for her security. The dark and crooked paths of cunning are unsearchable, and inconceivable to an honourable and elevated mind. (p. 84) ......

When you observe ... a gentleman's behaviour ... If his attachment is agreeable to you, I leave you to do as nature, good sense, and delicacy, shall direct you. If you love him, let me advise you never to discover to him the full extent of your love, no not although you marry him. (pp. 87-88) ......

I wish you to possess such high principles of honour and generosity as will render you incapable of deceiving, and at the same time to possess that acute discernment which may secure you against being deceived. (pp. 102-103) ......

A woman in this country, may easily prevent the first impressions of love, and every motive of prudence and delicacy should make her guard her heart against them, till such time as she has received the most convincing proofs of the attachment of a man of such merit, as will justify a reciprocal regard. (p. 103) ......

In short, I am of the opinion, that a married state, if entered into from proper motives of esteem and affection, will be the happiest for yourselves, make you most respectable in the eyes of the world, and the most useful members of society ...... I wish you to marry for no other reason but to make yourselves happier. (pp. 108-109) ......

There is one advice I shall leave you, to which I beg your particular attention. Before your affections come to be in the least engaged to any man, examine your tempers, your tastes, and your hearts, very severely, and settle in your own minds, what are the requisites to your happiness in a married state; and as it is almost impossible that you should get every thing you wish, come to a steady determination what you are to consider as essential, and what may be sacrificed. (pp. 114-115) ......

In matters of business, follow the advice of those who know them better than yourselves, and in whose integrity you can confide; but in matters of taste, that depend on your own feelings, consult no one friend whatever, but consult your own hearts. (p. 120) ......

If a gentleman makes his addresses to you, or gives you reason to believe he will do so, before you allow your affections to be engaged, endeavour, in the most prudent and secret manner, to procure from your friends every necessary piece of information concerning him; such as his character for sense, his morals, his temper, fortune, and family; whether it is distinguished for parts and worth, or for folly, knavery, and loathsome hereditary diseases. (p. 121) ......

Whatever your views are in marrying, take every possible precaution to prevent their being disappointed ...... If fortune, and the pleasures it brings, are your aim ... the principal security you can have for this will depend on your marrying a good-natured generous man, who despises money, and who will let you live where you can best enjoy that pleasure, that pomp and parade of life for which you married him. (p. 122) ......

Do not give way to a sudden sally of passion, and dignify it with the name of love. – Genuine love is not founded in caprice; it is founded in nature, on honourable views, on virtue, on similarity of tastes and sympathy of souls. (p. 126) ......

Endnotes

Abbreviations Used in Notes

Adm	Admiralty
ANQM	Archives nationales du Québec, Montreal
AO	Archives of Ontario, Toronto
Bacon Journal	Crawford, Mary M. "Mrs Lydia Bacon's Journal, 1811-1812." *Indiana Magazine of History*, Volume 40 (December 1944) 367-386; Volume 41 (March 1945) 59-79.
BECHS	Buffalo and Erie County Historical Society, Buffalo, New York
CHS	Connecticut Historical Society, Hartford, Connecticut
CLUM	Clements Library, University of Michigan, Ann Arbor, Michigan
Doc. Hist.	Cruikshank, Ernest A., ed. *Documentary History of the Campaigns upon the Niagara Frontier in 1812-1814* [titles vary slightly]. Welland: Tribune Press, 1896-1908, 9 vols.
DU	Duke University, Perkins Library, Durham, North Carolina
Kennon Letters	Kennon, Elizabeth Beverly. "Kennon Letters." *Virginia Magazine of History and Biography* 34 (April, July, October, 1926): 120-124;220-231;322-338; 35 (January, July 1927): 13-21; 287-292; 36 (April, July, October, 1928): 170-174; 213-238; 363-370; 37 (January, April, July, October 1929): 46-51; 143-153; 261-268; 335-338.
LAC	Library and Archives of Canada, Ottawa
LC	Library of Congress, Washington
MG	Manuscript Group
MHS	Maryland Historical Society, Baltimore
MM	McCord Museum, Montreal,
MTRL	Metropolitan Toronto Reference Library, Toronto
MVHS	Maumee Valley Historical Society, Maumee, Ohio
NAB	National Archives of Britain, Kew, Surrey
NAUS	National Archives of the United States, Washington
NFPL	Niagara Falls Public Library, Niagara Falls, Canada
NLS	National Library of Scotland, Edinburgh
NMM	National Maritime Museum, London
NWR	*Niles' Weekly Register*
PANS	Public Archives of Nova Scotia, Halifax
PRONI	Public Records Office of Northern Ireland, Belfast
PU	Princeton University, Firestone Library, Princeton, New Jersey
RG	Record Group
Rodgers	Library of Congress, Rodgers Family Papers, Correspondence
SCCIRO	Suffolk County Council Ipswich Record Office, Ipswich, Suffolk
SJ	Société Jersiaise, St. Helier, Jersey, Channel Islands
SUNY	State University of New York, Plattsburgh, NY
UG	University of Guelph, McLaughlin Library, Guelph, Canada
UNC	University of North Carolina, Chapel Hill
WO	War Office

Prologue: "A terrible commotion": War Comes to North America

1. "A New Recruiting Song," a variant of the ever popular "Yankee Doodle" appeared in the Pennsylvania newspaper *The Reporter* in November 1812.

2. Ernest A. Cruikshank, *A Memoir of Colonel the Honourable James Kerby, his Life in Letters* (Welland, 1931), 27. The express sent to Thomas Clark by American fur trader, John Jacob Astor, was a measure taken for the protection and safety of cargoes of furs coming down the Great Lakes.

3. William Kirby, *Annals of Niagara* (1896, reprinted Niagara Falls, 1972), 151.

4. Cruikshank, *Memoir of Kerby*, 20.

5. Elizabeth Kerr (c.1762-1794) was the eldest daughter of Sir William Johnson and Molly Brant. Because of their loyalty to Britain during the Revolutionary War, Molly, by then a widow, and her seven children were forced to flee with other Loyalists. They eventually settled in Upper Canada, where Elizabeth married Dr. Robert Kerr at Niagara in 1783, by whom she had five children. She died at the age of 32 while giving birth to her son, Robert J. Kerr.

6. Molly Brant or Konwatsi'tsiaiénni (meaning "someone lends her a flower") was probably born in 1736 to Christian Mohawk parents and grew up at Canajoharie in New York state. The Mohawks, easternmost nation of the Six Nations Iroquois Confederacy, had strong connections with former Dutch and English trading partners and Molly married Sir William Johnson, first superintendent of the northern aboriginals of British North America. She presided over their fine home, Johnson Hall, and as a highly intelligent woman at ease in both cultures was able to forge a consensus between her people and the British.

7. "Volunteers to Arms!", a proclamation by Brigadier-General Andrew Jackson, 7 March 1812, quoted in Robert Remini, *Andrew Jackson and the Course of American Empire 1767-1821* (New York, 1977), 169-170.

8. Abigail Smith Adams to John Adams, 23 September 1794 quoted in Kathleen Prindiville, *First Ladies* (New York, 1964), 39.

9. Abigail Smith Adams to Elizabeth Shaw, quoted in Elizabeth Evans, *Weathering the Storm: Women of the American Revolution* (New York, 1975), 30.

10. Abigail Smith Adams to Elizabeth Shaw, in Evans, *Weathering the Storm*, 30.

11. Maine was a district of Massachusetts until 1820, and Wisconsin was included in the Illinois Territory until 1818. Ethnologically, the American population at that time could be divided into three groups: whites; African-Americans, of which the majority were slaves; and aboriginal peoples.

12. Gaillard Hunt, *Life in America One Hundred Years Ago* (New York, 1914), 18. Despite these boasts, many Europeans did not know a great deal about the United States in 1812. Following the American struggle for freedom, culminating in the Revolutionary War, the concept of popular liberty had been discredited by the French Revolution, interest in it had waned and Europeans were preoccupied with the Napoleonic Wars.

13. Jack Larkin, *The Reshaping of Everyday Life 1790-1840* (New York, 1988), 15-16.

14. Untitled poem, quoted in Orsamus Turner, *Pioneer History of the Holland Purchase of Western New York* (Buffalo, 1849), 547.

15. Mary A. Wyman, *Selections from the Autobiography of Elizabeth Oakes (Prince) Smith* (New York, 1980), 48.

16. Felix de Beaujour quoted in Hunt, *Life in America*, 30.

17. Hunt, *Life in America*, 22.

18. Wyman, *Selections from the Autobiography of Elizabeth Oakes (Prince) Smith*, 46.

19. Abigail Smith Adams, quoted in Evans, *Weathering the Storm*, 5.

20. The law identified a woman as being one person with her husband. If she happened to live in a state other than Connecticut, he also had total control, legally, over her children. The one advantage American women enjoyed over English law was the legal recognition of antenuptial and postnuptial contracts. If these were drawn up and signed by both parties, they allowed a wife to retain control of her own real estate and private property. See Evans, *Weathering the Storm*, 2-3.

21. James J. Talman, ed., *Loyalist Narratives from Upper Canada* (Toronto, 1946), 87.

22. Eric W. Hounsom, *Toronto in 1810* (Toronto, 1970), 3-4.

23. Statistics vary but current estimates seem to indicate that of the half million Americans who had supported the British side to a greater or lesser extent during the Revolutionary War, between 60,000 and 100,000 chose to leave immediately after the war, and of these between 40,000 and 42,000 went to Nova Scotia and Lower Canada. Those who came to the British provinces in later years were possibly more at-

tracted by the prospect of land grants than other considerations.

24. John L. Field, ed., *Bicentennial Stories of Niagara-on-the-Lake* (Lincoln, Ont., 1981), 9-12.

25. Letter dated 15 April 1795 in Anonymous, *Canadian Letters: Description of a Tour thro' the Provinces of Lower and Upper Canada in the Course of the Years 1792 and 1793* (Montreal, 1912), 47.

26. Arthur Britton Smith ed., *Kingston! Oh Kingston!* (Kingston, 1987), 159.

27. John Duncan, *Travels through part of the United States and Canada in 1818 and 1819* (Glasgow, 1823), 152.

28. Pierre Berton, *The Invasion of Canada 1812-1813* (Toronto, 1980) 136.

29. Isaac Brock to Irving Brock, 19 February 1811, quoted in Ferdinand Brock Tupper, ed., *The Life and Correspondence of Major-General Sir Isaac Brock, K.B* (London, 1847), 92.

30. Jacques Viger, *Reminiscences of the War of 1812-14. Being portions of the Diary of a Captain of the Voltigeurs Canadiens while at Garrison in Kingston* (Montreal, 1895), 4.

31. John M. Duncan, quoted in Britton Smith, ed., *Kingston! Oh Kingston!*, 179.

32. Michael Smith. *A Geographical View of the Province of Upper Canada and Promiscuous Remarks on the Government* (Trenton, NJ, 1813) 47-48.

33. George Heriot, *Travels Through the Canadas*, (London, 1807; reprinted in 2 vols, Toronto, 1971), vol 1, 139.

34. According to their beliefs, the aboriginal peoples inhabited a universe divided into a sky world, the physical world and a nether world, and further subdivided into a series of categories across which they could only move safely with ritually-acquired sacred power. Survival was thought to depend upon the cooperation of spirit forces that inhabited other quarters of the universe and their most essential relations with plants, animals and the opposite sex required appeals to sacred power through proper ritual. See Gregory Evans Dowd, *A Spirited Resistance: The North American Indian Struggle for Unity, 1745-1815* (Baltimore, 1992), 6.

35. Thomas Ridout to his sister, 26 September 1811, in Mathilda Edgar, *Ten Years of Upper Canada in Peace and War, 1805-1815: Being the Ridout Letters* (London, 1891), 60.

36. Abigail Smith Adams to Mrs. Warren, 30 December 1812, in Adams, *Letters of Abigail Smith Adams*, 413.

37. MTRL, L16 A93, Anne Powell to George Murray, 10 Sep 1811.

38. MTRL, L16 A93, Anne Powell to George Murray, 22 Feb 1812.

39. Diary of Ely Playter, 27 June 1812, quoted in Edith G. Firth, ed., *The Town of York 1793-1815: A Collection of Documents of Early Toronto* (Toronto, 1962), 279.

40. William Henry Kilby, *Eastport and Passamaquoddy: A Collection of Historical and Biographical Sketches* (Eastport, Maine, 1982), 159.

41. Jean Hunter, 25-26 June 1812, in Anne Hunter and Elizabeth Bell, eds., *The Journal of General Sir Martin Hunter and Some Letters of his Wife, Lady Hunter* (Edinburgh, 1894), 265-266.

42. LAC, MG24 A57, Journal of Lady Katherine Sherbrooke, 28 June 1812.

43. LAC, MG24 A57, Journal of Lady Katherine Sherbrooke, 28 June 1812.

44. LAC, MG24, A9, Diary of Anne Elinor Prevost, 25 June 1812.

45. Elizabeth Hale to William Amherst, 29 June 1812 and 2 July 1805 in Roger Hall and S.W. Shelton, *The Rising Country: The Hale-Amherst correspondence 1799-1825* (Toronto, 2002), 186, 271.

46. George A. Seibel, *The Niagara Portage Road: 200 Years 1790-1990* (Niagara Falls, 1990), 141.

47. Franklin B. Hough, *A History of St. Lawrence and Franklin Counties, New York, from the Earliest Period to the Present Time* (Harrison, New York, 1970), 619.

48. Extract from a Buffalo newspaper dated 14 July 1812, quoted in Tupper, ed., *Life and Correspondence of Brock*, 204.

49. Hough, *History of St. Lawrence and Franklin Counties*, 620-621.

50. Susan Burnham Greeley, quoted in Talman, ed., *Loyalist Narratives*, 103.

51. Niagara Historical Society, No. 28, *Family History and Reminiscences of Early Settlers*, "Reminiscences of Mrs. Edward Pilkington", 6.

52. *NWR*, 27 June 1812, Vol. II, 285.

53. Turner, *History of the Holland Purchase*, 190.

54. Hough, *History of St. Lawrence and Franklin Counties*, 619.

55. Hough, *History of St. Lawrence and Franklin Counties, New York*, 619.

56. Turner, *History of the Holland Purchase*, 190.

57. John Patterson to Levina Patterson, 16 August 1812, in Florence and Mary Howard, eds., "The Letters of John Patterson, 1812-1813." *Pennsylvania Historical Magazine*, 23, 100.

58. Elizabeth Ellet, *Pioneer Women of the West* (New York, 1856), 309.

59. Tecumseh, pronounced by the native people as Tecumthé, was a chieftain of the Shawnee tribe

and his parents belonged to the panther clan. Tecumseh was almost certainly born on the Scioto River near Chillicothe, then the capital of the young state of Ohio. His exact date of birth is not known, but the most authoritative estimate puts it at 1768. A charismatic leader with outstanding military and political talents and a vision of a great Indian confederacy, he led the native peoples allied to Great Britain during the War of 1812 and was killed at the Battle of the Thames in 1813.

60. Robert S. Allen, *His Majesty's Indian Allies: British Indian Policy in the Defence of Canada, 1774-1815* (Toronto, 1992), 149-150.

61. Rosalie Stier Calvert to Henri J. Stier, June 1812, in Margaret Law Callcott, ed., *Mistress of Riversdale: The Plantation Letters of Rosalie Stier Calvert 1795-1821* (Baltimore, 1991), 251.

62. Elizabeth B. Kennon to Rachel Mordecai, 5 July 1812, in "Kennon Letters", *Virginia Historical Magazine*, Vol. XXXIV, No. 2 (April 1926), 129.

63. Elizabeth B. Kennon to Rachel Mordecai, 5 July 1812, in "Kennon Letters", Vol. XXXIV, No. 2 (April 1926), 129.

64. Dolley Madison to Anna Cutts 27 March 1812, in Lucia B. Cutts, ed., *Memoirs and Letters of Dolly Madison: wife of James Madison, President of the United States* (London and New York, 1971), 77.

65. Dolley Madison to Anna Cutts, 12 May 1812 in Cutts, ed., *Memoirs and Letters of Dolly Madison*, 79.

66. Sarah Anna Emery, ed., *Reminiscences of A Nonagenarian* (Newburyport, Mass., 1879), 274.

67. *The Richmond Enquirer*, 23 June 1812, 2.

68. Article, "War Against England," *NWR*, 27 June 1812.

69. *NWR*, 27 June 1812.

1: "The faithful wife, without debate": The Woman's World in 1812

1. "Hard is the Fortune," a traditional song popular in Britain and North America in the late eighteenth century.

2. Lee Holcombe, *Wives and Property: Reform of the Married Women's Property Law in Nineteenth-Century England* (Toronto, 1983), 18, 23.

3. Whether spinsters or widows, unmarried women enjoyed the same rights over property as men, with the single (but major) exception that possession of property did not entitle them to vote. As regards crime, English law imposed harsher penalties than American law. A woman found guilty of *petite* or small treason for murdering her husband could, for example, still be burned alive – at least this was the penalty in the Criminal Code but it was never used as by 1812, hanging was the standard method of capital punishment in Britain and her colonies.

4. Micheline Dumont, Michèle Jean, Marie Lavigne, Jennifer Stoddart, *Quebec Women: A History* (Toronto, 1987), 70-71.

5. Hunt, *Life in America*, 77.

6. Elizabeth Jane Errington, *Wives and Mothers School Mistresses and Scullery Maids: Working Women in Upper Canada, 1790-1840* (Montreal and Kingston, 1995), 235-236.

7. Poem, "What is Woman?", quoted in Beth Light and Alison Prentice, ed., *Pioneer & Gentlewomen of British North America* (Toronto, 1980), 218.

8. Eliza Rundell, *A New System of Domestic Cookery*, (New York, 1815), iii.

9. From "Martial's Quiet Life," by Henry Howard, Earl of Surrey, *Oxford Dictionary of Quotations*, 518:2.

10. Julia Delafield, *Biographies of Frances Lewis and Morgan Lewis* (New York, 1877), 64.

11. Henry Bradshaw Fearon, *Sketches of America: A Narrative of A Journey of Five Thousand Miles Through the Eastern and Western States of America* (London, 1818), 81.

12. Joseph Gubbins, 20 July 1811, in Howard Temperley, ed., *Lieutenant-Colonel Joseph Gubbins. New Brunswick Journals of 1811 & 1813* (Fredericton, 1980), 26.

13. Joseph Gubbins, 20 July 1811, in Temperley, ed., *Lieutenant-Colonel Joseph Gubbins*, 27.

14. LAC, MG24 F128 Vol. 1, Grant Papers, Jasper Grant to Mrs. Grant Sr., 1 Aug 1801.

15. LAC, MG24 F128 Vol. 1, Jasper Grant to Thomas Grant, 2 Feb 1808.

16. Rundell, *New System of Domestic Cookery*, iv-vi.

17. Rosalie Stier Calvert to Charles J. Stier, 23 July 1810, in Callcott, *Mistress of Riversdale*, 221.

18. Rosalie Stier Calvert to Isabelle Van Havre, undated, in Callcott, *Mistress of Riversdale*, 10.

19. L.H. Sigourney, *Letters of Life* (New York, 1867), 5, 99.

20. Sigourney, *Letters of Life*, 102. In the days before the connection between germs and disease was discovered, many housewives were not as concerned with cleanliness as might be expected. Floors, clothes and bedclothes were washed infrequently, and many poorer women, who only possessed one set of clothing, had to wear a cotton shift while they washed their outer garments.

21. Turner, *History of the Holland Purchase*, 316. In the early nineteenth century, houses that

would be regarded today as comfortable, sizeable and well-maintained were in a minority. Most North American homes were far smaller and more scantily furnished than is popularly believed.

22. Joseph Gubbins, 20 July 1811, in Temperley, ed., *Lieutenant-Colonel Joseph Gubbins*, 23.

23. Joseph Gubbins, 20 July 1811, 13 July 1811 in Temperley, ed., *Lieutenant-Colonel Joseph Gubbins*, 22-23.

24. Mary Ann Brevoort Bristol, "Reminiscences of the Northwest," *Wisconsin Historical Collections*, Vol. VIII (1879), 296.

25. Bristol, "Reminiscences of the Northwest," 294-295.

26. Dumont, *et al.*, *Quebec Women*, 88.

27. Bristol, "Reminiscences of the Northwest," 295.

28. Diamond Jenness, *The Indians of Canada* (Toronto, 1977), 292-293.

29. Emery, *Reminiscences of a Nonagenerian*, 7.

30. Emery, *Reminiscences of a Nonagenerian*, 7-8.

31. Wyman, ed., *Elizabeth Oakes Smith*, 16-17.

32. PANS, MG1 Vol. 1463E, Diary of Louisa Collins, 15, 17, 30 Aug 1815, 1, 7, 20 Sept 1815, 12 Oct 1815.

33. Sigourney, *Letters of Life*, 113-114.

34. James A. Beal, *Jefferson at Monticello: Memoirs of a Monticello Slave* (Charlottesville, 1981), 4; Thomas Jefferson Randolph to James Parton, 1 June 1868, in Milton E. Flower, *James Parton: The Father of Modern Biography* (Durham, 1951), 236-239. Sally (likely Sarah) Hemings (1773-1835) became the property of Thomas Jefferson as a baby, and probably helped to look after Mary Jefferson while still young. She accompanied Mary to Paris in 1787 as a member of the family household (Jefferson having been appointed American Minister to France at the time), and returned with the family to Virginia in 1789. Thereafter she seems to have remained at Monticello, where Jefferson had gardens and a 5,000-acre plantation worked by some 150 other slaves.

35. CHS, 19828-1909, George Howard Autobiography and Record Book, 10.

36. CHS, 19828-1909, George Howard Autobiography and Record Book, 10.

37. William Brown, "Recollections of Old Halifax," *Collections of the Nova Scotia Historical Society*, vol 13 (1908), 78.

38. LAC MG24 A57, Journal of Lady Katherine Sherbrooke, 1 July 1815.

39. LAC, MG24 A57, Journal of Lady Katherine Sherbrooke, 6 Apr 1812, 8 Oct 1812, 18 May 1813.

40. Larkin, *The Reshaping of Everyday Life*, 261-262.

41. Hunt, *Life in America*, 95.

42. Sigourney, *Letters of Life*, 6.

43. Thomas Jefferson, quoted in Michael Weishan, *The New Traditional Garden* (New York, 1999), 213.

44. LAC, MG19 F1, Garden book of Catherine Claus, 6 and 9 Apr 1806, 25 May 1806, 15 Apr 1807, 22 Apr 1809, 8-9 Aug 1806. War paid no regard to beautifully tended gardens and whilst Thomas Jefferson's property was far enough away from hostilities to suffer no harm, Catherine Claus's garden was destroyed, along with almost everything else in Newark, by an American occupying force in December 1813.

45. Sigourney, *Letters of Life*, 115.

46. Hunt, *Life In America*, 217-218.

47. Hunt, *Life In America*, 219-220.

48. Frederick Chamier, *The Life of a Sailor* (London, 1832), Vol. 2, 175.

49. John Lovett to Joseph Alexander, 12 June 1813, quoted in Catharina W.R. Bonney, *Legacy of Historical Gleanings* (Albany, 1875), 298.

50. Edwin C. Guillet, *Pioneer Arts and Crafts* (Toronto, 1960), 73.

51. Frances Phipps, *Colonial Kitchens, Their Furnishings, and Their Gardens* (New York, 1972), 250-251, 253-254, 257, 259.

52. Rundell, *New System of Domestic Cookery*, iv.

53. Hannah Glasse, née Allgood (1708-1770), was the London-born daughter of a clergyman. She married Peter Glasse, a solicitor, and had several children. When she wrote her famous book, she described herself as "Habit maker to HRH the Princess of Wales, in Tavistock St, Covent Garden."

54. Amelia Simmons, *American Cookery* (Poughkeepsie, New York, 1815), 1.

55. Amelia Simmons, quoted in Phipps, *Colonial Kitchens*, 124.

56. UG, McLaughlin Library, XR1 MS A210088, Hannah Jarvis, "Cookbook with Health Remedies", 18-19, 24-25.

57. Ellet, *Pioneer Women of the West*, 137.

58. William Dunlap, 9 Feb 1806 in Dunlap, *Diary of William Dunlap (1766-1839): The Memoirs of a Dramatist, Theatrical Manager, Painter, Critic, Novelist, and Historian* (reprinted New York, 1969), 387.

59. LAC, MG24 A57, Journal of Lady Katherine Sherbrooke, 11 Sep 1812.

60. Bristol, "Reminiscences of the Northwest," 304.

61. Sigourney, *Letters of Life*, 106.

62. Margaret Bayard Smith to Susan B. Smith, 4 Aug 1809, in Gaillard Hunt, ed., *The First For-*

ty Years of Washington Society portrayed by the Family Letters of Mrs. Samuel Harrison Smith (New York, 1906), 81-82.

63. LAC, MG24, C2, Diary of Joseph Willcocks, 1801-1803.

64. LAC, MG24, C2, Diary of Joseph Willcocks, 1801-1803.

65. Diary of Sarah Seaton, 12 Nov 1812, in Allen C. Clark, *Life and Letters of Dolly Madison* (Washington D.C., 1914), 138.

66. Michael Smith, *Geographical View of the Province of Upper Canada and Promiscuous Remarks on the Government* (Trenton, NJ, 1813), 42.

67. Wyman, *Elizabeth Oakes Smith*, 16.

68. Elizabeth Kennon to Samuel Mordecai, 13 June 1814, "Kennon Letters," Vol. XXXVII, No. 2 (April 1929), 148.

69. Elizabeth Kennon to Samuel Mordecai, 9 May 1814, "Kennon Letters," Vol. XXXVII, No. 1 (Jan 1929), 46.

70. Delafield, *Frances Lewis and Morgan Lewis*, 64.

71. A chemise was the basic article of underclothing that women of all classes wore until well into the nineteenth century. It could be long or short, and the more elegant type of chemise was made of fine linen, often with a ruffled trim to the sleeves and neck.

72. Ellet, *Pioneer Women of the West*, 137-138.

73. Linda Grant De Pauw and Conover Hunt, "*Remember the Ladies*": *Women in America, 1750-1815* (New York, 1976), 118.

74. *Nova Scotia Royal Gazette*, 6 May 1812, 2.

75. Anthony Benezet, quoted in De Pauw and Hunt, *Remember the Ladies*, 125.

76. Rosalie Stier Calvert to Henri J. Stier, 23 Nov 1813 in Callcott, *Mistress of Riversdale*, 259.

77. PANS, MG1, Letterbook, Catherine Byles to Rebecca Almon, 17 February 1813.

78. *Louisiana Gazette*, 10 Feb 1812, 2; 10 Sep 1814, 2.

79. *Report of the Task force on the Implementaton of Midwifery in Ontario* (Toronto, 1987) 198.

80. Among Hannah Jarvis's remedies is one entitled "Indian Cure for the Ague," which gives the following advice: "Take a dried Bullock-Gall – make into three small Pills – the size of a Pea – when the fit comes on – take one which will cause sickness – and a great perspiration – the second and third taken the same way – will cure the ague," See UG, XR1 MS A210088, "Cookbook with health remedies", 28.

81. Milo Milton Quaife, ed., *War on the Detroit: The Chronicles of Thomas Verchères de Boucherville and The Capitulation by an Ohio Volunteer* (Chicago, 1940), 104.

82. Rundell, *New System of Domestic Cookery*, iii.

83. Evans, *Weathering the Storm*, 1975), 20. Contraceptive devices, such as they were, were mainly used by prostitutes – other women were likely to know little of them.

84. Diary of Elisha Risdon, 17 Mar 1812, quoted in Carlton E. Sanford, *Early History of the Town of Hopkinton* (Boston, 1903), 265.

85. De Pauw and Hunt, *Remember the Ladies*, 38.

86. Sally G. McMillen, *Motherhood in the Old South: Pregnancy, Childbirth and Infant Rearing* (Baton Rouge, 1990), 45.

87. LAC MG24 F9, Diary of Major-General Louis De Watteville, 27 June 1810.

88. Charles White, *A Treatise on the Management of Pregnant and Lying In Women*, (Worcester, Mass., 1793) 85.

89. White, *Treatise*, 80.

90. McMillen, *Motherhood in the Old South*, 95.

91. White, *Treatise*, 83.

92. White, *Treatise*, 79.

93. Rosalie Stier Calvert to Isabelle Van Havre, 4 Dec 1804, in Callcott, *Mistress of Riversdale*, 103.

94. *Report of the Task Force on the Implementation of Midwifery in Ontario*, 199.

95. LAC, MG24 L8, "Ma Saberdache," Vol. V, Joseph-David Mermet to Jacques Viger, 28 Aug 1814, 274.

96. From "Spring," by Henry Howard, Earl of Surrey, *The Oxford Dictionary of Quotations*, 518:2.

97. Alexander Pope, "Epistle II. To a Lady," in Bonamy Dobrée, ed., *Alexander Pope's Collected Poems* (London, 1963), 233.

Picture Essay: What to Wear? Women's Clothing in the War of 1812 Period

1 Sources: Sue McLean, article, "*How to Dress for 1812*"; Linda Grant De Pauw and Conover Hunt, *Remember the Ladies*; K.B. Brett, *Women's Costume in Early Ontario*; Elizabeth McLellan, *Historic Dress in America 1607-1880*.

2: "Maidens here are sweetly singing": Love, Courtship, Marriage and Dangerous Liaisons

1. "The Day of Marriage," an American song dating to the first decade of the nineteenth century and published in Philadelphia, Box 108, Item 51, Lester Levy Collection, Milton Eisenhower Library, Johns Hopkins University, Baltimore.

2. James Nugent Boyle Bernardo Townshend, Captain, Royal Navy (1785-1842), was the fifth son of the lst Marquess Townshend of Raynham Hall, Norfolk, England, by his second wife. His father, a godson of King George I, had had a

long and distinguished army career and served under Major-General James Wolfe at Quebec in 1759 as a brigadier.

3. Clarence Cook, *A Girl's Life Eighty Years Ago: Selections from the Letters of Eliza Southgate Bowne* (New York, 1887), 47.

4. LAC, MG24, L8, "Ma Saberdache", Vol. 4, 22.

5. LAC, MG24, L8, "Ma Saberdache", Vol. 4, 24.

6. Marius Barbeau, *Jongleur Songs of Old Quebec* (New Brunswick, N.J, 1962), 65-67. In the final verse of the song, mother and daughter argue, the mother wanting to send her daughter to a convent and the daughter resisting.

7. Dr. John Gregory, *A Father's Legacy to his Daughters* (Edinburgh, 1793, reprinted New York, 1974), 42.

8. PANS, MG1, Almon Family Papers, Rebecca Byles to Catherine and Mary Byles, 17 January 1785.

9. From "Good-bye and How-d'ye-do," by The Hon. William Robert Spencer, *The Annual Register, or a View of the History, Politics and Literature, for the Year 1811* (London, 1825), 609.

10. MM, Acc. 1761, Papers of Sir John Johnson. From poem, "On meeting Maria after her absence at Quebec 2 Feb 1805," by Barnard Foord Bowes.

11. Le Couteur, 11 Nov 1813 in Donald E. Graves, ed., *Merry Hearts Make Light Days: The War of 1812 Journal of Lieutenant John Le Couteur, 104th Foot* (Ottawa, 1983), 150.

12. Le Couteur, 27 October 1815 in Graves, ed., *Merry Hearts*, 242.

13. Le Couteur, 27 Oct 1815, in Graves, ed., *Merry Hearts*, 242.

14. Lydia Bacon, 10 June 1812, "Bacon Journal," 63.

15. Emery, *Reminiscences*, 245.

16. Emery, *Reminiscences*, 247.

17. Wyman, *Elizabeth Oakes Smith*, 42.

18. Wyman, *Elizabeth Oakes Smith*, 42.

19. Ellen K. Rothman, *Hands and Hearts: A History of Courtship in America* (New York, 1984), 25.

20. Wyman, *Elizabeth Oakes Smith*, 90.

21. Wyman, *Elizabeth Oakes Smith*, 92.

22. CHS, 19628-1909, George Howard Autobiography and Record Book, 15. George and Sarah were married on 28 May 1810.

23. Rothman, *Hands and Hearts*, 30.

24. Rothman, *Hands and Hearts*, 29. Whereas customs in the British colonies remained much in line with those in Britain, by the early nineteenth century in America, parental approval for a match was becoming desirable rather than essential.

25. Brendan O'Brien, *Speedy Justice: The Tragic Last Voyage of His Majesty's Vessel Speedy* (Toronto, 1992), 92.

26. LAC, MG24, C1, Joseph Willcocks to his brother, 3 Nov 1800.

27. William Renwick Riddell, "Joseph Willcocks, Sheriff, Member of Parliament and Traitor," *Ontario Historical Society Papers and Records*, Vol. 24 (1927), 478.

28. LAC, MG24 L8, "Ma Saberdache", Vol. 4. Poem, "The Flatterer" by Joseph-David Mermet, 18-19.

29. Riddell, "Joseph Willcocks," 478.

30. Thomas G. Ridout to Thomas Ridout, 4 Sep 1813, in *Doc. Hist.* Vol. 7, 99.

31. LAC, MG40, M1, John Johnston to his mother, 23 July 1813.

32. Anonymous, "First Campaign of An A.D.C." *Military and Naval Magazine of the United States*, No. 12, 90.

33. Anonymous, "First Campaign of an A.D.C." No. 12, 90.

34. LAC, MG24, F3, William Jarvis to his parents, 28 Sep 1814.

35. Charles L. Leslie, *Memoirs of Col. Leslie: Whilst serving with the 29th Regiment in the Peninsula and the 60th Rifles in Canada* (Aberdeen, 1887), 289.

36. PRONI, T/1870/4, Samuel Holmes, "A Pedestrian Tour to the Falls of Niagara in Upper Canada", 180.

37. "First Campaign of An A.D.C." No. 6, 280.

38. "First Campaign of An A.D.C.", 280.

39. "First Campaign of An A.D.C.", 280-281.

40. Le Couteur, 3 Sep 1812, in Graves ed., *Merry Hearts*, 76.

41. Le Couteur, 3 Sep 1812 in Graves, ed., *Merry Hearts*, 76.

42. H. Perry Smith, *History of the City of Buffalo and Erie County* (New York, 1894), Vol. 2, 66.

43. Mordecai Myers, *Reminiscences. 1700-1814, Including Incidents in the War of 1812-1814* (Washington, 1900), 43.

44. Captain John Kincaid, *Random Shots From a Rifleman* (Staplehurst, Kent, 1998), 294.

45. Kincaid, *Random Shots*, 294.

46. Lieutenant Harry Smith, in G.C. Moore Smith, *The Autobiography of Lieutenant General Sir Harry Smith*, 71.

47. Smith, quoted in Smith, *Harry Smith*, 72.

48. Kincaid, *Random Shots*, 296.

49. James Parton, *Life of Andrew Jackson* (New York, 1861), Vol. 2, 268.

50. SUNY, Bailey Papers, Diary of the Reverend Eleazer Williams, 7 Oct 1812.

51. LAC, MG24, F90, Account of the Life of Sir William Howe Mulcaster, 39, 40-42.

52. Agnes Cossar, quoted in Sandor Antal, *A Wampum Denied: Procter's War of 1812* (Ottawa, 1997), 403. The couple were married in 1814.

53. AO, F662, MU 5856, William Hamilton Merritt to Catherine Prendergast, 4 Sep 1812, 9 Feb 1814.

54. AO, F662, MU 5856, Catherine Prendergast to William Merritt, 9 Nov 1814, 10 Dec 1814.

55. AO, F662, MU 5856, William Merritt to Catherine Prendergast, 23 Dec 1814.

56. Peter Ward, *Courtship, Love and Marriage in Nineteenth Century English Canada* (Montreal, 1990), 30-31.

57. *Louisiana Gazette*, 21 Feb 1812, 3.

58. *Louisiana Gazette*, 21 Feb 1812, 3.

59. John Strachan, quoted in Errington, *Wives and Mothers*, 25.

60. Remini, *Andrew Jackson and the Course of the American Empire 1767-1821*, 69.

61. *Poulson's Weekly Advertiser*, 3 May 1813, 3.

62. *Montreal Herald*, 26 Mar 1814, 3.

63. LAC, MG24, L3, Correspondence 1814, Vol. 15, Charles-Nicolas de Montanach to his father, 30 June 1814, 19.

64. LAC, MG24 L3, Correspondence 1814, Vol. 15, Charles-Nicolas de Montanach to his father, 30 June 1814, 19.

65. Emery, *Reminiscences*, 271.

66. Account from a Glasgow newspaper, quoted in Charlotte Gourley Robinson, *Pioneer Profiles of New Brunswick Settlers* (Belleville, 1980), 214.

67. *NWR*, 1812, Vol. III, 148.

68. *NWR*, 1812, Vol. III, 148.

69. *NWR*, 1812, Vol. III, 148. A pelisse was a light coat or cloak, often trimmed with fur.

70. Wyman, *Elizabeth Oakes Smith*, 43.

71. Emery, *Reminiscences*, 272.

72. *Connecticut Gazette*, 22 May 1814, 3.

73. Robinson, *Pioneer Profiles of New Brunswick Settlers*, 63.

74. Alphonse J. Deveau, ed., *Diary of a Frenchman: François Lambert Bourneuf's Adventures from France to Acadia 1787-1871* (Halifax, 1990), 99-100.

75. Ellet, *Pioneer Women of the West*, 139.

76. Ellet, *Pioneer Women of the West*, 140.

77. Ellet, *Pioneer Women of the West*, 140-141.

78. Edwin O. Wood, *Historic Mackinac: The Historical Picturesque and Legendary Features of the Mackinac Country* (New York, 1918), Vol. 2, 132.

79. Wood, *Historic Mackinac*, Vol. 2, 132.

80. Wood, *Historic Mackinac*, Vol. 2, 133.

81. Wood, *Historic Mackinac*, Vol. 2, 132.

82. As examples of the different native courtship and marriage customs, an alliance between a warrior of the Huron people and his chosen woman was preceded by his wooing her with presents. She and her parents were required to give their consent and at the wedding feast, all the women of the bride's village presented her with firewood for the following winter. In other traditions such as that of the Iroquois, marriage seems to have been more strictly regulated, with a young man's parents choosing his bride and arranging the match with her parents.

83. Le Couteur in Graves, ed., *Merry Hearts*, 156. Captain Robert Loring of the 104th Foot (1789-1848) was the personal ADC to Lieutenant General Gordon Drummond, Commander, Upper Canada from December 1813 to 1815 when he succeeded Sir George Prevost as commander in chief, British North America. Miss Mary Ann Campbell, was the daughter of Judge William Campbell of York.

84. Le Couteur in Graves, ed., *Merry Hearts*, 157. Lieutenant and Commander Alexander T. Dobbs, RN, promoted to that rank in 1814, married Mary, daughter of Colonel Richard Cartwright, (1759-1815), a Kingston merchant and one of the most prominent landowners and businessmen in eastern Upper Canada.

85. Mary Agnes Fitzgibbon, *A Veteran of 1812* (Toronto, 2000), 125.

86. Fitzgibbon, *Veteran of 1812*, 127.

87. Fitzgibbon, *Veteran of 1812*, 128.

88. Susanna Moodie, *Roughing it In The Bush* (1852, reprinted Toronto, 1989), 208. This custom was most common in cases where an old man married a young wife, or vice versa, or two older people married for the second or third time.

89. Moodie, *Roughing it In The Bush*, 208-209.

90. LAC, MG24, A57, Journal of Lady Katherine Sherbrooke, 7 June 1812.

91. "Reminiscences of Mrs. Edward Pilkington," 8. Edward Pilkington was quartermaster of the 100th Foot and his family owned an estate in Ireland.

92. Rothman, *Hands and Hearts*, 67.

93. Sarah Chester Williams, quoted in Rothman, *Hands and Hearts*, 63.

94. Elizabeth C. Barney Buel, ed., *Chronicles of a Pioneer School from 1792-1833, being the History of Miss Sarah Pierce and her Litchfield School* (Cambridge, Mass, 1903), 186-187.

95. LC, Rodgers Family Papers, I:14, Margaretta G. Wingate to Minerva Rodgers, 27 Apr 1809.

96. LC, Rodgers I:14, Margaretta G. Wingate to Minerva Rodgers, 27 Apr 1809.

97. Dean Swift, quoted in Hunt, *Life in America*, 80.

98. Hannah More, quoted in Hunt, *Life in America*, 81.

99. From poem, "Advice to Mrs. Mowat," by Anne Hecht, quoted in Grace Helen Mowat, *The Diverting History of a Loyalist Town: A Portrait of St. Andrews, New Brunswick* (Fredericton, 1953), 57.

100. Mowat, *History of a Loyalist Town*, 57.

101. Mowat, *History of a Loyalist Town*, 57.

102. Mowat, *History of a Loyalist Town*, 56.

103. *Connecticut Gazette*, 6 May 1812, 4.

104. Hunt, *Life in America*, 79.

105. Henri J. Stier to Rosalie Stier Calvert, 10 Nov 1804, in Callcott, *Mistress of Riversdale*, 114.

106. Elizabeth Kennon to Ellen Mordecai, 1 Mar 1814, "Kennon Letters," Vol. XXXVI, No. 3 (July 1928), 234.

107. Elizabeth Kennon to Ellen Mordecai, 1 Mar 1814, "Kennon Letters," Vol. XXXVI, No. 3 (July 1928), 234.

108. Elizabeth Kennon to Ellen Mordecai, 1 Mar 1814, "Kennon Letters," Vol. XXXVI, No. 3 (July 1928), 234.

109. LAC, MG24, L8, "Ma Saberdache", Vol. 4, 21.

110. Temperley, ed., *Lieutenant-Colonel Joseph Gubbins*, 16 July 1811, 17.

111. LAC, MG24, A9, Diary of Anne Elinor Prevost, 17 Feb 1813, 126.

112. LAC, MG24, A9, Diary of Anne Elinor Prevost, 17 Feb 1813, 126.

113. LAC, MG24, A9, Diary of Anne Elinor Prevost, 17 Feb 1813, 127. A cariole was a small, covered carriage driven by one horse.

114. LAC, MG24, A9, Diary of Anne Elinor Prevost, 17 Feb 1813, 124.

115. LAC, MG24, A9, Diary of Anne Elinor Prevost, 17 Feb 1813, 125.

116. LAC, MG24, A9, Diary of Anne Elinor Prevost, 17 Feb 1813, 125.

117. LAC, MG24, A9, Diary of Anne Elinor Prevost, 24 Apr 1813, 136.

118. LAC, RG8, IV, Vol. 78, No. 293, Mary Baker to Margaret Pacan, 30 June 1813.

119. *Royal Gazette and New Brunswick Advertiser*, 27 July 1812, 3.

120. *Connecticut Gazette*, 13 May 1812, 4.

121. *Connecticut Gazette*, 25 Mar 1812, 4.

122. *New York Evening Post*, 19 Dec 1812, 2.

123. *New York Evening Post*, 19 Dec 1812, 3.

124. Dumont, *et al. Quebec Women: A History*, 106.

125. Dumont *et al.*, *Quebec Women: A History*, 106.

126. Lieutenant P. McDonogh to his parents, 25 Apr 1813, in Frank H. Severance, ed., "Hero of Fort Erie: The Correspondence of Lieutenant P. McDonogh," *Publications of the Buffalo Historical Society* (Buffalo, 1902) Vol. V, 83.

127. LAC, RG 8 I, vol 1203-1/2, 14, Captain James Basden to Sir George Prevost, 2 Aug 1813.

128. LAC, RG 8I, vol 12031/2, 14, Captain James Basden to Sir George Prevost, 2 Aug 1813.

129. NAUS, RG 125, Roll 6, vol 4, Case 152, Proceedings of a Court Martial held at Sackets Harbor for the trial of Captain James Leonard, 1 Dec 1813.

130. NAUS, RG 125, Roll 6, vol 4, Case 152, Court Martial of James Leonard.

131. NAUS, RG 125, Roll 6, vol 4, Case 152, Court Martial of James Leonard.

132. NAUS, RG 125, Roll 6, vol 4, Case 152, Court Martial of James Leonard.

133. NAUS, RG 125, Roll 6, vol 4, Case 152, Court Martial of James Leonard.

134. NAUS, RG 125, Roll 6, vol 4, Case 152, Court Martial of James Leonard.

135. Chauncey to Leonard, 13 Apr 1813, in William F. Dudley, ed., *The Naval War of 1812. A Documentary History. Volume II. 1813* (Washington, 1992), 442-443.

136. Chauncey to Leonard, 13 Apr 1813, in Dudley, ed., *Naval War of 1812. A Documentary History. Volume II*, 442-443.

137. Chauncey to Leonard, 13 Apr 1813, in Dudley, ed., *Naval War of 1812. A Documentary History.* Volume II, 442-443.

138. NAUS, RG 125, Roll 6, vol 4, Case 152, Court Martial of Captain James Leonard.

139. "The Unfortunate Miss Bailey" or "Miss Bailey's Ghost" was a popular ballad in the late 18th and early 19th centuries. In one version, Miss Bailey returns to haunt the captain as a ghost, complaining that because of what she had done," the parson would not bury me." The captain, in a fit of conscience, gives the ghost "a five-pound note" and she then departs, happy in the knowledge that the money will "bribe the sexton for my grave," and that she will have a proper resting place.

140. John Green, *Vicissitudes of a Soldier's Life* (London, 1827), 53.

141. Le Couteur, 13 Nov 1814 in Graves, ed., *Merry Hearts*, 216.

142. From "Psyche" by Mrs. Tighe, *Annual Register*, 1811, 601-602.

3: "For their work continueth": Gainful Employment

1. "Sweet Poll of Plymouth," a traditional sailor's ballad from the eighteenth century, was sung by the actress Eleanora Darley at the special concert held in New London in January 1813 for Commodore Stephen Decatur and the crew of the USS *United States* to celebrate their victory over HMS *Macedonian*.
2. De Pauw and Hunt, *Remember the Ladies*, 64.
3. *Upper Canada Gazette*, 7 May 1808, 2.
4. Dumont, et. al., *Quebec Women*, 90.
5. Jacques Viger, *Reminiscences*, 3. Literally translated, the expression means "fork lunch."
6. William Dunlop, *Tiger Dunlop's Upper Canada* (Toronto, 1967), 17.
7. *Montreal Herald*, 15 May 1813, 3.
8. Fearon, *Sketches of America*, 45.
9. Fearon, *Sketches of America*, 7.
10. Lyman Spalding, *Recollections of the War of 1812 and Early Life in Western New York. No. 2.*(Lockport, New York, 1949), 14.
11. *Montreal Herald*, 28 May 1813, 2.
12. ANQM, TL32 S1 S51, Boite 10, Cour des Sessions de la Paix, Petition dated 6 Oct 1813. Madame Bouquin's petition to open a tavern was accompanied by a note from the regiment's commanding officer, Major-General Louis De Watteville, certifying "as to the truth of all her statements," and it was granted by the Montreal Court of Quarter Sessions.
13. SJ, Le Couteur-Sumner Papers, John Le Couteur to Philip Bouton, 24 Oct 1814.
14. Donald E. Graves, *Where Right and Glory Lead: The Battle of Lundy's Lane, 1814* (Toronto, 1997) 115-116.
15. Frank H. Severance, ed., "Recalling Pioneer Days," *Publications of the Buffalo Historical Society, Vol XXVI,* (Buffalo, New York, 1922), 216.
16. Severance, ed., "Recalling Pioneer Days", 189.
17. Severance, ed., "Recalling Pioneer Days", 188.
18. Severance, ed., "Recalling Pioneer Days", 188-189.
19. Notes by Captain Merritt, *Doc. Hist.*, Vol 6, 122.
20. PRONI, T/1870/4, Holmes, "Pedestrian Tour," 194.
21. PRONI, T/1870/4, Holmes, "Pedestrian Tour", 120-121.
22. PRONI, T/1870/4, Holmes, "Pedestrian Tour", 131-132.
23. Samuel White, *History of the American Troops, During the Late War, under the Command of Colonels Fenton and Campbell* (Baltimore, 1830), 29.
24. MTRL, Diary of Christopher Hagerman, 27 Nov 1813, 1-2.
25. Robinson, *Pioneer Profiles of New Brunswick Settlers*, 88-98.
26. Emery, *Reminiscences*, 275.
27. Emery, *Reminiscences*, 277. Efforts were made to control bootlegging and American militiamen were posted along the borders with Upper and Lower Canada, where people on both sides of the lines were on friendly terms. Orders were given to prevent the illicit transporting of goods but the militiamen were often unsuccessful.
28. *Boston Gazette*, 27 May 1813, 1.
29. Emery, *Reminiscences*, 277.
30. Emery, *Reminiscences*, 280.
31. *Poulsons Weekly Advertiser*, 11 Dec 1813, 4. Other examples of these early charitable organizations included the Washington Benevolent Society of Massachussetts and The Association for the Relief of Respectable, Aged, Indigent Females, formed in 1813 and probably the earliest effort to establish a home for poor, elderly women.
32. The translation reads, "the ladies of Charity directed by His Majesty to run the General Hospital," an institution dating from the French régime in North America.
33. Rosalie Stier Calvert to Isabelle Van Havre, 28 Sep 1804 in Callcott, *Mistress of Riversdale*, 101.
34. *Montreal Herald* 26 Mar 1813, 3.
35. "Old Inns and Coffee Houses of Halifax", *Collections of Nova Scotia Historical Society*, Vol. 22 (1933), 16. Dancing was an accomplishment that was generally approved of, even by someone as critical of "over-polishing" as Rosalie Stier Calvert. She had to admit it was the surest way for a young lady to be noticed in society.
36. LAC, MG19 F1, Claus Papers, Advertisement for the Montreal Ladies Seminary. Catherine Claus sent her daughter to this establishment.
37. LAC, MG19 F1, Claus Papers, Advertisement for the Montreal Ladies Seminary.
38. LAC, MG19 F1, Claus Papers, Advertisement for the Montreal Ladies Seminary.
39. Robinson, *Loyalist Pioneers*, 63-64.
40. Jean-Charlotte Berczy, née Jean-Charlotte Allamand (1760-1839), came from a cultured family. She arrived with her husband, William von Moll Berczy, in Upper Canada in 1794, where he became a captain in the York militia, an overseer of highways, and a building contractor. He was granted Markham township for settlement on condition that he build Yonge Street to run beyond the settlement. Having settled 77 families there by 1798, he ruined himself financial-

ly and went to Montreal, where his wife taught and he earned his living as a painter.

41. Patricia L. Parker, *Susanna Rowson* (Boston, 1986), 123.

42. Parker, *Susanna Rowson*, 122-123.

43. Cook, *A Girl's Life Eighty Years Ago*, iv-v.

44. Sigourney, *Letters of Life*, 190.

45. Sigourney, *Letters of Life*, 193.

46. Sigourney, *Letters of Life*, 194-195, 197.

47. *Richmond Enquirer*, 21 Dec 1813, 4.

48. Many girls remained illiterate or badly educated. Diaries such as that left by Louisa Collins, a farmer's daughter from Dartmouth, Nova Scotia, quoted in Chapter 1, demonstrate poor spelling and grammar, but it remained the belief of many that it was only necessary for girls to be useful in matters of housekeeping.

49. PANS, MG1, Vol. 479, Bishop Inglis to Dr. Morice, 18 Aug 1813.

50. *New York Evening Post*, 12 Apr 1813, 2.

51. *Richmond Enquirer*, 8 June 1813, 4.

52. *New York Evening Post*, 12 Apr 1813, 2.

53. *Richmond Enquirer*, 23 June 1812, 4.

54. *Richmond Enquirer*, 13 Dec 1813, 4.

55. *Upper Canada Gazette*, 21 Dec 1808, 2. Tailoring originally included gown making or mantua making, which required the skill of draping while the tailor made flat patterns.

56. *Poulsons Weekly Advertiser*, 15 Dec 1813, 21.

57. Rosalie Stier Calvert to Isabelle van Havre, 28 September 1804, in Callcott, *Mistress of Riversdale*, 100.

58. Rosalie Stier Calvert to Isabelle Van Havre, undated; Rosalie Stier Calvert to H.J. Stier, 25 Dec 1803 in Callcott, *Mistress of Riversdale*, 9, 65.

59. Temperley, ed., *Lieutenant Colonel Joseph Gubbins*, 20 July 1811, 26.

60. Delafield, *Frances Lewis and Morgan Lewis*, 196.

61. LAC RG8, IV, vol 138, No. 113., Vice-Admiralty Prize records.

62. *Upper Canada Gazette*, 7 May 1808, 2.

63. Robinson, *Pioneer Profiles*, 210.

64. Allen, *His Majesty's Indian Allies*, 182.

65. John E. McDowell, "Madame La Framboise", *Michigan History*, Vol. 56, Winter 1972, 280.

66. McDowell, "Madame La Framboise", 278.

67. John R. Bailey, *Mackinac* (Lansing, Michigan, 1895), 177-178.

68. McDowell, "Madame La Framboise", 273.

69. Edwin O. Wood, *Historic Mackinac*, Vol. 2, 124.

70. Rosalie Stier Calvert to Henri J. Stier, 19 May 1805 in Callcott, *Mistress of Riversdale*, 117.

71. Rosalie Stier Calvert to Isabelle van Havre, 10 Dec 1807 in Callcott, *Mistress of Riversdale*, 177.

In addition to supervising the running of her house, gardens and plantations, Rosalie made all her family's clothes and those of her servants, and all the soap and candles required. She also supervised the making of other foodstuffs such as jams, pickles and sausages.

72. Martha Ballard, 24 Apr 1789, in Laurel Thatcher Ulrich, *A Midwife's Tale: The Life of Martha Ballard, based on her diary, 1785-1812* (New York, 1991), 5.

73. Ulrich, *A Midwife's Tale*, 11. Of the books available on the subject, few were as popular as *English Herbals, or The English Physician Enlarged*, written by Nicholas Culpeper, apothecary-turned-physician. The book went through 23 editions from 1770 until its last printing in America in 1824. Although herbs certainly formed the solid basis of Martha Ballard's treatments, she also believed in the virtue of common garden plants and household items such as vinegar and soap. Unconcerned with the theory of treatment, her "empiric" approach occasionally extended to some unorthodox treatments, such as the healing power of cat's blood. Such treatments were quite accepted at a time when superstition still abounded.

74. Hounsom, *Toronto in 1810*, 115.

75. Stephen Keese Smith, quoted in Allan S. Everest, *Recollections of Clinton County and the Battle of Plattsburgh 1800-1840* (Plattsburg, 1964), 56.

76. Stephen Keese Smith, quoted in Everest, *Recollections of Clinton County*, 56.

77. Dunlop, *Tiger Dunlop's Upper Canada*, 25.

78. Dunlop, *Tiger Dunlop's Upper Canada*, 25.

79. Dunlop, *Tiger Dunlop's Upper Canada*, 26.

80. Dunlop, *Tiger Dunlop's Upper Canada*, 27.

81. James Mann, *Medical Sketches of the Campaigns of 1812,1813, 1814: to which are added surgical cases, observations on military hospitals and flying hospitals attached to a moving army* (Dedham, Mass., 1816), 51-52. Mann was in overall charge of the medical services of the American forces in upstate New York from early in the war, and worked to improve organisation, precautions to prevent sickness, general health through better diet and effective diagnoses and treatment of common conditions like pneumonia, rheumatism, and dysentery.

82. Military surgeons were assisted by surgeons mates who possessed some medical training and who would nonetheless be expected to operate on wounded soldiers under fire. See Charles Boutflower, *The Journal of an Army Surgeon during the Peninsular War* (Staplehurst, Kent, 1997), Introduction, i,viii,ix.

83. AO, MG23, HI 3, Vol. 2, Hannah Jarvis to Rev. Samuel Peters, 25 May 1815.

84. Parton, *Andrew Jackson*, Vol. 2, 234.

85. Dunbar Rowland, *Andrew Jackson's Campaign Against the British, or the Mississippi Territory in the War of 1812* (New York, 1926), 367.

86. Paul Litt, Ronald F. Williamson, Joseph W.A. Whitehorne, *Death at Snake Hill: Secrets from a War of 1812 Cemetery* (Toronto, 1993), 104. As an example of individual regimental staffing, the records of the 23rd United States Infantry Regiment hospital estimated that in August 1814 there were five women associated with it.

87. Dunlop, *Tiger Dunlop's Upper Canada*, 34.

88. General Notebook of William Beaumont, 27 April 1813, in Genevieve Miller, ed., *William Beaumont's Formative Years. Two Early Notebooks 1811-1821* (New York, 1946), 46.

89. Turner, *History of the Holland Purchase*, 191. Statistically, it was wounds to limbs that were most common and had to be quickly assessed, since the force of a musket ball produced dead tissue on impact which could spawn bacteria causing gas gangrene and tetanus. With no antibiotics to treat infected wounds and the danger of gangrene, amputation was the only recourse. For a summary and description of military medicine on the battlefield in the War of 1812, see Graves, *Where Right and Glory Lead*, 187-205.

90. B.H. Liddell Hart, ed., *The Letters of Private Wheeler 1809-1828* (London, 1951), 153.

91. William Horner, "Surgical Sketches: A Military Hospital at Buffalo, New York, in the Year 1814," *Medical Examiner and Record of Medical Service*, vol 16 (December 1852), 753.

92. With the Peninsular War acting as a catalyst, improvements emerged in the field of medicine that included brand new techniques in surgery, better hospital organisation, preventive measures to help guard soldiers from disease, better sanitation and hygiene, and a more humane system for the evacuation of casualties. See Richard L. Blanco, *Wellington's Surgeon General: Sir James McGrigor* (Durham, N.C., 1974), 142.

93. Emery, *Reminiscences*, 250. Moll Pitcher was a very famous psychic and fortune teller who lived in Massachussetts and was said to have inherited her gift from her father. She was so well respected that on one occasion, a crew deserted their ship before it set sail because Moll had predicted an ill-fated voyage. For more information see Michael Hyde, "Fortune Tellers, Witches and Such," *Davy Jones' Locker*, No. 47, December 2001.

94. Emery, *Reminiscences*, 250.

95. Emery, *Reminiscences*, 250.

96. Lyman Spalding, *Recollections of the War of 1812*, 4.

97. *Nova Scotia Gazette*, 12 Sep 1809.

98. William Dunlap, *Diary of William Dunlap (1766-1839): The Memoirs of a Dramatist, Theatrical Manager, Painter, Critic, Novelist, and Historian* (reprinted New York 1969), 365.

99. Dunlap, *Diary of William Dunlap*, 389.

100. William Dunlap, *History of the American Theatre* (London, 1833), Vol. 2, 211. Eleanora's sister, Elizabeth, married actor, William Twaits, who founded a theatre company in Philadelphia. Under her married name of Elizabeth Twaits, she was regarded as a distinguished actress in her own right.

101. Dunlap, *History of the American Theatre*, Vol. 2, 134. Sarah Ross, (1790-1854) was born in Saint John, New Brunswick. After her marriage in 1806 to Frederick Wheatley, an actor, she retired from the stage, returning to it later for financial reasons after her husband's business enterprises failed. She was noted for her artistic representation of old women.

102. Dunlap, *History of the American Theatre*, Vol. 2, 165; Vol. 1, 294.

103. Dunlap, *History of the American Theatre*, Vol. 1, 348.

104. *Boston Gazette*, 16 Dec 1812, 2.

105. Article, "A Finishing Compliment" in *NWR*, 1813, Vol. III, 314.

106. Article, "A Finishing Compliment" in *NWR*, 1813, Vol. III, 314.

107. "Poll of Plymouth," a popular sailors' song, told the story of a sailor pressed into service and forced to be parted from his new wife, Poll, for five years. The story had a sad ending, for just as his ship was due to sail for home, he was pressed onto another vessel and by the time he reached home, poor Poll had "languish'd, droop'd and died." See *Henry Livingston's Music Manuscript Book*, 53, at <www.iment.com/maida/fa107.milytree/henry/music>.

108. Rudyard Kipling, *Stalky & Co.* (London, 1899), ix.

4: "A stirring and restless life": Army Officers' Ladies

1. "The Gallant Hussar," a broadsheet ballad of the Napoleonic period.

2. University of North Carolina, Kirby-Smith Papers, Frances Webster to Lieutenant Edmund Kirby Smith, 2 June 1851.

3. Le Couteur, 23 May 1812, in Graves, ed., *Merry Hearts*, 59.

4. Le Couteur, 23 May 1812, in Graves, *Merry Hearts Make Light Days*, 59. Lieutenant John Le Couteur was an officer in the same regiment as "Mrs. P's" husband. He does not name the lady, discretion being the better part of valour at that time, but from to the *Army List* for that year, she is likely to have been Mrs. Procter, wife of Captain William Procter of the 104th Foot.

5. Jean Hunter, 27 Oct 1798, in Hunter and Bell, eds., *Journal of General Sir Martin Hunter*, 127. Jean Hunter was the daughter and heiress of a Scottish landed gentleman, who had married her husband in 1797 after his return from service in India and the West Indies. Promoted to the rank of Brigadier-General, he arrived in New Brunswick in 1803 tasked with raising a new regiment, The New Brunswick Fencibles. Jean joined him the following spring after giving birth to their third child.

6. Jean Hunter, 23 Sep 1805, in Hunter and Bell, eds., *Journal of General Sir Martin Hunter*, 160.

7. Jean Hunter, 1 Nov 1804, in Hunter and Bell, eds., *Journal of Sir Martin Hunter*, 217.

8. Jean Hunter, 2 Dec 1808, in Hunter and Bell, eds., *Journal of Sir Martin Hunter*, 217.

9. Jean Hunter, quoted in Temperley, ed., *Lieutenant Colonel Joseph Gubbins*, xv. Charlotte Gubbins was the daughter of a prosperous West Country merchant and Joseph Gubbins, the second son of a wealthy Irish landowner. "*Haut ton*" would translate as "lofty tone" or "superior taste."

10. Crisfield Johnson, *Centennial History of Erie County, New York: Being its Annals from the Earliest Recorded Events to the Hundredth Year of American Independence* (Buffalo, 1876), 208.

11. Stephen Jarvis, quoted in Talman, ed., *Loyalist Narratives*, 258-259.

12. Stephen Jarvis, quoted in Talman, ed., *Loyalist Narratives*, 259.

13. MVHS, "Memoirs of General John Elliot Hunt 1798-1877", 6.

14. Mary Stickney Green, "Reminiscences of Travel on the Maumee River in 1815", *Daily Toledo Blade*, 23 February 1867, 3.

15. Milo M. Quaife, *Chicago and the Old Northwest, 1673-1835*, 153, 178.

16. William B. Skelton, *An American Profession of Arms: The Army Officer Corps, 1784-1861* (Lawrence, Kansas, 1992), 40.

17. Under prevailing regulations governing the provision of firewood, baggage and accommodations, allowances for American officers were clearly laid out. A major-general, for example, was provided with four rooms and a kitchen; a field officer was allocated two rooms and a kitchen; and a captain, one room – but when commanding a post, a kitchen to himself. Baggage allowances, "when ordered on distant commands," were 1,000 lbs for general officers below the rank of major-general, 750 lbs for a colonel, 500 lbs for a major and 400 lbs for a captain and a surgeon. *An Act Establishing Rules and Articles for the Government of the Armies of the United States: With the Regulations of the War Department respecting the same*, 37, 42.

18. Captain Nathan Heald, quoted in Quaife, *Chicago and the Old Northwest*, 159.

19. LAC, MG24, F128, Jasper Grant to Thomas Grant, 3 Oct 1801.

20. LAC, MG24, F128, Jasper Grant to Thomas Grant, 12 Aug 1802.

21. LAC, MG24, F128, Jasper Grant to unnamed correspondent, 11 June 1802.

22. LAC, MG24, F128, Jasper Grant to Thomas Grant, 30 Sep 1802.

23. LAC, MG24, F128, Jasper Grant to Thomas Grant, 2 Feb 1808.

24. LAC, MG24, F128, Jasper Grant to Thomas Grant, 7 Aug 1808.

25. The officers' pavilion at Fort George is shown in a watercolour painting by Surgeon Edward Walsh of the 49th Foot, completed in 1815 and on display at the fort, as a pleasant, single-storey building with wainscotting, painted in yellow ochre. Fragments of bone china cups and pearlware saucers were located in excavations carried out at the fort in the summers of 1973 and 1974, providing evidence of the type of tableware used.

26. Isaac Brock to Irving Brock, 19 Feb 1811, in Tupper, ed., *Life and Correspondence of Brock*, 94.

27. Isaac Brock to Irving Brock, 10 Jan 1811, in Tupper, ed., *Life and Correspondence of Brock*, 87.

28. James Kempt to Isaac Brock, 17 Jan 1811, in Tupper, ed., *Life and Correspondence of Brock*, 90.

29. AO, MU2635, Military scrapbook, newspaper article, Feb 1815.

30. Turner, *Pioneer History of the Holland Purchase*, 190.

31. Sir James Turner, *Pallas Armata or Military Essayes of the Ancient Grecian Roman and Modern Art of War* (London, 1683), 276-277.

32. Thomas Reide, *The Staff Officer's Manual* (London, 1806), 3-4, 7.

33. H. De Watteville, *The British Soldier: His Dai-*

ly Life from Tudor to Modern Times (London, 1954), 172. The implication here is that deaths in battle left vacancies which were filled by the promotion of officers without purchase.

34. Stuart Sutherland, ed. *"A Desire of Serving and Defending My Country": The War of 1812 Journals of William Hamilton Merritt* (Toronto, 2001), 31 Oct 1814, 59.

35. Sutherland, ed., *Journals of William Merritt*, 9 Nov 1814, 2 Nov 1814, 59-60.

36. Reide, *Staff Officer's Manual*, 8.

37. Skelton, *American Profession of Arms*, 24.

38. Winfield Scott, quoted in Skelton, *Profession of Arms*, 30.

39. Nicolas Butley, ed., *The Reminiscences of Captain Gronow*, (London, 1977), 262.

40. Lydia Bacon, 10 June 1812, in "Bacon Journal," 63.

41. Lydia Bacon, 10 June 1812 in "Bacon Journal," 64.

42. Lydia Bacon, 10 June 1812, in "Bacon Journal," 65.

43. Lydia Bacon, 17 May 1812, in "Bacon Journal," 61.

44. Lydia Bacon, 15 May 1812 and 18 June 1812, in "Bacon Journal," 61, 64-65.

45. Lydia Bacon, 1 July 1812, in "Bacon Journal," 66.

46. NLS, MS 9303/62-74, "A Lady's Campaigns in Canada: Extracts from the Journal of a Subaltern's Wife written in Canada during the years 1812, 1813 and 1814", 1.

47. NLS, MS 9303/62-74, "A Lady's Campaigns", 2.

48. Le Couteur, 6 July 1815 in Graves, ed., *Merry Hearts*, 234.

49. DU, "Diary of John Lang, Lieutenant", 19-20 May 1813.

50. Patrick Finan, quoted in John Gellner, ed. *Recollections of the War of 1812: Three Eyewitness Accounts* (Toronto, 1964), 59.

51. Finan, quoted in Gellner, ed. *Recollections of the War of 1812*, 59.

52. LAC, MG24, G45, Vol. 10, Part I, Charles-Michel de Salaberry to his father, 29 Jan 1813.

53. ANQM, Nowlan Papers, Maurice Nowlan to Agathe Nowlan, 25 May 1813.

54. ANQM, Nowlan Papers, Maurice Nowlan to Agathe Nowlan, 5 June 1813.

55. ANQM, Nowlan Papers, Maurice Nowlan to Agathe Nowlan, 23 Sep 1813.

56. Lieutenant William MacEwen to Mrs. MacEwen, 3 July 1813, in *Doc.Hist.*, Vol.6, 174-175.

57. MacEwen to Mrs. MacEwen, 13 August 1813, in *Doc. Hist.*, Vol. 7, 14.

58. MacEwen to Mrs. MacEwen, 1 Mar 1814, in *Doc. Hist.*, Vol. 9, 266.

59. Thomas Verchères de Boucherville, quoted in Quaife, ed., *War on the Detroit*, 161-162.

60. Isaac Brock to the Military Secretary, York, 16 May 1812, in Tupper, ed., *Life and Correspondence of Brock*, 175.

61. LAC, MG24, I28, Alicia Cockburn to Charles Sandys, 4 Apr 1814.

62. LAC, MG24, I28, Alicia Cockburn to Charles Sandys, 20 Oct 1814.

63. LAC, MG24, I28, Alicia Cockburn to Charles Sandys, 28 June 1814.

64. LAC, MG24, I28, Alicia Cockburn to Charles Sandys, 28 June 1814.

65. Quoted in E.S. Turner, *Gallant Gentlemen: A Portrait of the British Officer 1800-1856* (London, 1956), 153.

66. Dunlop, *Tiger Dunlop's Upper Canada*, 20. The quote is from Shakespeare's Henry IV Part II, Act III Scene II, and the exact wording is: "Sir, pardon; a soldier is better accommodated than with a wife."

67. NLS, MS 9303/62-74, "A Lady's Campaigns", 3.

68. NLS, MS 9303/62-74, "A Lady's Campaigns", 5.

69. NLS, MS 9303/62-74, "A Lady's Campaigns", 5.

70. NLS, MS 9303/62-74, "A Lady's Campaigns", 6.

71. Ellet, *Pioneer Women of the West*, 321. Abigail Snelling was reunited with her husband at Buffalo later in the war.

72. At his court martial, held from December 1814 to January 1815, Major-General Henry Procter was charged with incompetence, cowardice, making faulty dispositions on the field of battle at Moraviantown in October 1814, and carelessness in conducting his retreat. He was acquitted of the former two charges, but found guilty of both the latter. Sentenced to be publicly reprimanded and suspended from pay and rank for a period of six months, Procter was also informed of the Prince Regent's "high disapprobation" of his conduct. The Prince remitted his suspension but the verdict was included in a general order to be read at the head of every regiment in the British army. For further details, see LAC MG13 which contains the transcript of the court martial from NAB, WO71/55. For comment on the court martial, see J.M. Hitsman, *The Incredible War of 1812: A Military History*, updated by Donald E. Graves (Toronto, 1999), 344n.

73. John Norton had been educated in Britain before enlisting in the British army in the hope of being posted to the land of his father's people. After deserting, he worked in the fur trade and as an interpreter and teacher in an aboriginal school, before allying himself with the British forces in the War of 1812. On Norton and his wife, see C.F. Klinck and J.J. Talman, *The Journal of Major John Norton, 1816* (Toronto, 1970).

74. DU, "Diary of John Lang", 22 August 1813.

75. Charles B. Brooks, *The Siege of New Orleans* (Seattle, 1961), 67. Lieutenant-Colonel Thomas Mullins' eldest brother, heir to the baronetcy and family seat of Burnham House, Dingle, was a graduate of Trinity College Dublin, and Member of Parliament for Dingle. Another brother was married to the daughter of the Gentleman Privy Chamber to Kings George II and III, and yet another, a clergyman, was married to an heiress.

76. Brooks, *New Orleans*, 110.

77. Brooks, *New Orleans*, 257-258, 267. The court martial of Lieutenant-Colonel the Honourable Thomas Mullins, held on 29 June 1815, required him to answer charges that included neglect, disobedience, and infamous conduct. See NAB, WO30, vol 49, 43.

78. Francis Markham, quoted in Turner, *Gallant Gentlemen*, frontispiece.

5: "Their fate unpitied, and unheard their name": Soldiers' Wives and Women

1. A broadsheet ballad of the Napoleonic period, with the substitution of "America" for "France" in the first verse, contained in Roy Palmer, ed., *The Rambling Soldier* (London, 1985), 250.

2. Liddell Hart, ed., *Letters of Private Wheeler*, 141.

3. Noel St. John Williams, *Judy O'Grady and the Colonel's Lady: The Army wife and the camp follower since 1660* (London, 1988), 9.

4. St. John Williams, *Judy O'Grady and the Colonel's Lady*, 10.

5. From recruiting poster, "Great Advantages to those who enlist for Capt. Liddell's Company of the Glengary Light Infantry Fencibles," D.E. Graves collection.

6. *Rules and Regulations for Cavalry* (London, 1795), 74, quoted in Richard Glover, *Peninsular Preparation. The Reform of the British Army. 1795-1809* (Cambridge, 1963), 221.

7. Bennett Cuthbertson, *A System for the Complete Interior Management and Oeconomy of a Battalion of Infantry* (London, 1779), 113. Although Cuthbertson wrote three decades before the War of 1812, the information in his book still applied to the British army of the Napoleonic period.

8. Cuthbertson, *Interior Oeconomy*, 113.

9. Cuthbertson, *Interior Oeconomy*, 113.

10. *An Act, establishing Rules and Articles for the Government of the Armies of the United States; with the Regulations of the War Department respecting the same* (Albany, 1812), 52.

11. *The Army Register of the United States ... Corrected Up to the 1st Day of June 1814* (Boston, 1814), 94.

12. LAC, RG5, A1 Vol 29, 8092-8102, Incorporated Militia of Upper Canada, Return of Wives and Children, 14 Mar 1814.

13. LAC, MG24 L8, "Ma Saberdache," Vol. 3, Captain Jacques Viger to Marie-Marguerite Viger, 23 Aug 1813. The translation of "*caquet-bon-bec*" would approximate to "chatterbox."

14. Piers Compton, *Colonel's Lady and Camp-Follower: The Story of Women in the Crimean War* (London, 1970), 23. The first official married quarters for British soldiers and their families were not provided until 1860.

15. Adjutant-General's Office, *General Regulations and Orders for the Army, 1811* (London, 1816, reprinted 1970), 409, General Order, 16 Jan 1815.

16. NAB, War Office 27 vol 133, Inspection Returns dated 1815.

17. Willa G. Cranton, *Women Beyond the Frontier: A Distaff View of Life at Fort Wayne* (Fort Wayne, 1977), 9.

18. Cranton, *Women Beyond the Frontier*, 9.

19. Charles Oman, *Wellington's Army* (1913 reprinted London 1993), 275-276.

20. Richard Holmes, *Redcoat: The British Soldier in the Age of Horse and Musket* (London, 2001), 186-187.

21. E.C. Kyte, "Fort Niagara in the War of 1812; Sidelights from an Unpublished Orderbook," *Canadian Historical Review*, 17 (1936), 379.

22. Kyte, "Fort Niagara in the War of 1812," 376, 24 Jan 1813.

23. Kyte, "Fort Niagara in the War of 1812," 376, 24 Jan 1813.

24. Kyte, "Fort Niagara in the War of 1812," 24 Jan 1813.

25. *Articles of War, Military Laws, and Rules and Regulations for the Army of the United States* (Washington, 1816), 84.

26. General Order, Camp Meigs, 1 Aug 1813 in Harlow Lindley, ed., *Fort Meigs and the War of 1812* (Columbus, 1975), 55.

27. De Watteville, *The British Soldier*, 124.

28. NMM, COD/6/4, Codrington to respective Captains, 3 Sep 1814. According to Captain Thomas Browne, an officer serving in the Peninsular War, many British army women were indeed reprehensible characters, given to licentiousness and marauding. Their behaviour resulted directly from the very harsh conditions and uncertainty of life, particularly when on active service. In an effort to survive in a system

in which they were virtually powerless, army women were routinely driven to marauding and other lawless acts. See Roger Buckley, ed., *The Napoleonic War Journal of Captain Thomas Henry Browne, 1807-1816* (London, 1987), 245.

29. *Articles of War, Military Laws, and Rules and Regulations for the Army of the United States* (Washington, 1816), 9, Article 2.

30. Cuthbertson, *Interior Oeconomy*, 83.

31. Cuthbertson, *Interior Oeconomy*, 21.

32. Cuthbertson, *Interior Oeconomy*, 19.

33. Holmes, *Redcoat*, 281. Bugle calls and drum beats were used to announce numerous aspects of army daily life, from Reveille to Last Post. Drummers and buglers invented little rhymes to remember the notes or rhythms, as the case might be. Over centuries, these became hallowed in the British and Commonwealth armies and were in use up to the period of the Second World War and later. Another example would be the call for guard mounting: "Come and do a picket, boys, come and do a guard; t'isn't very easy, boys, t'isn't very hard." See Donald E. Graves, *South Albertas: A Canadian Regiment at War* (Toronto, 1998), 92.

34. *An Act fixing the Military Peace Establishment of the United States, 1812.* Section 6, 52. In 1812 the daily food allowance of American soldiers consisted of a pound and a quarter of beef, or three quarters of a pound of pork, eighteen ounces of bread or flour, one gill of rum, whiskey, or brandy, with an allowance of two quarts of salt, four quarts of vinegar, four pounds of soap, and a pound and a half of candles to every hundred rations.

35. Major Patterson of 50th Foot, quoted in De Watteville, *The British Soldier*, 180.

36. Cranton, *Women Beyond the Frontier*, 5. There were some exceptions, and according to this book, research carried out at Fort Wayne found no references to women as cooks. Information gathered at that fort suggested that the soldiers prepared their own meals, either in a cook house or in their rooms on a rota system.

37. Buckley, ed. *Journal of Captain Thomas Henry Browne*, 324, Note 109.

38. LAC, MG24 L8, "Ma Saberdache," Vol. 3, Captain Jacques Viger to Marie-Marguerite Viger, 23 Aug 1813. "*Propre*" translates as "clean," and "*Ménagère, Cuisinière et Laveuse*," as "housewife, cook and laundress."

39. Garrison Orders 11 Jan 1798, 7 Dec 1798, 19 May 1811, 31 May 1804, at Fort Wayne, in Cranton, *Women Beyond the Frontier*, 3-4.

40. Colonel Wilbur Nye, quoted in Miller J. Stewart, "Army Laundresses: Ladies of the 'Soap Suds Row'", *Nebraska History*, Vol. 61 (1980), 422.

41. General George A. Forsyth, quoted in Stewart, "Army Laundresses", 431.

42. Cuthbertson, *Interior Oeconomy*, 16.

43. Cuthbertson, *Interior Oeconomy*, 16.

44. George Sheppard, "'Wants and Privations': Women and the War of 1812 in Upper Canada," *Social History* 28 (1995) 175. This rate was paid to wives of Incorporated Militia soldiers.

45. *Articles of War, Military Laws, and Rules and Regulations for the Army of the United States* (Washington, 1816), 84.

46. *The Army Register ... Corrected up to the 1st Day of June, 1814*, 80.

47. *Rules and Regulations of the Army for 1813.* Schedule of Monthly compensation of the Troops of the United States, 431, 435-436.

48. Adjutant General, *Regulations for Regimental Surgeons, &c., for the Better Management of the Sick in Regimental Hospitals* (London, 1799), 13.

49. *Regulations for Regimental Surgeons*, 13-14.

50. *Regulations for Regimental Surgeons*, 16-17.

51. *Regulations for Regimental Surgeons*, 37.

52. *Regulations for Regimental Surgeons*, 56. According to a "Diet and Ward Diet-Table," the daily food regime of a patient was one pint of oatmeal or rice gruel for breakfast, one pound of bread, one pound of meat and one quart of small beer for dinner, and one pint of broth for supper. Smaller portions for a "half" or "low" diet could also be prescribed. A milk diet consisted of one pint of milk for breakfast and supper, and one pint of broth and one pound of bread for dinner.

53. *General Regulations and Orders for the Army, 1811*, Regulations regarding Military Hospitals, 136.

54. *General Regulations and Orders for the Army, 1811*, General Order, 10 Apr 1813, 370.

55. General Order for Troops destined for Continental Service, 15 Apr 1807, quoted in Glover, *Peninsular Preparation*, 221n.

56. NAB, War Office 27, vol 133, Inspection Returns of the 2/8th Foot, 41st Foot, 2/89th Foot, 103rd Foot and 104th Foot, all dated 1815.

57. Joseph Donaldson. *Recollections of the Eventful Life of a Soldier* (1856, reprinted Staplehurst, Kent, 2000), 51-52.

58. Donaldson, *Recollections of the Eventful Life of a Soldier*, 52.

59. Donaldson, *Recollections of the Eventful Life of a Soldier*, 53.

60. Donaldson. *Recollections of the Eventful Life of a Soldier*, 56. Sergeant Donaldson was unable to find out what became of Sandy's wife. All he knew was that Sandy did not return from the war.

61. Buckley, ed., *Journal of Captain Browne*, 69.

62. William Keep to Samuel Keep, 8 Oct 1812 in Ian Fletcher, ed. *In the Service of the King: The Letters of William Thornton Keep at Home, Walcheren, and in the Peninsula*, 1810-1814 (Staplehurst, Kent, 1997), 102.

63. Oman, *Wellington's Army*, General Order of 26 Apr 1814, 276n.

64. Donaldson, *The Eventful Life of a Soldier*, 232.

65. Poster, 14th Light Dragoons, printed between 1803 and 1812, text quoted in "Old Recruiting Posters," *Journal of the Society for Army Historical Research*, vol 1 (1920), 120.

66. Rosanna Hickman to the Secretary of War, 9 Nov 1809, cited in Cranton, *Women Beyond the Frontier*, 8.

67. Mary Maloney to the Secretary of War, 1 Aug 1810, cited in Cranton, *Women Beyond the Frontier*, 8.

68. René Chartrand, *Canadian Military Heritage. Volume II, 1755-1971* (Ottawa, 1995), 126.

69. *General Regulations and Orders, 1811*, 255.

70. *General Regulations and Orders, 1811*, 256.

71. *General Regulations and Orders, 1811*, 258.

72. Adjutant-General, *General Regulation and Orders, 1804* (London, 1805) 99.

73. *General Regulation and Orders, 1804*, 102.

74. *General Regulation and Orders, 1804*, 107.

75. NAB, ADM37, vol 4338, Muster List of HMS *Leopard*, April–May 1814. There are indications that many women were young when they married soldiers and started their families. One survey carried out at Fort Wayne on the American frontier revealed that its women married between the ages of sixteen and nineteen. See Cranton, *Women Beyond the Frontier*, 14.

76. Lieutenant William Keep to Samuel Keep, 22 Oct 1812, in Fletcher, *In the Service of the King*, 109.

77. Jack Nasty-Face. *Nautical Economy or Forecastle Recollections of Events during the Last War, by a Sailor politely called by the officers of the Navy Jack Nasty-Face* (London, no date), 102.

78. LAC, MG24 F4 vol 1, Lieutenant-Colonel Cecil Bisshopp to Katherine Bisshopp, 9 Oct 1812.

79. Buckley, ed., *Journal of Captain Browne*, 74.

80. St. John Williams, *Judy O'Grady and the Colonel's Lady*, 44.

81. DU, Diary of John Lang, 17 June 1813.

82. Lydia Bacon, 19 May 1812, "Bacon Journal," 62.

83. John Lovett to John Alexander, 22 Sep 1812 in Bonney, *Historical Gleanings*, 237.

84. Viger, *Reminiscences of the War of 1812-14*, 14.

85. Lieutenant-Colonel George McFeely, 31 Dec 1813, in John C. Fredriksen, "Chronicle of Valour: The Journal of a Pennsylvania Officer in the War of 1812." *Western Pennsylvania Historical Magazine 676*, 268.

86. McFeely, 31 Dec 1813, in Fredriksen, "Chronicle of Valour," 268.

87. Maria Fergusson Sakovich, "Jane Ferguson: Immigrant, Pioneer, and Itinerant Wife in Upper Canada," *The Hay Bay Guardian*, Vol.13 (2005), 2, 4. Most administrative problems of this nature were resolved, but sometimes it took action at the highest level to do so. When several wives with the 104th Foot, for reasons of sickness or childbirth, were not able to travel with the regiment from New Brunswick to Lower Canada in 1814, they immediately had their rations cut. Sergeant Jabish Squiers sent a petition on behalf of his heavily pregnant wife to Lieutenant-General Sir George Prevost, asking him to intervene in the "distressed situation," and allow Mrs. Squiers to draw provisions for herself and her children. It was not long before rations were again issued to the destitute dependants of the 104th Foot. See Squires, *The 104th Regiment of Foot*, 141-142.

88. Joseph Gardner Swift. *The Memoirs of General Joseph Gardner Swift, LL.D* (Privately printed, 1890), 49.

89. Myers, *Reminiscences*, 41.

90. Dunlop, *Tiger Dunlop's Upper Canada*, 35.

91. Dunlop, *Tiger Dunlop's Upper Canada*, 35.

92. NMM, COD/6/4, Sir Edward Codrington to Jane Codrington, 15 January 1815.

93. *An Act Establishing Rules and Articles for the Government of the Armies of the United States* (Albany, 1812), 20.

94. *An Act Establishing Rules and Articles for the Government of the Armies of the United States, 1812*, 26.

95. *An Act Establishing Rules and Articles for the Government of the Armies of the United States, 1812*, 20.

96. Francis Seymour Larpent, *The Private Journal of Judge-Advocate Larpent* (Staplehurst, Kent, 2000), 8 Aug 1813, 226. As a matter of interest, the sutler's equivalent in the French army was called a *cantinière*, who was subject to different regulations, one of which was the fact that she had to be married to a soldier of the regiment

or battalion to which she was authorised to sell food and drink. If the husband of a *cantinière* was killed in action, she would often marry another enlisted man to retain her position and she, too, was required to sell her goods at a fair price on pain of confiscation. A *cantinière* also carried alcohol, usually brandy, in a *tonnelet*, a small barrel suspended from a wide leather strap. See Thomas Cardoza, "La Belle Cantinière: Women in the French Army, 1789-1913," *Proceedings. Western Society for French History* 1995, 45-54.

97. General order, 22 Apr 1813, Lindley, ed., *Fort Meigs and the War of 1812*, 11.

98. Larpent, *Journal*, 8 Aug 1813, 226.

99. Mrs. Fitzmaurice, *Recollections of A Rifleman's Wife At Home and Abroad* (London, 1851), 184-185.

100. From poem by John Wolcot, quoted in T.H. McGuffie, ed., *Peninsular Cavalry General (1811-1813): The Correspondence of Lieutenant-General Robert Ballard Long*, 260. Wolcot (1738-1819), was a physician who wrote satirical verse under the name Peter Pindar.

6: "The lass that loves a sailor": Naval Wives and Women

1. "The Lass that Loves a Sailor," written by Charles Dibdin, a London composer of the early nineteenth century, was popular throughout the English-speaking world.

2. *The Military Mentor, Being a Series of Letters recently written by a General Officer to his Son, on his Entering the Army: Comprising a Course of Elegant Instruction, calculated to unite the Characters and Accomplishments of the Gentleman and the Soldier*, (2 volumes,) Vol. 1, 45. This publication was designed as a series of homilies on military etiquette, behaviour and military subjects. As well as chapters on drinking, duelling, health and fitness, there was also guidance on the topic of love. Although written for a young man entering army service, some of its advice could as well be applied to naval officers. The work was translated and adapted from "*Conseils d'un militaire à son fils, par M. le baron d'A – – -*" who was Baron d'Anglesy, a colonel in the French army.

3. Rodgers, I:15, Ann Hull to Minerva Rodgers, 25 May 1813.

4. Jean Hunter, 27 Nov 1807, in Hunter and Bell, eds., *Journal of General Sir Martin Hunter*, 242. Anne Louise Emily Hardy, née Berkeley, was the eldest daughter of Vice-Admiral Sir George Berkeley. Her mother, Lady Emily, was the sister of Charles, 4th Duke of Richmond.

5. Jane Codrington to Edward Codrington, 4 Dec 1805, in Lady Bourchier, ed., *Memoir of the Life of Admiral Sir Edward Codrington* (London, 1873), 85.

6. Jane Codrington to Edward Codrington, 8 Dec 1805, in Bourchier, ed., *Memoir of the Life of Admiral Sir Edward Codrington*, 88.

7. Alexander Slidell Mackenzie, *The Life of Commodore Oliver Hazard Perry* (New York, 1841), 234.

8. David Curtis Skaggs, *Thomas Macdonough: Master of Command in the Early U.S. Navy* (Annapolis, 2003), 54.

9. Poem by Elizabeth Denning, quoted in Skaggs, *Thomas Macdonough*, 56.

10. Lucy Macdonough to Abbey Hortense Chew, quoted in Skaggs, *Thomas Macdonough*, 149.

11. James Tertius de Kay, *Chronicles of the Frigate Macedonian 1809-1922* (London, 2000), 72.

12. *Norfolk Gazette and Public Ledger*, 10 March 1806, 2.

13. Stephen Decatur to Edward Preble, 6 May 1806, quoted in Spencer Tucker, *Stephen Decatur: A Life Most Bold and Daring* (Annapolis, Maryland, 2005), 86.

14. Samuel Leech, *Thirty Years from Home, or A Voice from the Main Deck, being the experience of Samuel Leech* (Boston, 1843), 162. If Leech's memory was correct, this account is likely to have been true because by the time he wrote it, he had become a committed Christian. However, it is more probable that Susan interceded on behalf of the sailors occasionally rather than on a regular basis, as shipboard discipline had to be seen to be firmly maintained.

15. *Connecticut Gazette*, 12 June 1813, 4.

16. De Kay, *Chronicles of the Macedonian*, 86-90.

17. Philip Broke, quoted in Peter Padfield, *Broke and the Shannon* (London, 1968), 84.

18. Elizabeth Kennon to Rachel Mordecai, 5 July 1812, "Kennon Letters", Vol. XXXIV, No. 2, (April 1926), 126.

19. Elizabeth Kennon to Rachel Mordecai, 16 Oct 1812, "Kennon Letters", Vol. XXXIV, No. 3, (July 1926), 223.

20. Rodgers I:15, Sarah B. Sullivan to Minerva Rodgers, 2 Feb 1814.

21. Admiralty, *Regulations and Instructions Relating to His Majesty's Service at Sea …* (London, 1806), 144-145.

22. Admiralty, *Regulations and Instructions Relating to His Majesty's Service at Sea* (London, 1808), 145.

23. Naval regulations issued 22 Jan 1802, in *Naval Documents Related to the United States Wars with the Barbary Powers* (2 vols, Washington, 1940), Vol. 2, 33.

24. Journal of Midshipman Henry Wadsworth, 2 Apr 1803 in *Naval Documents Related to the United States Wars with the Barbary Powers*, Vol. 2, 387.

25. Journal of Midshipman Henry Wadsworth, 2 Apr 1803 in *Naval Documents Related to the United States Wars with the Barbary Powers*, Vol. 2, 387.

26. See David Cordingly, *Women Sailors and Sailors' Women. An Untold Maritime History* (New York, 2001), 88-108, for a discussion of this evidence.

27. NAB, ADM 37, vol 5631.

28. N.A.M. Rodger, *The Wooden World: An Anatomy of the Georgian Navy* (Glasgow, 1988), 78-82.

29. Rodger, *Wooden World*, 366.

30. Leech, *Thirty Years from Home*, 109, 229.

31. Roger Hart, *England Expects* (London, 1972), 20. Press gangs were only instituted in time of war and were not used between 1815 and 1833, when the practice was legally abolished.

32. LAC, RG5, A1, Vol. 36, A Complete Book of the Establishment of the Naval Hospital at Kingston, Upper, Canada, for the Year 1815.

33. George Watson in Henry Baynham, *From the Lower Deck: The Royal Navy 1780-1840* (Barre Mass, 1970), 118. The term "husband" was used loosely among sailors and port women at the time.

34. John Masefield, *Sea Life in Nelson's Time* (London, 1972), 91.

35. Jack Nasty-Face. *Nautical Economy*, 57.

36. Arthur Bryant, *The Years of Endurance* (London, 1948), 196.

37. Jack Nasty-Face, *Nautical Economy*, 57.

38. Leech, *Thirty Years from Home*, 112-113.

39. Leech, *Thirty Years from Home*, 41.

40. Masefield, *Sea Life in Nelson's Time*, 93.

41. Frederick Chamier, *The Life of a Sailor* (London, 1832), Vol. 1, 21, 29.

42. Nasty-Face, *Nautical Economy*, 68.

43. Masefield, *Sea Life in Nelson's Time*, 93.

44. Nasty-face, *Nautical Economy*, 63.

45. Chamier, *Life of a Sailor*, Vol. 2, 40.

7: "The sensations of a wife, and mother in times such as these": Binding Ties and Keeping in Touch

1. "All through the night," a traditional Welsh folk song, first published in 1784, with modern lyrics by Harold Boulton.

2. John Askin to William Dummer Powell, 25 Jan 1813, in *Doc. Hist.*, Vol. 5, 50-51.

3. The Reverend Dr. Mather Byles was a Loyalist minister from Connecticut who fled to Halifax during the Revolutionary War. He became the rector of Trinity Church, Saint John, New Brunswick.

4. PANS, MG1, Almon Family Papers 1724-1954, Letterbook of Mary and Catherine Byles 1808-1818, Mary and Catherine Byles to Anna Debrisay, 4 July 1812.

5. PANS, MG1, Almon Family Papers, Mary and Catherine Byles to Rebecca Almon, 4 July 1812.

6. PANS, MG1, Almon Family Papers, Rebecca Almon to Catherine and Mary Byles, 4 Aug 1812.

7. PANS, MG1, Almon Family Papers, Rebecca Almon to Catherine and Mary Byles, 5 Feb 1813.

8. PANS, MG1, Almon Family Papers, Rebecca Almon to Catherine and Mary Byles, 25 Feb 1814.

9. PANS, MG1, Almon Family Papers, Mary and Catherine Byles to Mather Brown, 7 Oct 1812.

10. PANS, Almon Family Papers, MG1, Mary and Catherine Byles to Rebecca Almon, 23 Oct 1812.

11. LAC, MG24, L3, Baby Collection, vol 15, Captain Paul-Théophile Pinsonnant to Louise Pinsonnant, undated, and 11 Nov 1812.

12. LAC, MG24, L3, Baby Collection, vol 15, Lieutenant Pierre Weilbrunner to Clotilde Weilbrunner, 22 June 1812.

13. MM, P.O10, Dessaulles Papers 1700-1950, Louis-Joseph Papineau to Rosalie Papineau, 7 July 1812.

14. MM, P.O10, Louis-Joseph Papineau to Rosalie Papineau, 7 July 1812.

15. MM, P.O10, Louis-Joseph Papineau to Rosalie Papineau, 27 Sep 1812.

16. William B. Atherton, *Narrative of the Suffering & Defeat of the North-Western Army, under General Winchester …* (Frankfort, 1842), 151.

17. Atherton, *Narrative of the Suffering & Defeat of the North-Western Army*, 151.

18. Atherton, *Narrative of the Suffering & Defeat of the North-Western Army*, 152.

19. *NWR*, 1812, vol II, 411.

20. Elizabeth Kennon to Rachel Mordecai, 15 Apr 1812, "Kennon Letters," Vol. XXXIII, No. 3 (July 1925), 273.

21. Elizabeth Kennon to Rachel Mordecai, 5 July 1812, "Kennon Letters," Vol. XXXIV, No. 2, (April 1926), 125; Elizabeth Kennon to Rachel Mordecai, 16 Oct 1812, Vol. XXXIV, No. 3, (July 1926), 221.

22. Elizabeth Kennon to Rachel Mordecai, 5 July 1812, "Kennon Letters," Vol. XXXIV, No. 2 (April 1926), 126.

23. Elizabeth Kennon to Rachel Mordecai, 14 Aug 1813, "Kennon Letters," Vol. XXXIV, No. 4, (October 1926), 327.

24. Elizabeth Kennon to Samuel Mordecai, 6 Nov 1813, "Kennon Letters," Vol. XXXIV, No. 4, (October 1926), 334.

25. Elizabeth Kennon to Rachel Mordecai, 21 July 1814, "Kennon Letters," Vol. XXXVII, No. 3, (July 1929), 266.

26. Elizabeth Kennon to Rachel Mordecai, 3 Dec 1814, "Kennon Letters," Vol. XXXVII, No. 4 (October 1929), 337.

27. Midshipman John Johnston R.N. to Jane Johnston, 28 Apr 1813, quoted in William S. Dudley, ed., *The Naval War of 1812, Volume II*, 1992), 444-445.

28. On 12 July 1813, Midshipman John Johnston was promoted to the rank of acting lieutenant in recognition of his valour in action during the British attack on Sackets Harbor in May 1813.

29. CLUM, Jacob Brown Papers, Jacob Brown to Pamela Brown, 24 Aug 1817.

30. Jacob Brown to Nathan Williams, 28 Jan 1818, quoted in John Morris, *Sword of the Border: Major General Jacob Jennings Brown, 1775-1828* (Kent, Ohio, 2000). 161.

31. Jacob Brown to Nathan Williams, 16 Aug 1819, quoted in Morris, *Sword of the Border*, 163.

32. LAC, MG24, G45, De Salaberry Papers, vol 10, Charles-Michel de Salaberry to Marie-Anne de Salaberry, 6 Oct 1813.

33. LAC, MG24, G45, vol 10, Charles-Michel de Salaberry to Marie-Anne de Salaberry, 6 Oct 1813.

34. LAC, MG24, G45, vol 10, Charles-Michel de Salaberry to Marie-Anne de Salaberry, 29 Oct 1813.

35. NMM, COD/6/4, Edward Codrington to Jane Codrington, 30 July 1814.

36. NMM, COD/6/4, Edward Codrington to Jane Codrington, 4 Jan 1815.

37. Rachel Jackson to Andrew Jackson, January 1813, quoted in Robert Remini, *Andrew Jackson and the Course of American Empire. 1767-1821* (New York, 1977), 174.

38. Andrew Jackson to Rachel Jackson, 15 Nov 1814, quoted in Robert V. Remini, *Andrew Jackson and the Course of the American Empire*, 245.

39. B. Smyth, *A History of the Lancashire Fusiliers (formerly the XX Regiment)* (Dublin, 1903), 328.

40. PRONI, D/2004/1A/3, Robert Ross to Elizabeth Ross, 28 Aug 1814.

41. PRONI, D/2004/1A/3, Robert Ross to Elizabeth Ross, 28 Aug 1814.

42. Edward Livingston to Louise Livingston, quoted in Louise Livingston Hunt, *Memoir of Mrs. Edward Livingston* (New York, 1886), 89.

43. Edward Livingston to Louise Livingston, quoted in Hunt, *Memoir of Mrs. Edward Livingston*, 89-90.

44. PU, CO.280, Livingston Family Papers, Edward Livingston to Louise Livingston, 6 Nov 1813.

45. Morgan Lewis to Gertrude Lewis, 1 Sep 1812, in Delafield, ed., *Frances Lewis and Morgan Lewis*, 74-75.

46. Morgan Lewis to Gertrude Lewis, 10 Dec 1812 in Delafield, ed., *Francis Lewis and Morgan Lewis*, 80.

47. Rodgers, I:14, Minerva Rodgers to John Rodgers, 26 Sep 1812.

48. Rodgers, I:14, Minerva Rodgers to John Rodgers, 17 Dec 1808.

49. Rodgers, I:14, Minerva Rodgers to John Rodgers, 25 Mar 1810.

50. Rodgers, I:13, John Rodgers to Minerva Rodgers, 18 July 1811.

51. Rodgers I:14, Minerva Rodgers to John Rodgers, 17 Mar 1810.

52. Rodgers, I:14, Minerva Rodgers to John Rodgers, 26 Sep 1812.

53. Rodgers, I:14, Minerva Rodgers to John Rodgers, 25 July 1810.

54. Rodgers II:2, Minerva Rodgers to John Rodgers, 11 Apr 1813.

55. Rodgers, I:14, Minerva Rodgers to John Rodgers, 9 Feb 1809.

56. Rodgers, I:13, John Rodgers to Minerva Rodgers, 16 June 1810.

57. Rodgers, I:14, Minerva Rodgers to John Rodgers, 22 Apr 1813.

58. Rodgers, II:2, Minerva Rodgers to John Rodgers, 25 Aug 1814.

59. Rodgers, II:2, Minerva Rodgers to John Rodgers, 12 Sep 1814.

60. Rodgers, II:2, Minerva Rodgers to John Rodgers, 12 Sep 1814.

61. William K. Beall, quoted in Berton, *Invasion of Canada*, 141.

62. ANQM, Maurice Nowlan Papers, Maurice to Agathe Nowlan, 22 Sep 1812.

63. ANQM, Maurice Nowlan Papers, Maurice to Agathe Nowlan, 23 July 1813.

64. ANQM, Maurice Nowlan Papers, Maurice to Agathe Nowlan 27 Sep 1813 and 24 Oct 1813.

65. ANQM, Maurice Nowlan Papers, Maurice to Agathe Nowlan, 16 Oct 1813.

66. ANQM, Maurice Nowlan Papers, Maurice to Agathe Nowlan, 18 Dec 1813.

67. CHS, 19628-1909, George Howard Autobiography and Record Book, 45.

68. CHS, 19628-1909, George Howard Autobiography and Record Book, George Howard to Sarah Howard, 8 Oct 1812.

69. CHS, 19628-1909, George Howard Autobiography and Record Book, 84.

70. CHS, 19628-1909, George Howard to Sarah Howard, 27 Apr 1814.

71. CHS, 19628-1909, Sarah Howard to George Howard, 26 Apr 1814.

72. SCCIRO, HA93/9/32-164, Philip Broke to Louisa Broke, 22 Sep 1812.

73. SCCIRO, HA93/9/32-164, Philip Broke to Louisa Broke, 11 June 1813.

74. The blue satin bag became bloodstained after Broke received his wound in battle. His First Lieutenant, Provo Wallis, the brother of Lady Elizabeth Townshend, removed the bag and gave it to his sister, who made a new one for the captain.

75. SCCIRO, HA93/9/32-164, Louisa Broke to Philip Broke, 11 July 1813.

76. Padfield, *Broke and the Shannon*, 241.

77. Solomon Van Rensselaer to Harriet Van Rensselaer, 21 Aug 1812, in Bonney, *Historical Gleanings*, 211.

78. Solomon Van Rensselaer to Abraham Van Vechten, 5 Sep 1812, in Bonney, *Historical Gleanings*, 227.

79. Harriet Van Rensselaer to Solomon Van Rensselaer, 6 Sep 1812, in Bonney, *Historical Gleanings*, 227.

80. Harriet Van Rensselaer to Solomon Van Rensselaer, 6 Sep 1812 in Bonney, *Historical Gleanings*, 227-228.

81. Solomon Van Rensselaer to Harriet Van Rensselaer, 10 Oct 1812, in Bonney, *Historical Gleanings*, 247.

82. John Patterson to Levina Patterson, 16 Aug 1812, in Florence and Mary Howard, eds., "Letters of John Patterson," 100.

83. John Patterson to Levina Patterson, 16 Aug 1812, in Howard, eds. "Letters of John Patterson," 101.

84. John Patterson to Levina Patterson, 12 Sep 1812, in Howard, eds., "Letters of John Patterson," 101.

85. John Patterson to Levina Patterson, 3 Oct 1812, in Howard, eds., "Letters of John Patterson," 103.

86. John Patterson to Levina Patterson, 18 Feb 1813, in Howard, eds., "Letters of John Patterson," 106.

87. John Patterson to Levina Patterson, 25 Apr 1813, in Howard, eds., "Letters of John Patterson," 108.

88. John Patterson to Levina Patterson, 25 Apr 1813, in Howard, eds., "Letters of John Patterson," 109. Patterson also mentioned in this letter his idea of approaching the Secretary of War

for permission to preach and to do "no duty nor fiteing." This provides a further indication that Patterson may have been a Quaker. Quakers took no part in war, their beliefs precluding it, and Levina Patterson may have been under pressure from her family and other Quakers not to contact her husband after his decision to join the army.

8: "The windings of the mazy dance": High Society

1. Poem written "on a select party" at Scott's Tavern, Cork, Ireland, *c.* 1740 in T.W. Moody and W.E. Vaughan, *A New History of Ireland* (Oxford, 1986), Vol. IV, 52.

2. Gregory, *Father's Legacy to his Daughters*, 26-27.

3. Jane Austen illustrates this point in her novel *Persuasion* by contrasting the behaviour of her characters, Eleanor and Marianne Dashwood – the former steady, thoughtful and controlled; the latter, impetuous and emotional.

4. From poem, "Imitation of Spencer," by John Keats in, *The Poetical Works of John Keats* (London, undated), 23-24.

5. Journal of Eliza Southgate, 11 July 1802, in Cook, ed., *A Girl's Life Eighty Years Ago*, 119. During her New England tour, Eliza met her future husband, Walter Bowne.

6. Thomas Jefferson's "Canons of Etiquette," which clearly demonstrated that European court rules of precedence had no place in his republic, included the following principles: (1) no titles were admitted and those of foreigners gave them no precedence; (2) at any public ceremony to which the Government invited foreign ministers and their families, no precedence or privilege was given to them other than the provision of a convenient seat or station with any other stranger invited, and with the families of the national ministers; (3) at dinner, in public or private, and on all other social occasions, a perfect equality would exist between those present, whether foreign or domestic, titled or untitled, in or out of office. See Cutts, ed., *Memoirs and Letters of Dolly Madison*, 30-31.

7. "Dolley" was James Madison's nickname for his wife, Dorothea being her full christian name. The name is spelled Dolly by some authors.

8. Margaret Bayard Smith to Susan B. Smith, March 1809 [no exact date given], in Gaillard Hunt, ed., *First Forty Years of Washington Society*, 58.

9. Katharine Anthony, *Dolly Madison: Her Life and Times* (Garden City, N.Y., 1949), vii, x.

10. At that time, Princeton University was called the College of New Jersey.

11. Kathleen Prindiville, *First Ladies*, 44.

12. Anne Hollingsworth Wharton, *Salons Colonial and Republican* (Philadelphia, 1900), 209.

13. Wharton, *Salons Colonial and Republican*, 192.

14. Conover Hunt-Jones, *Dolley and the "great little Madison"* (Washington, 1977), 35.

15. Anthony, *Dolly Madison*, 247.

16. Washington Irving to Henry Brevoort, 13 Jan 1811, in Clark, *Life and Letters of Dolly Madison*, 115.

17. Anthony, *Dolly Madison*, 124-125.

18. Anthony, *Dolly Madison*, 117, 125.

19. Dr. Mitchill, quoted in Mary Caroline Crawford, *Romantic Days in the Early Republic* (Boston, 1912), 178-179.

20. Dolley Madison to Phoebe Morris, 1811 [no exact date given], in Clark, *Life and Letters of Dolly Madison*, 122.

21. Dolley Madison to Joel Barlow, 15 Nov 1811, in Cutts, ed., *Memoirs and Letters of Dolly Madison*, 83.

22. Dolley Madison to Anna Barlow, quoted in Anthony, *Dolly Madison*, 235.

23. Dunlap, *Diary of William Dunlap*, 15 Feb 1806, 385.

24. Washington Irving to Henry Brevoort, 13 Jan 1811, in Clark, *Life and Letters of Dolly Madison*, 115.

25. Margaret Bayard Smith to Susan B. Smith, Mar 1809 [no exact date given], in Hunt, ed., *First Forty Years*, 58, 62.

26. Margaret Bayard Smith to Susan B. Smith, Mar 1809 [no exact date given], in Hunt, ed., *First Forty Years*, 62.

27. Constance McLaughlin Green, *Washington: Village and Capital, 1800-1878* (Princeton, 1962), 50.

28. Anne Hollingsworth Wharton, *Social life in the Early Republic* (Philadelphia, 1902), 86.

29. Margaret Bayard Smith to Jane Kirkpatrick, 13 Mar 1814, in Hunt, ed., *First Forty Years*, 97. Jane Kirkpatrick, Margaret Bayard Smith's sister, was herself a woman of literary accomplishments and the wife of Chief Justice Andrew Kirkpatrick of New Jersey.

30. Clark, *Life and Letters of Dolly Madison*, 256.

31. Margaret Bayard Smith to Jane Kirkpatrick, 20 July 1813, in Hunt, ed., *First Forty Years*, 91.

32. Diary of Mrs. Sarah Seaton, 12 Nov 1812, quoted in Clark, *Life and Letters*, 139.

33. Wharton, *Social Life in the Early Republic*, 135. Elizabeth Kortright Monroe, (1768-1830) was the daughter of one of the founders of the New York Chamber of Commerce. Her husband had earlier been posted to France as Minister Plenipotentiary and the couple had arrived in Paris during the French Revolution at the end of the so-called "Reign of Terror." It was here that Elizabeth acquired the nickname *"la belle Américaine."* She also accompanied her husband on his subsequent postings as American Minister to the Spanish court in Madrid and to the Court of St. James, London.

34. Wharton, *Social Life in the Early Republic*, 156.

35. E.F. Ellet, *Court Circles of the Republic, or the Beauties and Celebrities of the Nation* (Hartford, Conn. 1870), 117.

36. Swift, *Memoirs of General Joseph Gardner*, 11 Dec 1813, 124; Wharton, *Social Life in the Early Republic*, 141.

37. Wharton, *Social Life in the Early Republic*, 145. Mary Ann Caton, one of four sisters, married Robert Patterson, brother of Elizabeth Patterson Bonaparte. While abroad, she was much admired by the young Sir Arthur Wellesley, afterwards the Duke of Wellington, who regularly corresponded with her upon her return to America. When Robert Patterson died, Mary Ann married the Duke's elder brother, the Marquess of Wellesley, then Viceroy of India.

38. Phoebe Morris, 17 Feb 1812, in Wharton, *Social Life in the Early Republic*, 147.

39. James Parton, *Daughters of Genius: A Series of Sketches* (Philadelphia, 1888), 513.

40. Rosalie Stier Calvert to Madame H.J. Stier, Nov 1803, in Callcott, *Mistress of Riversdale*, 62. The British writer, Mary (Wollstonecraft) Godwin (1759-1797) had published a work in 1792 entitled *A Vindication of the Rights of Women*, in which she supported equality of the sexes in terms of education and the marriage relationship.

41. Elizabeth Patterson Bonaparte, quoted in Parton, *Daughters of Genius*, 513.

42. Margaret Bayard Smith, quoted in Anthony, *Dolly Madison*, 152.

43. Margaret Bayard Smith, quoted in Anthony, *Dolly Madison*, 152.

44. Rosalie Stier Calvert to Madame H.J. Stier, 2 Mar 1804, in Callcott, *Mistress of Riversdale*, 77.

45. Rosalie Stier Calvert to Madame H.J. Stier, 2 Mar 1804, in Callcott, *Mistress of Riversdale*, 78.

46. Margaret Bayard Smith, quoted in Anthony, *Dolly Madison*, 152.

47. Among the items listed in an undated inventory of Elizabeth Patterson Bonaparte's jewellery are: "some amber, Coral and Jet ... 1 Am-

ethyst necklace, earrings, diadem and pin … a coquil necklace bracelets clasp and pin … 1 pair of pearl bracelets … 1 diamond crown … 1 pair of emerald earings [sic]." Madame Bonaparte seemed to have a particular fondness for topaz, for the list also includes three pairs of topaz earrings, two topaz bracelets and sixteen topaz stones. See MHS, MS.142, Elizabeth Patterson Bonaparte Papers.

48. Sarah Seaton, quoted in Wharton, *Salons Colonial and Republican*, 204.

49. Wharton, *Social Life in the Early Republic*, 147.

50. MHS, MS.142, Elizabeth Patterson Bonaparte Papers.

51. Account of Mrs. B.H. Latrobe, quoted in de Kay, *Chronicles of the Macedonian*, 99.

52. J. Henley Smith, quoted in Hunt, ed., *First Forty Years*, v.

53. Monsieur Brissot de Warville, quoted in Wharton, *Social Life in the Early Republic*, 13.

54. Mary Allen, quoted in Wharton, *Social Life in the Early Republic*, 31.

55. Dr. Benjamin Rush, quoted in Wharton, *Social Life in the Early Republic*, 32.

56. From article, "Our Naval Victories," 4 Jan 1813, *NWR*, vol III, 312-313.

57. From article, "Our Naval Victories," 4 Jan 1813, *NWR*, Vol. III, 312-313. General John Armstrong was the Secretary of War.

58. Mary Williams to Deborah Ames Fisher, 29 Nov 1813, "Salem Social Life in the Early Nineteenth Century," *Historical Collections of the Essex Institute*, Vol. XXXVI, No. 2 (1900), 118.

59. Hunt, *Life in America*, 72.

60. Wharton, *Salons Colonial and Republican*, 228.

61. Monsieur De Montezlun, quoted in Robin Reilly, *The British at the Gates: The New Orleans Campaign in the War of 1812* (Toronto, 2002), 189.

62. Hunt, *Memoir of Mrs. Edward Livingston*, 27.

63. In another verse of the song is a reference to Major-General Sir Edward Pakenham, who commanded the British troops in the Battle of New Orleans. The song supposes that after winning the battle, Pakenham would enjoy the company of the ladies and help himself to the region's cotton production. In the event, the British suffered a terrible defeat and Pakenham was killed in action. As these lines from the song tell:

> They found, at last, 'twas vain to fight,
> Where lead was all the booty,
> And so they wisely took to flight
> And left us all our beauty.

64. Such New Orleans courtyards, protected from the fierce summer sun, served as perfect venues for meals. Many houses also had covered galleries on the first floor as walkways and places for sitting, eating and sleeping in hot weather.

65. Hunt, *Memoir of Mrs. Edward Livingston*, 214.

66. Vincent Nolte, *Fifty Years in Both Hemispheres, or Reminiscences of the Life of a Former Merchant* (New York, 1854), 317.

67. Sir John Coape Sherbrooke served in Nova Scotia in 1784-85 as a young captain of the 33rd Regiment of Foot and Arthur Wellesley later became its lieutenant-colonel. In the Peninsular War campaign of 1809, Sherbrooke as a local lieutenant-general was second in command to the then Sir Arthur Wellesley and commanded the troops of the British 1st Division. Following operations that year in Portugal and Spain, Wellesley's general orders of 18 August 1809 stated that Sherbrooke's conduct had entitled him to the "King's marked approbation". He was knighted in September 1809 and received the Talavera medal. See *Dictionary of National Biography* (Oxford, 1921), Vol. XVII, 70-71.

68. *The Times*, 21 June 1811, 3.

69. *The Times*, 21 June 1811, 3.

70. *The Times*, 20 June 1811, 2.

71. Margaret Atwood, *Canada's Illustrated Heritage. Days of the Rebels 1815-1840* (Toronto, 1977), 7. This is likely to be a reference to Mrs. Inglis, wife of the Right Reverend Charles Inglis, first Anglican Bishop of Nova Scotia.

72. Thomas H. Raddall, *Halifax, Warden of the North* (Garden City, NY, 1965), 137.

73. Leslie, *Military Memoirs of Col. Leslie*, 286, 289.

74. LAC, MG24, A57, Journal of Lady Katherine Sherbrooke, 4 Nov 1812. When calls were made and the lady of the house was not at home, it was the custom to leave a card displaying one's name.

75. LAC, MG24, A57, Journal of Lady Katherine Sherbrooke, 29 Oct 1811.

76. Literally translated means "a fire of joy," celebratory gunfire, usually in honour of a Royal birthday or to mark a victory.

77. LAC, MG24, A57, Journal of Lady Katherine Sherbrooke, 1 June 1814. Such public events were a signal for all manner of people to appear, including women of of the *demi-monde*, who were seen among the spectators in their flamboyant attire, and no doubt given a suitably wide berth by those ladies who considered themselves superior.

78. William Moorsom, *Letters from Nova Scotia* (London, 1830), 26.

79. Squires, *104th Regiment of Foot*, 103.

80. Squires, *104th Regiment of Foot*, 103.

81. Le Couteur, 13 July 1812, in Graves, ed., *Merry Hearts*, 72-73.

82. Le Couteur, 31 Dec 1812, in Graves, ed., *Merry Hearts*, 78.

83. Among new arrivals to Fredericton was a Captain John Jenkins, a "tall, fine looking young officer" of the Glengarry Light Infantry Fencibles who became town major in the summer of 1813. Penelope Winslow and the captain, who had lost an arm in action at Ogdensburg, New York, were married in 1814. William Odber Raymond, ed., *Winslow Papers, A.D. 1776-1826* (Boston, 1972), 677n.

84. Temperley, ed., *Lieutenant-Colonel Joseph Gubbins*, 9 Aug 1811, 60.

85. Temperley, ed., *Lieutenant-Colonel Joseph Gubbins*, 20 July 1811, 37.

86. LAC, MG24, A9, Diary of Anne Elinor Prevost, Oct 1812, 130.

87. George M. Wrong, *A Canadian Manor and Its Seigneurs: The Story of A Hundred Years 1761-1861* (Toronto, 1908), 107. Colonel John Nairne, father of Christine "Rusty" Nairne, had fought with the forces of Major-General James Wolfe at Quebec in 1759.

88. Elizabeth Frances Hale, née Amherst, was the daughter of William Amherst, a former ADC to King George III, Governor of St. John's Newfoundland and Adjutant-General of His Majesty's forces. His brother Jeffery had been Commander-in-Chief of British Forces in North America during the Seven Years' War.

89. LAC, MG24, A9, Diary of Anne Elinor Prevost. 21.

90. LAC, MG24, A9, Diary of Anne Elinor Prevost, 1 Oct 1811, 76-77.

91. According to Anne Elinor Prevost, the Baroness de Longueuil was "a queer-looking little roly-poly person," who was "abounding in good nature, but did not speak English." See LAC, MG24, A9, Diary of Anne Elinor Prevost, December 1811, 70

92. The young ladies in question were Elizabeth Grant, a Miss Bailey and Ann Bruyères, the daughter of Lieutenant-Colonel Ralph Bruyères, who commanded the Royal Engineers in the Canadas.

93. LAC, MG24, I28, Alicia Cockburn Letters, Alicia Cockburn to Charles Sandys, 16 Mar 1813.

94. LAC, MG24, A9, Diary of Anne Elinor Prevost, Dec 1813, 164.

95. LAC, MG24, A9, Diary of Anne Elinor Prevost,

29 Dec 1813, 114; 7 Jan 1813, 120; 18 Jan 1813, 121.

96. LAC, MG24, A9, Diary of Anne Elinor Prevost, 6 Dec 1812, 111.

97. LAC, MG24, A9, Diary of Anne Elinor Prevost, Dec 1813, 164.

98. LAC, MG24, A9, Diary of Anne Elinor Prevost, 7 Jan 1814, 166.

99. LAC, MG24, B16, Andrew Cochran Papers, Cochran to his mother, 14 Jan 1814.

100. Tupper, ed., *Life and Correspondence of Brock*, 68.

101. Duncan, *Travels through part of the United States and Canada*, Vol. 2, 171-172.

102. Joseph Bouchette, *Topographical Description of the Province of Lower Canada* (London, 1815), 208.

103. Isaac Ogden was a Loyalist from a prominent New York family, and a judge of the Court of King's Bench in Montreal.

104. Colonel Edward Baynes to Brock, 6 Sep 1810, in Tupper, ed., *Life and Correspondence of Brock*, 81.

105. Le Couteur, 25 Feb 1815 in Graves, ed., *Merry Hearts*, 224.

106. Thornton to Brock, 4 Oct 1810, in Tupper, ed., *Life and Correspondence of Brock*, 84.

107. LAC, MG24, H4, Journal of John Slade.

108. LAC, MG 24, I 29, Diary of James Pringle, 81st Foot.

109. DU, Diary of John Lang, 29 May 1813.

110. DU, Diary of John Lang, 6 June 1813.

111. DU, Diary of John Lang, 21 June 1813.

112. Lieutenant-Colonel John O'Neill, 19th Dragoon Guards, served in the Canadas from May 1813 to February 1815 and was in action during the Plattsburgh campaign of 1814.

113. DU, Diary of John Lang, 23 June 1813.

114. DU, Diary of John Lang, 23 June 1813.

115. DU, Diary of John Lang, 15 July 1813. Things were just as lively when Lieutenant John Le Couteur was in Montreal at the end of the war. He was introduced to the "genteelest circles," and enjoyed "all sorts of entertainments, Balls, dinner & Country parties." It was, he decided "a most agreeable quarter," and "a delightful sejour for a Soldier." Le Couteur, March and April 1815 in Graves, ed., *Merry Hearts*, 227-229.

116. LAC, MG 19, F1, Claus Papers, vol 17. Bassanio in "The Merchant of Venice," Act 2 Scene 2. Interestingly, the preceding few lines run as follows:

Thou art too wild, too rude, and bold of voice;-

Parts that become thee happily enough,

And in such eyes as ours appear not faults;
But where thou art not known, why, there
    they show
Something too liberal.

117. LAC, MG 19, F1, Claus Papers, vol 17. Romeo in "Romeo and Juliet," Act 1, Scene 5. A few lines further on in this speech, Romeo says, "For I ne'er saw true beauty till this night" alluding yet again to the exceptional looks of Julia de Rottenburg.

118. LAC, MG 19, F1, Claus Papers, vol 17. Macbeth in "Macbeth," Act 1, Scene 7. Early in 1814, Elizabeth Grant married Lieutenant Charles-Nicolas de Montenach of De Meuron's Regiment (see Chapter 2), and her irrepressible spirit is captured in this quote.

119. Atwood, *Days of the Rebels 1815-1840*, 11.

120. Laurent Quetton de St. George (1771-1821) a French Royalist who had come to Canada in 1798 and received lands in the French royalist colony at Windham, opened a shop at York. He also carried on extensive business and owned stores in York, Queenston, Fort Erie, Lundy's Lane, Dundas, Amherstburg, Kingston and Niagara, as well as Indian trading posts on Lakes Simcoe and Couchiching.

121. MTRL, L16, A93, Anne Powell to George Murray, 4 Sep 1807.

122. Anne Powell to George Murray, 19 Jan 1806, quoted in Firth, ed., *Town of York 1793-1815*, 270.

123. Anne Powell to George Murray, 19 Jan 1806, quoted in Firth, ed., *Town of York 1793-1815*, 271.

124. Firth, ed., *Town of York 1793-1815*, lxxxv.

125. General Account of Subscription Assemblies, 1814, in Firth, ed., *The Town of York, 1793-1815*, 325-236.

126. Le Couteur, 1 Jan 1814, in Graves, ed., *Merry Hearts*, 155.

127. Le Couteur, 1 Jan 1814, in Graves, ed., *Merry Hearts*, 155.

128. Elizabeth Beverley Kennon to Rachel Mordecai, 15 Apr 1812, "Kennon Letters," Vol. XXXIII, No. 3, 274.

9: "Vicissitudes and commotions": Women and the War in the Northern Theatre

1. From *"Chansons militaires de 1812"* by E-Z Massicotte, *Le Bulletin des Récherches Historiques*, Vol. XXXVI, May 1930, No. 5. p. 277. This verse is taken from a song written either in France or Lower Canada. If the latter, it would certainly date from the War of 1812. The original French reads:

Tous les braves courent aux armes,
Adieu! je quitte ce séjour,
J'emporte au milieu des alarmes
Le souvenir de nos amours.
Ma devise? En amant fidèle,
Je prendrai, madame: l'honneur!
Lorsque je combattrai pour elle,
Je suis certain d'être vainqueur.

2. Major-General Henry Dearborn to Julia Wingate, quoted in Lossing, *Pictorial Field-Book of the War of 1812*, 219n.

3. Dwight H. Kelton, *Annals of Mackinac 1843-1906* (Detroit, 1888), 79. In 1814 the Americans tried to recapture the fort on Mackinac Island but their efforts were unsuccessful and it remained in British hands until the end of the War of 1812.

4. Lossing, *Pictorial Field-Book*, 304n.

5. Lossing, *Pictorial Field-Book*, 307.

6. Thomas Verchères de Boucherville in Quaife, ed., *War on the Detroit*, 107-108.

7. Electra Sheldon, *Early History of Michigan from the First Settlement to 1815* (New York, 1856), 398.

8. Sheldon, *Early History of Michigan*, 399.

9. Sheldon, *Early History of Michigan*, 399.

10. Sheldon, *Early History of Michigan*, 400.

11. Lydia Bacon, "Bacon Journal," 16 Aug 1812.

12. "Bacon Journal," 16 Aug 1812.

13. "Bacon Journal," 16 Aug 1812.

14. Ellet, *Pioneer Women of the West*, 315.

15. "Bacon Journal," 16 Aug 1812.

16. Ellet, *Pioneer Women of the West*, 315.

17. Ellet, *Pioneer Women of the West*, 315.

18. Brian Leigh Dunnigan, *Frontier Metropolis: Picturing Early Detroit, 1701-1838* (Detroit, 2001), 74, 110, 136, 205.

19. Sheldon, *Early History of Michigan*, 400.

20. Sheldon, *Early History of Michigan*, 400-401.

21. Sheldon, *Early History of Michigan*, 401.

22. G.M. Fairchild, ed., *Journal of an American Prisoner at Fort Malden and Quebec in the War of 1812*, (Quebec, 1909), 9.

23. Susan Burnham Greeley, in Talman, ed., *Loyalist Narratives*, 93. After travelling by boat under a flag of truce to Black Rock, Susan was able to reach Hopkinton, New York, where she had relatives. Lydia Bacon and her husband, Josiah, travelled aboard a British ship to the Niagara River, and thence by road to Newark, where they found themselves sharing a carriage with the vanquished Brigadier-General William Hull. After being paroled, Lydia's husband took his wife across the border and safely home to New England.

24. "Manitou" was the great spirit believed by the Algonkian peoples of the Northwest to inhabit both animate beings and inanimate objects.

25. Bristol, "Reminiscences of the Northwest," 299.

26. Ellet, *Pioneer Women of the West*, 303-304. Five hundred dollars was paid for the release of the children, and an apology was made for the murder of Mrs. Snow.

27. Lossing, *Pictorial Field-Book*, 313.

28. Wallace A. Brice, *History of Fort Wayne* (Fort Wayne, Indiana, 1868), 22-23.

29. Sheldon, *Early History of Michigan*, 405.

30. Sheldon, *Early History of Michigan*, 405.

31. Sheldon, *Early History of Michigan*, 405.

32. Sheldon, *Early History of Michigan*, 405.

33. Sheldon, *Early History of Michigan*, 407.

34. Bristol, "Reminiscences of the Northwest," 297.

35. "Reminiscences of Early Buffalo and the Vicinity," *Buffalo Courier Express*, Vol. 2, 159.

36. Lieutenant-Colonel Thomas Bligh St. George, Inspecting Field Officer of militia in the Canadas.

37. William F. Coffin, *1812: The War and Its Morals: A Canadian Chronicle*, (Montreal, 1864), 203.

38. Coffin, *1812: The War and Its Morals*, 203.

39. Sugden, *Tecumseh*, 21-22.

40. Glenn Tucker, *Tecumseh, Vision of Glory* (New York, 1956), 62.

41. Sugden, *Tecumseh*, 99.

42. Tupper, ed., *Life and Correspondence of Brock*, 396.

43. Tecumseh, quoted on website <www:/native-longhouse.com>.

44. Robert J. Foley, *The War of 1812: Niagara Story*. Vol. 2 (Niagara Falls, 1994), Vol. 2., 22.

45. Klinck and Talman, eds., *Journal of Major John Norton*, 306.

46. Lieutenant-Colonel George McFeely to General Smyth, 25 Nov 1812, in *Doc. Hist.*, Vol 4, 233.

47. Lossing, *Pictorial Field-Book*, 427n.

48. Merritt, 27 May 1813, in Sutherland, ed., *Journals of William Merritt*, 5.

49. Merritt, 27 May 1813, in Sutherland, ed., *Journals of William Merritt*, 5.

50. Anonymous. "First Campaign of An A.D.C.", *Military and Naval Magazine of the United States* Vol.I. No.5, 206.

51. Anonymous. "First Campaign of An A.D.C.", *Military and Naval Magazine of the United States* Vol.I. No.5, 206.

52. Merritt, 6 July 1813, in Sutherland, ed, *Journals of William Merritt*, 9.

53. John H. Thompson, *Jubilee History of Thorold Township and Town* (Thorold, 1897), 98.

54. Thompson, *Jubilee History of Thorold*, 98.

55. R.I. Warner, "Memoirs of Captain John Lampman and his Wife Mary Secord," *Welland County Historical Society Papers and Records*, Vol. III (1921), 128-129.

56. Cruikshank, "A Memoir of The Honourable James Kerby, his Life in Letters," *Welland County Historical Society Papers and Records*, (1931), Vol. IV., 27-28.

57. Merritt, 19 June 1813, in Sutherland, ed. *Journals of William Merritt*," 8.

58. Merritt, 19 June 1813, in Sutherland, ed., *Journals of William Merritt*, 8.

59. Merritt, 19 June 1813, in Sutherland, ed., *Journals of William Merritt*, 8.

60. Mary Agnes Fitzgibbon, *Veteran of 1812*, 76-77.

61. Article from *Montreal Gazette*, 6 July 1813, in *Doc. Hist.*, 1813, Vol. 6, 117.

62. George McClure, *Causes of the Destruction of the American Towns on the Niagara Frontier and Failure of the Campaign of the Fall of 1813* (Bath, NY, 1817), 19.

63. Richard Merritt, Nancy Butler, and Michael Power, ed. *The Capital Years: Niagara-on-the-Lake 1792-1796* (Toronto and Oxford, 1991), 165. Among those whose names appear on a list of Newark residents who lost homes and property were Dr. Robert Kerr, Colonel William Claus and his wife Catherine, and some ten women.

64. Janet Carnochan, *History of Niagara*, 35.

65. LAC, RG 8 I, vol 681, 217, Murray to Vincent, 12 Dec 1813.

66. Mrs. McFarland's large brick house still stands today on the Niagara Parkway and is an historic site.

67. LAC, RG 8 I, vol 83, Major-General James Wilkinson to Sir George Prevost, 28 Jan 1814.

68. *Report of the Loyal and Patriotic Society of Upper Canada*, (Montreal, 1817) 391.

69. BECHS, F129B8B6928, Local History Scrapbook, vol 9, article "Hard Times: A True Incident of Life on the Niagara Frontier in 1813," 157.

70. BECHS, F129B8B6928, Local History Scrapbook, vol 9, article "Hard Times," 157.

71. Henry W. Hill, *Municipality of Buffalo, New York: A History 1720-1923* (New York, 1923), Vol. I, 148.

72. Robert W. Bingham, *The Cradle of the Queen City: A History of Buffalo to the Incorporation of the City* (Buffalo, 1931), 330.

73. William Ketchum, *An Authentic and Comprehensive History of Buffalo*, (Buffalo, New York, 1865), Vol. 1, 303.

74. Daniel R. Porter, "Jacob Porter Norton: A Yankee on the Niagara Frontier in 1814." *Niagara Frontier (Buffalo & Erie County Historical Society)*, Vol. 12 (1965), 53.

75. Bingham, *Cradle of the Queen City*, 328-329.

76. Smith, *History of the City of Buffalo*, Vol. 2, 61.

77. Johnson, *Centennial History*, 255.

78. Louis L. Babcock, *The War of 1812 on the Niagara Frontier* (Buffalo, 1927), 252.

79. Johnson, *Centennial History of Erie County*, 255.

80. Bingham, *Cradle of the Queen City*, 331.

81. Smith, *History of the City of Buffalo*, Vol. 2, 65.

82. Hill, *Municipality of Buffalo*, Vol. 1, 148.

83. Babcock, *War of 1812 on the Niagara Frontier*, 252.

84. Smith, *History of City of Buffalo*, Vol. 2. 65, Johnson, *Centennial History of Erie County*, 258, and Bingham, *Cradle of the Queen City*, 333, also note that this event took place. Judge Ebenezer Walden was a presiding judge for Erie County.

85. Frank H. Severance, ed., *Publications of the Buffalo Historical Society, Vol XXVI, Recalling Pioneer Days*, "Our Tavern in the Log House," 224-226.

86. Johnson, *History of Erie County*, 261.

87. Turner, *History of the Holland Purchase*, 601.

88. Turner, *History of the Holland Purchase*, 603.

89. Merritt, 9 July 1814, in Sutherland, ed., *Journals of William Merritt*, 41.

90. Merritt, 9 July 1814, in Sutherland, ed., *Journals of William Merritt*, 41.

91. Hannah Jenoway to her sister-in-law. 14 Sep 1814, in *Doc. Hist.*, Vol. 2, 231.

92. Hannah Jenoway to her sister-in-law, 14 Sep 1814, in *Doc. Hist.*, Vol. 2, 231.

93. Hannah Jenoway to her sister-in-law, 14 Sep 1814, in *Doc. Hist.*, Vol. 2, 231. Hannah survived her ordeals and by mid-September 1814 was living in a cottage her husband had built for his family at Fort George, complete with a horse and carriage.

94. George Landmann, *Adventures and Recollections of Colonel Landmann, late of the Corps of Royal Engineers* (London, 1852), Vol. II, 145-146.

95. Procter to Talbot, 23 Sep 1813, quoted in Glenn Stott, *Greater Evils: The War of 1812 in Southwestern Ontario* (Arkona, Ontario, 2001), 34.

96. Thomas Verchères de Boucherville, in Quaife, ed., *War on the Detroit*, 159.

97. Stott, *Greater Evils*, 126.

98. NAUS, RG 107, Micro 221, reel 51, Lieutenant-Colonel John B. Campbell to Secretary of War John Armstrong, 18 May 1814.

99. Amelia Ryerse in Talman, ed., *Loyalist Narratives*, 147-148.

100. Stott, *Greater Evils*, 133. In a return of property destroyed by the Americans at Long Point on 15 and 16 May 1814, Mrs. Sarah Ryerse lost her house, mill and distillery, valued at £2,500, and was the only widow to register her losses. See Stott, 135.

101. White, *History of the American Troops during the Late War*, 11-12.

102. Eyewitness description by Aletta Rapelje quoted in Stuart Rammage, *The Militia Stood Alone: Malcom's Mills. 6 November, 1814* (Penticton, 2000), 124.

103. Stott, *Greater Evils*, 148.

104. Rammage, *The Militia Stood Alone*, 124.

105. N.M. Breckenridge, *Some Account of the Settlement in Upper Canada of Robert Baldwin the Emigrant*, (York, 1859), 25-26.

106. Penelope Beikie to John Macdonell, 5 May 1813, in Firth, ed., *Town of York, 1793-1815*, 299.

107. Penelope Beikie to John Macdonell, 5 May 1813, in Firth, ed., *Town of York, 1793-1815*, 300.

108. Morris Zaslow, *The Defended Border: Upper Canada and the War of 1812* (Toronto, 1964), 253. As the Receiver-General of Upper Canada, Prideaux Selby had a considerable sum of public money which was kept in his house, and which he was determined the Americans should not have. On the advice of members of the provincial Executive Council his daughter, Elizabeth Derenzy, moved it to a safer place.

109. Patrick Finan in *Doc. Hist.*, Vol. 5 207-211.

110. Breckenridge, *Some Account of the Settlement in Upper Canada of Robert Baldwin the Emigrant*, 26.

111. John Strachan to Dr. James Brown, 26 Apr 1813, in George W. Spragge, *The John Strachan Letter Book: 1812-1834* (Toronto, 1946), 295.

112. Statement of William Dummer Powell in Firth, ed., *Town of York 1793-1815*, 301-302.

113. Penelope Beikie, quoted in Carl Benn, *Historic Fort York 1793-1993* (Toronto, 1993), 60.

114. Penelope Beikie to John Macdonnell, 5 May 1813, in Firth, ed., *Town of York, 1793-1815*, 299-300.

115. MTRL, L16, A93, Anne Powell to William Dummer Powell, 10 May 1813.

116. MTRL, L16, A93, Anne Powell to William Dummer Powell, 10 May 1813.

117. MTRL, L16, A93, Anne Powell to William Dummer Powell, 10 May 1813.

118. Le Couteur, 29 May 1813, in Graves, ed., *Merry Hearts*, 118.

119. *Kingston Gazette*, 7 Nov 1812, 3.

120. Article in *Buffalo Gazette*, 22 Sep 1812, quoted in *Doc. Hist.* 1812, Vol 3, 287-288.

121. Mrs. York to her brother, 26 Feb 1813, quoted in Hough, *History of St. Lawrence and Franklin Counties*, 634.

122. Mrs. York to her brother, 26 Feb 1813, quoted in Hough, *History of St. Lawrence and Franklin Counties*, 634. The British attack on Ogdensburg put an end to American raids along the St. Lawrence and Ogdensburg remained without any military defence for the remainder of the war.

123. AO, F996, Jane Stuart to James Stuart, 20 Oct 1813.

124. AO, F996, Jane Stuart to James Stuart, 20 Oct 1813.

125. Historical Society of Pennsylvania, Robert Carr Diary, General Order, 4 Nov 1813 quoted in Donald E. Graves, *Field of Glory: The Battle of Crysler's Farm, 1813* (Toronto, 1999), 124.

126. "First Campaign of an A.D.C.," No. 13, 258-259, quoted in Graves, *Field of Glory*, 151.

127. Extract of a letter from Plattsburgh, 14 Aug 1813, in *Columbian Centinel* 25 Aug 1813, 2.

128. Letter dated 3 Aug 1813, in *Columbian Centinel*, 14 Aug 1813, 2.

129. Letter dated 3 Aug 1813, in *Columbian Centinel*, 14 Aug 1813, 2.

130. Allan Everest, *The War of 1812 in the Champlain Valley* (Syracuse, 1981), 169.

131. Everest, ed., *Recollections of Clinton County*, 18.

132. Everest, ed., *Recollections of Clinton County*, 19.

133. Everest, ed., *Recollections from Clinton County*, 19-20.

10: "The anguish of such hours": The Atlantic and Gulf Coasts

1. The song "Hail Columbia" dates from the War of 1812.

2. Wyman, *Elizabeth Oakes Smith*, 27.

3. Lieutenant Henry Napier, 11 June 1814, in Walter Muir Whitehill, ed., *New England Blockaded in 1814: The Journal of Henry Edward Napier* (Salem, 1939), 24.

4. Napier, 11 June 1814, in Whitehill, ed., *New England Blockaded*, 24.

5. Napier, 13 June 1814 in Whitehill, ed., *New England Blockaded*, 25.

6. Napier, 13 June 1814 in Whitehill, ed., *New England Blockaded*, 25.

7. Napier, 13 June 1814 in Whitehill, ed., *New England Blockaded*, 26.

8. Kilby, *Eastport and Passamaquoddy*, 420.

9. Kilby, *Eastport and Passamaquoddy*, 420.

10. William Henry Kilby, "A New England Town Under Martial Law," *New England Magazine*, Vol. XIV (1896), 691.

11. David Zimmerman, *Coastal Fort: A History of Fort Sullivan Eastport, Maine* (Moose Island, Maine, 1984), 58-59.

12. Maxwell Vesey, "A Strange Interlude in Border History," *Dalhousie Review*, Volume XXX (1941), 417.

13. Vesey, "Strange Interlude in Border History," 421.

14. George A. Wheeler, *Castine Past and Present: The Ancient Settlement of Pentagöet and the Modern Town* (Boston, 1896), 49-50.

15. Wheeler, *Castine Past and Present*, 51.

16. Wheeler, *Castine Past and Present*, 52.

17. Wheeler, *Castine Past and Present*, 53.

18. Rear-Admiral Sir George Cockburn, born into an old Scottish family, was the second of the five sons of Sir James and Lady Augusta Cockburn. The first and fifth sons, James and Francis, became generals in the British Army and colonial governors. The third son, William, became Dean of York, and the fourth son achieved high rank in the consular service. A famous portrait of Lady Augusta and her three eldest sons, James, George and William, by Sir Joshua Reynolds, hangs in the National Gallery, London.

19. James Pack, *The Man who burned the White House: Admiral Sir George Cockburn, 1772-1853* (Emsworth, Hampshire, 1987), 145.

20. James Jones Wilmer, *Narrative Respecting the Conduct of the British from their first landing on Spesutia Island, till their progress to Havre de Grace* (Baltimore, 1813), 9-10.

21. The town reputedly received the name Havre de Grace, or "Harbour of Mercy," from the Marquis de Lafayette, who passed through in the area in the 1780s and extolled its beauty.

22. Rodgers, I:16, Memoir of Minerva Denison Rodgers, 12.

23. Wilmer, *Narrative Respecting the Conduct of the British*, 16; Report on British attack at Havre de Grace, *NWR*, 22 May 1813, Vol. IV, 195.

24. Wilmer, *Narrative Respecting the Conduct of the British*, 13, 26.

25. Report on British attack at Havre de Grace, *NWR*, 22 May 1813, Vol. IV, 195.

26. Lossing, *Pictorial Field-Book*, 672n. The fire was extinguished with considerable effort.

27. Lieutenant J.R.N. Scott, quoted in Pack, *The Man who burned the White House*, 153.

28. Letter of unidentified correspondent, 7 May 1813, *NWR*, Vol. IV, 196.

29. Notice of 14 May 1813, in *NWR*, Vol. IV, 197.

With the issue of this notice, a deputation from Havre de Grace went to see the mayor and city council of Baltimore to request relief and assistance for their town.

30. Wilmer, *Narrative Respecting the Conduct of the British*, 17, 20.

31. Wilmer, *Narrative Respecting the Conduct of the British*, 30.

32. Untitled newspaper article, 22 Nov 1855, displayed in <www.kittyknight.com>.

33. Untitled newspaper article, 22 November 1855, displayed in <www.kittyknight.com>.

34. Verse appearing in <www.kittyknight.com>.

35. Wilmer, *Narrative Respecting the Conduct of the British*, 20. These ladies were entertained to dinner. So late was the hour when it was over that the ship's carpenter "gave up his room to the females," and they spent the night aboard the British ship. According to this account Miss Oliver was successful in obtaining "some parts of her effects."

36. Dolley Madison to Hannah Gallatin, 7 Jan 1814, quoted in Henry Adams, *History of the United States During the Administration of James Madison 1813-1817* (New York, 1930), Vol. 7, 379-380.

37. Chamier, *Life of a Sailor*, Vol. 2, 128.

38. Chamier, *Life of a Sailor*, Vol. 2, 128.

39. Chamier, *Life of a Sailor*, Vol. 2, 133.

40. Eleanor Jones to Dolley Madison, 23 Aug 1814, in Cutts, ed. *Memoirs and Letters of Dolly Madison*, 105.

41. "A Colored Man's Reminiscences of James Madison" by Paul Jennings, *White House History*, Vol. 1, No. 1 (1983), 50.

42. Dolley Madison to Anna Cutts, 23 Aug 1814, in Cutts, ed., *Memoirs and Letters of Dolly Madison*, 110.

43. Dolley Madison to Anna Cutts, 23 Aug 1814, in Cutts, ed., *Memoirs and Letters of Dolly Madison*, 109.

44. "A Colored Man's Reminiscences of James Madison" by Paul Jennings, *White House History*, Vol. 1, No. 1 (1983), 47.

45. Rosalie Stier Calvert to Isabelle van Havre, 30 Aug 1814, in Callcott, *Mistress of Riversdale*, 271.

46. Dolley Madison to Anna Cutts, 23 Aug 1814, in Cutts, ed., *Memoirs and Letters of Dolly Madison*, 110.

47. Dolley Madison to Anna Cutts, 23 Aug 1814, in Cutts, ed., *Memoirs and Letters of Dolly Madison*, 109-110.

48. Dolley Madison to Anna Cutts, 23 Aug 1814, in Cutts, ed., *Memoirs and Letters of Dolly Madison*, 110-111.

49. Dolley Madison to Anna Cutts, 23 August 1814 in Cutts, ed., *Memoirs and Letters of Dolly Madison*, 111. George Washington's portrait was deposited for safe keeping at a farmhouse just outside Georgetown. Several months later, Dolley confessed to her friend Mary Latrobe that on that day, she had been "so unfeminine as to be free from fear," and wished she "could have had a cannon" pointing out of every window. Dolley Madison to Mary Latrobe, 3 Dec 1814 in Clark, *Life and Letters*, 166.

50. It is of note that the accounts of Mrs. Thornton and Mrs. Bayard Smith have been used by historians. There is a gap in Mrs. Thornton's journal, however, at the time of the actual British occupation, which suggests that she was unable to write during those days, and that she and her husband had their papers and valuables sent out of the city when the situation became critical.

51. Walter Lord, *The Dawn's Early Light* (New York, 1972), 102.

52. Anthony S. Pitch, *The Burning of Washington: The British Invasion of 1814* (Annapolis, Maryland, 1998), 88.

53. Pitch, *Burning of Washington*, 89.

54. Lord, *Dawn's Early Light*, 102; Pitch, *The Burning of Washington*, 98.

55. Green, *Washington: Village and Capital 1800-1878*, 61. In 1812, the Washington city council imposed the requirement that every free African-American register and carry a certificate of freedom, without which a person could be jailed as a runaway slave.

56. W.B. Bryan, ed. "Diary of Mrs. William Thornton. Capture of Washington by the British." *Columbia Historical Society Proceedings* 19 (1916), 175.

57. Pitch, *Burning of Washington*, 115. Camphor, a substance obtained from the Asian or Australian laurel, was regarded as having a soothing effect in cases of "nervous excitement" and a calming influence upon "hysteria, nervousness and neuralgia." See Maud Grieve, *A Modern Herbal* (London, 1931).

58. Mary Hunter to Susan Cuthbert, 30 Aug 1814, in "The Burning of Washington, D.C.," *New York Historical Society Bulletin*, Vol. 8, No. 3 (Oct 1924), 82.

59. James Ewell, *Planters and Mariner's Medical Companion* (Philadelphia, 1816), 638-639.

60. Charles J. Ingersoll, *Historical Sketch of the Second War between the United States of America and Great Britain* (Philadelphia, 1849), Vol. 2, 186.

61. Ingersoll, *Historical Sketch of the Second War*, Vol. 1, 200.

62. Bryan, ed. "Diary of Mrs. William Thornton," 172.

63. Mary Hunter to Susan Cuthbert, 30 Aug 1814, in "The Burning of Washington, D.C.," 82.

64. Mary Hunter to Susan Cuthbert, 30 Aug 1814, in "The Burning of Washington, D.C.," 82-83.

65. George Gleig, *The Campaigns of the British Army at Washington & New Orleans* (1847, reprinted East Ardsley, Yorkshire, 1972), 71-72.

66. Gleig, *Campaigns of the British Army*, 76.

67. Bryan, ed. "Diary of Mrs. William Thornton," 27 Aug 1814, 177.

68. Dolley Madison to Mary Latrobe, 3 Dec 1814, in Clark, *Life and Letters*, 166. James and Dolley Madison found a temporary home at the Octagon House, a property loaned to them by the French Minister, Monsieur Serrurier.

69. Bryan, ed., "Diary of Mrs. William Thornton," 28 Aug 1814, 178.

70. Margaret Bayard Smith to Jane Kirkpatrick, 30 Aug 1814, in Hunt, ed., *First Forty Years*, 110.

71. Margaret Bayard Smith to Jane Kirkpatrick, 30 Aug 1814, in Hunt, ed., *First Forty Years*, 114. After an initial wave of accusations and recriminations on the part of Washington citizens, anger soon gave way to a new sympathy for the beleaguered President James Madison, and an awareness that this experience, hard though it was, had had a sobering effect upon the city.

72. Pitch, *Burning of Washington*, 209.

73. Notes of Hezekiah Niles, 12 Sep 1814, Huntingdon Library. This incident is also noted in Lossing, *Pictorial Field-Book*, 956n.

74. John Blair Linn, *Annals of the Buffalo Valley, Pennsylvania, 1755-1855,* (Harrisburg, 1877), pp 420-421.

75. Sally Johnston, Beth Miller and Pat Pilling, *The Star-Spangled Banner Flag House,* (Lawrenceburg, 1999), 5.

76. Johnston, Miller and Pilling, *Star-Spangled Banner Flag House*, 17.

77. Johnston, Miller and Pilling, *Star-Spangled Banner Flag House*, 1, 4-5; Caroline Pickersgill Purdy to Georgiana Armistead Appleton, 9 Sep 1876, Star-Spangled Banner Flag House Collection, Baltimore.

78. Johnston, Miller and Pilling, *Star-Spangled Banner Flag House*, 2.

79. Gleig, *Campaigns of the British Army*, 109.

80. Parton, *Andrew Jackson*, Vol. 2, 60-61. This reference is to the sexual assault on American women at the town of Hampton, Virginia, by troops

under British command, which occurred in 1813. See Chapter 12.

81. Louise Livingston to Mrs. Montgomery, 12 Jan 1815, in Hunt, *Memoir of Mrs. Edward Livingston*, 59-61.

82. Parton, *Andrew Jackson*, Vol. 2, 271-272.

83. Parton, *Andrew Jackson*, Vol. 2, 272.

84. Parton, *Andrew Jackson*, Vol. 2, 273.

85. Parton, *Andrew Jackson*, Vol. 2, 274.

11: "Boldly I did fight ... although I'm but a wench": Women as Combatants, Agents and Prisoners of War

1. "The Pretty Drummer Boy," a traditional ballad dating to the Napoleonic Wars or before.

2. AO, MU.2635, Military Scrapbook, newspaper article, "The Manchester Heroine," December 1814.

3. See Nadezhda Durova, *The Cavalry Maid: The Memoirs of a Woman Soldier of 1812* (Ann Arbor, Michigan, 1988).

4. On women sailors and marines in the Royal Navy, see David Cordingly, *Women Sailors and Sailors' Women. An Untold Maritime History* (New York, 2001) and Suzanne Stark, *Female Tars: Women Aboard Ship in the Age of Sail* (London, 1996).

5. "The Monthly Register of Naval Events," July 1802, in Nicholas Tracy, *The Naval Chronicle: The Contemporary Record of the Royal Navy at War* (London, 1999), Vol. III, 80. One of the sisters was eventually wounded by a splinter in the side and "her sex being discovered, she was discharged" and returned to England. The other sister contracted a fever and thinking she might not live, confided her secret to one of the ship's officers. The discovery "gave tenderness to the esteem" he had felt for the young "sailor" and his attentions aided her recovery. Love blossomed, they were married and returned to live the rest of their days in England.

6. AO, MU.2635, Military Scrapbook, newspaper article, "The Manchester Heroine," December 1814.

7. *Annual Register*, Sep 1815, quoted in Stark, *Female Tars: Women Aboard Ship in the Age of Sail*, 87.

8. John C. Fredriksen, *Surgeon of the Lakes. The Diary of Dr. Usher Parsons, 1812-1814,* (Erie County Historical Society, Erie, Pennsylvania, 2000), 5, entry 28 Sep 1812.

9. LAC, RG8 I, vol 694A, General Entry Book of American Prisoners of War, June 1813, No. 240, 16.

10. William S. Dudley, ed. *The Naval War of 1812: A Documentary History. Vol. II* (Washington, D.C., 1992), 601.

11. Dudley, ed., *Naval War of 1812, Vol. II.*, 602.

12. Report dated 17 July 1813 in *NWR*, Vol. IV, 325. This same report also appeared in *The Royal Gazette and New Brunswick Advertiser* of 27 July 1813.

13. See Daniel A. Cohen, *The Female Marine and Related Works: Narratives of Cross-Dressing and Urban Vice in America's Early Republic* (Amherst, Mass., 1997).

14. A.A. Hoehling, *Women Who Spied: True Stories of Feminine Espionage from the American Revolution to the Present Day* (New York, 1967), xii.

15. *Report of the Loyal and Patriotic Society of Upper Canada* (Montreal, 1817), 253.

16. LAC, RG 5 B3, Upper Canada Land Petitions, Petition of Anna Maria Grenville dated 15 July 1834.

17. Sutherland, ed., *Journals of William Merritt*, 7.

18. Sutherland, ed., *Journals of William Merritt*, 7.

19. Ruth McKenzie, *Laura Secord: The Legend and the Lady* (Toronto, 1971), 19.

20. McKenzie, *Laura Secord*, 29.

21. McKenzie, *Laura Secord*, 47-48.

22. McKenzie, *Laura Secord*, 48-49.

23. McKenzie, *Laura Secord*, 49.

24. Colin M. Coates and Cecilia Morgan, *Heroines and History: Representations of Madeleine de Verchères and Laura Secord* (Toronto, 2002), 125.

25. McKenzie, *Laura Secord*, 50.

26. Coates and Morgan, *Heroines and History*, 119.

27. Coates and Morgan, *Heroines and History*, 119. James Fitzgibbon attested by means of a signed certificate in 1837 that Laura Secord walked from her house, "near the village of St. David's," using a "circuitous route of about twenty miles," to "aquaint me that the enemy intended to attempt, by surprise, to capture a detachment of the 49th Regiment, then under my command, she having obtained such knowledge from good authority," but without giving further details. Mary Agnes Fitzgibbon, *A Veteran of the War of 1812*, 84. Fitzgibbon had also made a much briefer statement on 24 February 1820 stating categorically that Mrs. Secord came to him two days before the engagement with Boerstler and that she arrived at his headquarters, "about sunset of an excessively warm day, after having walked twelve miles," which tends to indicate that Laura had, in fact, set out from St. David's, where she had relatives, and not Queenston. See

LAC, RG5 A1, Upper Canada Sundries, vol 46.

28. Coates and Morgan, *Heroines and History*, 129.

29. Laura Secord's Narrative, 1855, *Doc. Hist.* 1813, Vol. 6, 127.

30. Laura Secord's Narrative, *Doc. Hist.* 1813, Vol. 5, 127-128.

31. Laura Secord, quoted in Coates and Morgan, *Heroines and History*, 127.

32. Le Couteur, 24 June 1813, in Graves, ed., *Merry Hearts*, 126.

33. Coates and Morgan, *Heroines and History*, 129.

34. Coates and Morgan, *Heroines and History*, 151, 153.

35. James Tertius De Kay, *The Battle of Stonington: Torpedoes, Submarines and Rockets in the War of 1812* (Annapolis, Maryland, 1990) 123.

36. Commodore Stephen Decatur to Secretary of the Navy William Jones, 18 June 1813 in Dudley, ed., *Naval War of 1812, Vol. II*, 139.

37. *NWR*, Vol. IV, 10 July 1813, 304.

38. De Kay, *Battle of Stonington*, 97.

39. De Kay, *Battle of Stonington*, 83-85.

40. Sheppard, "Wants and Privations," 178.

41. Sheppard, "Wants and Privations," 178. Such women may have decided to offer hospitality to the enemy to safeguard themselves from any trouble, for at the very least, soldiers short of food or supplies were likely to help themselves to whatever they could find.

42. "Bacon Journal," 16 Aug 1812, 72.

43. "Bacon Journal," 17 Aug 1812, 75.

44. "Bacon Journal," 17 Aug 1812, 79.

45. Lydia Barker Hayward, "The Escape of Lydia Hayward," *The Hay Bay Guardian*, No.5 (1997), 2.

46. Hayward, "Escape of Lydia Hayward," 4.

47. Hayward, "Escape of Lydia Hayward," 7.

48. Hayward, "Escape of Lydia Hayward," 7.

49. Hayward, "Escape of Lydia Hayward," 9.

50. Hayward, "Escape of Lydia Hayward," 9. Lydia and Joshua Hayward settled in Adams, New York, and survived the war unharmed.

51. Fredriksen, ed., "Chronicle of Valour: The Journal of a Pennsylvania Officer in the War of 1812," 244-245.

52. Le Couteur, 10 Sep 1813, in Graves, ed., *Merry Hearts*, 133. The translations of the French expressions read, "under my guard," and "spying in uniform," respectively.

53. Charles J. Dutton, *Oliver Hazard Perry* (New York, 1935), 244.

54. Dutton, *Oliver Hazard Perry*, 244.

55. Dutton, *Oliver Hazard Perry*, 245.

12: "Worthless is the laurel steeped in female tears": Privations, Poverty, Bereavement and Crime

1. "The Bonny Light Horseman," a British song clearly dating back to the early nineteenth century, if not before, from Palmer, *The Rambling Soldier*, 252.

2. Joseph Gubbins, 20 July 1811, in Temperley, ed., *Lieutenant-Colonel Joseph Gubbins*, 27.

3. Joseph Gubbins, 20 July 1811, in Temperley, ed., *Lieutenant-Colonel Joseph Gubbins*, 27.

4. AO, F536, Lieutenant-Colonel Benoni Wiltse to Colonel Joel Stone, 13 Apr 1813.

5. Smith, *Geographical View of the Province of Upper Canada*, 98-99.

6. Alexander Wood to James Leslie, 11 Nov 1812 and 29 Aug 1812, quoted in Firth, ed., *Town of York, 1793-1815*, lxxxviii.

7. Smith, *Geographical View of the Province of Upper Canada*, 98.

8. Thomas Verchères de Boucherville, quoted in Quaife, ed., *War on the Detroit*, 133.

9. John Howison, *Sketches of Upper Canada, Domestic, Local and Characteristic* (Edinburgh, 1825), 94.

10. William Dummer Powell to Mrs. Warren, 12 Oct 1815, quoted in Firth, ed., *The Town of York, 1795-1815*, lxxxix.

11. Breckinridge, *Some Account of the Settlement in Upper Canada of Robert Baldwin*, 29.

12. As the war progressed, people became increasingly reliant on what they could hunt, fish and gather. Fish was abundant at that time for reports from the war period talk of immense quantities of salmon, and shoals of bass, trout and pickerel, not to mention pike and sturgeon in the Great Lakes. Rabbits, small game birds and wild berries served as other sources of food.

13. DU, Diary of John Lang, 19 May 1813, 22 May 1813. The farming methods of the *habitants* of Lower Canada normally only produced enough food for their own needs, and by 1813 the people there were living very frugally according to Lieutenant Lang. A Briton like Lang, who had come from a country which had been at the peak of agricultural production, achieved through more than three generations of experimentation, was bound to remark on the contrast.

14. PANS, MG1, Almon Family Papers, Catherine and Mary Byles to Mrs. Brooke, 21 Sep 1812.

15. AO, F996, Jane Stuart to James Stuart, 7 Feb 1814. James Stuart was Solicitor-General of Lower Canada and a representative in the Lower Canada Legislative Assembly.

16. AO, F996, Jane Stuart to James Stuart, 7 Feb 1814.

17. Emery, *Reminiscences of a Nonagenarian*, 275.

18. Emery, *Reminiscences of a Nonagenarian*, 275.

19. Phebe Hammond to John Champlin, Mar 1813, LAC, RG8 IV, Vice-Admiralty Prize Courts, vol 84, 38976.

20. Phebe Hammond to John Champlin, Mar 1813, LAC, RG8, IV, vol 84, 38976. Phebe Hammond's letter was one of several being carried by the American sloop, *Fame*, when she was captured by the Nova Scotian privateer, *Sir John Sherbrooke*, on 1 Apr 1813. The *Fame* was condemned as a lawful prize by the Vice Admiralty Court and unfortunately, Phebe's letter did not reach its destination.

21. Unnamed British officer, quoted in Carlton E. Sanford, *Early History of the Town of Hopkinton* (Boston, 1903), 89.

22. Sheppard, "'Wants and Privations,'" 166.

23. CHS, 19628-1909, George Howard Autobiography and Record Book, 11.

24. Tupper, ed., *Life and Correspondence of Brock*, 197. Some former Americans living in Upper Canada refused to take the oath and were imprisoned. Many, however, decided to take it, reasoning that if their service in the militia helped to shorten the war, they would be able to return all the sooner to their struggling families.

25. Kenneth Scott, *British Aliens in the United States during the War of 1812* (Baltimore, 1979), 292-293, 361-365. British citizens in the United States were required to give their name, age, occupation, place of residence, details of the other members of their family, and the length of time they had been living there. Reports on alien residents were filed in Maine, New Hampshire, Vermont, Massachusetts, Rhode Island, Connecticut, New York, New Jersey, Delaware, Pennsylvania, Maryland, Virginia, North and South Carolina, Georgia, Louisiana, Ohio, Kentucky, East and West Tennessee, Illinois and Mississippi.

26. Scott, *British Aliens in the United States during the War of 1812*, 1, 2, 12.

27. NAUS, RG 59, Records of the Department of States, War of 1812 Papers, vol 8, reels 1575 and 1576, U.S. Marshals' Return of Enemy Aliens and Prisoners of War (Part II). Returns of the Department of State of British subjects who reported themselves to the Marshal of Virginia (4-11 Apr 1813), the Marshal of Pennsylvania (1

and 30 June 1814) and the Marshal for the District of New York (7 July 1812, and 21 December-23 January 1813.

28. NAUS, RG 59, Records of the Department of State, War of 1812 Papers, vol 8, reel 1576, Orders dated 6 February 1813 and 23 February 1813.

29. Merritt, 7 Oct 1813, in Sutherland, ed., *Journals of William Merritt*, 12.

30. Merritt, 7 Oct 1813, in Sutherland, ed., *Journals of William Merritt*, 12.

31. Merritt, 9 Oct 1813, in Sutherland, ed., *Journals of William Merritt*, 12.

32. Merritt, in Sutherland, ed., *Journals of William Merritt*, 13.

33. Merritt, in Sutherland, ed., *Journals of William Merritt*, 15.

34. Merritt, in Sutherland, ed., *Journals of William Merritt*, 15.

35. Moore Smith, ed. *Autobiography of Lieutenant-General Sir Harry Smith*, 182-183.

36. Moore Smith, ed. *Autobiography of Lieutenant-General Sir Harry Smith*, 204.

37. Moore Smith, ed. *Autobiography of Lieutenant-General Sir Harry Smith*, 217.

38. *Bath Chronicle*, 17 Nov 1814, 3.

39. Moore Smith, ed., *Autobiography of Sir Harry Smith*, 223.

40. Moore Smith, ed., *Autobiography of Sir Harry Smith*, 260.

41. Susan Burnham Greeley in Talman, ed., *Loyalist Narratives*, 101.

42. AO, F434, Thomas G. Ridout to Thomas Ridout, 1 Nov 1813, 256. The corduroy bottom of a road, made by laying logs to help prevent vehicles from sinking into the mud, often collapsed and sometimes it took hours to raise a coach from the mire. On many roads taverns were located about a mile apart because progress was so slow that travellers needed to make frequent stops.

43. Rodgers, I:13, Minerva Rodgers to John Rodgers, 24 Apr 1813.

44. Ellet, *Pioneer Women of the West*, 323.

45. Duncan, *Travels through part of the United States and Canada*, Vol.1, 51.

46. Letter dated 3 Feb 1813, in *NWR*, Vol. III, 396.

47. Garrett Glen Clift, *Remember the Raisin! Kentucky and Kentuckians in the battles and massacre at Frenchtown, Michigan Territory, in the War of 1812* (Frankfort, Kentucky, 1961), 150.

48. Clift, *Remember the Raisin*, 114-115.

49. Le Couteur, 27 July 1814, in Graves, ed., *Merry Hearts*, 176.

50. Sir John Johnson to Colonel William Claus, in Earle Thomas, *Sir John Johnson: Loyalist Baronet* (Toronto, 1986), 158.

51. Verse from poem "Death of Mr. Job Hoisington," by Elder A. Turner, in *Publications of the Buffalo Historical Society*, Vol. II (Buffalo, 1880), 392.

52. Anonymous, *Centennial History of the Fredonia Baptist Church 1808-1908* (Buffalo, 1908), 30.

53. *Centennial History of the Fredonia Baptist Church*, 30.

54. *Centennial History of the Fredonia Baptist Church*, 30-31.

55. *Centennial History of the Fredonia Baptist Church*, 31.

56. NFPL, Local History Collection of the War of 1812, General file, "Reminders of the Past" by Eva Elliott Tolan, undated article, *Niagara Falls Review*, 1963. The author is grateful to Dr. Katherine McKenna for information on the relationship between John Macdonell and Mary Powell.

57. Dunlop, *Tiger Dunlop's Upper Canada*, 51.

58. Chamier, *Life of a Sailor*, Vol. 2, 139.

59. Chamier, *Life of a Sailor*, Vol. 2, 139.

60. Anonymous, *Biographical Memoir of the Late Sir Peter Parker, Baronet, Captain of H.M. Ship Menelaus* (London, 1815), 69.

61. *Memoir of Sir Peter Parker*, 69.

62. LAC, MG24, A57, Journal of Lady Katherine Sherbrooke, 29 Sep 1814.

63. Anne Ilbert, quoted in Berton, *The Invasion of Canada*, 251.

64. Mary Williams to Deborah Ames Fisher, 20 Sep 1813, in "Salem Social Life," 112.

65. Mary Williams to Deborah Ames Fisher, 20 Sep 1813, in "Salem Social Life," 113.

66. Charles Pingey, *A Narrative of a few of the Scenes and Incidents that occured in the Sanguinary and Cruel War of 1812-14 between England and the United States*, (Norway, 1853), 11.

67. Pingey, *Narrative of a few of the Scenes and Incidents*, 11.

68. Parton, *Andrew Jackson*, Vol. 2, 281-282.

69. Parton, *Andrew Jackson*, Vol. 2, 287. Later examination of evidence suggests that presidential authorisation for six months of duty had not been made to the governor of Tennessee and that the men's departure from camp "was not desertion, but a lawful going home after they had done their part as citizen soldiers". See Parton, Vol. 2, 293.

70. Parton, *Andrew Jackson*, Vol. 2, 278.

71. Parton, *Andrew Jackson*, Vol. 2, 278-279.

72. AO, F955, Edward McMahon to Thomas Merritt, 20 Sep 1814.

73. George Sheppard, *Plunder Profits and Paroles: A Social History of the War of 1812 in Upper Canada* (Montreal and Kingston, 1994), 167.

74. Sheppard, *Plunder, Profit, and Paroles*, 168.

75. Sheppard, *Plunder, Profit, and Paroles*, 169.

76. LAC, RG5, A1, vol 19, James McNabb to Richard Cartwright, 7 Apr 1814 with attached depositions by Captain John Meyers and others dated 6 Apr 1814.

77. LAC, RG5, A1, vol 19, Examination of Captain John M. Meyers and others.

78. LAC, RG5, A1, vol 19, McNabb to Cartwright, 7 Apr 1814.

79. *Connecticut Gazette*, 17 June 1812, 2.

80. *Connecticut Gazette*, 17 June 1812, 3.

81. Kilby, "A New England Town Under Martial Law," 695.

82. Kilby, *Eastport and Passamaquoddy*, 189.

83. Joseph Gubbins, 16 July 1811, in Temperley, ed., *Lieutenant-Colonel Joseph Gubbins*, 17.

84. Statistics from Old Bailey website at <www.old-baileyonline.org>.

85. Dumont et al., *Quebec Women: A History*, 100.

86. *Dictionary of Canadian Biography*, vol 9, Strachan entry; Carl Benn, "A Georgian Parish, 1797-1839," in William Cooke, ed., *The Parish and Cathedral of St. James*, Toronto (Toronto, 1998), 16.

87. NAB, CO42, vol 23, Beckwith to Goulburn, 31 Mar 1813.

88. *NWR*, Vol. IV, 24 July 1813, 332-333.

89. Article in *Norfolk Herald*, quoted in *NWR*, Vol. IV, 24 July 1813, 333.

90. Article in *Norfolk Herald*, quoted in *NWR*, Vol. IV, 24 July 1813.

91. Article, "The Monsters at Hampton," in *NWR*, Vol. IV, 24 July 1813, 333.

92. Donald E. Graves, "'Worthless is the laurel steeped in female tears': An Investigation into the Outrages Committed by British Troops at Hampton, Virginia, in 1813," *Journal of the War of 1812*, Vol VII, No 1 (Winter 2002), 23.

93. *NWR*, Vol. IV, 28 Aug 1813, 419.

94. *NWR*, Vol. IV, 28 Aug 1813, 419.

95. *NWR*, Vol. IV, 28 Aug 1813, 419.

96. Taylor to Beckwith, 1 July 1813, quoted in Graves, "Worthless is the laurel steeped in female tears," 23.

97. Brown, "Recollections of Old Halifax," 77-78.

98. James Hamilton, *The Life, and Dying Confessions of James Hamilton, executed for the Murder of Major Benjain Birdsall, November 6, 1818 at Albany* (New York, 1818), 20.

99. Hamilton, *Dying Confessions*, 20.

100. Hamilton, *Dying Confessions*, 20.

101. *Upper Canada Guardian*, 15 Apr 1810, 2.

102. *Upper Canada Guardian*, 15 Apr 1810, 2.

103. *Upper Canada Guardian*, 15 Apr 1810.

104. Lossing, *Pictorial Field-Book*, 618.

105. Lossing, *Pictorial Field-Book*, 619.

106. Gregory, *Father's Legacy to His Daughters*, 20-21.

107. PRONI, T/1870/4, Holmes, "Pedestrian Tour," 83.

108. PRONI, T/1870/4, Holmes, "Pedestrian Tour," 84-85.

109. Lord, *Dawn's Early Light*, 179.

110. Hamilton, *Dying Confessions*, 7.

111. Matthew Hale Smith, quoted in Timothy Gilfoyle, *City of Eros: New York City, Prostitution and the Commercialization of Sex, 1790-1920* (New York, 1992), 49.

112. LAC, RG19, vol 4358, Claim 1714, Testimony of Peter Wheeler.

113. Henry Mayhew and Peter Quennell, *London's Underground* (London 1969), 48.

114. *1811 Dictionary of the Vulgar Tongue: A Dictionary of Buckish Slang, University Wit, and Pickpocket Eloquence* (reprinted, Northfield, Ill., 1971), 5, 35, 78, 63, 153,1 97, 210. Although the compiler of the expressions contained in this dictionary assumed its circulation would be confined almost exclusively to the lower orders of society, it became popular among young men of fashion. Such expressions found a use partly because they enabled men to talk about the seamier side of life without causing any embarassment or discomfort to the better class of woman.

115. Cordingly, *Women Sailors*, 15.

116. *Montreal Herald*, 19 Mar 1812, 3.

117. Dumont et al., *Quebec Women*, 35.

13: "The blessings of peace": The End of the War and Afterwards

1. Song sung at the Harvard College peace celebration, March 1815, reprinted in the *Columbian Centinel*, 25 Mar 1815.

2. The Octagon House was a spacious mansion on the corner of Washington's New York Avenue and 18th Street, built in 1798 by Colonel John Tayloe of Virginia.

3. Clark, *Life and Letters of Dolly Madison*, 209.

4. Susan Burnham Greeley, in Talman, ed., *Loyalist Narratives*, 253.

5. Wyman, *Elizabeth Oakes Smith*, 30.

6. CHS, 19628-1909, George Howard Autobiography and Record Book, 13 Feb 1815.

7. CHS, 19628-1909, George Howard Autobiography and Record Book, 13 Feb 1815.

8. M.A. De Wolfe Howe, *The Articulate Sisters: Passages from the Journals and Letters of the Daughters of President Josiah Quincy of Harvard University* (Cambridge, Mass., 1946), 12.

9. De Wolfe Howe, *Articulate Sisters*, 12-13.

10. *Columbia Centinel*, 25 Feb 1814, 2.

11. De Wolfe Howe, *Articulate Sisters*, 14-15.

12. De Wolfe Howe, *Articulate Sisters*, 15.

13. LAC, MG24, A57, Journal of Lady Katherine Sherbrooke, 19 Feb 1815.

14. LAC, MG24, A57, Journal of Lady Katherine Sherbrooke, 2 Mar 1815, 15 Mar 1815.

15. PRONI, T/1870/4, Holmes, "Pedestrian Tour," 211.

16. Le Couteur, 25 Feb 1815 in Graves, ed., *Merry Hearts*, 222.

17. Le Couteur, 25 Feb 1815, in Graves, ed., *Merry Hearts*, 223.

18. Parton, *Andrew Jackson*, Vol. 2, 325-326.

19. Gleig, *Campaigns of the British Army*, 194.

20. The *Louisiana Gazette* of 21 February 1815, for example, contained an editorial stating that some people did not like the terms of peace and that "those who were resolved not to like the treaty" were already making their voices heard, with the result that "our coffee houses rang with discontent." Given that it was human nature to find fault, the *Gazette* begged its readers to "suspend all fault finding until we have *a full view of the whole ground.*" Andrew Jackson added weight to this by saying, "Peace, whenever it shall be re-established on full and honourable terms, is an event in which both nations ought to rejoice."

21. *NWR*, 11 Mar 1815, Vol. VII, 433.

22. J.L.H. Henderson, ed., *John Strachan: Documents and Opinions* (Toronto, 1969), 17.

23. Delafield, *Frances Lewis and Morgan Lewis*, 111-112.

24. *NWR*, 4 Mar 1815, Vol. VII, 426.

25. *Montreal Herald*, 11 Mar 1815, 3.

26. *Montreal Herald*, 11 Mar 1815, 3.

27. Le Couteur, Apr 1815, in Graves, ed., *Merry Hearts*, 229.

28. *Montreal Herald*, 11 Mar 1815, 3.

29. *Montreal Herald*, 11 Mar 1815, 3.

30. "Reminiscences of Mrs. Edward Pilkington," 7.

31. PRONI, T/1870/4, Holmes, "Pedestrian Tour," 205.

32. "Reminiscences of Mrs. Edward Pilkington," 7.

33. PANS, MG1, Almon Family Papers, Rebecca Almon to Mary and Catherine Byles, 8 Apr 1815.

34. Elizabeth Kennon to Rachel Mordecai, 21 July 1814, "Kennon Letters," Vol. XXXVII, No. 3 (July 1929), 267.

35. MTRL, L16 A93, Anne Powell to George Murray, 7 Apr 1815.

36. Rosalie Stier Calvert to Charles J. Stier, 10 Mar 1815, in Callcott, *Mistress of Riversdale*, 278.

37. Rosalie Stier Calvert to Henri J. Stier, 20 Mar 1815 in Callcott, *Mistress of Riversdale*, 279.

38. Within this number were slaves and their children who had responded to a proclamation issued in the spring of 1814 by Vice-Admiral Sir Alexander Cochrane to American slaves who wished to "withdraw therefrom, with a view to entering into His Majesty's Service, or of being received as Free Settlers into some of His Majesty's Colonies." According to a list sent by Admiral Cockburn to Admiral Cochrane on 9 May 1814, there were aboard the transport HMS *Lord Collingwood* 36 men, 48 women and 67 children, a total of 151 refugees. See Michael J. Crawford, ed., *The Naval War of 1812: A Documentary History, Volume III*, (Washington, D.C., 2002,) 60-66.

39. Howison, *Sketches of Upper Canada*, 96.

40. *Kingston Chronicle*, 20 Sep 1822, 2.

41. Dowd, *Spirited Resistance*, 107.

42. Dowd, *Spirited Resistance*, 108.

43. Letter from unnamed correspondent to Christine Nairne, 17 Mar 1815, quoted in Wrong, *A Canadian Manor and Its Seigneurs*, 170.

44. Thomas Verchères de Boucherville, in Quaife, ed., *War on the Detroit*, 168-169, 171.

45. *Report of the Loyal and Patriotic Society of Upper Canada*, 1.

46. *Report of the Loyal and Patriotic Society*, 231.

47. *Report of the Loyal and Patriotic Society*, 239.

48. *Report of the Loyal and Patriotic Society*, 241.

49. *Report of the Loyal and Patriotic Society*, 245, 249.

50. *Report of the Loyal and Patriotic Society*, 257.

51. *Report of the Loyal and Patriotic Society*, 259.

52. *Report of the Loyal and Patriotic Society*, 283.

53. *Report of the Loyal and Patriotic Society*, 289.

54. Babcock, *War of 1812 on the Niagara Frontier*, 251.

55. Babcock, *War of 1812 on the Niagara Frontier*, 256, 283-284.

56. Babcock, *War of 1812 on the Niagara Frontier*, 257-266.

57. Babcock, *War of 1812 on the Niagara Frontier*, 267-268.

58. Babcock, *War of 1812 on the Niagara Frontier*, 297.

59. Babcock, *War of 1812 on the Niagara Frontier*, 292, 294-297.

60. Babcock, *War of 1812 on the Niagara Frontier*, 298.

61. Babcock, *War of 1812 on the Niagara Frontier*, 316.

62. *Report of the Loyal and Patriotic Society*, 385.

63. LAC, MG19, F1, vol 17, Account of Property lost by the Honourable William Claus by the enemy at Niagara, between 27th May and the 13th December 1813 inclusive, 101, 106.

64. Statement of Major Givins's Losses, contained in Firth, ed., *The Town of York 1793-1815*, 301.

65. LAC, RG19, E5(a), vol 4358, Jessup claim.

66. *An Act, establishing Rules and Articles for the Government of the Armies of the United States with the Regulations of the War Department Respecting the Same*, 66.

67. Mary Boardman Crowninshield to her mother, 2 Jan 1816, in Francis Boardman Crowninshield, ed., *Letters of Mary Boardman Crowninshield 1815-1816* (Cambridge, Mass., 1905), 35-36.

68. Mary Boardman Crowninshield to her mother, March 1816, in Crowninshield, ed., *Letters of Mary Boardman Crowninshield*, 61-62.

69. Mary Boardman Crowninshield to her mother, March 1816, in Crowninshield, ed., *Letters of Mary Boardman Crowninshield*, 62.

70. Fearon, *Sketches of America*, 294.

71. Mary Boardman Crowninshield to her mother, 6 Apr 1816, in Crowninshield, ed., *Letters of Mary Boardman Crowninshield*, 66-67.

72. Le Couteur, 25 Feb 1815, in Graves, ed., *Merry Hearts*, 223.

Epilogue: "A chaplet of unfading laurels":
The Fates of Women and Men

1. Alexander Mackenzie, *Life of Commodore Oliver Hazard Perry*, (New York, 1841), 234.

2. Skaggs, *Thomas Macdonough*, 200.

3. Charles Paullin, *Commodore John Rodgers: Captain, Commander and Senior Officer of the American Navy, 1773-1838* (Cleveland, Ohio, 1910), 368-369.

4. De Pauw and Hunt, *Remember the Ladies*, 149.

5. Elizabeth Patterson Bonaparte to William Patterson, quoted in Anthony, *Dolley Madison*, 155.

6. William Patterson, quoted in Parton, *Daughters of Genius*, 516.

7. Wyman, *Autobiography of Elizabeth Oakes Prince Smith*, 90.

8. Keith R. Widder, "Magdelaine LaFramboise, Fur Trader and Educator," in Rosalie Troester, ed., *Historic Women of Michigan: A Sesquitennial Celebration* (Detroit, 1987), 8.

9. Vivian Moore, "A Pocahontas of Michigan," *Michigan History*, Vol. 15 (1931), 79.

10. Ellet, *Pioneer Women of the West*, 302-303.

11. Abigail Smith Adams to John Quincy Adams, in Janet Whitney, *Abigail Adams* (Westport, Conn, 1947), 324.

12. Sakovich, "Jane Ferguson," 8-9.

13. Hunter and Bell, eds., *Journal of General Sir Martin Hunter*, 290.

14. The Marquess of Anglesey, *One Leg: The Life and Letters of Henry William Paget First Marquess of Anglesey, K.G., 1768-1845* (London, 1961), 317.

15. Frank B. Risteen, Sr. "Children of Sir John Johnson & Lady Mary Johnson." *Ontario History Society Quarterly Journal*, Vol. LXIII, No. 2 (June 1971), 99-100.

16. Klinck and Talman, eds., *Journal of Major John Norton*, lxxxii.

17. Klinck and Talman, eds., *Journal of Major John Norton*, xci.

18. Klinck and Talman, eds., *Journal of Major John Norton*, xcii-xciv.

19. Elma E. Gray, *Wilderness Christians: The Moravian Mission to the Delaware* (Toronto, 1956), 214-215.

20. Talman, ed., *Loyalist Narratives*, 98.

21. Talman, ed., *Loyalist Narratives*, 358-359.

22. Book of Job, Chapter 1, verse 21.

23. James Kerby to Charles Askin, 1 Apr 1809, quoted in Cruikshank, *Memoir of Col. The Honourable James Kerby*, 13.

24. Atherton, *Narrative of the Suffering & Defeat*, 148-149.

25. Richard Cobbold, *Mary Anne Wellington: The Soldier's Daughter, Wife and Widow* (London, 1846), Vol. 2, 278.

Bibliography

PRIMARY SOURCES

Archival

Archives nationales du Québec, Montreal
  Maurice Nowlan Fonds: Correspondence, 1811-1813
  TL32 S1 S51, Boîte 10: Documentation du Cour des Sessions de la Paix, Dossiers, April 1815
Archives of Ontario, Toronto
  F434. Ridout Family papers
  F536. Joel Stone Family papers
  F662. William Hamilton Merritt papers.
  F995. Sir Gordon Drummond papers
  F996. Stuart Family Papers. File 6.
  MU2635. Military Scrapbook
  MU5856. Merritt Papers
  MS 842. Journal of a Staff Officer
Buffalo & Erie County Public Library, Special Collections, Buffalo, NY
  F129B8B6928, Local History Scrapbook, Vol. 9.
Clements Library, University of Michigan, Ann Arbor
  Jacob Jennings Brown Papers
Connecticut Historical Society, Hartford
  19628-1909: George Howard Autobiography and Record Book.
Decatur House, Washington, DC.
  Papers and correspondence of Stephen and Susan Decatur
Duke University, Perkins Library, Durham, North Carolina
  27706 Diary of Lieutenant John Lang, 19th Light Dragoons
Huntington Library, Marino, California
  Hezekiah Niles Papers, "Battle of Baltimore, 12 September 1814"
Johns Hopkins University, Milton Eisenhower Library, Baltimore
  Lester Levy Collection
Library and Archives of Canada, Ottawa
  Manuscript Group 19
    F1. Claus Family Papers. 1810-1816
  Manuscript Group 23
    H13. Correspondence of Hannah Peters Jarvis
  Manuscript Group 24
    A9. Diary of Anne Elinor Prevost

A57. Journal of Lady Katherine Sherbrooke
B16. Andrew Cochran Papers
C2. Willcocks Diary and Correspondence
F4. Bisshopp Papers
F9. De Watteville Papers
F95. Mulcaster Papers
F128. Jasper Grant Papers
G45. De Salaberry Papers
H4. Journal of John Slade, 1814-1815
H78. Diary of Thomas Porter, 1811-1812
I28. Alicia Cockburn and Charles Sandys Correspondence
I29. Diary of James Pringle
L3. Baby Collection, Correspondence, 1812-1814
L8. Jacques Viger Fonds, "Ma Saberdache," vols 3, 4 and 5
  Manuscript Group 40
    M1. Correspondence of John Johnston, 1813-1815
  Record Group 4
    B28. Secretary and Provincial Secretary Correspondence Lower Canada and Canada East, 1763-1867, Volume 69
  Record Group 5
    A1. Civil Secretary's Correspondence, Upper Canada, Upper Canada Sundries, 1813-1814
    Volume 19, 7738-8287, 8196-8197
  Record Group 8 I, British Military Records
  Record Group 8 IV, Vice Admiralty Court of Nova Scotia
  Record Group 19
    E5(a) Board of Claims for War Losses, Volume 4358
Library of Congress, Washington, DC
  Rodgers Family Papers
Maryland Historical Society, Baltimore
  MS142. Elizabeth Patterson Bonaparte Papers, 1785-1879
Maumee Valley Historical Society, Maumee, Ohio
  John Elliot Hunt Papers
McCord Museum of Canadian History, Montreal
  P.010 Dessaulles Fonds, File 9: Letters of Louis-Joseph Papineau to Rosalie Papineau Dessaulles, 1803-1857

M.21410 Letters of Major-General Barnard Bowes and Major James Johnson, 1810-1812
Metropolitan Toronto Reference Library, Toronto
L16 A93. William Dummer Powell Papers. Correspondence of Anne Powell 1807-1816
Journal of Christopher Hagerman, 1813-1814
National Archives of Britain, Kew, England
Admiralty 37, vol 4338: Muster Lists, HMS *Confiance*, 1814
Colonial Office 42: Canada, Original Correspondence, 1808-1815
War Office 4: Secretary-at-War, Out-letters, 1814-1815
vol 1029: Out-letters, 1814-1815
vol 469: Claims of Wounded Officers 1812-1813
vol 470: Claims of Wounded Officers 1813-1814
vol 471: Claims of Wounded Officers 1814-1815
War Office 23: Royal Hospital Chelsea: Admission Books, Registers and Papers, 1702-1933
vol 105: Register of Awards 1815-1856
vol 123: Compassionate Allowances, Royal Bounty & Relief Fund, 1815-1827
War Office 25: Secretary of State for War, and Related Bodies, Registers
vol 3069: Register of Warrants 1815-1818
vol 3110: Compassionate Papers 1812-1813
vol 748: Returns of Officers' Services
vol 3995: Register of Annual Bounty to Officers' Widows
War Office 27: Office of the Commander-in-Chief:Inspection Returns
vol 126: 40th Foot, 1814 lst Half Year
vol 127: 41st-103rd Foot, 1814, lst Half Year
vol 128: 104th Foot, 1814 lst Half Year
vol 129: 59th Foot, 1814, 2nd Half Year
vol 130: 60th Foot, 1814, 2nd Half Year
vol 134: 50th Foot, 1815 lst Half Year
War Office 30: Miscellaneous Papers
vol 49: Register of Warrants
War Office 81: Judge Advocate General's Office
vol 52: Letter Books
National Archives of the United States, Washington, DC
Record Group 59, War of 1812 Papers of the Department of State 1789-1815. Reel 8. U.S. Marshals' Returns of Enemy Aliens and Prisoners of War, 1812-1815 (Part II), Microfilms 1575 and 1576
Record Group 107, Secretary of War, Registered Series, Letters Received
Record Group 125, Records of the Judge Advocate General, Navy. Court Martial of Captain James Leonard, 1813
National Library of Scotland, Edinburgh

MS 9303/62-74. "A Lady's Campaigns in Canada: Extracts from the Journal of a Subaltern's Wife written in Canada during the years 1812, 1813 and 1814"
National Maritime Museum, London, England
COD/6/4 Papers of Sir Edward Codrington
New York Historical Society, New York
Manuscript Division
John M. O'Connor Papers
Miscellaneous Hunter Manuscripts
Niagara Falls Public Library, Niagara Falls, Canada
Local History Collection
Princeton University, Firestone Library, Princeton, New Jersey
CO280. Livingston Family Papers, Box 52 F23 and F24
Letters of Edward and Louise Livingston
Public Archives of Nova Scotia, Halifax
Manuscript Group 1
Volume 1463E. Diary of Louisa Collins
Volumes 10-17A. Almon Family Papers 1724-1954
Volume 479. Letters & Journal of Bishop Inglis 1785-1814
Manuscript Group 9
Volume 43. Halifax & Districts of Nova Scotia, Scrapbook
Public Record Office, Northern Ireland, Belfast
D/2004/1A/3. Papers of Major-General Robert Ross
T/1870/4. Samuel Holmes: "A Pedestrian Tour to the Falls of Niagara in Upper Canada"
Société Jersiaise, St. Helier, Jersey, Channel Islands
Le Couteur-Sumner Papers: Diaries of Sir John Le Couteur: No.1 July 1815-February 1818
State University of New York, Plattsburgh, NY
Bailey Papers: Diary of the Reverend Eleazer Williams
Suffolk County Council Ipswich Record Office, Ipswich, Suffolk
HA93/9/32-164: De Saumarez Collection. Correspondence of P.B.V. Broke and Louisa Broke.
United Church Archives, Victoria University, Toronto
Journal of the Reverend George Ferguson
University of Guelph, McLaughlin Library, Guelph, Ontario
John Macintosh Duff Collection: Hannah Jarvis Papers, 1811: XR1 MS A210088, Cookbook with health remedies
University of North Carolina, Durham
Davis Library, Southern Historical Collection: 404 Edmund Kirby-Smith Papers 1796-1906

Period Newspapers and Periodicals

Annual Register, or a View of the History, Politics, and Literature, for the Year 1811

Bath Chronicle, 1814

Boston Gazette, 1812-1815

Buffalo Evening News, 1813-1814

Buffalo Gazette, 1813-1815

Columbian Centinel, 1813-1815

Connecticut Gazette, 1812-1815

Kingston Chronicle, 1822

Kingston Gazette, 1812-1815

Ladies Monthly Museum or Polite Repository of Amusements and Instruction, Vol. XVII, 1814.

Louisiana Gazette and New Orleans Daily Advertiser, 1812-1815

Montreal Gazette, 1813-1814

Montreal Herald, 1811-1815

New York Evening Post, 1812-1815

Niles' Weekly Register. Vol.I, September 1811-March 1812; Vol.II, March-September 1812; Vol.III, September 1812-March 1813; Vol.IV, March-September 1813; Vol.V, September 1813-March 1814; Vol. VI, March-September 1814; Vol. VII, September 1814-March 1815; Vol. VIII March-September 1815

Norfolk Gazette and Public Ledger, 1806

Nova Scotia Royal Gazette, 1811-1813

Poulson's Weekly Advertizer, 1813

Quebec Gazette, 1811-1812

Repository of Arts, Literature, Commerce, Manufactures, Fashions and Politics, The. Second Series. Vol. I, No. 1.

Richmond Enquirer, 1812-1813

Royal Gazette and New Brunswick Advertizer, 1812

The Times [London], 1811-1813

Upper Canada Gazette, 1808-1811.

Upper Canada Guardian and Freeman's Gazette, 1810

Published Document Collections

Brannan, John, ed.. *Official Letters of the Military and Naval Officers of the United States During the War with Great Britain in the Years 1812, 13, 14 & 15.* Washington: Way & Gideon, 1823.

Firth, Edith G, ed. *The Town of York 1793-1815. A Collection of Documents of Early Toronto.* Toronto: The Champlain Society, 1962

Crawford, Michael J., ed. *The Naval War of 1812: A Documentary History. Volume III.* Washington, D.C: The Naval Historical Center, 2002.

Cruikshank, Ernest A., ed. *Documentary History of the Campaigns upon the Niagara Frontier in 1812-1814* [titles vary slightly]. Welland: Tribune Press, 1896-1908, 9 vols.

———, ed. *Documents Relating to the Invasion of Canada and the Surrender of Detroit, 1812.* Ottawa: Dominion Archives, 1913, reprinted New York, Arno Press, 1971.

Naval Documents Related to the United States' Wars with the Barbary Powers. Washington: Government Printing Office, 9 vols, 1939-1944.

Dudley, William S., ed. *The Naval War of 1812: A Documentary History. Volume II.* Washington, D.C.: Naval Historical Center, Department of the Navy, 1992.

Published Correspondence, Diaries, Journals and Memoirs

Adams, Charles Francis, ed. *Letters of Mrs. Adams, the Wife of John Adams.* Boston: Wilkins, Carter & Company, 1848.

Anonymous. *Canadian Letters: Description of a Tour thro' the Provinces of Lower and Upper Canada in the Courses of the Years 1792 & 1793.* Montreal; E.A. Marchand, 1912

———, "First Campaign of An A.D.C.", *Military and Naval Magazine of the United States* Vol. I. No. 1, 1833: 153-162; No. 2, July 1833: 257-267; No. 5, 1834: 200-210; No. 6, 1834: 278-288; No. 8, June 1834: 258-266; No. 9, July 1834: 329-338; No. 10, August 1834: 437-446; No. 11, September 1834: 26-34; No. 12, April 1835: 85-93; No. 13, June 1835: 253-261.

Atherton, William. *Narrative of the Suffering & Defeat of the North-Western Army, under General Winchester.* Frankfort, Kentucky: A.G. Hodges, 1842.

Beall, William K., "Journal of William K. Beall, July-August 1812," *American Historical Review*, Volume 17 (July 1912), No. 4, 783-808.

Bentley, Nicolas., ed. *Selections from the Reminiscences of Captain Gronow.* London: Folio Society, 1977

Bonney, Catherina W.R. (Catharine Rensselaer), ed. *Legacy of Historical Gleanings.* Albany, New York: J. Munsell, 1875.

Bouchette, Joseph. *Topographical Description of the Province of Lower Canada with remarks upon Upper Canada.* London: W. Faden, 1815.

Bourchier, Lady, ed. *Memoir of the Life of Admiral Sir Edward Codrington.* London: Longman, Green and Co., 1873, 2 vols.

Boutflower, Charles. *The Journal of an Army Surgeon during the Peninsular War.* Staplehurst, Kent: Spellmount 1997.

Bristol, Mary Ann Brevoort, "Reminiscences of the Northwest," *Wisconsin Historical Collections*, Volume VIII (1879), 293-308.

Bryan, W.B. ed. "Diary of Mrs. William Thornton. Capture of Washington by the British." *Columbia Historical Society Proceedings* 19 (1916) 173-182.

Buckley, Roger N., ed., *The Napoleonic War Journal of Captain Thomas Henry Browne 1807-1816.* London: Army Records Society, 1987.

Callcott, Margaret Law, ed. *Mistress of Riversdale: The Plantation Letters of Rosalie Stier Calvert, 1795-1821.* Baltimore and London: Johns Hopkins University Press, 1991.

Casselman, Alexander Clark, ed. *Richardson's War of 1812.* Toronto: Coles Publishing Company Limited, Facsimile edition 1974.

Chamier, Frederick. *The Life of a Sailor.* London: R. Bentley, 1832, 2 vols.

Clark, Allen C., ed. *Life and Letters of Dolly Madison.* Washington, D.C. Press of W.F. Roberts Company, 1914.

Cook, Clarence, ed. *A Girl's Life Eighty Years Ago: Selections from the Letters of Eliza Southgate Bowne.* New York: Charles Scribner, 1887.

Cooper, John Spencer. *Rough Notes of Seven Campaigns, 1809-1815.* Staplehurst, Kent: Spellmount, 1996.

Crawford, Mary M., ed., "Mrs Lydia Bacon's Journal, 1811-1812," *Indiana Magazine of History,* Volume 40 (December 1944) 367-386; Volume 41 (March 1945) 59-79.

Crowninshield, Francis Boardman, ed. *Letters of Mary Boardman Crowninshield 1815-1816.* Cambridge, Ma.: Riverside Press, 1905.

Cruikshank, E.A., ed., "A Memoir of Colonel The Honourable James Kerby, His Life in Letters." *Welland County Historical Society Papers and Records,* Volume IV (1931), 17-37.

Cutts, Lucia B., ed. *Memoirs and letters of Dolly Madison, wife of James Madison, President of the United States.* Boston: Houghton Mifflin & Co., 1886.

Deveau, J. Alphonse. ed. *Diary of a Frenchman: François Lambert Bourneuf's Adventures from France to Acadia 1787-1871.* Halifax: Nimbus Publishing, 1990.

De Wolfe Howe, M.A., ed. *The Articulate Sisters: Passages from the Journals and Letters of the Daughters of President Josiah Quincy of Harvard University.* Cambridge, Mass: Harvard University Press, 1946.

Donaldson, Joseph. *Recollections of the Eventful Life of a Soldier.* 1853, reprinted Staplehurst, Kent: Spellmount, 2000.

Dulles, Charles W. ed., "Extracts from the Diary of Joseph Heatly Dulles." *Pennsylvania Magazine of History & Biography* 35 (October 1925), 80-83.

Duncan, John. *Travels through part of the United States and Canada in 1818 and 1819* (2 volumes), Glasgow: Hurst Robinson & Co., Oliver & Boyd, and Wardlaw & Cunningham, 1823, 2 vols.

Dunlap, William. *Diary of William Dunlap (1766-1839): The Memoirs of a Dramatist, Theatrical Manager, Painter, Critic, Novelist, and Historian.* Reprinted New York/London: Benjamin Bloom, 1969, 2 vols.

Dunlop, William. *Tiger Dunlop's Upper Canada.* Toronto: McClelland and Stewart, 1967.

Durova, Nadezhda. *The Cavalry Maid: The Memoirs of a Woman Soldier of 1812.* Ardis, Ann Arbor, Michigan, 1988.

Edgar, Matilda. *Ten Years of Upper Canada in Peace and War, 1805-1815: Being the Ridout Letters.* London: T. Fisher Unwin, 1891.

Emery, Sarah Anna ed. *Reminiscences of A Nonagenarian.* Newburyport, Mass. William H. Huse, 1879.

Everest, Allan S. ed. *Recollections of Clinton County and the Battle of Plattsburgh 1800-1840.* Plattsburgh, NY: Clinton County Historical Association, 1964.

Ewart, James. *James Ewart's Journal.* Cape Town: C. Struik, 1970.

Fairchild, G.M. ed. *Journal of an American Prisoner at Fort Malden and Quebec in the War of 1812,* Quebec: Daily Telegraph Printing Co., 1909.

Fearon, Henry Bradshaw. *Sketches of America: A Narrative of A Journey of Five Thousand Miles Through the Eastern and Western States of America.* London: Longman, Hurst, Rees, Orme and Brown, 1818.

Fisher, Deborah Ames, "Salem Social Life in the Early Nineteenth Century. Familiar Letters written between 1812 and 1831 from Friends in Salem to a Salem school girl removed to Ohio," *Historical Collections of the Essex Institute,* Volume XXXVI, No. 2 (April 1900), 105-127.

Fitzmaurice, Mrs. *Recollections of A Rifleman's Wife At Home and Abroad.* London: Hope and Co., 1851.

Fletcher, Ian, ed. *In the Service of the King: The Letters of William Thornton Keep at Home, Walcheren, and in the Peninsula, 1810-1814.* Staplehurst, Kent: Spellmount, 1997.

Fredriksen, John C. ed., "Chronicle of Valour: The Journal of a Pennsylvania Officer in the War of 1812." *Western Pennsylvania Historical Magazine* 676 (July 1984), 243-284.

———, *Surgeon of the Lakes: The Diary of Dr. Usher Parsons 1812-1814.* Erie, Pennsylvania: Erie County Historical Society, 2000.

Gellner, John, ed. *Recollections of the War of 1812: Three Eyewitness Accounts.* Toronto: Baxter, 1964.

Gleig, George R. *The Campaigns of the British Army at Washington & New Orleans.* Reprinted: East Ardsley, Yorkshire: EP Publishing Limited, 1972.

Grattan, William. *Adventures with the Connaught Rangers, 1809-1814.* London: 1902, reprinted Greenhill, 1989.

Graves, Donald E., ed. *Merry Hearts Make Light Days: The War of 1812 Journal of Lieutenant John Le Couteur, 104th Regiment of Foot.* Ottawa: Carleton University, 1993.

Greeley, Susan Burnham, "Sketches of the Past," *Ontario Historical Society Papers & Records*, Volume XXIII (1926), 243-260.

Green, John. *Viccissitudes of a Soldier's Life*. London: Simpkin & Marshall, 1827.

Green, Mary Stickney, "Reminiscences of Travel on the Maumee River in 1815," *Daily Toledo Blade*, 23 February 1867.

Hall, Roger, and Shelton, S.W. *The Rising Country: The Hale-Amherst correspondence 1799-1825*. Toronto: Champlain Society, 2002.

Hamilton, James. *The Life, and Dying Confessions of James Hamilton, executed for the Murder of Major Benjain Birdsall, Nov 6, 1818 at Albany*. New York: Printing Store, corner of Wall and Broad Streets, 1818.

Hayward, Lydia Barker, "The Escape of Lydia Hayward (taken from Narrative of Mrs. Lydia [Barker] Hayward, including the Life, Experience, Call to the Ministry and Extensive Travels of Her Husband, the late Elder Joshua Hayward," *The Hay Bay Guardian*, No.5 (1997), 2-10.

Heriot, George. *Travels Through the Canadas*. London, 1807, reprinted Toronto: Coles, 1971. 2 vols.

Hibbert, Christopher, ed. *Captain Gronow: His Reminiscences of Regency and Victorian Life 1810-60*. London: Kyle Cathie, 1991.

Horner, William, "A Military Hospital at Buffalo New York in the year 1814," *The Medical Examiner and Record of Medical Science*, No XCVI (December 1852), 753-774.

Howard, Florence and Howard, Mary, eds. "The Letters of John Patterson, 1812-1813." *Pennsylvania Historical Magazine*, 23 (July 1940), 99-109.

Howison, John. *Sketches of Upper Canada, Domestic, Local and Characteristic*. Edinburgh: Oliver and Boyd, 1825.

Hunt, Gaillard, ed. *The First Forty Years of Washington Society portrayed by the Family Letters of Mrs. Samuel Harrison Smith*. New York: Scribner's, 1906.

Hunt, Louise Livingston, ed. *Memoir of Mrs. Edward Livingston with Letters Hitherto Unpublished*. New York: Harper & Brothers, 1886.

Hunter, Anne and Bell, Elizabeth, eds. *The Journal of General Sir Martin Hunter and Some Letters of his Wife, Lady Hunter*. Edinburgh: The Edinburgh Press, 1894.

Hunter, Mary, "The Burning of Washington, D.C.", *New York Historical Society Bulletin*, Volume 8, No. 3, (October 1924), 80-83.

Jennings, Paul, "A Coloured Man's Reminiscences of James Madison," *White House History*, vol 1, No. 1 (1983), 46-51.

Kennon, Elizabeth Beverly. "Kennon Letters." *Virginia Magazine of History and Biography* 34 (April, July, October, 1926): 120-124; 220-231; 322-338; 35 (January, July 1927): 13-21; 287-292; 36 (April, July, October, 1928): 170-174; 213-238; 363-370; 37 (January, April, July, October 1929): 46-51; 143-153; 261-268; 335-338.

Kincaid, John. *Random Shots From a Rifleman*. Staplehurst, Kent: Spellmount, 1998.

Klinck, Carl F. and Talman, James J., eds. *The Journal of Major John Norton, 1816*. Toronto: Champlain Society, 1970.

Kyte, E.C., ed., "Fort Niagara in the War of 1812," *Canadian Historical Review*, 17 (1936), 373-384.

Landmann, George. *Adventures and Recollections of Colonel Landmann, late of the Corps of Royal Engineers*. London: Colburn and Co., 1852, 2 vols.

Larpent, Francis Seymour. *The Private Journal of Judge-Advocate Larpent attached to the Headquarters of Lord Wellington during the Peninsular War, from 1812 to its close*. 1854, reprinted Staplehurst, Kent: Spellmount, 2000.

Leech, Samuel. *Thirty Years from Home, or A Voice from the Main Deck, being the experience of Samuel Leech*. Boston: Tappan & Dermet, 1843.

Leslie, Charles L. *Memoirs of Col. Leslie: Whilst serving with the 29th Regiment in the Peninsula and the 60th Rifles in Canada*. Aberdeen: Aberdeen University, 1887.

Liddell Hart, Captain B.H., ed. *The Letters of Private Wheeler 1809-1828*. London: Michael Joseph, 1951.

Lindley, Harlow, ed. *Fort Meigs and the War of 1812. Orderly Book of Cushing's Company and Personal Diary of Captain Daniel Cushing*. Columbus: Ohio Historical Society, 1975

Malcomson, Robert ed. *Sailors of 1812: Memoirs and Letters of Naval Officers on Lake Ontario*. Youngstown, New York: Old Fort Niagara Association, 1997.

Mann, James. *Medical Sketches of the Campaigns of 1812,1813, 1814: to which are added surgical cases, observations on military hospitals and flying hospitals attached to a moving army*. Dedham, Mass: H. Mann & Co., 1816.

McClure, George. *Causes of the Destruction of the American Towns on the Niagara Frontier and Failure of the Campaign of the Fall of 1813*. Bath, NY: 1817.

McGuffie, T.H. ed. *Peninsular Cavalry General 1811-1813*. London: George G. Harrap & Co., 1951.

Miller, Genevieve, ed. *William Beaumont's Formative Years. Two Early Notebooks 1811-1821*. New York: Henry Schuman, 1946.

Moore Smith, G.C., ed. *The Autobiography of Lieutenant General Sir Harry Smith*. London: John Murray, 1901.

Myers, Mordecai. *Reminiscences 1780-1814. Including Incidents in the War of 1812-14.* Washington, D.C.: The Crane Company, 1900.

Nasty-Face, Jack. *Nautical Economy or Forecastle Recollections of Events during the Last War, by a Sailor politely called by the officers of the Navy Jack Nasty-Face.* London: no date.

Nevens, William. *Forty Years at Sea, or a Narrative of the Adventures of William Nevens.* Portland, Maine: S.H. Colesworthy, 1847.

Nolte, Vincent. *Fifty Years in Both Hemispheres, or Reminiscences of the Life of a Former Merchant.* New York: Redfield, 1854.

O'Reilly, Isabelle M., ed., "Hero of Fort Erie: The Correspondence of Lieutenant P. McDonogh," *Publications of the Buffalo Historical Society*, Vol. V (1902), 63-93

Pilkington, Mrs Edward, "Reminiscences of Mrs. Edward Pilkington, *Family History and Reminiscences of Early Settlers* No 28, 5-9, Niagara Historical Society, Niagara-on-the-Lake, 1915.

Pingey, Charles. *A Narrative of a few of the Scenes and Incidents that occured in the Sanguinary and Cruel War of 1812-14 between England and the United States.* Norway: Advertiser Press, 1853.

Porter, Daniel R., ed., "Jacob Porter Norton: A Yankee on the Niagara Frontier in 1814," *Niagara Frontier*, Vol. 12 (1965), 51-57.

Quaife, Milo Milton, ed. *War on the Detroit: The Chronicles of Thomas Verchères de Boucherville and The Capitulation by an Ohio Volunteer.* Chicago: The Lakeside Press, 1940.

Raymond, William Odber, ed. *Winslow Papers, A.D. 1776-1826.* St. John, New Brunswick: Sun Printing, 1901.

Severance, Frank, H., ed. "Recalling Pioneer Days," *Publications of the Buffalo Historical Society*, Vol XXVI (1922).

Sigourney, Lydia H. *Letters of Life 1791-1865.* New York: Arno Press, 1980.

Smith, Michael. *A Geographical View of the Province of Upper Canada and promiscuous remarks on the Government.* Trenton: Moore and Lake; William & David Robinson, 1813.

Spalding, Lyman. *Recollections of the War of 1812 and Early Life in Western New York. No. 2.* Lockport, New York: Niagara County Historical Society, 1949.

Spragge, George W. ed. *The John Strachan Letter Book: 1812-1834.* Toronto: Ontario Historical Society, 1946.

Surtees, William. *Twenty-five Years in the Rifle Brigade.* London: Greenhill, 1996.

Sutherland Stuart, ed. "A Desire of Serving and Defending My Country": The War of 1812 journals of William Hamilton Merritt.* Toronto: Iser Publications, 2001.

Swift, Joseph Gardner. *The Memoirs of General Joseph Gardner Swift, LL.D.* Privately printed, 1890.

Talman, James J., ed. *Loyalist Narratives from Upper Canada.* New York: Greenwood Press, 1969.

Temperley, Howard., ed. *Lieutenant-Colonel Joseph Gubbins: New Brunswick Journals of 1811 and 1813.* Fredericton: New Brunswick Heritage Publications, 1980.

Tracy, Nicolas, ed., *The Naval Chronicle; The Contemporary Record of the Royal Navy at War. Consolidated Edition. Volume III, 1804-1806.* London: Chatham, 1999

Tupper, Ferdinand Brock, ed. *The Life and Correspondence of Major-General Sir Isaac Brock, K.B.* London: Simpkin, Marshall & Co., 1847.

Turner, Elder, Death of Mr. Job Hoisington," *Publications of the Buffalo Historical Society*, Vol. IX. Buffalo, vol 2 (1880), 392.

Viger, Jacques. *Reminiscences of the War of 1812-14. Being portions of the Diary of a Captain of the Voltigeurs Canadiens while at Garrison in Kingston.* Kingston: News Printing Company, 1895.

Warner, R.I., ed., "Memoirs of Captain John Lampman and his Wife Mary Secord," *Welland County Historical Society Papers and Records*, Volume III (1927), 126-134.

White, Samuel. *History of the American Troops During the War, under the command of Colonels Fenton and Campbell.* Rochester, New York: C. Mann, 1896.

Whitehill, Walter Muir, ed. *New England Blockaded in 1814: The Journal of Henry Edward Napier.* Salem: Peabody Museum, 1939.

Wilmer, James Jones. *Narrative Respecting the Conduct of the British from their first landing on Spesutia Island, till their progress to Havre de Grace.* Baltimore: P. Mauro, 1813.

Wyman, Mary A., ed. *Selections from the Autobiography of Elizabeth Oakes (Prince) Smith.* New York: Arno Press, 1980.

Period Books on Medicine, Domestic Matters and Gardening

Culpeper, Nicolas. *Culpeper's English Physician and Complete Herbal ... with Notes ... by E. Sibley.* London: 1798.

Ewell, James. *Planter's and Mariner's Medical Companion.* Philadelphia: Anderson & Meehan, 1816.

Glasse, Hannah. *The Art of Cookery, Made Plain and Easy.* First American edition published Alexandria, Virginia, 1805. Reprinted: Bedford, Mass: Applewood Books, 1997.

Gregory, John. *A Father's Legacy to his Daughters.* 1774. Reprinted New York: Garland Publishers, 1974.

Rundell, Eliza. *A New System of Domestic Cookery, formed upon the principles of Economy and adapted to the use of private families throughout the United States by a Lady.* New York: R. McDermut & D.S. Arden, 1815.

Simmons, Amelia. *American Cookery or the Art of Dressing Viands, Fish, Poultry and Vegetables and the best mode of making puff-pastes, pies, tarts, pudding, custards and preserves and all kinds of Cakes from the Imperial Plumb to plain cake. Adapted this country, and all grades of life.* Poughkeepsie, New York: Paraclete Potter, 1815.

White, Charles. *A Treatise on the Management of Pregnant and Lying-in Women and the Means of Curing, but more especially of the principal Disorders to which they are liable.* Worcester, Mass: Isaiah Thomas, 1793.

Period Military Manuals, Regulations and Treatises

Cuthbertson, Bennett. *A System for the Complete Interior Management and Oeconomy of A Battalion of Infantry.* London: J. Millan, 1779.

Great Britain, Admiralty. *Regulations and Instructions Relating to His Majesty's Service at Sea.* London: Admiralty, 1806

————, *Regulations and Instructions Relating to His Majesty's Service at Sea.* London: Admiralty, 1808

————, War Office. *Articles of War. Rules and Articles for the Better Government of His Majesty's Horse and Foot Guards and all other of His Majesty's Forces in Great Britain and Ireland, Dominions Beyond the Seas, and Foreign Parts, From the 24th Day of March, 1778.* London: Charles Eyre and William Strachan, 1778

————, War Office. *General Regulations and Orders for the Army.* Cork: A. Edwards, 1805.

————, War Office. *General Regulations and Order for the Army 1811.* Facsimile edition, Frederick Muller Ltd., 1970.

————, War Office. *Regulations for Regimental Surgeons, &c., for the Better Management of the Sick in Regimental Hospitals.*

The Military Mentor, being a Series of Letters recently written by a General Officer to his son on entering the Army: Comprising a Course of Elegant Instruction, calculated to unite the Characters and Accomplishments of the Gentleman and the Soldier. London, printed for Richard Phillips, 1804, 2 vols.

Reide, Thomas. *The Staff Officer's Manual.* London, T. Egerton, 1806.

United States, War Department. *An Act Establishing Rules and Articles for the Government of the Armies of the United States; with the Regulations of the War Department respecting the same.* Albany: Websters and Skinners, 1812.

————. *An Act fixing the Military Peace Establishment of the United States.* Albany: Websters and Skinners, 1812.

————. *Articles of War, Military Laws and Rules and Regulations for the Army of the United States.* Adjutant and Inspector General's Office: E. de Krafft, 1816.

————. *The Army Register of the United States.* Boston: Chester Stebbins, 1814.

————. *Rules and Regulations for the Army for 1813.* Washington: 1813.

SECONDARY SOURCES

Biographical Encyclopedias, Registers and Dictionaries

Debrett's Peerage & Baronetage, 106th Edition. Crans, Switzerland: Burke's Peerage (Genealogical Books) Ltd., 1999.

Dictionary of American Biography. New York; Scribner, 1958-1962, 22 vols.

Dictionary of Canadian Biography. Toronto: University of Toronto Press, Vols. V-IX, 1976-1988.

[Grose, Francis]. *1811 Dictionary of the Vulgar Tongue: A Dictionary of Buckish Slang, University Wit and Pickpocket Eloquence.* Northfield, Ill. Digest Books Inc., 1971.

Morgan, Henry James, ed. *Types of Canadian Women and of Women who are or have been connected with Canada,* Volume I. Toronto: William Briggs, 1903.

O'Byrne, William R., ed. *A Naval Biographical Dictionary.* London: John Murray, 1849.

Oxford Dictionary of Quotations. Oxford: University Press, 1941.

Stephen, Leslie and Sidney Lee, eds. *Dictionary of National Biography,* Volumes II, IV, IX, XVII, XVIII. Oxford: Oxford University Press, 1921

Sutherland, Stuart, ed. *His Majesty's Gentlemen: A Directory of British Regular Army Officers of the War of 1812.* Toronto: Iser Publications, 2000.

Published Books

Adams, Henry. *History of the United States During the Administration of James Madison 1813-1817.* New York: A.C. Boni, 1930, 4 vols.

Allen, Robert S. *His Majesty's Indian Allies: British Indian Policy in the Defence of Canada, 1774-1815.* Toronto: Dundurn Press, 1992.

Ames, William E. *A History of the National Intelligencer.* Chapel Hill: University of North Carolina, 1972.

Anglesey, The Marquess of, F.S.A. *One-Leg: The Life*

and Letters of Henry William Paget First Marquess of Anglesey, K.G., 1768-1845. London: Jonathan Cape, 1961.

Anonymous. A Biographical Memoir of the Late Sir Peter Parker, Baronet, Captain of H.M. Ship Menelaus. London: Longman, Hurst, Rees, Orme, and Brown, 1815.

Antal, Sandor. A Wampum Denied: Procter's War of 1812. Ottawa: Carleton University, 1997.

Anthony, Katharine. Dolly Madison: Her Life and Times. Garden City, NY: Doubleday, 1949.

Atwood, Margaret. Canada's Illustrated Heritage. Days of the Rebels 1815-1840. Toronto: Natural Science, 1977.

Babcock, Louis L. The War of 1812 on the Niagara Frontier. Buffalo, New York: Buffalo Historical Society, 1927.

Bailey, John R., Mackinac, formerly Michilimackinac. Lansing, Michigan: D.D. Thorp, 1895.

Bamfield, Veronica. On the Strength: The Story of the British Army Wife. London and Tonbridge: Charles Knight & Company Ltd., 1974.

Barbeau, Marius. Jongleur Songs of Old Quebec, New Brunswick, NJ: Rutgers University, 1962.

Baynham, Henry. From the Lower Deck: The Royal Navy 1780-1840. Barre Mass: Barre Publishers, 1970.

Bear, James A. Jefferson at Monticello. Charlottesville: University of Virginia, 1981.

Benn, Carl. The Iroquois in the War of 1812. Toronto: University of Toronto, 1998.

———. Historic Fort York 1793-1993. Toronto: Natural Heritage/Natural History, 1993.

Benn, Carl, Giles Bryant, William Cooke, Paul Friesen, Alan Hayes, C. Thomas McIntire and Shirley Morriss. The Parish and Cathedral of St James', Toronto 1797-1997. Toronto: St. James' Cathedral, 1998.

Berton, Pierre, The Invasion of Canada 1812-1813, Toronto: McClelland & Stewart, 1980.

Bingham, Robert W. The Cradle of the Queen City: A History of Buffalo to the Incorporation of the City. Buffalo: Buffalo Historical Society, 1931

Blanco, Richard L. Wellington's Surgeon General: Sir James McGrigor. Durham, N.C.: Duke University, 1974.

Brice, Wallace A. History of Fort Wayne. Fort Wayne: D.W. Jones, 1868.

Brooks, Charles B. The Siege of New Orleans. Seattle: University of Washington Press, 1961.

Bryant, Arthur. The Years of Endurance, 1973-1802. London: Collins, 1948.

Buel, Elizabeth C. Barney, ed. Chronicles of a Pioneer School from 1792-1833, being the History of Miss Sarah Pierce and her Litchfield School. Cambridge,

Mass: University Press, 1903.

Calver, William Louis, and Bolton, Reginald Pelham. History Written with Pick and Shovel. New York: New York Historical Society, 1950.

Carnochan, Janet. History of Niagara. Toronto: William Briggs, 1914.

Centennial History of the Fredonia Baptist Church 1808-1908. Buffalo: The Matthews Northrup Works, 1908

Chartrand, René. Canadian Military Heritage. Volume II 1755-1871. Montreal: Art Global, 1995.

Clark, Anna. Women's Silence, men's violence: sexual assault in England, 1770-1845. New York: Pandora, 1987.

Clift, Garrett Glen. Remember the Raisin! Kentucky and Kentuckians in the battles and massacre at Frenchtown, Michigan Territory, in the War of 1812. Frankfort, Kentucky: Kentucky Historical Papers, 1961.

Coates, Colin M. and Morgan, Cecilia. Heroines and History: Representations of Madeleine de Verchères and Laura Secord. Toronto: University of Toronto, 2002.

Cobbold, Richard. Mary Anne Wellington: The Soldier's Daughter, Wife and Widow. London: H. Coulbourn, 1846, 2 vols.

Coffin, William F. 1812: The War, And Its Moral: A Canadian Chronicle. Montreal: John Lovell, 1864.

Cohen, Daniel A. The Female Marine and Related Works: Narratives of Cross-Dressing and Urban Vice in America's Early Republic. Amherst, Mass: University of Massachusetts, 1997.

Compton, Piers. Colonel's Lady and Camp-Follower: The Story of Women in the Crimean War. London: Robert Hale, 1970.

Cordingly, David. Women Sailors and Sailors' Women: An Untold Maritime History. New York: Random House, 2001.

Cranton, Willa G. Women Beyond the Frontier: A Distaff View of Life at Fort Wayne. Historic Fort Wayne, 1977.

Crary, Catherine S. The Price of Loyalty: Tory Writings from the Revolutionary Era. New York: McGraw Hill, 1973.

Crawford, Mary. Romantic Days in the Early Republic. Boston: Little, Brown, 1912.

De Kay, James Tertius. The Battle of Stonington: Torpedoes, Submarines and Rockets in the War of 1812. Annapolis, Maryland: The Naval Institute Press, 1990.

———. Chronicles of the Frigate Macedonian 1809-1922. London: W.W. Norton & Company, 2000.

Delafield, Julia. Biographies of Frances Lewis and Morgan Lewis. New York: A. Randolph, 1877.

De Pauw, Linda Grant and Hunt, Conover. "Remember the Ladies": Women in America, 1750-1815. New York: Viking Press, 1976.

De Watteville, H. *The British Soldier: His Daily Life from Tudor to Modern Times.* London: J.M. Dent, 1954.

Dowd, Gregory Evans. *A Spirited Resistance: The North American Indian Struggle for Unity, 1745-1815.* Baltimore, Johns Hopkins University, 1992.

Dumont, Micheline, Michèle Jean, Marie Lavigne and Jennifer Stoddart. *Quebec Women: A History.* Toronto: Women's Press, 1987.

Dunnigan, Brian Leigh. *Frontier Metropolis: Picturing Early Detroit, 1701-1838.* Detroit: Wayne State University, 2001.

Dutton, Charles J. *Oliver Hazard Perry.* New York: Longmans Green & Co., 1935.

Ellet, Mrs. E.F. *The Court Circles of the Republic, or the Beauties and Celebrities of the Nation.* Hartford, Conn.: Hartford Publishing, 1870.

———. *Pioneer Women of the West.* New York: Charles Scribner, 1856.

Errington, Elizabeth Jane. *Wives and Mothers School Mistresses and Scullery Maids: Working Women in Upper Canada, 1790-1840.* Montreal and Kingston: McGill-Queen's University Press, 1995.

Evans, Elizabeth. *Weathering the Storm: Women of the American Revolution.* New York: Charles Scribner, 1975.

Everest, Allan S. *The War of 1812 in the Champlain Valley.* Syracuse: Syracuse University Press, 1981.

Field, John L. ed. *Bicentennial Stories of Niagara-on-the-Lake.* Lincoln: Rannie Publications, 1981.

Fitzgibbon, Mary Agnes. *A Veteran of 1812.* Toronto, 1898: reprinted Prospero Books, 2000.

Flower, Milton. *James Parton: The Father of Modern Biography.* Durham, NC: Duke University, 1951.

Foley, Robert. *The War of 1812: Niagara Story.* Volume 2. Niagara Falls: The Haunted Press, 1994.

George, Christopher. *Terror on the Chesapeake: The War of 1812 on the Bay.* Shippensburg, PA: White Mane Books, 2000.

Gilfoyle, Timothy. *City of Eros: New York City, Prostitution and the Commercialization of Sex, 1790-1920.* New York, W.W. Norton, 1992.

Gillett, Mary C. *The Army Medical Department, 1775-1818.* Washington, D.C.: Center of Military History, United States Army, 1981.

Glover, Richard. *Peninsular Preparation.* Cambridge: Cambridge University Press, 1963.

Graves, Donald E. *Where Right and Glory Lead! The Battle of Lundy's Lane, 1814.* Toronto: Robin Brass Studio, 1997.

———. *South Albertas: A Canadian Regiment at War.* Toronto: Robin Brass Studio, 1998.

———. *Field of Glory: The Battle of Crysler's Farm, 1813.* Toronto: Robin Brass Studio, 1999.

Gray, Elma E. *Wilderness Christians: The Moravian Mission to the Delaware.* Toronto: Macmillan, 1956.

Green, Constance McLaughlin. *Washington: Village and Capital, 1800-1878.* Princeton, NJ: Princeton University Press, 1962.

Guillet, Edwin C. *Pioneer Social Life.* Toronto: The Ontario Publishing Company Ltd., 1938.

———. *Pioneer Arts and Crafts.* Toronto: University of Toronto, 1960.

Guitard, Michelle. *The Militia of the Battle of Châteauguay: A Social History.* Ottawa: Parks Canada, 1983.

Harvey, A.D. *Sex in Georgian England: Attitudes and Prejudices from the 1720s to the 1820s.* London: Phoenix Press, 2001.

Hart, Roger. *England Expects.* London: Wayland, 1972.

Henderson, J.L.H. ed. *John Strachan: Documents and Opinions.* Toronto: McClelland and Stewart, 1969.

Hickey, Donald R. *Don't Give Up the Ship! Myths of the War of 1812.* Toronto: Robin Brass Studio, 2006.

Hill, Henry Wayland. *Municipality of Buffalo, New York: A History 1720-1923.* Volume I. Lewis. New York: Lewis Historical Publishing Co., 1923.

Hitsman, J.M. *The Incredible War of 1812.* Updated by Donald E. Graves. Toronto: Robin Brass Studio, 1999

Hoehling, A.A. *Women Who Spied: True Stories of Feminine Espionage from the American Revolution to the Present Day.* Lanham, MD: Madison Books, 1993.

Holcombe, Lee. *Wives and Property: Reform of the Married Women's Property Law in Nineteenth-Century England.* Toronto: University of Toronto Press, 1983.

Holmes, Richard. *Redcoat: The British Soldier in the Age of Horse and Musket.* London: Harper Collins, 2001.

Hough, Franklin B. *A History of St. Lawrence and Franklin Counties, New York, from the Earliest Period to the Present Time.* Harrison, NY: Harbor Hill Books, 1970.

Hounsom, Eric Wilfrid. *Toronto in 1810.* Toronto: Ryerson Press, 1970.

Hunt, Gaillard. *Life In America One Hundred Years Ago.* New York: Harper & Brothers, 1914.

Hunt-Jones, Conover. *Dolley and the "great little Madison".* Washington: American Institute of Architects Foundation, 1977.

Ingersoll, Charles J. *Historical Sketch of the Second War between the United States of America and Great Britain.* Philadelphia: Lea & Blanchard, 1849, 2 vols.

Jenness, Diamond. *The Indians of Canada.* Toronto: University of Toronto Press, 1977.

Johnson, Crisfield. *Centennial History of Erie County, New York: Being its Annals from the Earliest Recorded Events to the Hundredth Year of American Independence.* Buffalo: Matthews & Warren, 1876.

Johnston, Sally, Beth Miller and Pat Pilling. *The Star-*

Spangled Banner House: Home of America's Flag. Lawrenceburg, Indiana: R.L. Ruehrwein, 1999.

Johnston, Winston. *The Glengarry Light Infantry, 1812-1816: who were they and what did they do in the war?* Charlottetown: Benson Publishing, 1998.

Keats, John. *The Poetical Works of John Keats.* London: Frederick Warne and Co., Undated.

Kelton, Dwight H. *Annals of Mackinac 1843-1906.* Detroit: Detroit Free Press Printing Co., 1888.

Ketchum, William. *An Authentic and Comprehensive History of Buffalo.* 2 vols., Buffalo: Rockwell, Baker and Hill, 1865.

Kilby, William Henry. *Eastport and Passamaquoddy: A Collection of Historical and Biographical Sketches.* Eastport, Maine: E.E. Shead, 1982.

Kipling, Rudyard. *Stalky & Co.* London: Macmillan, 1899.

Larkin, Jack. *The Reshaping of Everyday Life 1790-1840.* New York, Harper & Row, 1988.

Leavitt, Thaddeus. *History of Leeds and Grenville.* Belleville: Mike Silk Screening Limited, 1972.

Light, Beth and Alison Prentice, eds. *Pioneer and Gentlewomen of British North America 1713-1867.* Toronto: New Hogtown Press, 1980.

Linn, John. *Annals of Buffalo Valley, Pennsylvania. 1755-1855.* Harrisburg: Lane & Haupt, 1877.

Litt, Paul, Ronald F. Williamson and Joseph Whitehorne *Death at Snake Hill: Secrets from a War of 1812 Cemetery.* Toronto: Dundurn Press, 1993.

Lord, Walter. *The Dawn's Early Light.* New York: W.W. Norton, 1972.

Lossing, Benson J. *The Pictorial Field-Book of the War of 1812.* Glendale, NY: 1869 reprinted Benchmark Publishing Corporation, 1970.

Low, Donald A. *The Regency Underworld.* Stroud, Glos: Sutton Publishing, 2000.

Mackenzie, Alexander Slidell. *The Life of Commodore Oliver Hazard Perry.* New York: Harper, 1841.

Maclean, Virginia. *A Short-Title Catalogue of Household and Cookery Books published in the English Tongue, 1701-1800.* London: Prospect Books, distributed by University of Virginia Press, 1981.

Malcomson, Robert. *Lords of the Lake: The Naval War on Lake Ontario 1812-1814.* Toronto: Robin Brass Studio, 1998.

Masefield, John. *Sea Life in Nelson's Time.* London: Sphere Books, 1972.

Mayhew, Henry and Peter Quennell. *London's Underground,* London: Spring Books, 1969.

McClellan, Elisabeth. *History of American Costume 1607-1870.* New York: Tudor Publishing Company, 1969.

———. *Historic Dress in America 1607-1870.* New York: Arno Press, 1977

McKenzie, Ruth. *Laura Secord: The Legend and the Lady.* Toronto: McClelland and Stewart, 1971.

McMillen, Sally G. *Motherhood in the Old South: Pregnancy, Childbirth and Infant Rearing.* Baton Rouge: Louisiana State University Press, 1990.

Merritt, Richard, Nancy Butler and Michael Power. eds. *The Capital Years: Niagara-on-the-Lake 1792-1796.* Toronto and Oxford: Dundurn Press, 1991.

Moodie, Susanna. *Roughing it in the Bush, or Life in Canada.* London: 1852, reprinted McClelland & Stewart, Toronto, 2000.

Moody, T.W. and W.E. Vaughan. *A New History of Ireland.* Oxford: Clarendon, 1986, 9 vols.

Morris, John D. *Sword of the Border: Major General Jacob Jennings Brown, 1775-1828.* Kent, Ohio: Kent State University Press, 2000.

Mowat, Grace Helen. *The Diverting History of a Loyalist Town: A Portrait of St. Andrews, New Brunswick.* St. Andrews, NB: Charlotte County Cottage Craft, 1932.

Norton, Mary Beth. *Liberty's Daughters: The Revolutionary Experience of American Women, 1750-1800.* Boston: Little Brown & Company, 1980.

O'Brien, Brendan. *Speedy Justice: The Tragic Last Voyage of His Majesty's Vessel Speedy.* Toronto: University of Toronto Press, 1992.

Oman, Charles. *Wellington's Army.* 1913 reprinted London: Greenhill 1993.

Ontario, Government of. *Report of the Task Force on Midwifery in Ontario.* Toronto: The Task Force, 1987.

Osborne, Peter. *Harbledown Heritage.* Harbledown Conservation Association, 2000.

Pack, James. *The Man who burned the White House: Admiral Sir George Cockburn, 1772-1853.* Emsworth, Hampshire: Kenneth Mason, 1987.

Padfield, Peter. *Broke and the Shannon.* London: Hodder and Stoughton, 1968.

Palmer, Roy, ed. *The Rambling Soldier.* London: Alan Sutton, 1985.

Parker, Patricia L. *Susanna Rowson.* Boston: Twayne Publishers, 1986.

Parton, James. *Daughters of Genius: A Series of Sketches.* Philadelphia: Hubbard Brothers, 1888.

———. *Life of Andrew Jackson.* New York: Mason Brothers, 1861, 3 vols.

Perry Smith H. *History of the City of Buffalo and Erie County,* Syracuse, NY: D. Mason & Co., 1894, 2 vols.

Phipps, Frances. *Colonial Kitchens, Their Furnishings, and Their Gardens.* New York: Hawthorn Books, 1972.

Pitch, Anthony S. *The Burning of Washington: The British Invasion of 1814.* Annapolis, Maryland: Naval Institute Press, 1998.

Potter-Mackinnon, Janice. *While The Women Only*

Wept: Loyalist Refugee Women. Montreal and Kingston: McGill-Queen's University Press, 1993.

Prindiville, Kathleen. *First Ladies*. New York: Macmillan Company, 1964.

Reilly, Robin. *The British at the Gates: The New Orleans Campaign in the War of 1812*. Toronto: Robin Brass Studio, 2002.

Rodger, N.A.M. *The Wooden World: An Anatomy of the Georgian Navy*. Glasgow: Fontana Press, 1988.

Rowland, Eron. *Andrew Jackson's Campaign Against the British, or the Mississippi Territory in the War of 1812*. New York: Macmillan, 1926.

Quaife, Milo. *Chicago and the Old Northwest, 1673-1835: A Study of the evolution of the northwestern frontier, together with a history of Fort Dearborn*. Chicago: University of Chicago, 1913.

Quennell, Peter. *London's Underworld: being selections from "those that will not work" the fourth volume of "London labour and the London poor"*. London: Spring Books, 1966.

Raddall, Thomas H. *Halifax: Warden of the North*. Garden City, NY: Doubleday, 1965.

Rammage, Stuart. *The Militia Stood Alone: Malcom's Mills, 6 November 1814*. Penticton: Valley Publications, 2000.

Remini, Robert V. *Andrew Jackson and the Course of the American Empire 1767-1821*. New York: Harper & Row, 1977.

Robinson, Charlotte Gourley. *Pioneer Profiles of New Brunswick Settlers*. Belleville: Mika Publishing, 1980.

Rothman, Ellen K. *Hands and Hearts: A History of Courtship in America*. New York: Basic Books, 1984.

Sanford, Carlton E. *Early History of the Town of Hopkinton*. Boston: The Bartlett Press, 1903.

Scott, Kenneth. *British Aliens in the United States during the War of 1812*. Baltimore: Genealogical Publishing, 1979.

Seibel, George A. *The Niagara Portage Road: 200 Years 1790-1990*. Niagara Falls, Canada: City of Niagara Falls, 1990.

Senior, Elinor Kyte. *From Royal Township to Industrial City: Cornwall 1784-1984*. Belleville: Mika Publishing, 1983.

Shakespeare, William. *The Complete Works of William Shakespeare*. New York: Avenil Books, 1975.

Sheldon, Electra. *The Early History of Michigan from the first settlement to 1815*. New York, A.S. Barnes & Company, 1856.

Sheppard, George. *Plunder, Profit, and Paroles: A Social History of the War of 1812 in Upper Canada*. Montreal and Kingston: McGill Queen's University Press, 1994.

Skaggs, David Curtis. *Thomas Macdonough: Master of Command in the Early U.S. Navy*. Annapolis, MD: Naval Institute Press, 2003.

Skelton, William B. *An American Profession of Arms: The Army Officer Corps, 1784-1861*. Lawrence, Kansas: University of Kansas, 1992.

Smith, Arthur Britton, ed. *Kingston! Oh Kingston!*. Kingston: Brown & Martin, 1987.

Smyth, B. *A History of the Lancashire Fusiliers (formerly the XX Regiment)* (2 volumes). Dublin: Sackville Press, 1903.

Squires, W. Austin. *The 104th Regiment of Foot (The New Brunswick Regiment) 1803-1817*. Fredericton: Brunswick Press, 1962.

St. John Williams, Noel. *Judy O'Grady and the Colonel's Lady: The Army wife and the camp follower since 1660*. London: Brassey, 1988.

Stott, Glenn. *Greater Evils: The War of 1812 in Southwestern Ontario*. Arcona, Ontario: G. Stott Publishing, 2001.

Sugden, John. *Tecumseh: A Life*. New York: Henry Holt and Company, 1997.

Thomas, Earle. *Sir John Johnson: Loyalist Baronet*. Toronto: Dundurn Press, 1986.

Thompson, John H. *Jubilee History of Thorold township and town*. Thorold: The Thorold Post, 1897-98.

Tucker, Glenn. *Tecumseh: Vision of Glory*. Indianapolis: Bobbs-Merrill, 1956

Tucker, Spencer. *Stephen Decatur: A Life Most Bold and Daring*. Annapolis: Naval Institute Press, 2005.

Turner, E.S. *Gallant Gentlemen: A Portrait of the British Officer 1800-1856*. London: Michael Joseph, 1956.

Turner, James. *Pallas Armata or Military Essayes of the Ancient Grecian Roman and Modern Art of War*. London: Richard Chiswell, 1683.

Turner, Orsamus. *Pioneer History of the Holland Purchase of Western New York*. Buffalo: Jewett, Thomas & Co, 1849.

Turner, Wesley B. *British Generals in the War of 1812: High Command in the Canadas*. Montreal and Kingston: McGill-Queen's University Press, 1999.

Ulrich, Laurel Thatcher. *A Midwife's Tale: The Life of Martha Ballard, based on her diary, 1785-1812*. New York: Vintage Books, 1990.

Ward, Peter. *Courtship, Love and Marriage in Nineteenth Century English Canada*. Montreal: McGill-Queen's University Press, 1990.

Weishan, Michael. *The New Traditional Garden*. New York: The Ballantyne Publishing Group, 1999.

Wetherell, J.E., ed. *The Prisoner of Chillon and Selections from Childe Harold's Pilgrimage*. Toronto: W.J. Gage & Co., 1889.

Wharton, Anne Hollingsworth. *Salons Colonial and Republican*. Philadelphia & London: J.B. Lippincott, 1900

———. *Social Life in the Early Republic*. Philadelphia: J.B. Lippincott, 1902.

Wheeler, George Augustus. *Castine Past and Present: The Ancient Settlement of Pentagöet and the Modern Town*. Boston: Rockwell and Churchill Press, 1896.

Whitehorne, Joseph A. *The Battle for Baltimore 1814*. Baltimore: Nautical & Aviation Publishing, 1997.

Whitney, Janet. *Abigail Adams*. Westport, Conn: Greenwood Press, 1947.

Wilder, Patrick A. *The Battle of Sackett's Harbour*. Baltimore: Nautical and Aviation Publishing, 1994.

Wilson, Bruce. *As She Began: An illustrated introduction to Loyalist Ontario*. Toronto and Charlottetown: Dundurn Press, 1981.

Wohler, J. Patrick. *Charles de Salaberry: Soldier of the Empire, Defender of Quebec*. Toronto: Dundurn Press, 1984.

Wood, Edwin O. *Historic Mackinac: The Historical Picturesque and Legendary Features of the Mackinac Country*. New York: Macmillan, 1918, 2 vols.

Wrong, George M. *A Canadian Manor and Its Seigneurs: The Story of A Hundred Years 1761-1861*. Toronto: Macmillan, 1908

Zaslow, Morris. *The Defended Border: Upper Canada and the War of 1812*. Toronto: Macmillan of Canada, 1964.

Zimmerman, David. *Coastal Fort: A History of Fort Sullivan, Eastport, Maine*. Eastport, Maine: Border Historical Society, 1984.

Published Articles

Brown, William, "Recollections of Old Halifax," *Nova Scotia Historical Society*, Volume XIII (1908).

Cardoza, Thomas, "*La Belle Cantinière*: Women in the French Army, 1789-1913," *Proceedings. Western Society for French History* (1995), 45-54.

Graves, Donald E., "Worthless is the laurel steeped in female tears: An Investigation into the Outrages Committed by British Troops at Hampton, Virginia, in 1813," *Journal of the War of 1812*, Volume VII, No. 1 (Winter 2002), 4-23.

Heriot, J.C.A., "Major-General, The Hon. Frederick George Heriot, C.B.", *The Canadian Antiquarian and Numismatic Journal*, Volume VIII (1911), No. 2, 49-72.

Hyde, Michael, "Fortune Tellers, Witches and Such," *Davy Jones' Locker* No. 47 (December 2001).

Johnson, Jean, "Ancestry and Descendants of Molly Brant," *Ontario Historical Society Quarterly Journal*, Volume LXIII, No. 2 (June 1971), 86-102.

Kilby, William Henry, "A New England Town Under Martial Law," *New England Magazine*, Volume XIV (Winter 1896), 685-698.

Lord, Norman C. ed., "The War on the Canadian Frontier 1812-1814: Letters written by Sergeant James Commins, 8th Foot," *Journal of the Society for Army Historical Research*, Volume 18 (1939), 199-211.

McDowell, John E., "Madame La Framboise," *Michigan History*, Volume 56 (Winter 1972), 271-286.

———, "Therese Schindler of Mackinac: Upward Mobility in the Great Lakes Fur Trade," *Wisconsin Magazine of History*, Volume 61, No. 2 (Winter 1977-1978), 125-143.

Massicotte, E.-Z., "Chansons Militaires de 1812," *Le Bulletin des Recherches Historiques*, Volume XXXVI, No. 5 (May 1930), 188-191.

Moore, Vivian Lyon, "A Pocahontas of Michigan," *Michigan History Magazine*, Volume 15 (1931), 71-79.

Mullane, George, "Old Inns and Coffee Houses of Halifax," *Collections of Nova Scotia Historical Society*, Volume 22 (1933), 1-24.

"Old Recruiting Posters," *Journal of the Society of Army Historica Research*, Vol. 1 (1920), 120-123.

Riddell, William Renwick, "Joseph Willcocks, Sheriff, Member of Parliament and Traitor," *Ontario Historical Society Papers and Records*, Volume 24 (1927), 475-489.

Risteen, Frank B., "Children of Sir John Johnson & Lady Mary Johnson," *Ontario History Society Quarterly Journal*, Volume LXIII, No. 2 (June 1971), 93-102.

Sakovich, Maria Fergusson, "Jane Ferguson: Immigrant, Pioneer, and Itinerant Wife in Upper Canada," *The Hay Bay Guardian*, Volume 13 (2005), 2-9.

Sheppard, George, "'Wants and Privations': Women and the War of 1812 in Upper Canada," *Social History 28* (1995), 159-179.

Stewart, Miller, "Army Laundresses: Ladies of the 'Soap Suds Row'," *Nebraska History*, Volume 61 (1980), 421-426.

Turner, Elder A., ed., "Death of Mr. Job Hoisington," *Publications fo the Buffalo Historical Society*, Vol. II (1880), 2.

Vesey, Maxwell, "A Strange Interlude in Border History," *Dalhousie Review*, Volume XXX (1941) 417-424.

Widder, Keith R., "Magdelaine LaFramboise, Fur Trader and Educator," in Rosalie Troester, ed., *Historic Woman of Michigan: a sesquicentennial celebration*. Lansing, Michigan: Michigan Women's Studies Association, 1987.

Internet Sources

[Knight, Kitty] <www.kittyknight.com>

[Old Bailey Courthouse] <www:oldbaileyonline.org>

[Tecumseh] <www.nativelonghouse.com>

Index